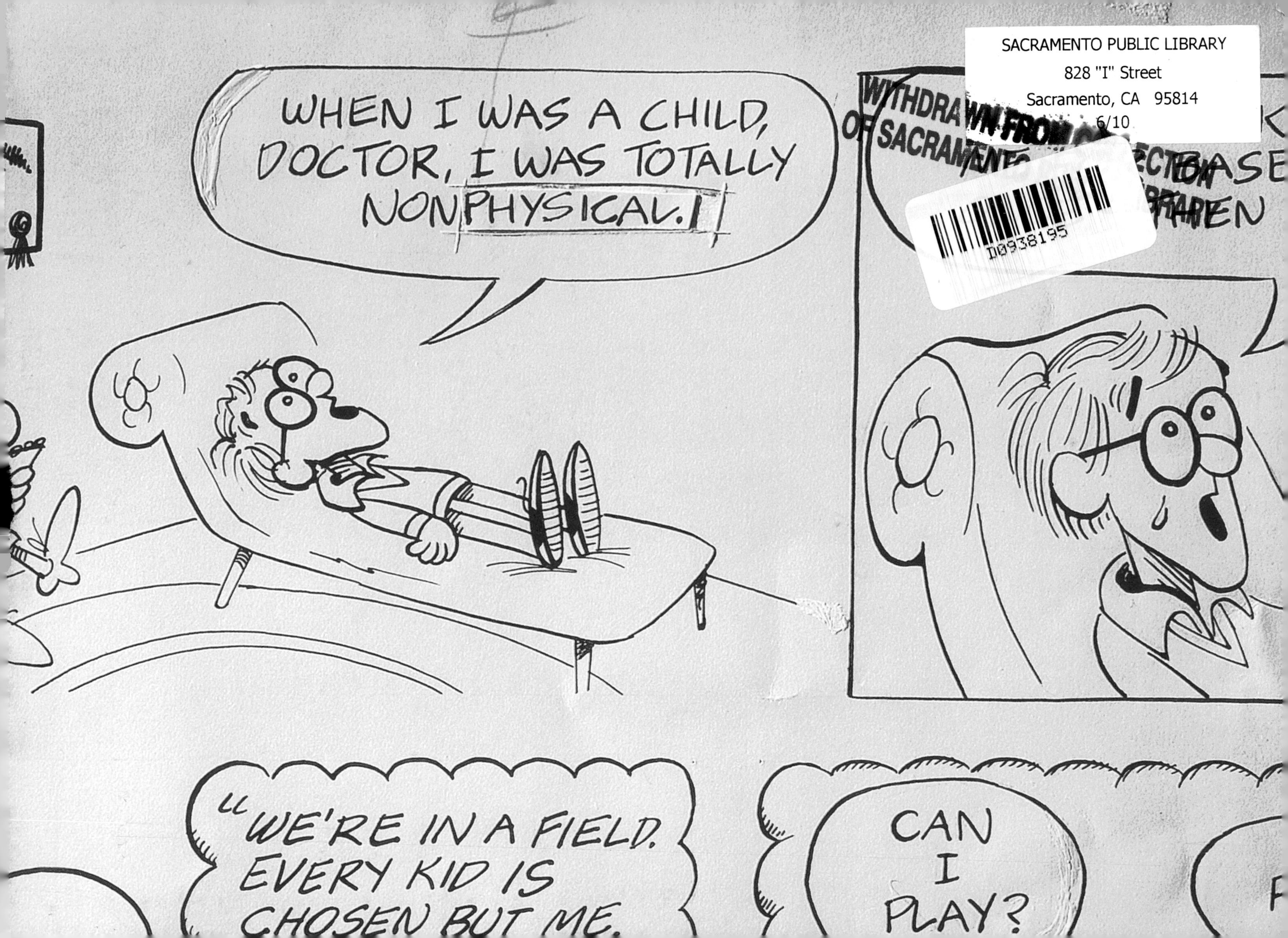
WHEN I WAS A CHILD, DOCTOR, I WAS TOTALLY NONPHYSICAL.
“WE'RE IN A FIELD. EVERY KID IS CHOSEN BUT ME.
CAN I PLAY?

Dread & Superficiality

DREAD

& Superficiality

Woody Allen as Comic Strip

Written & Illustrated by Stuart Hample

Introduction by R. Buckminster Fuller

Abrams ComicArts, New York

Cast of Characters

Woody

Woody's Father

Woody's Mother

Woody's Nephew

Woody's Shrink

Woody's Agent

Woody's Women

Contents

To Jack Rollins,
Great and Wonderful Comedy Wizard,
Man of Consummate Integrity and Openhearted Pal,
who allowed me to follow him into all those
so-called dressing rooms-cum-kitchens.

Acknowledgments

Special thanks to Lucy Shelton Caswell of the Ohio
State University Cartoon Research Library & Museum;
the patient John Peter Ferry, keeper of the Bucky Fuller
legacy; and at Abrams ComicArts, Sofia Gutiérrez and
designer Neil Egan. All these folks were of inestimable
help with the assembly of this book. Finally, but for
editor Charlie Kochman's intrepidity, and the endless
generosity of Woody Allen, the book wouldn't exist at all.

"Cartoonist Walks Into a Bar…"

PART I: HOW I MET WOODY

It's arguable that my disdain for having to flog lawn furniture played a small part in how I met Woody Allen.

In 1955, to maintain my sanity, I fled a difficult situation in Boston working with Al Capp, creator of the comic strip "Li'l Abner," and joined a Buffalo ad agency. Being an art director wasn't as electrifying as hanging with Capp—a capricious, creative whirlwind—but it was considerably more serene.

Also humdrum.

One example, of many: I was conscripted to attend a convention in Chicago on behalf of a patio furniture client. To alleviate the boredom of pimping the life-enhancing virtues of chrome at the Merchandise Mart, my final evening in town I went, seeking laughs, to Mr. Kelly's, a well-known supper club on Rush Street. The poster outside listed a new comedy act called Nichols & May. Assuming they had to be at least as funny as a furniture show, I went in. The room was smoky, and so boisterous you could barely hear the pianist playing in the background. Most of the boozy crowd wore name tags. Two stools stood side by side on the tiny, murky stage.

Blackout!

Abruptly, the piano music ceased.

A spotlight hit one stool. A twentysomething fellow with golden hair and baby-pink cheeks sat on it. He pantomimed inserting a coin into a pay phone and dialing.

A second spot hit the other stool. A slim, raven-haired young woman materialized. She pantomimed plugging into a phone operator's board. *"In-fer-MAY-shee-un!"* she said in a jaded voice.

"Operator," Mike Nichols said, "I'd like the number for a George Kaplan, at forty-four eleven Hugenot-Walloon Drive."

"Kaplan?" Elaine May responded tonelessly, "That is K as in knife, A as in aardvark, P as in *pneu-MUN-ya*, L as in luscious, A as in aardvark again, N as in newelpost, Kaplan?"

"Uh . . . uh . . . I think so," Mike said uncertainly. "Yes . . ." Nichols and May were off on their lost-dime sketch. I was hooked.

Later in the set, Nichols invited the audience to suggest a style for an improvisation. Someone called out, "Shakespeare." When Nichols asked for an opening line, a smashed conventioneer rose unsteadily and shouted, "THE LAMP SHOW!" Nichols's face went slack; this dreary cue predestined a heavy-weather lift-off. Nevertheless, he and Elaine took flight and landed laughs.

But . . . *the lamp show?*

Between sets I slipped outside, determined to forge a show-offy opening line for the improv Nichols would request in the second set. I would be more than just another ad agency schmuck. I would be the dazzling comedian's collaborator!

Back inside. Second set. Mike's cue. I was ready: "Madame, if you get one more drop of chicken fat on my Gutenberg Bible, I shall have you ejected from the Andalusian Room of the Audubon Society for life." The audience roared. "Sir," Nichols said, laughing, "would you repeat that?"

When the set finished, Mike and Elaine came over to chat briefly; Mike soon left with his then-wife, singer Pat Scot (yes, only one "t"), but Elaine stayed to schmooze till the joint closed. I told her I was writing material for a wannabe-comedian friend in Buffalo named Frank Buxton, who needed representation. Elaine graciously gave me the

Above: King Features publicity photo of Stuart Hample and Woody Allen (1976).

Below: *Improvisations to Music,* Mike Nichols & Elaine May debut record album from Mercury Records (1959).

name of her manager, Jack Rollins. Back in Buffalo, I phoned Rollins in New York, using Elaine's name as a battering ram. Claiming Frank and I planned to visit Manhattan (a momentary improv), I asked if he'd listen to Frank's act. Rollins said yes. A week later at the Nola Studio on 57th Street, with Elaine in the audience, Rollins listened—and accepted Frank as a client.

Frank was a pale, blue-eyed, Waspy, Tom Poston lookalike with blond body hair. His performing outfit was an Oxford button-down shirt, rep striped tie, and tweed blazer. One night some months later, after Frank scored at the Blue Angel (then the premier cabaret showcase for comics in America), Rollins took us to Lindy's, the iconic Broadway deli famous for its cheesecake, overstuffed sandwiches, and comedian's table, where big-name comics shpritzed zingers at one another. Rollins introduced Frank to the table as his newest client. Fat Jack "the Laughmaster" Leonard, the first insult comedian (likely he was Don Rickles's inspiration), eyeballed Frank: "What's your act, kid—ya come out and do accounting?"

Two years later the ad agency transferred me to Manhattan. Still eager to be around comedians, I convinced Rollins to take me along on his nightly rounds of the comedy clubs while he nurtured his stable of funny people.

One of them was a mild-mannered, twenty-five-year-old, bespectacled redhead with chalk-white skin like the underbelly of a frog ("I don't tan, I *stroke*") named Woody Allen, who gave the impression of a sociology student inimical to body building. This Woody fellow was the exact opposite of the Laughmaster.

While Fat Jack strode the stage commandingly like a mastodon on steroids, Woody stood deathly still, outwardly disinclined to be performing at all. Fat Jack stabbed the air with his salami-sized forefinger, assertively firing off his put-downs at machine gun speed ("There's nothing wrong with you that reincarnation won't cure!"), loud enough to be heard in the next borough. Woody, on the other hand, white-knuckled the mic for support, and stammered self-deprecatingly ("My only regret in life is that I'm not someone else"). Fat Jack rambled wildly, free of concept, goal, point of view, subtext, or single line of thought, aiming his incendiary one-liners like buckshot at anyone within his line of

fire. Woody modestly offered a tightly focused, hyperintelligent, angst-ridden narrative of his life's failures in the form of bent therapy sessions ("I'd like to review for you some of the outstanding incidents of my private life to put them in perspective"). Although audiences went wild over Fat Jack, few, in the beginning, were able to assimilate Woody's literate, groundbreaking subtextual memoirs ("I phoned my psychiatrist and told him I was depressed and going to commit suicide by jumping from the top of the Empire State Building. He said, 'That's fine, but you'll have to pay for the sessions you miss.'").

I saw Woody perform, sometimes for no pay, at such comedy clubs in Greenwich Village as the Bitter End and Upstairs at the Duplex, on occasion falling flat. There was the night he got no laughs. Working, for God's sake, for no money, or maybe fifty bucks, and not a single laugh. None. Yes, Woody Allen! Not a snicker, a titter, a chortle (except from Rollins and me at the rear of the room). The material, of course, was singularly original, luminously funny—the same stuff that later, when Woody was a name, nourished audiences hungry for laughter. But that night there was zero connection between performer and patrons.

Death to a stand-up.

Afterward, in the so-called dressing room (a forlorn little kitchen), Woody was despondent. Rollins lit up a Cuban Montecristo and said, "What went wrong, Wood?" "The audience was hostile," Woody said. Rollins exhaled blue smoke thoughtfully. "An audience has to like you, to connect with you emotionally before they'll laugh at your jokes. They sensed that you were fighting them." He bit off a speck of cigar leaf, spat it into a waste bin, and continued, "Could you come out and do your act, just for yourself, regardless of whether you get laughs or not?" Woody wasn't sure. Jack urged him to try it for at least twenty performances. (I didn't have a tape recorder with me at the time, so this dialogue isn't exact; but it's as close to what was said as memory permits, and emotionally on the mark according to discussions I've subsequently had with Rollins.)

Dissolve to montage: Woody performing in clubs.

Superimpose calendar: Pages float off one by one.

Above: Hample's sketch of Jack Rollins, Woody's manager from the start—their contract is based on nothing more than a handshake.

Following Rollins's advice, Woody doggedly performed, week after week after week. Gradually he gained confidence, until the audience was his plaything. (You surely know the rest of the story.)

PART II: WORKING WITH WOODY

Fade out on 1956.

Fade in on 1975—a pretty good year. President Nixon was gone. A gaggle of his hired guns were in the slammer as punishment for the Watergate caper. The United States pulled out of Vietnam. Charlie Chaplin was knighted. I had sold to Field Enterprises a comic strip called "Rich and Famous."

That was the good news.

The not-so-good news: "Rich and Famous" failed to make me either. I remained a peon in an ad agency, turning out the strip at night. Days I ground out TV commercials for a cigarette brand furtively peddling cancer. If I had had to continue in that mind-numbing job for very much longer, I would have cracked and become a mass murderer.

What to do?

My dream: Find an alternate way to put food on the table, keep a roof over my family, and kiss the ad biz good-bye.

SHAZAM! A Light Bulb Epiphany.

It occurred to me that Woody's persona—feeling alone in an uncaring universe, striking out with women, being humiliated by his parents (I knew the terrains), all these subjects offered with some of the funniest ripostes this side of Oscar Wilde—might make a terrific comic strip (an area I also knew), and spring me from servitude as an ad hack!

Hmmm. How would Woody, who, at thirty-nine, was wildly successful—he'd already written and acted in *What's New Pussycat?*, then the highest-grossing comedy in movie history; written, directed, and starred in *Take the Money and Run*; *Bananas*; *Play It Again, Sam*; *Everything You Always Wanted to Know About Sex* (**But Were Afraid to Ask*); *Sleeper*; and *Love and Death*; acted in *The Front*; authored two Broadway hits, *Don't Drink the Water* and *Play It Again, Sam*; was editing a movie titled *Anhedonia*, which, renamed *Annie Hall*, would later snag four Oscars, including (in com-

petition with *Star Wars*) Best Picture—how would he react to my notion? I ran a test scene in my head:

Me: (On fantasy phone) Woody, I have an idea for a comic strip based on you. Possible?

Woody: Sorry. Up to my neck writing a movie, editing another movie. Writing a piece for the *New Yorker*. Don't need the money. Try me next year.

So I asked him in person.

Woody was intrigued enough to say, "Show me some sketches." I based my drawings on how he looked in his late twenties when we'd first met.

Above: Sunday page of "Rich and Famous," the comic strip Hample was writing and illustrating while he was doing "Inside Woody Allen" (December 5, 1976).

He okayed the Woody cartoon character (even had it animated for a sequence in the film he was working on at the time, *Annie Hall*), and said, "What about the jokes?"

I brought jokes. He speedily riffled through them. "Maybe," he said casually, "I could help you with the jokes."

OH. MY. GOD! Woody Allen offered to HELP. ME. WITH. THE. JOKES!

Assuming he was offering to *write* the jokes, I wanted to holler, MY SAVIOR! Instead, I said, softly, "Okay." Which was more appropriate, since his help turned out instead to be dozens of pages of jokes and abbreviations of jokes he had written and compiled during his stand-up years. Some were mere shards, such as "Muscles in their hair," or "Tied me to Jewish star—uncomfortable crucifixion." Others were even more minimal subject descriptions: "Bull fighting," "Astrology." (Woody occasionally served as my Rosetta Stone to translate the hieroglyphs.)

There were also longer notations:

"I'm ignorant when it comes to politics. All I know is two men run against each other and the one who gets the most votes doesn't necessarily win."

"Sketch—man breaking up with female ape after his evolution."

"N.Y. Psychoanalytic Institute—ten most wanted list."

"Underground movie—newsreels of Vietnam. Show them backward and for an hour and a half it looks like we're winning the war."

"I was born Jewish and a Democrat. I didn't know which one was my religion."

There were also scenes written out like little playlets:

"Freud could not order blintzes. He was ashamed to say the word. He'd go into an appetizer store and say, 'Let me have some of those crepes with cheese in the middle.' And the grocer would say, 'Do you mean blintzes, Herr Professor?' And Freud would turn all red and run out through the streets of Vienna, his cape flying. Furious, he founded psychoanalysis and made sure it wouldn't work."

Woody gave his consent to adapt any of these loose lines for the strips, and said I could pirate material from his books, movies, plays, and stand-up material.

Based on Woody's famous public persona, King Features Syndicate agreed to publish the feature. They requested six weeks of sample strips so they could start selling to newspapers. Using Woody's humor scraps as a springboard, I began to churn out the required daily and Sunday strips. To assure the initial quality of the work, for a number of weeks I went each Saturday to Woody's Fifth Avenue penthouse, where he judged the material and offered suggestions on how to develop characters and pace gags and constantly pleaded with me to maintain high standards—always urging me not to settle for anything less than top-drawer material.

During this pre-publication period, the syndicate's PR department dispatched announcement releases to the media.

One Saturday I showed Woody a copy of the influential Brazilian newspaper *Folha de S.Paulo*, excited that the strip and his photo were featured on the front page. "I don't read Portuguese," he said in jest. "Doesn't matter," I said, "it's obvious that you're esteemed beyond the United States. This is sensational publicity." He peered at the article: "For a nice change, I don't see *Juif* anywhere." I pressed on, hyping the value of international acclaim: "At minimum, this is evidence of how admired you are in Brazil." Woody shrugged. "Why am I always popular in countries with one-crop economies?"

There was one wildly advantageous publicity bonanza that almost fell apart. During the time Woody was editing *Annie Hall*, *People* magazine agreed to do a cover story on the impending strip. *People* editor Dick Stolley sought to set up a photo shoot. Instead Woody volunteered to supply the cover photo. In the editing room he handed me a photograph to deliver to Stolley. It showed Woody looking as solemn as an undertaker, shot by his production photographer, Brian Hamill. Stolley turned it down on the basis that a photo of a cover subject smiling netted the publication a higher percentage of newsstand sales than a glum one. Woody's serious expression, he said, was too downbeat. I told Woody that Stolley wanted him smiling. Woody said Hamill was his friend and *People* would have to use the Hamill photo, or he didn't want to go ahead with the story. A PR opportunity was about to go up in smoke. But I dodged the bullet with a Solomonic solution: I drew a cartoon of Woody and superimposed it on his shoulder in the photo to lighten his grim visage. Unable to sign the cartoon but avid to stamp it as mine, I craftily left my mark: Woody's shoelaces form my initials, S. H.

Above: Cover (photograph by Brian Hamill) and first page of *People* magazine article (October 4, 1976) announcing the launch of "Inside Woody Allen." Note the S. H. initials on Woody's shoes—Hample's ploy for being identified as the artist.

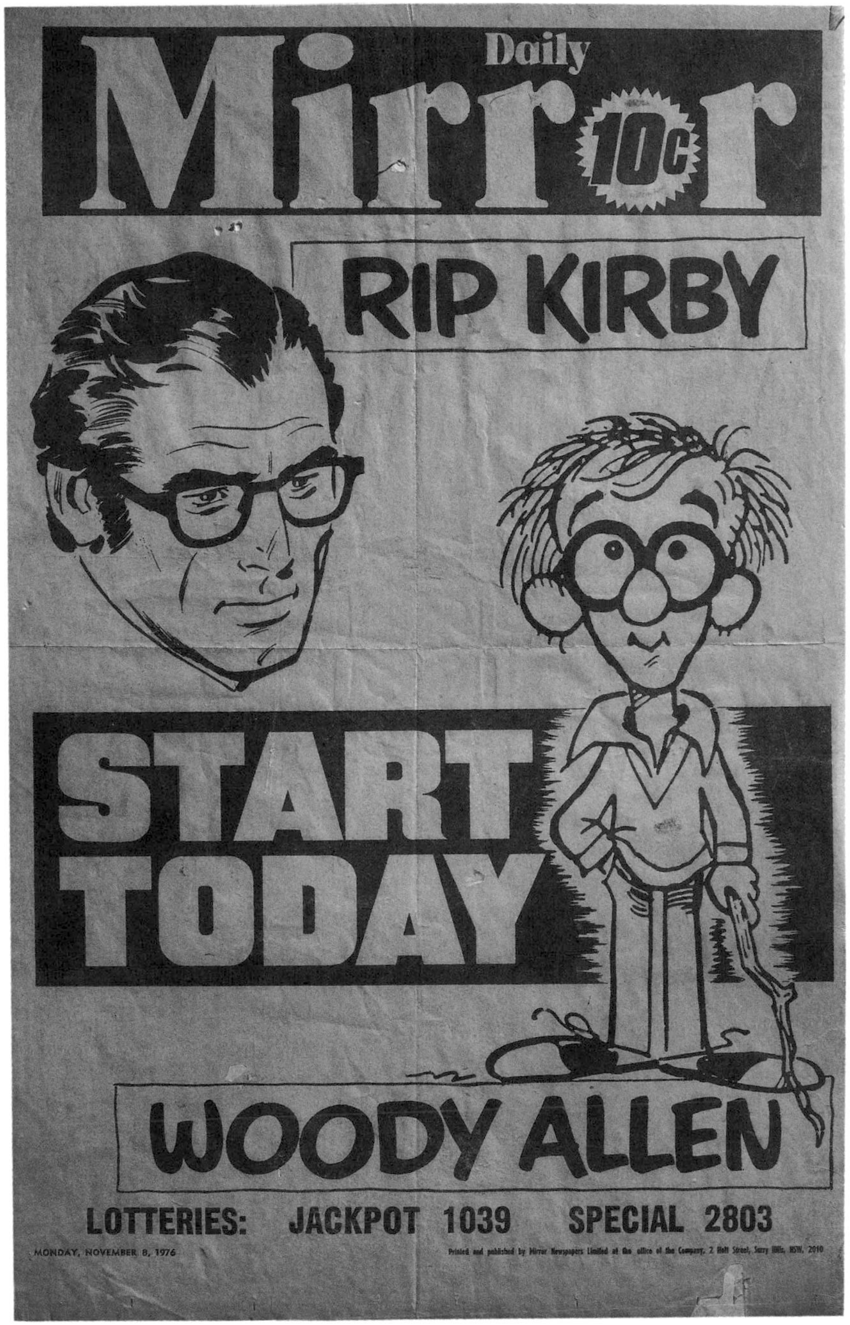
Daily
Mirror
10c
RIP KIRBY
START TODAY
WOODY ALLEN
LOTTERIES: JACKPOT 1039 SPECIAL 2803
MONDAY, NOVEMBER 8, 1976

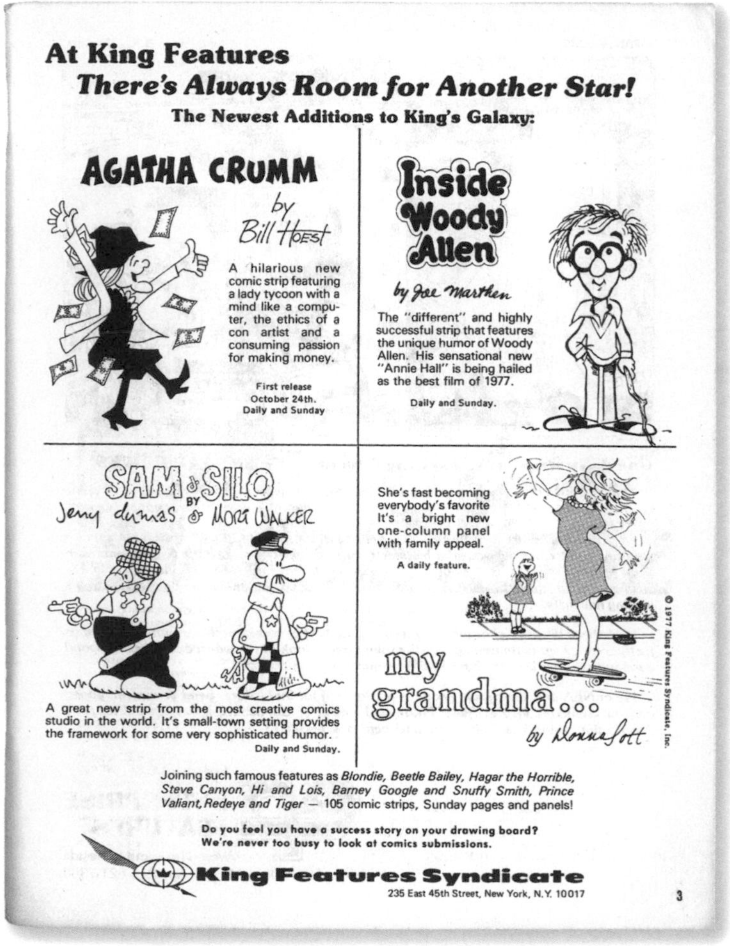
At King Features
There's Always Room for Another Star!
The Newest Additions to King's Galaxy:
AGATHA CRUMM
by Bill Hoest
A hilarious new comic strip featuring a lady tycoon with a mind like a computer, the ethics of a con artist and a consuming passion for making money.
First release October 24th. Daily and Sunday
Inside Woody Allen
by Joe Marthen
The "different" and highly successful strip that features the unique humor of Woody Allen. His sensational new "Annie Hall" is being hailed as the best film of 1977.
Daily and Sunday.
SAM & SILO
BY Jerry Dumas & Mort Walker
A great new strip from the most creative comics studio in the world. It's small-town setting provides the framework for some very sophisticated humor.
Daily and Sunday.
She's fast becoming everybody's favorite It's a bright new one-column panel with family appeal.
A daily feature.
my grandma...
by Donna Lott
© 1977 King Features Syndicate, Inc.
Joining such famous features as Blondie, Beetle Bailey, Hagar the Horrible, Steve Canyon, Hi and Lois, Barney Google and Snuffy Smith, Prince Valiant, Redeye and Tiger — 105 comic strips, Sunday pages and panels!
Do you feel you have a success story on your drawing board?
We're never too busy to look at comics submissions.
King Features Syndicate
235 East 45th Street, New York, N.Y. 10017
3

Far left: Australian promotional poster for "Inside Woody Allen," which appeared in the *Daily Mirror* (November 8, 1976).

Left: King Features ad from *Cartoonist Profiles* no. 35 (September 1977). In issue no. 38 (June 1978), editor Jud Hurd interviewed Stuart Hample about "Inside Woody Allen."

Below: The first "Inside Woody Allen" comic strip (October 4, 1976).

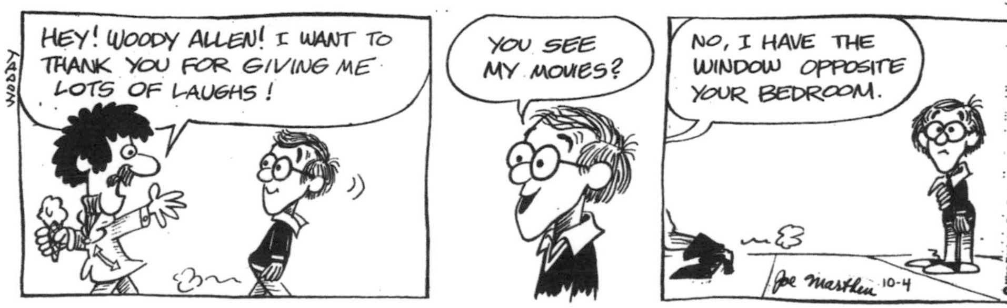
HEY! WOODY ALLEN! I WANT TO THANK YOU FOR GIVING ME LOTS OF LAUGHS!
YOU SEE MY MOVIES?
NO, I HAVE THE WINDOW OPPOSITE YOUR BEDROOM.
Joe Marthen 10-4

These two strips were based on gags from Woody Allen's notebook of collected jokes (see opposite page).

Unpublished strip

October 22, 1981

Took a philosophy program...

Truth, Beauty, Advanced Truth, Inter., Intro to God, guest lecturer...

~~Students required to start a new religion (term project)~~ ✓

FOR DAILY ★ It's like trying to teach painting...Emotional Sensitivity One ~~AND~~ and Two... ✓
Introduction to Greatness...lectures will be given in how to lead a tragic
life...students must ~~mix~~ bring in at least one painting that will live forever
and their own ear...

Grade advisor asked me what I wanted to do? I said I want to solve the manifold
ramifications of existence...he put in Mani Ram..One and Two...

Metaphysics...cheated soul of boy next to me

Got out...sat in room, thought...tree falls, make a sound if I'm not
there...took a lunch break...continued...

Discuss meaning of life and ~~death~~, became insurance man...
★ *I THOUGHT* *I WAS.* ← *FOR PRIVATE JOURNAL Darly*
He ~~does not think~~, therefore ~~he is not~~...

Partnership...Philosophers Incorporated...I supplied 66% of the ideas...
got a store...put in chairs... and thought...

I thought about life and man's existence, Herb thought about death and
eternity, and Jerry thought about how we were going to get the rent each
month (Dick - Pavlow)....not too many customers...occasionally guy pop in off
street and say, hey, do you think a system of moral ethics is dependent on
individual free will? We wouldn't get too many of those...thank God for the
cigarette machine...

Slogan: For the best of all possible worlds, use philosophy...

TV Quiz show..Russell, Satre, KGarry Moore...take members from audience and
force them to make existential decision...Mrs. Elsie Clinton of N.J., for
two thousand is there a Supreme Diety who created the universe and gave man
a soul? You have sixty seconds..(Groucho music)...Yes? Ohhh..I'm sorry...
the correct answer is no...

Above: Cover (right) and page from the first volume of Woody Allen's
notebook of collected jokes, often used as the basis for strip gags. See
opposite and page 20 for three that were developed into dailies.

Woody okayed the drawing. The cover story ran.

Preliminary sales of "Inside Woody Allen" were unprec-
edented; at that time the most successful beginning of any
strip ever. Before publication 460 papers signed up, whereas
"Peanuts" had begun with a mere six. (We all know the end
of *that* story, too!)

However, there was one small complication: my comic
strip "Rich and Famous." I hadn't told Field Enterprises
about the forthcoming Woody strip. And since my services
were contractually exclusive to them, they could proscribe
me from drawing "Inside Woody Allen." To camouflage
my duplicity I employed the pseudonym Joe Marthen—
combined parts of the names of my children, Joe, Martha,
and Henry (this explains its appearance on some strips
from 1976 to 1977). After the feature was launched and flying, I gave up "Rich and Famous," killed off Joe Marthen, and
signed my own name on "Inside Woody Allen." In the indus-
try, there was a soupçon of chatter about why Marthen, the

original Woody strip artist, was replaced by Stuart Hample. Lambiek.net, a Dutch Internet site about comics, wrote: "Joe Marthen was the comic artist of the comic 'Inside Woody Allen,' about the obsessions and insecurities of the famous actor. Joe Marthen drew the series in the period 1976–77, after which it was taken over by Stuart Hample."

As recently as 2004, a querulous piece appeared on an Internet site devoted to comic strip news, opinion, and esoterica: "Joe Marthen—is he or isn't he Stuart Hample?"

But it didn't matter what name was on the drawings; the name that brought the feature to life was Woody Allen.

Accordingly, on October 4, 1976, the strip was launched (see page 11). Woody, the pen-and-ink protagonist, just as in many of his early movies, was angst-ridden, flawed, fearful, insecure, inadequate, pessimistic, urban, single, lustful, rejected by women—often after a round of pretentious dialectics. And he was cowed by mechanical objects, and a touch misanthropic. The comic strip Woody was also at odds with his antagonistic parents; committed his inner thoughts and existential panic to a personal journal; discussed his free-floating angst in regular sessions with his passive-aggressive psychotherapist, Dr. Ilsa Fobick; was threatened by large, often armed, dangerous men; and employed his modest size to communicate physical impotence the way Chaplin, in the guise of the Little Tramp, suffered humiliation.

This was particularly apt, since Chaplin is the only other real person (also an esteemed movie writer and director) upon whom a comic strip has been based; in his case, actually, four. A strip, "Charlie Chaplin's Comic Capers," was licensed in 1915 by Chaplin to the *Chicago Herald*, whose publisher assigned the feature in 1918 to Elzie Segar—who subsequently became famous as the creator of Popeye.

Another strip, called "Pa's Imported Son-in-Law," written and illustrated by Ed Carey, began in 1916.

Two other strips about the Little Tramp also circulated about this time, when Chaplin, only four years into his movie career, was rapidly taking America by storm.

Chaplin's connection to these features was exclusively through his granting a license to produce them. Whereas Woody, also in no way the creator of the strip based on his persona, did serve occasionally in an advisory capacity.

While I benefited from the strip, I often wondered why Woody and Jack Rollins, his manager, gave the concept a green light. The answer came to me in 1977 when Woody related the following anecdote: He had cast the actress Mary Beth Hurt to play a part in his movie *Interiors*. As a young woman who had come from the boonies to seek a career in the big, hazardous city, Ms. Hurt regularly phoned her mother in Iowa (Marshalltown, home also of the late actress Jean Seberg) to reassure her that she was safe and happy. During one of those calls, Mary Beth proudly announced that she was going to play one of Diane Keaton's sisters in a movie "by somebody you probably haven't heard of, a director named Woody Allen." "I know about him," said her mother, "he's in the funny pages." Rollins, keen to expand the size of his client's movie audiences beyond the populous urban areas of New York, Los Angeles, Philadelphia, Boston, Chicago, Miami, etc., figured that more tickets might be sold to Woody's movies if his image was disseminated daily out in the heartland via the newspapers with their vast readership.

More evidence of Rollins's astute management of Woody's career: Early in the life of the strip, we had a serious inquiry from CBS about the possibility of creating a half-hour animated sitcom. (This, obviously, was years before the advent of *The Simpsons, Family Guy*, etc.) I was gung-ho. But this time Woody & Company vetoed the suggestion; like cutting back a plant to maintain healthy growth, and knowing a weekly Woody TV show would use his voice and persona in a medium that's a first cousin to movies, Rollins wisely elected to minimize rather than maximize Woody's image so as not to vitiate his power at the box office. As Woody put it, "Let me vitiate it in my own way."

Eventually, much as a sitcom requires a staff to churn out material to meet the never-ending demand for jokes, I took on a handful of writers. The star, by far, was David Weinberger, a brilliant twenty-six-year-old PhD candidate in philosophy (now a visionary Harvard professor), who had submitted some jokes out of the blue and won instant praise from Woody ("His gags are very clever, philosophical, and funny"). A classic Weinberger gag: Woody randomly tosses three pennies on the floor and muses, "I threw the I Ching . . . and got the hexagram: 'Shove off, Jewboy'" (see page 18).

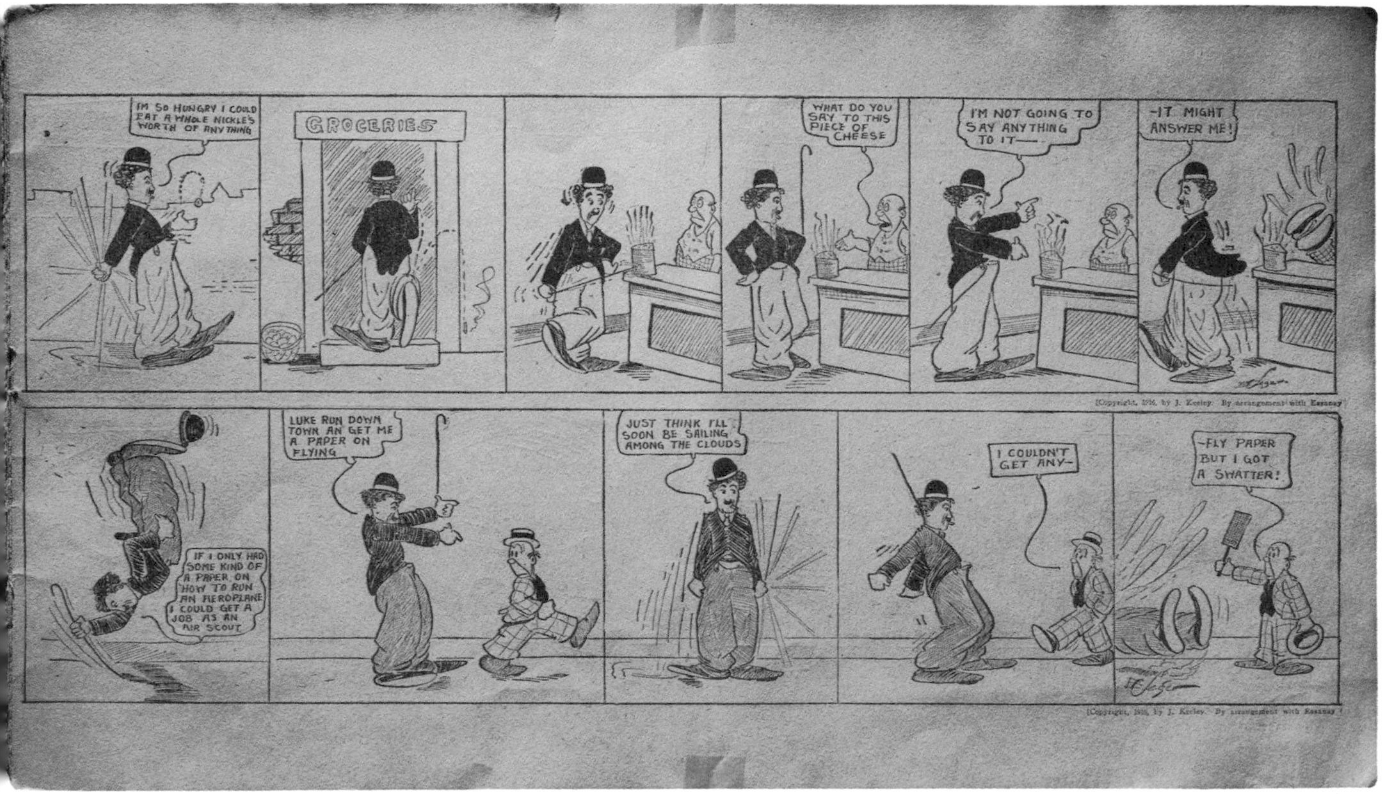
I'M SO HUNGRY I COULD EAT A WHOLE NICKLE'S WORTH OF ANYTHING
GROCERIES
WHAT DO YOU SAY TO THIS PIECE OF CHEESE
I'M NOT GOING TO SAY ANYTHING TO IT—
-IT MIGHT ANSWER ME!
IF I ONLY HAD SOME KIND OF A PAPER ON HOW TO RUN AN AEROPLANE I COULD GET A JOB AS AN AIR SCOUT
LUKE RUN DOWN TOWN AN GET ME A PAPER ON FLYING
JUST THINK I'LL SOON BE SAILING AMONG THE CLOUDS
I COULDN'T GET ANY-
-FLY PAPER BUT I GOT A SWATTER!

Above: Charlie Chaplin comic strips (1917) by Elzie Segar, who would later go on to create the iconic character Popeye.

The syndicate censor altered it to "Shove off, shorty," emasculating the witty, knife-edged commentary. This bowdlerization metastasized into a pesky, continuing problem, part of a schizophrenic air that hovered over the feature in its formative months. Like all new strips, unfamiliar to readers, it lost a few newspapers along the way. The folks at King Features became nervous. I started receiving notes of caution from the comics editor:

- Go easy on God references so we don't offend Bible Belt readers.

- Don't do gags with Woody in night clubs; they compare unfavorably with his live performances.

- Change the name of your character "Death" to "Fate." I'd rather you not use Death until the strip is solid and you can do anything. [Woody to me: "Better to call him Death. A character named Death can be quite funny. You have to take some chances. It'll be more alive if you use Death. Besides, you don't want just another strip that succeeds, do you?"]

Woody always envisioned I'd give him a wisecracking, zeitgeisty cartoon that would deal with human relationships, politics, and social commentary ("Doonesbury," born in 1970, was popular and, in my mind, a lodestar). Woody wanted his strip to appeal to the public by being amusing, but also intelligent. Still, certain things militated against this: (a) the syndicate wanted a feature with mass appeal, and (b) my over-eagerness to please them and keep the strip going, thus appeasing their criticism (considering the relentless progression of weekly closing dates a feature must be fed, I suppose it's a stretch to expect any comic strip's gags to be A-plus every day).

When the anxious syndicate honchos demanded more of a standard meat-and-potatoes style (among the enormously successful strips they syndicated—and still do—are "Beetle Bailey," "Blondie," and "Hägar the Horrible"), with gags and subjects accessible to the largest possible readership in the biggest number of newspapers, Woody's response was that an artist has to follow his own intuition rather than obey some huckster driven by readership surveys attempting to replicate what most other strips are like. This is borne out by my notes from a meeting with Woody on December 21, 1976, during which he said:

> Papers who might not want it would be millstones, and in the long run we will gain more than we will lose by establishing an identity; my tendency would be to risk being more offensive and deal with our strengths—offbeat and intelligent. After four or five months, they'll profit from it. And all of us could at least feel we have a small but very worthwhile following. You do have to risk not winning a certain acceptance, but we should go for offbeat. It takes longer but it's a stronger base from which to operate. I feel you're better off to do this and they will end up liking it better. I always believe that if

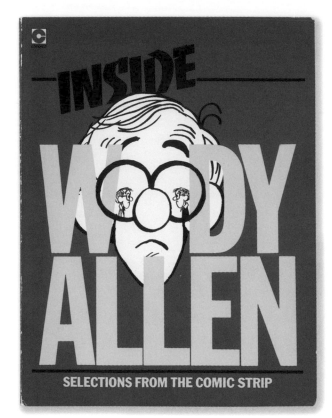

British

British

German

"Inside Woody Allen" was syndicated internationally by King Features. In 1978, Random House published a collection of strips, *Non-Being and Somethingness* (above). Shown here are the various foreign editions.

Dutch

German

Portuguese

Spanish

Spanish

"I THREW THE I CHING..."

"...AND GOT THE HEXAGRAM:"

"'SHOVE OFF, JEWBOY.'"

relationship between Lil Abner and Daisy Mae, are very involving and not just gags. A world needs to be created, peopled by real and original characters—who score visually because of your drawings and their humanity.

A suggestion:

Perhaps one theme for five days running (i.e.: Pogo's presidential campaign). [I'd done this in "Rich and Famous."]

Another Woody reminder:

We need more strips I'm not in, such as Fobick and her husband. My folks. My lovers. They must have their own personalities. What about the bitch girl? "Here it is three in the afternoon and I haven't hurt anybody yet." "Pogo" was the only truly great strip. It was not afraid to be different, non-commercial, because in the end that's how one winds up the most commercial.

And another:

We must not just use jokes that exploit my image—jokes should have genuine insights. Don't pander. Try not to be run-of-the-mill. Don't be afraid to be far-out. Lead your audience; don't look to them to lead you. Resist easy jokes that are expected. You could have a unique thing going—the terminology of the strip is different. The characters have distinctive speech patterns. The concerns and interests are apparently, though not really, intellectual. Therefore the gags must not be commercial. I really think it can spell the difference between people saying "You gotta see this strip—it's worthwhile" and "It's amusing—but just another strip."

Herewith, a number of Woody's comments from our conceptual meetings near the beginning, some of which were

DEATH

MY INITIAL HEAVY-HANDED CONCEPTION, DRAWN TO RESEMBLE LOU JACOBI, AN ACTOR WOODY SOMETIMES EMPLOYED

THIS VERSION WAS DRAWN TO REFLECT WOODY'S MORE SUBTLE, WITTY NOTION

I love a thing, 90 percent of the time there will be some people out there who also like it.

Woody's scribblings to me from 1977 and 1978 on strips I sent weekly at the start of the process for his approval, offer suggestions for keeping the overall tone up to snuff. (Note to aspiring comedians, gag writers, and professors: The following contains nuggets for a seminar on humor.)

The key is developing *people.* That silly cartoon of me surrounded by Fobick, Helmholtz [European philosopher], Laura [Woody's then-girlfriend], Bernie [his agent], etc. means nothing if they exist only to feed straight lines. They must have desires—goals—so we are interested in them. I still feel you must be daring. That's always been my most commercial thrust. I feel, as you know, that calling the character "Fate" instead of "Death," is a dopey concession and mistake for us, for as it appears to be "softer" it makes the strip less vivid. The strip can probably exist on the level of "cute" little jokes each day, but if you really want to involve the readers, it needs more substance—more plot in a sense. A joke, whether with Bernie or Laura or Fobick, is still just a joke. But ideas like, say, Al Capp's Sadie Hawkins Day, or the Shmoo, or the

This page: "Inside Woody Allen" Sunday pages as they appeared in the comics section on November 11, 1979, and June 29, 1980.

Above: In the New York *Daily News* (November 13, 1976) "Inside Woody Allen" and "Rex Morgan, M.D." (by Marvin Bradley and Frank Edgington) sometimes appeared on the same page. This strip was based on a gag from Woody Allen's notebook of collected jokes (see page 13).

Opposite: Pencil rough of a Dr. Fobick strip before inking. See note on bottom right about change of location.

not implemented, partly because of, as aforementioned, the syndicate's desire for the strip to be less "intellectual" and (full disclosure) my failings as a steward of Woody's vision.

Need more character engagement—instead of jokes being free-floating, they must be jokes on the way to character development. What will really make it go are real stories of people interacting in comic situations, and the laughs come on the way to a larger comic idea. Jokes are like the decorations on the Christmas tree—but it's a beautiful tree you need to start with. Only then can you hang baubles on it. (Sorry for the disgusting metaphor.)

My character now exists too much for the joke—to zing with a one-liner. He should be more identifiable—with emotion. The reader should become more involved.

Maybe the strip should be more real so the reader can more easily hook in with the problems. The characters are not sufficiently human. If it helps, you can use real names—

"Hello, this is Diane Keaton, is Woody there?" Or Louise Lasser—

Louise: Gee, even though we've been divorced for eight years, I still call you with problems, right?

Woody: What's the matter?

Louise: Did you watch *Mary Hartman* last night? Do you think the girl who played LuLu Belle is prettier than I am?

Put more involving ideas in the strip. Use my publicly perceived life. [Prescient: Larry David does this in *Curb Your Enthusiasm*.] My sister's kids ask me, "Are you a millionaire? How does it feel to be famous?" Have me watch *Mary Hartman* "for personal reasons."

Somebody wants to see *Bananas* with me. I say, "How can I watch a movie I'm in? What kind of an ego do you think I have?" Or "I'm going to Dick Cavett's house for the weekend." Or "I have a date with Diane Keaton." Or mention *Bananas* instead of saying, "I made a film"—be specific. Have me take the President's wife to a Martha Graham recital. [Woody actually took Betty Ford to such an event; when a reporter sought a comment, Woody, wearing a tuxedo and white sneakers, said, "We're just good friends."]

Please don't make me so masochistic. I'm not in life. Trying and failing is funny. Masochism is not.

In all cases go for the esoteric reference—it's more me. I've always been willing to lose half my audience with esoteric references, and you know what? They're always smarter than me and know my references and more. Never underestimate them. Despite Nixon.

I notice the content of the strip often drops beneath the level of humor I would do. I can tell this because the syndicate is not complaining about the content. Always a bad sign. I feel it's not sophisticated enough. You have to mediate between being too shocking and too banal. The Sunday pages don't violate the sexual and religious taboos. TV is even broader than

newspapers—look at *All in the Family, Mary Hartman*, etc.—they fly in the teeth of convention. Resign yourself—we'll never get a mass audience anyway. I'm not suggesting going crazy—but if the papers can't run these, then they have not bought my humor.

Meanwhile, syndicate executives, as they had since the strip's inception, continued to fire off cautionary critiques:

• Aim at the broad base. The strip is now too highbrow, philosophical.

• Minimize sophisticated gags.

• Be more comic-strip oriented to develop a new Woody Allen audience.

- There's too much emphasis on maintaining the Woody Allen screen character's integrity versus the comic-strip character.

- Let's not have such an emphasis on therapy jokes.

When the director of sales told me we'd just lost a paper in California because the editor felt the strip dealt too much with rejection, disappointment with life, and sometimes even God, Woody said, "I take that as a compliment. If a comic persona can reveal the pain, then that is a mark of how deep the humor is. In the long run, that's what gives it dimension. Of course, if the depressing stuff overwhelms the strip, then you have nothing. But I think you can look at the strips and they're far from symphonies of gloom. I will never please the big market guys. They labor under the delusion that they must aim at the lowest common denominator, but they're wrong. I have never cared about being popular and I won't start now. What's the worst thing that can happen? So they'll cancel the strip."

I felt like a schizophrenic living in a split level at the intersection of two state lines. But patches of equilibrium returned periodically, courtesy of Woody's steadfast sense of irony. One Saturday after we finished our meeting, he said, "I'm getting a ride to my therapist's. If you want to come

along I'll have my guy take you home." We went down in the elevator and climbed into a waiting automobile. I noticed the ubiquitous floppy fedora he habitually wore (to conceal his identity from the masses so he wouldn't be swamped with requests for autographs or otherwise hassled) resting on the armrest between us. Woody told his chauffeur to take me wherever I wanted to go after he got out at his psychotherapist's. After a ten-minute drive the car rolled down Fifth Avenue to a sleek apartment building directly across from the Metropolitan Museum and pulled to a stop in front of a canopy. The broad sidewalk was empty. Woody sat unmoving, chatting amiably. But then, when a gaggle of pedestrians appeared walking north on Fifth, he jammed the protective floppy hat on his head and dashed from the car into the building, barely escaping the curious stares of the passersby. The driver took me across Central Park to the unfashionable West side. There, replays of the floppy hat scene resonated in my unconscious.

A few days later I drew the strip at the bottom of this page (which ran on January 1, 1981).

When Woody came upon it among the week's batch, he simply said, "Very perceptive."

As you look at the collection of strips in the pages that follow and discover that some of the references are outdated, be aware that the feature ran a generation and a half

ago, from 1976 to 1984. During its life Carter and Reagan occupied the Oval Office. The Equal Rights Amendment was having trouble being passed. The movies *10* and *Ordinary People* are mentioned in a gag. The TV series *Dallas* was riding high. There's a strip about pollution in the Hudson, which today, thanks to Pete Seeger's Hudson River sloop *Clearwater* and the group's annual Hudson River Revival events, is now almost perfectly healthy.

IN A NUTSHELL: WHAT IT WAS LIKE TO WORK WITH WOODY

If there was any juicy dish, if the experience had been thorny, you wouldn't have to yank out my fingernails to force me to blab. (Working in the '50s with a different celebrated humorist on another comic strip was a train wreck; his name is in this piece, right up front.) But it was smooth sailing with Woody. Already an international icon, virtually the only director with final cut, the darling of the American moviegoing smart set, clearly the Big Dog in the project, he was nonetheless a paragon: modest, efficient, dependable, focused, loyal, generous to a fault, incisive, serious, and, no surprise, witty. But quietly so. He is never "on." Even when an archetypal Allen quip slips out, there are no eye rolls, no Johnny smirks, no grandstanding, no bada-boom! Woody is grounded, authentic. (Due to good psychotherapy?)

Note that he doesn't hang out with comics, doesn't seek the limelight at benefits and awards shows, doesn't demand that his name be above the title. An integral clue to who he is: There's no Woody Allen Room at the Friars Club.

He also has incredibly clean hands.

And there was a special bonus to the collaboration: It was through him that I discovered See's lollipops.

Finally, keep in mind that though Woody's DNA might be detected by a dogged forensic expert here and there on the tone of this enterprise, he did not write the comic strip. If he had, it probably would have had a smaller audience, but it would have been a hell of a lot funnier.

—Stuart Hample
New York City
2009

Introduction by R. Buckminster Fuller

Cast of Characters

Tetru

Tetrahedron:
Could Be Bucky

Summa

Octahedron:
Girl Student

Cum

Icosahedron:
Boy Student

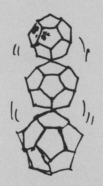

Bigbang

Dodecahedron:
Science Hypothesis

Solidstate

Cube:
Science Hypothesis

Woody

Woody:
Woody

1

HOW COME UNIVERSE?
HOW ELSE WOODY ALLEN?

2

WHO DONE IT?
WOODY HIMSELF SAYS:
"NO WAY TO PROVE GOD."?
WHO ELSE WANTED WOODY
ENOUGH TO CONCEIVE UNIVERSE?

*Woody's audience gaining
one million per week.
1.000.000 x 50 x 80 =
4,000,000,000 =
4 Billion

5

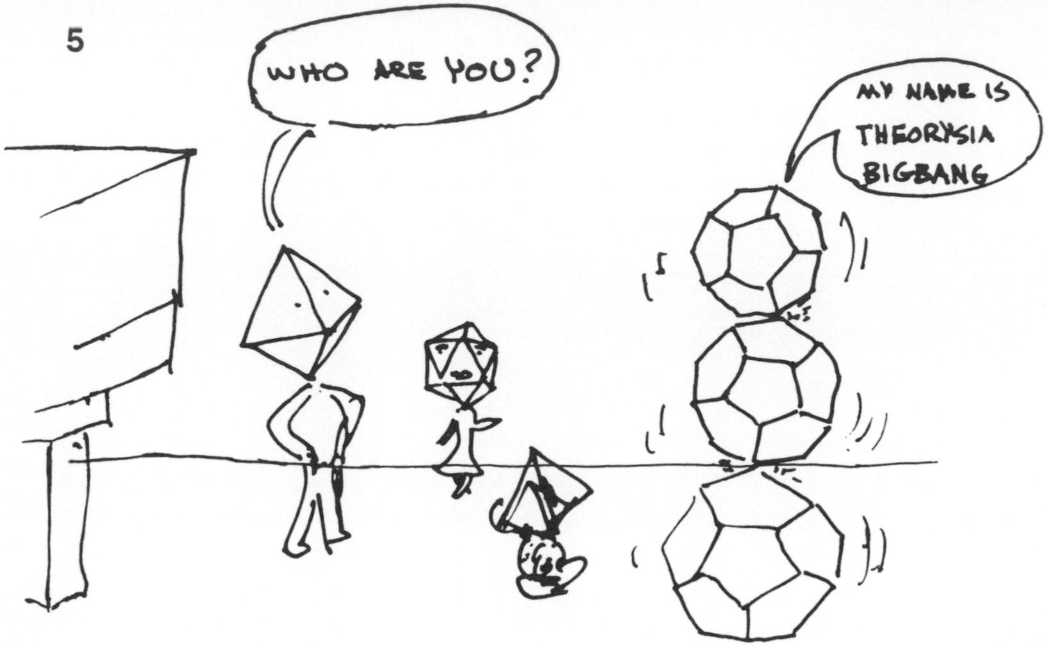
WHO ARE YOU?
MY NAME IS THEORYSIA BIGBANG

6

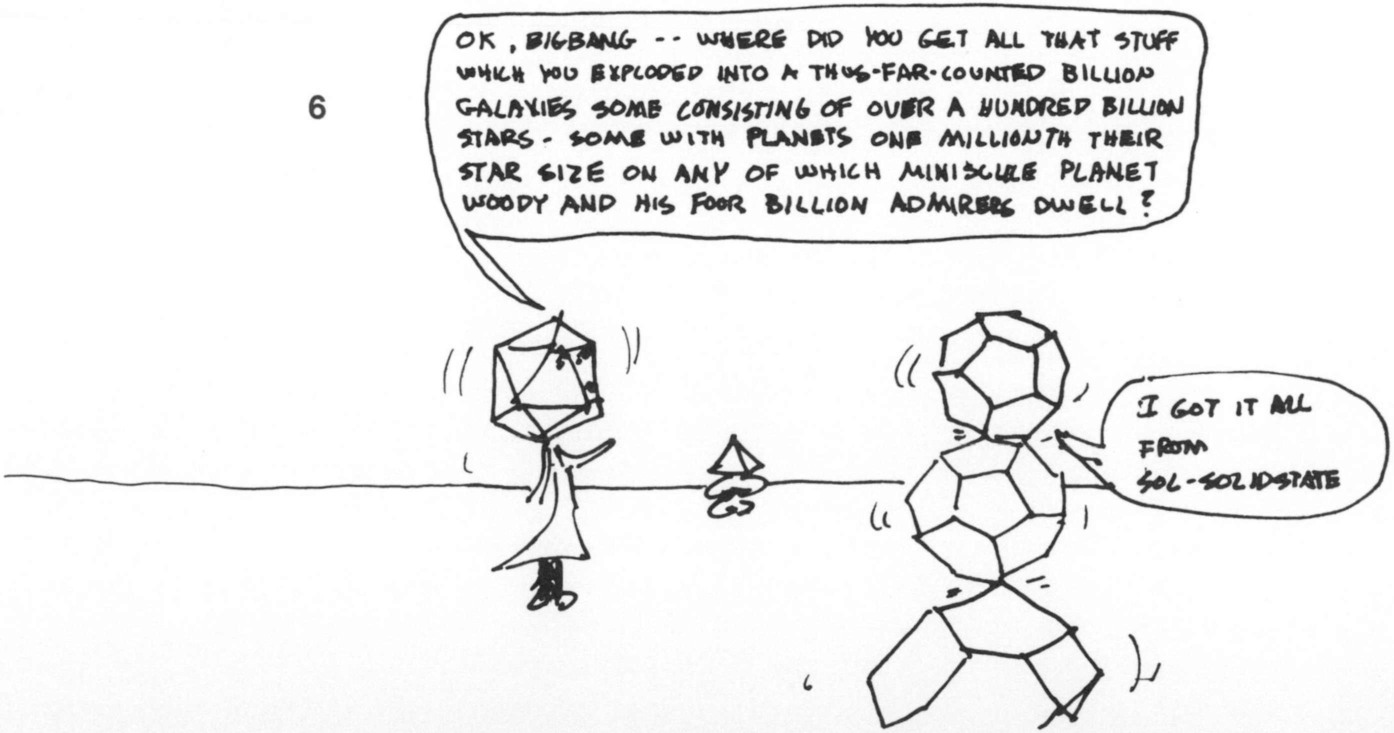
OK, BIGBANG -- WHERE DID YOU GET ALL THAT STUFF WHICH YOU EXPLODED INTO A THUS-FAR-COUNTED BILLION GALAXIES SOME CONSISTING OF OVER A HUNDRED BILLION STARS - SOME WITH PLANETS ONE MILLIONTH THEIR STAR SIZE ON ANY OF WHICH MINISCULE PLANET WOODY AND HIS FOUR BILLION ADMIRERS DWELL?
I GOT IT ALL FROM SOL-SOLIDSTATE

7

We gave her case the reducio-ad-absurdum from the complex to the simplex - we'll give you the same treatment but from the simplex to the complex. OK Solid State--your turn "Bigbang says she does her great thing with all your little things. The average human consists of 8 octillion atoms - written as 8 followed by 28 zeros. Average human beings of all ages weigh 150 pounds. The largest passenger ship ever made weighed 85 thousand tons. The largest ocean going oil tanker fully loaded weighs a million tons.

8

The four billion Earthian humans weigh three hundred million tons-- equal to three hundred super tankers. Planet Earth weighs two trillion times the weight of all humanity. Star Sun weighs a million times planet Earth. Our Milky Way Galaxy weighs one hundred billion times star Sun and all the thus far discovered galaxies weigh a billion times our Milky Way Galaxy--

9

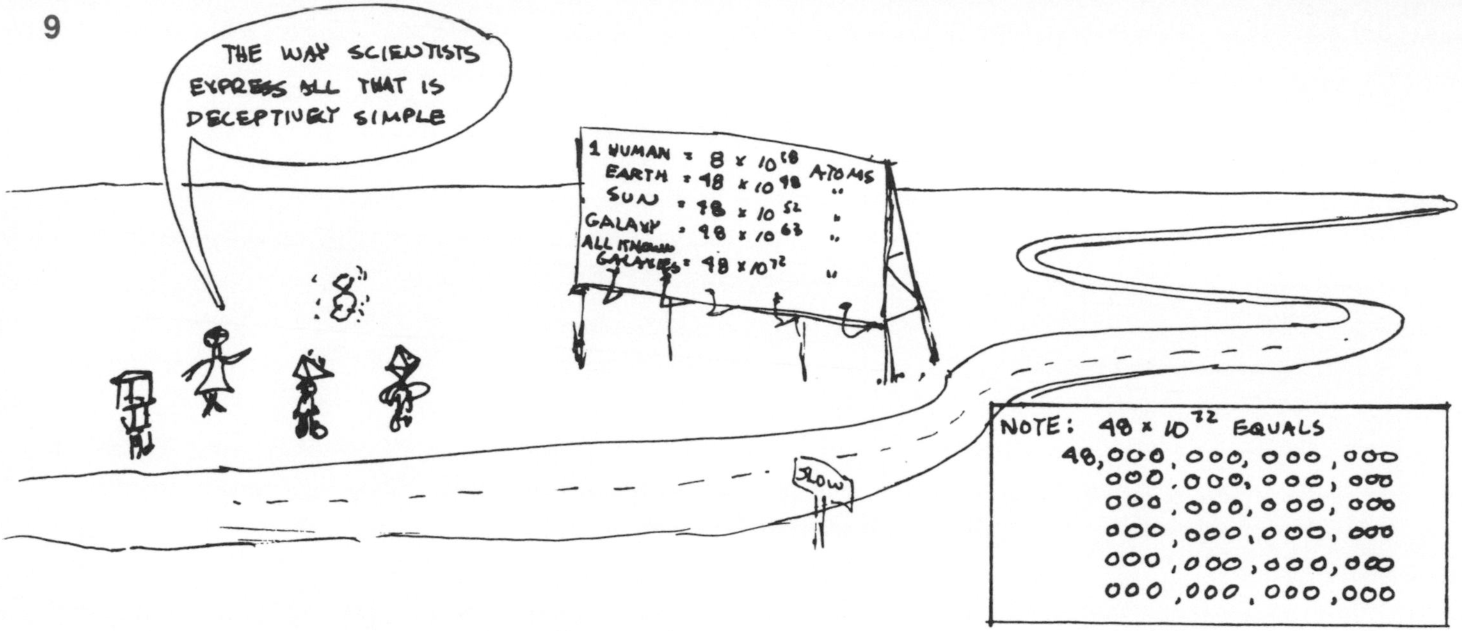

THE WAY SCIENTISTS EXPRESS ALL THAT IS DECEPTIVELY SIMPLE
1 HUMAN = 8 x 10^28 ATOMS
EARTH = 48 x 10^48 "
SUN = 48 x 10^52 "
GALAXY = 48 x 10^63 "
ALL KNOWN GALAXIES = 48 x 10^72 "
SLOW
NOTE: 48 x 10^72 EQUALS
48,000,000,000,000
000,000,000,000
000,000,000,000
000,000,000,000
000,000,000,000
000,000,000,000

10

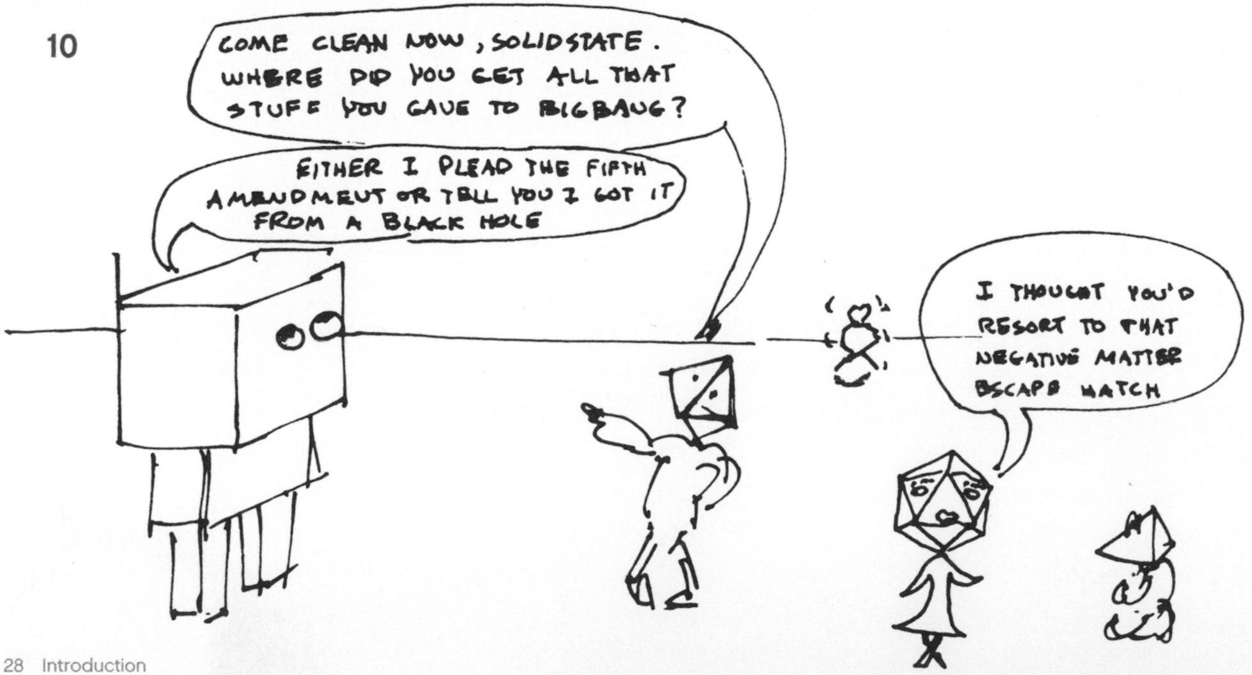

COME CLEAN NOW, SOLIDSTATE. WHERE DID YOU GET ALL THAT STUFF YOU GAVE TO BIGBANG?
EITHER I PLEAD THE FIFTH AMENDMENT OR TELL YOU I GOT IT FROM A BLACK HOLE
I THOUGHT YOU'D RESORT TO THAT NEGATIVE MATTER ESCAPE HATCH

12

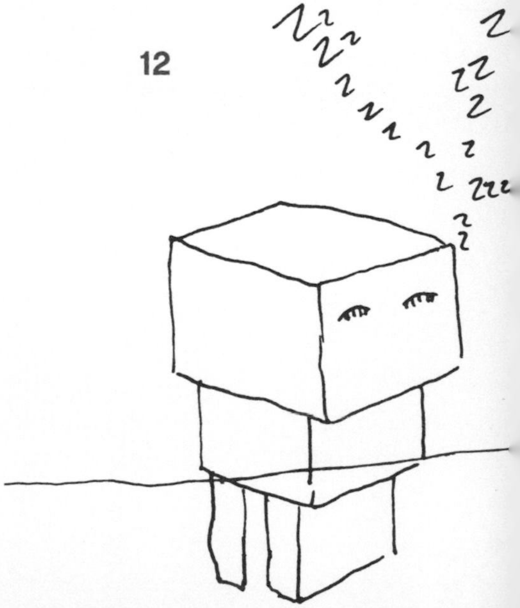

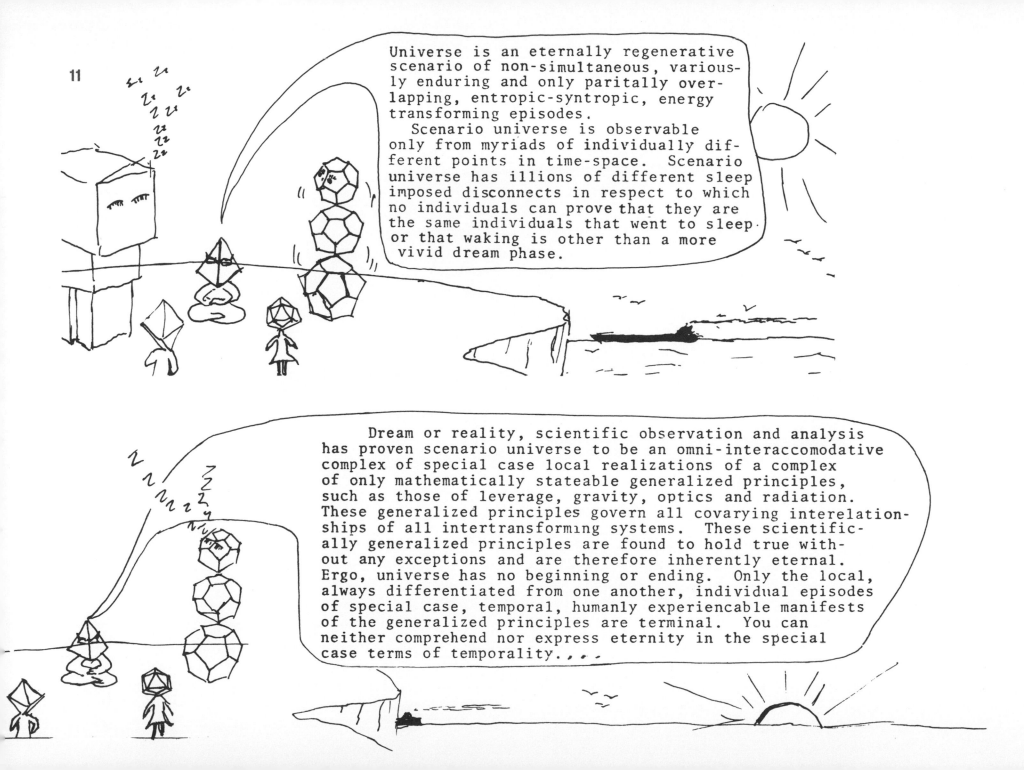

Universe is an eternally regenerative
scenario of non-simultaneous, various-
ly enduring and only paritally over-
lapping, entropic-syntropic, energy
transforming episodes.
  Scenario universe is observable
only from myriads of individually different points in time-space. Scenario
universe has illions of different sleep
imposed disconnects in respect to which
no individuals can prove that they are
the same individuals that went to sleep
or that waking is other than a more
vivid dream phase.

  Dream or reality, scientific observation and analysis
has proven scenario universe to be an omni-interaccomodative
complex of special case local realizations of a complex
of only mathematically stateable generalized principles,
such as those of leverage, gravity, optics and radiation.
These generalized principles govern all covarying interelation-
ships of all intertransforming systems. These scientific-
ally generalized principles are found to hold true without any exceptions and are therefore inherently eternal.
Ergo, universe has no beginning or ending. Only the local,
always differentiated from one another, individual episodes
of special case, temporal, humanly experiencable manifests
of the generalized principles are terminal. You can
neither comprehend nor express eternity in the special
case terms of temporality. . . .

13

14

To comprehend scenario universe in conradistinction to the
one frame of a moving picture, for instance a picture of a
it takes many frames to convince us that the butterfly is
of frames to disclose butterflies' interfunctioning with
of frames to elucidate the regenerative interfunctioning
and a thousand generations of human experience historians
and supporting such a phenomenon as humans, their physical
which human minds may deduce, comprehend and employ cosmic
varsity team functioning as local-universe harvesting moni
ever disclose to any one individual what it is all about
eternally regenerative, is the only 100% efficient system
humans to separate individual viewpoints ergo, designs us

BUTTERFLY

classical "One Big Simultaneous Thing" universe we first note that
caterpillar, does not tell us it is going to become a butterfly and
flying - millions of frames to disclose how the butterfly flies: billions
planet Earth's ecological regeneration of its sentient life; quadrillions
of planet Earth's ecology with cosmic regeneration; quintillions of frames
to piece together the total cosmic strategy's raision-d'etre for evolving
and metaphysical information apprehending and storing organisms from
generalized principles aboard planet Earth, thus to fuffill their cosmic
tors and local universe problem solvers - but no number of frames will
and how come. One thing is clear and that is that the universe, being
and is therefore a magnificent design which deliberately confines we
to be limited and not to be GOD.

15

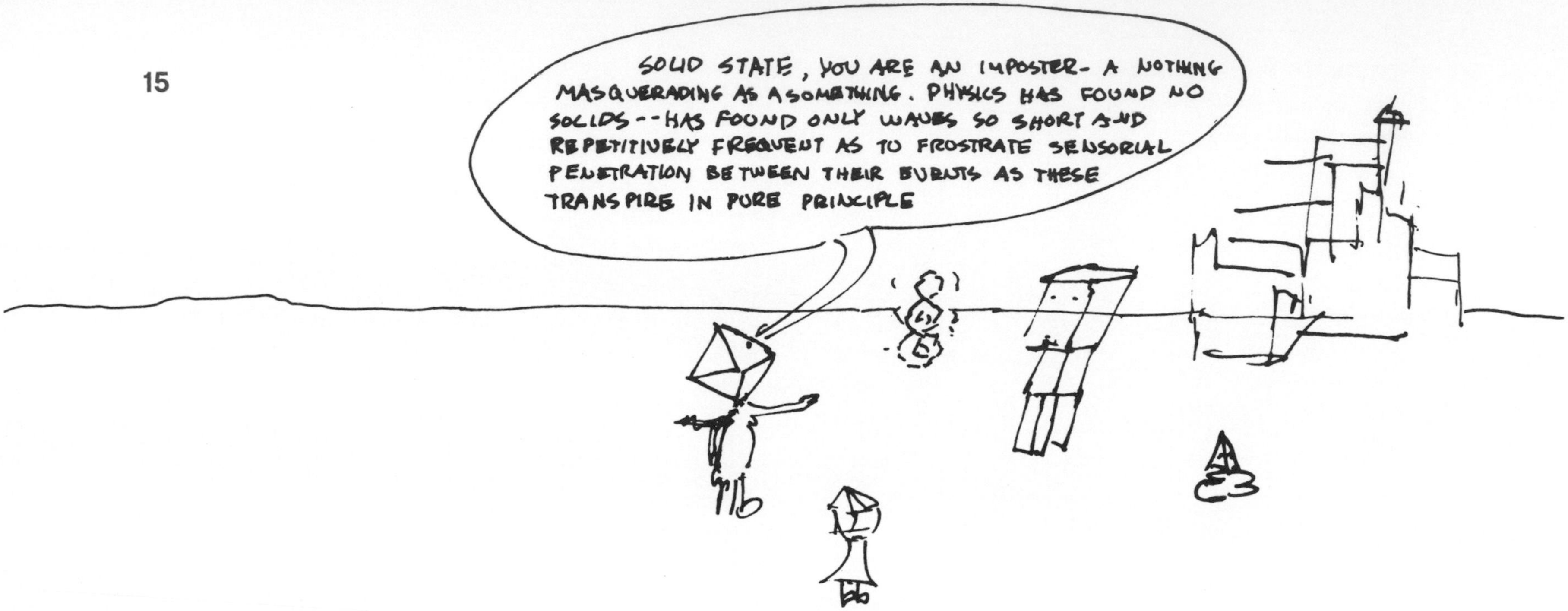
SOLID STATE, YOU ARE AN IMPOSTER- A NOTHING MASQUERADING AS A SOMETHING. PHYSICS HAS FOUND NO SOLIDS--HAS FOUND ONLY WAVES SO SHORT AND REPETITIVELY FREQUENT AS TO FROSTRATE SENSORIAL PENETRATION BETWEEN THEIR EVENTS AS THESE TRANSPIRE IN PURE PRINCIPLE

16

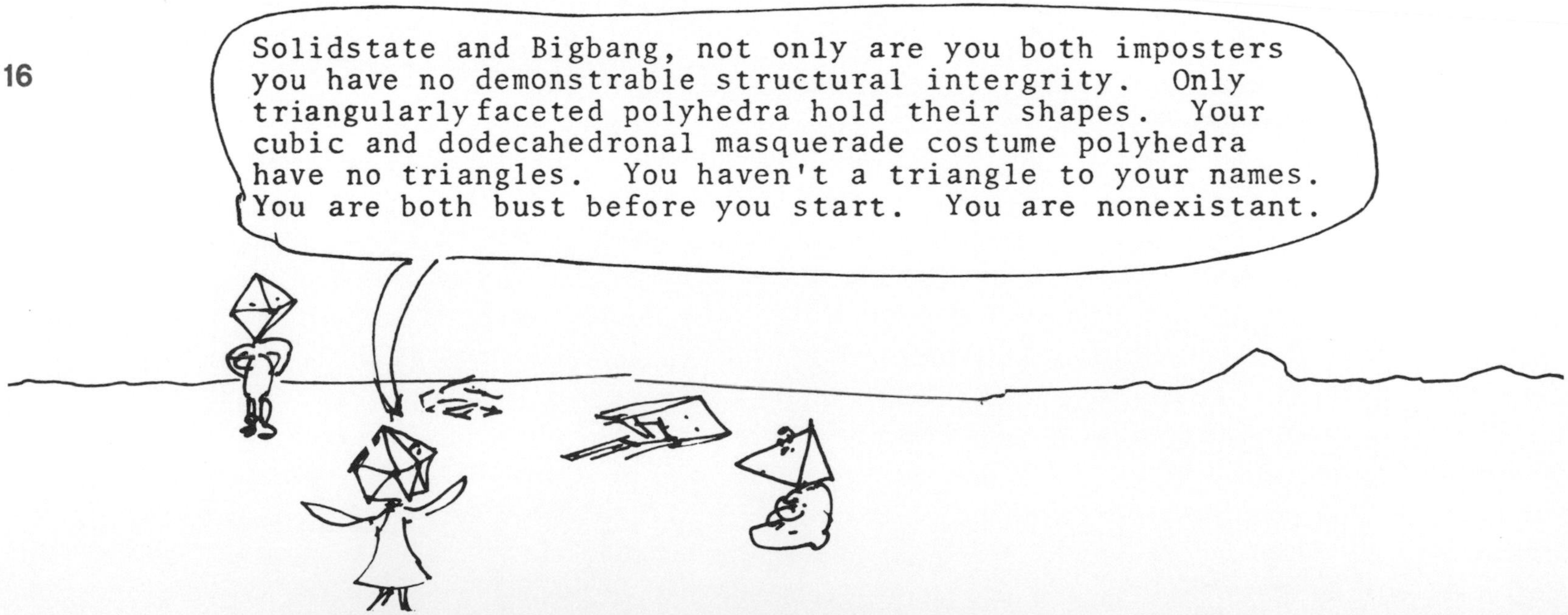
Solidstate and Bigbang, not only are you both imposters you have no demonstrable structural intergrity. Only triangularly faceted polyhedra hold their shapes. Your cubic and dodecahedronal masquerade costume polyhedra have no triangles. You haven't a triangle to your names. You are both bust before you start. You are nonexistant.

17

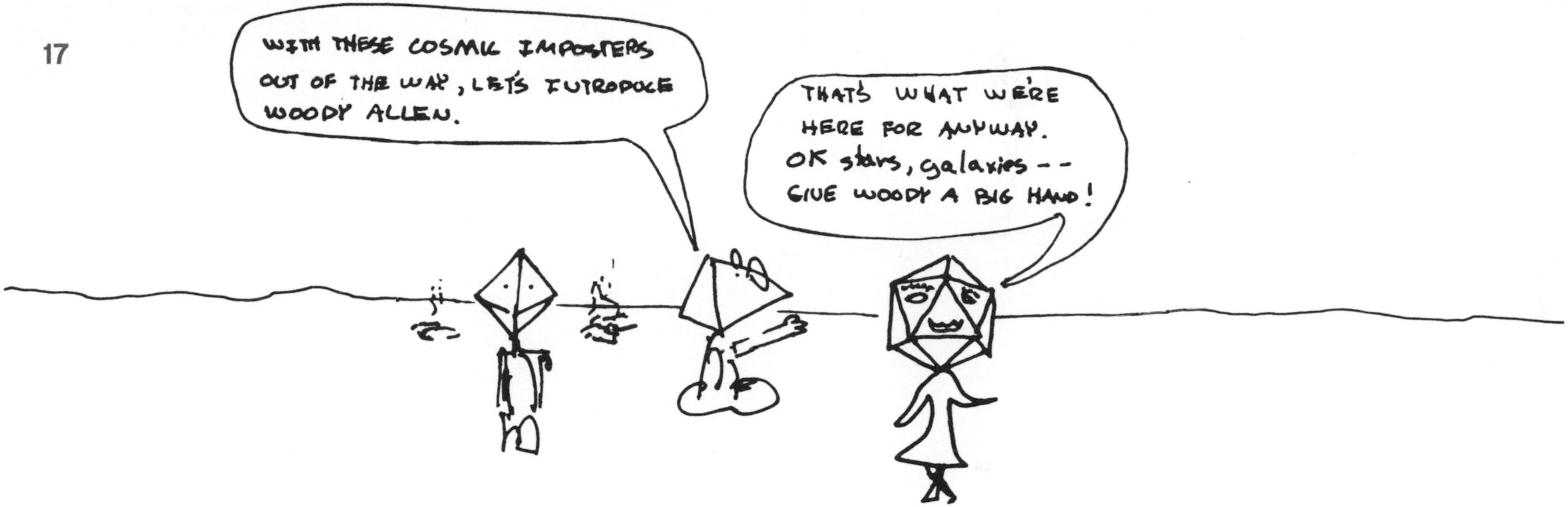
WITH THESE COSMIC IMPOSTERS OUT OF THE WAY, LET'S INTRODUCE WOODY ALLEN.
THAT'S WHAT WE'RE HERE FOR ANYWAY. OK stars, galaxies -- GIVE WOODY A BIG HAND!

18

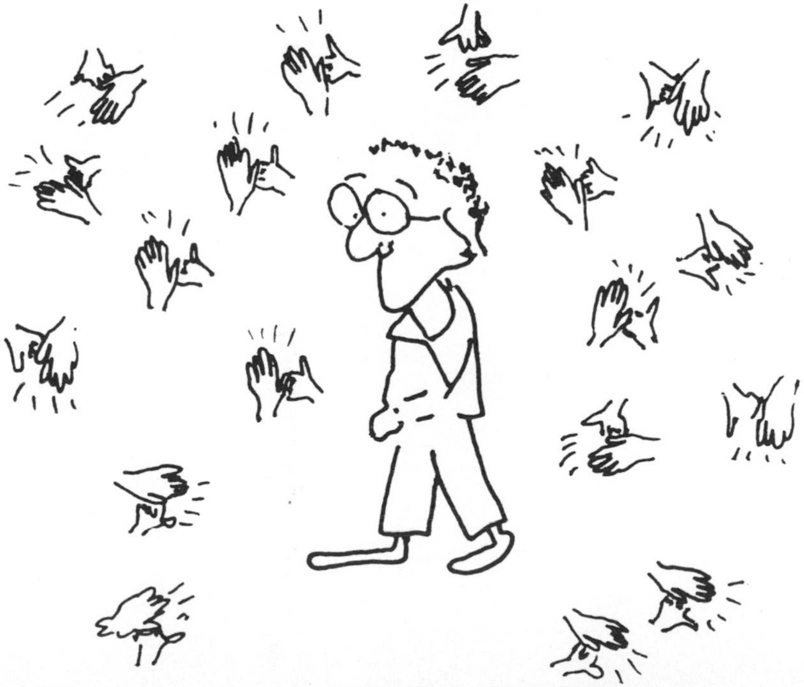

19 Woody is the master of ceremonies in what may be the last act of humans on Planet Earth or the first act of Humans in Universe. Human muscle is nothing in the cosmic energy scheme - Human minds are cosmically operative. Humans are included in universe for their mind capability function in support of the integrity of eternally regenerative universe. As of what is known as 1977 human muscle, cunning and guns are in control of human affairs. Two individuals are paid over a million dollars by T.V. producers for punching each others' heads for ten minutes... Earthian humans are going through their final ten yearexam as to whether they qualify to continue in universe. If physical power persists, we fail; if mind takes command, we qualify.

20 THE EINSTEIN SCHOOL OF SCIENTISTS DECLARE: "ALL THAT IS PHYSICAL IS ENERGY EITHER ASSOCIATIVE AS MATTER OR DISSASSOCIATIVE AS RADIATION WITH ONE TRANSFORMABLE INTO THE OTHER

THE SCIENTISTS ALSO SAID: "ALL PHYSICAL ENERGY CAN MOVE INSTRUMENT POINTERS EITHER GRAVITATIONALLY OR ELECTROMAGNETICALLY."

AND IT FOLLOWS THAT "ANY AND ALL THE EXPERIENCES THAT DO NOT MOVE INSTRUMENT POINTERS ARE METAPHYSICAL."

21

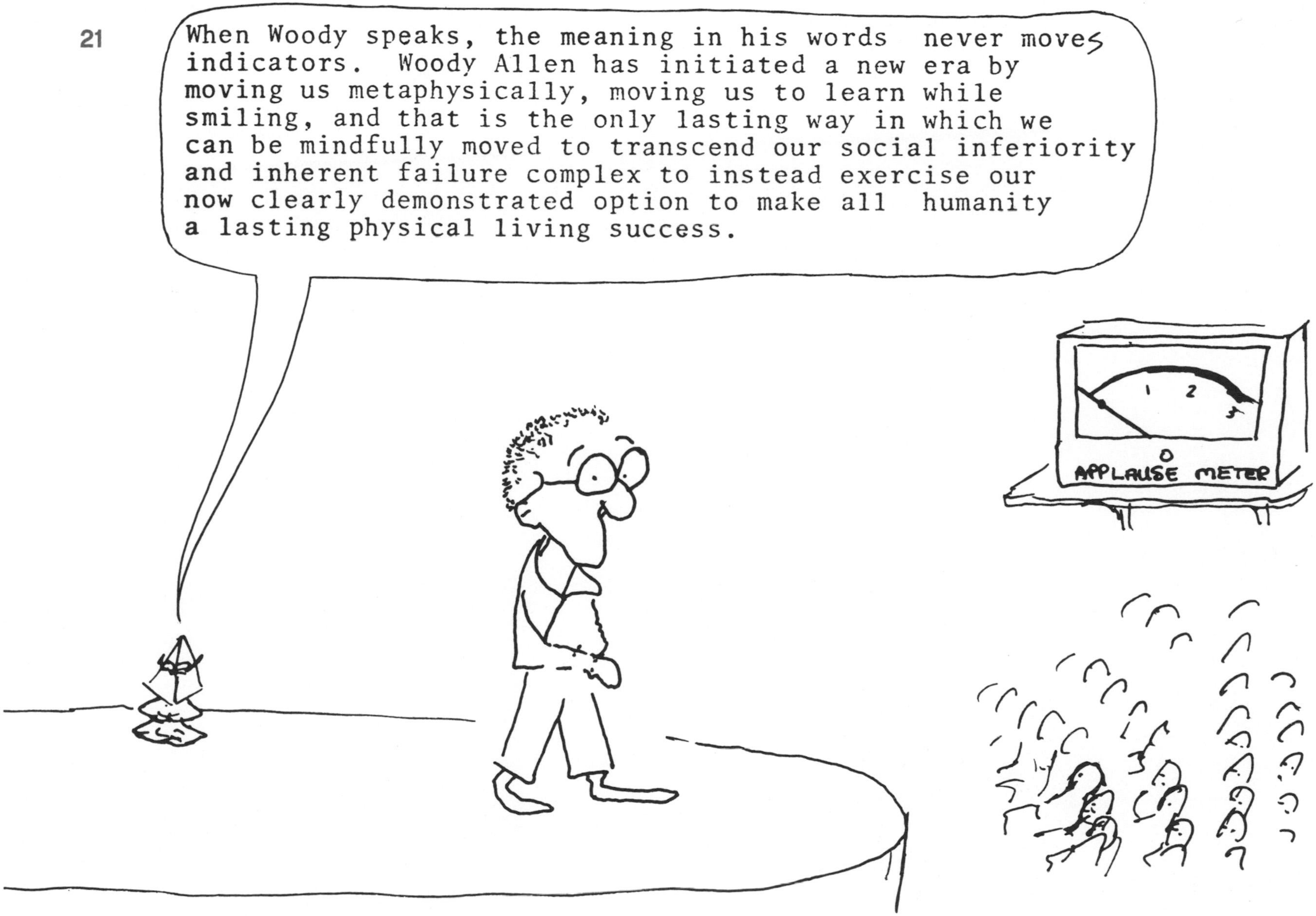
When Woody speaks, the meaning in his words never moves indicators. Woody Allen has initiated a new era by moving us metaphysically, moving us to learn while smiling, and that is the only lasting way in which we can be mindfully moved to transcend our social inferiority and inherent failure complex to instead exercise our now clearly demonstrated option to make all humanity a lasting physical living success.
APPLAUSE METER

Worms in a Cosmic Plan

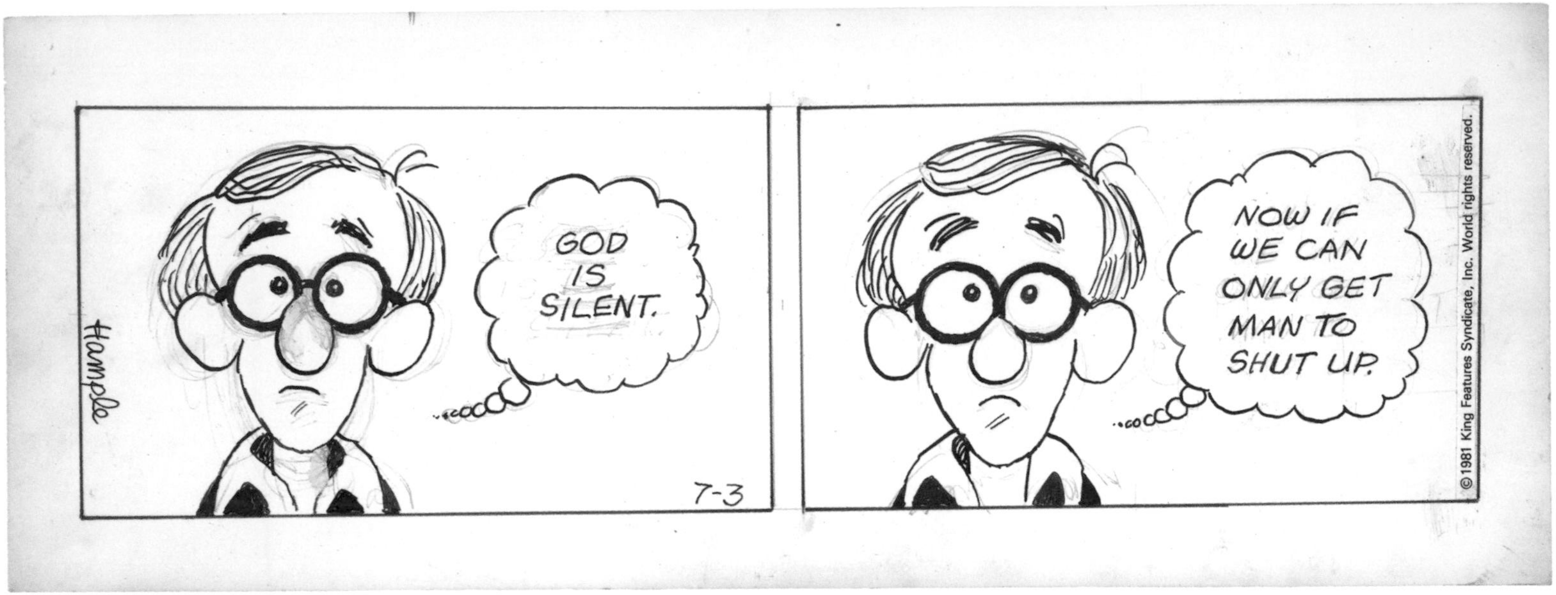
Hample
GOD IS SILENT.
7-3
NOW IF WE CAN ONLY GET MAN TO SHUT UP.
© 1981 King Features Syndicate, Inc. World rights reserved.

July 3, 1981

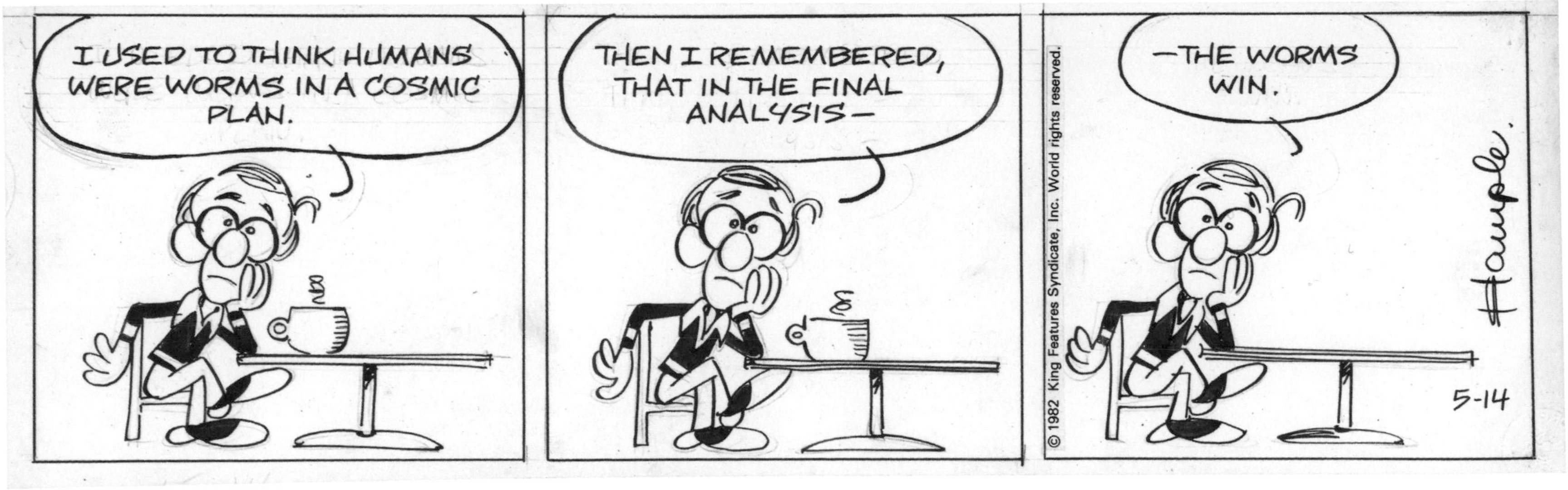
I USED TO THINK HUMANS WERE WORMS IN A COSMIC PLAN.
THEN I REMEMBERED, THAT IN THE FINAL ANALYSIS—
© 1982 King Features Syndicate, Inc. World rights reserved.
—THE WORMS WIN.
Hample.
5-14

May 14, 1982

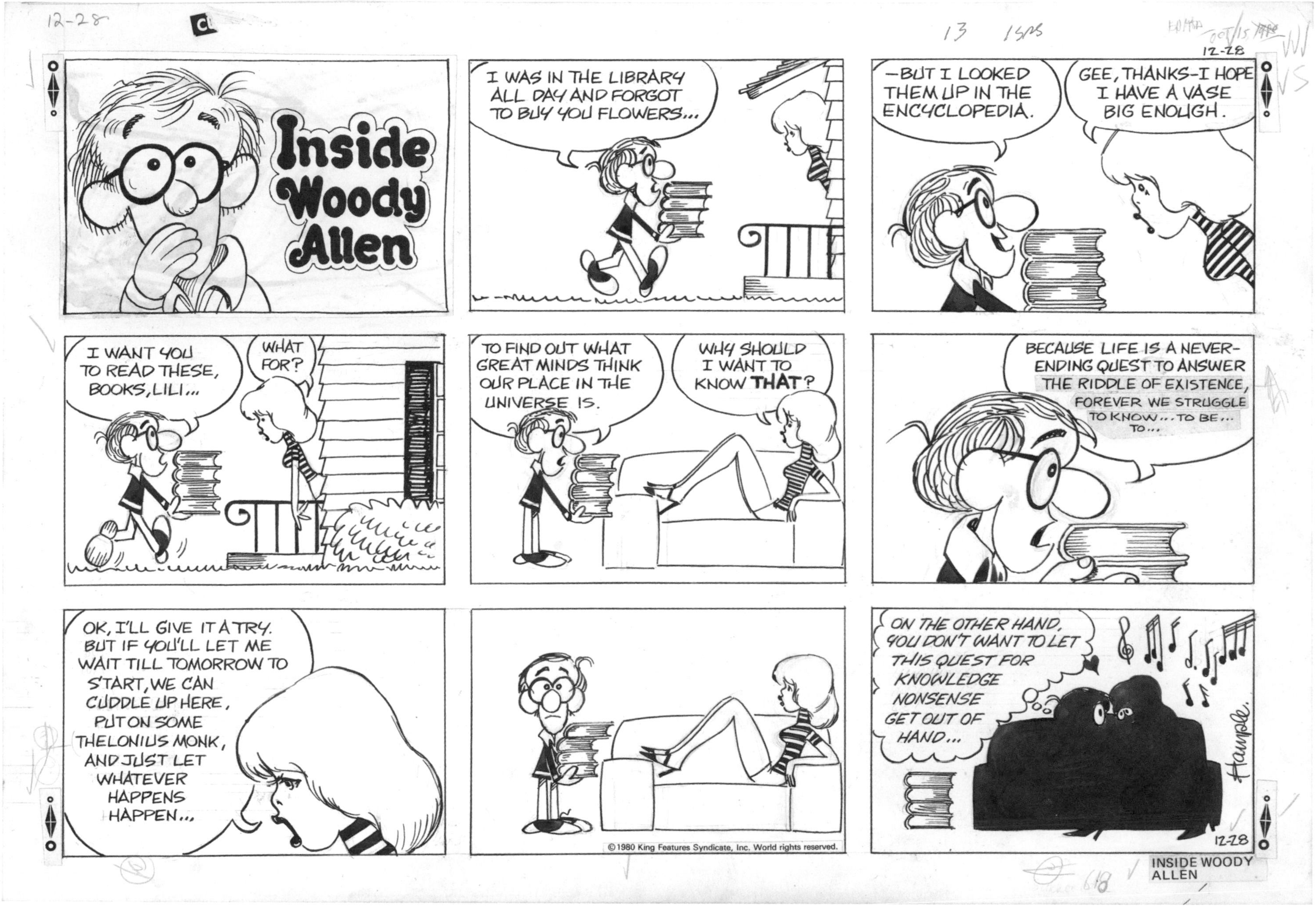
Inside Woody Allen
I WAS IN THE LIBRARY ALL DAY AND FORGOT TO BUY YOU FLOWERS...
—BUT I LOOKED THEM UP IN THE ENCYCLOPEDIA.
GEE, THANKS—I HOPE I HAVE A VASE BIG ENOUGH.
I WANT YOU TO READ THESE, BOOKS, LILI...
WHAT FOR?
TO FIND OUT WHAT GREAT MINDS THINK OUR PLACE IN THE UNIVERSE IS.
WHY SHOULD I WANT TO KNOW THAT?
BECAUSE LIFE IS A NEVER-ENDING QUEST TO ANSWER THE RIDDLE OF EXISTENCE, FOREVER WE STRUGGLE TO KNOW... TO BE... TO...
OK, I'LL GIVE IT A TRY. BUT IF YOU'LL LET ME WAIT TILL TOMORROW TO START, WE CAN CUDDLE UP HERE, PUT ON SOME THELONIUS MONK, AND JUST LET WHATEVER HAPPENS HAPPEN...
© 1980 King Features Syndicate, Inc. World rights reserved.
ON THE OTHER HAND, YOU DON'T WANT TO LET THIS QUEST FOR KNOWLEDGE NONSENSE GET OUT OF HAND...
Hample
12-28
INSIDE WOODY ALLEN

December 28, 1980. The first two panels of each Sunday page were written to accomodate newspapers that printed the gag in three rows. For papers where space was limited, the first row was dropped without affecting the rest of the strip.

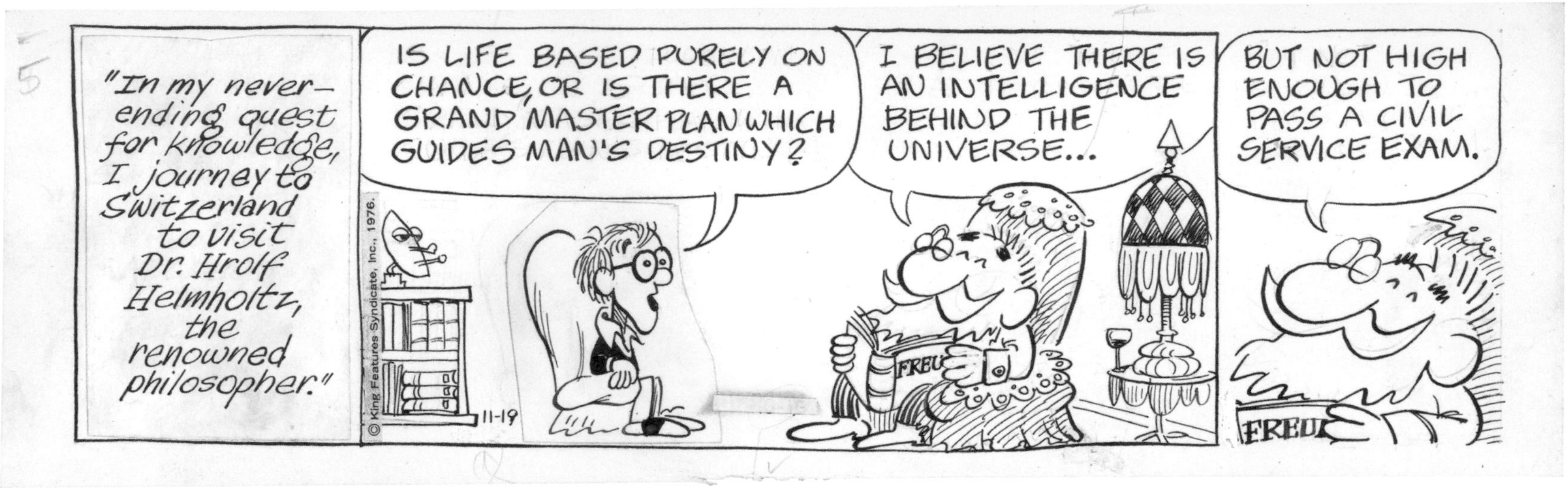
"In my never-ending quest for knowledge, I journey to Switzerland to visit Dr. Hrolf Helmholtz, the renowned philosopher."
IS LIFE BASED PURELY ON CHANCE, OR IS THERE A GRAND MASTER PLAN WHICH GUIDES MAN'S DESTINY?
I BELIEVE THERE IS AN INTELLIGENCE BEHIND THE UNIVERSE...
BUT NOT HIGH ENOUGH TO PASS A CIVIL SERVICE EXAM.
© King Features Syndicate, Inc., 1976.
11-19

November 19, 1976

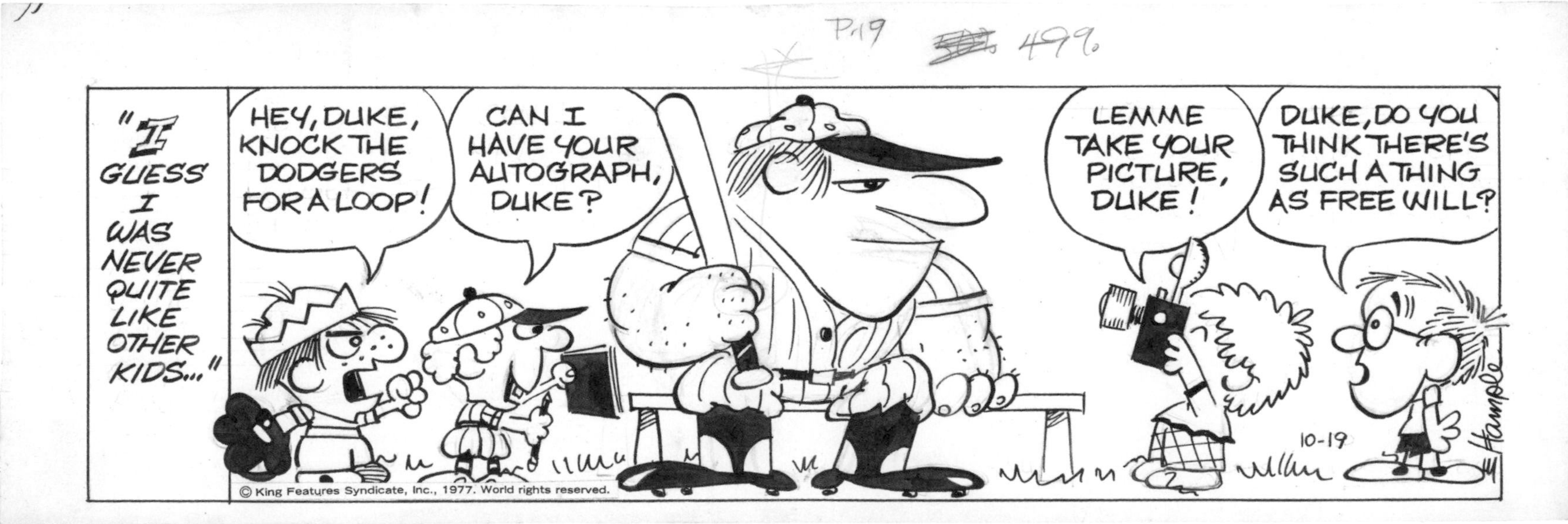
"I GUESS I WAS NEVER QUITE LIKE OTHER KIDS..."
HEY, DUKE, KNOCK THE DODGERS FOR A LOOP!
CAN I HAVE YOUR AUTOGRAPH, DUKE?
LEMME TAKE YOUR PICTURE, DUKE!
DUKE, DO YOU THINK THERE'S SUCH A THING AS FREE WILL?
10-19
Hample
© King Features Syndicate, Inc., 1977. World rights reserved.

October 19, 1977

Inside Woody Allen

AFTER A BIG MEAL THERE'S NOTHING LIKE READING.

I WONDER IF THEY HAVE ANY BOOKS ON FOOD POISONING.

WHAT IS TIME, UNCLE WOODY?

WELL, ARISTOTLE THOUGHT TIME MIGHT BE A QUANTITY.

WAS HE RIGHT?

PUT IT LIKE THIS: HIS TIME SHOP FAILED WHEN HE FOUND OUT HE COULDN'T GIFT WRAP IT

PLATO THOUGHT PERHAPS TIME WAS A CONTAINER IN WHICH EVENTS OCCURRED.

KANT CALLED TIME "THE A PRIORI FORM OF INTERNAL INTUITION" BUT THIS WAS TOO LONG, SO HE NICKNAMED IT "TIME."

THE EXISTENTIALISTS PREFER TO THINK OF TIME NOT AS MERE UNIFORM HOURS AND MINUTES, BUT AS THE TIME WE EXPERIENCE. LIFE AND DEATH ARE TIMES. SO ARE THE SEASONS. AND YET...

YAWN

10-15

SORRY TO INTERRUPT, BUT WHEN DO YOU GET TO THE PART ABOUT THE BIG HAND AND THE LITTLE HAND?

Hample

WOODY ALLEN

October 15, 1978

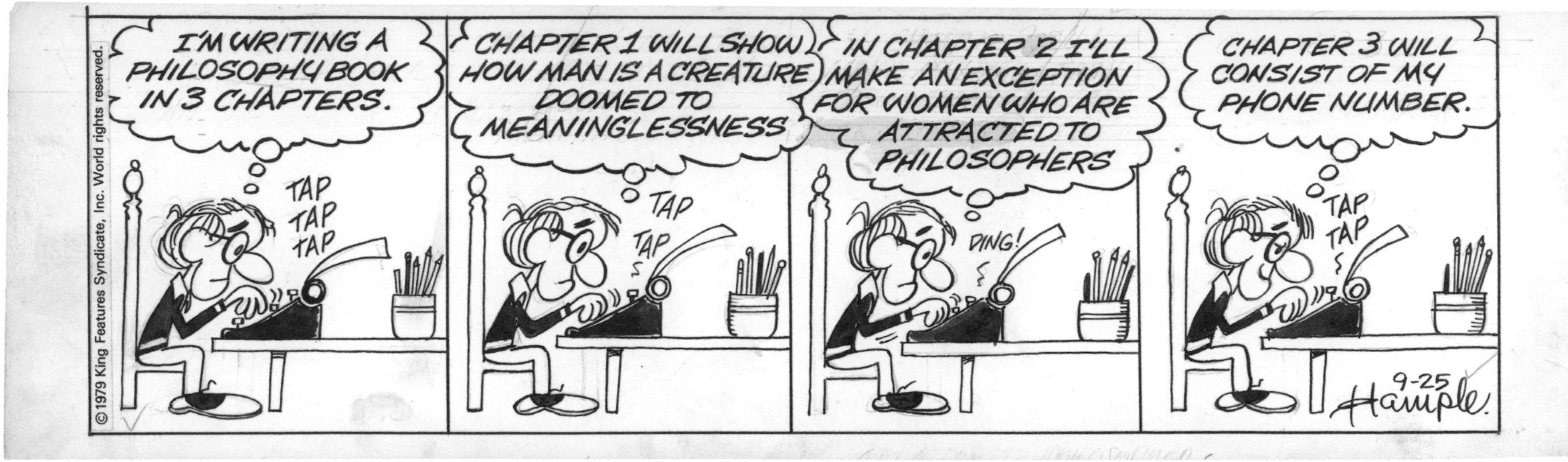

I'M WRITING A PHILOSOPHY BOOK IN 3 CHAPTERS.
TAP TAP TAP
CHAPTER 1 WILL SHOW HOW MAN IS A CREATURE DOOMED TO MEANINGLESSNESS
TAP TAP
IN CHAPTER 2 I'LL MAKE AN EXCEPTION FOR WOMEN WHO ARE ATTRACTED TO PHILOSOPHERS
DING!
CHAPTER 3 WILL CONSIST OF MY PHONE NUMBER.
TAP TAP
9-25
Hample.
© 1979 King Features Syndicate, Inc. World rights reserved.

September 25, 1979

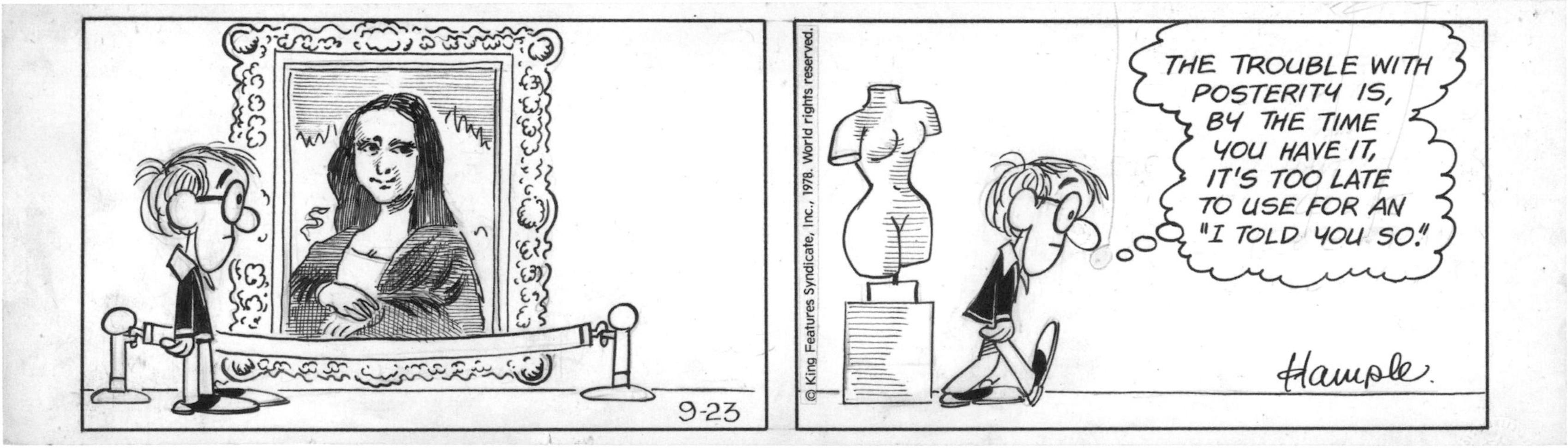

9-23
THE TROUBLE WITH POSTERITY IS, BY THE TIME YOU HAVE IT, IT'S TOO LATE TO USE FOR AN "I TOLD YOU SO."
Hample.
© King Features Syndicate, Inc., 1978. World rights reserved.

September 23, 1978

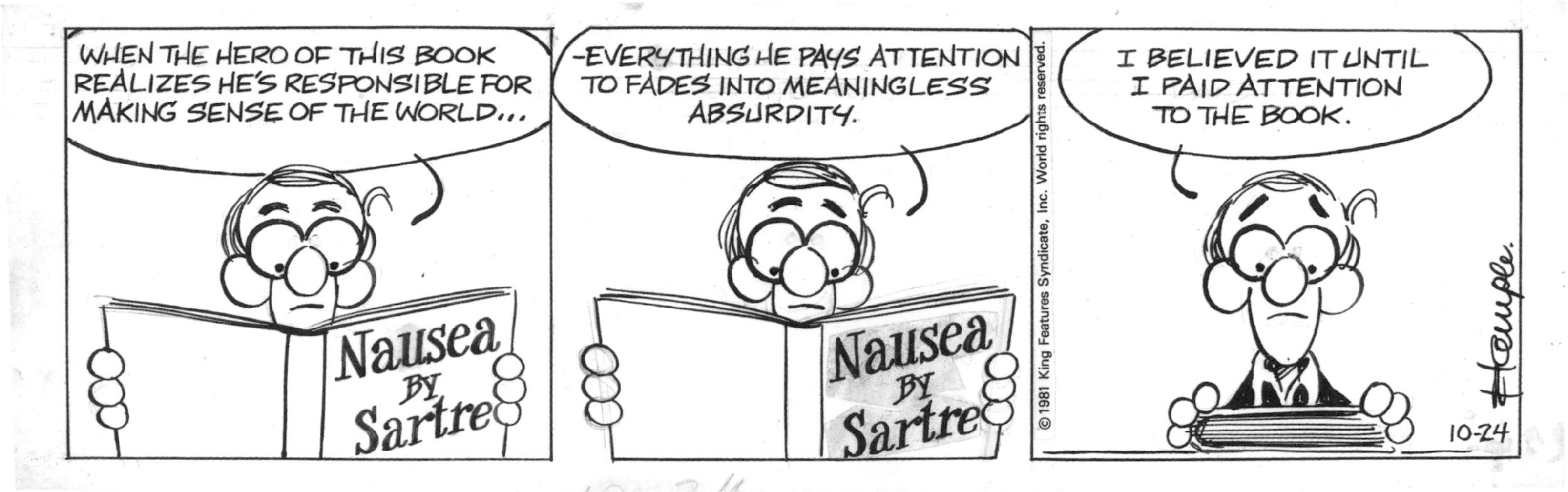
WHEN THE HERO OF THIS BOOK REALIZES HE'S RESPONSIBLE FOR MAKING SENSE OF THE WORLD...
Nausea BY Sartre
-EVERYTHING HE PAYS ATTENTION TO FADES INTO MEANINGLESS ABSURDITY.
Nausea BY Sartre
© 1981 King Features Syndicate, Inc. World rights reserved.
I BELIEVED IT UNTIL I PAID ATTENTION TO THE BOOK.
Hample
10-24

October 24, 1981

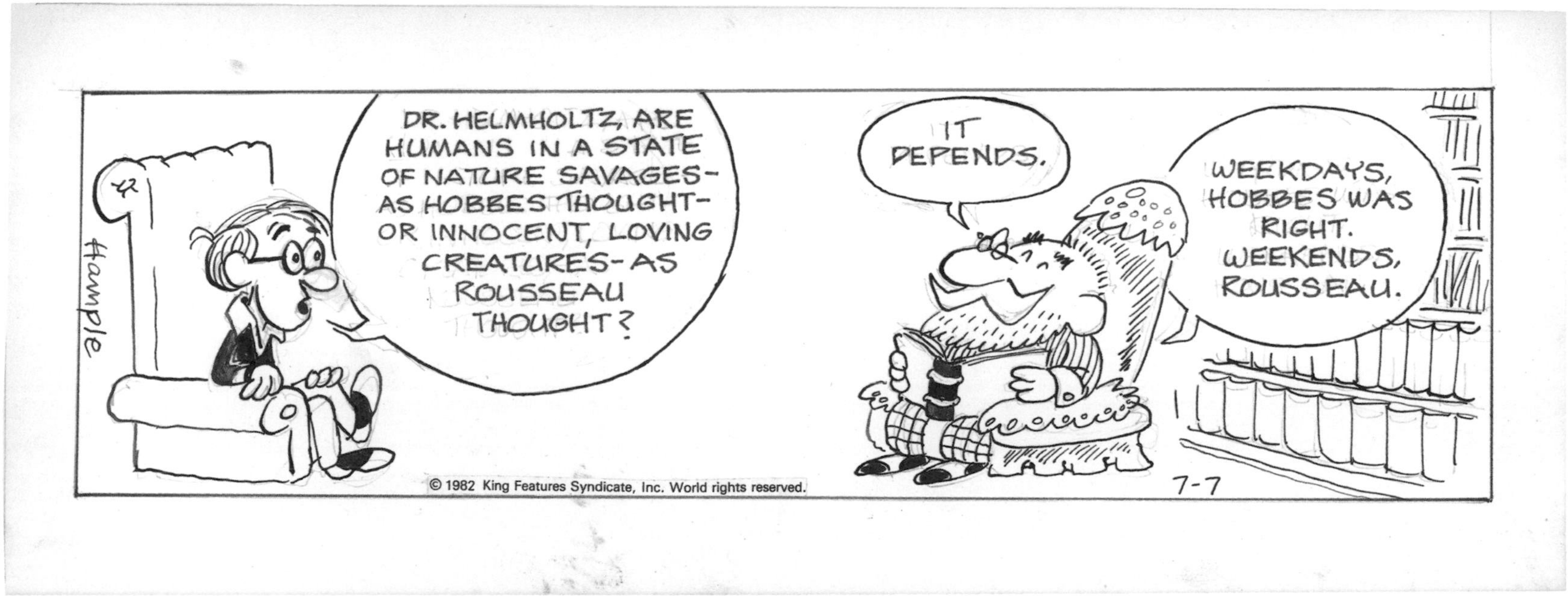
Hample
DR. HELMHOLTZ, ARE HUMANS IN A STATE OF NATURE SAVAGES- AS HOBBES THOUGHT- OR INNOCENT, LOVING CREATURES- AS ROUSSEAU THOUGHT?
IT DEPENDS.
WEEKDAYS, HOBBES WAS RIGHT. WEEKENDS, ROUSSEAU.
© 1982 King Features Syndicate, Inc. World rights reserved.
7-7

July 7, 1982

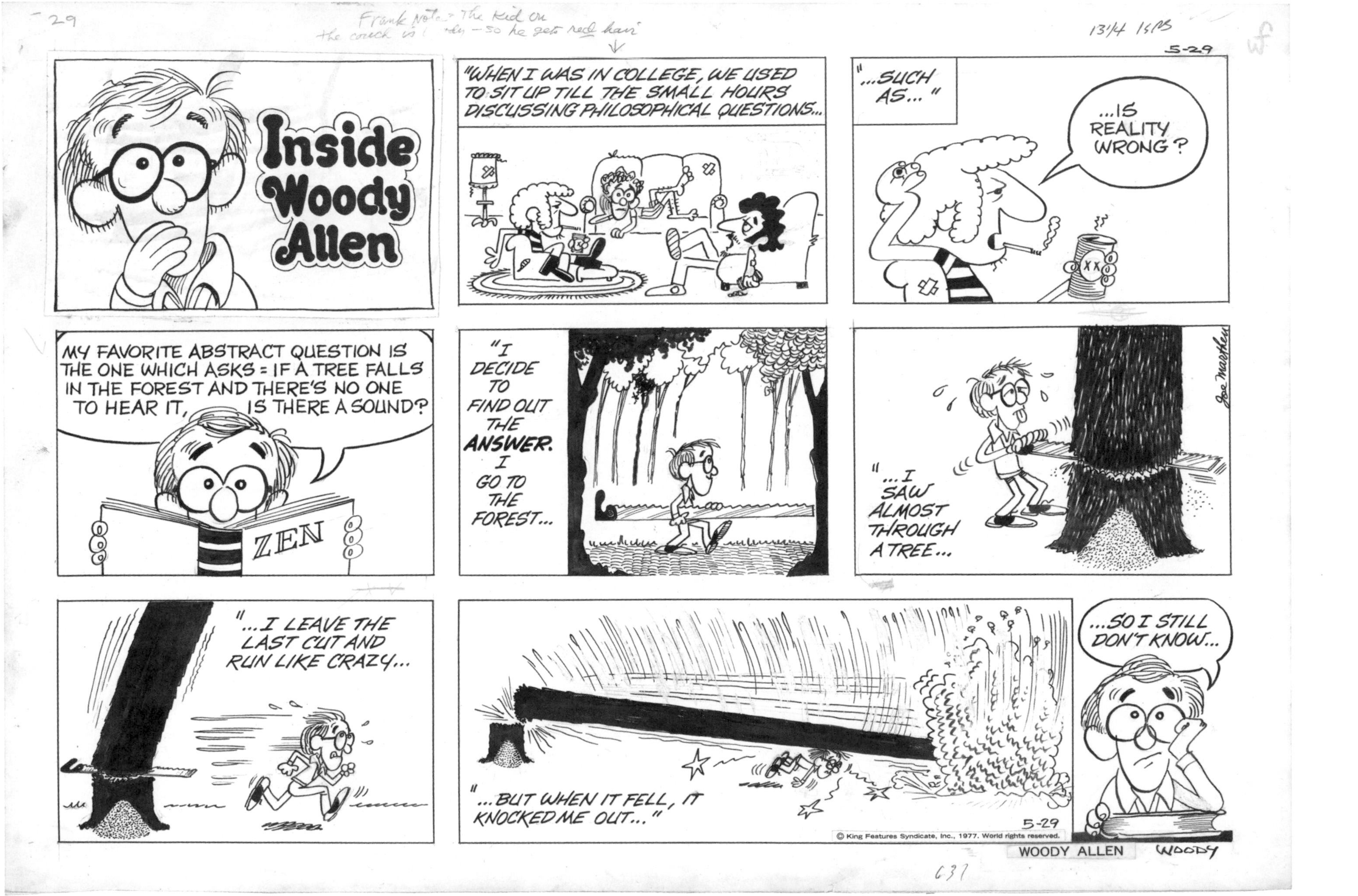
Inside Woody Allen
"WHEN I WAS IN COLLEGE, WE USED TO SIT UP TILL THE SMALL HOURS DISCUSSING PHILOSOPHICAL QUESTIONS...
"...SUCH AS..."
...IS REALITY WRONG?
MY FAVORITE ABSTRACT QUESTION IS THE ONE WHICH ASKS = IF A TREE FALLS IN THE FOREST AND THERE'S NO ONE TO HEAR IT, IS THERE A SOUND?
ZEN
"I DECIDE TO FIND OUT THE ANSWER. I GO TO THE FOREST...
"...I SAW ALMOST THROUGH A TREE...
Joe Marthen
"...I LEAVE THE LAST CUT AND RUN LIKE CRAZY...
"...BUT WHEN IT FELL, IT KNOCKED ME OUT..."
...SO I STILL DON'T KNOW...
5-29
© King Features Syndicate, Inc., 1977. World rights reserved.
WOODY ALLEN
WOODY

May 29,1977

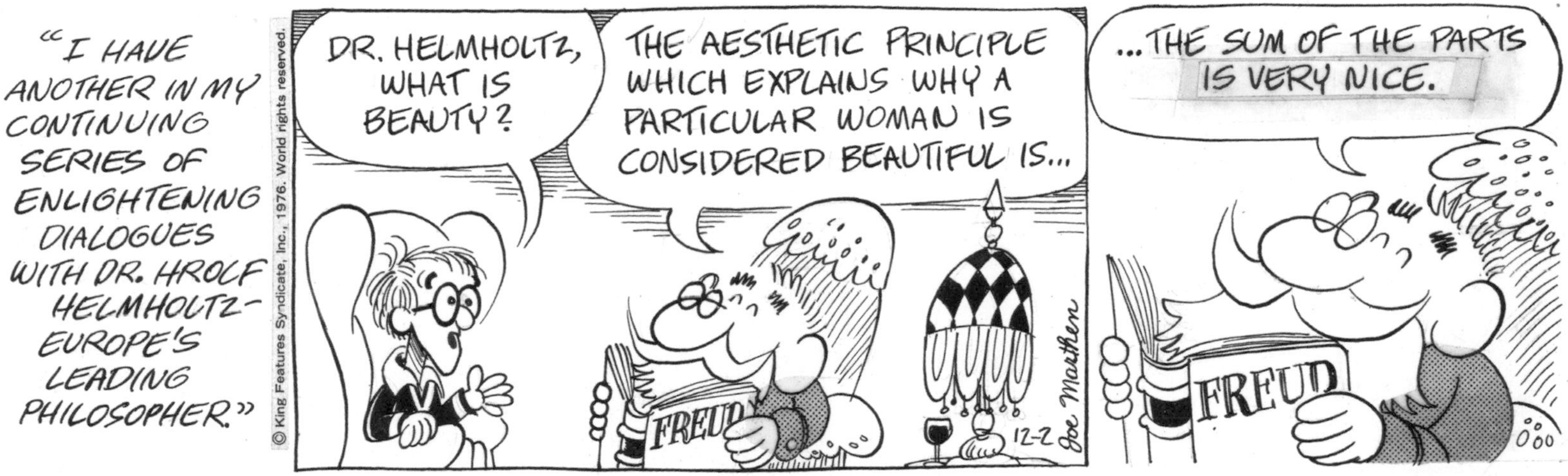
"I HAVE ANOTHER IN MY CONTINUING SERIES OF ENLIGHTENING DIALOGUES WITH DR. HROLF HELMHOLTZ-EUROPE'S LEADING PHILOSOPHER."
© King Features Syndicate, Inc., 1976. World rights reserved.
DR. HELMHOLTZ, WHAT IS BEAUTY?
THE AESTHETIC PRINCIPLE WHICH EXPLAINS WHY A PARTICULAR WOMAN IS CONSIDERED BEAUTIFUL IS...
FREUD
12-2
Joe Marthen
...THE SUM OF THE PARTS IS VERY NICE.
FREUD

December 2, 1976

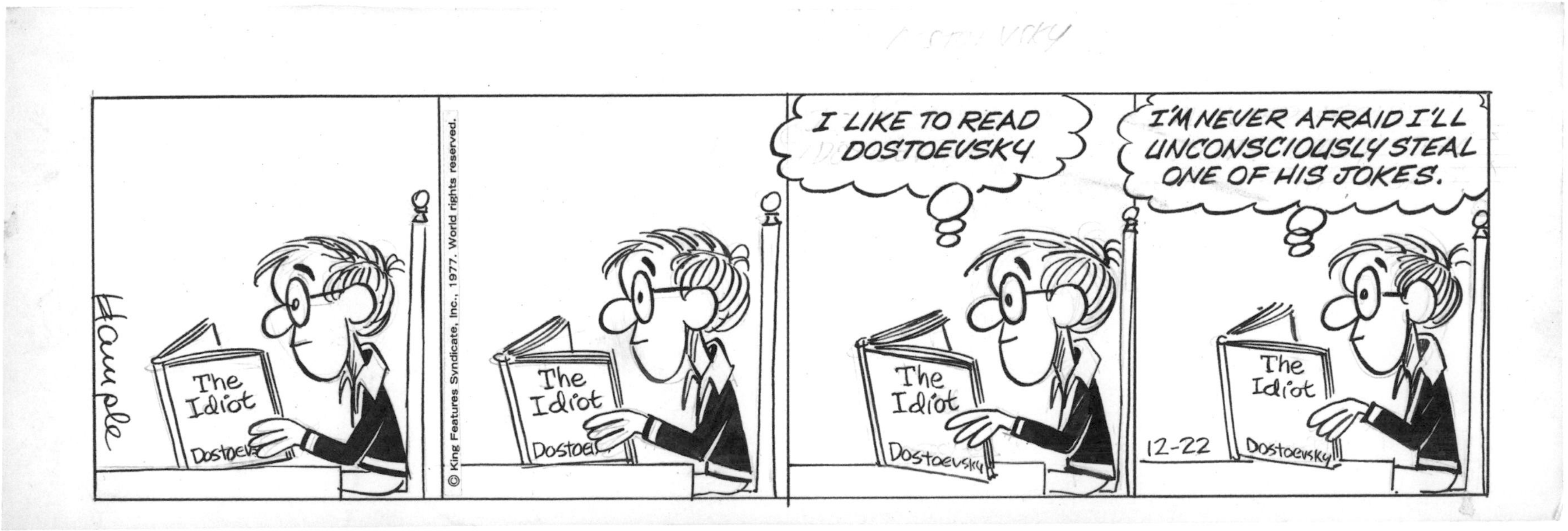
Hample
The Idiot
Dostoevsky
© King Features Syndicate, Inc., 1977. World rights reserved.
I LIKE TO READ DOSTOEVSKY
I'M NEVER AFRAID I'LL UNCONSCIOUSLY STEAL ONE OF HIS JOKES.
12-22

December 22, 1977

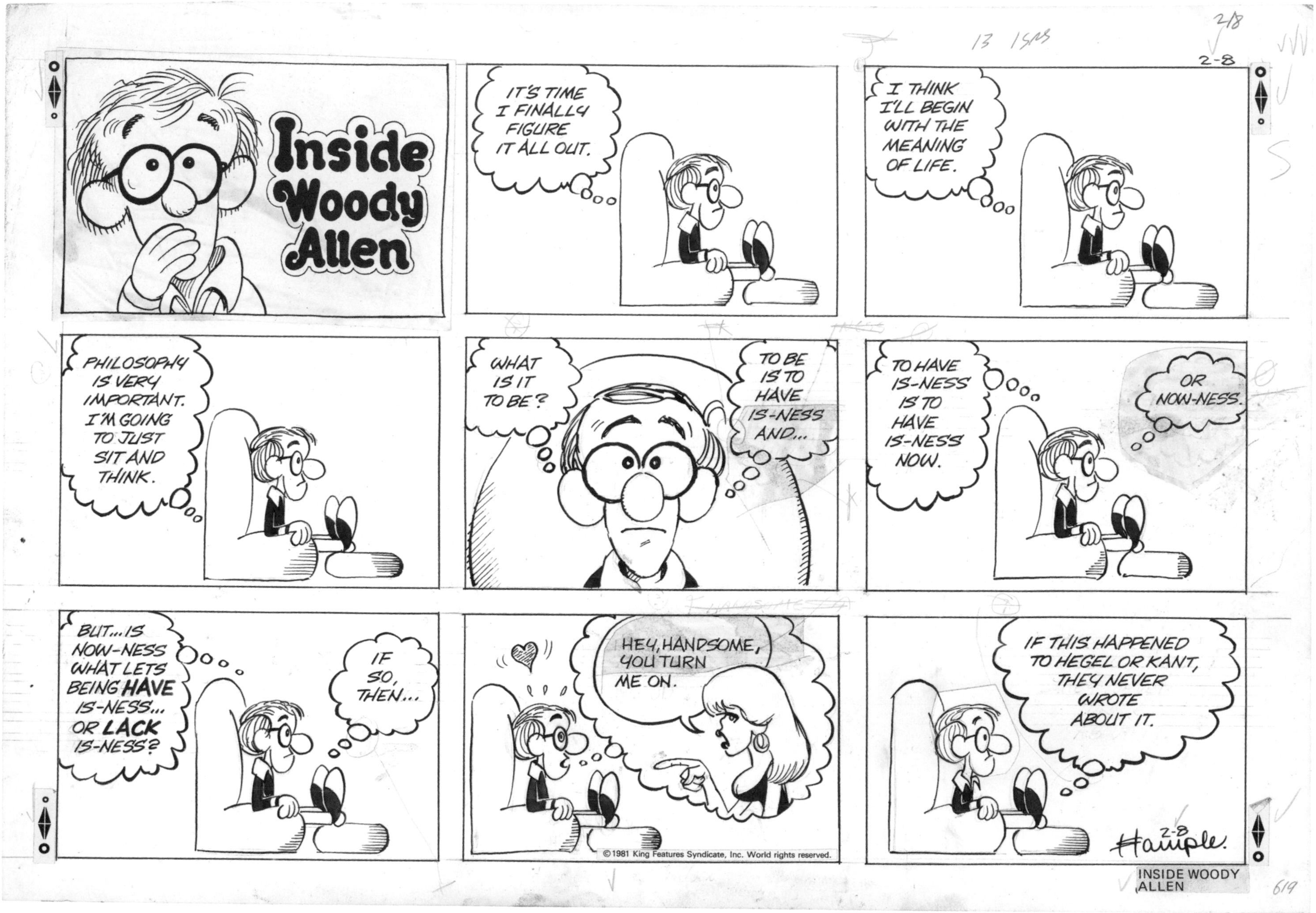
Inside Woody Allen
IT'S TIME I FINALLY FIGURE IT ALL OUT.
I THINK I'LL BEGIN WITH THE MEANING OF LIFE.
PHILOSOPHY IS VERY IMPORTANT. I'M GOING TO JUST SIT AND THINK.
WHAT IS IT TO BE?
TO BE IS TO HAVE IS-NESS AND...
TO HAVE IS-NESS IS TO HAVE IS-NESS NOW.
OR NOW-NESS.
BUT...IS NOW-NESS WHAT LETS BEING **HAVE** IS-NESS... OR **LACK** IS-NESS?
IF SO, THEN...
HEY, HANDSOME, YOU TURN ME ON.
IF THIS HAPPENED TO HEGEL OR KANT, THEY NEVER WROTE ABOUT IT.
©1981 King Features Syndicate, Inc. World rights reserved.
Hample.
INSIDE WOODY ALLEN

February 8, 1981

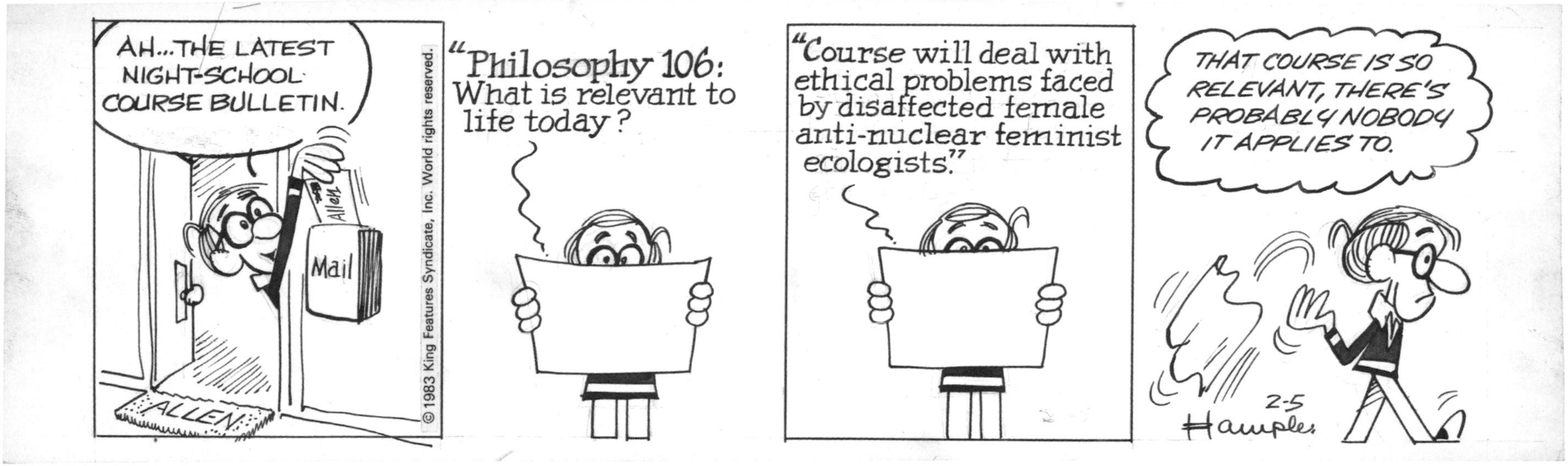
AH...THE LATEST NIGHT-SCHOOL COURSE BULLETIN.
Allen
Mail
ALLEN
© 1983 King Features Syndicate, Inc. World rights reserved.
"Philosophy 106: What is relevant to life today?
"Course will deal with ethical problems faced by disaffected female anti-nuclear feminist ecologists."
THAT COURSE IS SO RELEVANT, THERE'S PROBABLY NOBODY IT APPLIES TO.
2-5
Hampler

February 5, 1983

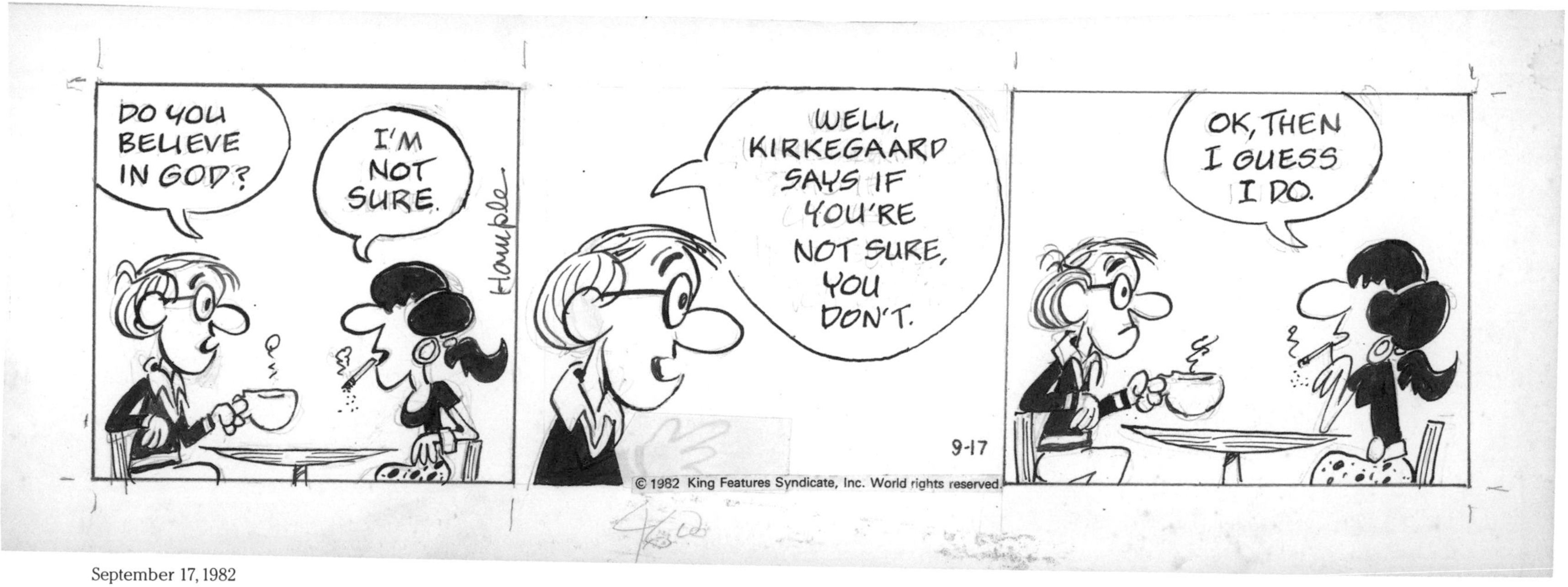
DO YOU BELIEVE IN GOD?
I'M NOT SURE.
Hample
WELL, KIRKEGAARD SAYS IF YOU'RE NOT SURE, YOU DON'T.
9-17
© 1982 King Features Syndicate, Inc. World rights reserved.
OK, THEN I GUESS I DO.

September 17, 1982

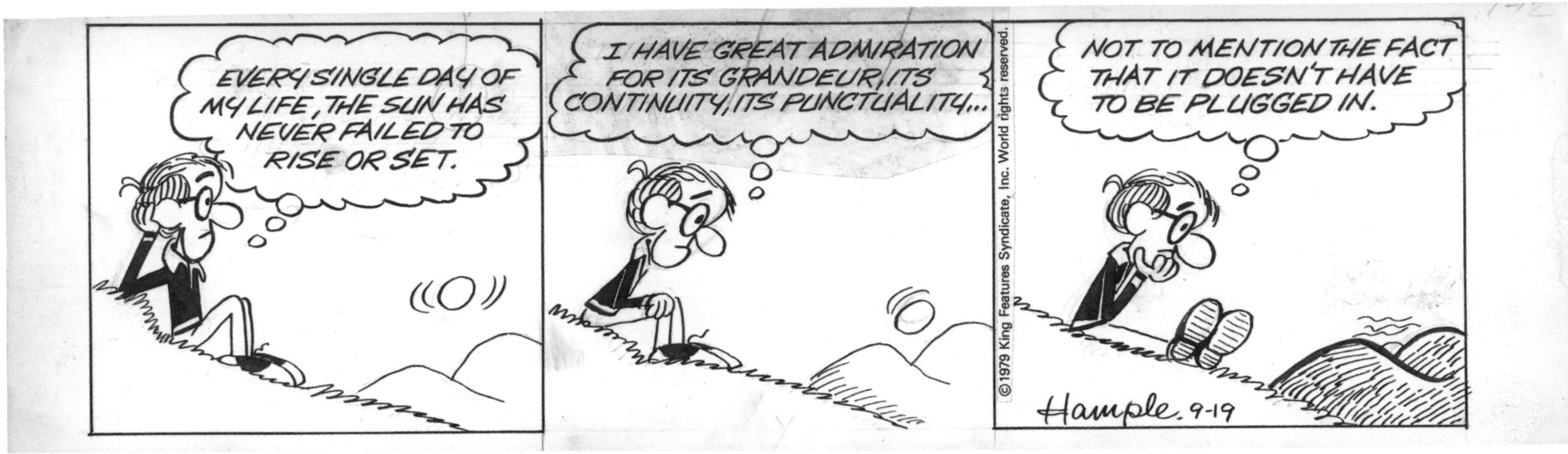
EVERY SINGLE DAY OF MY LIFE, THE SUN HAS NEVER FAILED TO RISE OR SET.
I HAVE GREAT ADMIRATION FOR ITS GRANDEUR, ITS CONTINUITY, ITS PUNCTUALITY...
NOT TO MENTION THE FACT THAT IT DOESN'T HAVE TO BE PLUGGED IN.
© 1979 King Features Syndicate, Inc. World rights reserved.
Hample 9-19

September 19, 1979

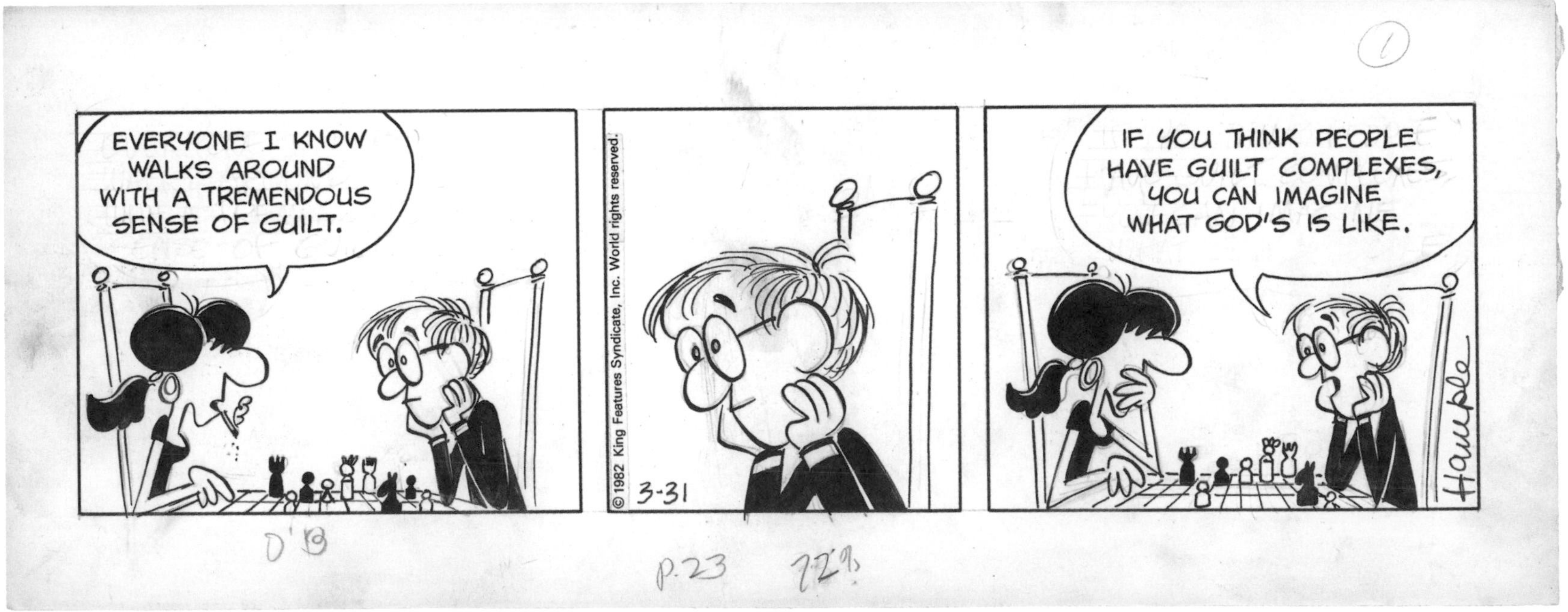
EVERYONE I KNOW WALKS AROUND WITH A TREMENDOUS SENSE OF GUILT.
© 1982 King Features Syndicate, Inc. World rights reserved.
3-31
IF YOU THINK PEOPLE HAVE GUILT COMPLEXES, YOU CAN IMAGINE WHAT GOD'S IS LIKE.
Hample

March 31, 1982

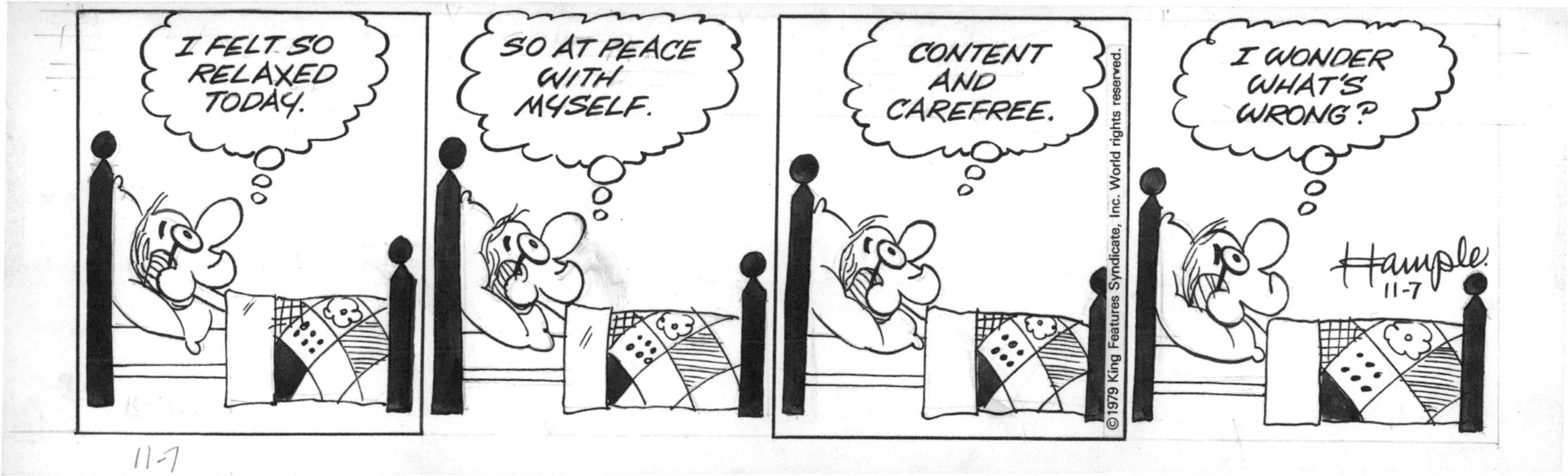
I FELT SO RELAXED TODAY.
SO AT PEACE WITH MYSELF.
CONTENT AND CAREFREE.
I WONDER WHAT'S WRONG?
©1979 King Features Syndicate, Inc. World rights reserved.
Hample 11-7
11-7

November 7, 1979

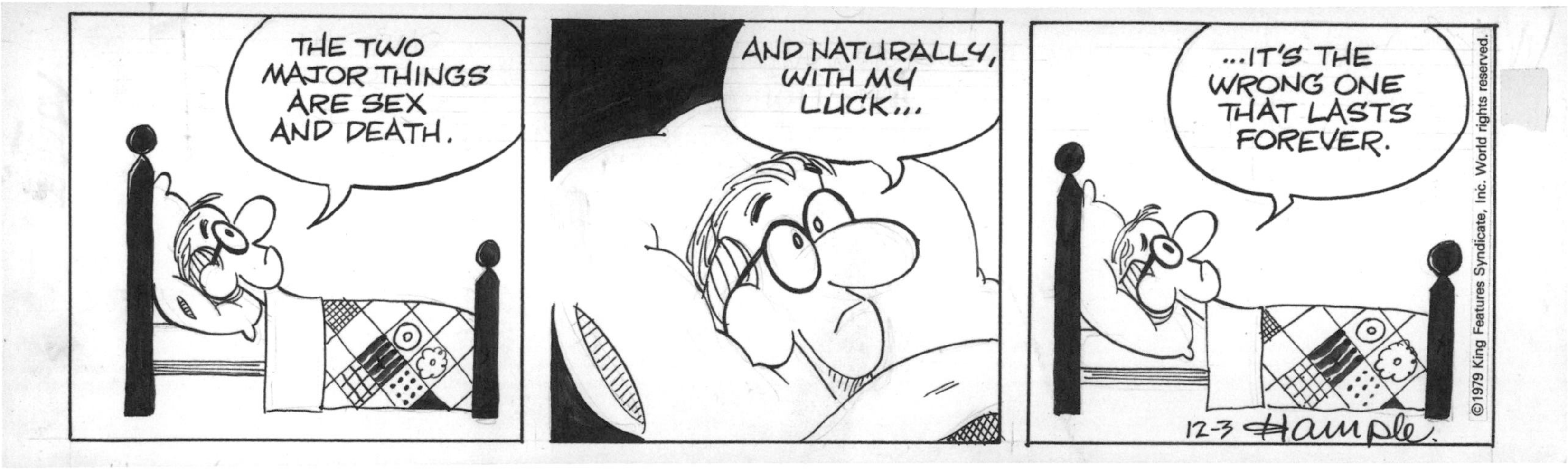
THE TWO MAJOR THINGS ARE SEX AND DEATH.
AND NATURALLY, WITH MY LUCK...
...IT'S THE WRONG ONE THAT LASTS FOREVER.
©1979 King Features Syndicate, Inc. World rights reserved.
12-3 Hample

December 3, 1979

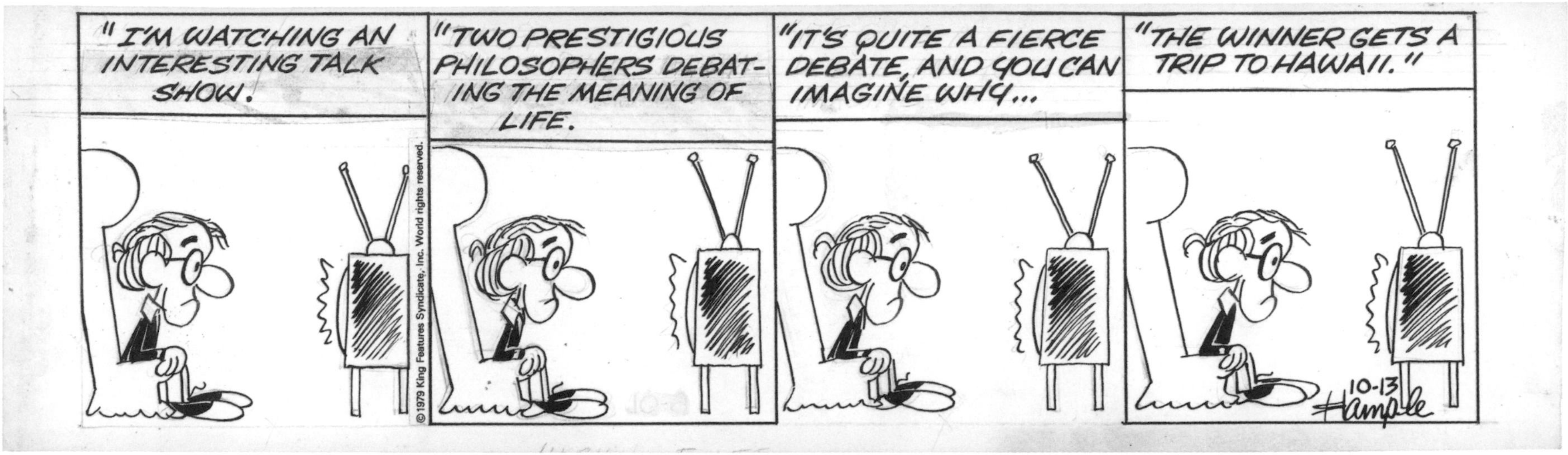
"I'M WATCHING AN INTERESTING TALK SHOW.
"TWO PRESTIGIOUS PHILOSOPHERS DEBATING THE MEANING OF LIFE.
"IT'S QUITE A FIERCE DEBATE, AND YOU CAN IMAGINE WHY...
"THE WINNER GETS A TRIP TO HAWAII."
10-13 Hample
© 1979 King Features Syndicate, Inc. World rights reserved.

October 13, 1979

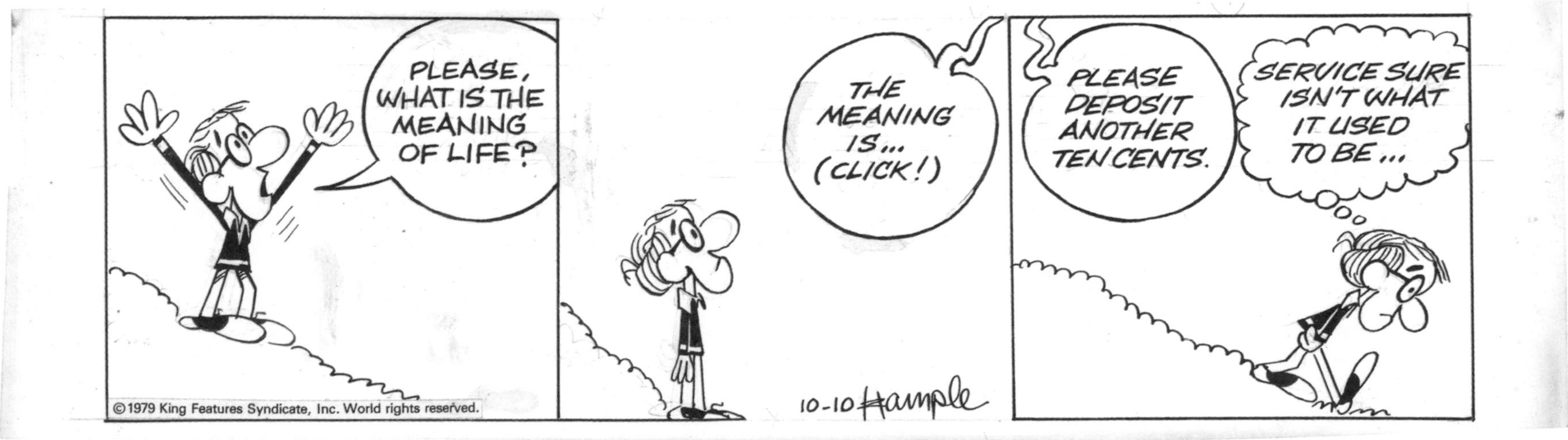
PLEASE, WHAT IS THE MEANING OF LIFE?
THE MEANING IS... (CLICK!)
PLEASE DEPOSIT ANOTHER TEN CENTS.
SERVICE SURE ISN'T WHAT IT USED TO BE...
10-10 Hample
© 1979 King Features Syndicate, Inc. World rights reserved.

October 10, 1979

Every Time She Had an Orgasm, Her Nose Grew Longer

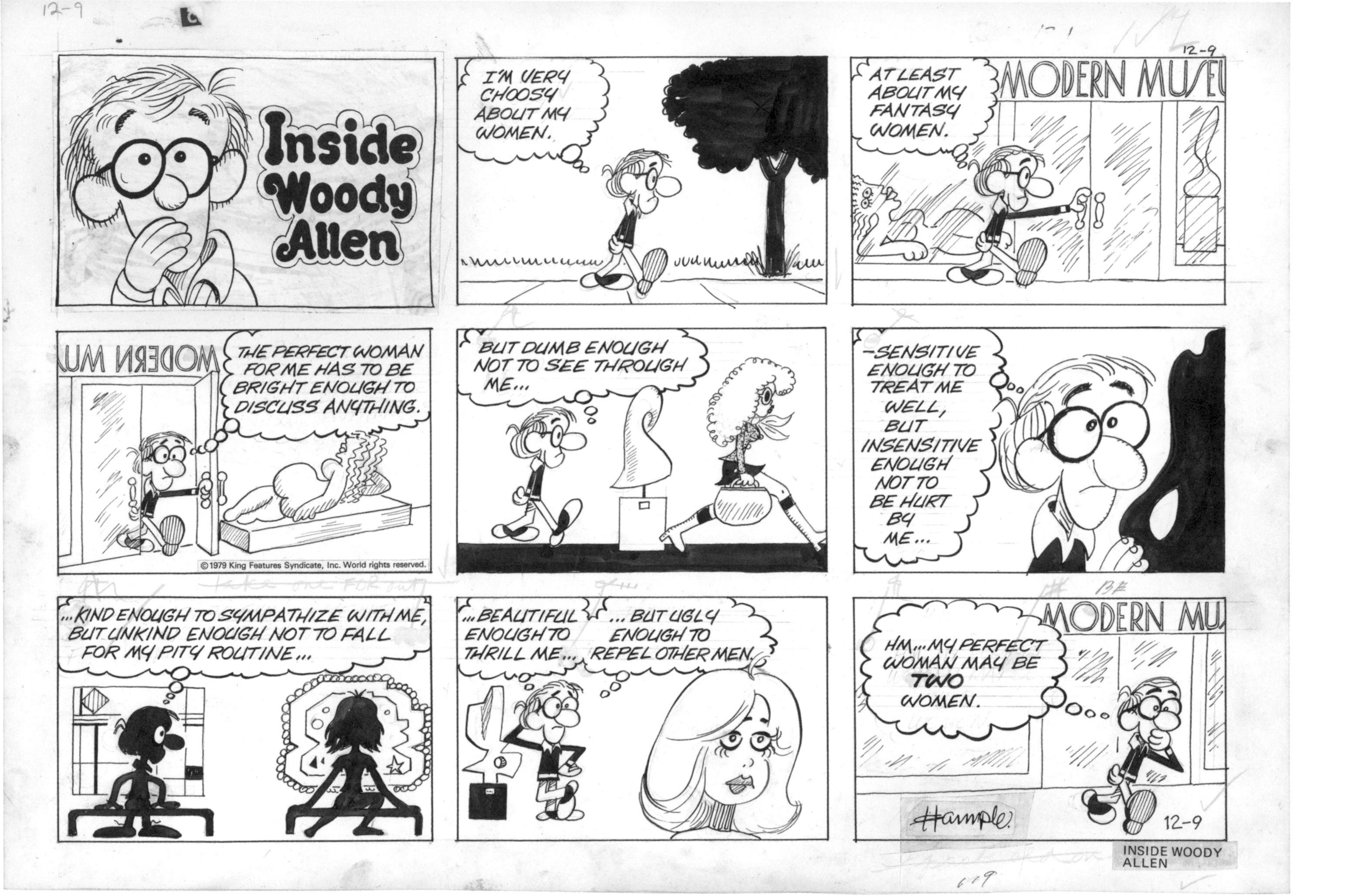

Inside Woody Allen
I'M VERY CHOOSY ABOUT MY WOMEN.
AT LEAST ABOUT MY FANTASY WOMEN.
MODERN MUSEU
MODERN MU
THE PERFECT WOMAN FOR ME HAS TO BE BRIGHT ENOUGH TO DISCUSS ANYTHING.
©1979 King Features Syndicate, Inc. World rights reserved.
BUT DUMB ENOUGH NOT TO SEE THROUGH ME...
-SENSITIVE ENOUGH TO TREAT ME WELL, BUT INSENSITIVE ENOUGH NOT TO BE HURT BY ME...
...KIND ENOUGH TO SYMPATHIZE WITH ME, BUT UNKIND ENOUGH NOT TO FALL FOR MY PITY ROUTINE...
...BEAUTIFUL ENOUGH TO THRILL ME...
...BUT UGLY ENOUGH TO REPEL OTHER MEN.
MODERN MU
HM...MY PERFECT WOMAN MAY BE TWO WOMEN.
Hample
12-9
INSIDE WOODY ALLEN

December 9, 1979

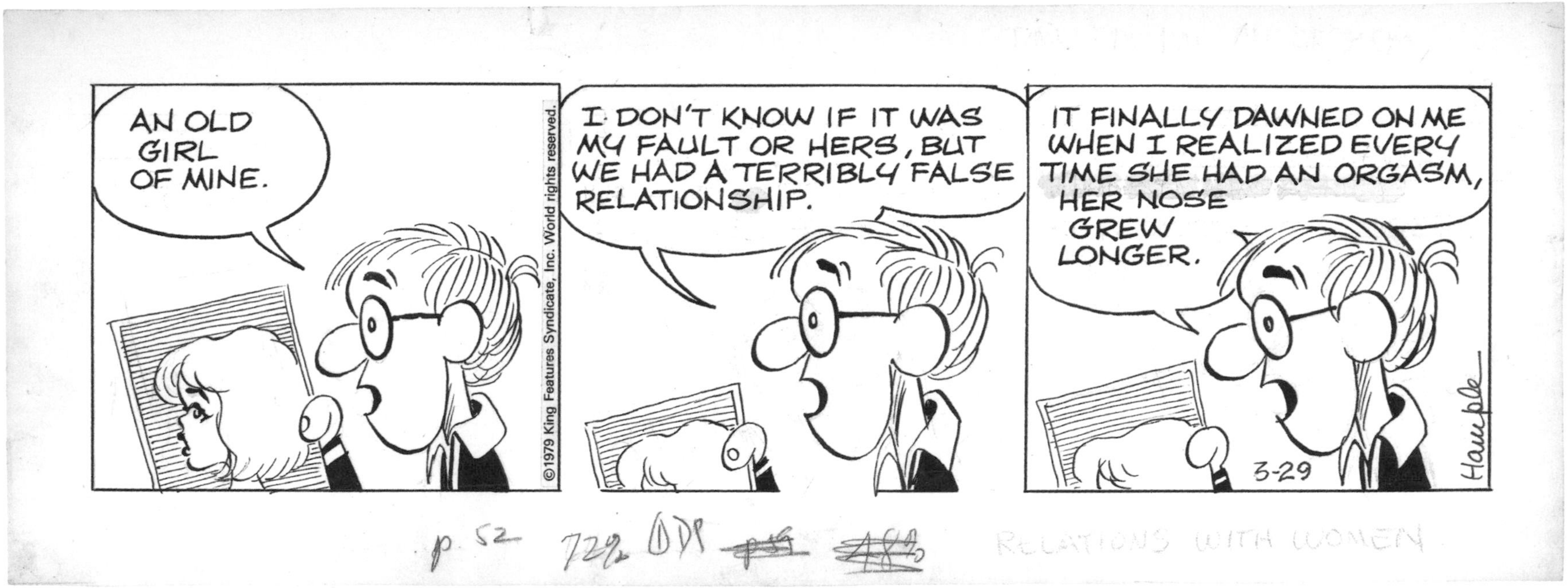
AN OLD GIRL OF MINE.
©1979 King Features Syndicate, Inc. World rights reserved.
I DON'T KNOW IF IT WAS MY FAULT OR HERS, BUT WE HAD A TERRIBLY FALSE RELATIONSHIP.
IT FINALLY DAWNED ON ME WHEN I REALIZED EVERY TIME SHE HAD AN ORGASM, HER NOSE GREW LONGER.
3-29
Hample
p. 52
RELATIONS WITH WOMEN

March 29, 1979

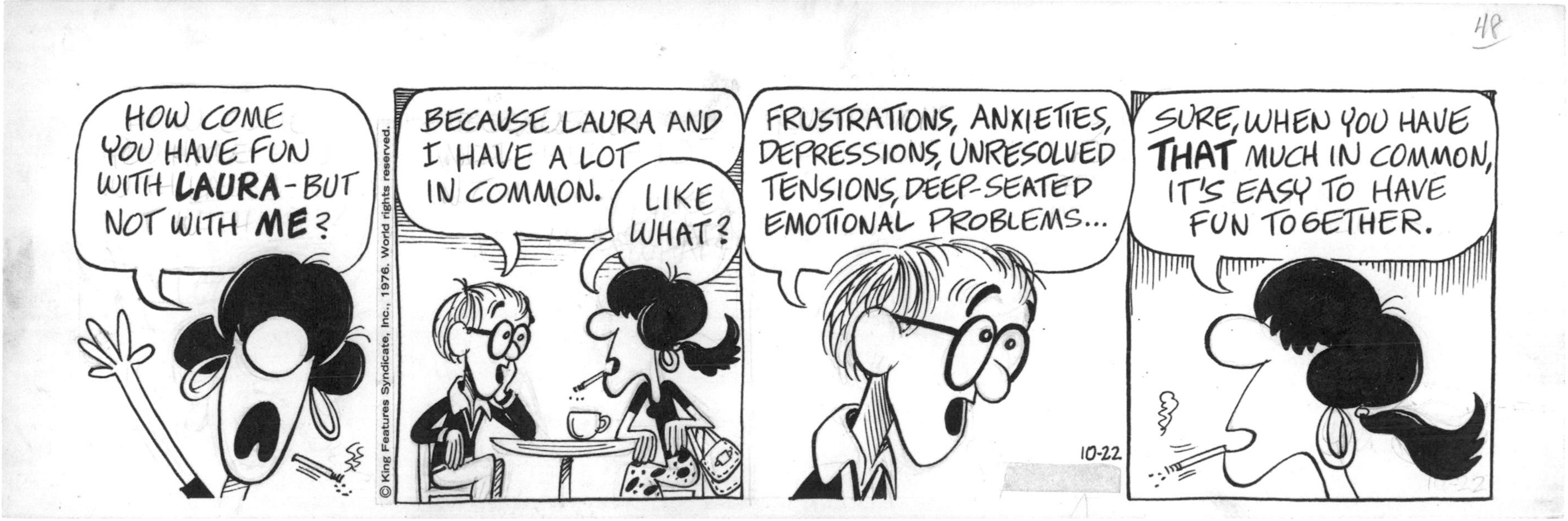
48
HOW COME YOU HAVE FUN WITH **LAURA**-BUT NOT WITH **ME**?
© King Features Syndicate, Inc., 1976. World rights reserved.
BECAUSE LAURA AND I HAVE A LOT IN COMMON.
LIKE WHAT?
FRUSTRATIONS, ANXIETIES, DEPRESSIONS, UNRESOLVED TENSIONS, DEEP-SEATED EMOTIONAL PROBLEMS...
10-22
SURE, WHEN YOU HAVE **THAT** MUCH IN COMMON, IT'S EASY TO HAVE FUN TOGETHER.

October 22 , 1976

June 12, 1983. Hample's guides for coloring of Sunday pages were indicated on tissue overlay taped to the black-and-white drawings. The letters YBR stand for the primary colors yellow, blue, and red, which are mixed by the printer to produce orange, green, purple, etc.; the numbers refer to intensity of hue.

THE LIFE OF THE MIND IS SO EXCITING.

IT DEFINITELY COMES IN A CLOSE SECOND

AH, A FINE DAY TO BE READING "POETRY JOURNAL."

Poetry Journal

Bzzzz

HOW RARE TO FIND SOME WILLING TO TAKE THE EFFORT TO READ THAT WHICH CAN EXPAND ONE'S AESTHETIC HORIZONS...

Bzzzz

Poetry Journal

...INSTEAD OF FILLING UP ON THE VAPID, JEJUNE NULLITIES WE FIND AROUND US PASSING AS ENTERTAINMENT

Bzzzz

Poetry

POW!

Bzzzz

I BROUGHT "POETRY REVIEW" BECAUSE I HATE TO GET "SOAP OPERA DIGEST" FULL OF FLIES.

SOAP OPERA DIGEST

I WONDER IF T.S. ELIOT HAD THIS MUCH TROUBLE MEETING WOMEN...

Hample. 6-12

INSIDE WOODY ALLEN

June 12, 1983

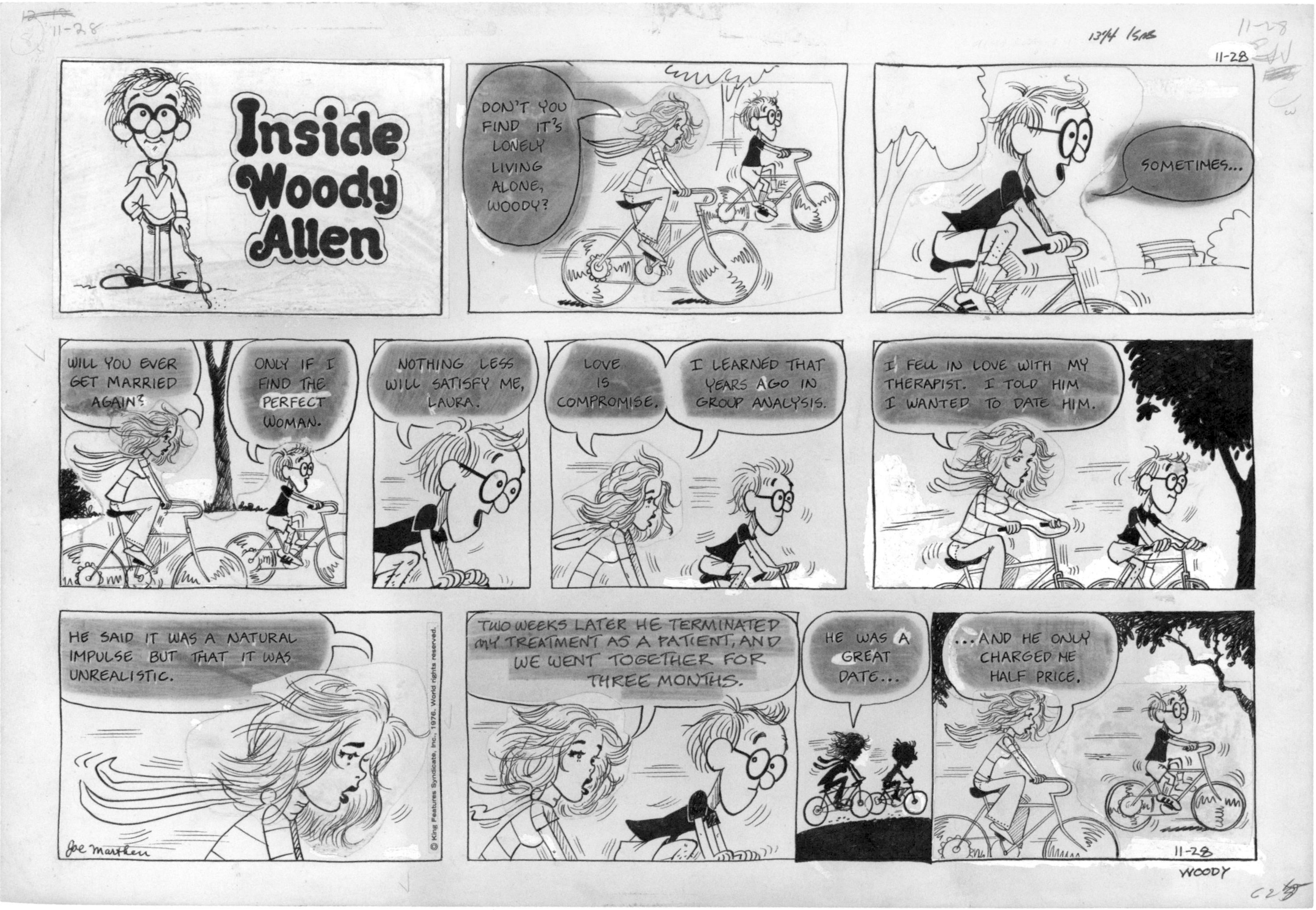
Inside Woody Allen
DON'T YOU FIND IT'S LONELY LIVING ALONE, WOODY?
SOMETIMES...
WILL YOU EVER GET MARRIED AGAIN?
ONLY IF I FIND THE PERFECT WOMAN.
NOTHING LESS WILL SATISFY ME, LAURA.
LOVE IS COMPROMISE.
I LEARNED THAT YEARS AGO IN GROUP ANALYSIS.
I FELL IN LOVE WITH MY THERAPIST. I TOLD HIM I WANTED TO DATE HIM.
HE SAID IT WAS A NATURAL IMPULSE BUT THAT IT WAS UNREALISTIC.
© King Features Syndicate, Inc., 1976. World rights reserved.
Joe Martin
TWO WEEKS LATER HE TERMINATED MY TREATMENT AS A PATIENT, AND WE WENT TOGETHER FOR THREE MONTHS.
HE WAS A GREAT DATE...
...AND HE ONLY CHARGED ME HALF PRICE.
11-28
WOODY

November 28, 1976

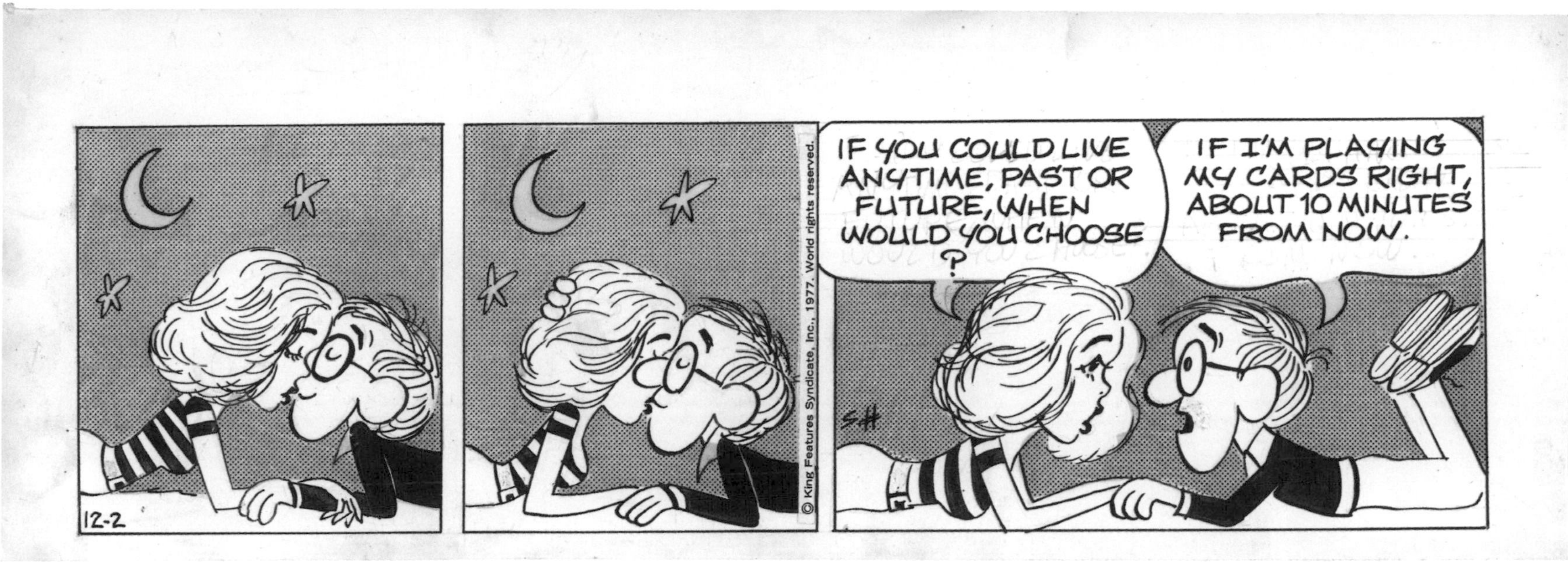
12-2
© King Features Syndicate, Inc., 1977. World rights reserved.
IF YOU COULD LIVE ANYTIME, PAST OR FUTURE, WHEN WOULD YOU CHOOSE ?
IF I'M PLAYING MY CARDS RIGHT, ABOUT 10 MINUTES FROM NOW.
S.H.

December 2, 1977

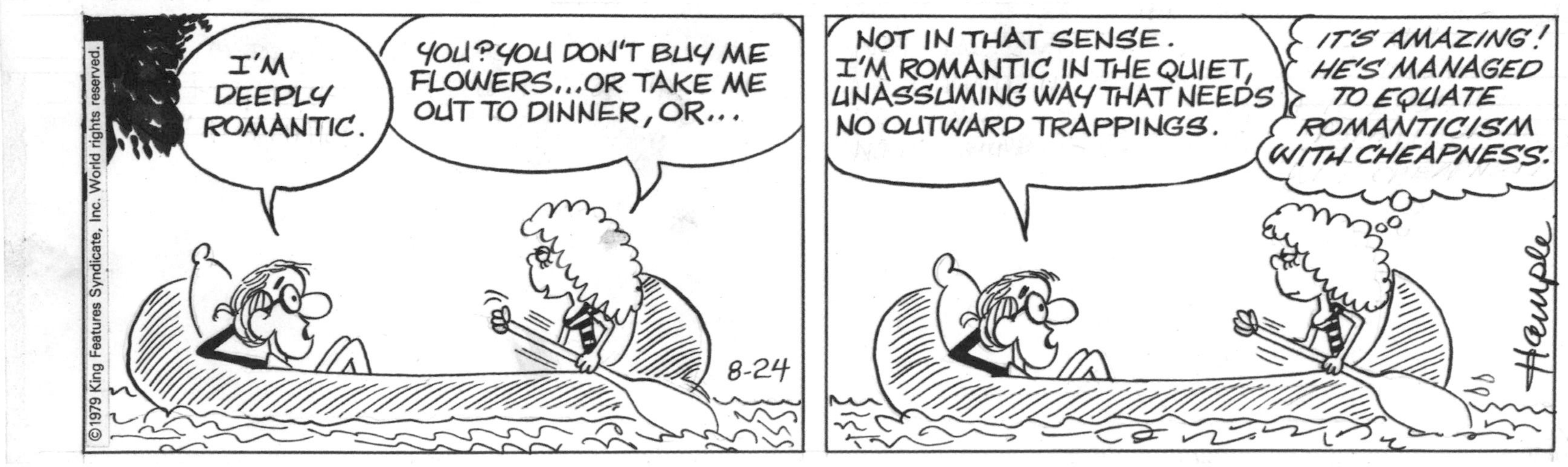
© 1979 King Features Syndicate, Inc. World rights reserved.
I'M DEEPLY ROMANTIC.
YOU? YOU DON'T BUY ME FLOWERS...OR TAKE ME OUT TO DINNER, OR...
8-24
NOT IN THAT SENSE. I'M ROMANTIC IN THE QUIET, UNASSUMING WAY THAT NEEDS NO OUTWARD TRAPPINGS.
IT'S AMAZING! HE'S MANAGED TO EQUATE ROMANTICISM WITH CHEAPNESS.
Hample

August 24, 1979

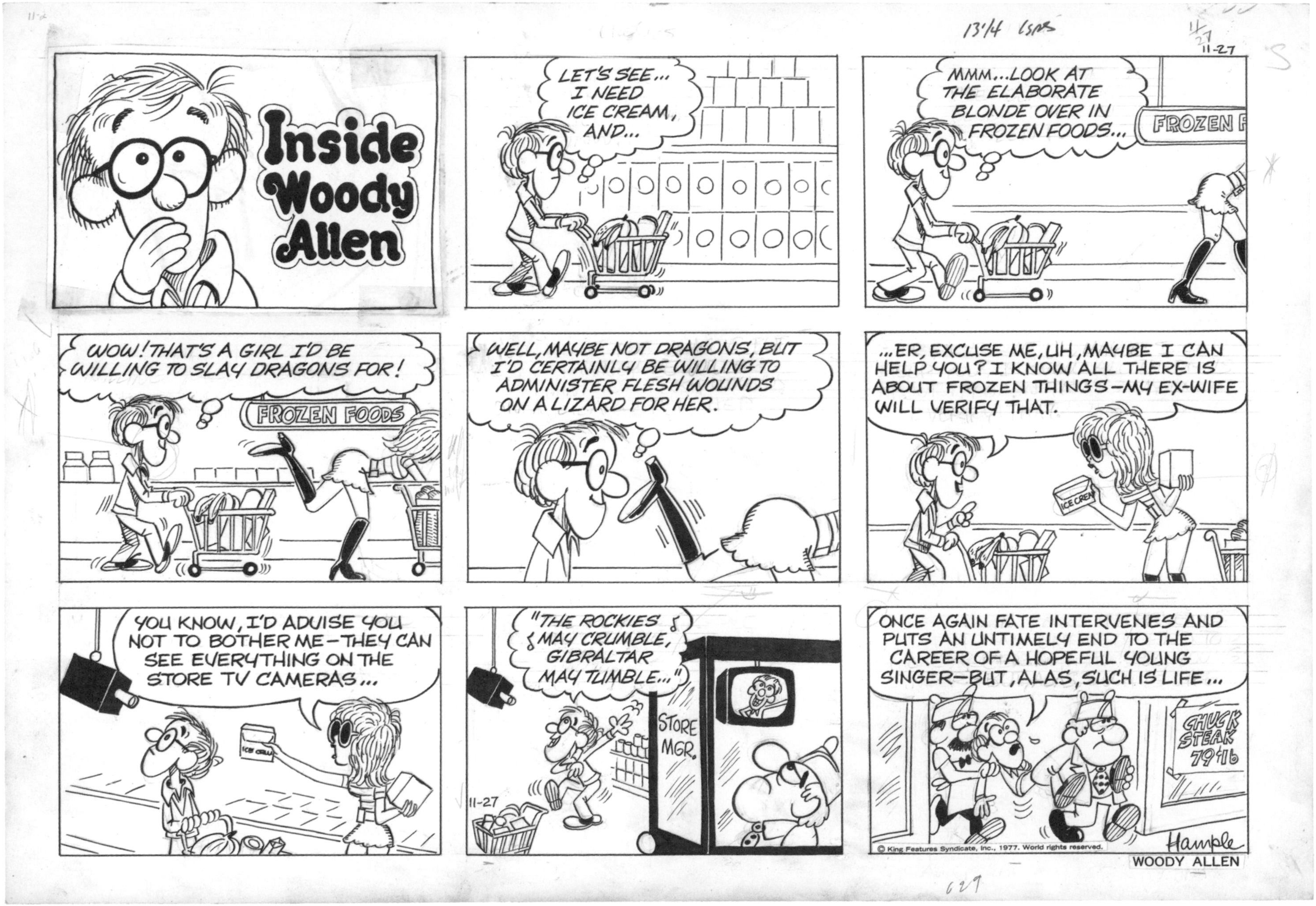
Inside Woody Allen
LET'S SEE... I NEED ICE CREAM, AND...
MMM...LOOK AT THE ELABORATE BLONDE OVER IN FROZEN FOODS...
FROZEN F
WOW! THAT'S A GIRL I'D BE WILLING TO SLAY DRAGONS FOR!
FROZEN FOODS
WELL, MAYBE NOT DRAGONS, BUT I'D CERTAINLY BE WILLING TO ADMINISTER FLESH WOUNDS ON A LIZARD FOR HER.
...ER, EXCUSE ME, UH, MAYBE I CAN HELP YOU? I KNOW ALL THERE IS ABOUT FROZEN THINGS—MY EX-WIFE WILL VERIFY THAT.
YOU KNOW, I'D ADVISE YOU NOT TO BOTHER ME—THEY CAN SEE EVERYTHING ON THE STORE TV CAMERAS...
"THE ROCKIES MAY CRUMBLE, GIBRALTAR MAY TUMBLE..."
STORE MGR.
ONCE AGAIN FATE INTERVENES AND PUTS AN UNTIMELY END TO THE CAREER OF A HOPEFUL YOUNG SINGER—BUT, ALAS, SUCH IS LIFE...
CHUCK STEAK 79¢ lb
Hample
© King Features Syndicate, Inc., 1977. World rights reserved.
WOODY ALLEN

November 27, 1977

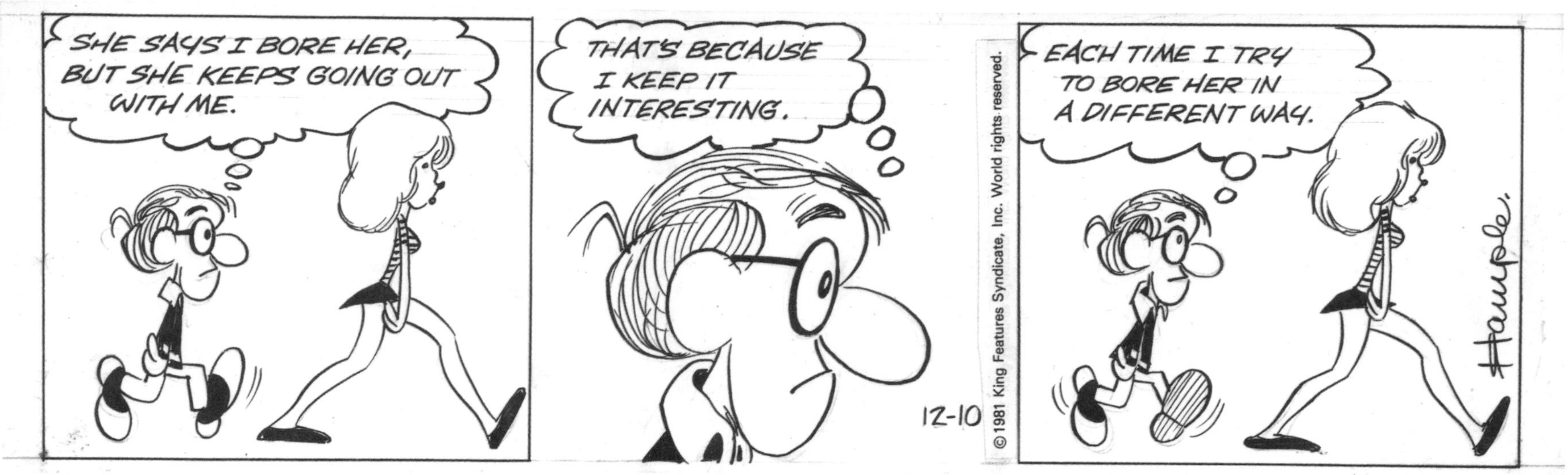
SHE SAYS I BORE HER, BUT SHE KEEPS GOING OUT WITH ME.
THAT'S BECAUSE I KEEP IT INTERESTING.
12-10
© 1981 King Features Syndicate, Inc. World rights reserved.
EACH TIME I TRY TO BORE HER IN A DIFFERENT WAY.
Hample

December 10, 1981

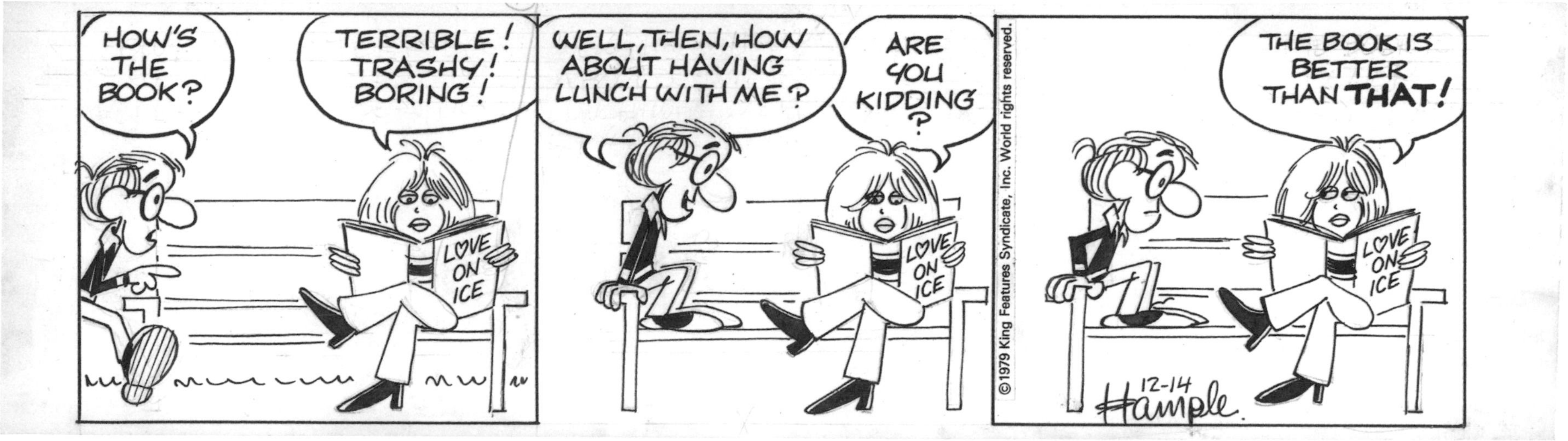
HOW'S THE BOOK?
TERRIBLE! TRASHY! BORING!
LOVE ON ICE
WELL, THEN, HOW ABOUT HAVING LUNCH WITH ME?
ARE YOU KIDDING?
© 1979 King Features Syndicate, Inc. World rights reserved.
THE BOOK IS BETTER THAN THAT!
12-14
Hample

December 14, 1979

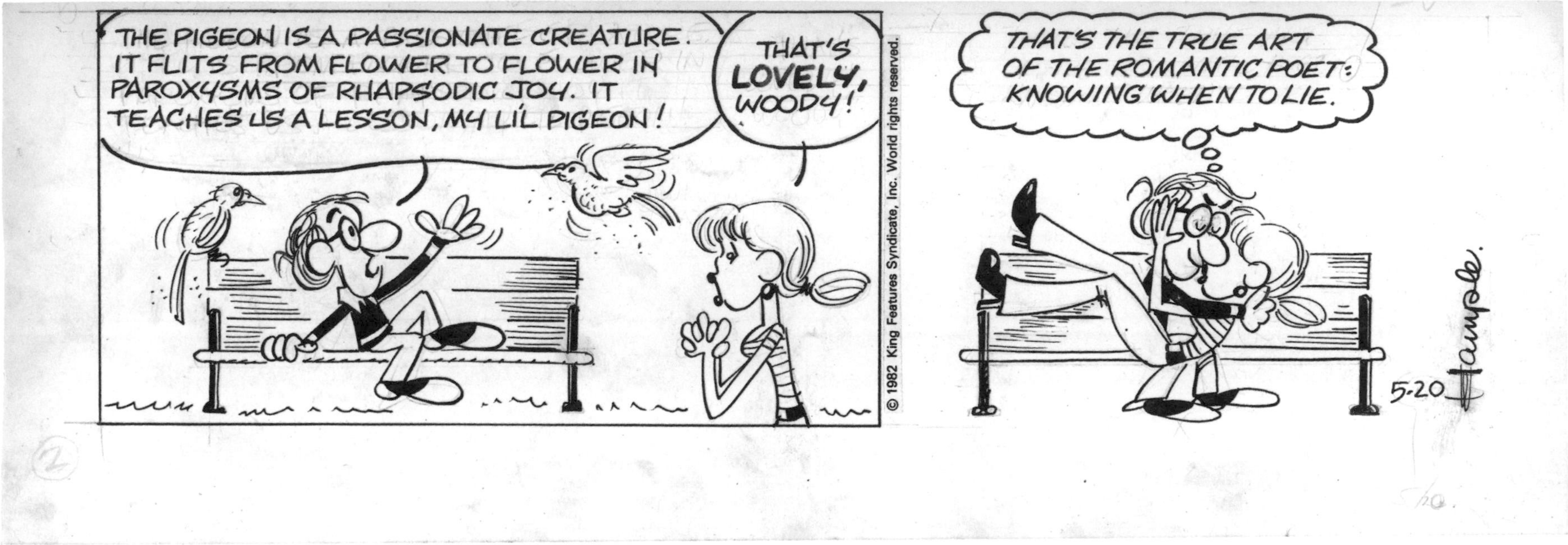

THE PIGEON IS A PASSIONATE CREATURE. IT FLITS FROM FLOWER TO FLOWER IN PAROXYSMS OF RHAPSODIC JOY. IT TEACHES US A LESSON, MY LIL PIGEON!
THAT'S LOVELY, WOODY!
© 1982 King Features Syndicate, Inc. World rights reserved.
THAT'S THE TRUE ART OF THE ROMANTIC POET: KNOWING WHEN TO LIE.
5-20

May 20, 1982

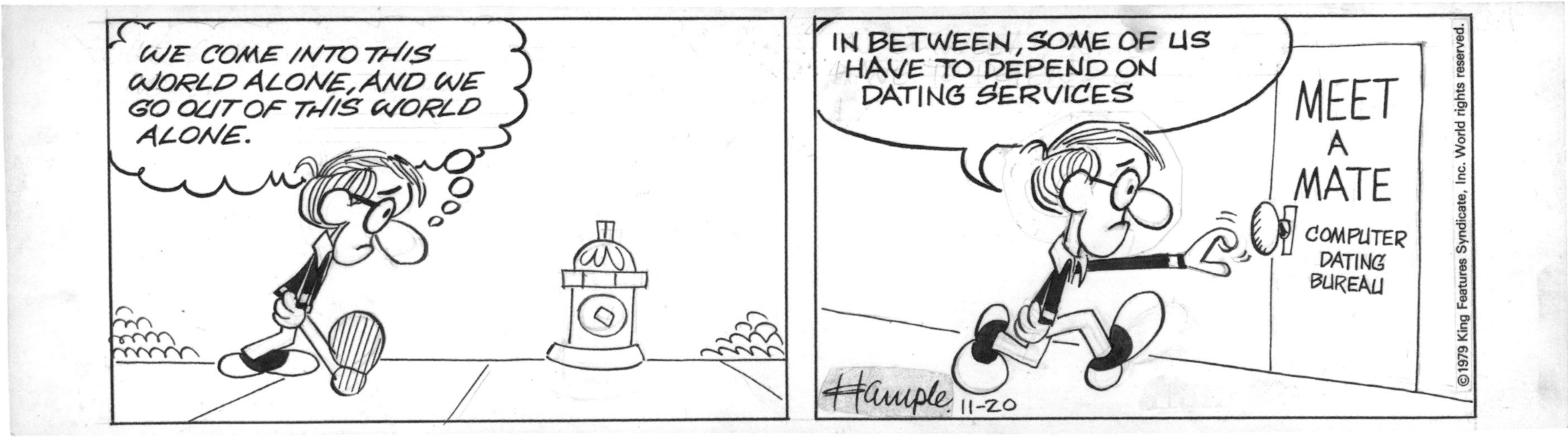

WE COME INTO THIS WORLD ALONE, AND WE GO OUT OF THIS WORLD ALONE.
IN BETWEEN, SOME OF US HAVE TO DEPEND ON DATING SERVICES
MEET A MATE
COMPUTER DATING BUREAU
© 1979 King Features Syndicate, Inc. World rights reserved.
Hample 11-20

November 20, 1979

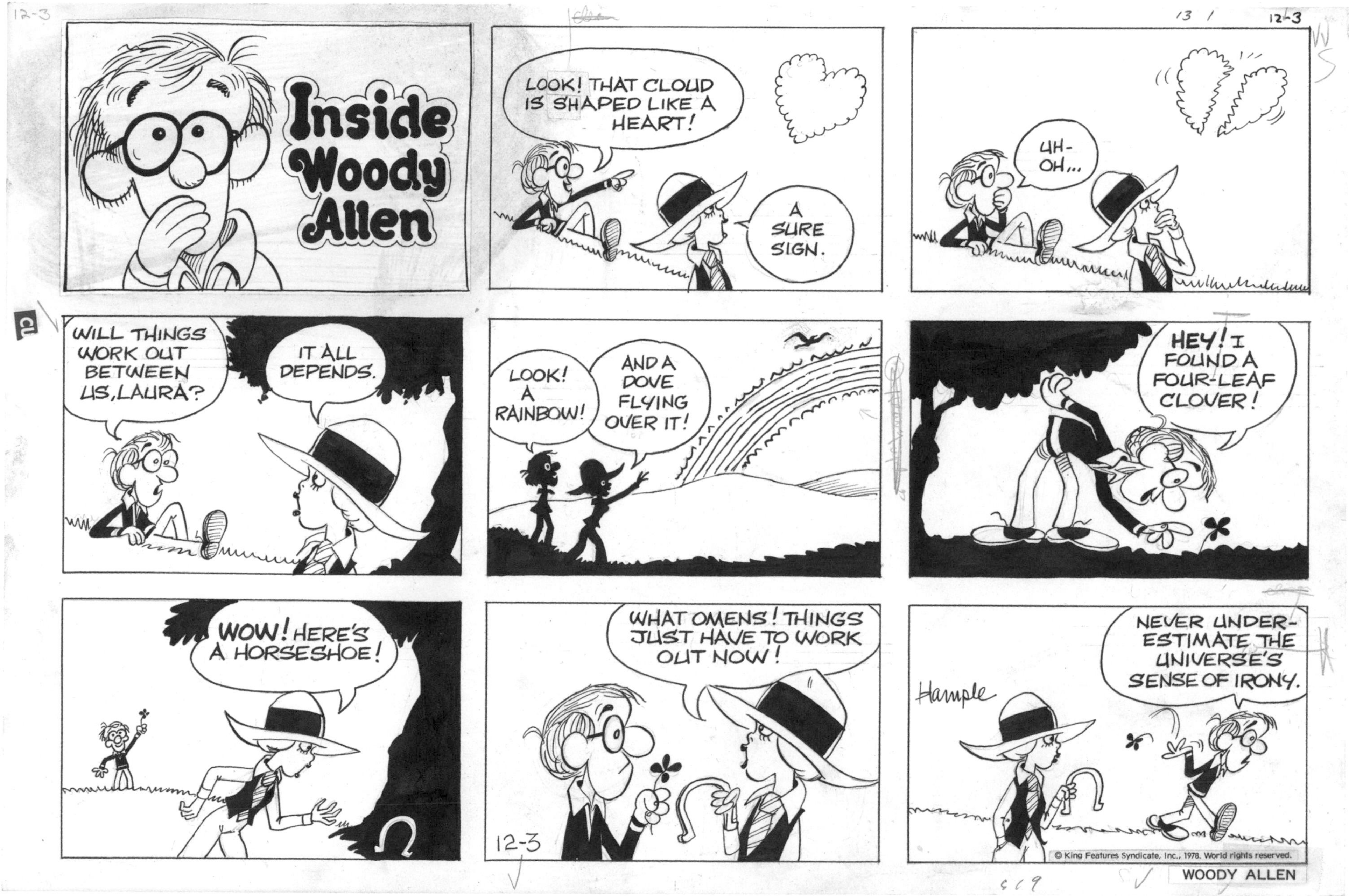
Inside Woody Allen
LOOK! THAT CLOUD IS SHAPED LIKE A HEART!
A SURE SIGN.
UH-OH...
WILL THINGS WORK OUT BETWEEN US, LAURA?
IT ALL DEPENDS.
LOOK! A RAINBOW!
AND A DOVE FLYING OVER IT!
HEY! I FOUND A FOUR-LEAF CLOVER!
WOW! HERE'S A HORSESHOE!
WHAT OMENS! THINGS JUST HAVE TO WORK OUT NOW!
NEVER UNDER-ESTIMATE THE UNIVERSE'S SENSE OF IRONY.
Hample
© King Features Syndicate, Inc., 1978. World rights reserved.
WOODY ALLEN

December 3, 1978

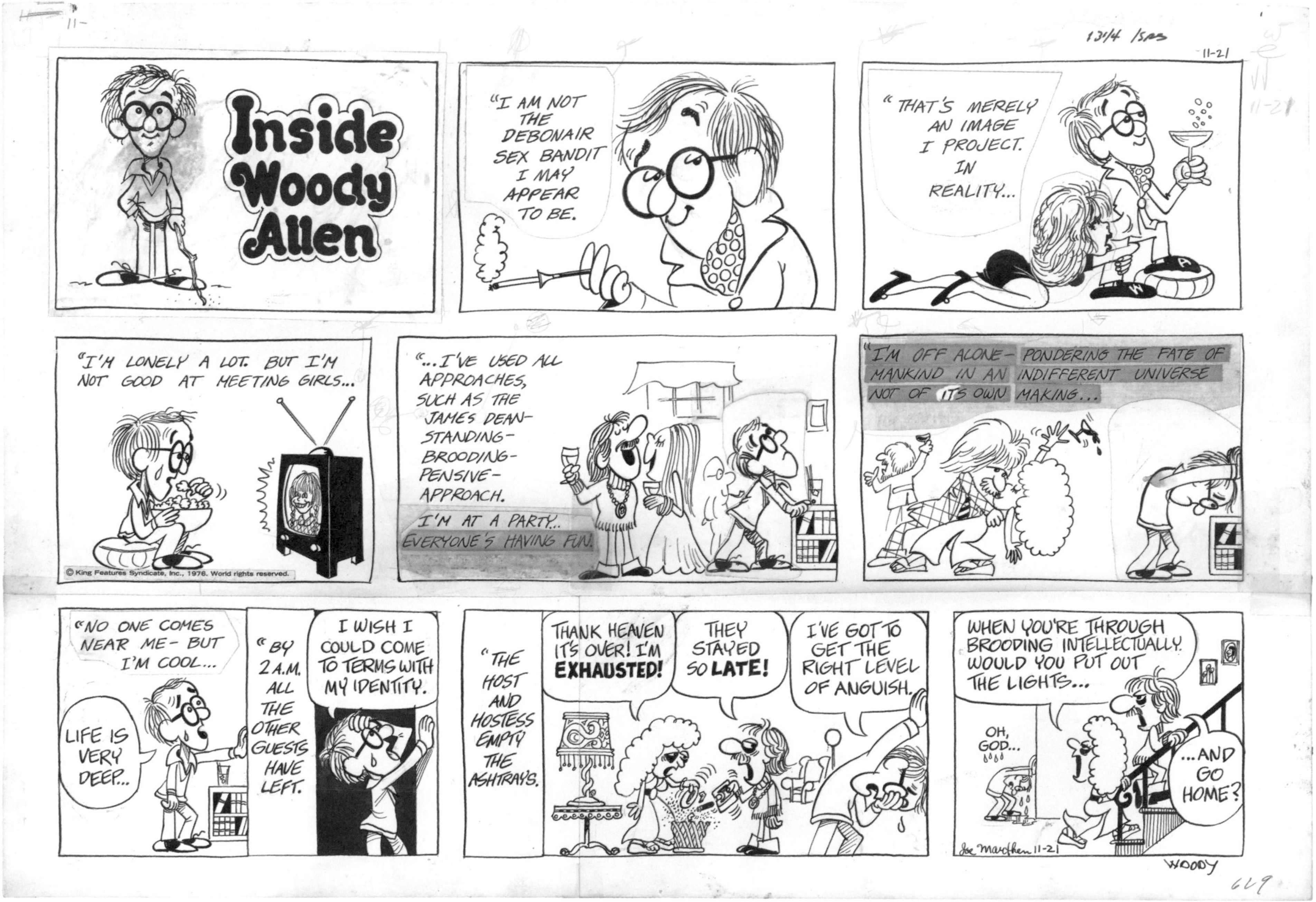
Inside Woody Allen
"I AM NOT THE DEBONAIR SEX BANDIT I MAY APPEAR TO BE.
"THAT'S MERELY AN IMAGE I PROJECT. IN REALITY...
"I'M LONELY A LOT. BUT I'M NOT GOOD AT MEETING GIRLS...
© King Features Syndicate, Inc., 1976. World rights reserved.
"...I'VE USED ALL APPROACHES, SUCH AS THE JAMES DEAN-STANDING-BROODING-PENSIVE-APPROACH.
I'M AT A PARTY... EVERYONE'S HAVING FUN.
"I'M OFF ALONE- PONDERING THE FATE OF MANKIND IN AN INDIFFERENT UNIVERSE NOT OF ITS OWN MAKING...
"NO ONE COMES NEAR ME- BUT I'M COOL...
LIFE IS VERY DEEP...
"BY 2 A.M. ALL THE OTHER GUESTS HAVE LEFT.
I WISH I COULD COME TO TERMS WITH MY IDENTITY.
"THE HOST AND HOSTESS EMPTY THE ASHTRAYS.
THANK HEAVEN IT'S OVER! I'M EXHAUSTED!
THEY STAYED SO LATE!
I'VE GOT TO GET THE RIGHT LEVEL OF ANGUISH.
WHEN YOU'RE THROUGH BROODING INTELLECTUALLY WOULD YOU PUT OUT THE LIGHTS...
OH, GOD...
...AND GO HOME?
WOODY

November 21, 1976

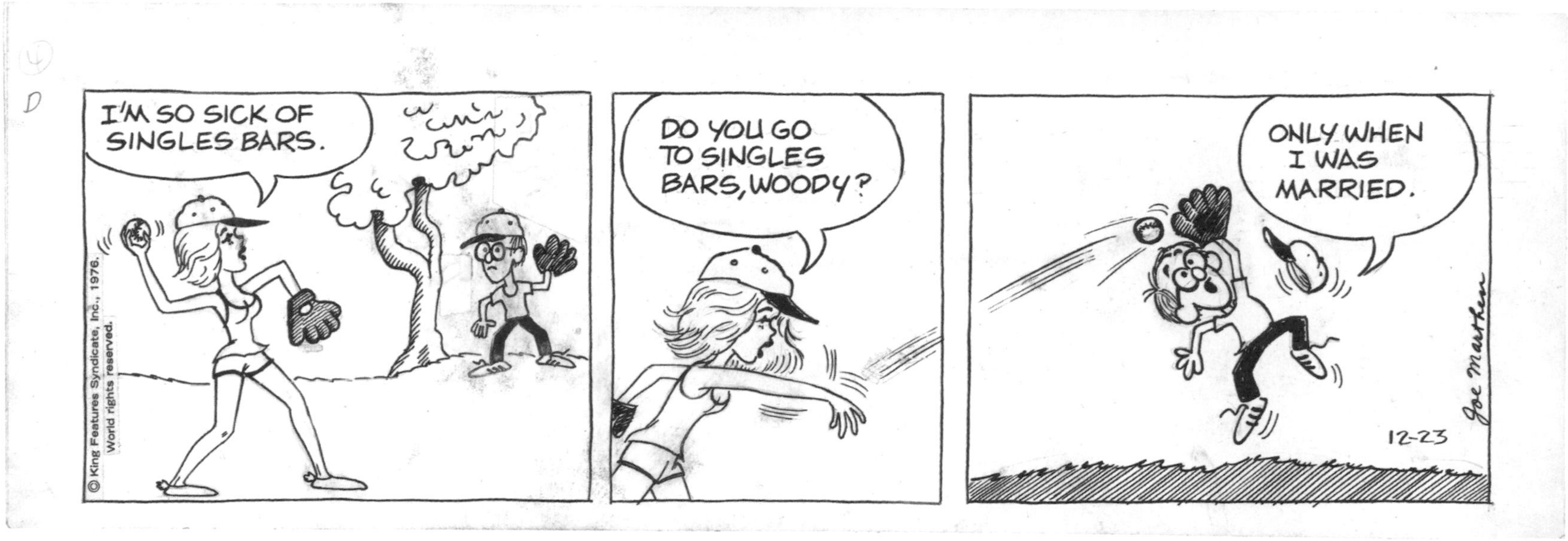
I'M SO SICK OF SINGLES BARS.
DO YOU GO TO SINGLES BARS, WOODY?
ONLY WHEN I WAS MARRIED.
© King Features Syndicate, Inc., 1976. World rights reserved.
12-23

December 23, 1976

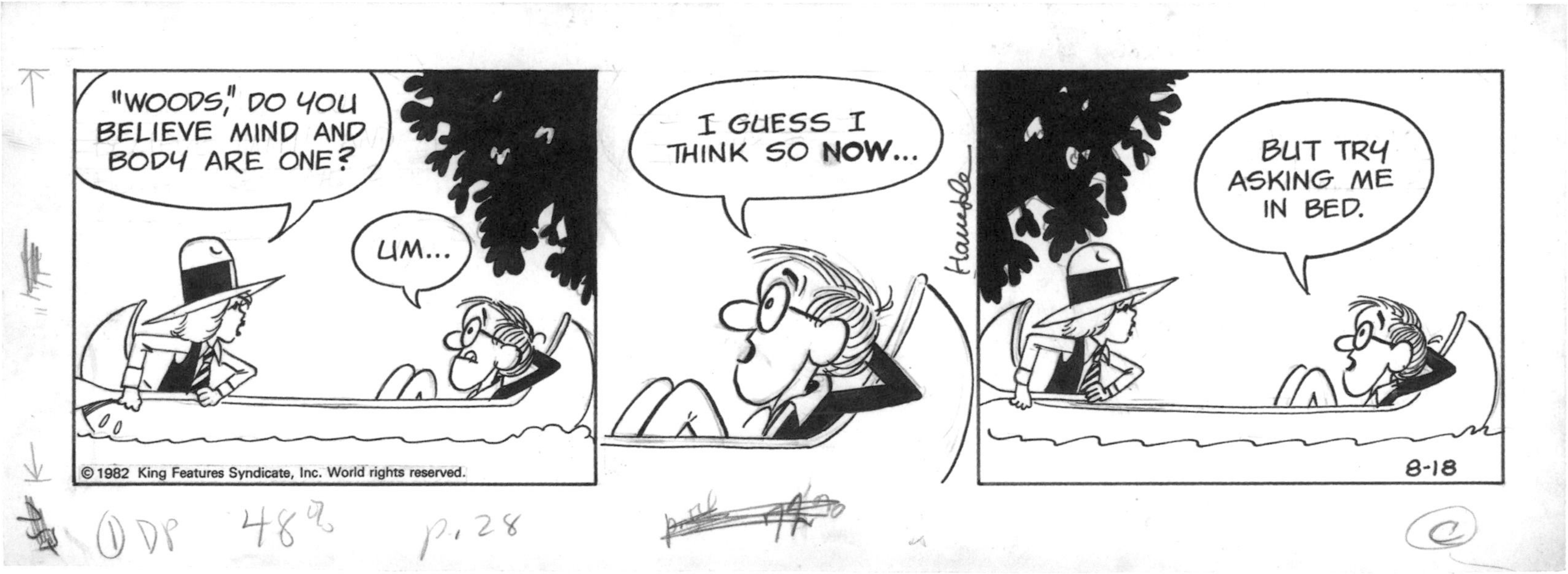
"WOODS," DO YOU BELIEVE MIND AND BODY ARE ONE?
UM...
I GUESS I THINK SO NOW...
BUT TRY ASKING ME IN BED.
© 1982 King Features Syndicate, Inc. World rights reserved.
8-18

August 18, 1982

SYLVAN & BEN= WOULD YOU BE HAPPIER ___ A "FAMILY"
13/4-LSP   PAGE AT THIS POINT ?

October 30, 1977

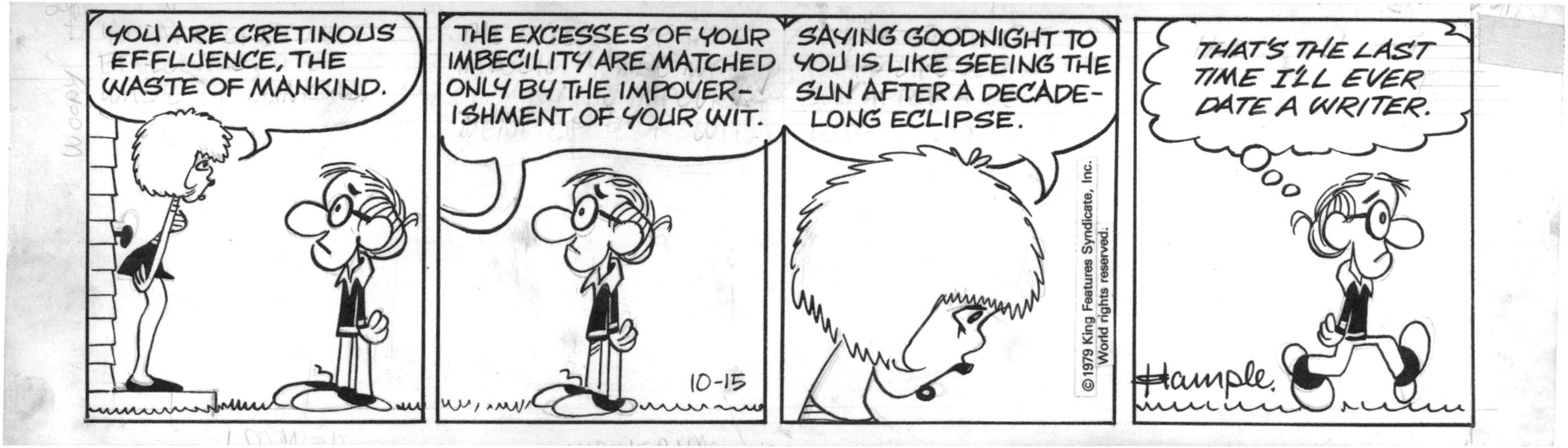
YOU ARE CRETINOUS EFFLUENCE, THE WASTE OF MANKIND.
THE EXCESSES OF YOUR IMBECILITY ARE MATCHED ONLY BY THE IMPOVER-ISHMENT OF YOUR WIT.
SAYING GOODNIGHT TO YOU IS LIKE SEEING THE SUN AFTER A DECADE-LONG ECLIPSE.
10-15
© 1979 King Features Syndicate, Inc. World rights reserved.
THAT'S THE LAST TIME I'LL EVER DATE A WRITER.
Hample.

October 15, 1979

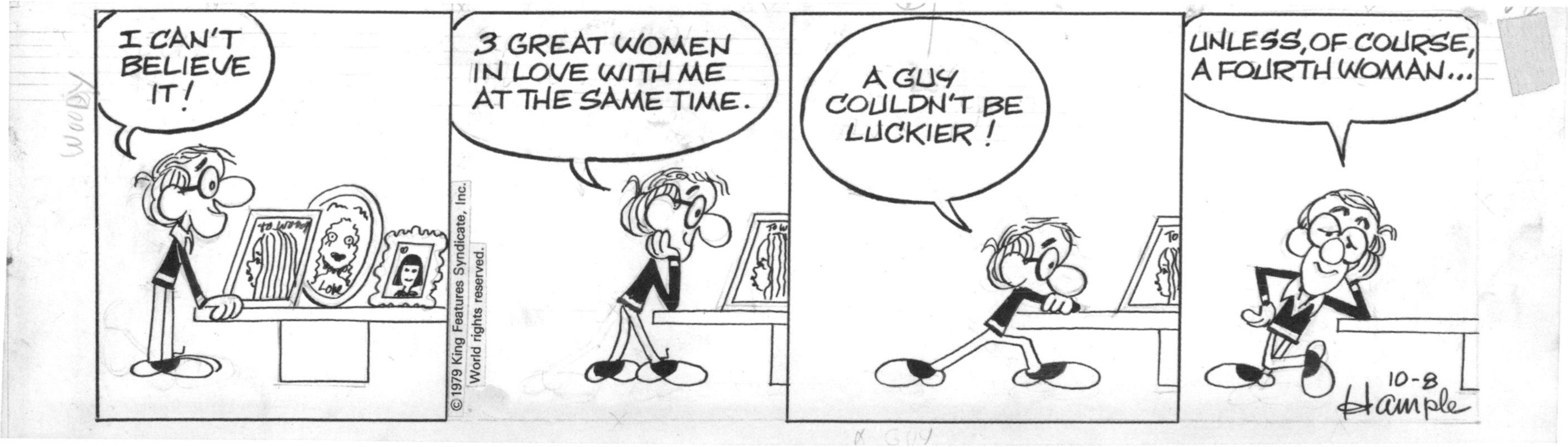
I CAN'T BELIEVE IT!
© 1979 King Features Syndicate, Inc. World rights reserved.
3 GREAT WOMEN IN LOVE WITH ME AT THE SAME TIME.
A GUY COULDN'T BE LUCKIER!
UNLESS, OF COURSE, A FOURTH WOMAN...
10-8
Hample

October 8, 1979

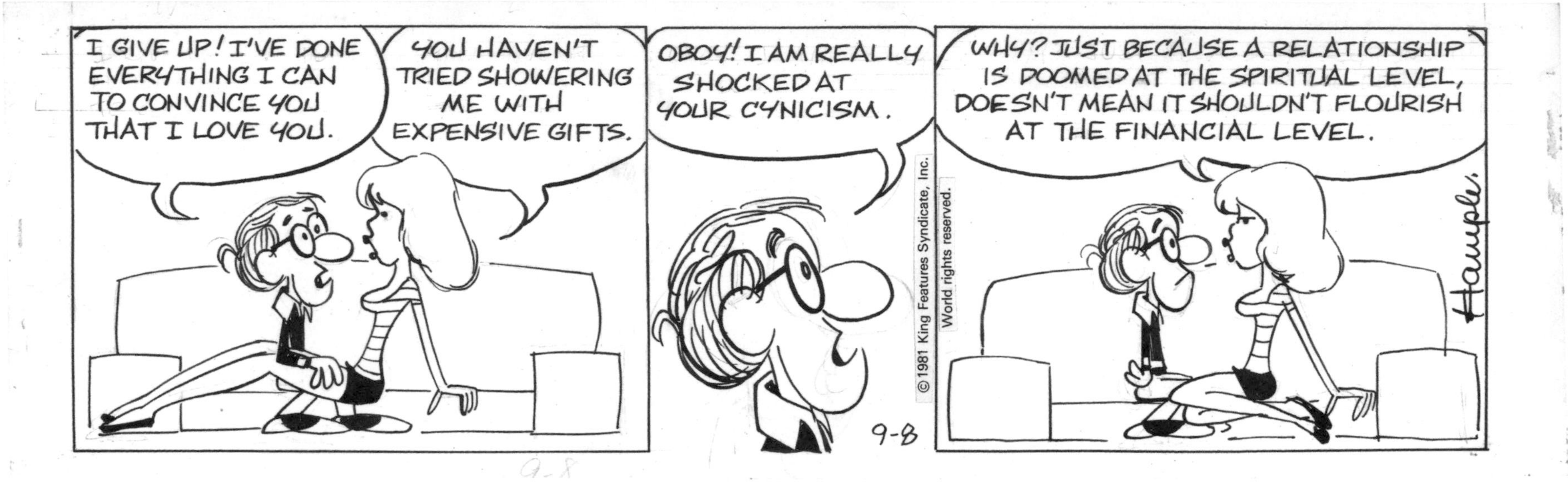
I GIVE UP! I'VE DONE EVERYTHING I CAN TO CONVINCE YOU THAT I LOVE YOU.
YOU HAVEN'T TRIED SHOWERING ME WITH EXPENSIVE GIFTS.
OBOY! I AM REALLY SHOCKED AT YOUR CYNICISM.
© 1981 King Features Syndicate, Inc. World rights reserved.
9-8
WHY? JUST BECAUSE A RELATIONSHIP IS DOOMED AT THE SPIRITUAL LEVEL, DOESN'T MEAN IT SHOULDN'T FLOURISH AT THE FINANCIAL LEVEL.
Hample

September 8, 1981

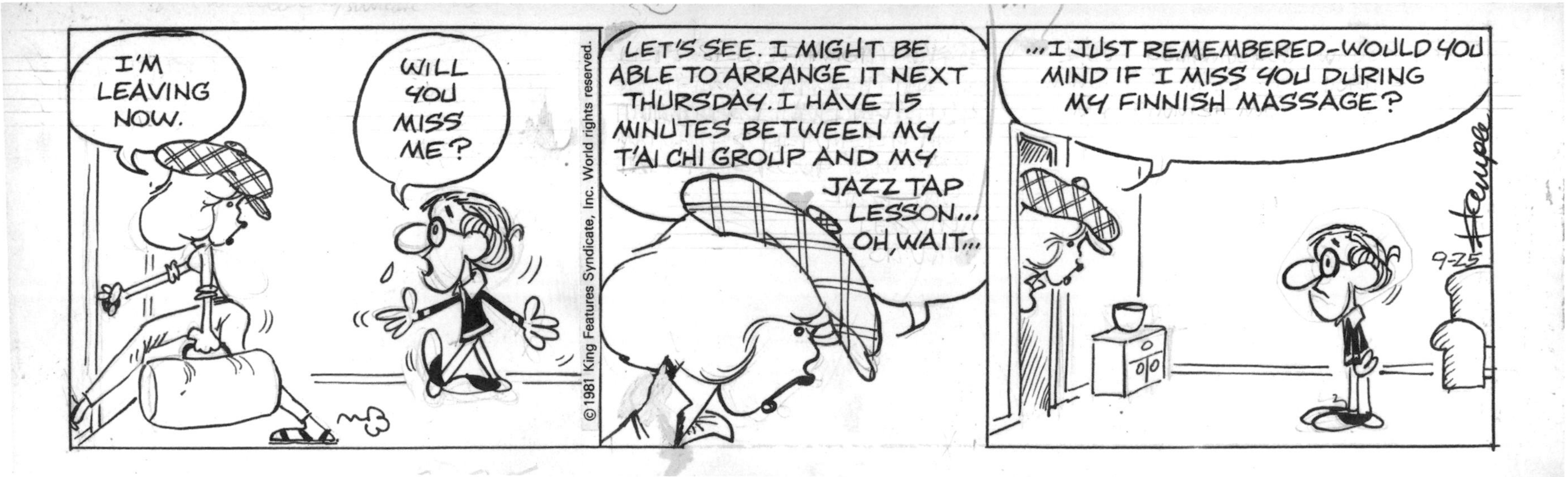
I'M LEAVING NOW.
WILL YOU MISS ME?
© 1981 King Features Syndicate, Inc. World rights reserved.
LET'S SEE. I MIGHT BE ABLE TO ARRANGE IT NEXT THURSDAY. I HAVE 15 MINUTES BETWEEN MY T'AI CHI GROUP AND MY JAZZ TAP LESSON... OH, WAIT...
...I JUST REMEMBERED-WOULD YOU MIND IF I MISS YOU DURING MY FINNISH MASSAGE?
9-25
Hample

September 25, 1981

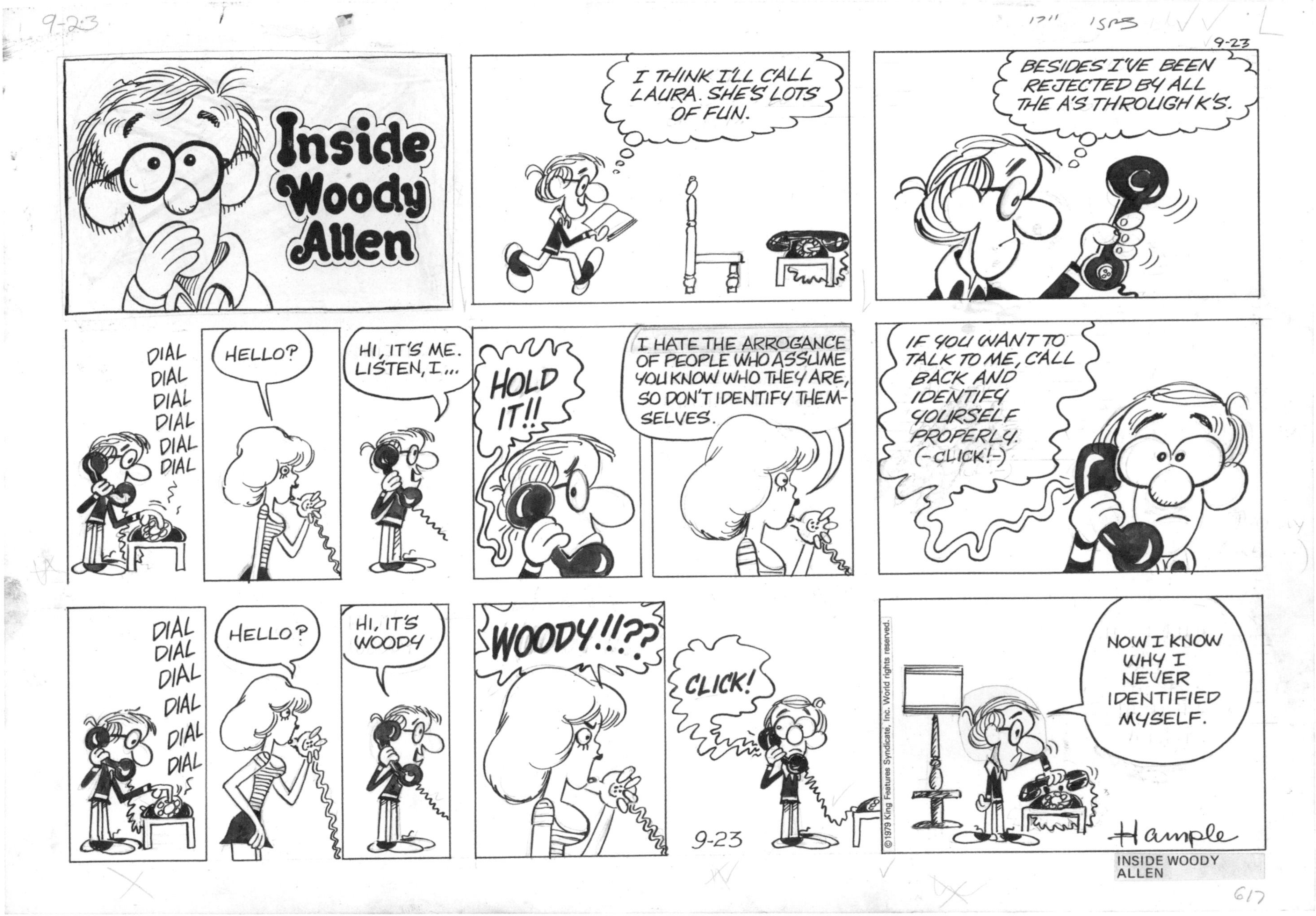

Inside Woody Allen
I THINK I'LL CALL LAURA. SHE'S LOTS OF FUN.
BESIDES I'VE BEEN REJECTED BY ALL THE A'S THROUGH K'S.
DIAL DIAL DIAL DIAL DIAL DIAL
HELLO?
HI, IT'S ME. LISTEN, I...
HOLD IT!!
I HATE THE ARROGANCE OF PEOPLE WHO ASSUME YOU KNOW WHO THEY ARE, SO DON'T IDENTIFY THEMSELVES.
IF YOU WANT TO TALK TO ME, CALL BACK AND IDENTIFY YOURSELF PROPERLY. (-CLICK!-)
DIAL DIAL DIAL DIAL DIAL DIAL
HELLO?
HI, IT'S WOODY
WOODY!!??
CLICK!
NOW I KNOW WHY I NEVER IDENTIFIED MYSELF.
©1979 King Features Syndicate, Inc. World rights reserved.
Hample
INSIDE WOODY ALLEN
9-23

September 23, 1979

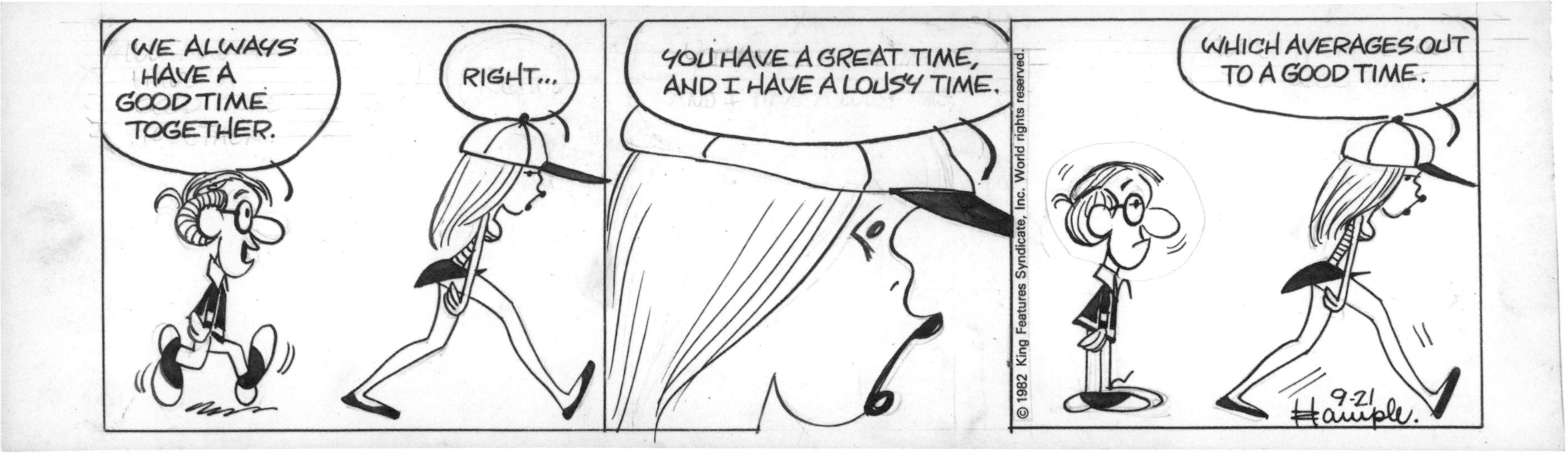
WE ALWAYS HAVE A GOOD TIME TOGETHER.
RIGHT...
YOU HAVE A GREAT TIME, AND I HAVE A LOUSY TIME.
© 1982 King Features Syndicate, Inc. World rights reserved.
WHICH AVERAGES OUT TO A GOOD TIME.
9-21
Hample.

September 21, 1982

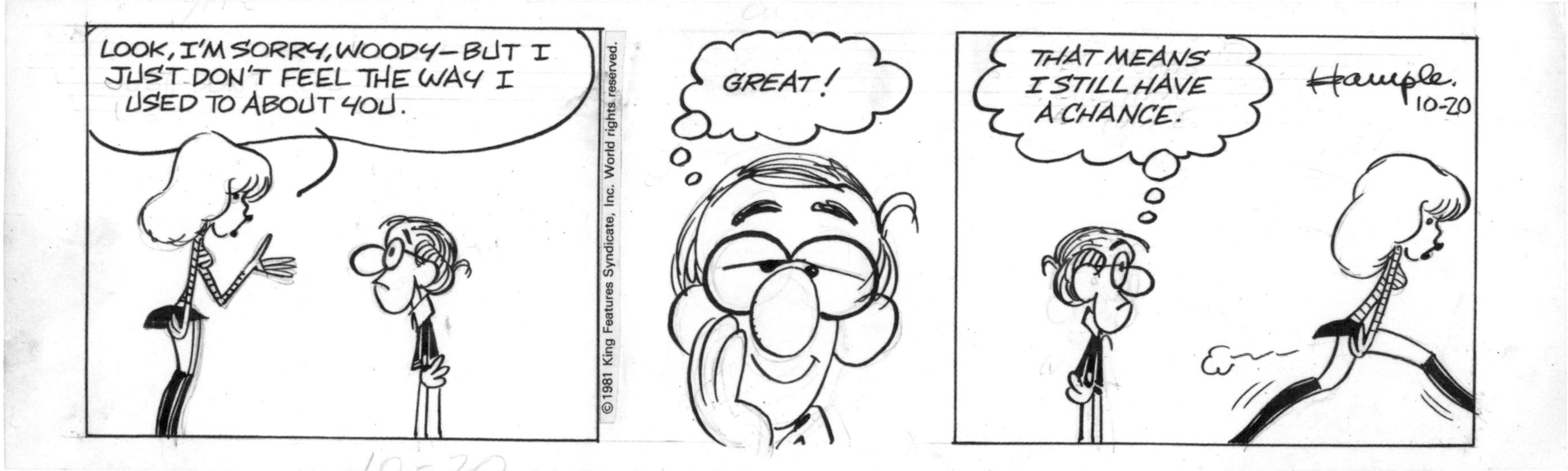
LOOK, I'M SORRY, WOODY—BUT I JUST DON'T FEEL THE WAY I USED TO ABOUT YOU.
© 1981 King Features Syndicate, Inc. World rights reserved.
GREAT!
THAT MEANS I STILL HAVE A CHANCE.
Hample.
10-20

October 20, 1981

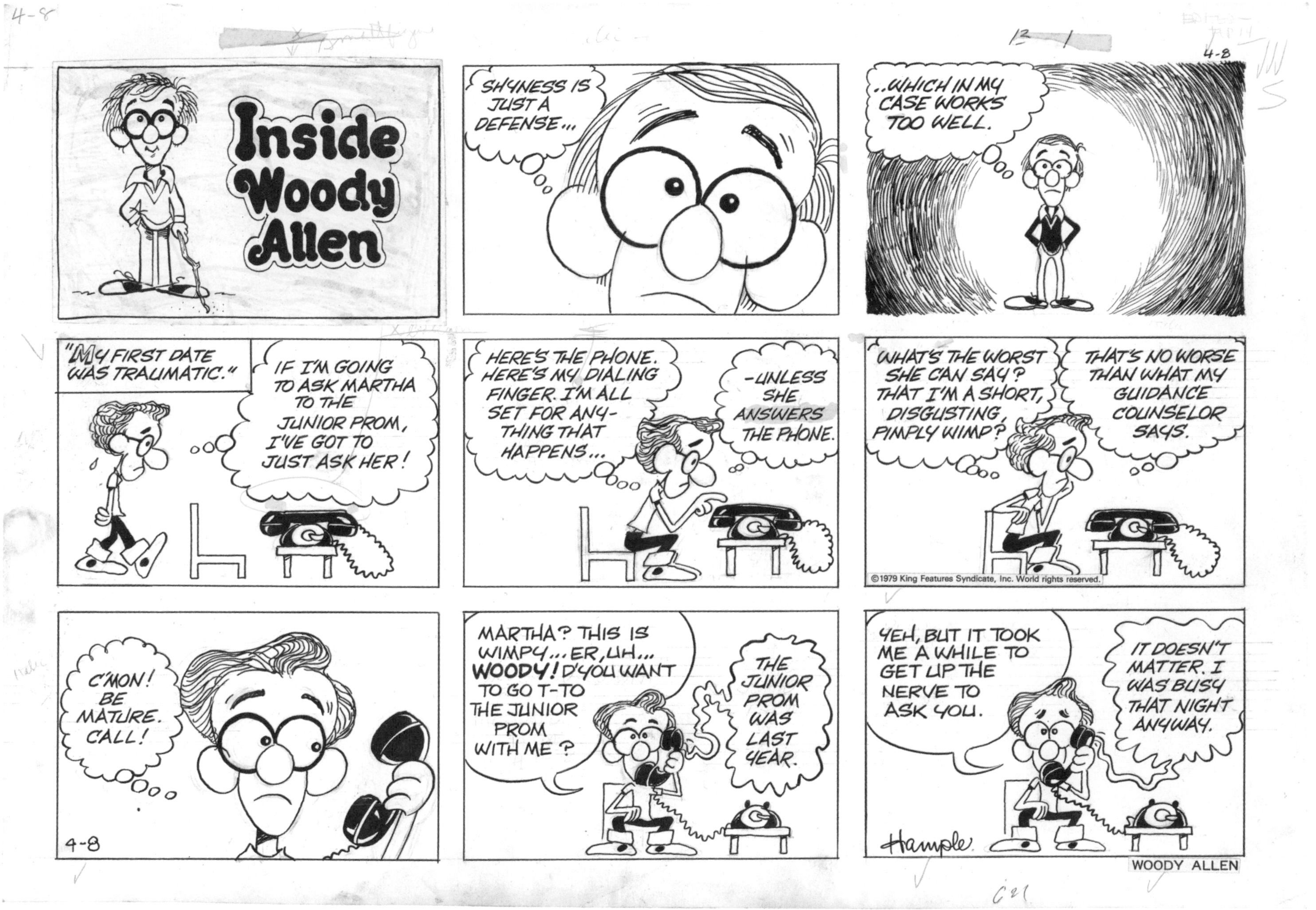
Inside Woody Allen
SHYNESS IS JUST A DEFENSE...
..WHICH IN MY CASE WORKS TOO WELL.
"MY FIRST DATE WAS TRAUMATIC."
IF I'M GOING TO ASK MARTHA TO THE JUNIOR PROM, I'VE GOT TO JUST ASK HER!
HERE'S THE PHONE. HERE'S MY DIALING FINGER. I'M ALL SET FOR ANY-THING THAT HAPPENS...
-UNLESS SHE ANSWERS THE PHONE.
WHAT'S THE WORST SHE CAN SAY? THAT I'M A SHORT, DISGUSTING, PIMPLY WIMP?
THAT'S NO WORSE THAN WHAT MY GUIDANCE COUNSELOR SAYS.
©1979 King Features Syndicate, Inc. World rights reserved.
C'MON! BE MATURE. CALL!
4-8
MARTHA? THIS IS WIMPY... ER, UH... WOODY! D'YOU WANT TO GO T-TO THE JUNIOR PROM WITH ME?
THE JUNIOR PROM WAS LAST YEAR.
YEH, BUT IT TOOK ME A WHILE TO GET UP THE NERVE TO ASK YOU.
IT DOESN'T MATTER. I WAS BUSY THAT NIGHT ANYWAY.
Hample
WOODY ALLEN

April 8, 1979

Inside Woody Allen

"I LEARNED EVERYTHING I KNOW ABOUT HANDLING DAMES FROM HUMPHREY BOGART.

I'D LOVE AN ICE CREAM.

THIS TIME, KID, YOU PAY.

UM...

ICE CRE

"THE FIRST HUMPHREY BOGART FILM I EVER SAW WAS 'THE MALTESE FALCON' AND I IDENTIFIED INSTANTLY WITH PETER LORRE.

BOGART FESTIVA

ONE.

"THE IMPULSE TO BE A SNIVELING, GREASY, LITTLE WEASEL APPEALED TO ME ENORMOUSLY.

"THE SECOND TIME I SAW 'THE MALTESE FALCON' I WAS 15 AND MY HEART WENT DIRECTLY TO BOGART.

"WHEN THE MASTER—IN LOVE WITH MARY ASTOR—TURNED HER IN TO THE COPS AND SAID:

I HOPE THEY DON'T HANG YOU BY THAT PRETTY NECK, SHWEETHEART...

"I WAS HOOKED FOR LIFE.

"WHY COULDN'T I HAVE THAT SAME ATTITUDE WHEN GIRLS TURNED ME DOWN?

ME? GO OUT WITH YOU?? AH HA HA HA...!!!

"NOW, YEARS LATER, I STILL WORSHIP BOGART. HE WAS TOUGH, BRILLIANT, HONEST AND LOVED BY EVERY WOMAN HE EVER CALLED 'SHWEETHEART...'"

...JUST LIKE ME.

8-17 Hample.

INSIDE WOODY ALLEN

August 17, 1980

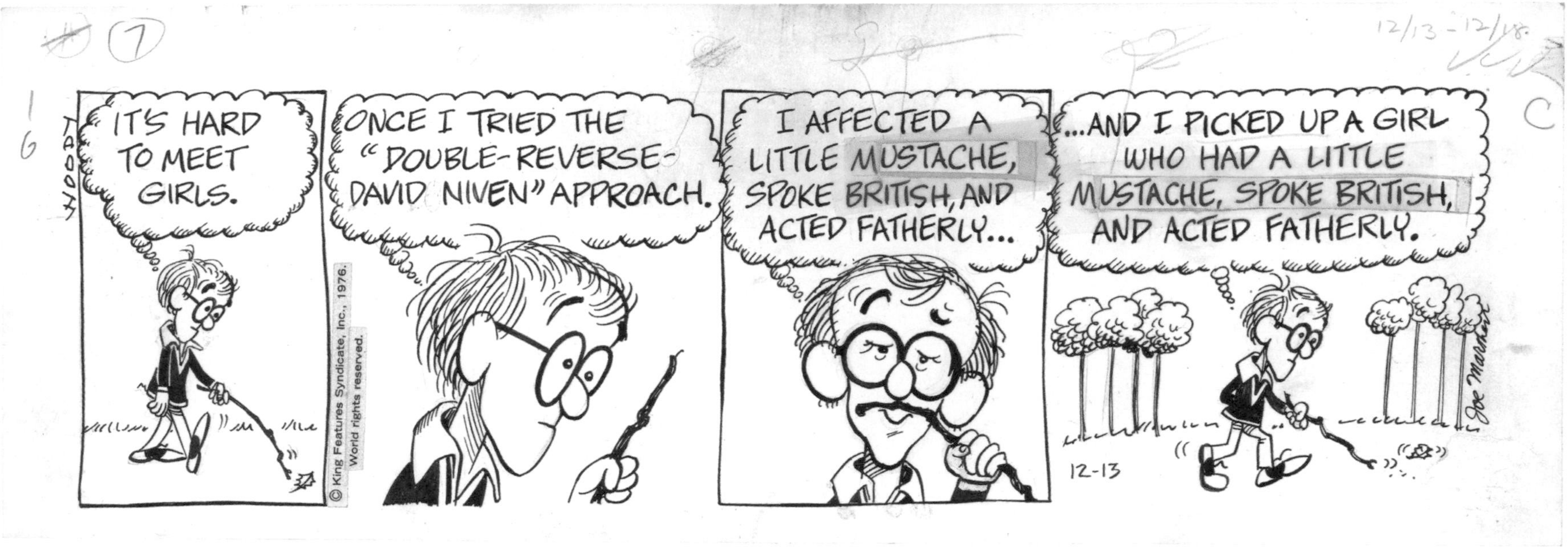
IT'S HARD TO MEET GIRLS.
ONCE I TRIED THE "DOUBLE-REVERSE-DAVID NIVEN" APPROACH.
© King Features Syndicate, Inc., 1976. World rights reserved.
I AFFECTED A LITTLE MUSTACHE, SPOKE BRITISH, AND ACTED FATHERLY...
...AND I PICKED UP A GIRL WHO HAD A LITTLE MUSTACHE, SPOKE BRITISH, AND ACTED FATHERLY.
12-13

December 13, 1976

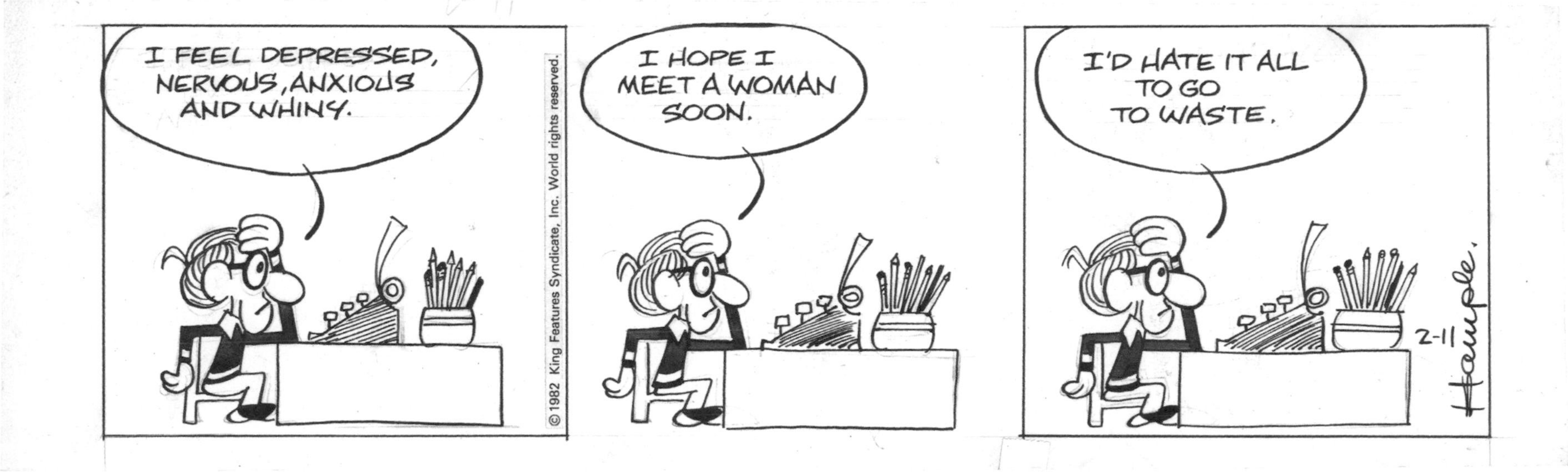
I FEEL DEPRESSED, NERVOUS, ANXIOUS AND WHINY.
© 1982 King Features Syndicate, Inc. World rights reserved.
I HOPE I MEET A WOMAN SOON.
I'D HATE IT ALL TO GO TO WASTE.
2-11
Hample.

February 11, 1982

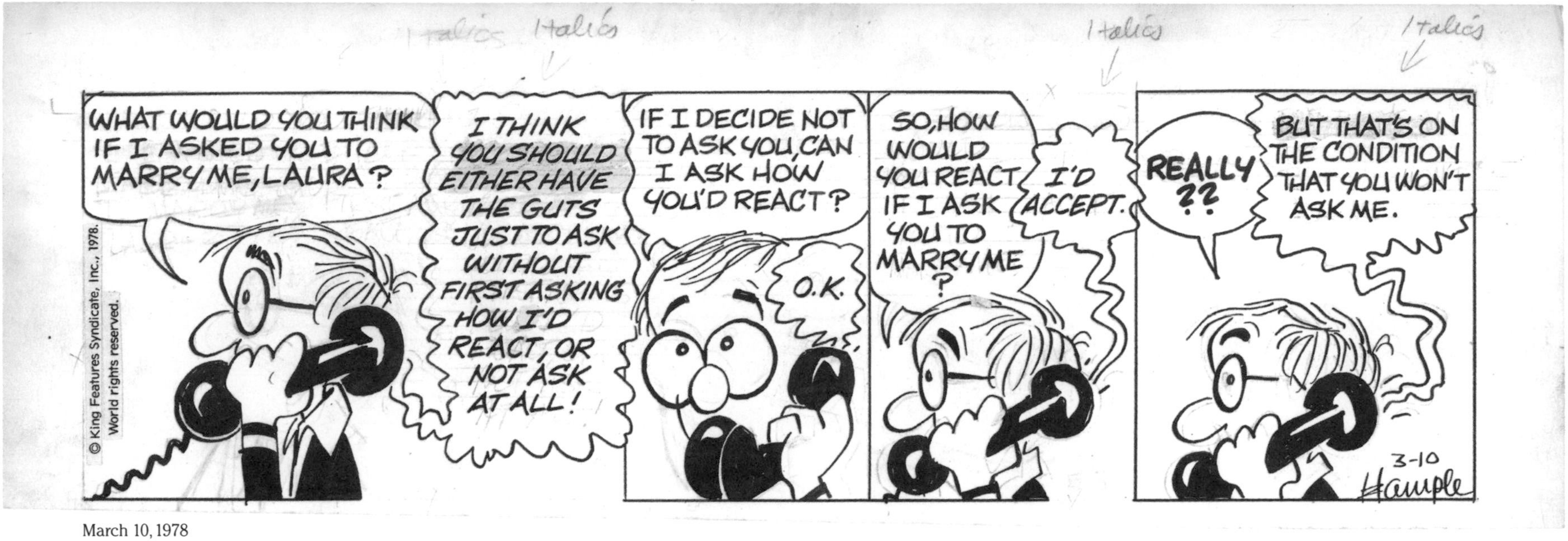
Italics
Italics
Italics
Italics
WHAT WOULD YOU THINK IF I ASKED YOU TO MARRY ME, LAURA?
I THINK YOU SHOULD EITHER HAVE THE GUTS JUST TO ASK WITHOUT FIRST ASKING HOW I'D REACT, OR NOT ASK AT ALL!
IF I DECIDE NOT TO ASK YOU, CAN I ASK HOW YOU'D REACT?
O.K.
SO, HOW WOULD YOU REACT IF I ASK YOU TO MARRY ME?
I'D ACCEPT.
REALLY??
BUT THAT'S ON THE CONDITION THAT YOU WON'T ASK ME.
© King Features Syndicate, Inc., 1978. World rights reserved.
3-10
Hample

March 10, 1978

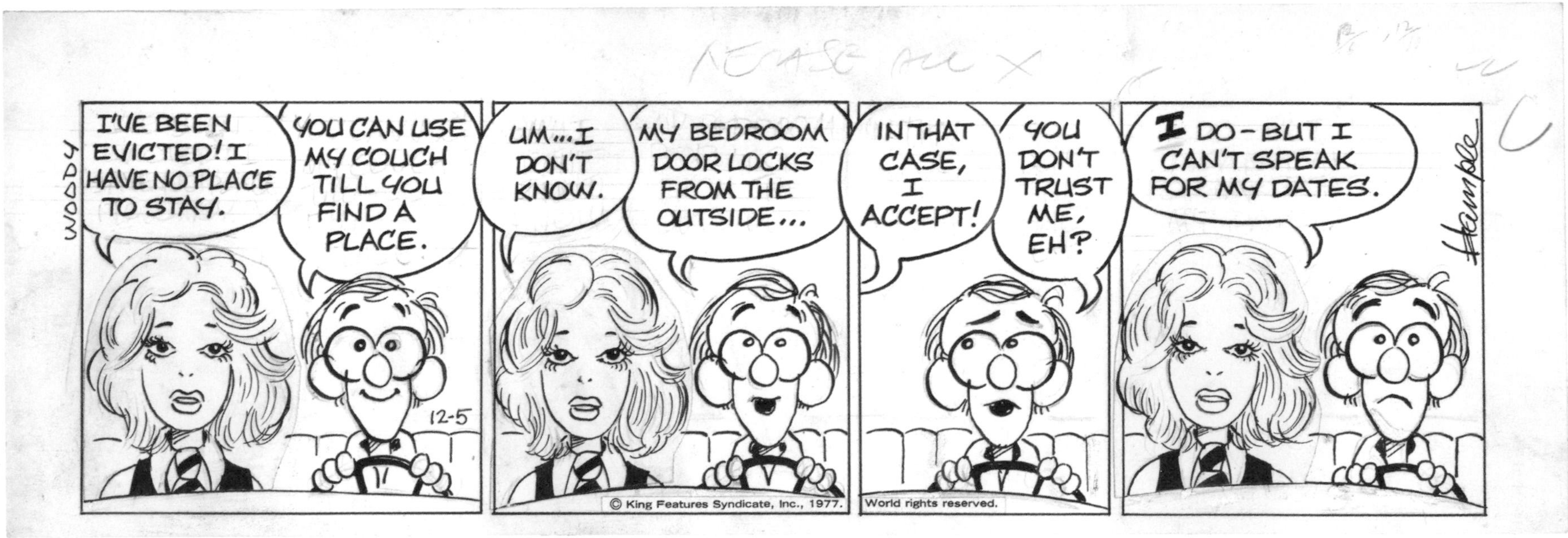
WOODY
I'VE BEEN EVICTED! I HAVE NO PLACE TO STAY.
YOU CAN USE MY COUCH TILL YOU FIND A PLACE.
UM...I DON'T KNOW.
MY BEDROOM DOOR LOCKS FROM THE OUTSIDE...
IN THAT CASE, I ACCEPT!
YOU DON'T TRUST ME, EH?
I DO - BUT I CAN'T SPEAK FOR MY DATES.
12-5
© King Features Syndicate, Inc., 1977.
World rights reserved.
Hample

December 5, 1977

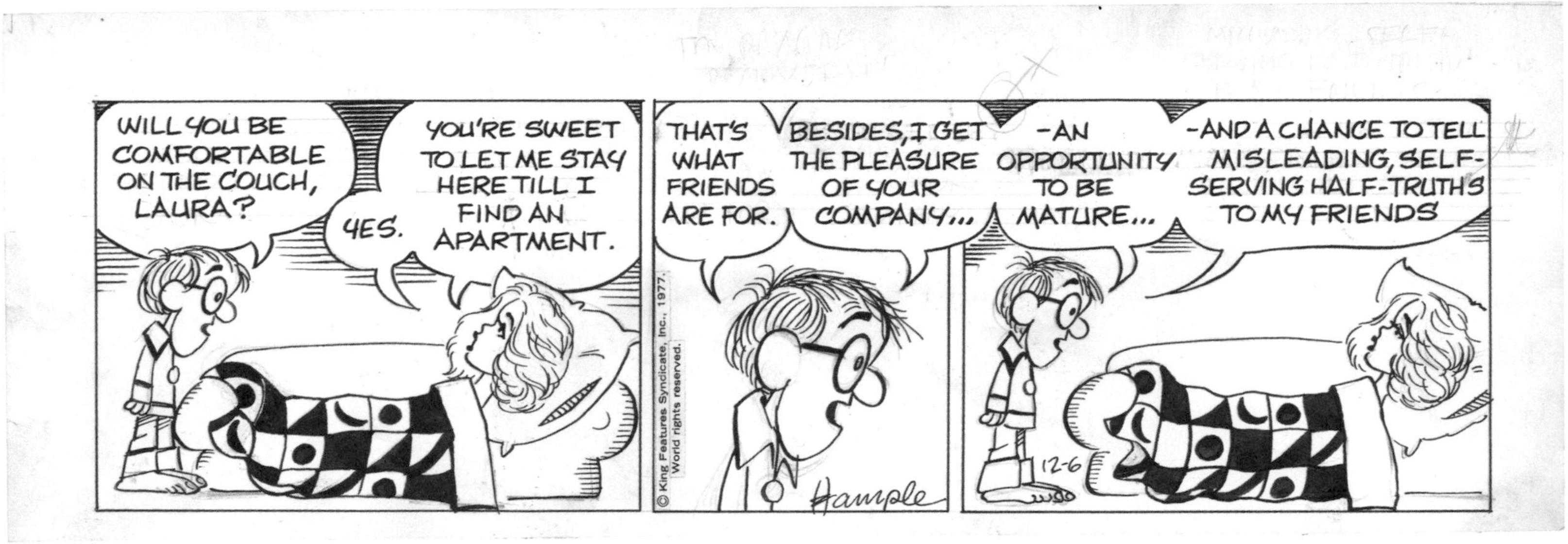
WILL YOU BE COMFORTABLE ON THE COUCH, LAURA?
YES.
YOU'RE SWEET TO LET ME STAY HERE TILL I FIND AN APARTMENT.
THAT'S WHAT FRIENDS ARE FOR.
BESIDES, I GET THE PLEASURE OF YOUR COMPANY...
-AN OPPORTUNITY TO BE MATURE...
-AND A CHANCE TO TELL MISLEADING, SELF-SERVING HALF-TRUTHS TO MY FRIENDS
© King Features Syndicate, Inc., 1977. World rights reserved.
Hample
12-6

December 6, 1977

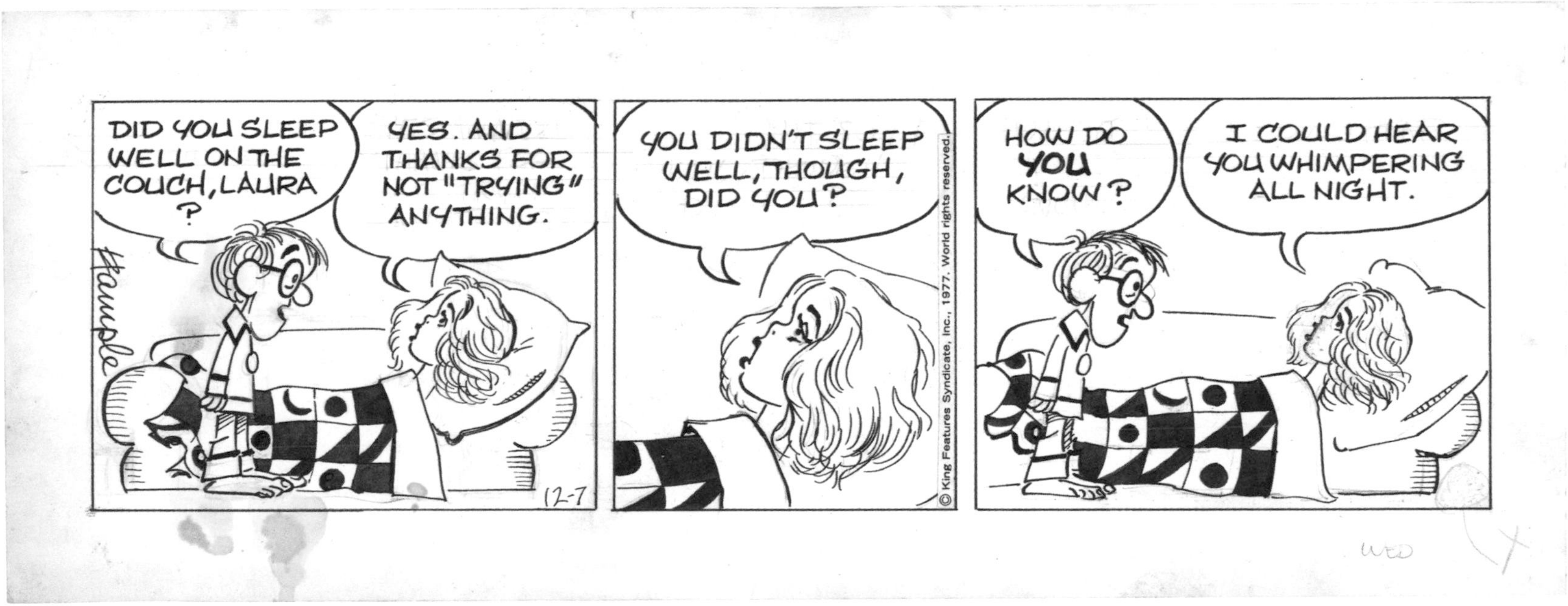
DID YOU SLEEP WELL ON THE COUCH, LAURA?
YES. AND THANKS FOR NOT "TRYING" ANYTHING.
YOU DIDN'T SLEEP WELL, THOUGH, DID YOU?
HOW DO **YOU** KNOW?
I COULD HEAR YOU WHIMPERING ALL NIGHT.
© King Features Syndicate, Inc., 1977. World rights reserved.
Hample
12-7

December 7, 1977

January 11, 1981

Every Time She Had an Orgasm, Her Nose Grew Longer

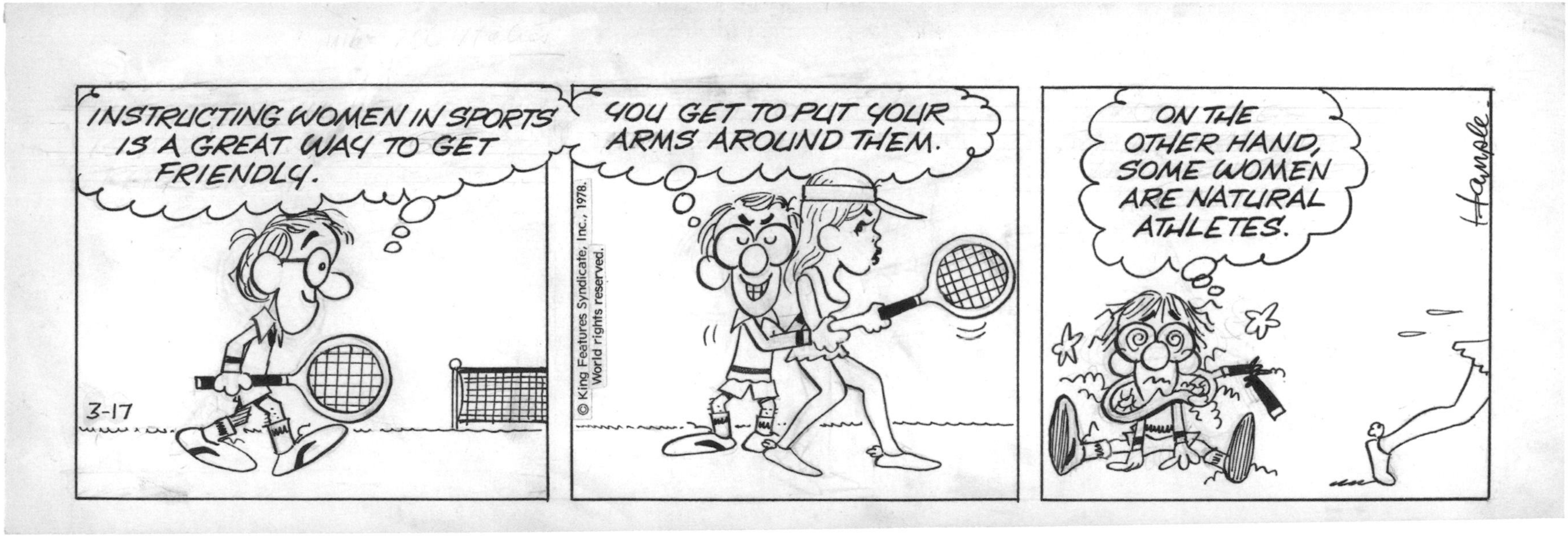
INSTRUCTING WOMEN IN SPORTS IS A GREAT WAY TO GET FRIENDLY.
3-17
YOU GET TO PUT YOUR ARMS AROUND THEM.
© King Features Syndicate, Inc., 1978. World rights reserved.
ON THE OTHER HAND, SOME WOMEN ARE NATURAL ATHLETES.
Hample

March 17, 1978

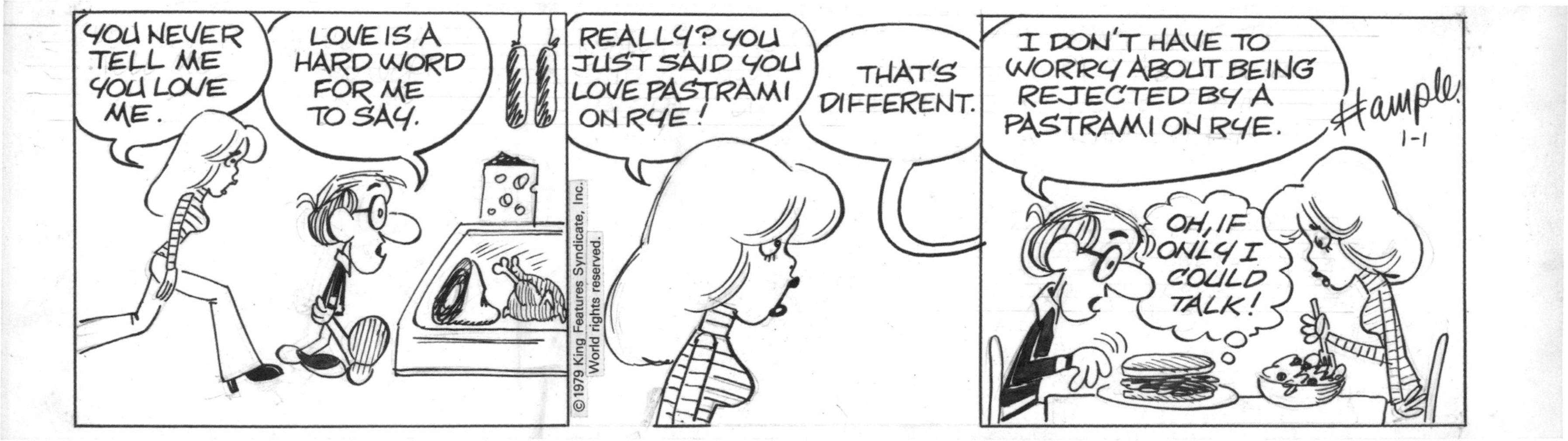
YOU NEVER TELL ME YOU LOVE ME.
LOVE IS A HARD WORD FOR ME TO SAY.
© 1979 King Features Syndicate, Inc. World rights reserved.
REALLY? YOU JUST SAID YOU LOVE PASTRAMI ON RYE!
THAT'S DIFFERENT.
I DON'T HAVE TO WORRY ABOUT BEING REJECTED BY A PASTRAMI ON RYE.
Hample
1-1
OH, IF ONLY I COULD TALK!

January 1, 1979

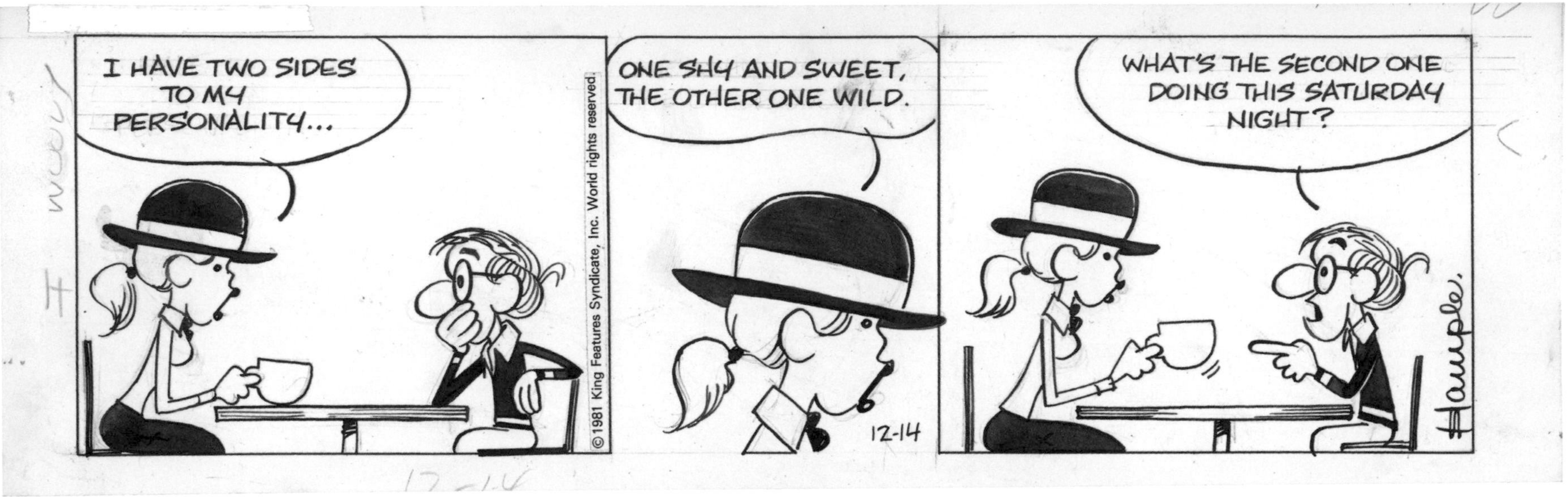
I HAVE TWO SIDES TO MY PERSONALITY...
ONE SHY AND SWEET, THE OTHER ONE WILD.
WHAT'S THE SECOND ONE DOING THIS SATURDAY NIGHT?
12-14
Hample.
© 1981 King Features Syndicate, Inc. World rights reserved.

December 14, 1981

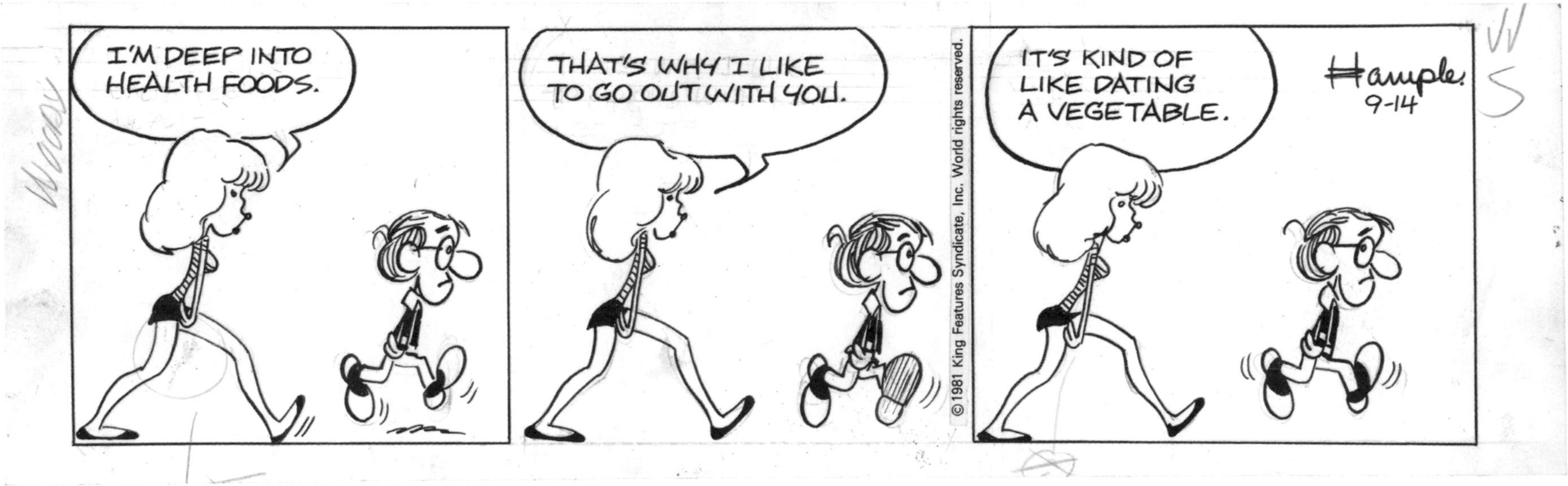
I'M DEEP INTO HEALTH FOODS.
THAT'S WHY I LIKE TO GO OUT WITH YOU.
IT'S KIND OF LIKE DATING A VEGETABLE.
Hample.
9-14
© 1981 King Features Syndicate, Inc. World rights reserved.

September 14, 1981

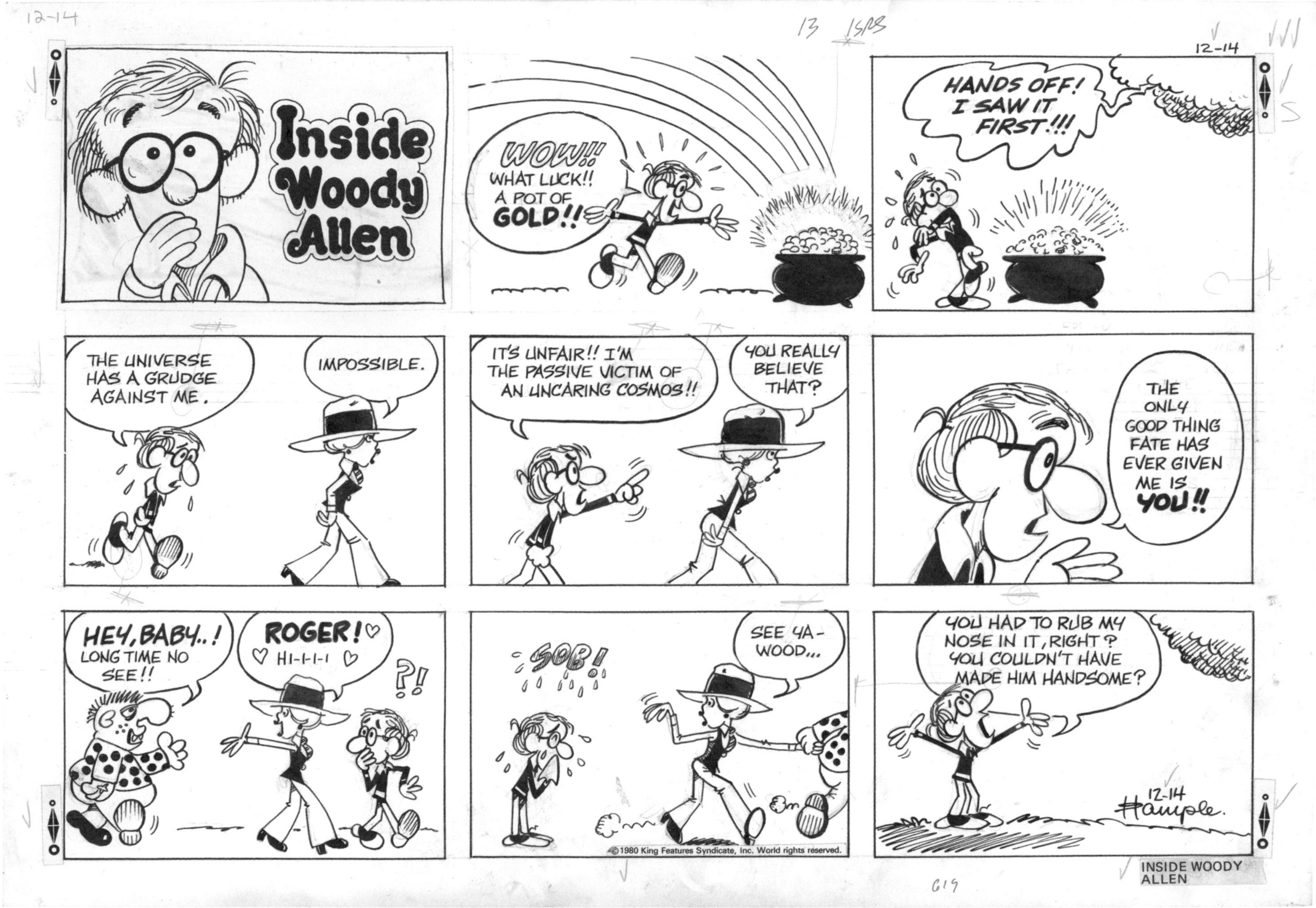

Inside Woody Allen
WOW!! WHAT LUCK!! A POT OF GOLD!!
HANDS OFF! I SAW IT FIRST!!!
THE UNIVERSE HAS A GRUDGE AGAINST ME.
IMPOSSIBLE.
IT'S UNFAIR!! I'M THE PASSIVE VICTIM OF AN UNCARING COSMOS!!
YOU REALLY BELIEVE THAT?
THE ONLY GOOD THING FATE HAS EVER GIVEN ME IS YOU!!
HEY, BABY..! LONG TIME NO SEE!!
ROGER! ♡ ♡ HI-I-I-I ♡
?!
SOB!
SEE YA-WOOD...
YOU HAD TO RUB MY NOSE IN IT, RIGHT? YOU COULDN'T HAVE MADE HIM HANDSOME?
12-14 Hample.
©1980 King Features Syndicate, Inc. World rights reserved.
INSIDE WOODY ALLEN

December 14, 1980

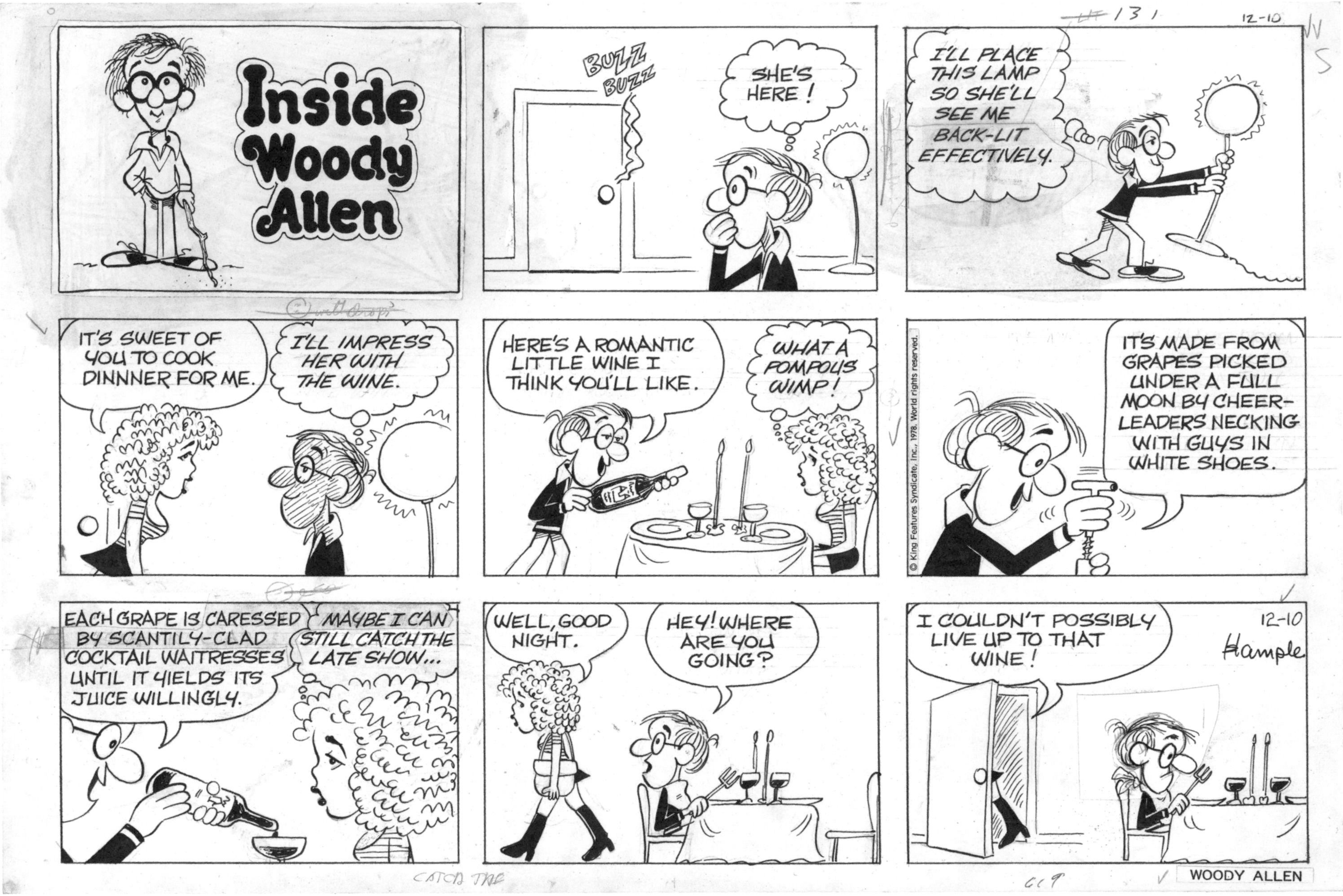
#131
12-10
Inside Woody Allen
BUZZ BUZZ
SHE'S HERE!
I'LL PLACE THIS LAMP SO SHE'LL SEE ME BACK-LIT EFFECTIVELY.
IT'S SWEET OF YOU TO COOK DINNNER FOR ME.
I'LL IMPRESS HER WITH THE WINE.
HERE'S A ROMANTIC LITTLE WINE I THINK YOU'LL LIKE.
WHAT A POMPOUS WIMP!
© King Features Syndicate, Inc., 1978. World rights reserved.
IT'S MADE FROM GRAPES PICKED UNDER A FULL MOON BY CHEER-LEADERS NECKING WITH GUYS IN WHITE SHOES.
EACH GRAPE IS CARESSED BY SCANTILY-CLAD COCKTAIL WAITRESSES UNTIL IT YIELDS ITS JUICE WILLINGLY.
MAYBE I CAN STILL CATCH THE LATE SHOW...
WELL, GOOD NIGHT.
HEY! WHERE ARE YOU GOING?
I COULDN'T POSSIBLY LIVE UP TO THAT WINE!
12-10
Hample
WOODY ALLEN

December 10, 1978

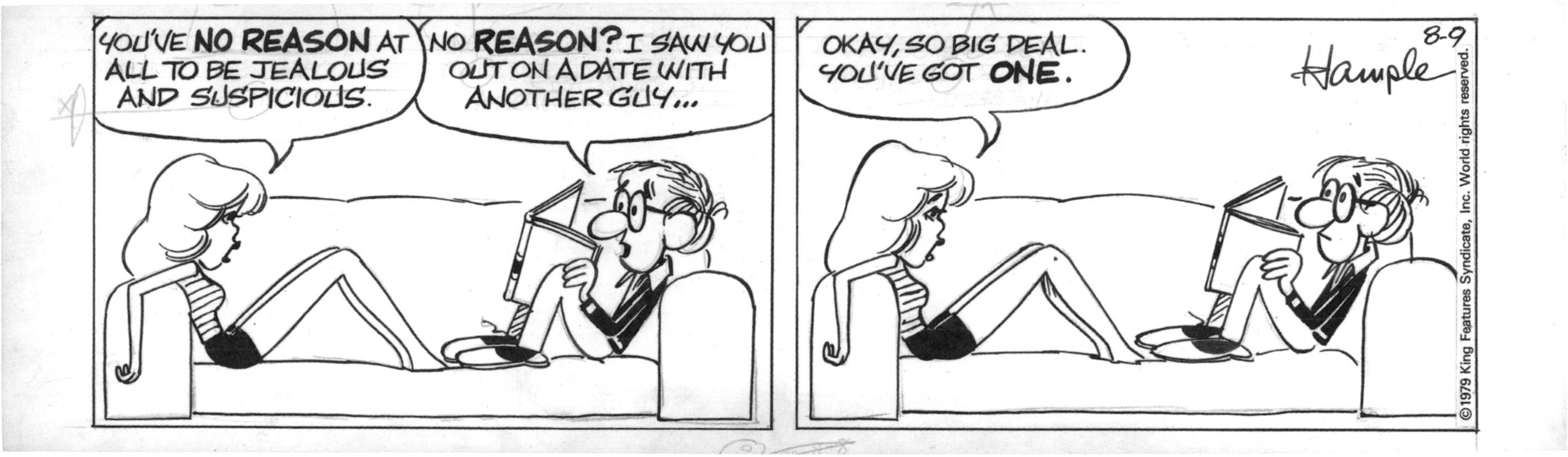
YOU'VE NO REASON AT ALL TO BE JEALOUS AND SUSPICIOUS.
NO REASON? I SAW YOU OUT ON A DATE WITH ANOTHER GUY...
OKAY, SO BIG DEAL. YOU'VE GOT ONE.
8-9
Hample
© 1979 King Features Syndicate, Inc. World rights reserved.

August 9, 1979

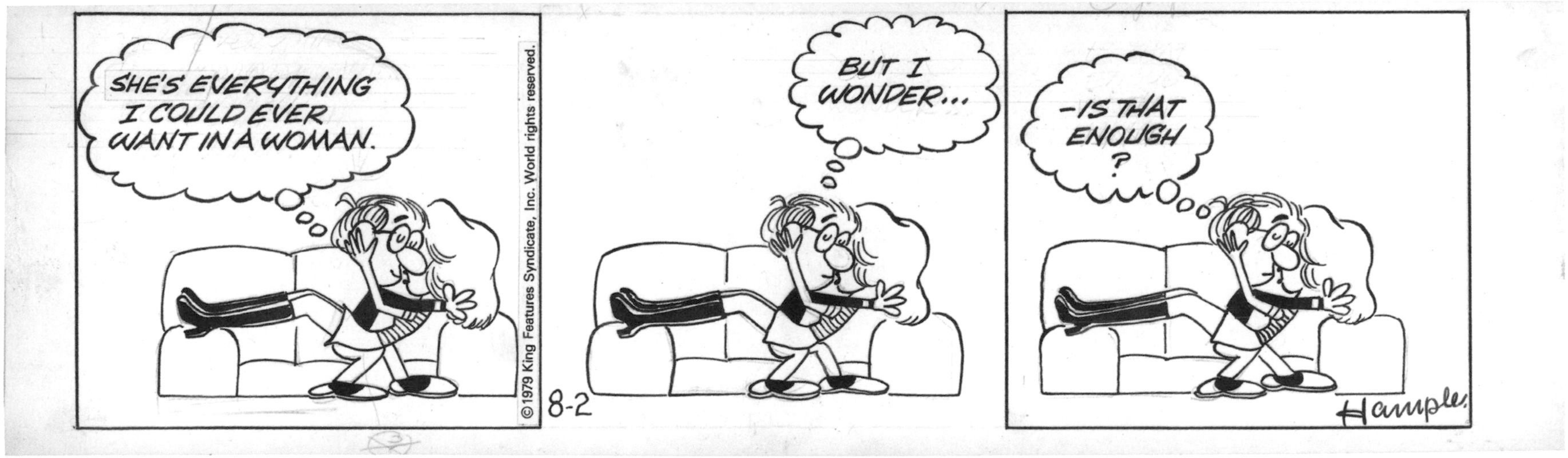
SHE'S EVERYTHING I COULD EVER WANT IN A WOMAN.
© 1979 King Features Syndicate, Inc. World rights reserved.
8-2
BUT I WONDER...
-IS THAT ENOUGH ?
Hample

August 2, 1979

Inside Woody Allen

THIS PLACE IS CRAWLING WITH ELIGIBLE BACHELORETTES...

...AND ONE FANTASTIC HUNK O'MAN...

WOW! THIS LAUNDROMAT IS DEFINITELY "SCORE COUNTRY"

IT'S LIKE LOOKING AT THE MENU OF A FINE RESTAURANT...

...HARD TO SETTLE ON JUST ONE DISH.

MAYBE I SHOULDN'T JUST SETTLE FOR ONE...YEAH, WHY LIMIT MYSELF? I'VE GOT ENOUGH ANIMAL MAGNETISM TO SATISFY EVERYONE HERE.

EXCUSE ME, GIRLS, I NOTICE WE ALL USE THE SAME BRAND OF SOAP.

SINCE WE OBVIOUSLY HAVE SO MUCH IN COMMON, I THOUGHT PERHAPS YOU'D ALL LIKE TO COME UP TO MY PLACE TONIGHT AND COMPARE NOTES ON PERMANENT PRESS.

IF YOU ASK ME, A SIMPLE "NO" WOULD'VE BEEN SUFFICIENT...

WOODY ALLEN

September 4, 1977

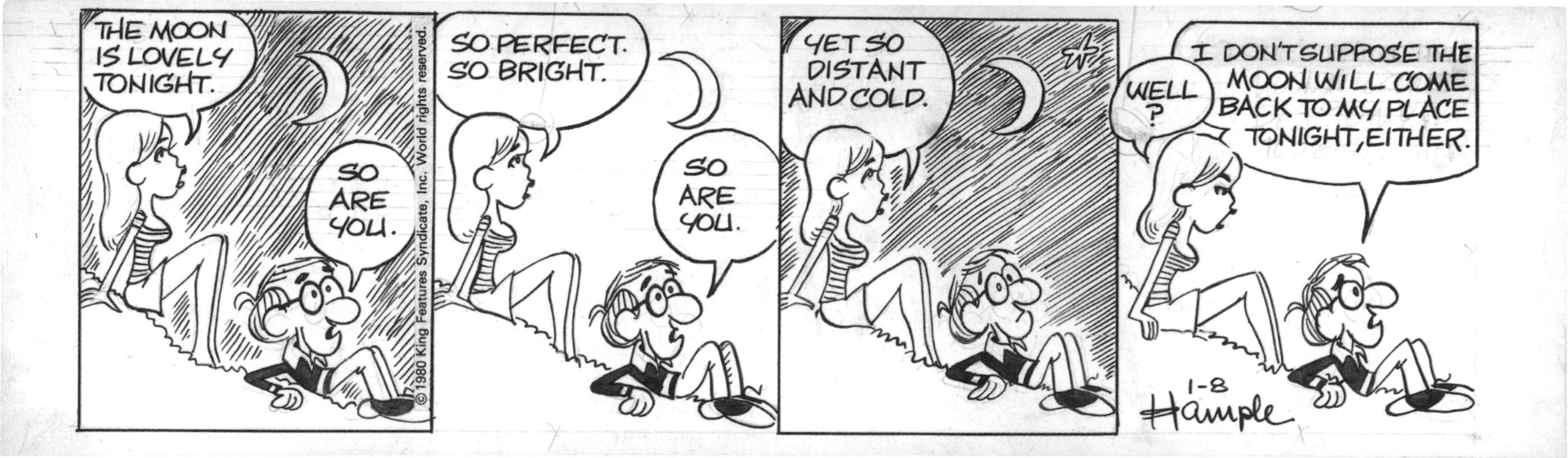
THE MOON IS LOVELY TONIGHT.
SO ARE YOU.
© 1980 King Features Syndicate, Inc. World rights reserved.
SO PERFECT. SO BRIGHT.
SO ARE YOU.
YET SO DISTANT AND COLD.
WELL ?
I DON'T SUPPOSE THE MOON WILL COME BACK TO MY PLACE TONIGHT, EITHER.
1-8
Hample

January 8, 1980

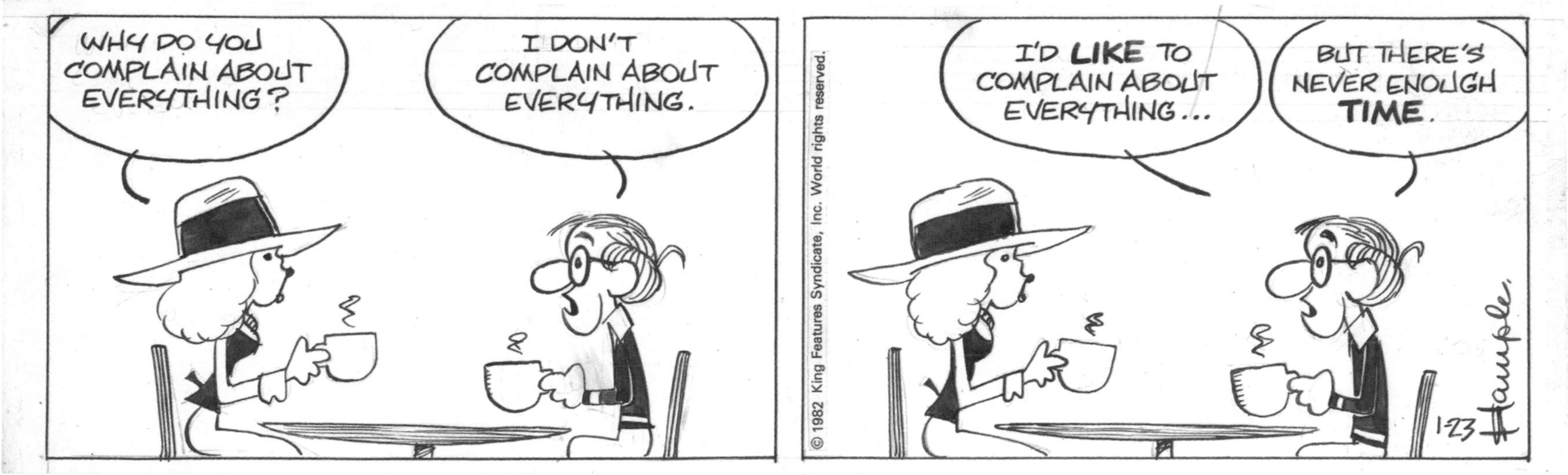
WHY DO YOU COMPLAIN ABOUT EVERYTHING?
I DON'T COMPLAIN ABOUT EVERYTHING.
© 1982 King Features Syndicate, Inc. World rights reserved.
I'D **LIKE** TO COMPLAIN ABOUT EVERYTHING...
BUT THERE'S NEVER ENOUGH **TIME**.
1-23
Hample

January 23, 1982

Inside Woody Allen

WHEN I WAS A KID, I DIDN'T HAVE THE ANIMAL MAGNETISM I HAVE TODAY.

AS A MATTER OF FACT, THE ONLY KIND OF DATE I COULD GET WAS A BLIND DATE.

"THE FIRST BLIND DATE I EVER HAD TURNED OUT TO BE THE GIRL VOTED IN OUR YEARBOOK MOST LIKELY TO GROW UP LOOKING LIKE HER MOTHER.

Muriel Plotnik

"SHE DID HAVE A KEEN SENSE OF SMELL, THOUGH. THE POLICE WOULD CALL HER IN TO TRACK DOWN A CRIMINAL WHEN THEIR BLOODHOUND HAD THE DAY OFF.

SNIF SNIF

© King Features Syndicate, Inc., 1977. World rights reserved.

"BUT I WAS ALWAYS A TERRIFIC ESCORT... MY IDEA OF SPENDING BIG WAS CALLING ON THE GIRL WITH A DOZEN ROSES...

"TAKING HER TO DINNER, ORCHESTRA SEATS FOR A TOP PLAY, THEN DANCING TILL 3 A.M. AT A NIGHTCLUB.

I NEVER **DID** ANY OF THOSE THINGS—THAT WAS JUST MY **IDEA**.

"I ONLY HAD ENOUGH MONEY TO TAKE HER DOWN TO THE DRUGSTORE AND HAVE HER WEIGHED ON ONE OF THOSE SCALES THAT ALSO GIVES YOUR FORTUNE.

7-31

"THEN WE'D SPEND THE REST OF THE NIGHT READING THAT..."

WOODY ALLEN

July 31, 1977

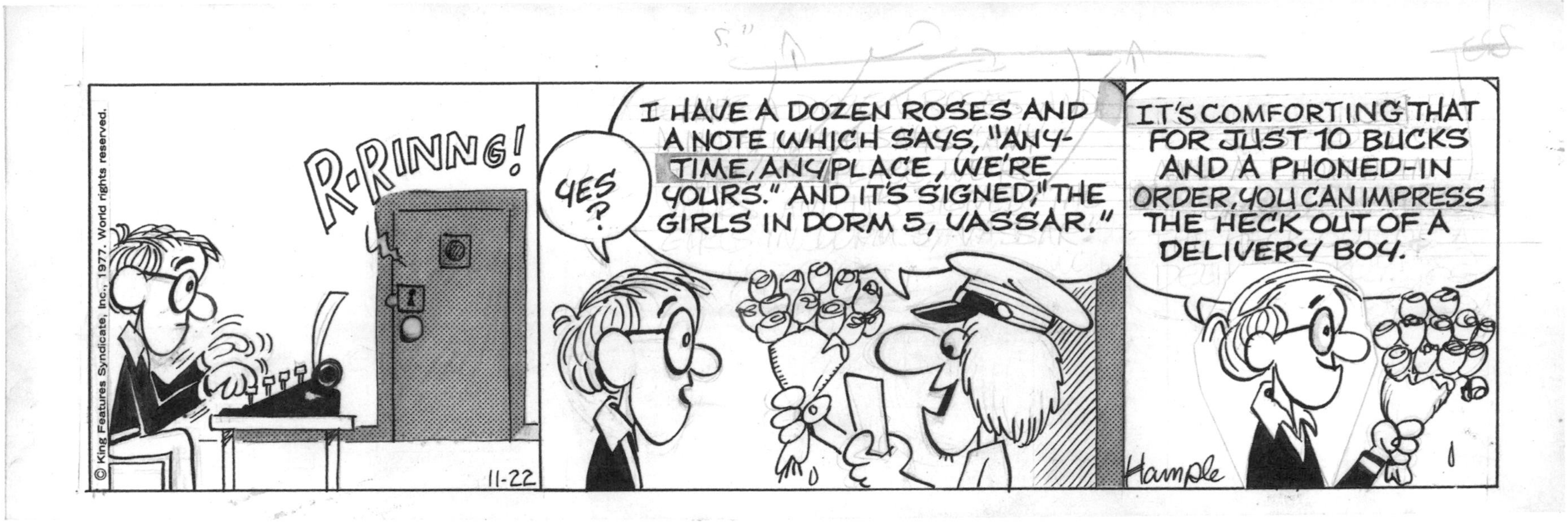
© King Features Syndicate, Inc., 1977. World rights reserved.
R-RINNG!
11-22
YES?
I HAVE A DOZEN ROSES AND A NOTE WHICH SAYS, "ANY-TIME, ANYPLACE, WE'RE YOURS." AND IT'S SIGNED, "THE GIRLS IN DORM 5, VASSAR."
IT'S COMFORTING THAT FOR JUST 10 BUCKS AND A PHONED-IN ORDER, YOU CAN IMPRESS THE HECK OUT OF A DELIVERY BOY.
Hample

November 22, 1977

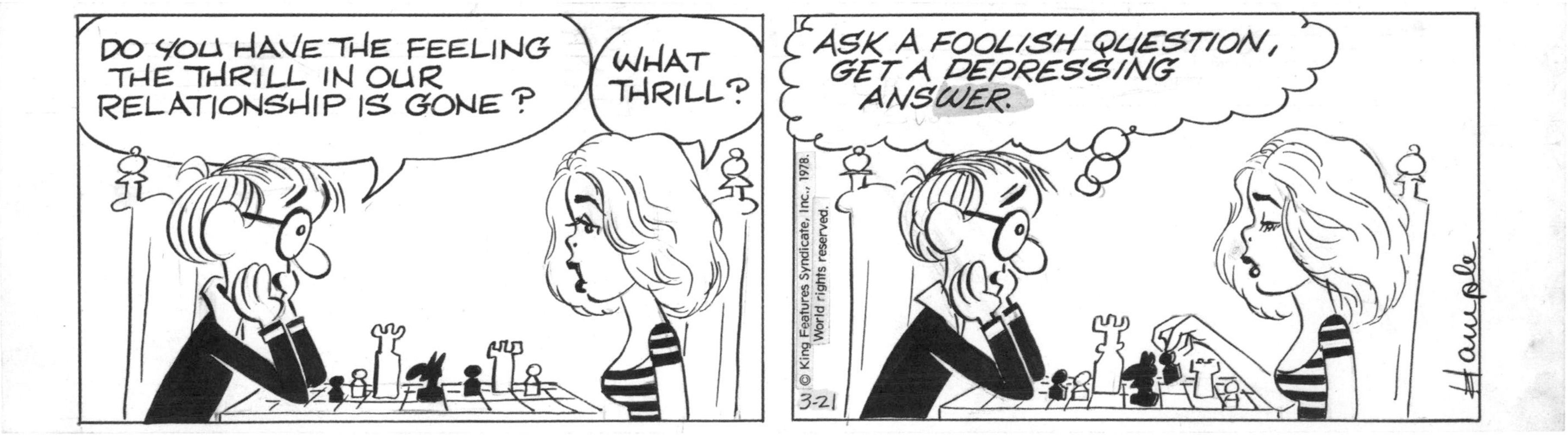
DO YOU HAVE THE FEELING THE THRILL IN OUR RELATIONSHIP IS GONE?
WHAT THRILL?
© King Features Syndicate, Inc., 1978. World rights reserved.
3-21
ASK A FOOLISH QUESTION, GET A DEPRESSING ANSWER.
Hample

March 21, 1978

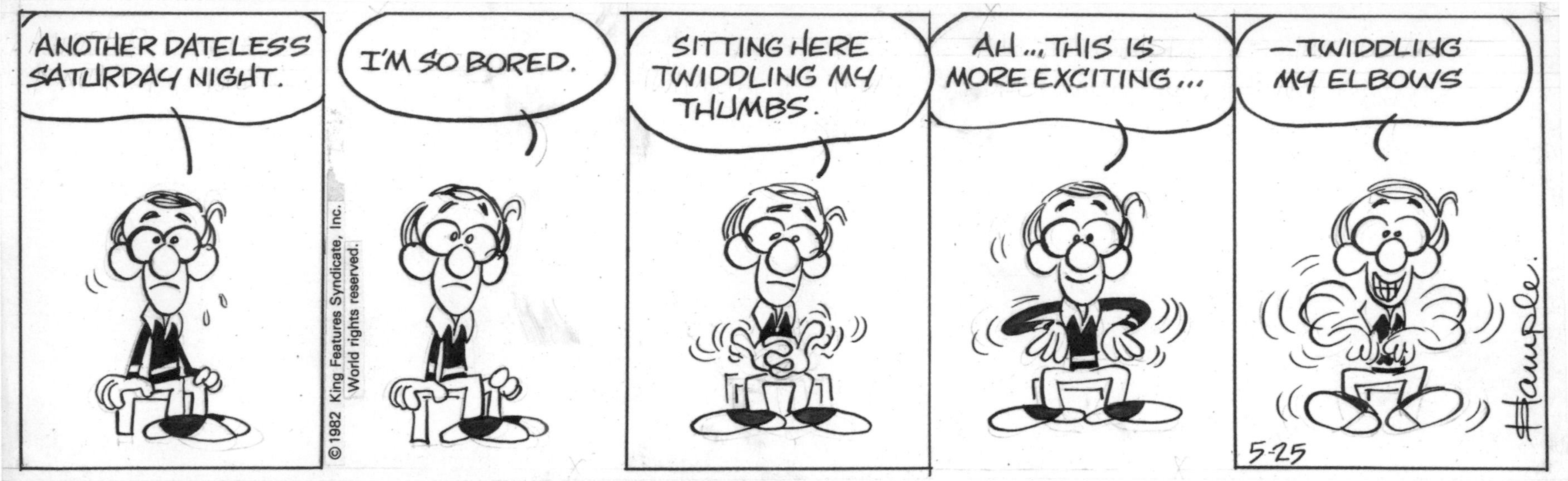
ANOTHER DATELESS SATURDAY NIGHT.
I'M SO BORED.
SITTING HERE TWIDDLING MY THUMBS.
AH ... THIS IS MORE EXCITING ...
—TWIDDLING MY ELBOWS
© 1982 King Features Syndicate, Inc. World rights reserved.
5-25
Hample

May 25, 1982

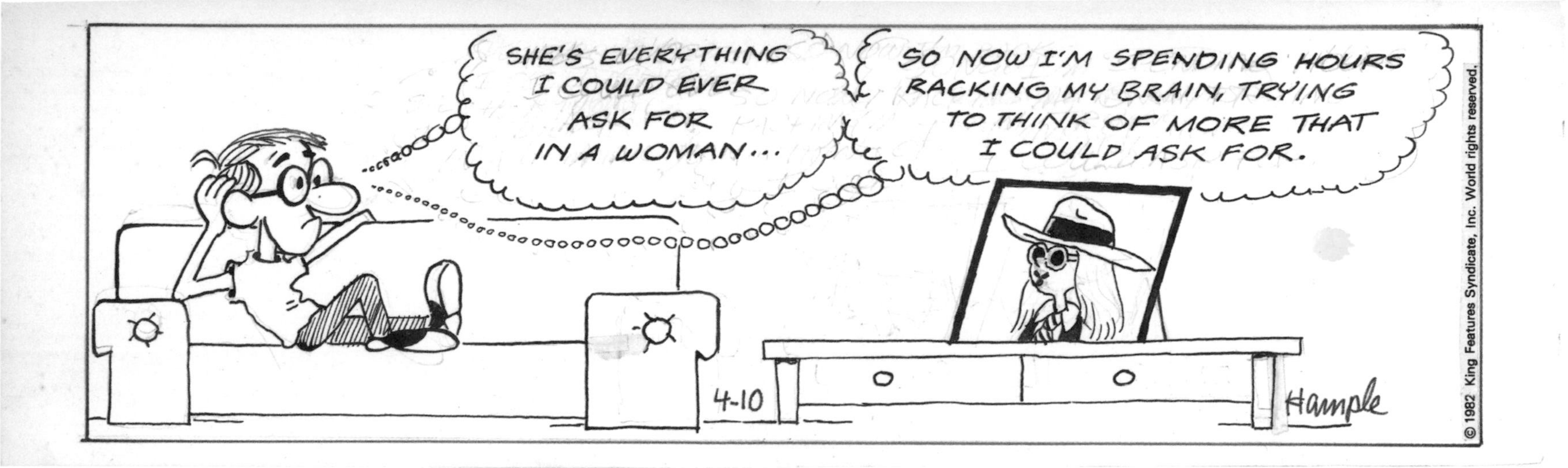
SHE'S EVERYTHING I COULD EVER ASK FOR IN A WOMAN...
SO NOW I'M SPENDING HOURS RACKING MY BRAIN, TRYING TO THINK OF MORE THAT I COULD ASK FOR.
4-10
Hample
© 1982 King Features Syndicate, Inc. World rights reserved.

April 10, 1982

...EXCEPT THE PART WHERE YOUR EYES LIGHT UP AND YOU BEGIN TO GIGGLE...

July 2, 1978

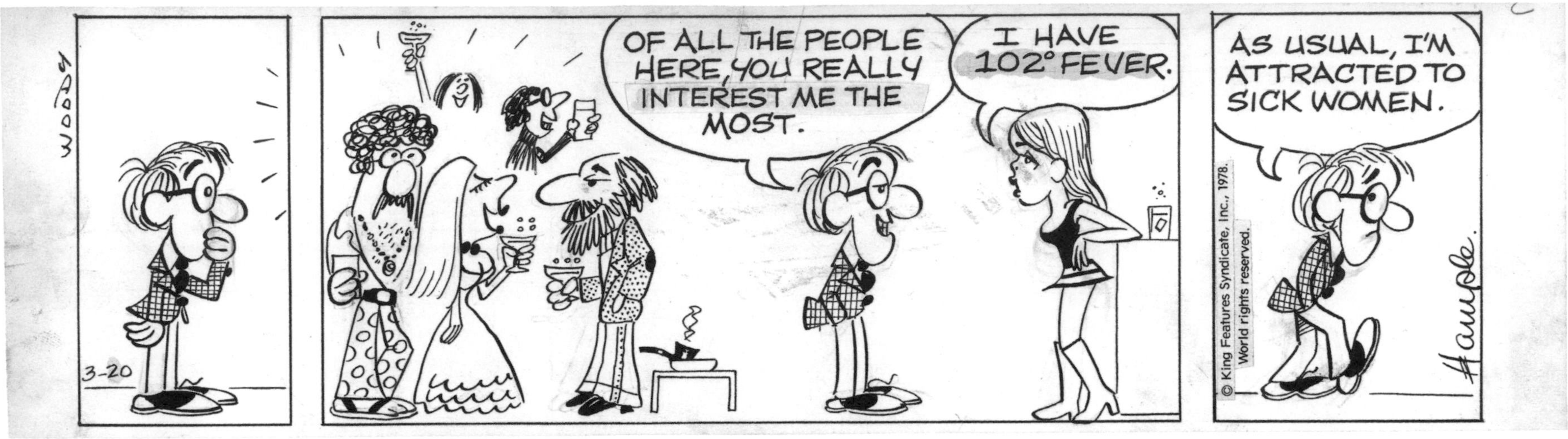
WOODY
3-20
OF ALL THE PEOPLE HERE, YOU REALLY INTEREST ME THE MOST.
I HAVE 102° FEVER.
AS USUAL, I'M ATTRACTED TO SICK WOMEN.
© King Features Syndicate, Inc., 1978. World rights reserved.
Hample

March 20, 1978

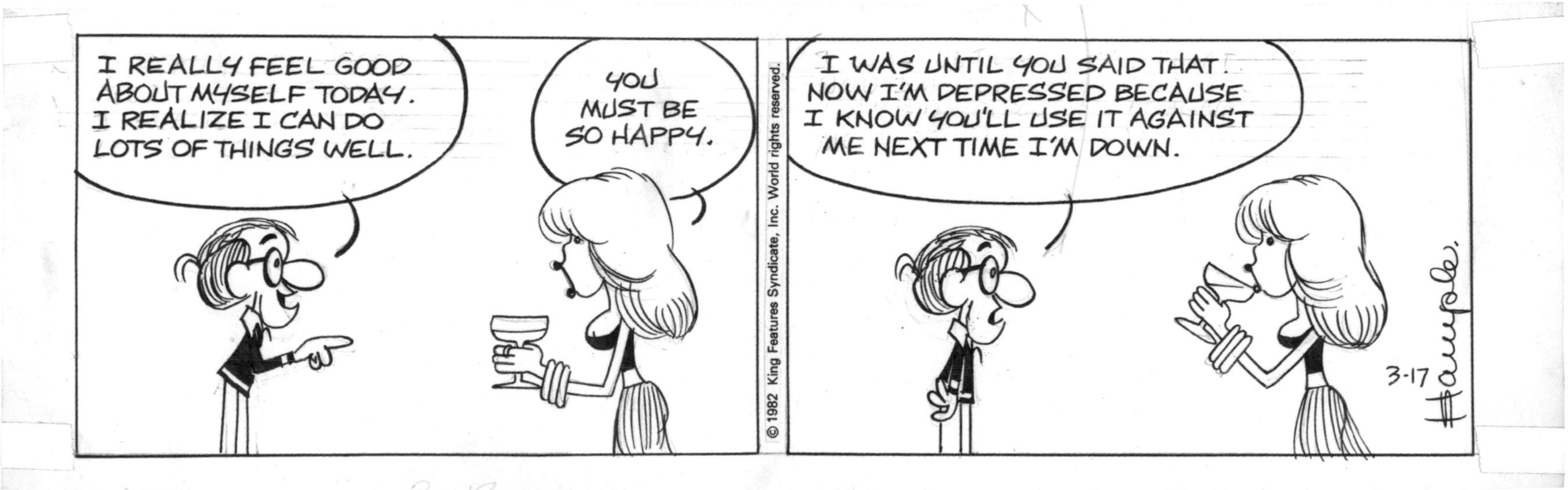
I REALLY FEEL GOOD ABOUT MYSELF TODAY. I REALIZE I CAN DO LOTS OF THINGS WELL.
YOU MUST BE SO HAPPY.
© 1982 King Features Syndicate, Inc. World rights reserved.
I WAS UNTIL YOU SAID THAT. NOW I'M DEPRESSED BECAUSE I KNOW YOU'LL USE IT AGAINST ME NEXT TIME I'M DOWN.
3-17
Hample

March 17, 1982

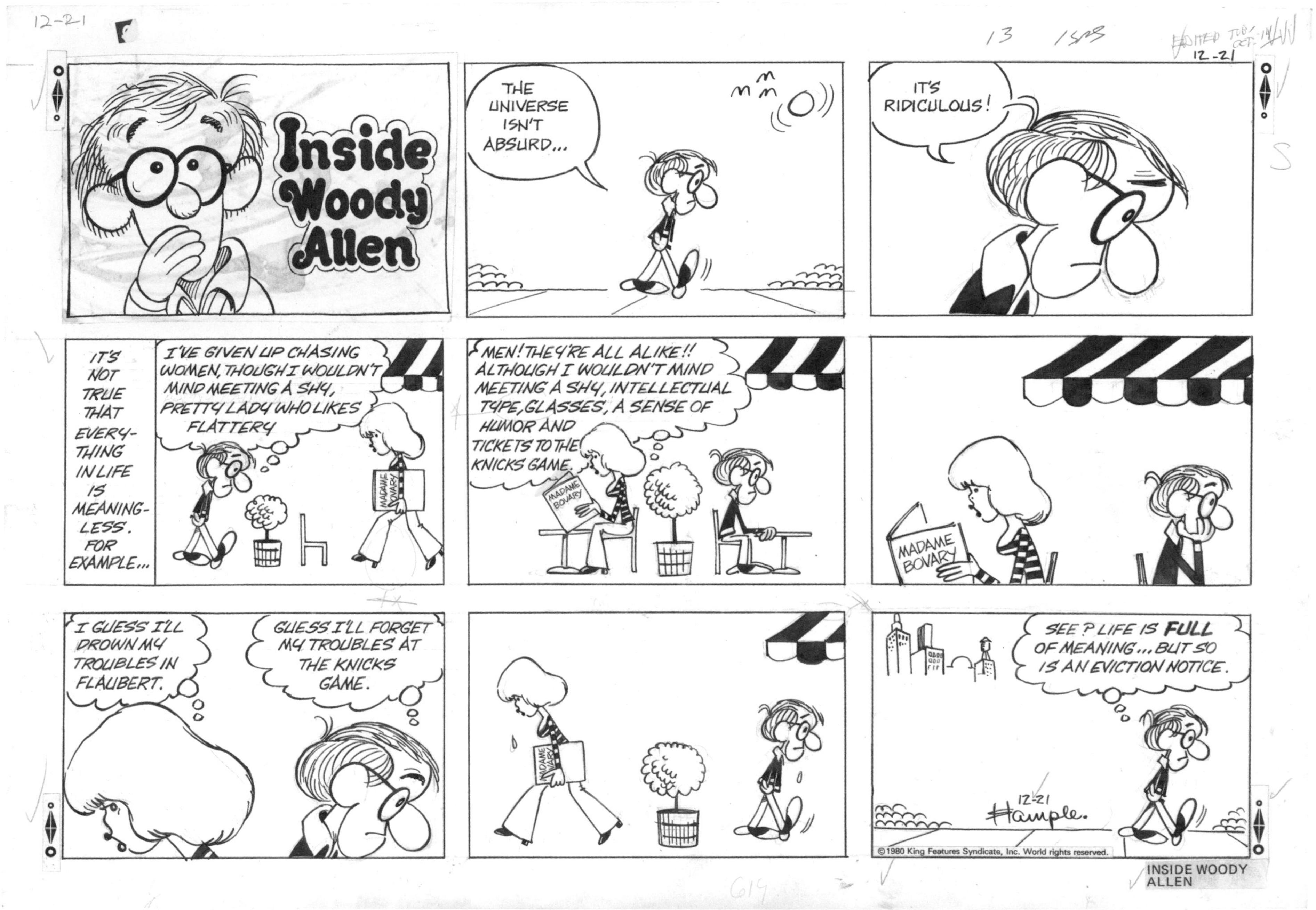
Inside Woody Allen
THE UNIVERSE ISN'T ABSURD...
M M M
IT'S RIDICULOUS!
IT'S NOT TRUE THAT EVERY-THING IN LIFE IS MEANING-LESS. FOR EXAMPLE...
I'VE GIVEN UP CHASING WOMEN, THOUGH I WOULDN'T MIND MEETING A SHY, PRETTY LADY WHO LIKES FLATTERY
MADAME BOVARY
MEN! THEY'RE ALL ALIKE!! ALTHOUGH I WOULDN'T MIND MEETING A SHY, INTELLECTUAL TYPE, GLASSES, A SENSE OF HUMOR AND TICKETS TO THE KNICKS GAME.
MADAME BOVARY
MADAME BOVARY
I GUESS I'LL DROWN MY TROUBLES IN FLAUBERT.
GUESS I'LL FORGET MY TROUBLES AT THE KNICKS GAME.
MADAME BOVARY
SEE? LIFE IS **FULL** OF MEANING... BUT SO IS AN EVICTION NOTICE.
12-21
Hample.
©1980 King Features Syndicate, Inc. World rights reserved.
INSIDE WOODY ALLEN

December 21, 1980

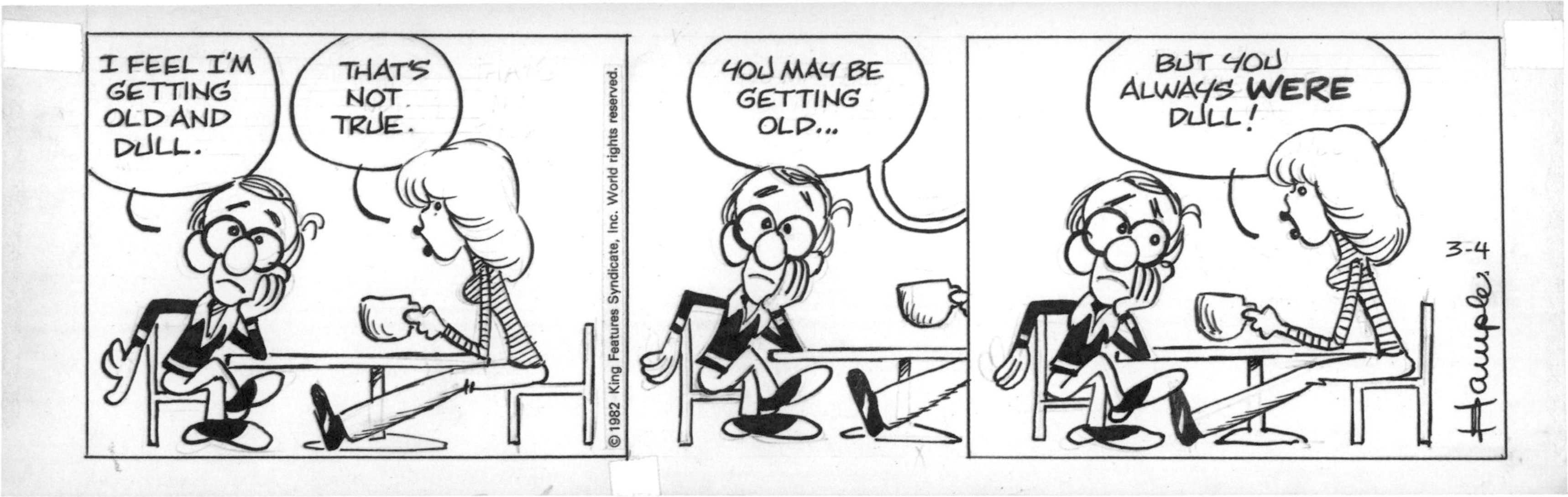
I FEEL I'M GETTING OLD AND DULL.
THAT'S NOT TRUE.
© 1982 King Features Syndicate, Inc. World rights reserved.
YOU MAY BE GETTING OLD...
BUT YOU ALWAYS WERE DULL!
3-4
Hample

March 4, 1982

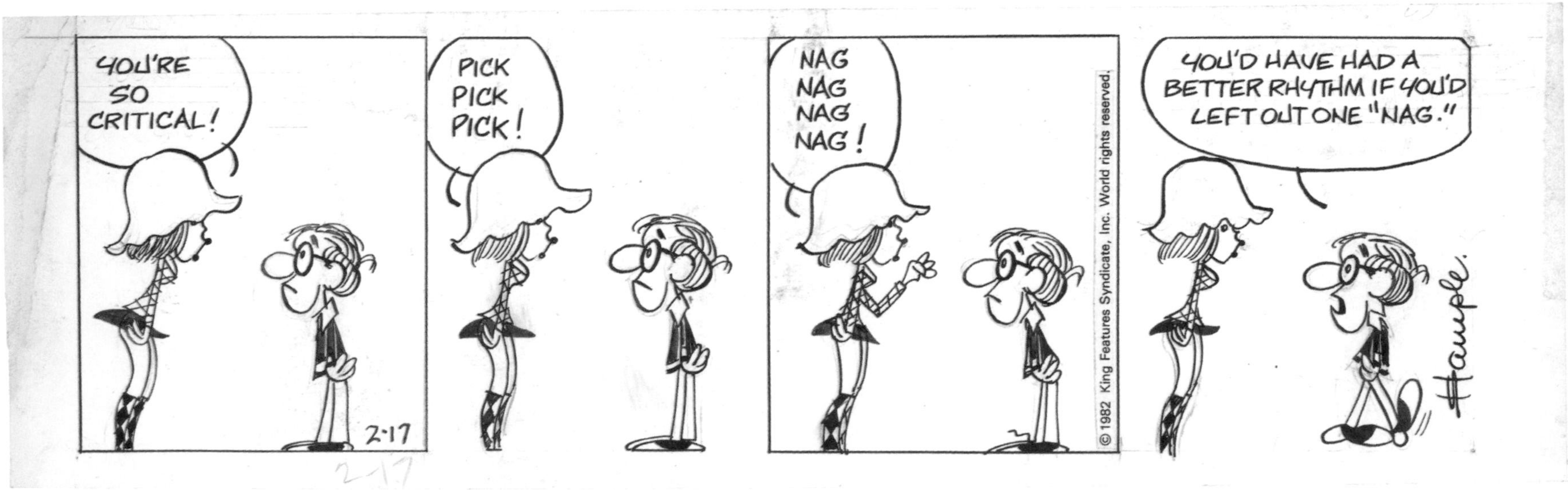
YOU'RE SO CRITICAL!
2·17
PICK PICK PICK!
NAG NAG NAG NAG!
© 1982 King Features Syndicate, Inc. World rights reserved.
YOU'D HAVE HAD A BETTER RHYTHM IF YOU'D LEFT OUT ONE "NAG."
Hample

February 17, 1982

Inside Woody Allen

ALL MEN ARE CREATED EQUAL.

—YET SOMEHOW, WOMEN MANAGE TO CHOOSE AMONG US.

SETH, THERE'S A LOT I CAN TEACH YOU ABOUT TYPES OF WOMEN.

THIS ONE'S AN INTELLECTUAL. GOES TO A BERGMAN FILM AND TAKES NOTES.

THAT ONE'S VERY VAIN. INHALES HER FOOD TO AVOID SMEARING HER LIPSTICK

POETIC TYPE. TRANSMUTES PAIN INTO VERSE, AND VICE VERSA. YOU TRY TO NECK WITH HER AND SHE GETS INSPIRED TO WRITE A POEM ABOUT LARKS SINGING AND THE LOWLY MOTH.

© King Features Syndicate, Inc., 1978. World rights reserved.

WHY DO YOU CATEGORIZE AND STEREOTYPE, UNCLE WOODY? WOULDN'T IT BE BETTER TO TREAT PEOPLE AS UNIQUE INDIVIDUALS?

11-5

FORGET IT! IT'S MUCH LESS PAINFUL TO BE REJECTED BY A STEREOTYPE!

Hample

WOODY ALLEN

November 5, 1978

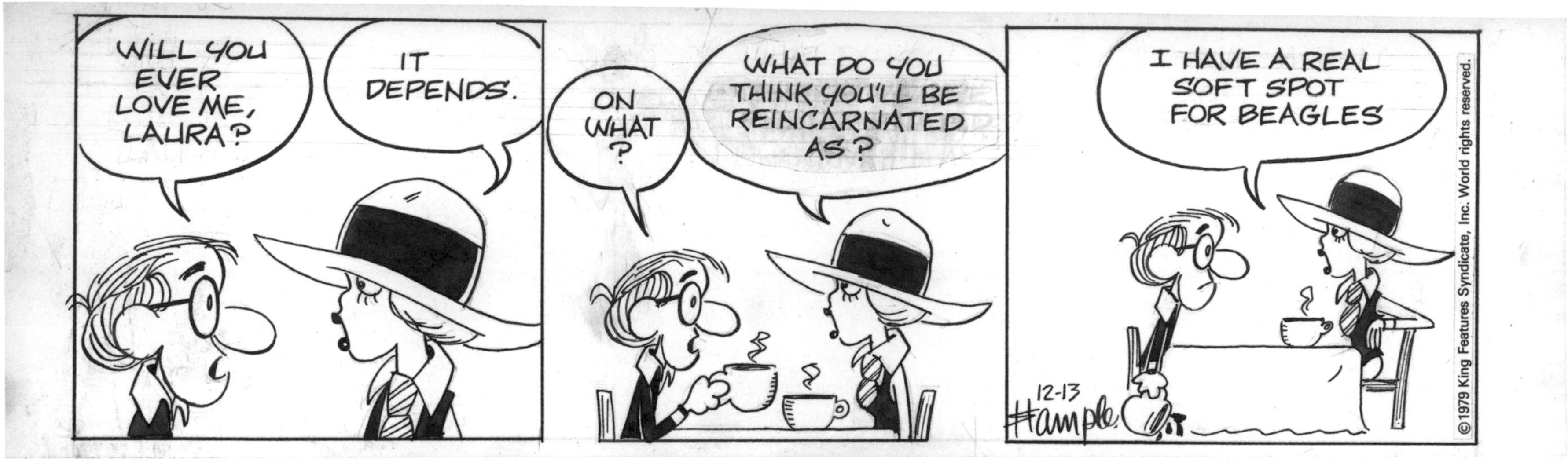
WILL YOU EVER LOVE ME, LAURA?
IT DEPENDS.
ON WHAT?
WHAT DO YOU THINK YOU'LL BE REINCARNATED AS?
I HAVE A REAL SOFT SPOT FOR BEAGLES
12-13
Hample
© 1979 King Features Syndicate, Inc. World rights reserved.

December 13, 1979

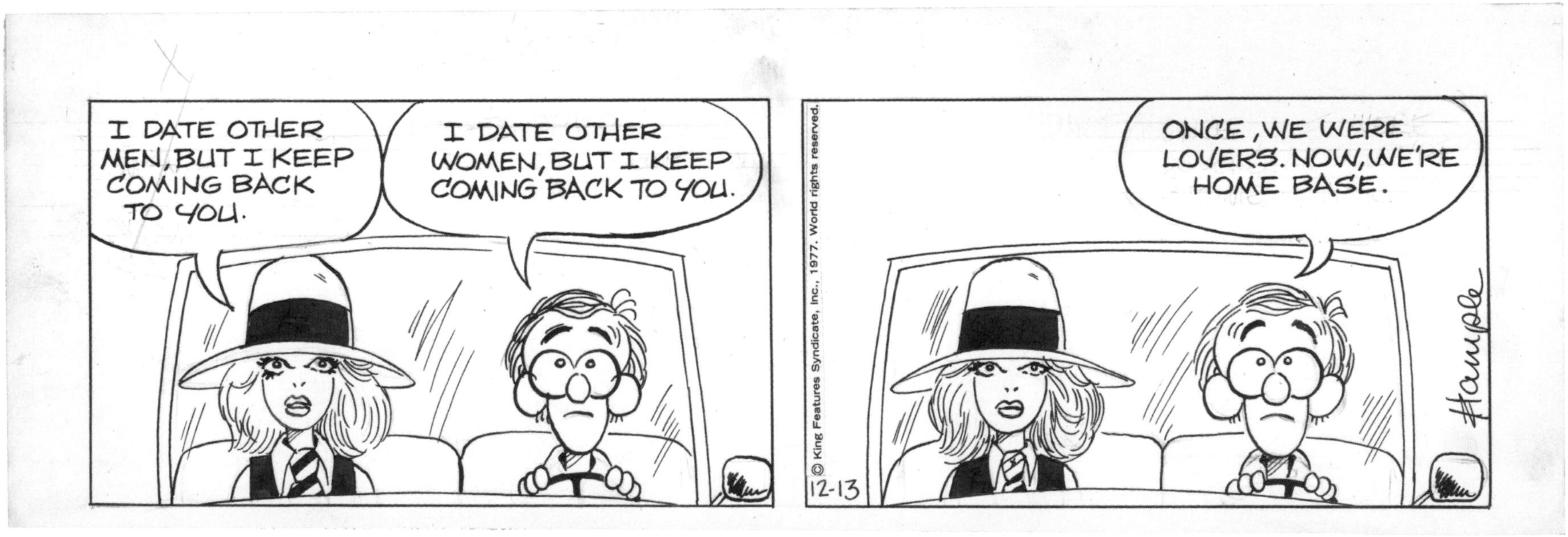
I DATE OTHER MEN, BUT I KEEP COMING BACK TO YOU.
I DATE OTHER WOMEN, BUT I KEEP COMING BACK TO YOU.
© King Features Syndicate, Inc., 1977. World rights reserved.
12-13
ONCE, WE WERE LOVERS. NOW, WE'RE HOME BASE.
Hample

December 13, 1977

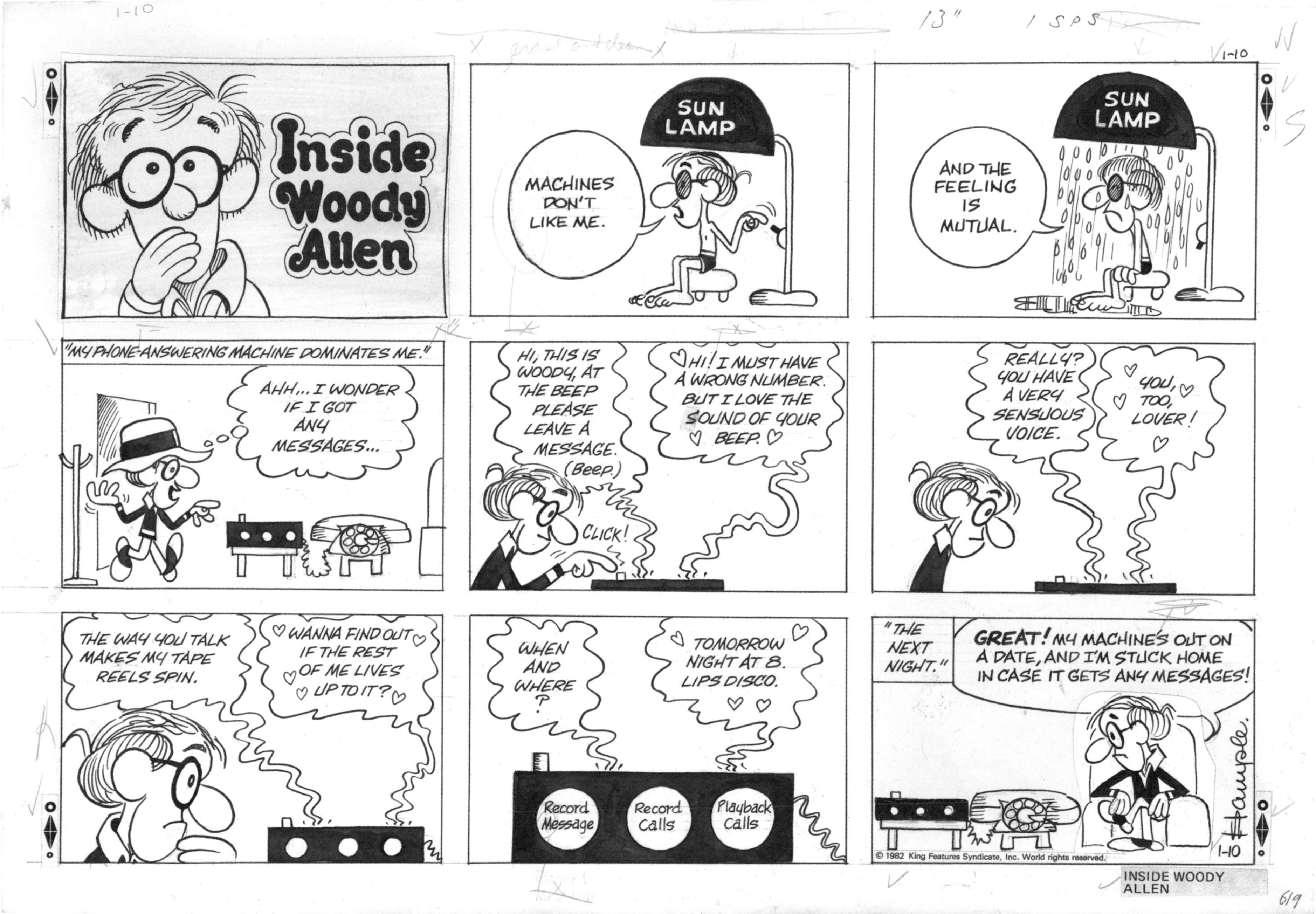
Inside Woody Allen
SUN LAMP
MACHINES DON'T LIKE ME.
SUN LAMP
AND THE FEELING IS MUTUAL.
"MY PHONE-ANSWERING MACHINE DOMINATES ME."
AHH... I WONDER IF I GOT ANY MESSAGES...
HI, THIS IS WOODY, AT THE BEEP PLEASE LEAVE A MESSAGE. (Beep.)
CLICK!
HI! I MUST HAVE A WRONG NUMBER. BUT I LOVE THE SOUND OF YOUR BEEP.
REALLY? YOU HAVE A VERY SENSUOUS VOICE.
YOU, TOO, LOVER!
THE WAY YOU TALK MAKES MY TAPE REELS SPIN.
WANNA FIND OUT IF THE REST OF ME LIVES UP TO IT?
WHEN AND WHERE?
TOMORROW NIGHT AT 8. LIPS DISCO.
Record Message
Record Calls
Playback Calls
"THE NEXT NIGHT."
GREAT! MY MACHINE'S OUT ON A DATE, AND I'M STUCK HOME IN CASE IT GETS ANY MESSAGES!
© 1982 King Features Syndicate, Inc. World rights reserved.
1-10
INSIDE WOODY ALLEN

January 10, 1982

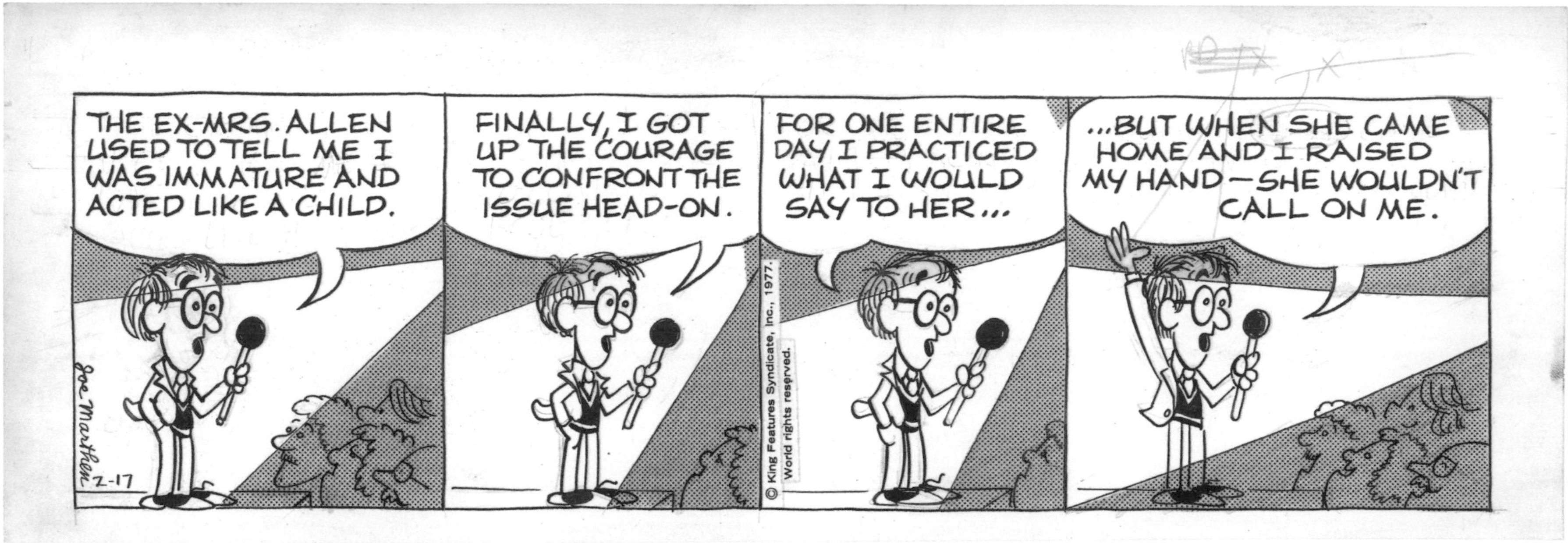
THE EX-MRS. ALLEN USED TO TELL ME I WAS IMMATURE AND ACTED LIKE A CHILD.
FINALLY, I GOT UP THE COURAGE TO CONFRONT THE ISSUE HEAD-ON.
FOR ONE ENTIRE DAY I PRACTICED WHAT I WOULD SAY TO HER...
...BUT WHEN SHE CAME HOME AND I RAISED MY HAND—SHE WOULDN'T CALL ON ME.
Joe Martin 2-17
© King Features Syndicate, Inc., 1977. World rights reserved.

February 17, 1977

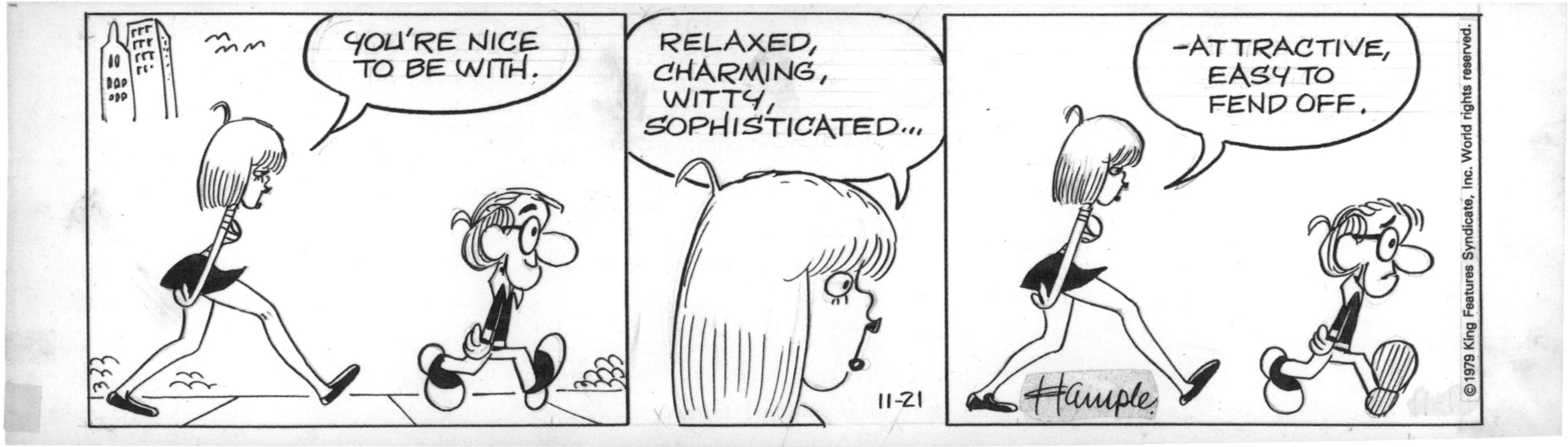
YOU'RE NICE TO BE WITH.
RELAXED, CHARMING, WITTY, SOPHISTICATED...
11-21
-ATTRACTIVE, EASY TO FEND OFF.
Hample
©1979 King Features Syndicate, Inc. World rights reserved.

November 21, 1979

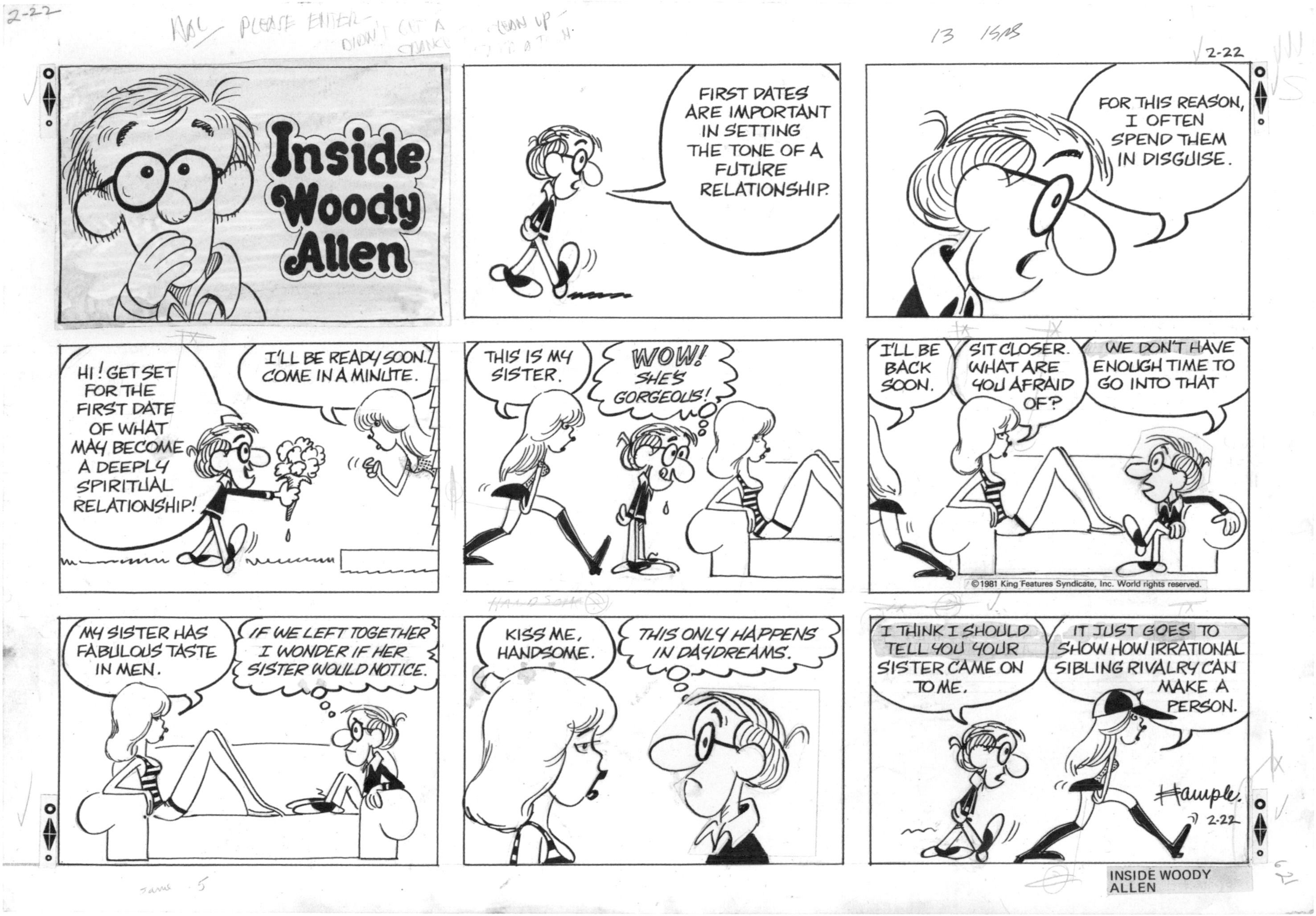
Inside Woody Allen
FIRST DATES ARE IMPORTANT IN SETTING THE TONE OF A FUTURE RELATIONSHIP.
FOR THIS REASON, I OFTEN SPEND THEM IN DISGUISE.
HI! GET SET FOR THE FIRST DATE OF WHAT MAY BECOME A DEEPLY SPIRITUAL RELATIONSHIP!
I'LL BE READY SOON. COME IN A MINUTE.
THIS IS MY SISTER.
WOW! SHE'S GORGEOUS!
I'LL BE BACK SOON.
SIT CLOSER. WHAT ARE YOU AFRAID OF?
WE DON'T HAVE ENOUGH TIME TO GO INTO THAT
© 1981 King Features Syndicate, Inc. World rights reserved.
MY SISTER HAS FABULOUS TASTE IN MEN.
IF WE LEFT TOGETHER I WONDER IF HER SISTER WOULD NOTICE.
KISS ME, HANDSOME.
THIS ONLY HAPPENS IN DAYDREAMS.
I THINK I SHOULD TELL YOU YOUR SISTER CAME ON TO ME.
IT JUST GOES TO SHOW HOW IRRATIONAL SIBLING RIVALRY CAN MAKE A PERSON.
Hample
2-22
INSIDE WOODY ALLEN

February 22, 1981

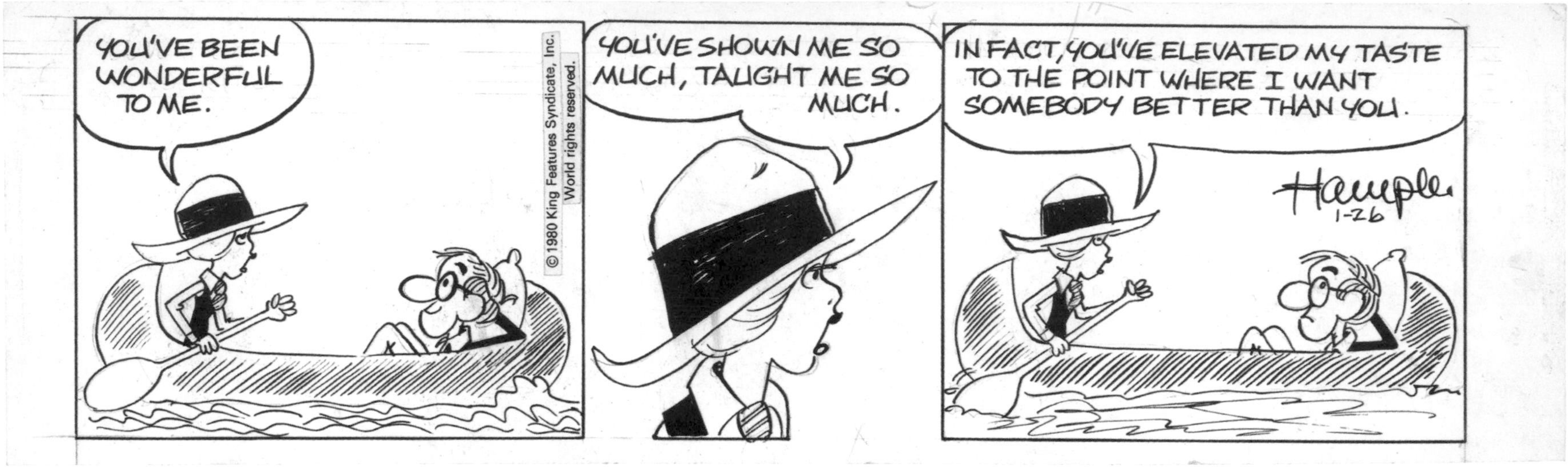
YOU'VE BEEN WONDERFUL TO ME.
© 1980 King Features Syndicate, Inc. World rights reserved.
YOU'VE SHOWN ME SO MUCH, TAUGHT ME SO MUCH.
IN FACT, YOU'VE ELEVATED MY TASTE TO THE POINT WHERE I WANT SOMEBODY BETTER THAN YOU.
Hample
1-26

January 26, 1980

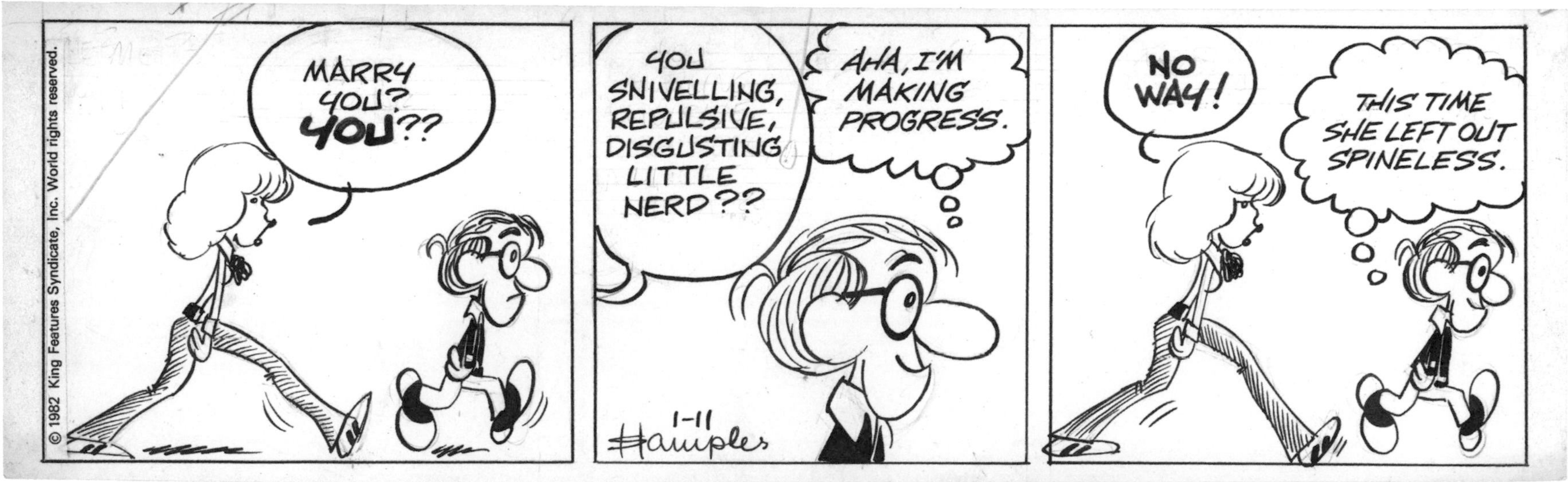
© 1982 King Features Syndicate, Inc. World rights reserved.
MARRY YOU? YOU??
YOU SNIVELLING, REPULSIVE, DISGUSTING LITTLE NERD??
AHA, I'M MAKING PROGRESS.
1-11
Hamples
NO WAY!
THIS TIME SHE LEFT OUT SPINELESS.

January 11, 1982

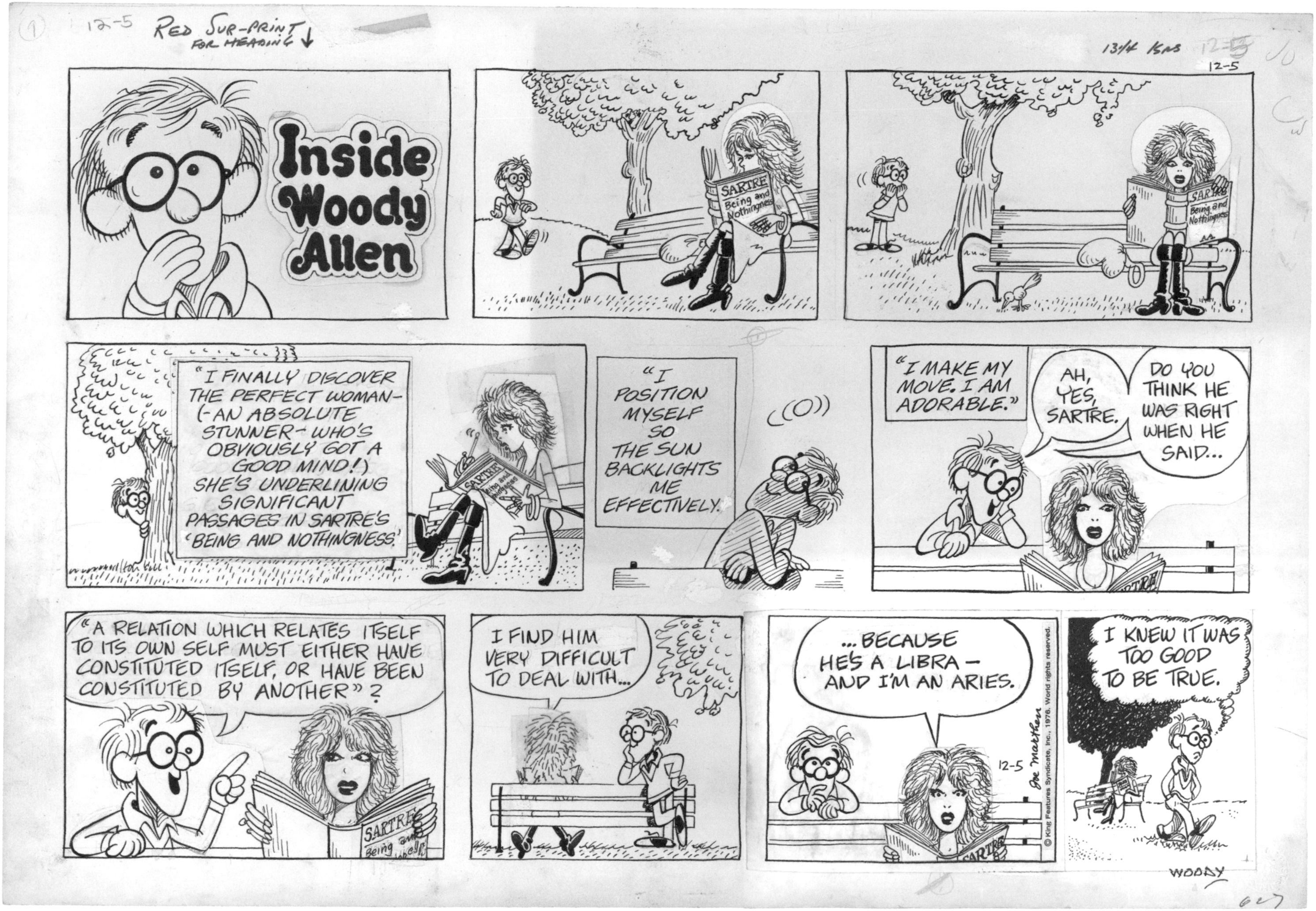
12-5
RED SUR-PRINT FOR HEADING
13 1/4 ISNS
12-5
Inside Woody Allen
SARTRE Being and Nothingness
"I FINALLY DISCOVER THE PERFECT WOMAN-(-AN ABSOLUTE STUNNER-WHO'S OBVIOUSLY GOT A GOOD MIND!) SHE'S UNDERLINING SIGNIFICANT PASSAGES IN SARTRE'S 'BEING AND NOTHINGNESS.'
"I POSITION MYSELF SO THE SUN BACKLIGHTS ME EFFECTIVELY.
"I MAKE MY MOVE. I AM ADORABLE."
AH, YES, SARTRE.
DO YOU THINK HE WAS RIGHT WHEN HE SAID...
"A RELATION WHICH RELATES ITSELF TO ITS OWN SELF MUST EITHER HAVE CONSTITUTED ITSELF, OR HAVE BEEN CONSTITUTED BY ANOTHER"?
I FIND HIM VERY DIFFICULT TO DEAL WITH...
...BECAUSE HE'S A LIBRA - AND I'M AN ARIES.
I KNEW IT WAS TOO GOOD TO BE TRUE.
© King Features Syndicate, Inc., 1976. World rights reserved.
WOODY

December 5, 1976

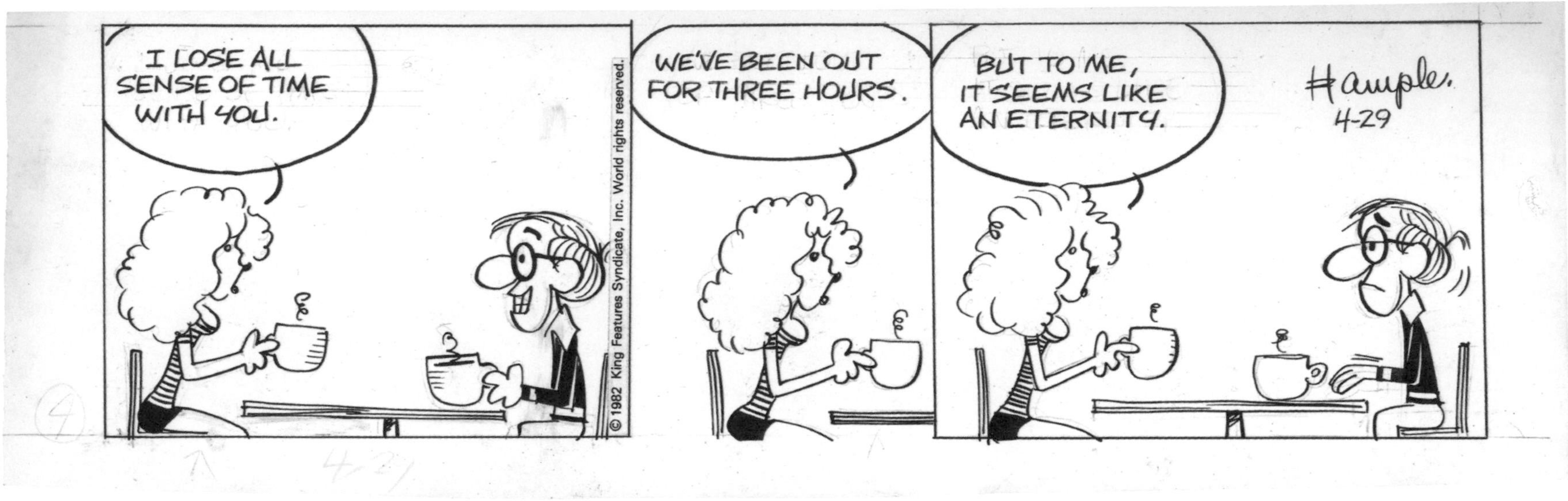
I LOSE ALL SENSE OF TIME WITH YOU.
© 1982 King Features Syndicate, Inc. World rights reserved.
WE'VE BEEN OUT FOR THREE HOURS.
BUT TO ME, IT SEEMS LIKE AN ETERNITY.
Hample
4-29

April 29, 1982

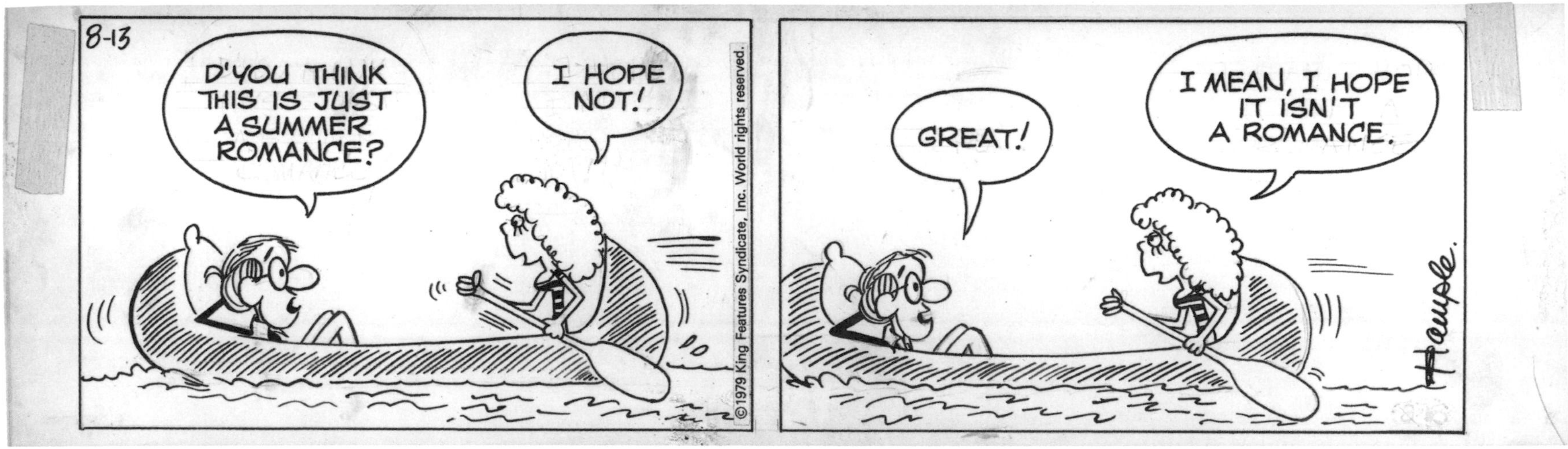
8-13
D'YOU THINK THIS IS JUST A SUMMER ROMANCE?
I HOPE NOT!
© 1979 King Features Syndicate, Inc. World rights reserved.
GREAT!
I MEAN, I HOPE IT ISN'T A ROMANCE.
Hample

August 13, 1979

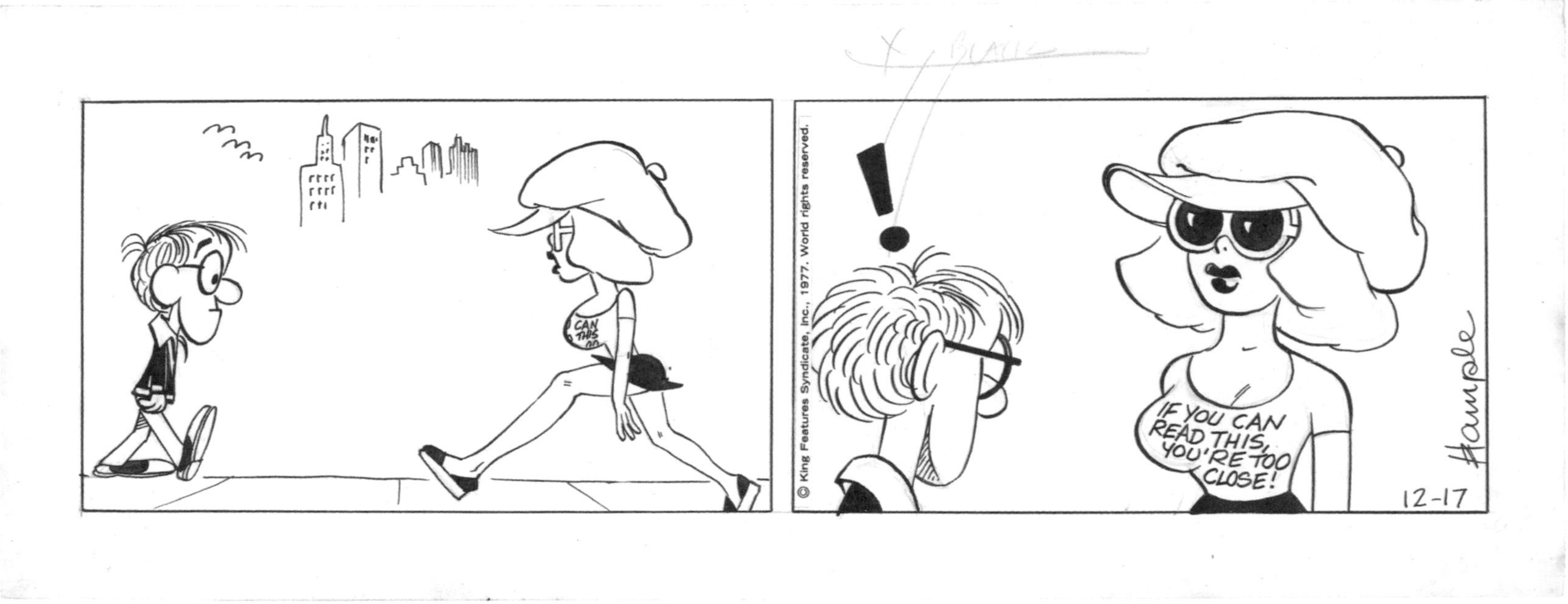
© King Features Syndicate, Inc., 1977. World rights reserved.
!
IF YOU CAN READ THIS, YOU'RE TOO CLOSE!
Hample
12-17

December 17, 1977

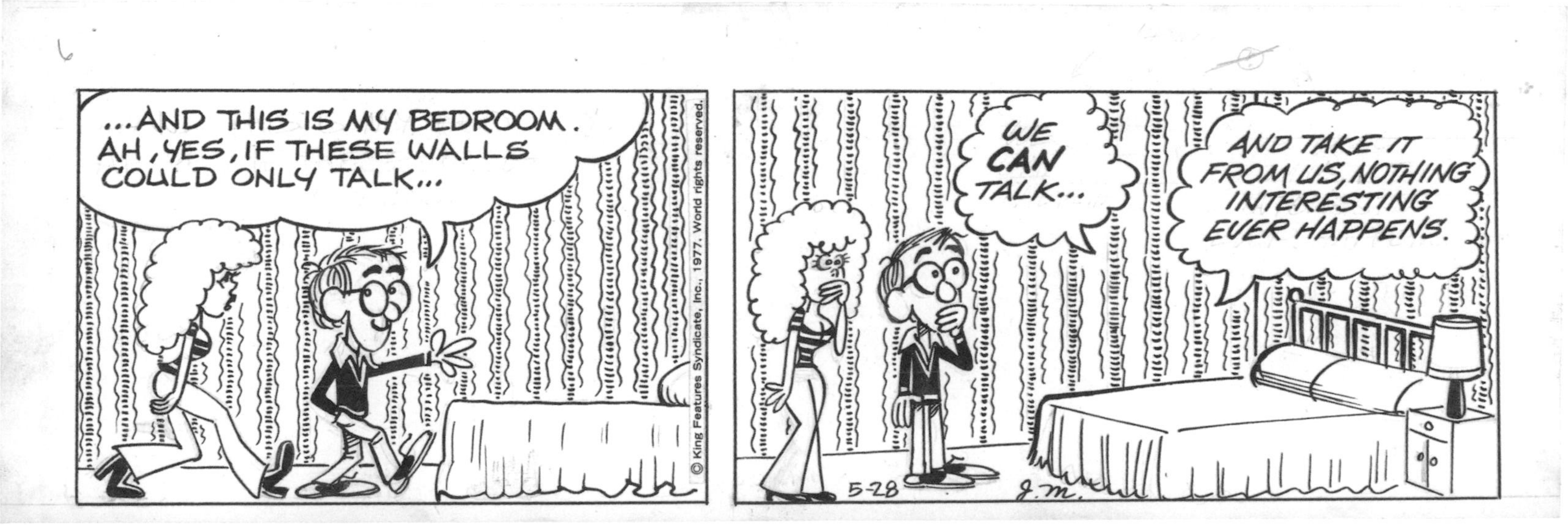
...AND THIS IS MY BEDROOM. AH, YES, IF THESE WALLS COULD ONLY TALK...
© King Features Syndicate, Inc., 1977. World rights reserved.
WE CAN TALK...
AND TAKE IT FROM US, NOTHING INTERESTING EVER HAPPENS.
5-28

May 28, 1977

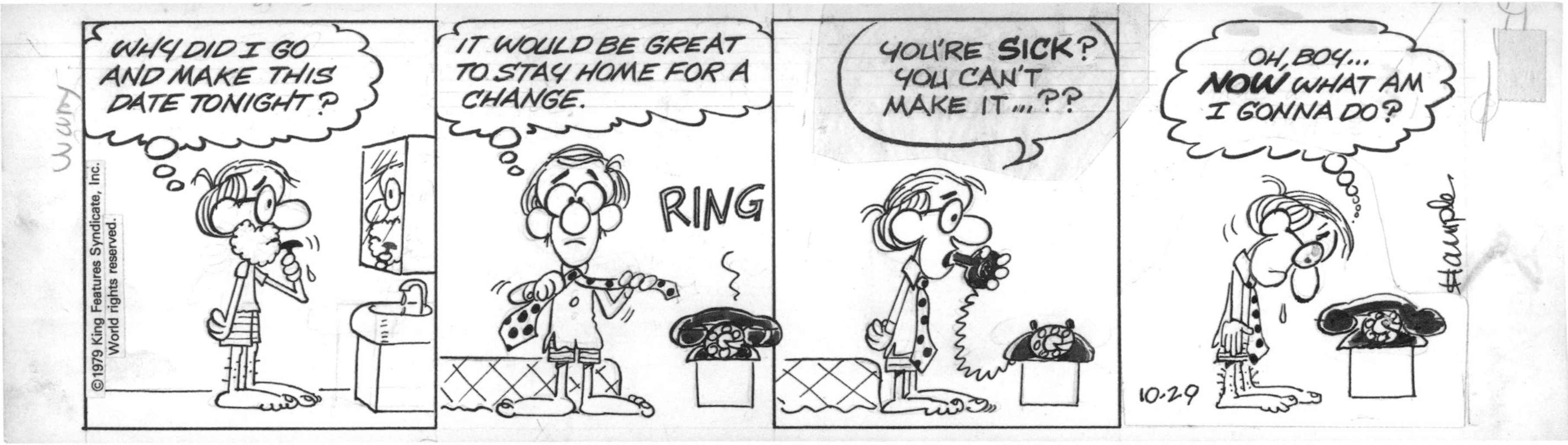
WHY DID I GO AND MAKE THIS DATE TONIGHT?
©1979 King Features Syndicate, Inc. World rights reserved.
IT WOULD BE GREAT TO STAY HOME FOR A CHANGE.
RING
YOU'RE SICK? YOU CAN'T MAKE IT...??
OH, BOY... NOW WHAT AM I GONNA DO?
10-29
Hample

October 29, 1979

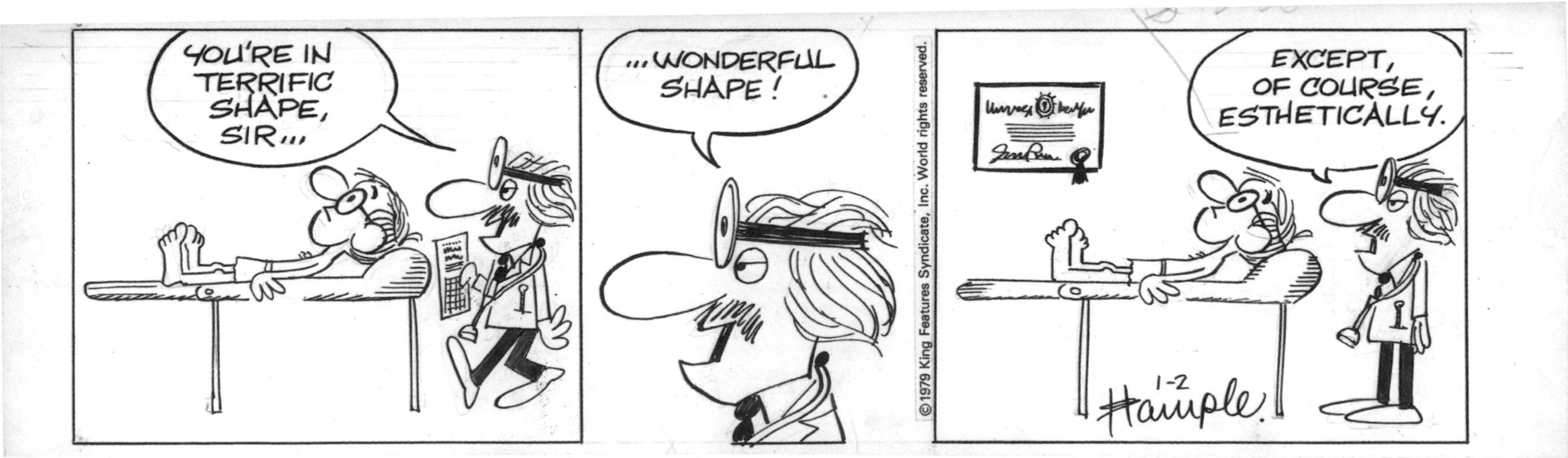
YOU'RE IN TERRIFIC SHAPE, SIR...
...WONDERFUL SHAPE!
©1979 King Features Syndicate, Inc. World rights reserved.
EXCEPT, OF COURSE, ESTHETICALLY.
1-2
Hample

January 2, 1979

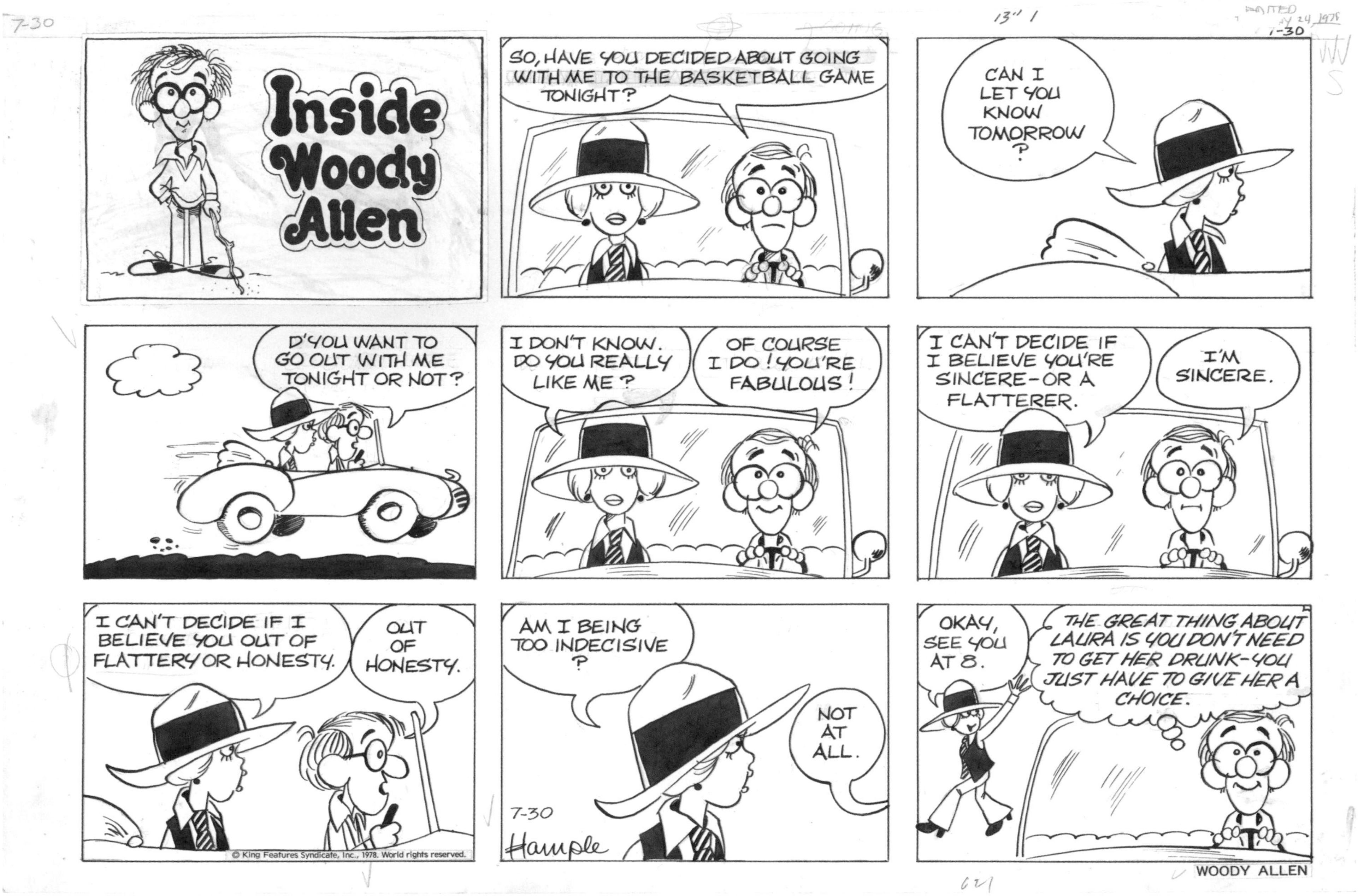

Inside Woody Allen
SO, HAVE YOU DECIDED ABOUT GOING WITH ME TO THE BASKETBALL GAME TONIGHT?
CAN I LET YOU KNOW TOMORROW?
D'YOU WANT TO GO OUT WITH ME TONIGHT OR NOT?
I DON'T KNOW. DO YOU REALLY LIKE ME?
OF COURSE I DO! YOU'RE FABULOUS!
I CAN'T DECIDE IF I BELIEVE YOU'RE SINCERE—OR A FLATTERER.
I'M SINCERE.
I CAN'T DECIDE IF I BELIEVE YOU OUT OF FLATTERY OR HONESTY.
OUT OF HONESTY.
AM I BEING TOO INDECISIVE?
NOT AT ALL.
OKAY, SEE YOU AT 8.
THE GREAT THING ABOUT LAURA IS YOU DON'T NEED TO GET HER DRUNK—YOU JUST HAVE TO GIVE HER A CHOICE.
7-30
Hample
WOODY ALLEN
© King Features Syndicate, Inc., 1978. World rights reserved.

July 30, 1978

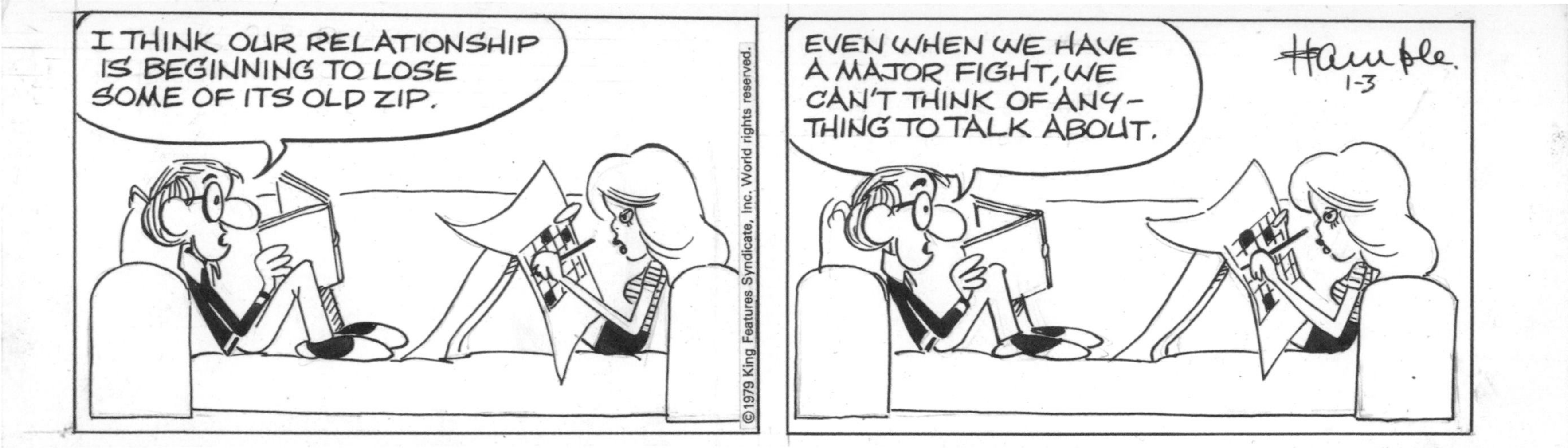
I THINK OUR RELATIONSHIP IS BEGINNING TO LOSE SOME OF ITS OLD ZIP.
© 1979 King Features Syndicate, Inc. World rights reserved.
EVEN WHEN WE HAVE A MAJOR FIGHT, WE CAN'T THINK OF ANY-THING TO TALK ABOUT.
Hample
1-3

January 3, 1979

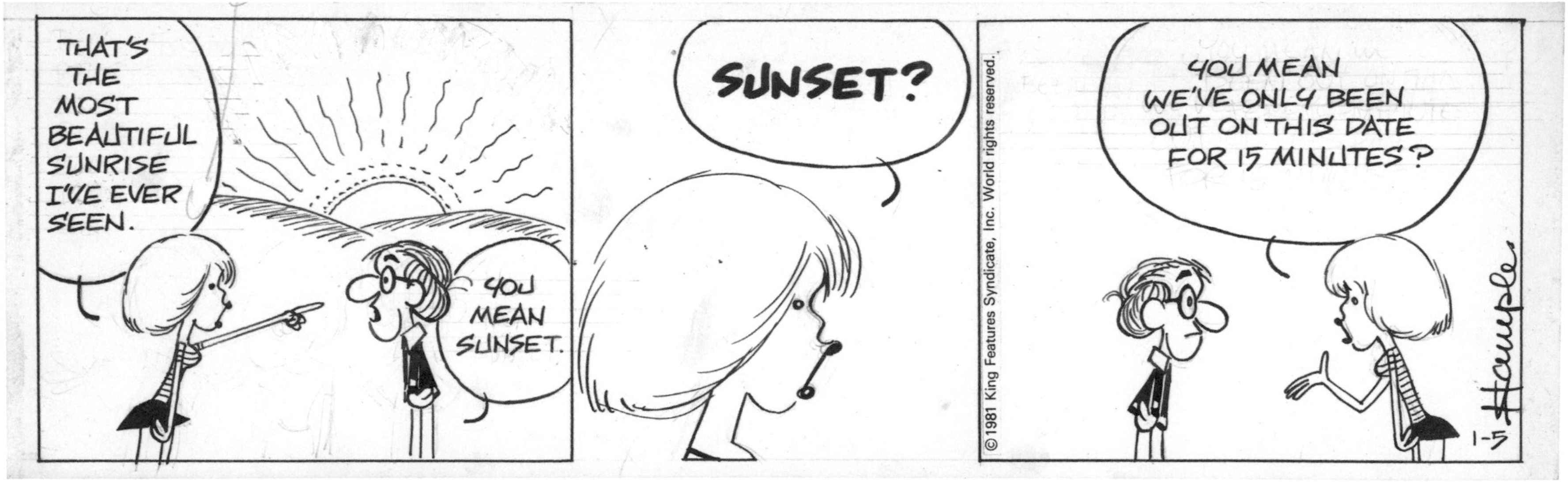
THAT'S THE MOST BEAUTIFUL SUNRISE I'VE EVER SEEN.
YOU MEAN SUNSET.
SUNSET?
© 1981 King Features Syndicate, Inc. World rights reserved.
YOU MEAN WE'VE ONLY BEEN OUT ON THIS DATE FOR 15 MINUTES?
Hample
1-5

January 5, 1981

3

My Face Is My Passport

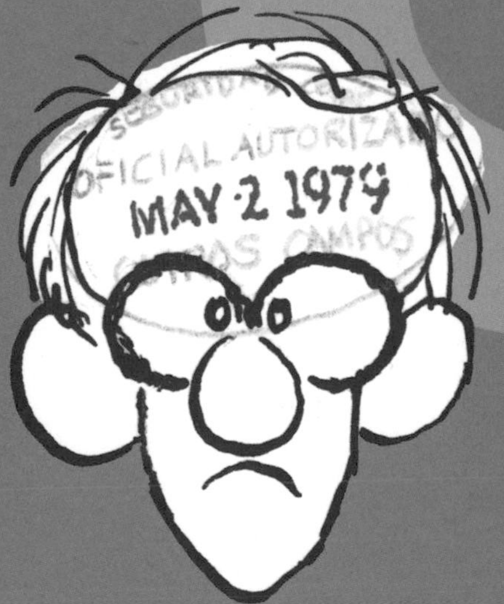
MAY 2 1979

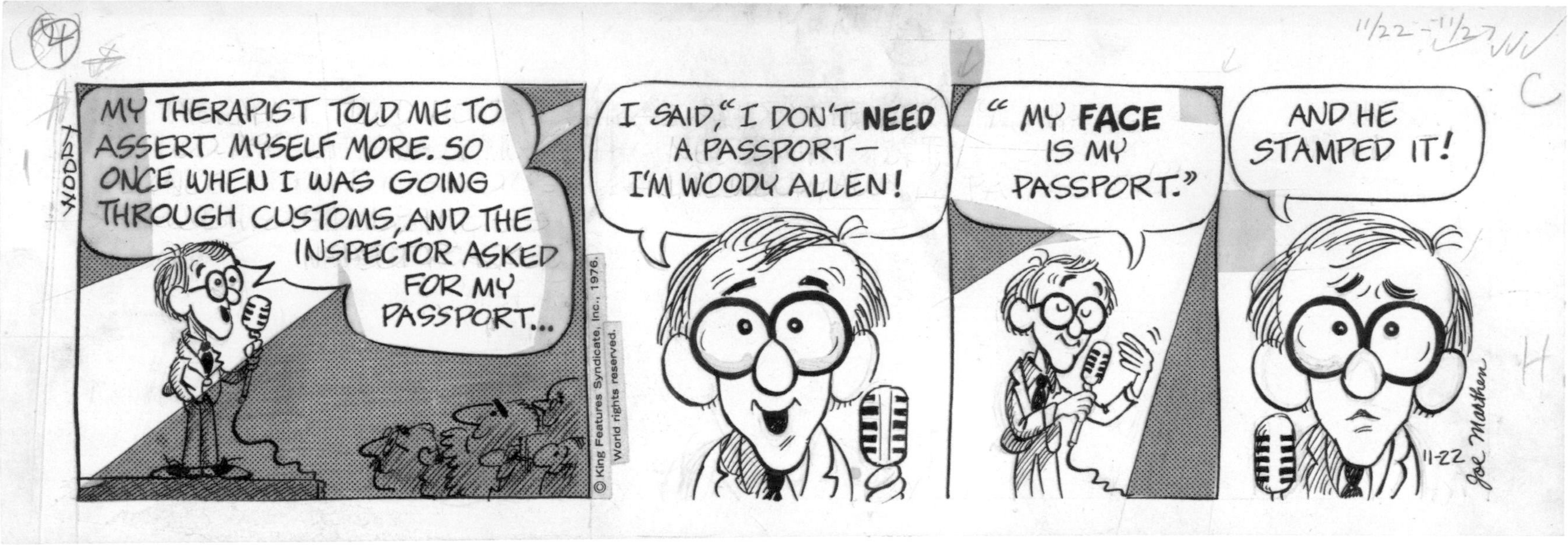
WOODY
MY THERAPIST TOLD ME TO ASSERT MYSELF MORE. SO ONCE WHEN I WAS GOING THROUGH CUSTOMS, AND THE INSPECTOR ASKED FOR MY PASSPORT...
© King Features Syndicate, Inc., 1976. World rights reserved.
I SAID, "I DON'T **NEED** A PASSPORT— I'M WOODY ALLEN!
" MY **FACE** IS MY PASSPORT."
AND HE STAMPED IT!
11-22
Joe Marthen

November 22, 1976

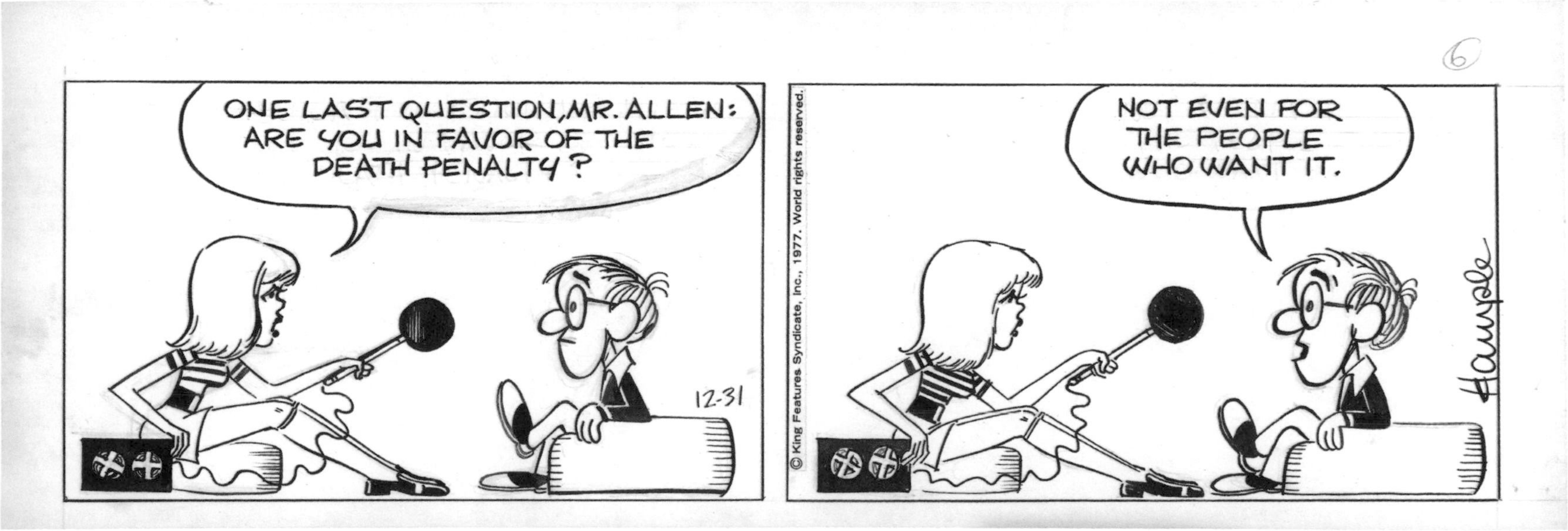
ONE LAST QUESTION, MR. ALLEN: ARE YOU IN FAVOR OF THE DEATH PENALTY?
12-31
© King Features Syndicate, Inc., 1977. World rights reserved.
NOT EVEN FOR THE PEOPLE WHO WANT IT.

December 31, 1977

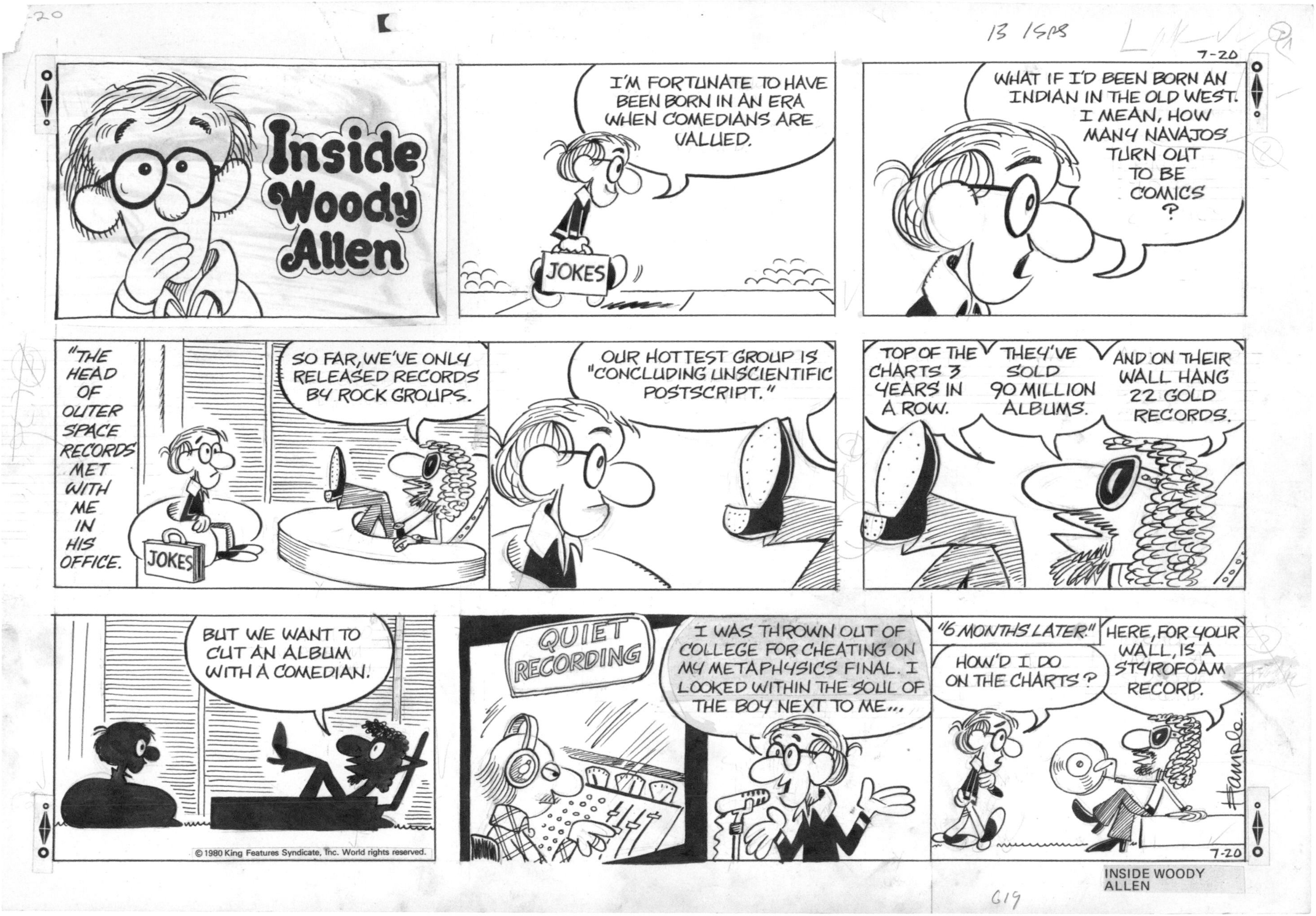

Inside Woody Allen
I'M FORTUNATE TO HAVE BEEN BORN IN AN ERA WHEN COMEDIANS ARE VALUED.
JOKES
WHAT IF I'D BEEN BORN AN INDIAN IN THE OLD WEST. I MEAN, HOW MANY NAVAJOS TURN OUT TO BE COMICS?
"THE HEAD OF OUTER SPACE RECORDS MET WITH ME IN HIS OFFICE.
SO FAR, WE'VE ONLY RELEASED RECORDS BY ROCK GROUPS.
JOKES
OUR HOTTEST GROUP IS "CONCLUDING UNSCIENTIFIC POSTSCRIPT."
TOP OF THE CHARTS 3 YEARS IN A ROW.
THEY'VE SOLD 90 MILLION ALBUMS.
AND ON THEIR WALL HANG 22 GOLD RECORDS.
BUT WE WANT TO CUT AN ALBUM WITH A COMEDIAN.
© 1980 King Features Syndicate, Inc. World rights reserved.
QUIET RECORDING
I WAS THROWN OUT OF COLLEGE FOR CHEATING ON MY METAPHYSICS FINAL. I LOOKED WITHIN THE SOUL OF THE BOY NEXT TO ME...
"6 MONTHS LATER."
HOW'D I DO ON THE CHARTS?
HERE, FOR YOUR WALL, IS A STYROFOAM RECORD.
Hample
7-20
INSIDE WOODY ALLEN

July 20, 1980

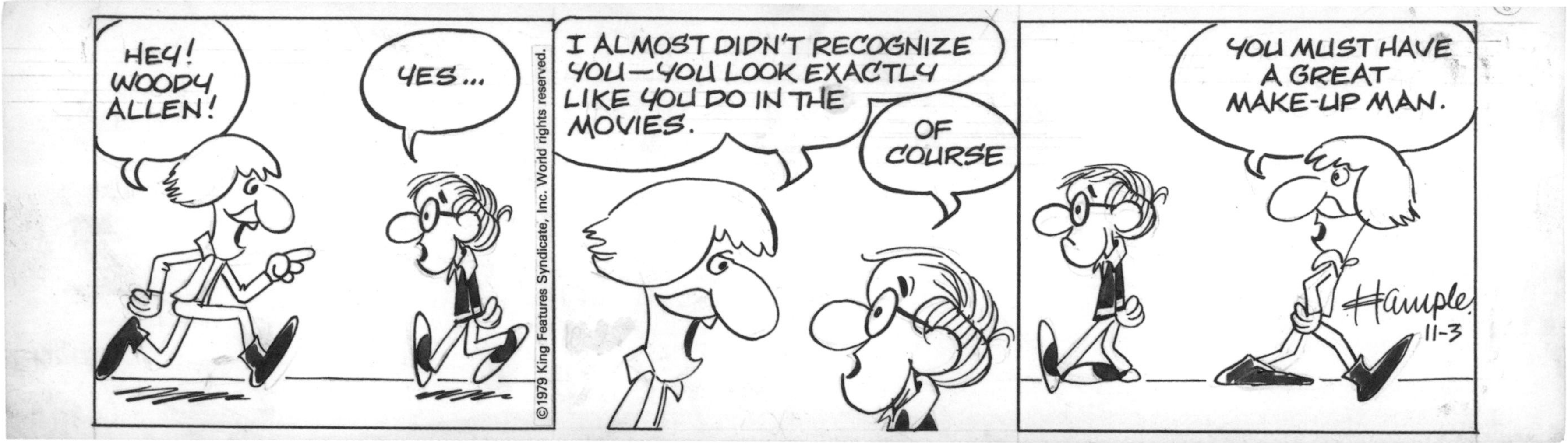
HEY! WOODY ALLEN!
YES...
©1979 King Features Syndicate, Inc. World rights reserved.
I ALMOST DIDN'T RECOGNIZE YOU—YOU LOOK EXACTLY LIKE YOU DO IN THE MOVIES.
OF COURSE
YOU MUST HAVE A GREAT MAKE-UP MAN.
Hample
11-3

November 3, 1979

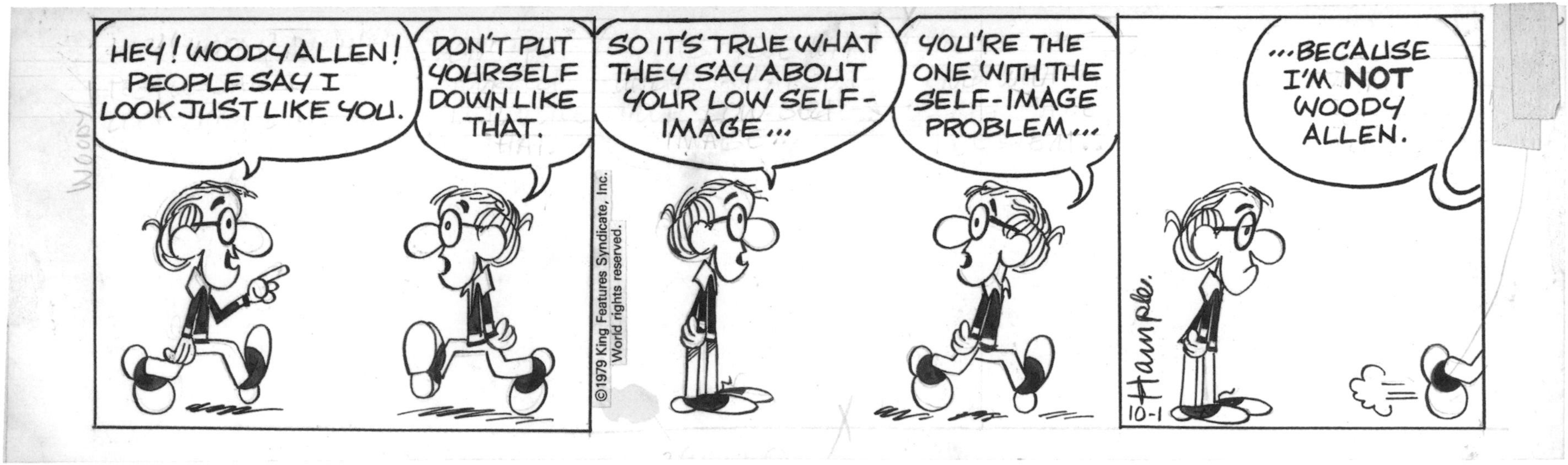
HEY! WOODY ALLEN! PEOPLE SAY I LOOK JUST LIKE YOU.
DON'T PUT YOURSELF DOWN LIKE THAT.
©1979 King Features Syndicate, Inc. World rights reserved.
SO IT'S TRUE WHAT THEY SAY ABOUT YOUR LOW SELF-IMAGE...
YOU'RE THE ONE WITH THE SELF-IMAGE PROBLEM...
Hample
10-1
...BECAUSE I'M **NOT** WOODY ALLEN.

October 1, 1979

Inside Woody Allen

AH, WITH THESE DARK GLASSES AND FAKE MUSTACHE, NO ONE WILL RECOGNIZE ME.

RINGS

YES?

HI, SYBIL, IT'S ME, WOODY!

COME IN AND TAKE OFF THAT STUPID DISGUISE. EVERYONE AT THE PARTY WANTS TO MEET THE FAMOUS WOODY ALLEN.

I DON'T WANT TO TRADE ON MY FAME. I ONLY WANT FRIENDS WHO LIKE ME FOR MYSELF.

INTRODUCE ME AS IRA GLICKMAN, SAY I'M A... A DENTIST FROM BUFFALO.

SCARLETT, I'D LIKE YOU TO MEET—ER—IRA GLICKMAN. IRA'S A DENTIST FROM BUFFALO.

PLEASED TO MEET YOU, IRA.

—NOW, IF YOU'LL EXCUSE ME, I HAVE TO GO GET A PIECE OF HERRING.

OKAY, INTRODUCE ME BY MY REAL NAME...

I GUESS I'M MORE HARD UP THAN I THOUGHT.

3-28 Hample

INSIDE WOODY ALLEN

March 28, 1982

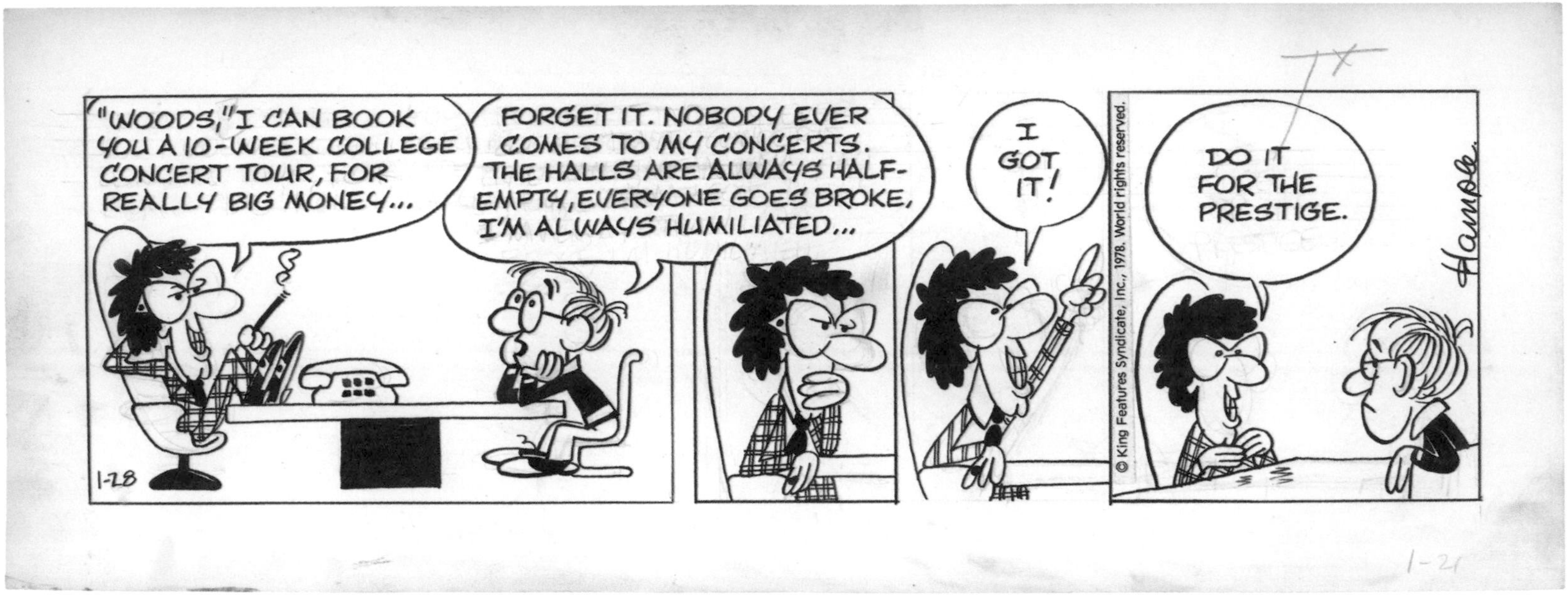
"WOODS," I CAN BOOK YOU A 10-WEEK COLLEGE CONCERT TOUR, FOR REALLY BIG MONEY...
FORGET IT. NOBODY EVER COMES TO MY CONCERTS. THE HALLS ARE ALWAYS HALF-EMPTY, EVERYONE GOES BROKE, I'M ALWAYS HUMILIATED...
I GOT IT!
DO IT FOR THE PRESTIGE.
1-28
© King Features Syndicate, Inc., 1978. World rights reserved.
Hample

January 28, 1978

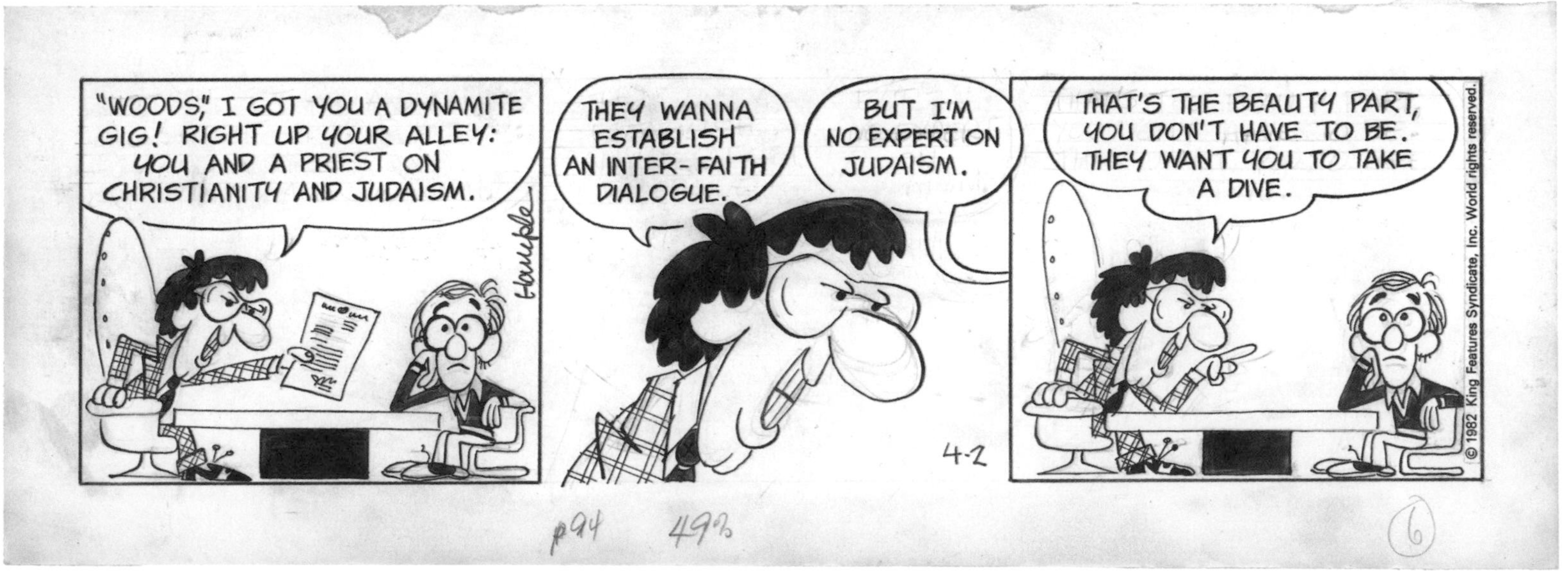
"WOODS," I GOT YOU A DYNAMITE GIG! RIGHT UP YOUR ALLEY: YOU AND A PRIEST ON CHRISTIANITY AND JUDAISM.
THEY WANNA ESTABLISH AN INTER-FAITH DIALOGUE.
BUT I'M NO EXPERT ON JUDAISM.
THAT'S THE BEAUTY PART, YOU DON'T HAVE TO BE. THEY WANT YOU TO TAKE A DIVE.
4-2
© 1982 King Features Syndicate, Inc. World rights reserved.
Hample

April 2, 1982

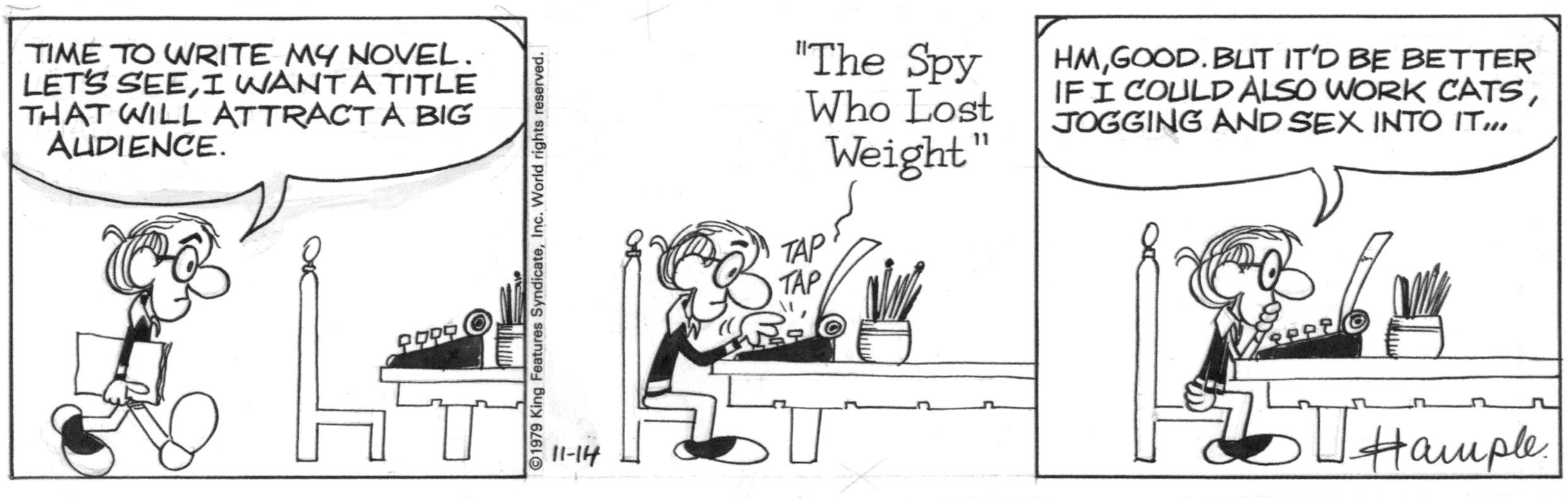

TIME TO WRITE MY NOVEL. LET'S SEE, I WANT A TITLE THAT WILL ATTRACT A BIG AUDIENCE.
©1979 King Features Syndicate, Inc. World rights reserved.
11-14
"The Spy Who Lost Weight"
TAP TAP
HM, GOOD. BUT IT'D BE BETTER IF I COULD ALSO WORK CATS, JOGGING AND SEX INTO IT...
Hample

November 14, 1979

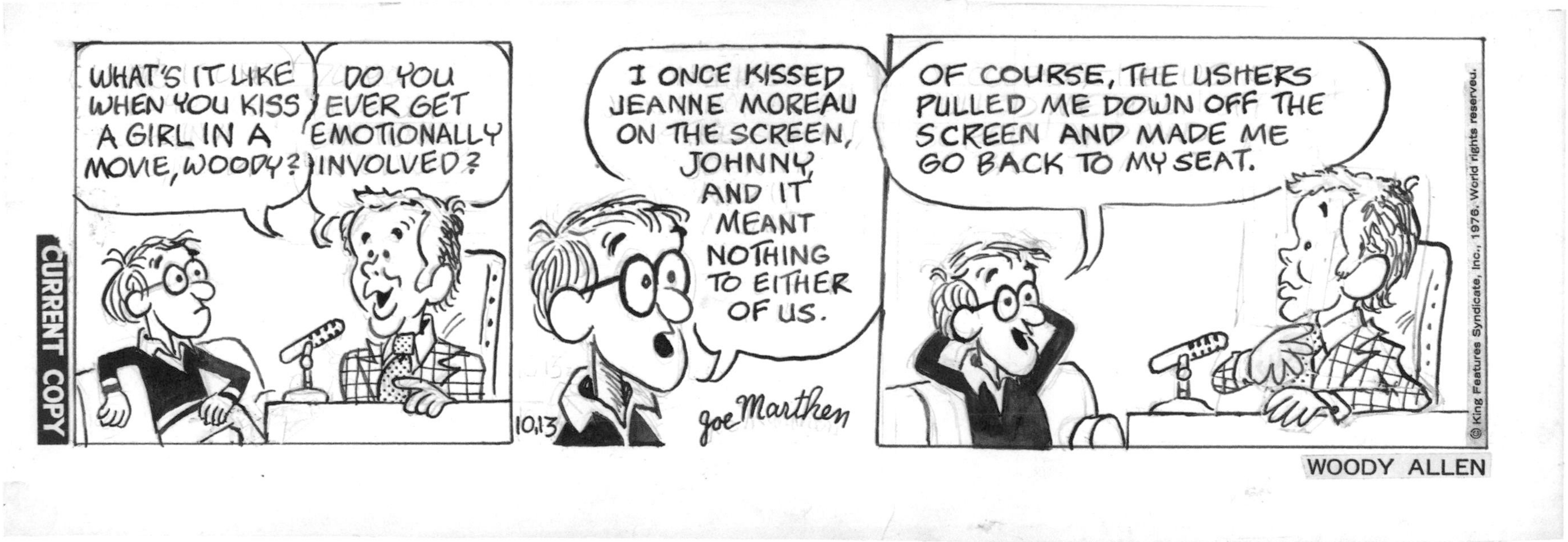

CURRENT COPY
WHAT'S IT LIKE WHEN YOU KISS A GIRL IN A MOVIE, WOODY?
DO YOU EVER GET EMOTIONALLY INVOLVED?
I ONCE KISSED JEANNE MOREAU ON THE SCREEN, JOHNNY, AND IT MEANT NOTHING TO EITHER OF US.
10,13
Joe Marthen
OF COURSE, THE USHERS PULLED ME DOWN OFF THE SCREEN AND MADE ME GO BACK TO MY SEAT.
© King Features Syndicate, Inc., 1976. World rights reserved.
WOODY ALLEN

October 13, 1976

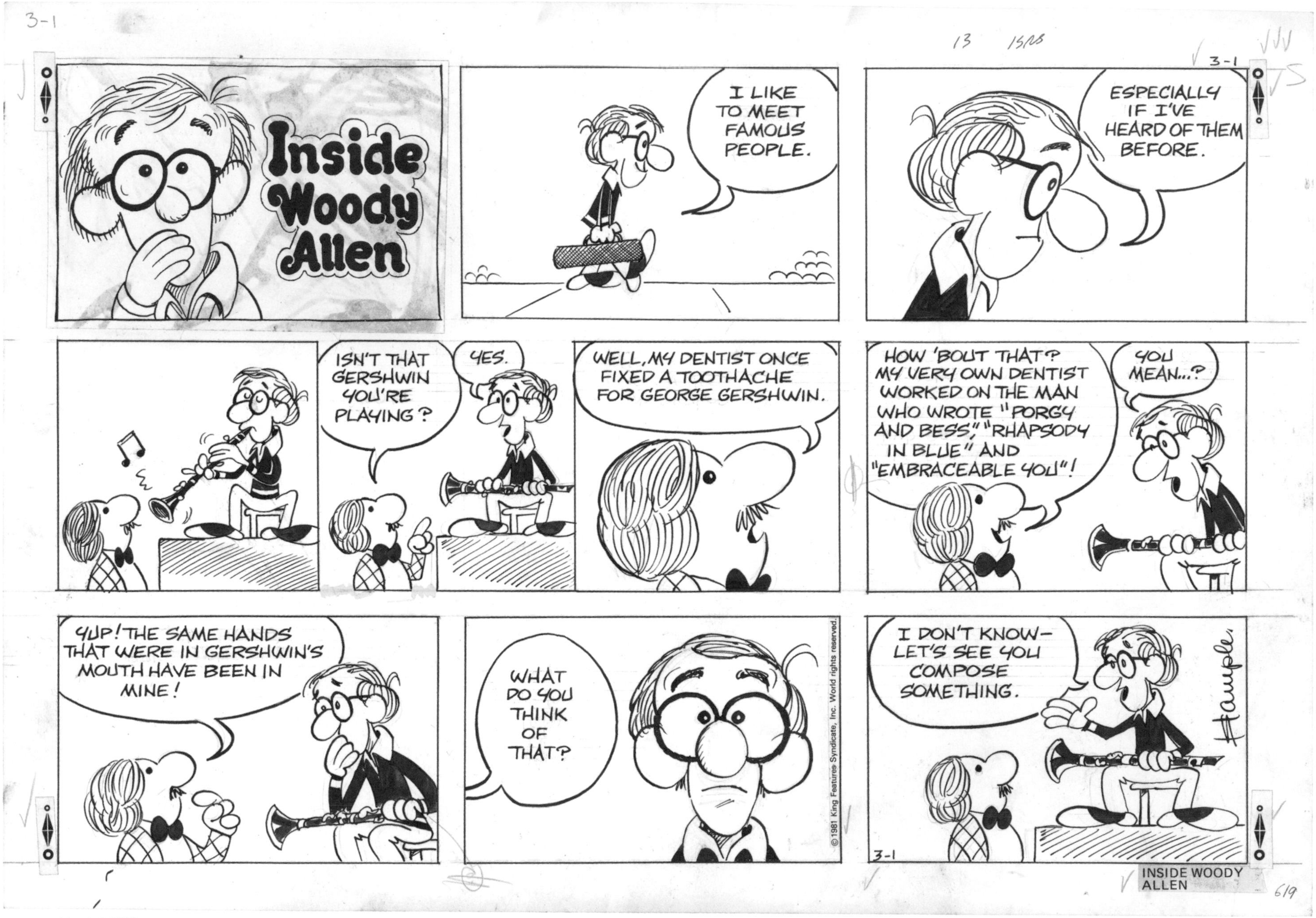
3-1
13 15R8
3-1
Inside Woody Allen
I LIKE TO MEET FAMOUS PEOPLE.
ESPECIALLY IF I'VE HEARD OF THEM BEFORE.
ISN'T THAT GERSHWIN YOU'RE PLAYING?
YES.
WELL, MY DENTIST ONCE FIXED A TOOTHACHE FOR GEORGE GERSHWIN.
HOW 'BOUT THAT? MY VERY OWN DENTIST WORKED ON THE MAN WHO WROTE "PORGY AND BESS," "RHAPSODY IN BLUE" AND "EMBRACEABLE YOU"!
YOU MEAN...?
YUP! THE SAME HANDS THAT WERE IN GERSHWIN'S MOUTH HAVE BEEN IN MINE!
WHAT DO YOU THINK OF THAT?
©1981 King Features Syndicate, Inc. World rights reserved.
3-1
I DON'T KNOW– LET'S SEE YOU COMPOSE SOMETHING.
Hample
INSIDE WOODY ALLEN
619

March 1, 1981

Rationalizations & Narcissism

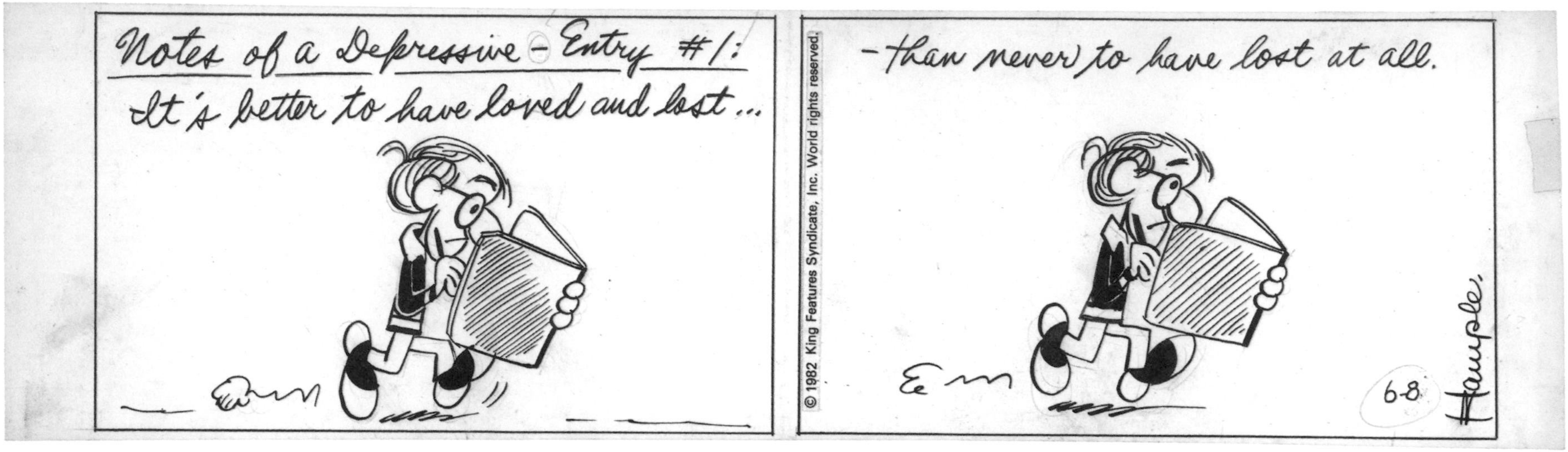
Notes of a Depressive - Entry #1:
It's better to have loved and lost...
- than never to have lost at all.
© 1982 King Features Syndicate, Inc. World rights reserved.
6-8
Hample.

June 8, 1982

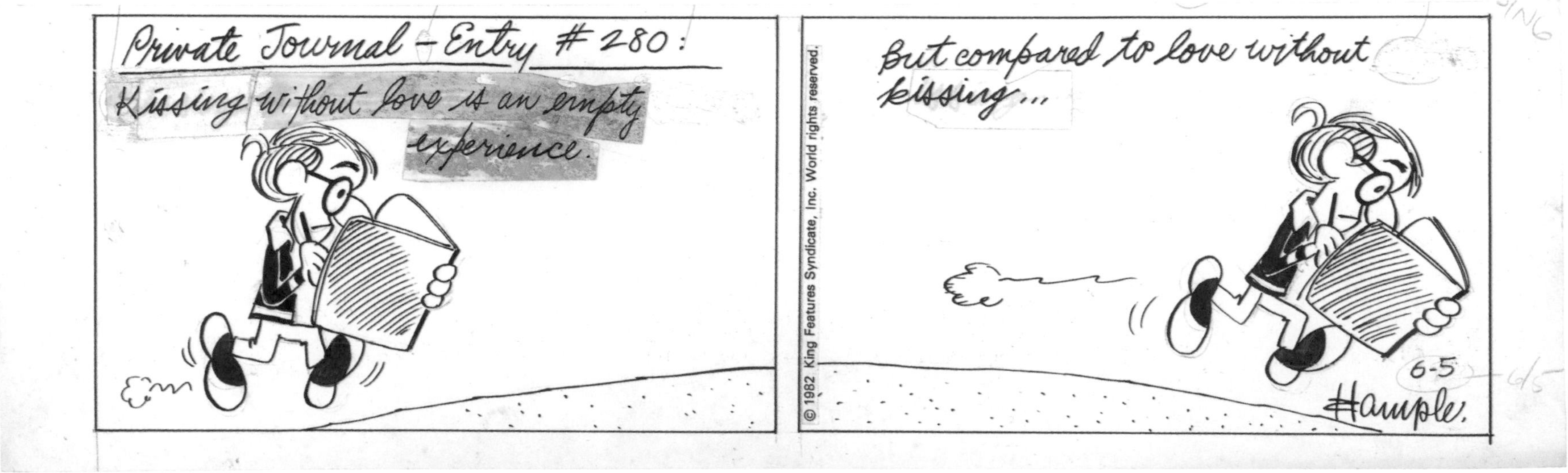
Private Journal - Entry # 280:
Kissing without love is an empty experience.
But compared to love without kissing...
© 1982 King Features Syndicate, Inc. World rights reserved.
6-5
Hample.

June 5, 1982

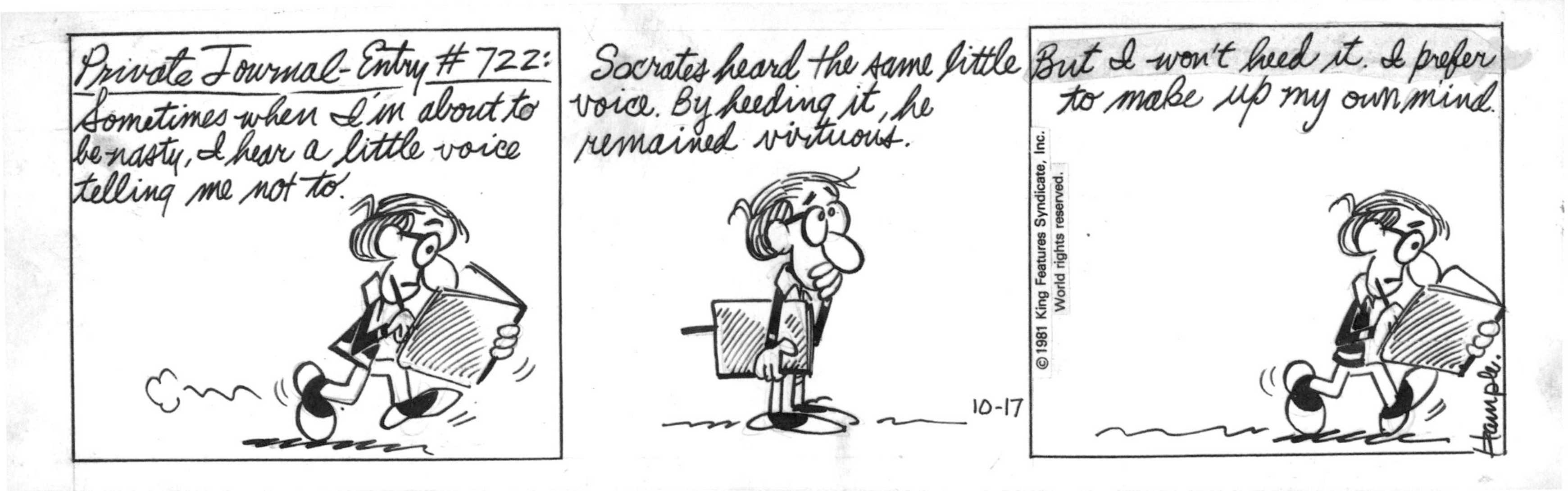
Private Journal-Entry #722: Sometimes when I'm about to be nasty, I hear a little voice telling me not to.
Socrates heard the same little voice. By heeding it, he remained virtuous.
10-17
But I won't heed it. I prefer to make up my own mind.
© 1981 King Features Syndicate, Inc. World rights reserved.
Hample.

October 17, 1981

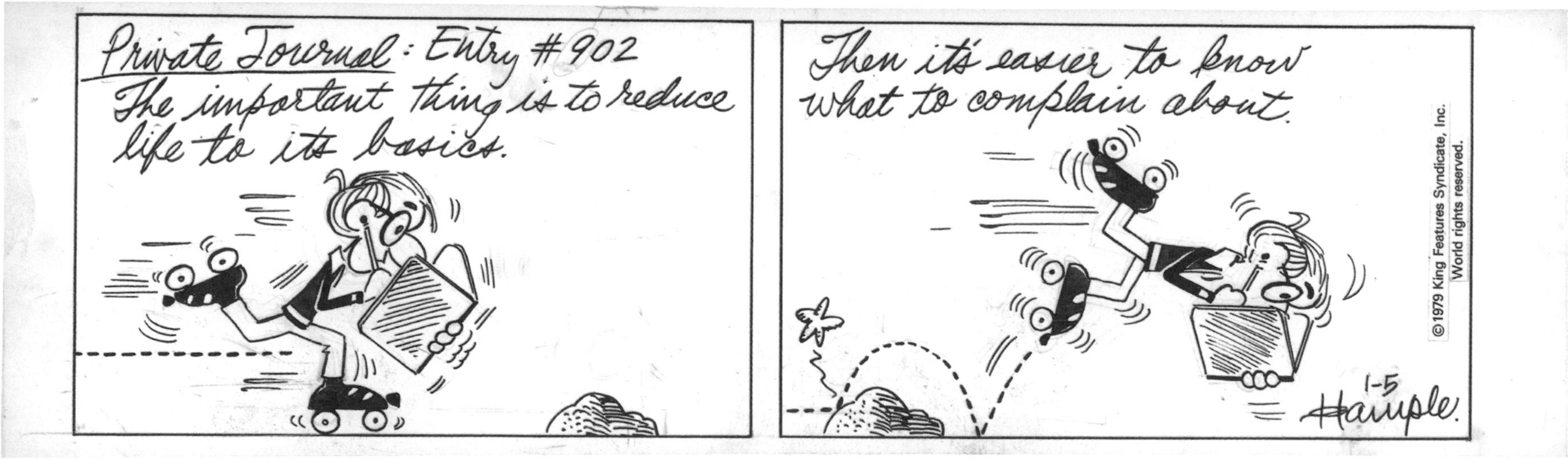
Private Journal: Entry #902 The important thing is to reduce life to its basics.
Then it's easier to know what to complain about.
© 1979 King Features Syndicate, Inc. World rights reserved.
1-5
Hample.

January 5, 1979

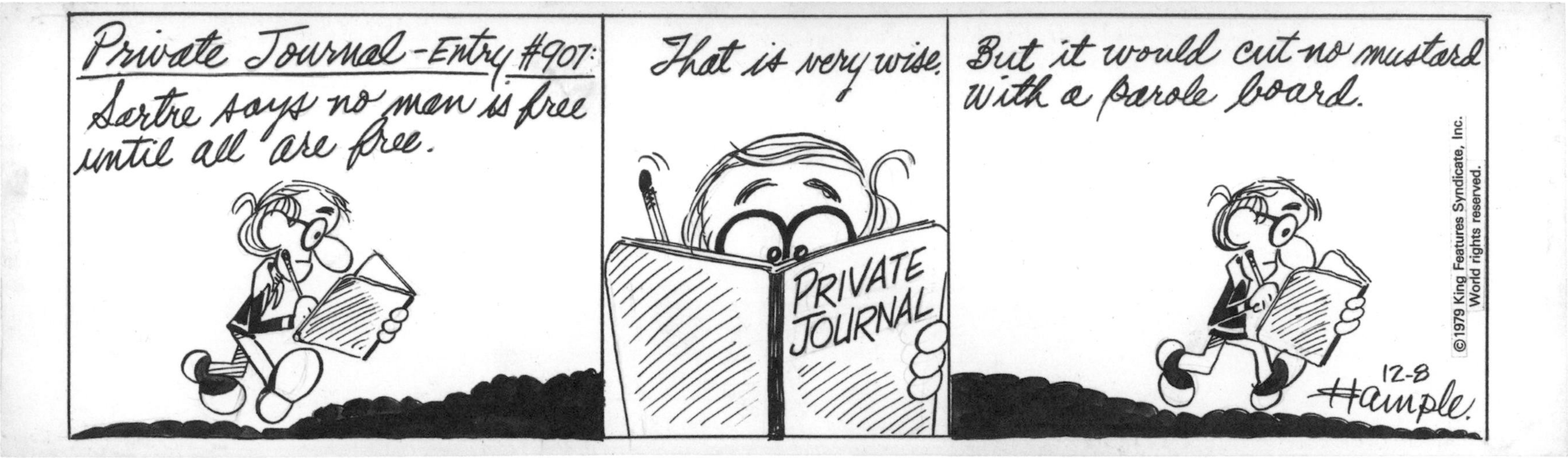
Private Journal - Entry #907:
Sartre says no man is free until all are free.
That is very wise.
PRIVATE JOURNAL
But it would cut no mustard with a parole board.
© 1979 King Features Syndicate, Inc. World rights reserved.
12-8
Hample.

December 8, 1979

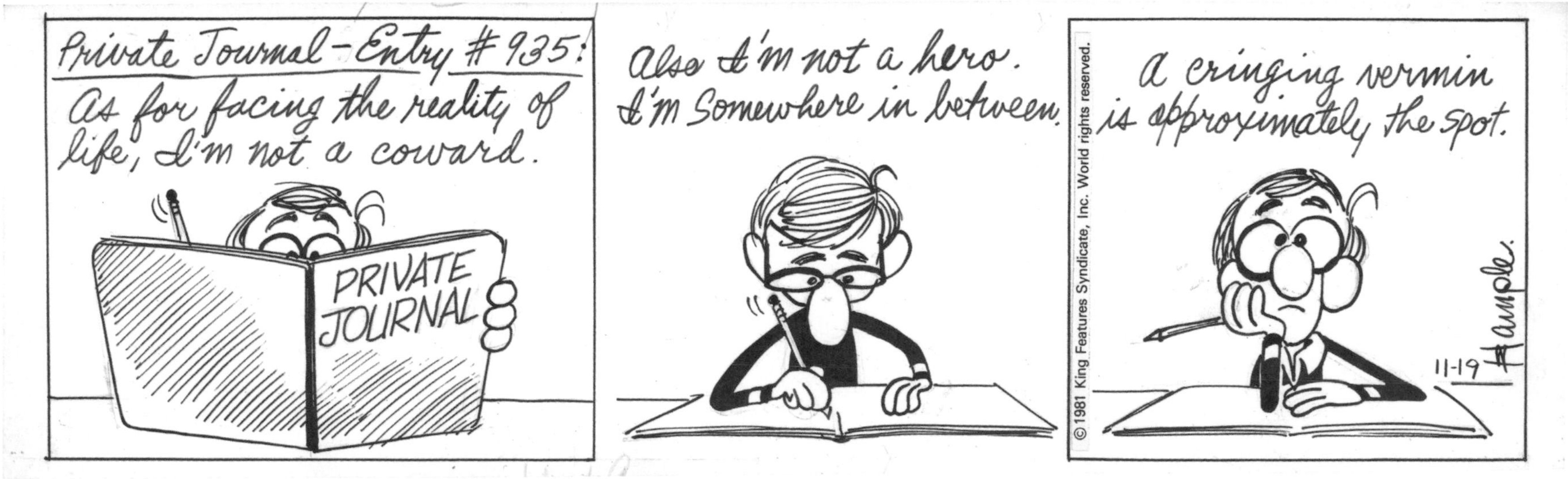
Private Journal - Entry # 935:
As for facing the reality of life, I'm not a coward.
PRIVATE JOURNAL
Also I'm not a hero. I'm Somewhere in between.
© 1981 King Features Syndicate, Inc. World rights reserved.
A cringing vermin is approximately the spot.
11-19
Hample.

November 19, 1981

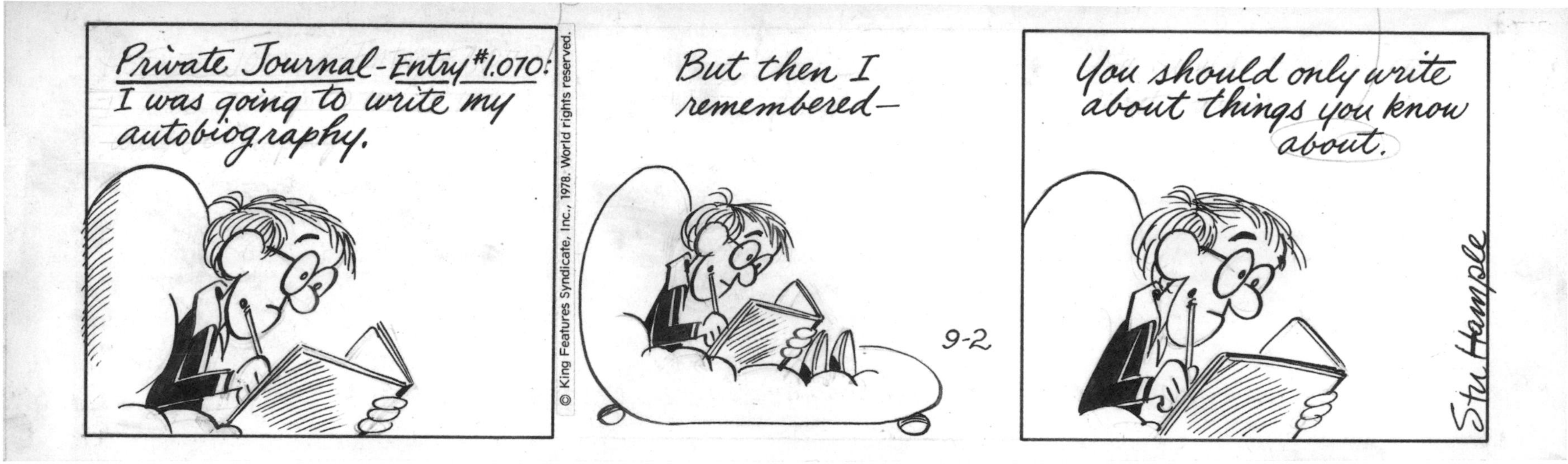
Private Journal-Entry #1,070: I was going to write my autobiography.
But then I remembered—
You should only write about things you know about.
9-2
Stu Hample
© King Features Syndicate, Inc., 1978. World rights reserved.

September 2, 1978

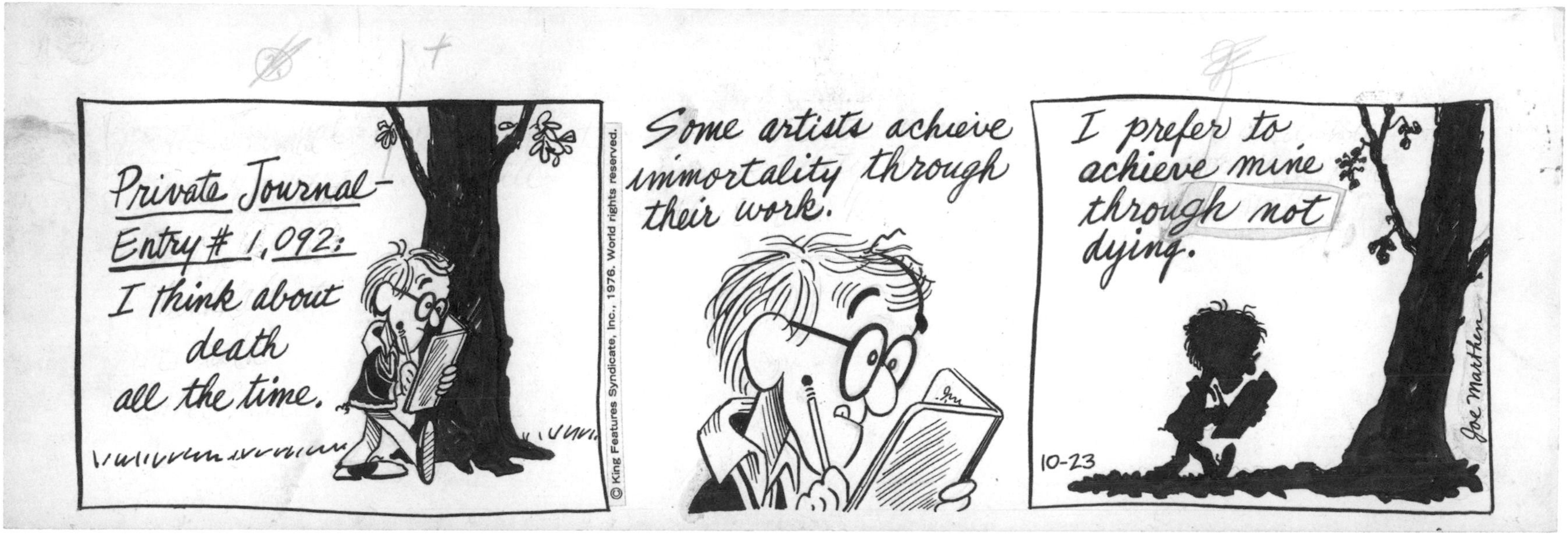
Private Journal-Entry # 1,092: I think about death all the time.
Some artists achieve immortality through their work.
I prefer to achieve mine through not dying.
10-23
Joe Martin
© King Features Syndicate, Inc., 1976. World rights reserved.

October 23, 1976

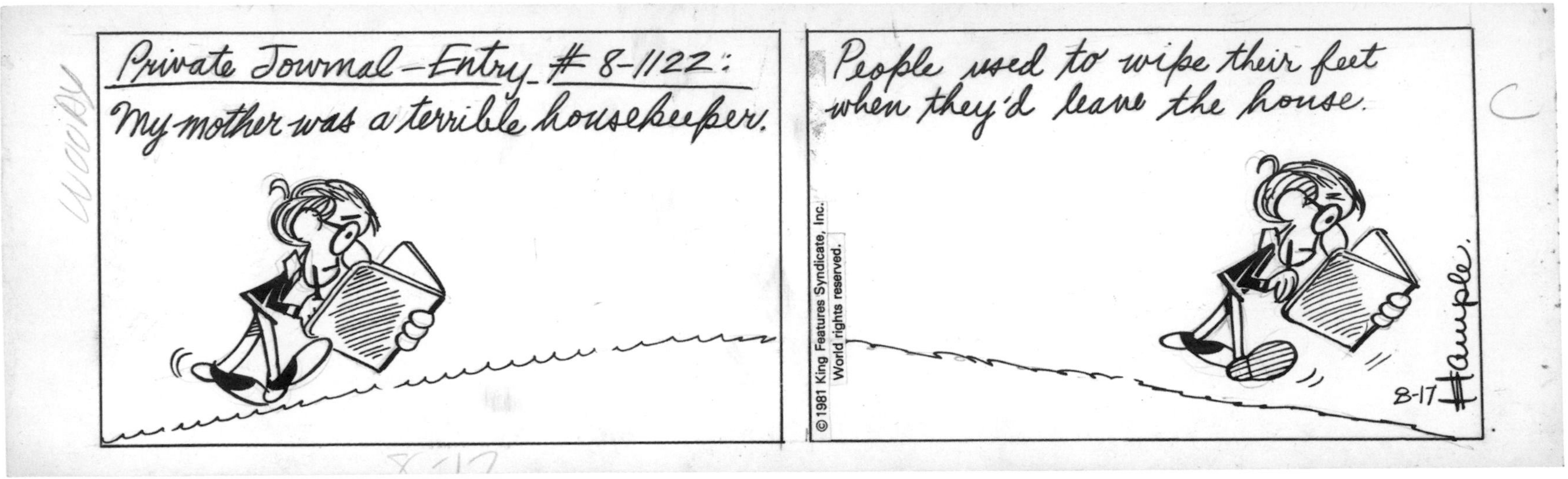
Private Journal—Entry #8-1122:
My mother was a terrible housekeeper.
People used to wipe their feet when they'd leave the house.
©1981 King Features Syndicate, Inc. World rights reserved.
8-17 Hample.

August 17, 1981

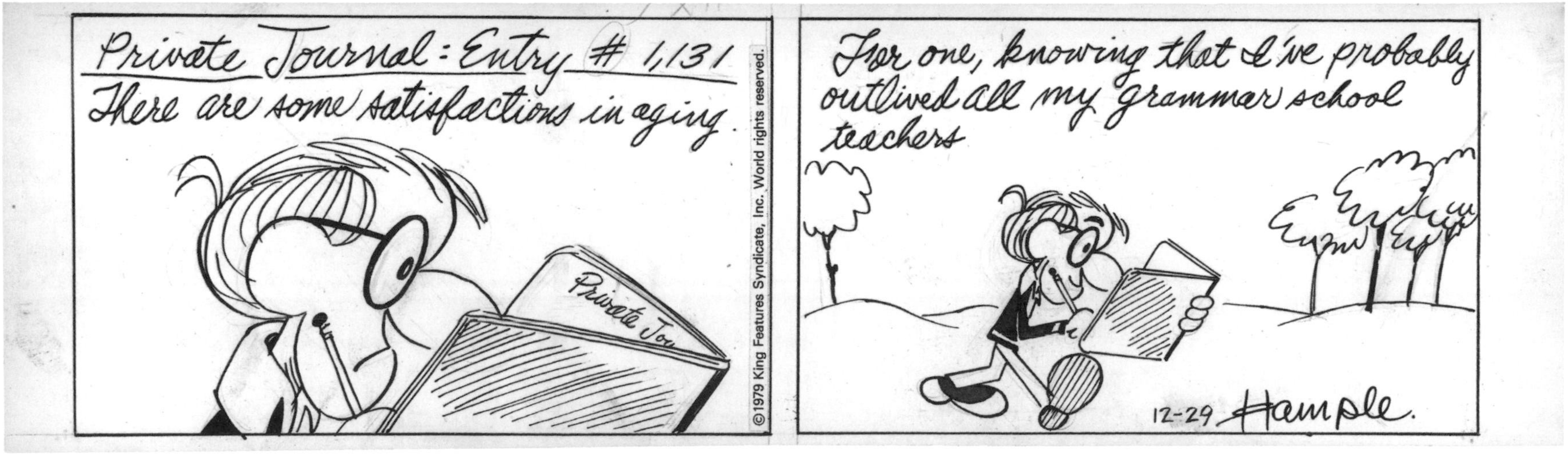
Private Journal: Entry #1,131
There are some satisfactions in aging.
Private Jou
©1979 King Features Syndicate, Inc. World rights reserved.
For one, knowing that I've probably outlived all my grammar school teachers
12-29 Hample.

December 29, 1979

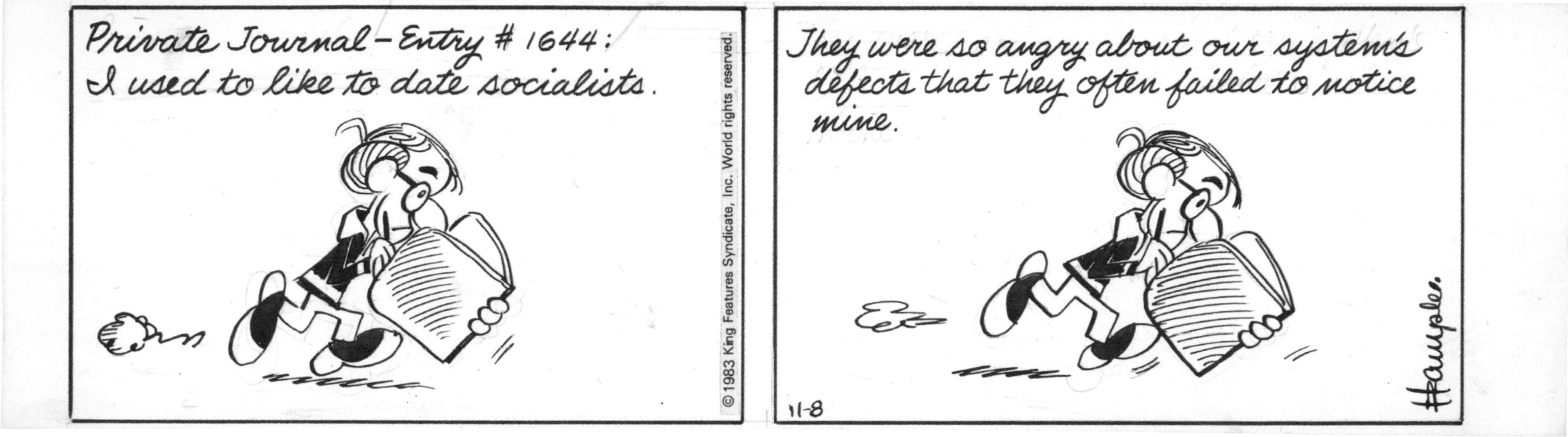
Private Journal – Entry # 1644:
I used to like to date socialists.
©1983 King Features Syndicate, Inc. World rights reserved.
They were so angry about our system's defects that they often failed to notice mine.
11-8
Hampler

November 8, 1983

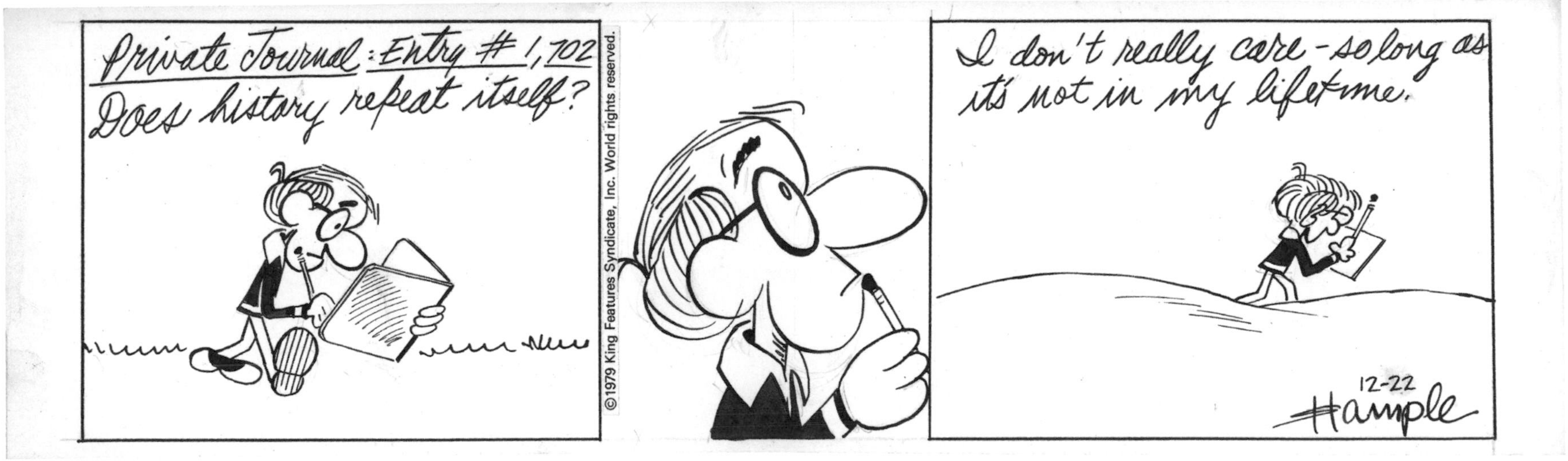
Private Journal: Entry # 1,702
Does history repeat itself?
©1979 King Features Syndicate, Inc. World rights reserved.
I don't really care – so long as it's not in my lifetime.
12-22
Hample

December 22, 1979

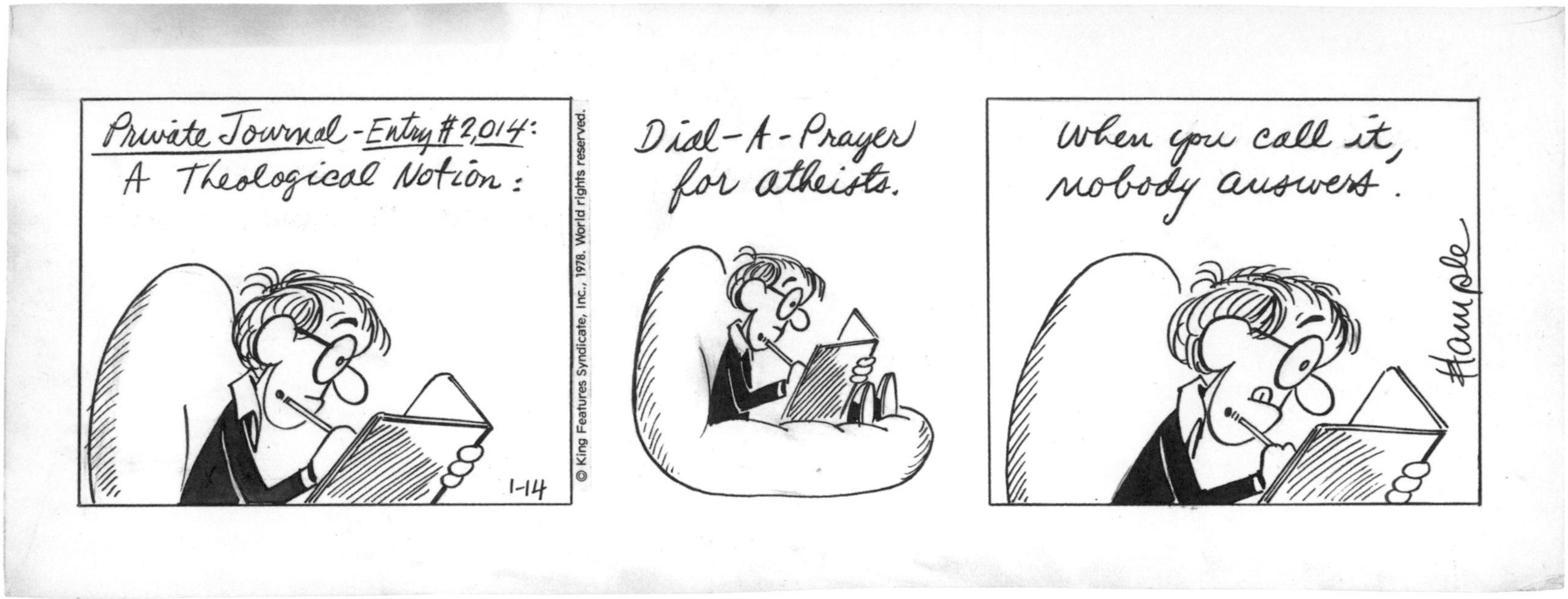
Private Journal - Entry #2,014:
A Theological Notion:
Dial-A-Prayer
for atheists.
When you call it,
nobody answers.
Hample
1-14
© King Features Syndicate, Inc., 1978. World rights reserved.

January 14, 1978

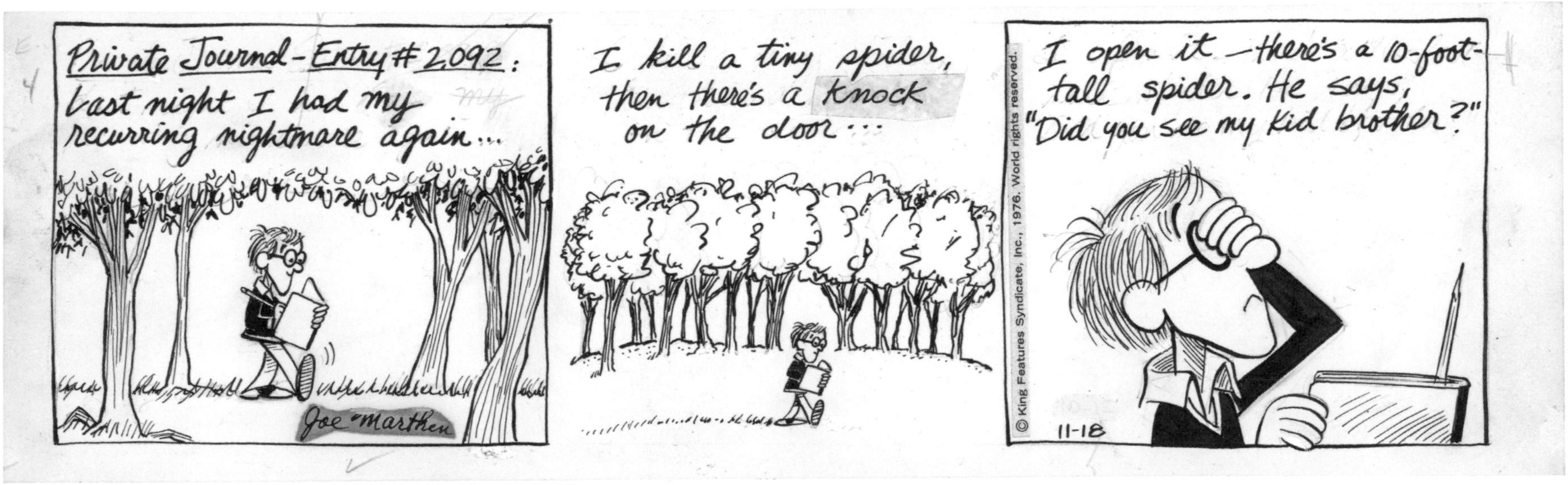
Private Journal - Entry # 2,092:
Last night I had my
recurring nightmare again...
Joe Marthen
I kill a tiny spider,
then there's a knock
on the door...
I open it — there's a 10-foot-
tall spider. He says,
"Did you see my kid brother?"
11-18
© King Features Syndicate, Inc., 1976. World rights reserved.

November 18, 1976

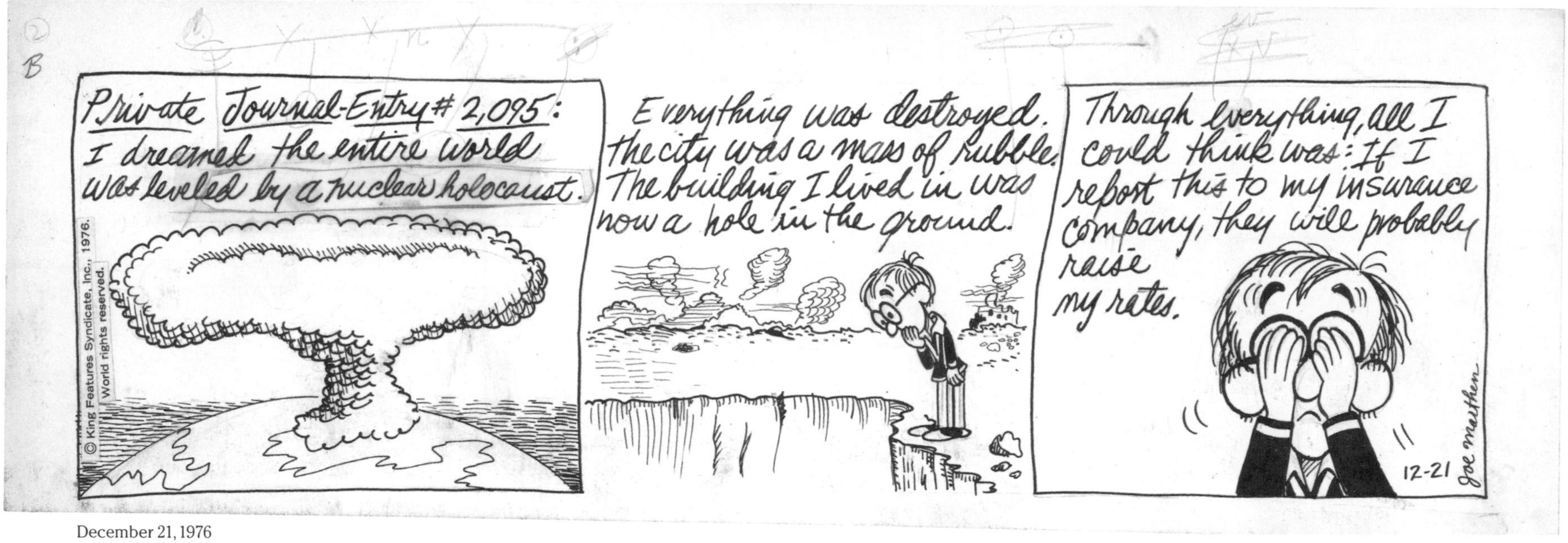
Private Journal-Entry # 2,095: I dreamed the entire world was leveled by a nuclear holocaust.
© King Features Syndicate, Inc., 1976. World rights reserved.
Everything was destroyed. The city was a mass of rubble. The building I lived in was now a hole in the ground.
Through everything, all I could think was: If I report this to my insurance company, they will probably raise my rates.
12-21
Joe Martin
December 21, 1976

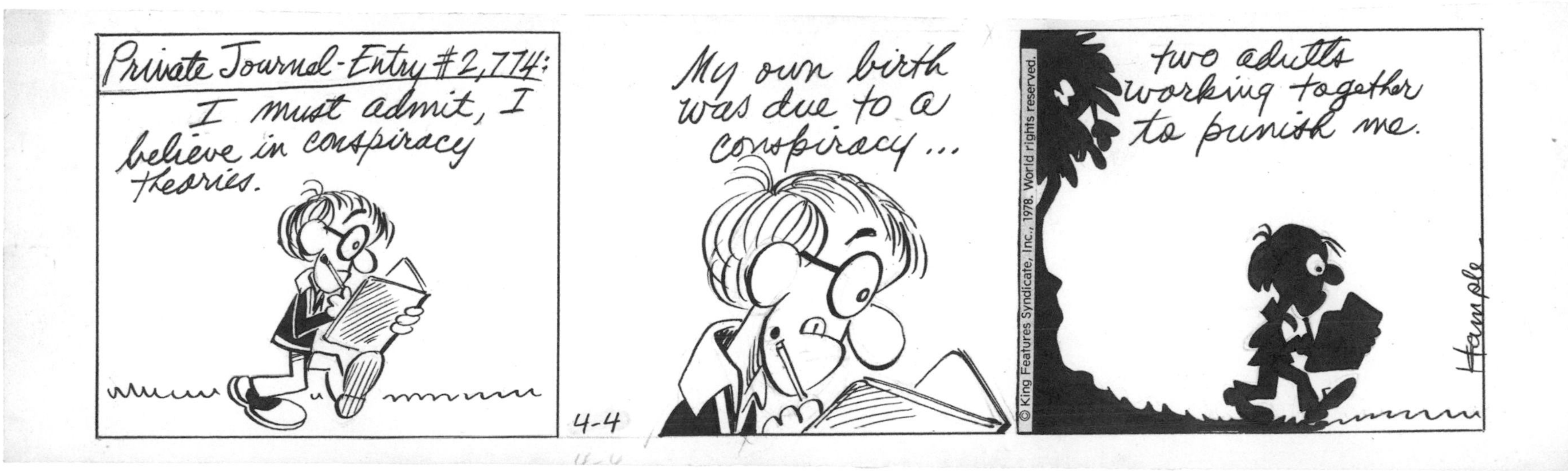
Private Journal-Entry # 2,774: I must admit, I believe in conspiracy theories.
4-4
My own birth was due to a conspiracy...
two adults working together to punish me.
© King Features Syndicate, Inc., 1978. World rights reserved.
Hample
April 4, 1978

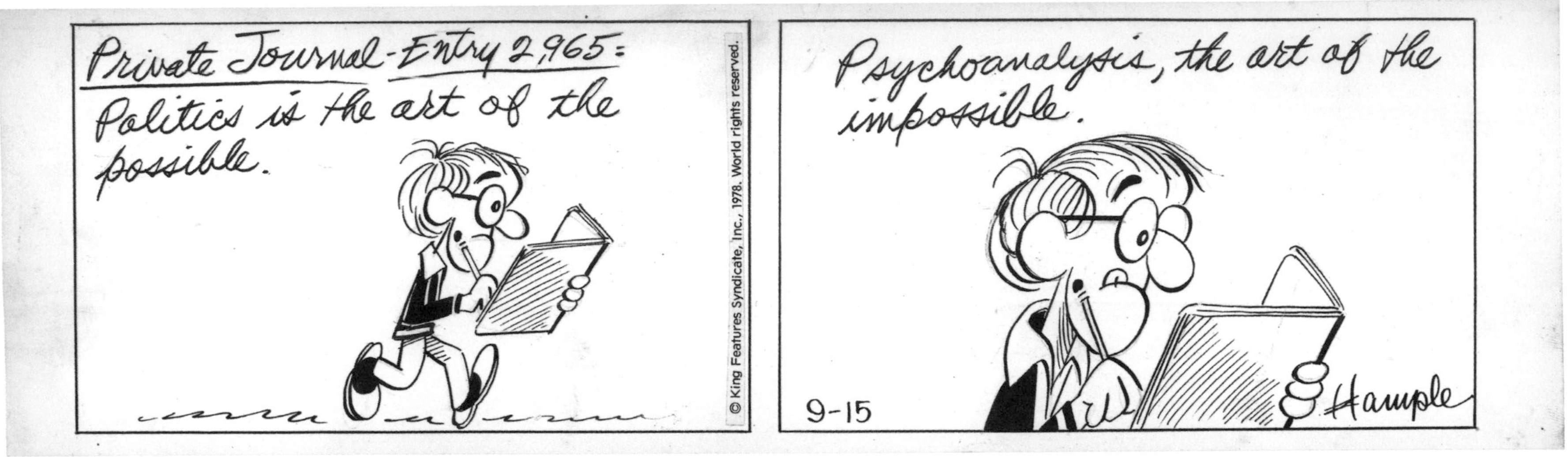
Private Journal-Entry 2,965:
Politics is the art of the possible.
© King Features Syndicate, Inc., 1978. World rights reserved.
Psychoanalysis, the art of the impossible.
9-15
Hample

September 15, 1978

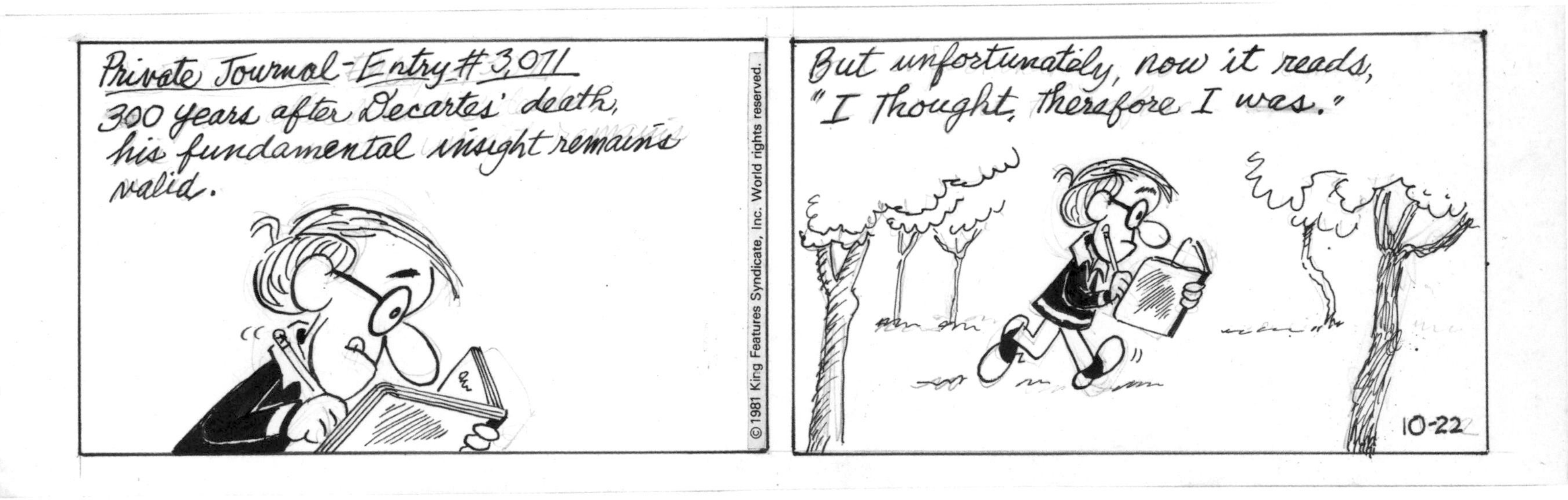
Private Journal-Entry #3,071
300 years after Decartes' death, his fundamental insight remains valid.
© 1981 King Features Syndicate, Inc. World rights reserved.
But unfortunately, now it reads, "I thought, therefore I was."
10-22

October 22, 1981

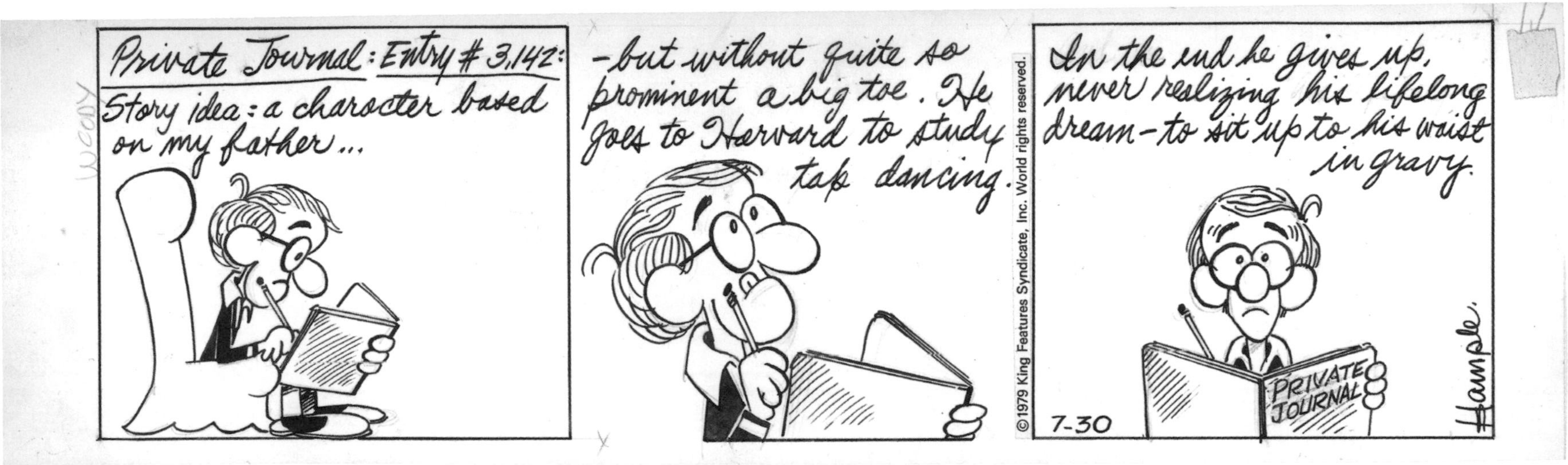
Private Journal: Entry # 3,142:
Story idea: a character based on my father...
-but without quite so prominent a big toe. He goes to Harvard to study tap dancing.
In the end he gives up, never realizing his lifelong dream-to sit up to his waist in gravy.
PRIVATE JOURNAL
© 1979 King Features Syndicate, Inc. World rights reserved.
7-30
Hample

July 30, 1979

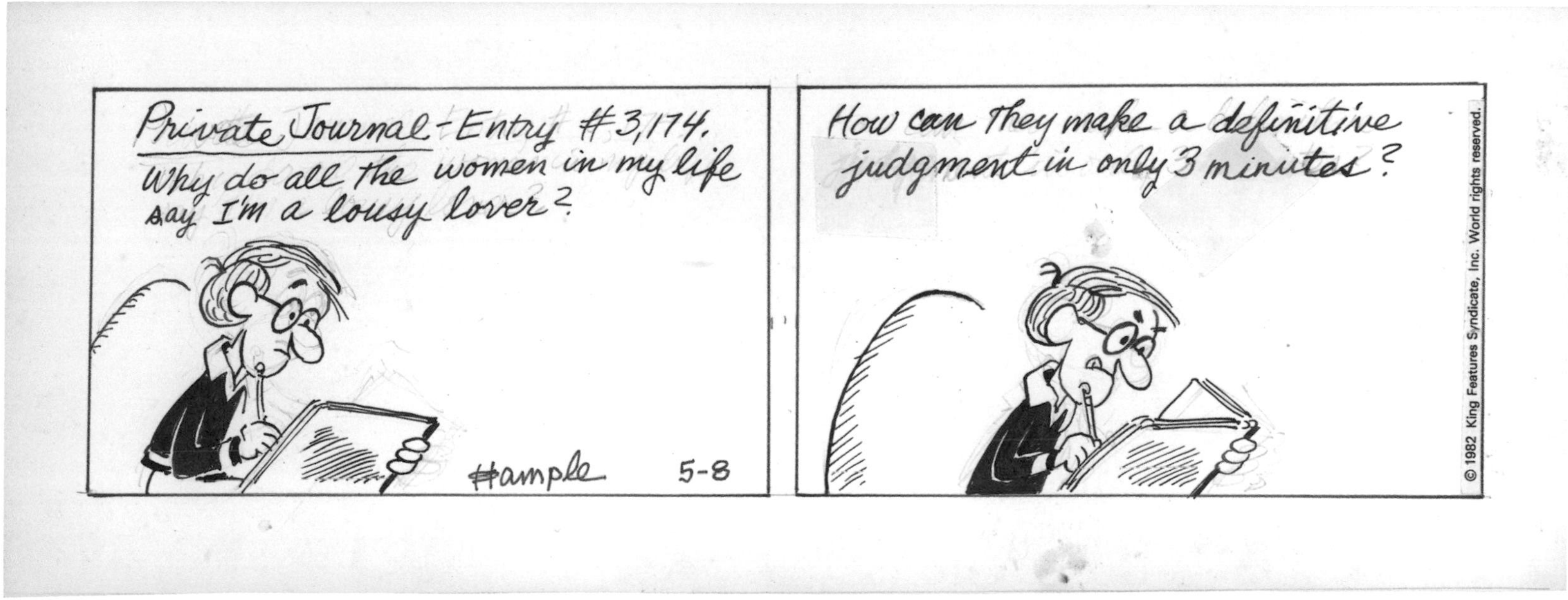
Private Journal-Entry #3,174.
Why do all the women in my life say I'm a lousy lover?
Hample
5-8
How can they make a definitive judgment in only 3 minutes?
© 1982 King Features Syndicate, Inc. World rights reserved.

May 8, 1982

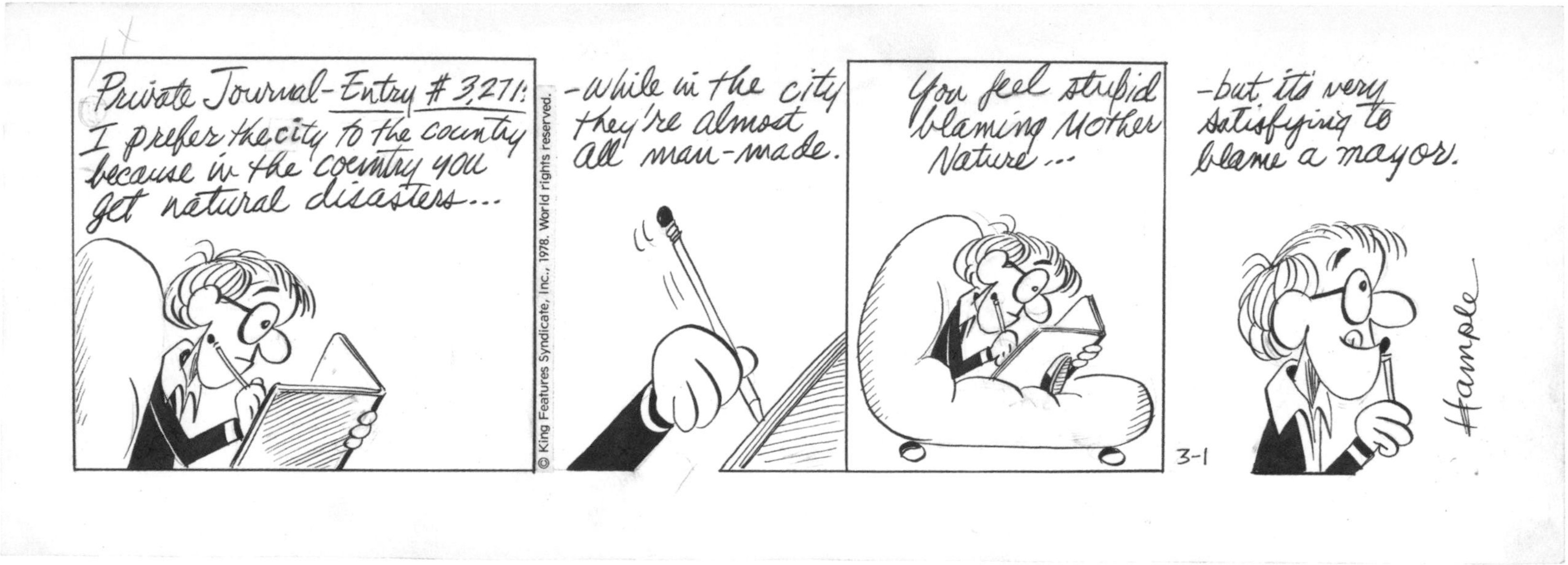
Private Journal-Entry #3,271:
I prefer the city to the country because in the country you get natural disasters...
-while in the city they're almost all man-made.
You feel stupid blaming Mother Nature...
-but it's very satisfying to blame a mayor.
© King Features Syndicate, Inc., 1978. World rights reserved.
3-1
Hample

March 1, 1978

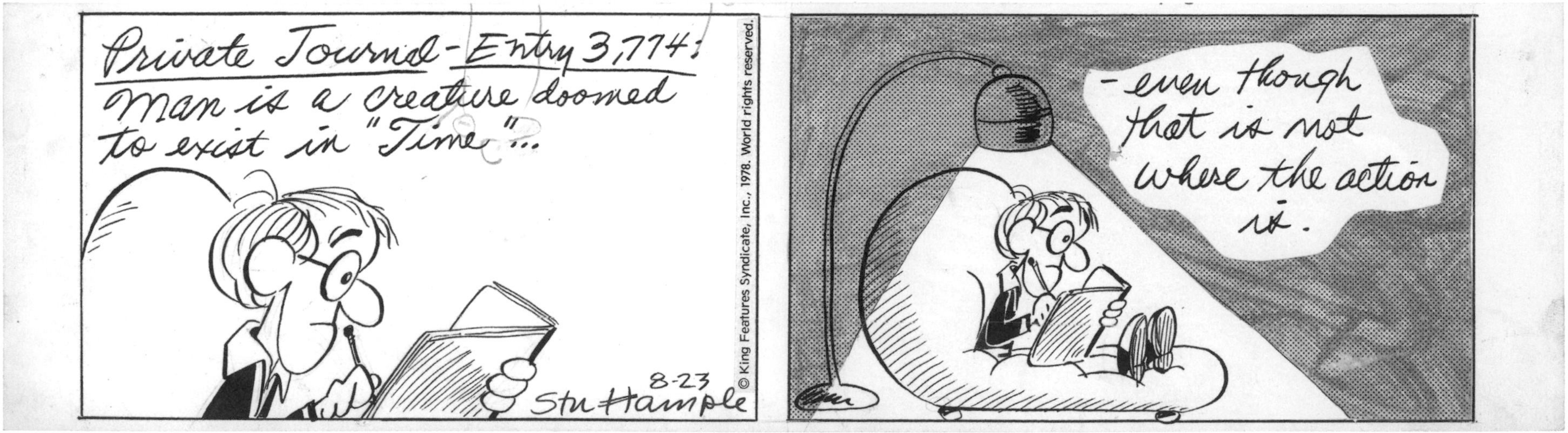
Private Journal-Entry 3,774:
Man is a creature doomed to exist in "Time"...
-even though that is not where the action is.
© King Features Syndicate, Inc., 1978. World rights reserved.
8-23
Stu Hample

August 23, 1978

Private Journal - Entry # 4066:
Love is the answer to everything.

But apparently not for more than a few weeks at a time.

9-22

September 22, 1981

Private Journal: Entry # 4,790
I don't pick the wrong women.

My problem is, it's wrong women who are right for me.

11-6

November 6, 1979

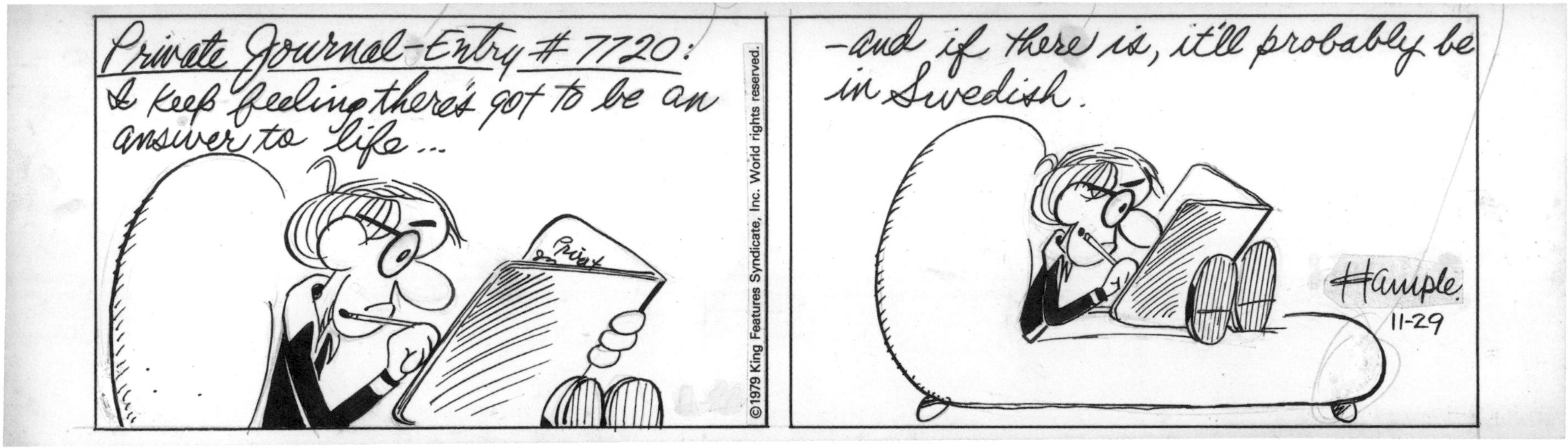
Private Journal-Entry #7720:
I keep feeling there's got to be an answer to life...
-and if there is, it'll probably be in Swedish.
Hample.
11-29
© 1979 King Features Syndicate, Inc. World rights reserved.

November 29, 1979

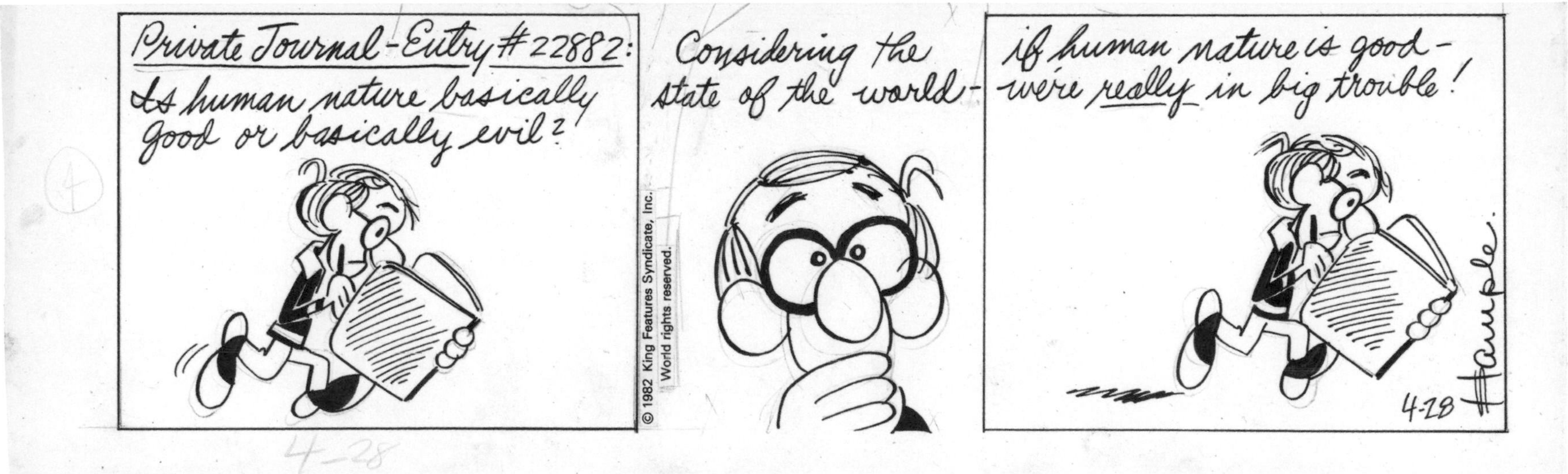
Private Journal-Entry #22882:
Is human nature basically good or basically evil?
Considering the state of the world-
if human nature is good-we're really in big trouble!
Hample
4-28
© 1982 King Features Syndicate, Inc. World rights reserved.

April 28, 1982

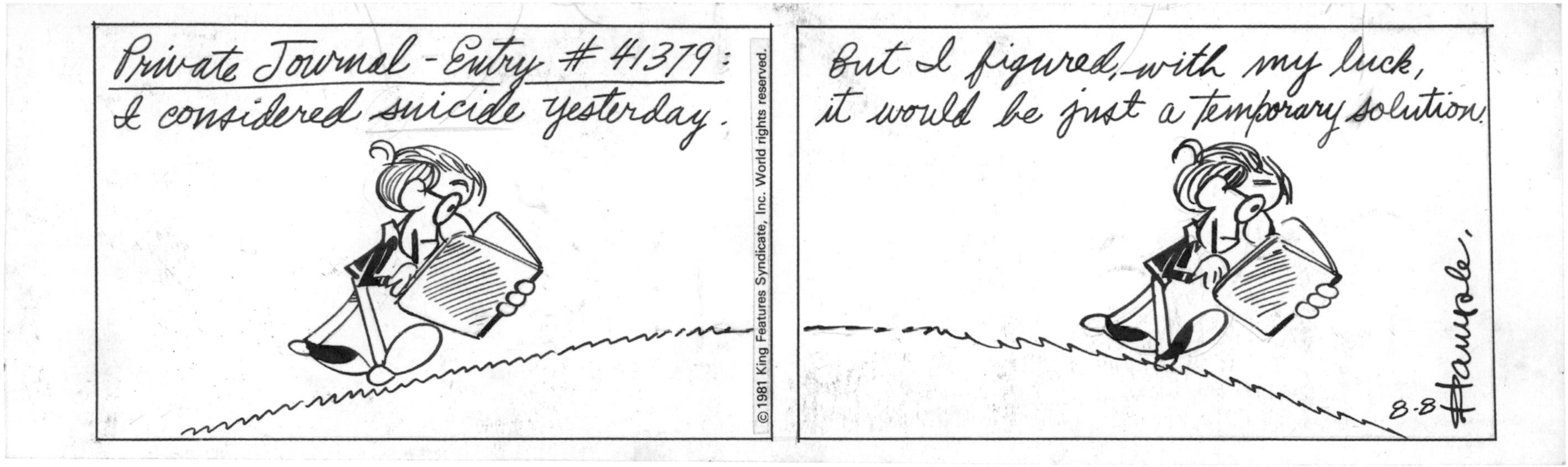
Private Journal - Entry #41379:
I considered suicide yesterday.
© 1981 King Features Syndicate, Inc. World rights reserved.
But I figured, with my luck,
it would be just a temporary solution.
8-8
Hample

August 8, 1981

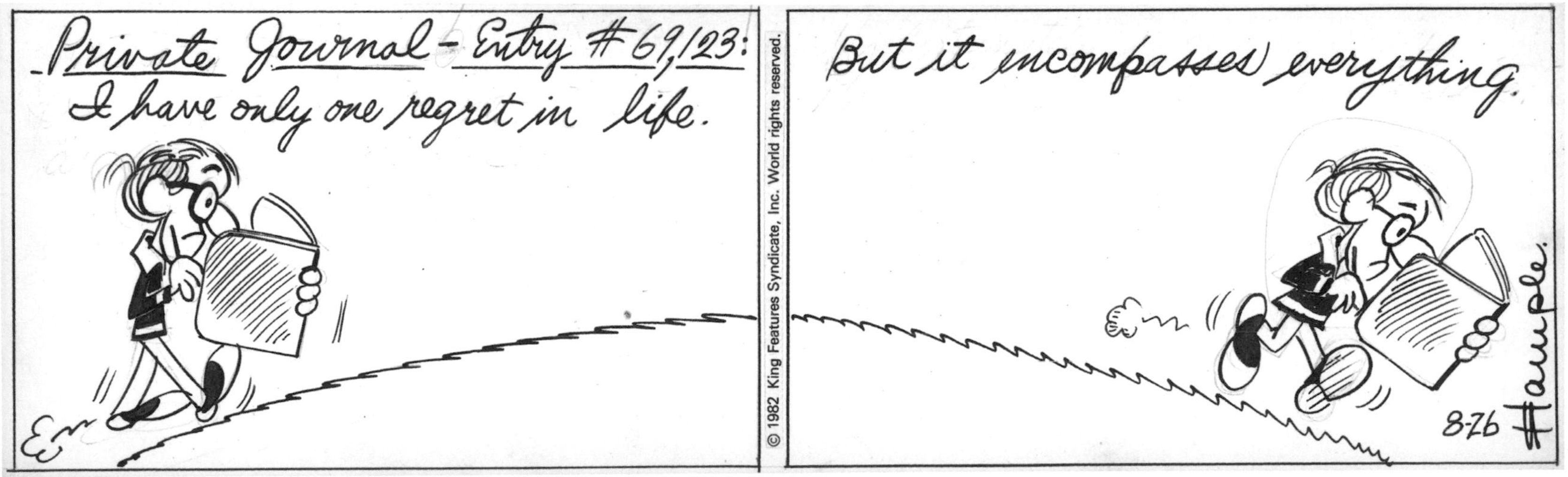
Private Journal - Entry #69,123:
I have only one regret in life.
© 1982 King Features Syndicate, Inc. World rights reserved.
But it encompasses everything.
8-26
Hample

August 26, 1982

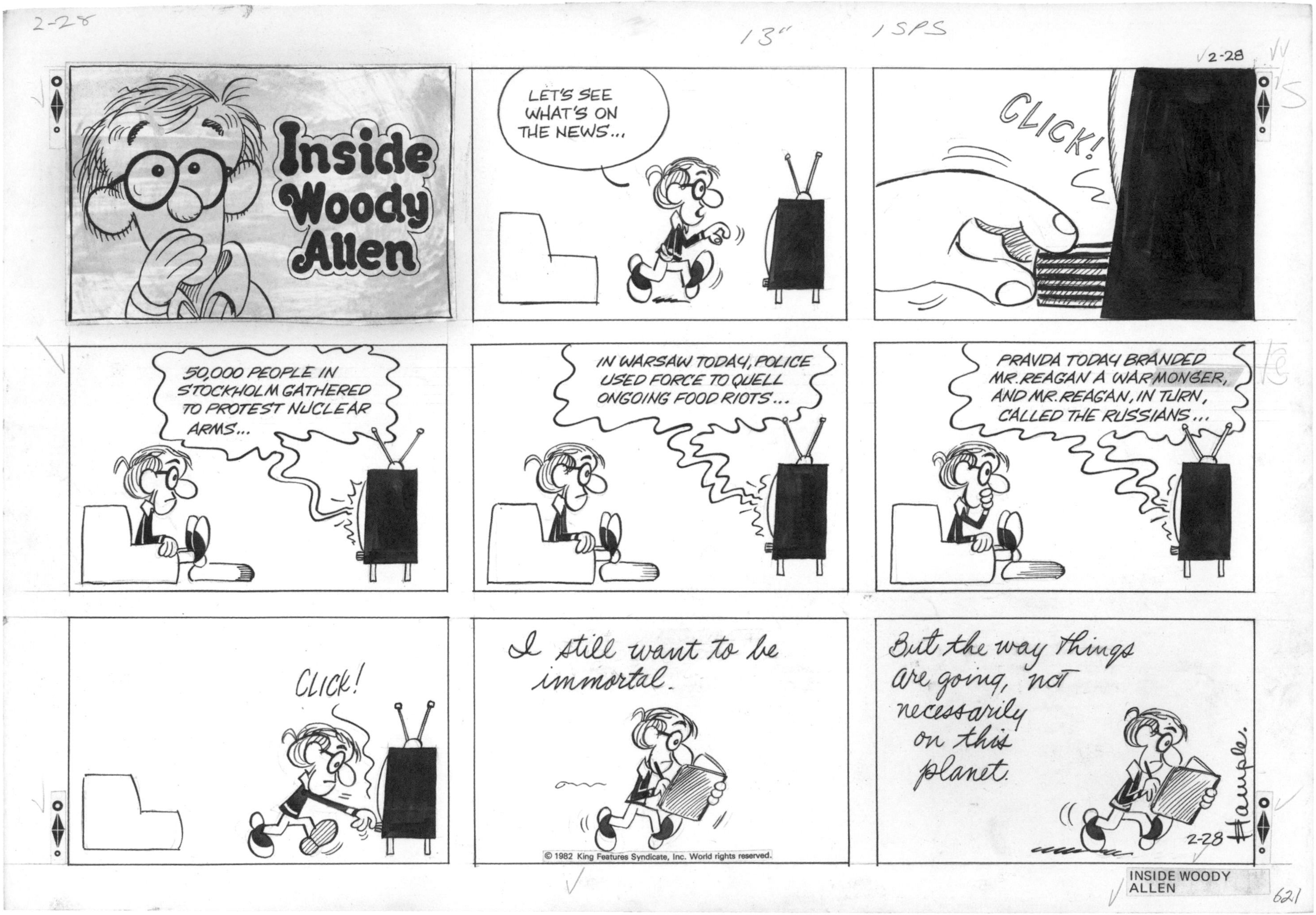
2-28
13"
1SPS
Inside Woody Allen
LET'S SEE WHAT'S ON THE NEWS...
2-28
CLICK!
50,000 PEOPLE IN STOCKHOLM GATHERED TO PROTEST NUCLEAR ARMS...
IN WARSAW TODAY, POLICE USED FORCE TO QUELL ONGOING FOOD RIOTS...
PRAVDA TODAY BRANDED MR. REAGAN A WARMONGER, AND MR. REAGAN, IN TURN, CALLED THE RUSSIANS...
CLICK!
I still want to be immortal.
But the way things are going, not necessarily on this planet.
Hample
2-28
© 1982 King Features Syndicate, Inc. World rights reserved.
INSIDE WOODY ALLEN
621

February 28, 1982

5 Freud's Last Resort

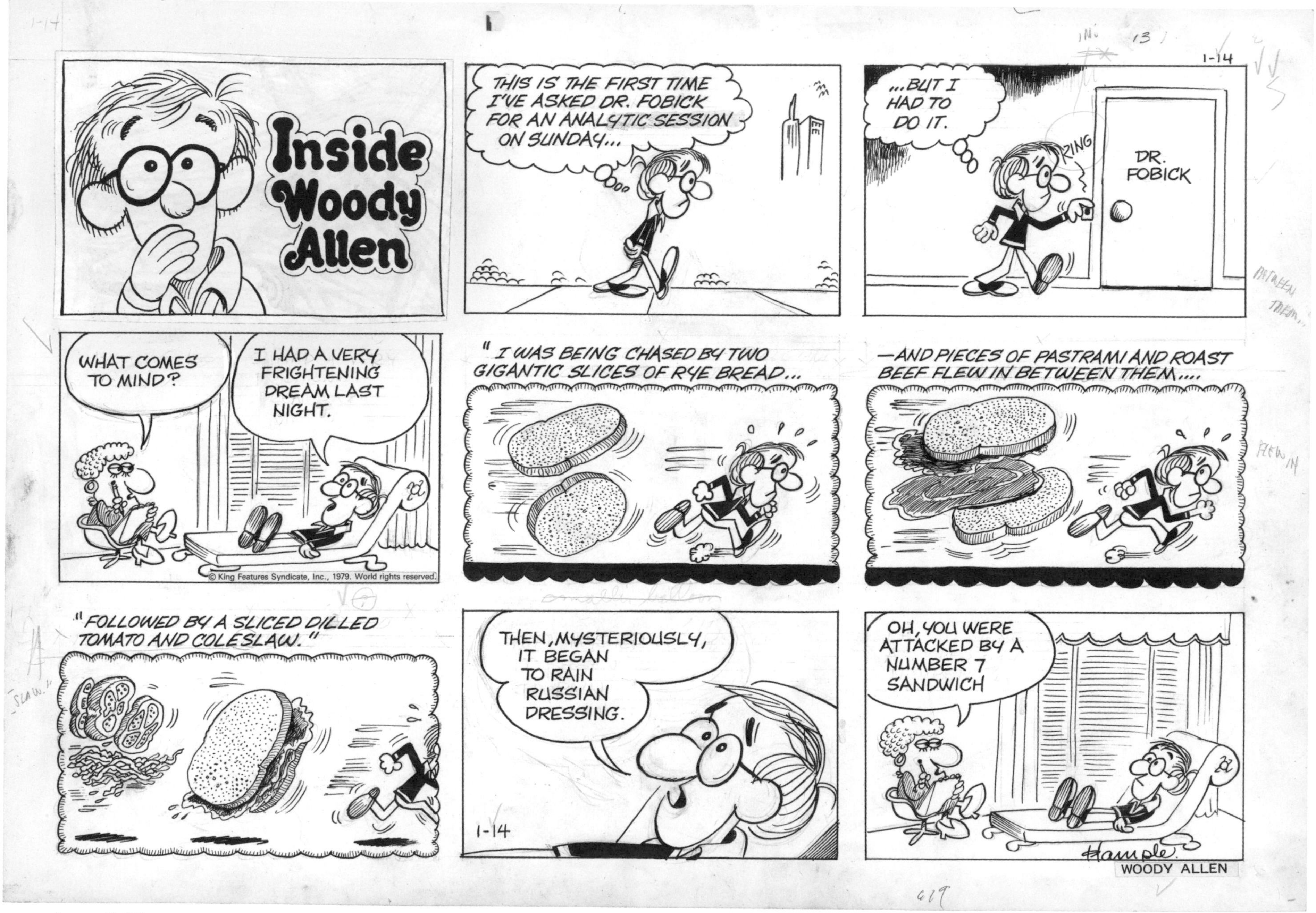
Inside Woody Allen
THIS IS THE FIRST TIME I'VE ASKED DR. FOBICK FOR AN ANALYTIC SESSION ON SUNDAY...
1-14
...BUT I HAD TO DO IT.
ZING
DR. FOBICK
WHAT COMES TO MIND?
I HAD A VERY FRIGHTENING DREAM LAST NIGHT.
© King Features Syndicate, Inc., 1979. World rights reserved.
"I WAS BEING CHASED BY TWO GIGANTIC SLICES OF RYE BREAD...
—AND PIECES OF PASTRAMI AND ROAST BEEF FLEW IN BETWEEN THEM....
"FOLLOWED BY A SLICED DILLED TOMATO AND COLESLAW."
THEN, MYSTERIOUSLY, IT BEGAN TO RAIN RUSSIAN DRESSING.
1-14
OH, YOU WERE ATTACKED BY A NUMBER 7 SANDWICH
Hample
WOODY ALLEN

January 14, 1979

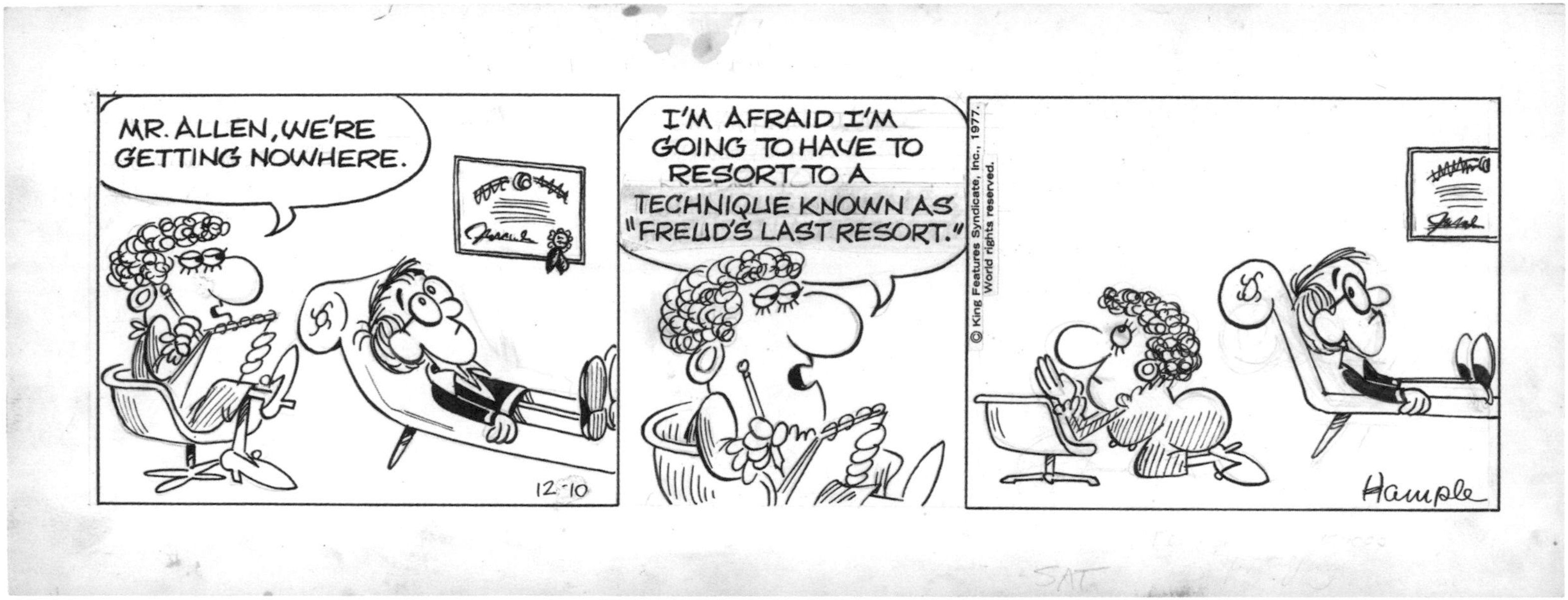
MR. ALLEN, WE'RE GETTING NOWHERE.
12-10
I'M AFRAID I'M GOING TO HAVE TO RESORT TO A TECHNIQUE KNOWN AS "FREUD'S LAST RESORT."
© King Features Syndicate, Inc., 1977. World rights reserved.
Hample

December 10, 1977

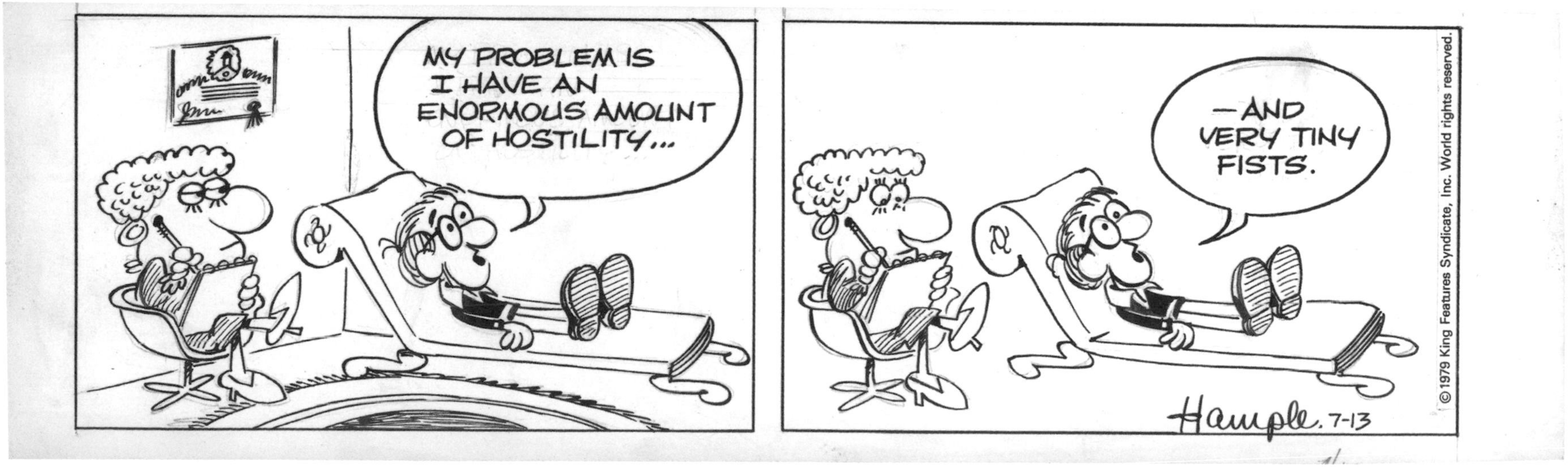
MY PROBLEM IS I HAVE AN ENORMOUS AMOUNT OF HOSTILITY...
—AND VERY TINY FISTS.
© 1979 King Features Syndicate, Inc. World rights reserved.
Hample. 7-13

July 13, 1979

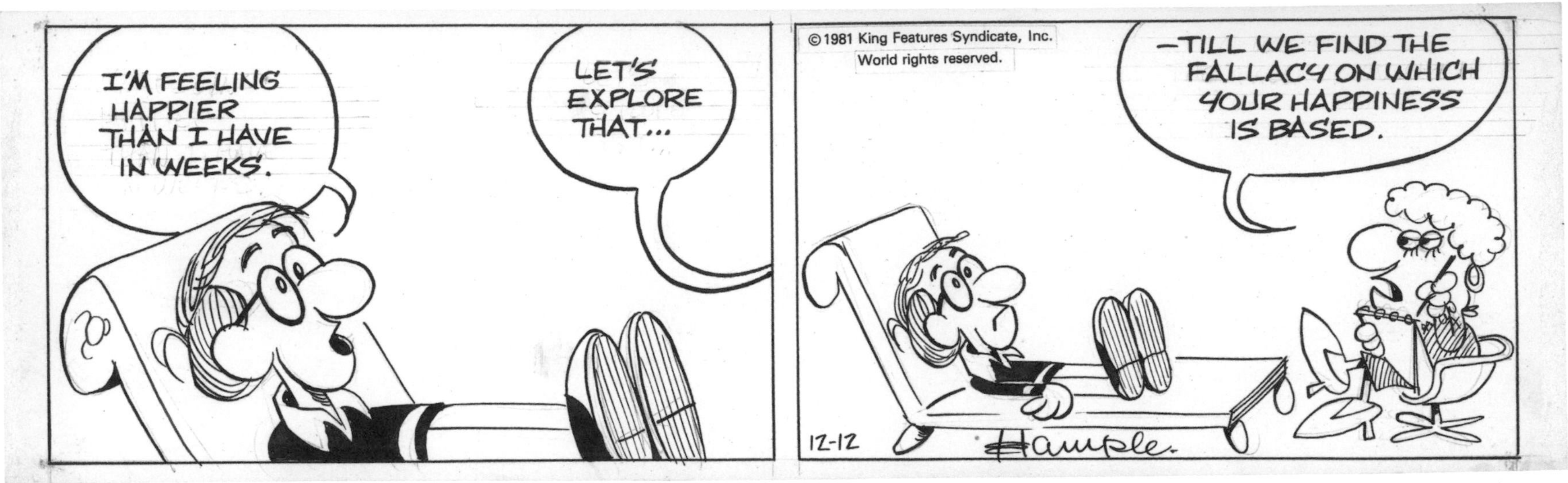
I'M FEELING HAPPIER THAN I HAVE IN WEEKS.
LET'S EXPLORE THAT...
© 1981 King Features Syndicate, Inc. World rights reserved.
–TILL WE FIND THE FALLACY ON WHICH YOUR HAPPINESS IS BASED.
12-12
Hample.

December 12, 1981

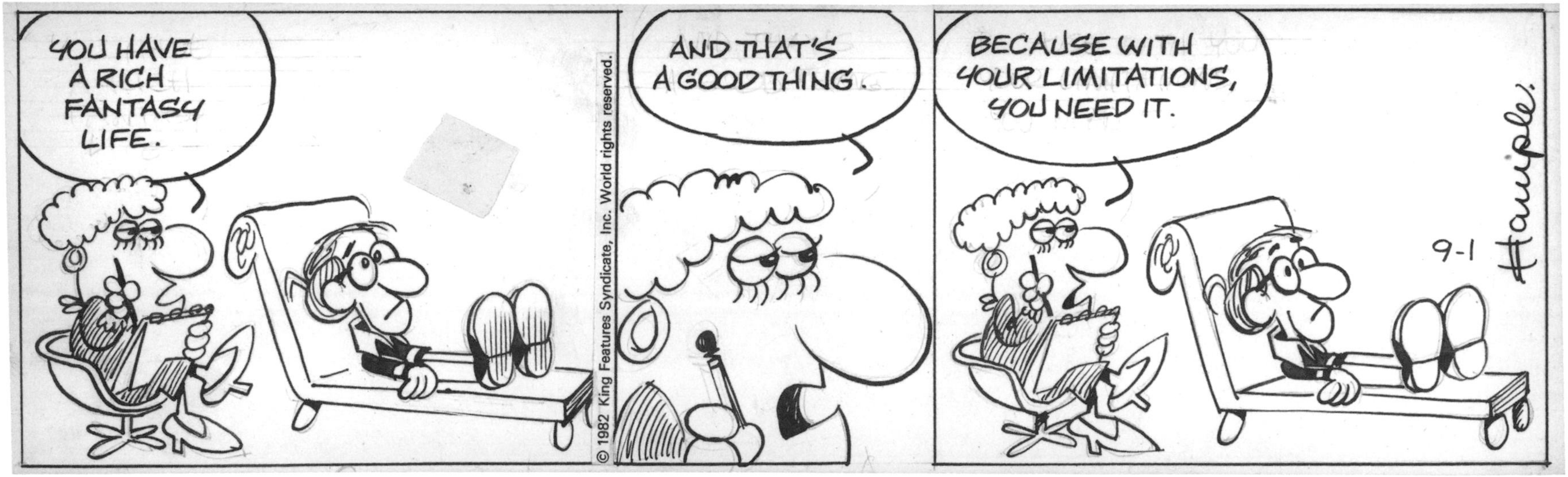
YOU HAVE A RICH FANTASY LIFE.
© 1982 King Features Syndicate, Inc. World rights reserved.
AND THAT'S A GOOD THING.
BECAUSE WITH YOUR LIMITATIONS, YOU NEED IT.
9-1
Hample.

September 1, 1982

Inside Woody Allen

342

I'M MR. ALLEN—FOR DR. FOBICK...

1-16

ER... MR. ALLEN, DR. FOBICK SAID TO TELL YOU SHE'LL BE RIGHT BACK...

THANKS.

WHILE YOU'RE WAITING, I JUST WANT TO SAY THAT YOU'VE GIVEN ME MANY HOURS OF JOY.

OH, YOU'RE A FAN OF MINE, HUH?

I'LL SAY! I NEVER MISS A SESSION.

342

WHAT?

WHEN YOU GO UP AND TALK TO THE DOCTOR ABOUT YOUR PRIVATE LIFE, I LEAVE THE INTERCOM ON.

OH?

I TELL YOU, EVERY DOORMAN ON THE BLOCK COMES TO LISTEN...

YOU'RE VERY POPULAR AROUND HERE.

GEE, I HAD NO IDEA I HAD AN AUDIENCE OUT THERE...

...I GUESS THOSE T.V. RATINGS WERE WRONG AFTER ALL....

1-16

WOODY

January 16, 1977

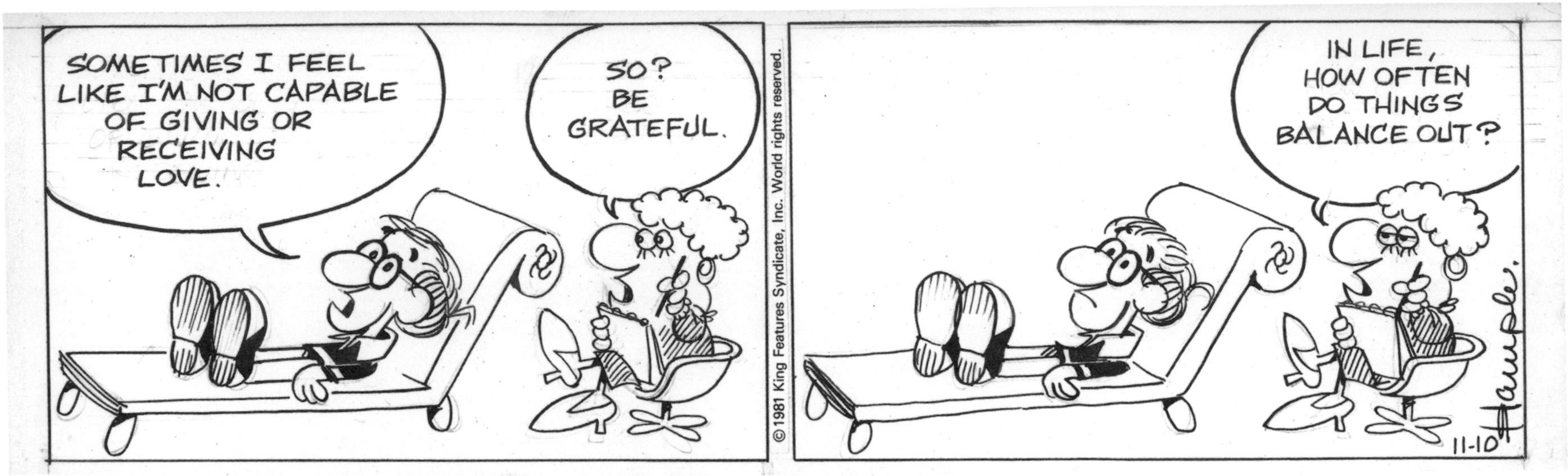
SOMETIMES I FEEL LIKE I'M NOT CAPABLE OF GIVING OR RECEIVING LOVE.
SO? BE GRATEFUL.
IN LIFE, HOW OFTEN DO THINGS BALANCE OUT?
© 1981 King Features Syndicate, Inc. World rights reserved.
Hample
11-10

November 10, 1981

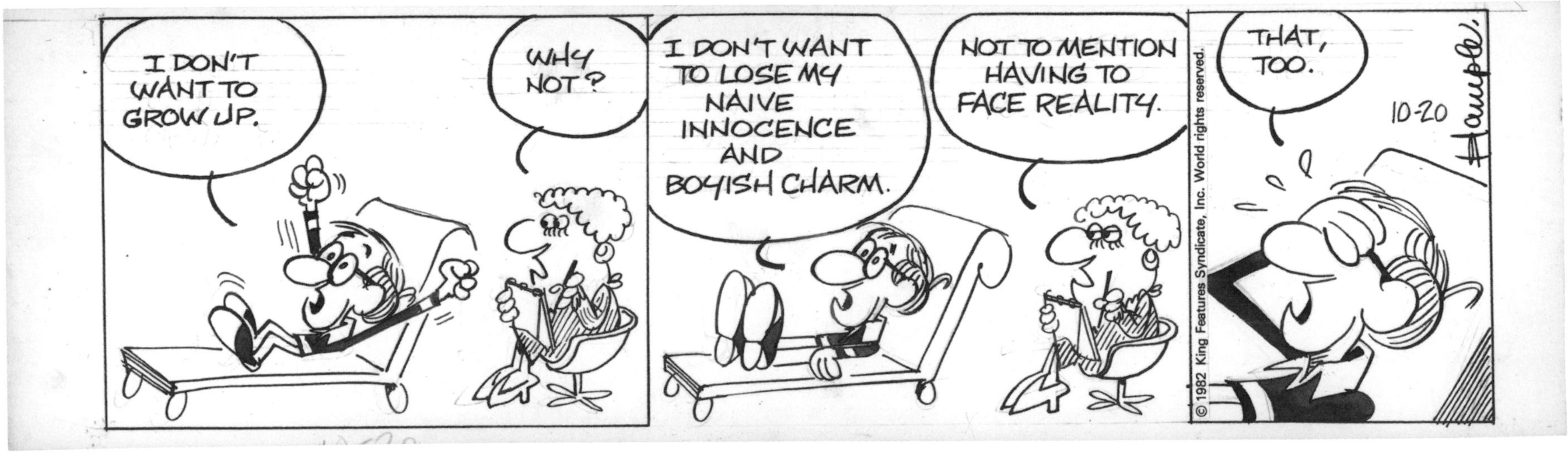
I DON'T WANT TO GROW UP.
WHY NOT?
I DON'T WANT TO LOSE MY NAIVE INNOCENCE AND BOYISH CHARM.
NOT TO MENTION HAVING TO FACE REALITY.
THAT, TOO.
© 1982 King Features Syndicate, Inc. World rights reserved.
Hample
10-20

October 20, 1982

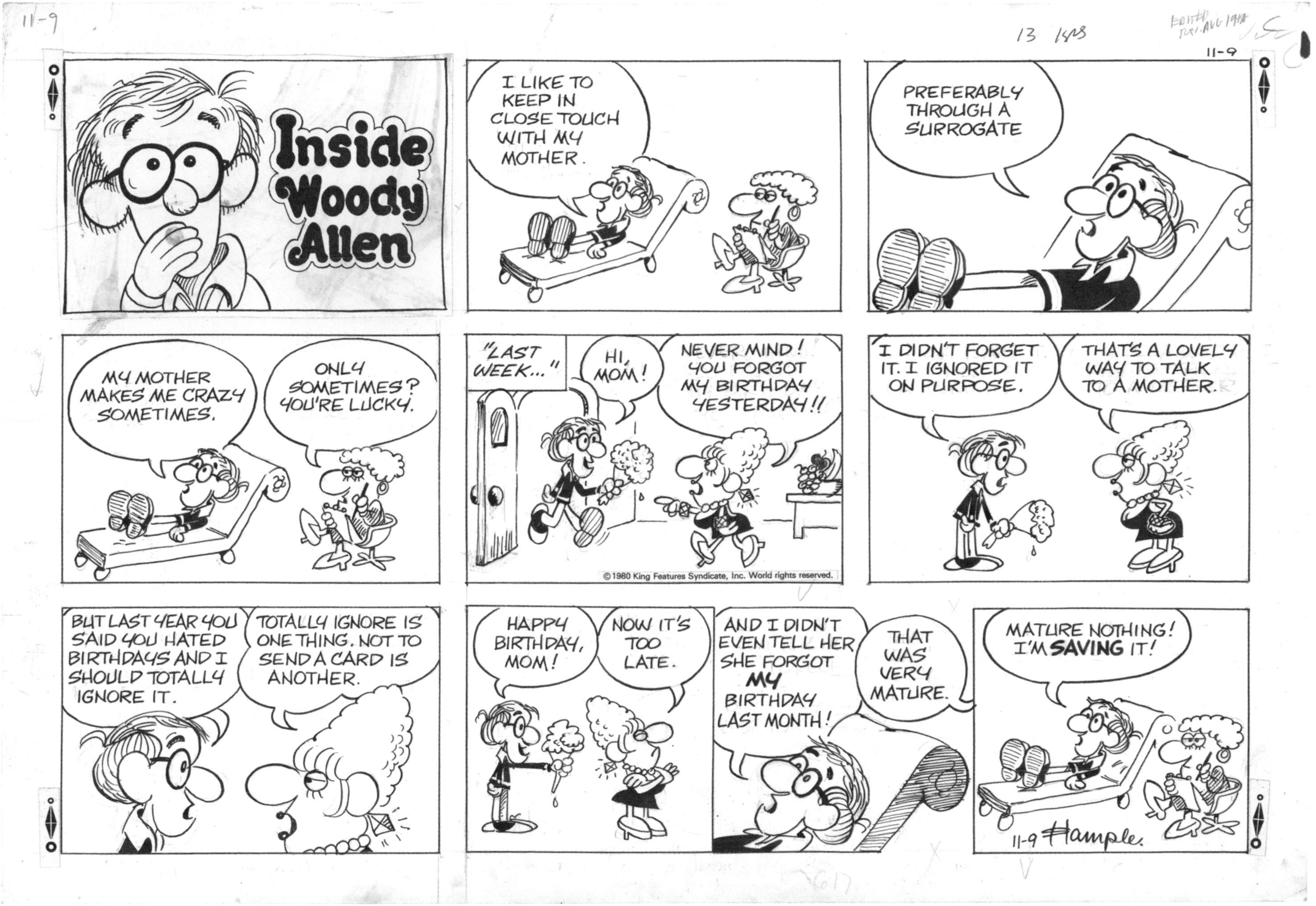
Inside Woody Allen
I LIKE TO KEEP IN CLOSE TOUCH WITH MY MOTHER.
PREFERABLY THROUGH A SURROGATE
MY MOTHER MAKES ME CRAZY SOMETIMES.
ONLY SOMETIMES? YOU'RE LUCKY.
"LAST WEEK..."
HI, MOM!
NEVER MIND! YOU FORGOT MY BIRTHDAY YESTERDAY!!
© 1980 King Features Syndicate, Inc. World rights reserved.
I DIDN'T FORGET IT. I IGNORED IT ON PURPOSE.
THAT'S A LOVELY WAY TO TALK TO A MOTHER.
BUT LAST YEAR YOU SAID YOU HATED BIRTHDAYS AND I SHOULD TOTALLY IGNORE IT.
TOTALLY IGNORE IS ONE THING. NOT TO SEND A CARD IS ANOTHER.
HAPPY BIRTHDAY, MOM!
NOW IT'S TOO LATE.
AND I DIDN'T EVEN TELL HER SHE FORGOT MY BIRTHDAY LAST MONTH!
THAT WAS VERY MATURE.
MATURE NOTHING! I'M SAVING IT!
11-9 Hample.

November 9, 1980

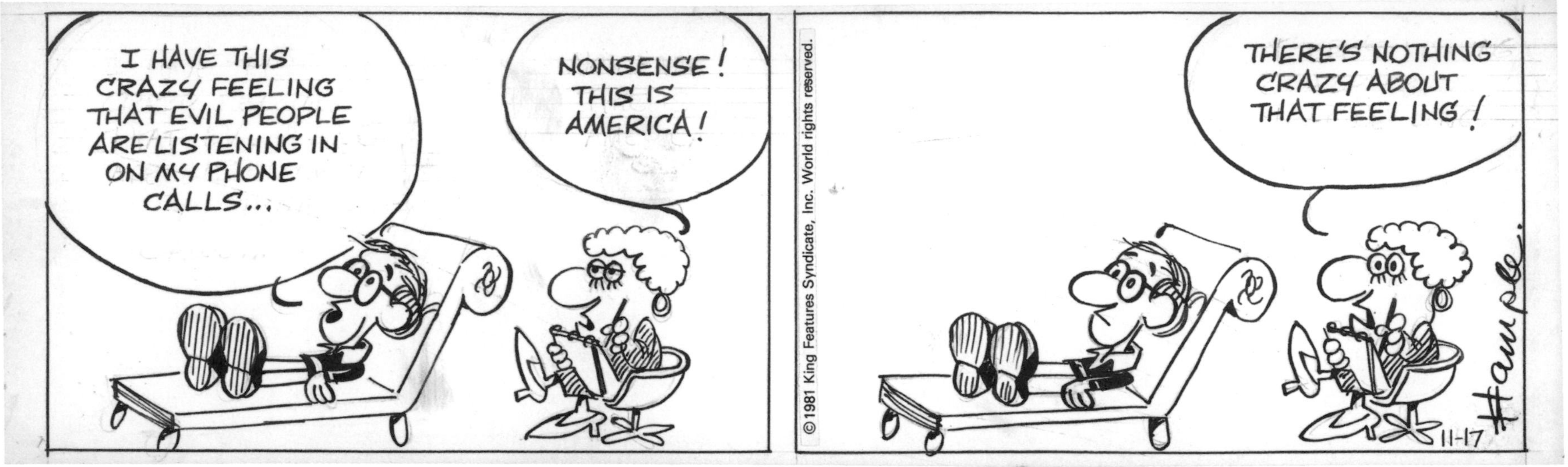
I HAVE THIS CRAZY FEELING THAT EVIL PEOPLE ARE LISTENING IN ON MY PHONE CALLS...
NONSENSE! THIS IS AMERICA!
THERE'S NOTHING CRAZY ABOUT THAT FEELING!
© 1981 King Features Syndicate, Inc. World rights reserved.
Hample
11-17

November 17, 1981

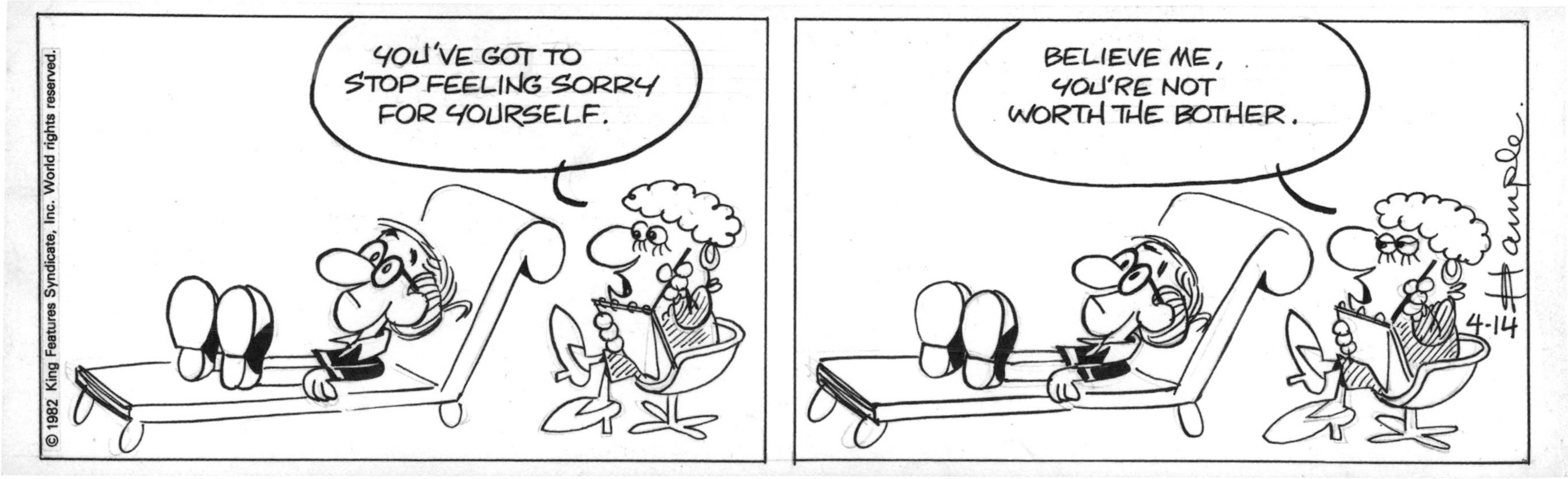
YOU'VE GOT TO STOP FEELING SORRY FOR YOURSELF.
BELIEVE ME, YOU'RE NOT WORTH THE BOTHER.
© 1982 King Features Syndicate, Inc. World rights reserved.
Hample
4-14

April 14, 1982

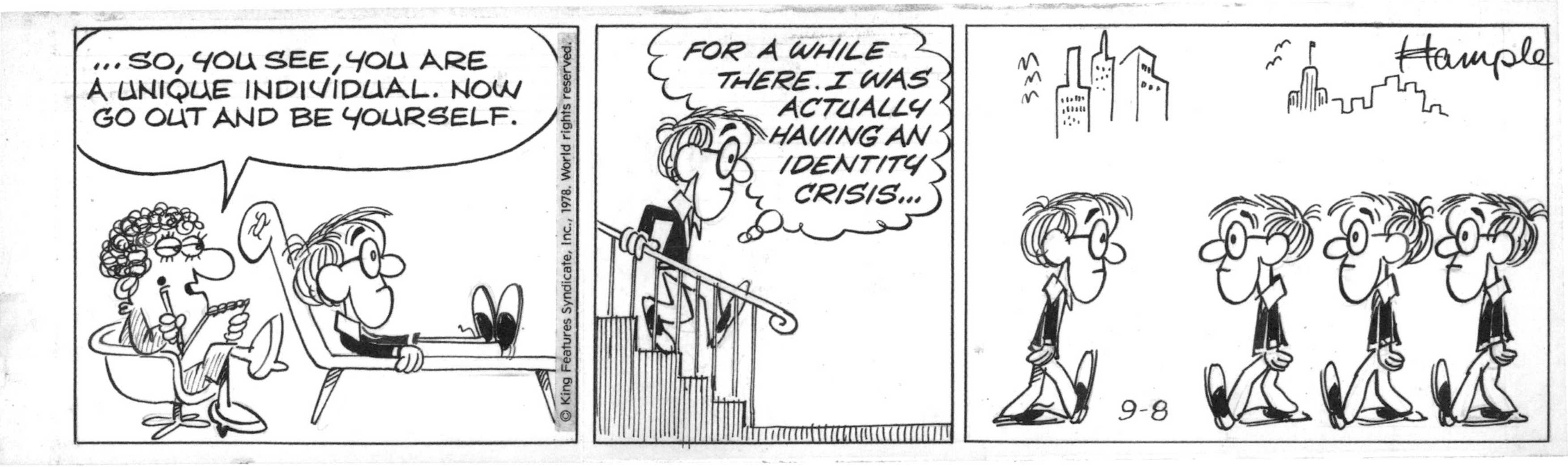
... SO, YOU SEE, YOU ARE A UNIQUE INDIVIDUAL. NOW GO OUT AND BE YOURSELF.
© King Features Syndicate, Inc., 1978. World rights reserved.
FOR A WHILE THERE. I WAS ACTUALLY HAVING AN IDENTITY CRISIS...
Hample
9-8

September 8, 1978

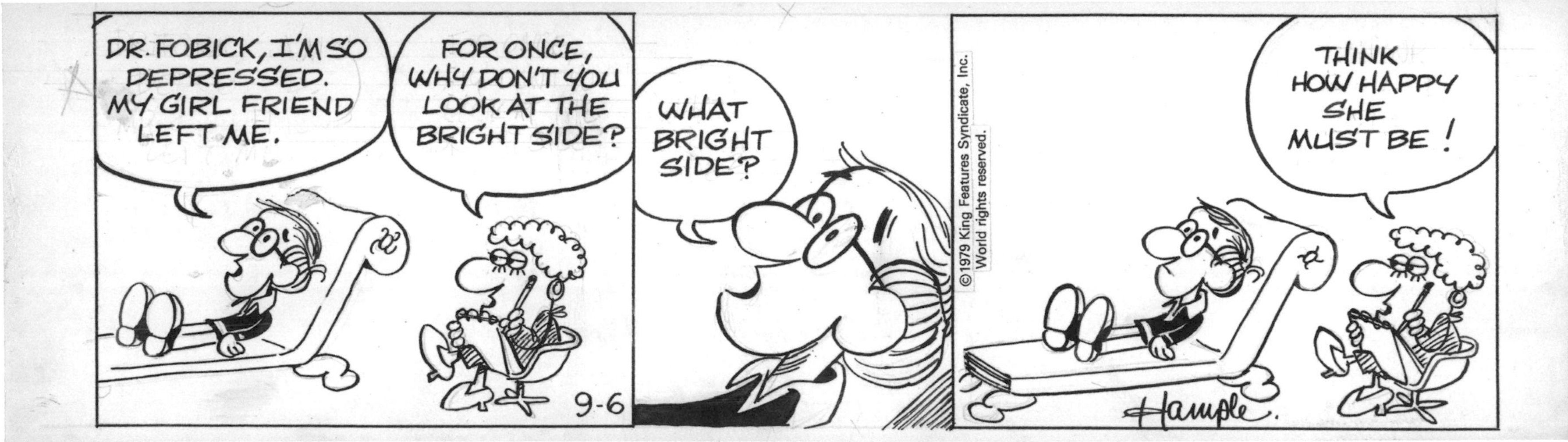
DR. FOBICK, I'M SO DEPRESSED. MY GIRL FRIEND LEFT ME.
FOR ONCE, WHY DON'T YOU LOOK AT THE BRIGHT SIDE?
9-6
WHAT BRIGHT SIDE?
©1979 King Features Syndicate, Inc. World rights reserved.
THINK HOW HAPPY SHE MUST BE!
Hample.

September 6, 1979

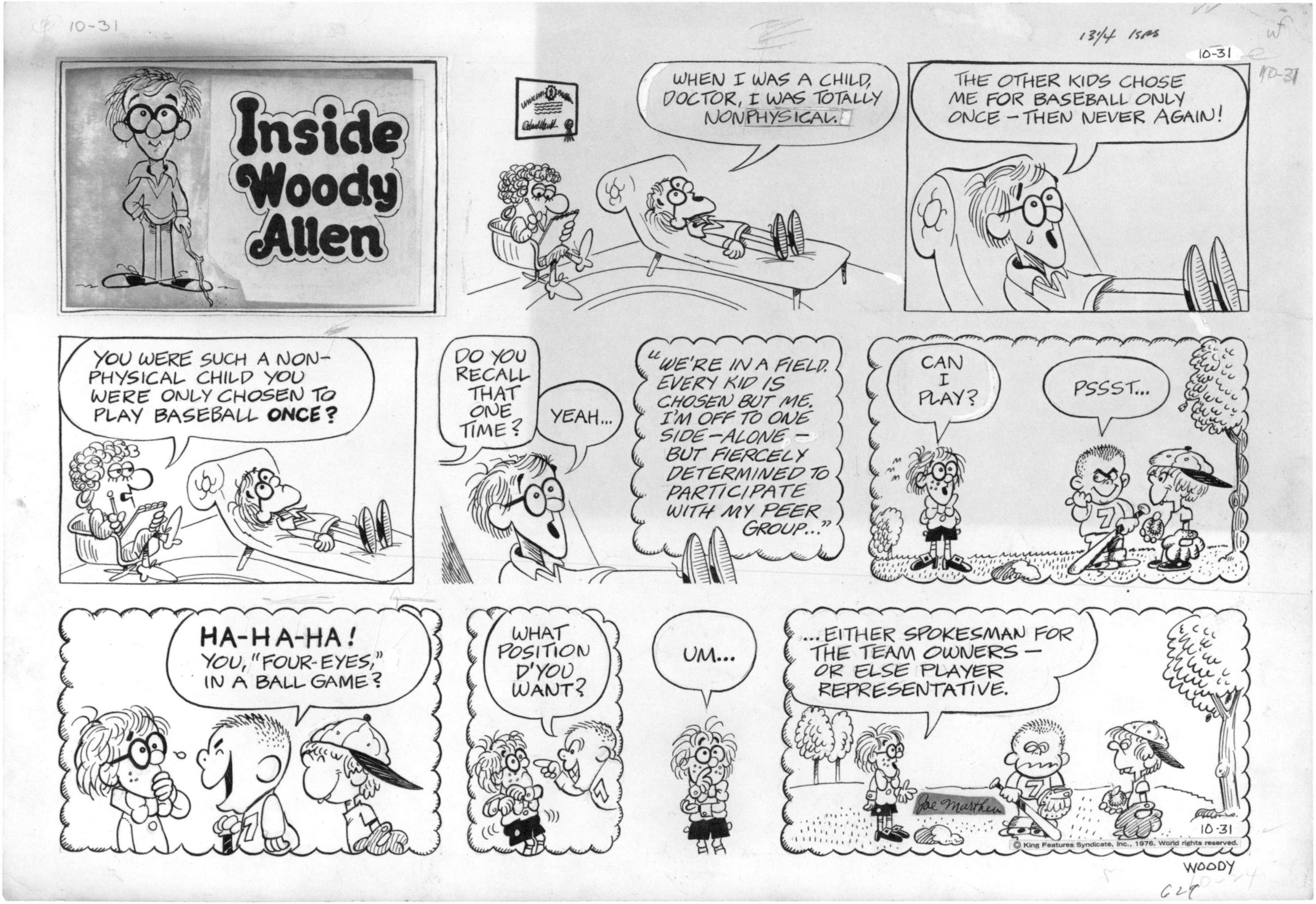
Inside Woody Allen
WHEN I WAS A CHILD, DOCTOR, I WAS TOTALLY NONPHYSICAL.
THE OTHER KIDS CHOSE ME FOR BASEBALL ONLY ONCE – THEN NEVER AGAIN!
YOU WERE SUCH A NON-PHYSICAL CHILD YOU WERE ONLY CHOSEN TO PLAY BASEBALL ONCE?
DO YOU RECALL THAT ONE TIME?
YEAH...
"WE'RE IN A FIELD. EVERY KID IS CHOSEN BUT ME. I'M OFF TO ONE SIDE–ALONE.– BUT FIERCELY DETERMINED TO PARTICIPATE WITH MY PEER GROUP..."
CAN I PLAY?
PSSST...
HA-HA-HA! YOU, "FOUR-EYES," IN A BALL GAME?
WHAT POSITION D'YOU WANT?
UM...
...EITHER SPOKESMAN FOR THE TEAM OWNERS – OR ELSE PLAYER REPRESENTATIVE.
© King Features Syndicate, Inc., 1976. World rights reserved.
WOODY

October 31, 1976

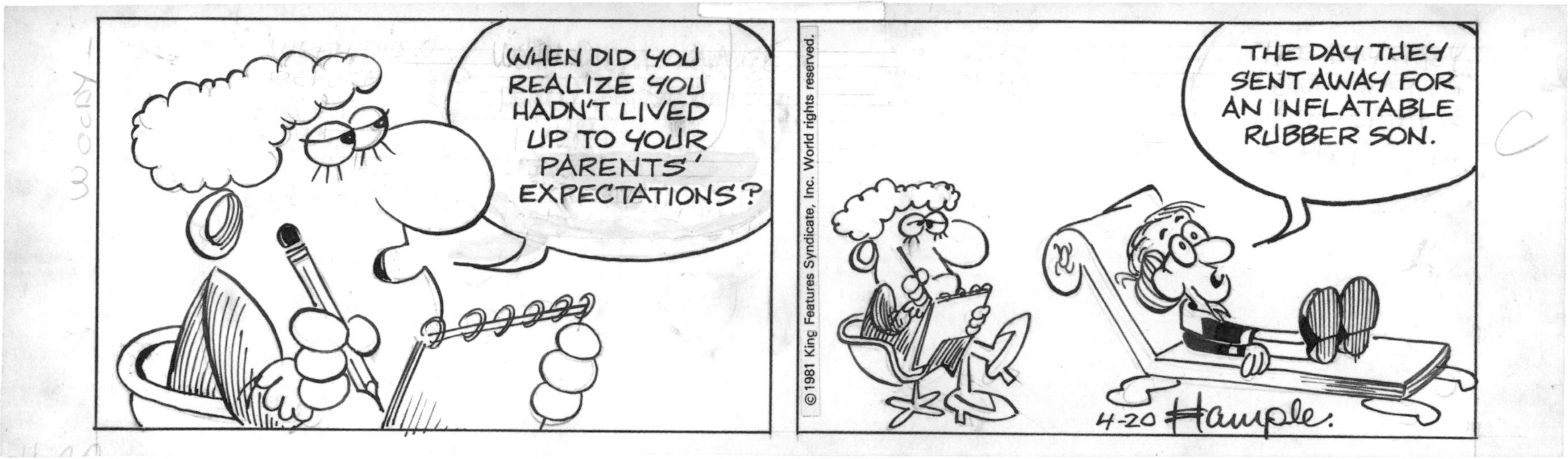

WHEN DID YOU REALIZE YOU HADN'T LIVED UP TO YOUR PARENTS' EXPECTATIONS?
THE DAY THEY SENT AWAY FOR AN INFLATABLE RUBBER SON.
© 1981 King Features Syndicate, Inc. World rights reserved.
4-20 Hample.

April 20, 1981

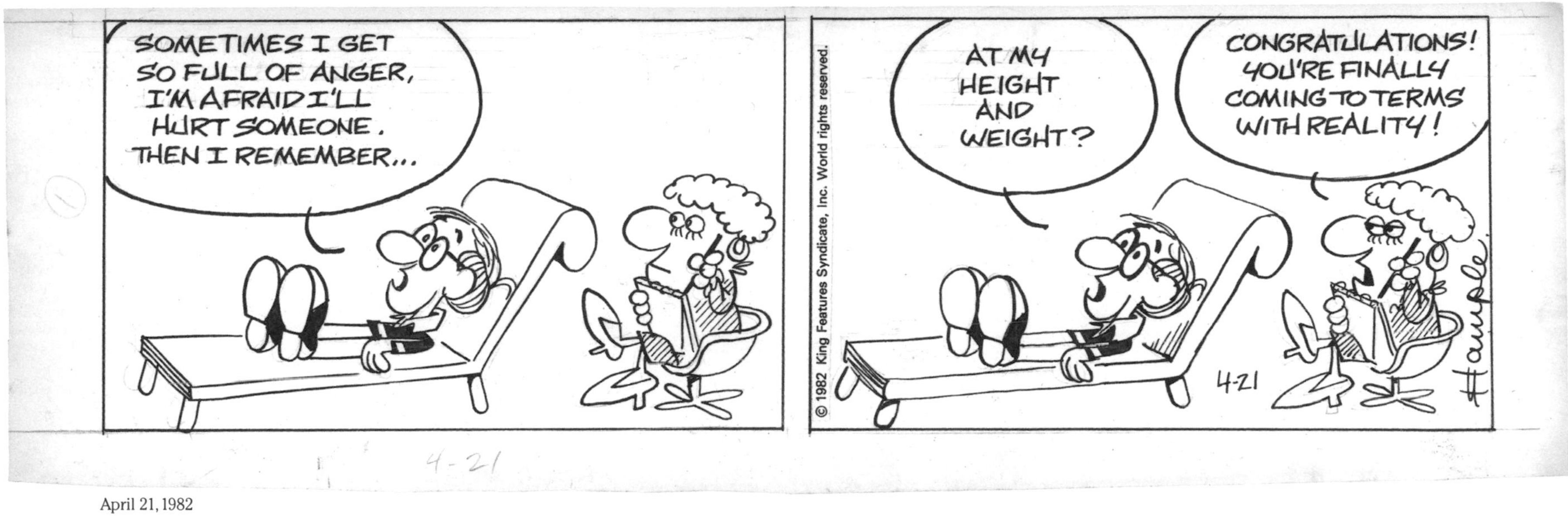

SOMETIMES I GET SO FULL OF ANGER, I'M AFRAID I'LL HURT SOMEONE. THEN I REMEMBER...
AT MY HEIGHT AND WEIGHT?
CONGRATULATIONS! YOU'RE FINALLY COMING TO TERMS WITH REALITY!
© 1982 King Features Syndicate, Inc. World rights reserved.
4-21 Hample

April 21, 1982

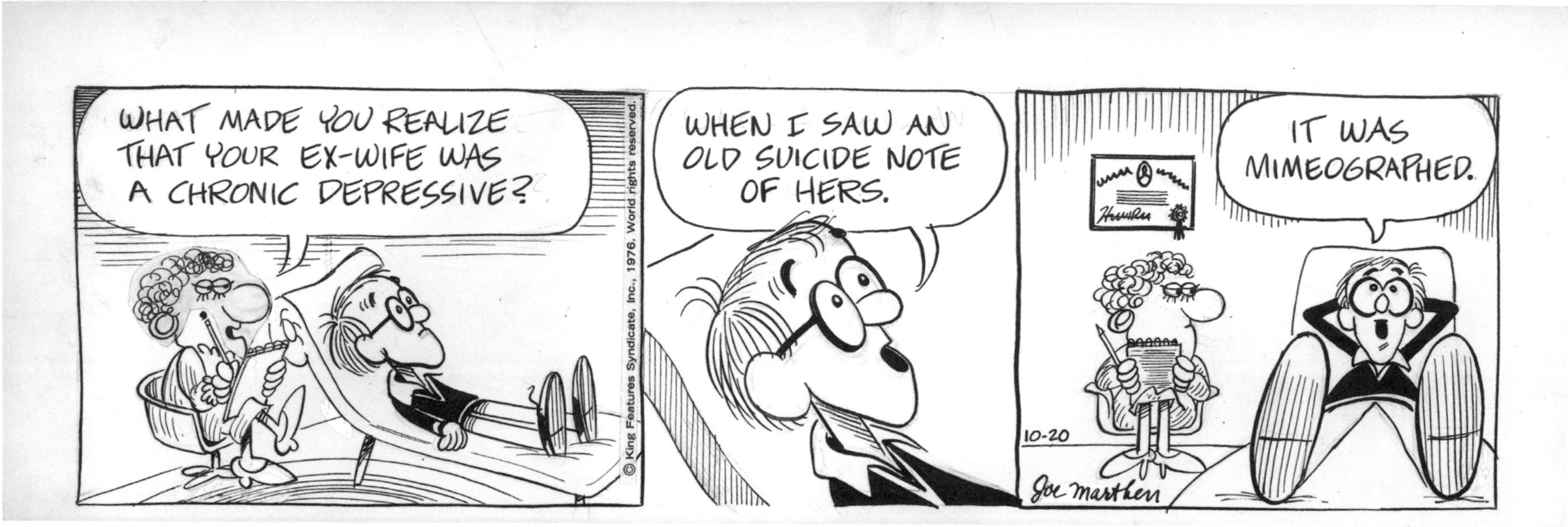
WHAT MADE YOU REALIZE THAT YOUR EX-WIFE WAS A CHRONIC DEPRESSIVE?
© King Features Syndicate, Inc., 1976. World rights reserved.
WHEN I SAW AN OLD SUICIDE NOTE OF HERS.
IT WAS MIMEOGRAPHED.
10-20
Joe Martin

October 20, 1976

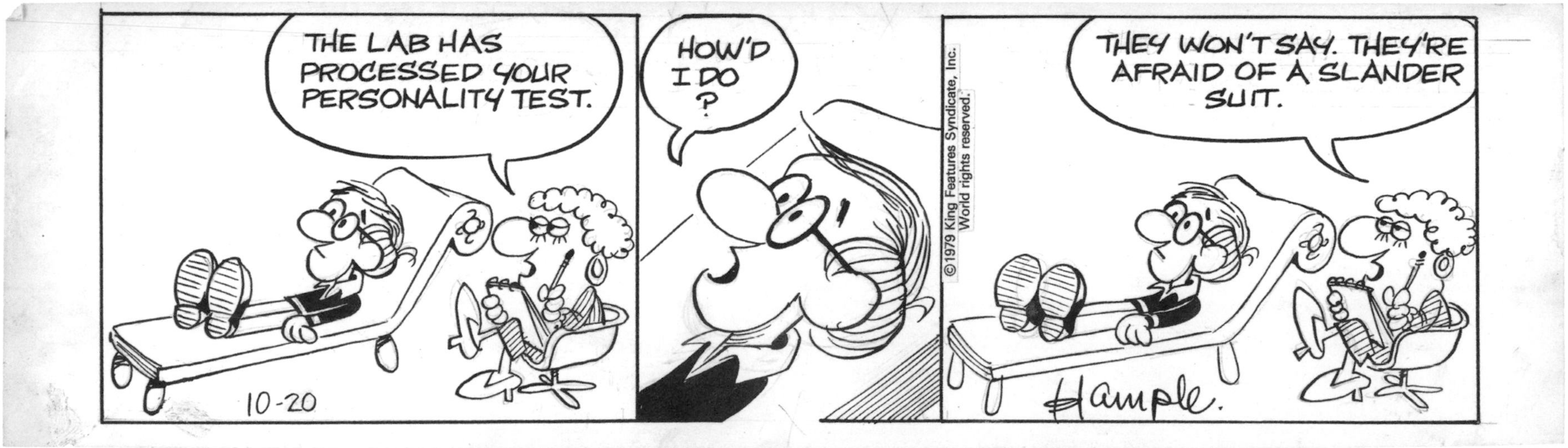
THE LAB HAS PROCESSED YOUR PERSONALITY TEST.
10-20
HOW'D I DO ?
© 1979 King Features Syndicate, Inc. World rights reserved.
THEY WON'T SAY. THEY'RE AFRAID OF A SLANDER SUIT.
Hample.

October 20, 1979

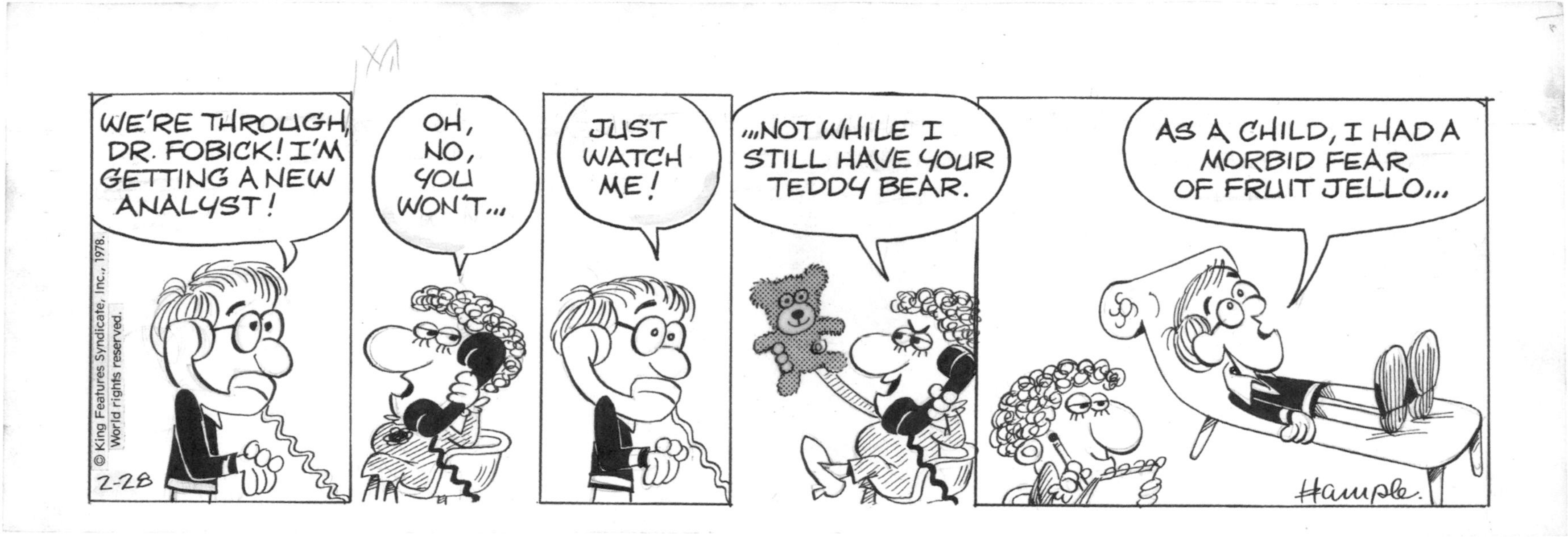
WE'RE THROUGH, DR. FOBICK! I'M GETTING A NEW ANALYST!
OH, NO, YOU WON'T...
JUST WATCH ME!
...NOT WHILE I STILL HAVE YOUR TEDDY BEAR.
AS A CHILD, I HAD A MORBID FEAR OF FRUIT JELLO...
© King Features Syndicate, Inc., 1978. World rights reserved.
2-28
Hample.

February 28, 1978

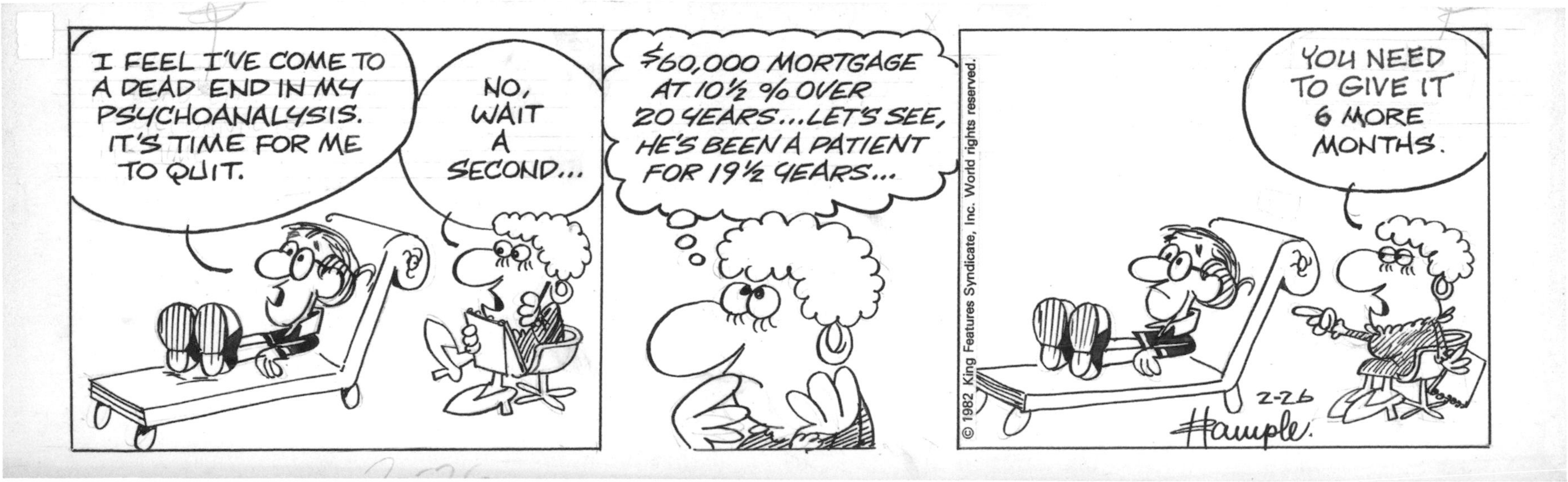
I FEEL I'VE COME TO A DEAD END IN MY PSYCHOANALYSIS. IT'S TIME FOR ME TO QUIT.
NO, WAIT A SECOND...
$60,000 MORTGAGE AT 10½ % OVER 20 YEARS...LET'S SEE, HE'S BEEN A PATIENT FOR 19½ YEARS...
YOU NEED TO GIVE IT 6 MORE MONTHS.
© 1982 King Features Syndicate, Inc. World rights reserved.
2-26
Hample.

February 26, 1982

September 18, 1983

Inside Woody Allen

AH, IT'S 3 PM, ORDINARILY TIME FOR ME TO BE LYING ON MY ANALYST'S COUCH.

BUT THANKS TO ELECTRONIC WIZARDRY, I'M BEING ANALYZED IN ABSENTIA.

WOODY, WHAT ARE YOU DOING AT MY PARTY?

AREN'T YOU SUPPOSED TO BE AT YOUR PSYCHIATRIST'S AT THIS HOUR?

YES...

– BUT SHE DOESN'T LIKE TO LISTEN TO NEW STUFF DURING HOT WEATHER.

© 1983 King Features Syndicate, Inc. World rights reserved.

SHE RUNS THE BEST OF MY ANALYTIC SESSIONS IN SUMMER RE-RUNS.

SO I DON'T HAVE TO GO IN AND REPEAT.

INSIDE WOODY ALLEN

September 18, 1983

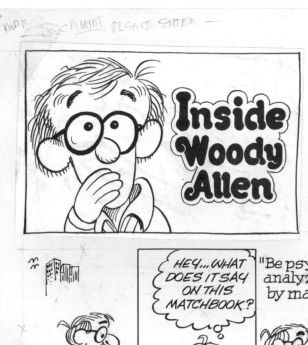

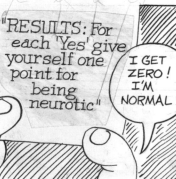

INSIDE WOODY ALLEN

January 6, 1980

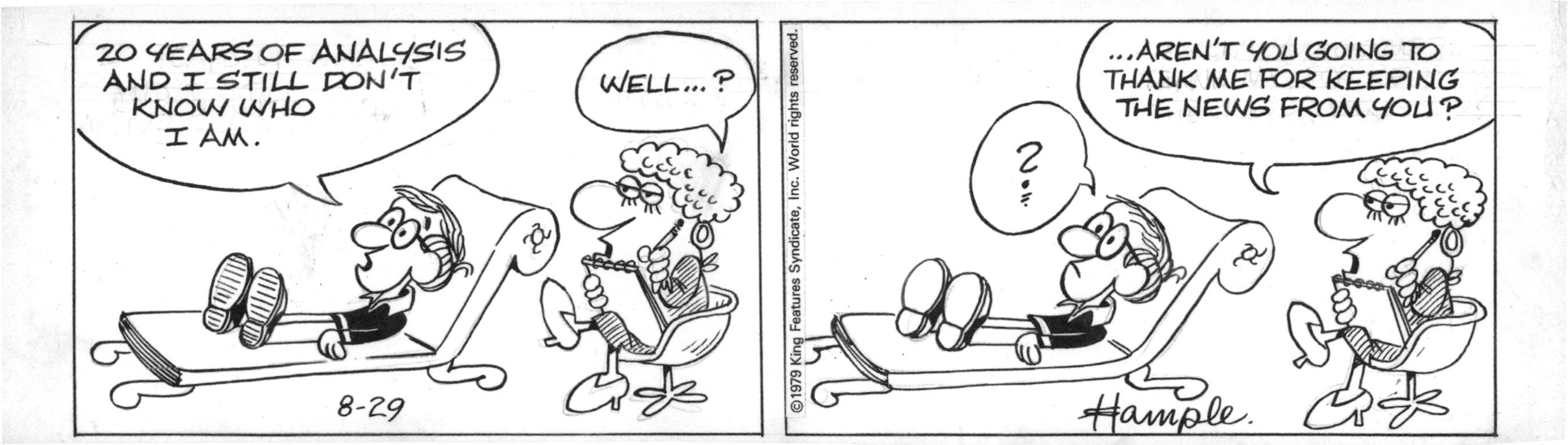
20 YEARS OF ANALYSIS AND I STILL DON'T KNOW WHO I AM.
WELL...?
8-29
©1979 King Features Syndicate, Inc. World rights reserved.
?
...AREN'T YOU GOING TO THANK ME FOR KEEPING THE NEWS FROM YOU?
Hample.

August 29, 1979

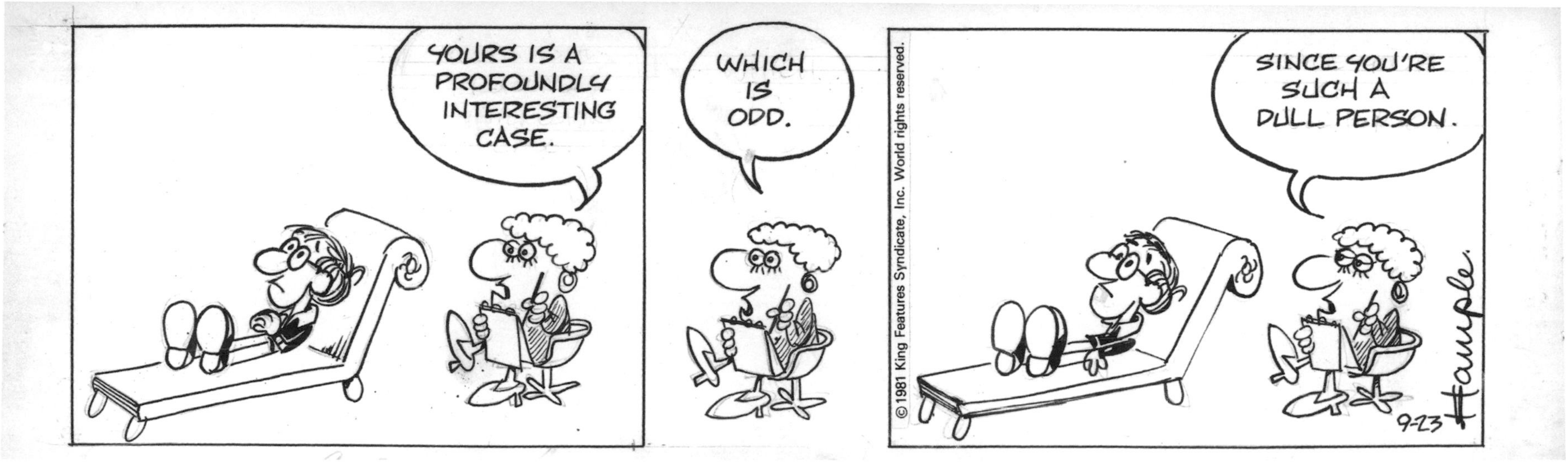
YOURS IS A PROFOUNDLY INTERESTING CASE.
WHICH IS ODD.
©1981 King Features Syndicate, Inc. World rights reserved.
SINCE YOU'RE SUCH A DULL PERSON.
Hample
9-23

September 23, 1981

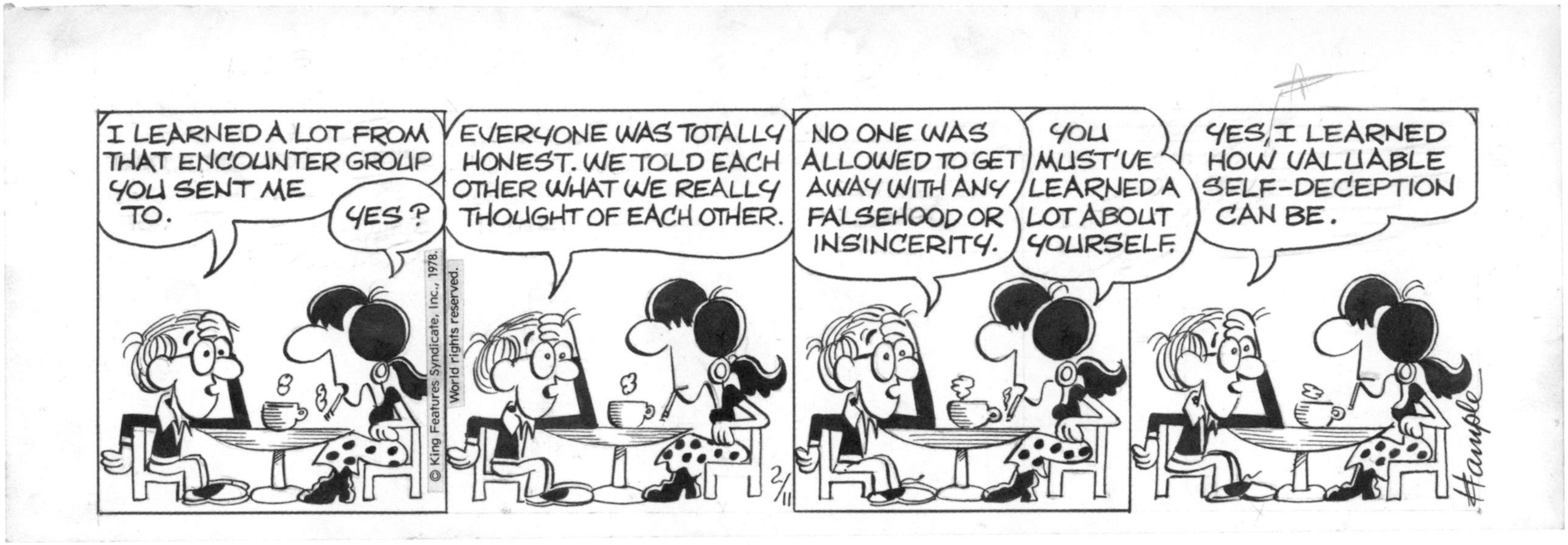
I LEARNED A LOT FROM THAT ENCOUNTER GROUP YOU SENT ME TO.
YES?
© King Features Syndicate, Inc., 1978. World rights reserved.
EVERYONE WAS TOTALLY HONEST. WE TOLD EACH OTHER WHAT WE REALLY THOUGHT OF EACH OTHER.
2/11
NO ONE WAS ALLOWED TO GET AWAY WITH ANY FALSEHOOD OR INSINCERITY.
YOU MUST'VE LEARNED A LOT ABOUT YOURSELF.
YES, I LEARNED HOW VALUABLE SELF-DECEPTION CAN BE.
Hample

February 11, 1978

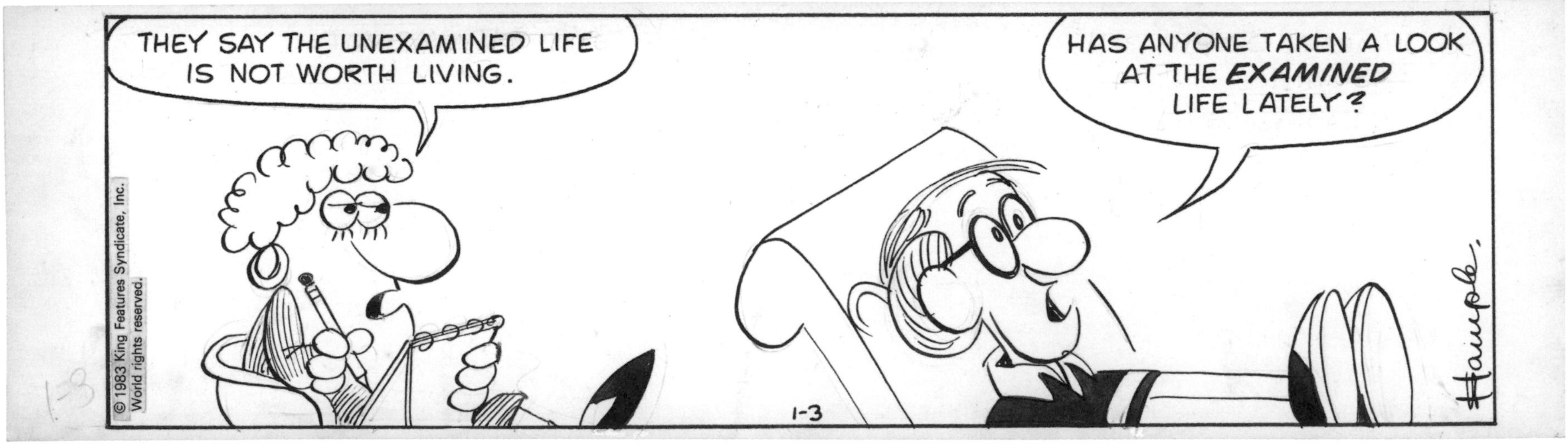
THEY SAY THE UNEXAMINED LIFE IS NOT WORTH LIVING.
HAS ANYONE TAKEN A LOOK AT THE *EXAMINED* LIFE LATELY?
© 1983 King Features Syndicate, Inc. World rights reserved.
1-3
Hample

January 3, 1983

Inside Woody Allen

"DR. SIGMUND NERF, CREATOR OF 'PRIMAL EGO THERAPY,' MAINTAINS THAT HE WOULD GLADLY TRADE THE ACCOMPLISHMENTS OF A LIFETIME...

Life of Dr. Nerf

"—IF HE COULD ONLY GET RID OF HIS RASH.

Life of Dr. Nerf

"I ONCE TRIED 'PRIMAL EGO THERAPY,' A METHOD WHICH HAS ATTRACTED MANY FAMOUS FILM STARS...

Institute for
P.E.T.
Primal Ego Therapy

"—WHO CLAIM IT CHANGED THEM FASTER AND IN A DEEPER WAY THAN EVEN THE ASTROLOGY COLUMNS.

TO BEGIN, I DEMAND THAT YOU GIVE UP YOUR EGO!

"FORCED TO CROUCH UNDER A TABLE FOR SEVENTY-TWO HOURS MY RESISTANCE GRADUALLY CRUMPLED.

"EVENTUALLY, I, AND SEVERAL CHIMPANZEES, PERFORMED 'HAMLET' ON ROLLER SKATES.

"AFTERWARDS, I WAS LOCKED IN A CLOSET AND TICKLED BY EXPERTS UNTIL CUMULATIVE SIDE EFFECTS TOOK THEIR TOLL ON MY PERCEPTION.

HAHAHAHA
HAHAHAH

"I WAS FINALLY RELEASED WHEN I COULD NO LONGER TELL THE DIFFERENCE BETWEEN MY BROTHER AND TWO POACHED EGGS."

HEY, IRA, WHERE'S THE $500 YOU OWE ME?

3-7

INSIDE WOODY ALLEN

March 7, 1982

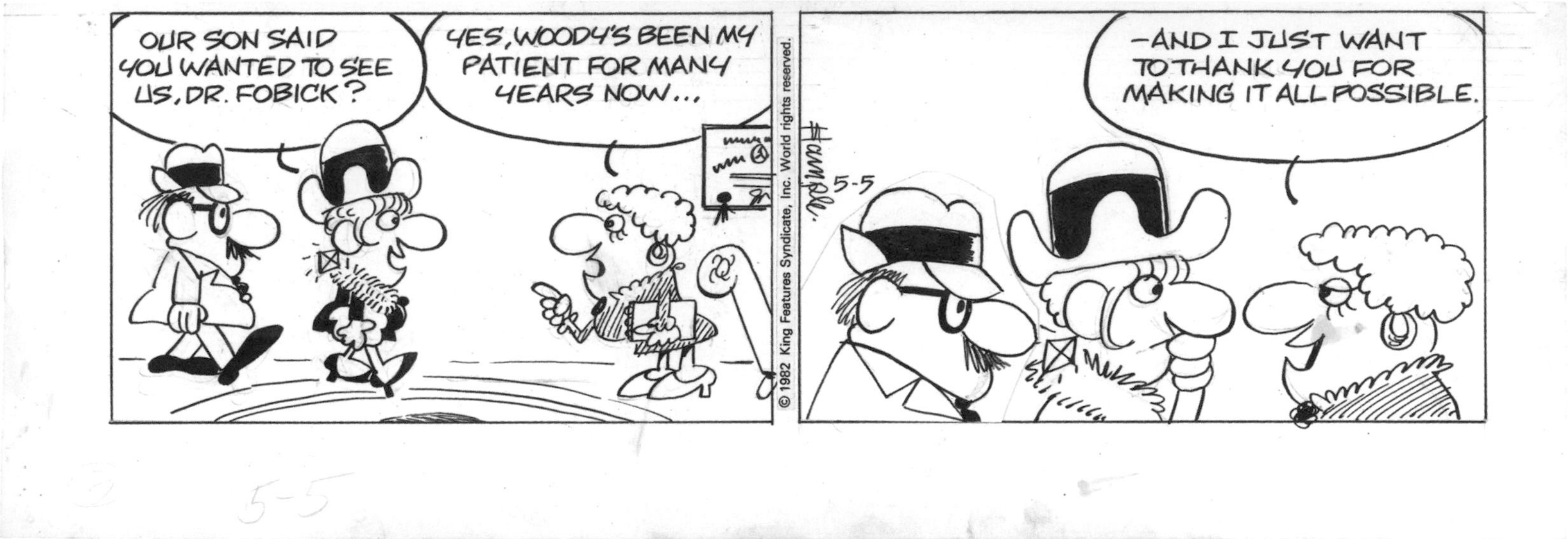
OUR SON SAID YOU WANTED TO SEE US, DR. FOBICK?
YES, WOODY'S BEEN MY PATIENT FOR MANY YEARS NOW...
© 1982 King Features Syndicate, Inc. World rights reserved.
Hample.
5-5
–AND I JUST WANT TO THANK YOU FOR MAKING IT ALL POSSIBLE.
5-5

May 5, 1982

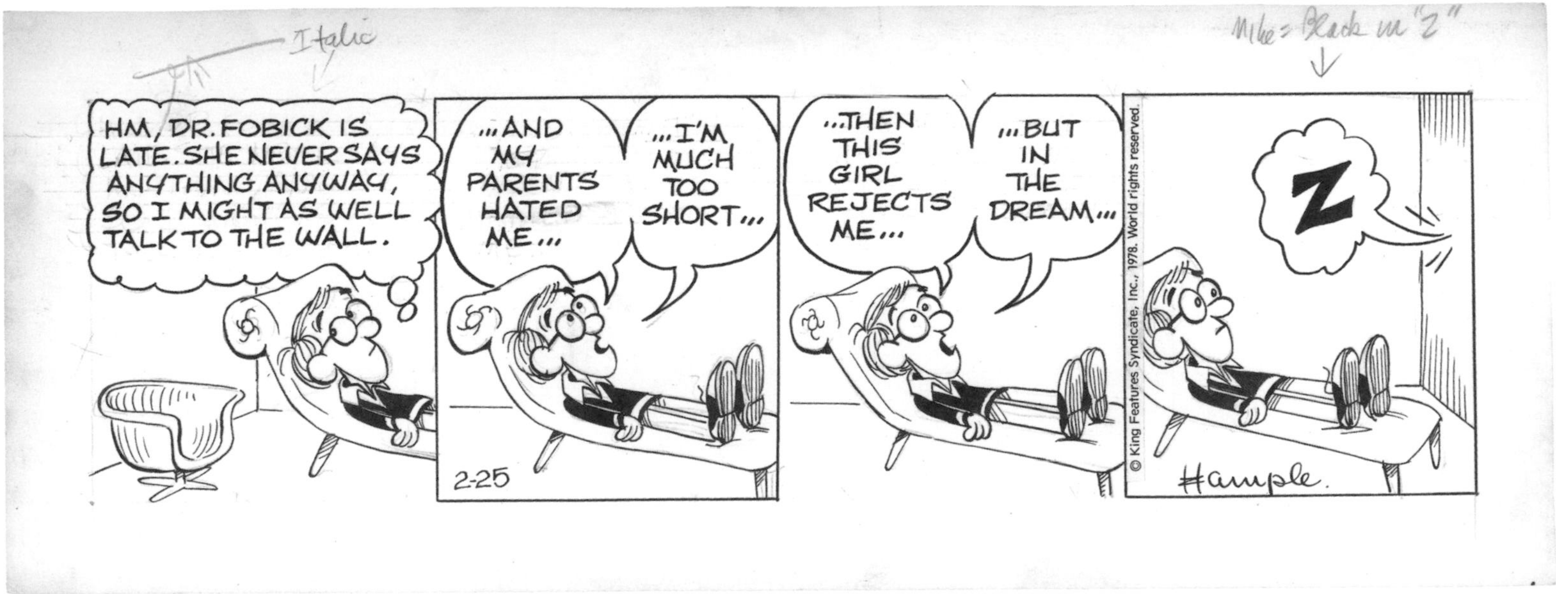
Italic
Mike = Black in "Z"
HM, DR. FOBICK IS LATE. SHE NEVER SAYS ANYTHING ANYWAY, SO I MIGHT AS WELL TALK TO THE WALL.
...AND MY PARENTS HATED ME...
...I'M MUCH TOO SHORT...
2-25
...THEN THIS GIRL REJECTS ME...
...BUT IN THE DREAM...
© King Features Syndicate, Inc., 1978. World rights reserved.
Z
Hample.

February 25, 1978

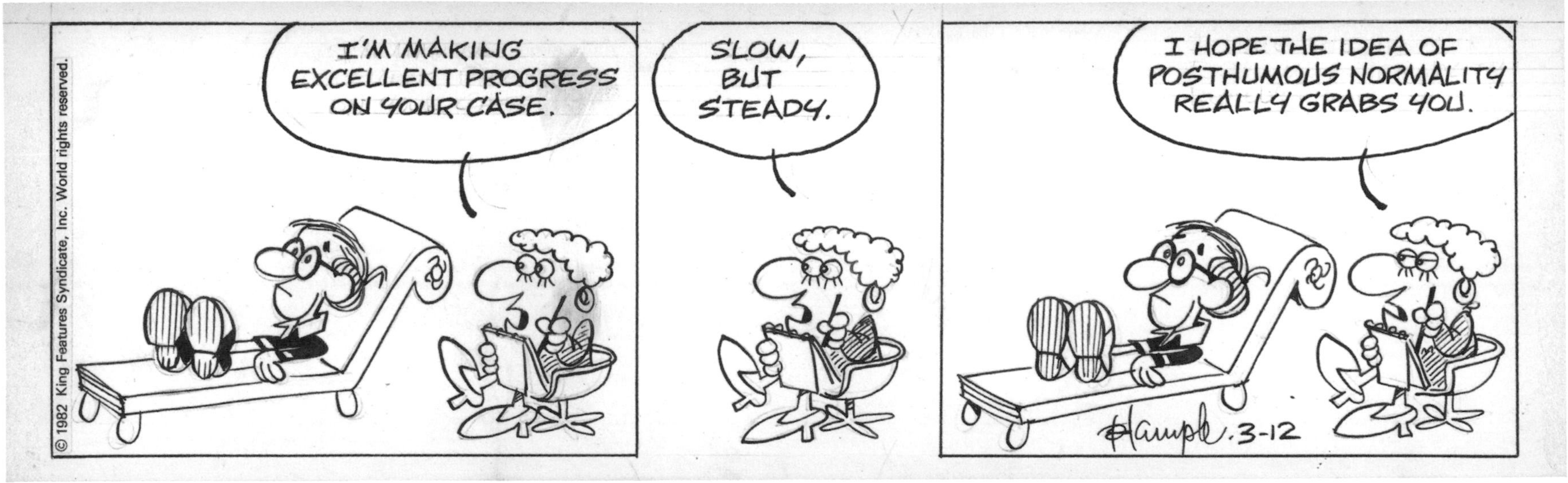
I'M MAKING EXCELLENT PROGRESS ON YOUR CASE.
SLOW, BUT STEADY.
I HOPE THE IDEA OF POSTHUMOUS NORMALITY REALLY GRABS YOU.
Hample. 3-12
© 1982 King Features Syndicate, Inc. World rights reserved.

March 12, 1982

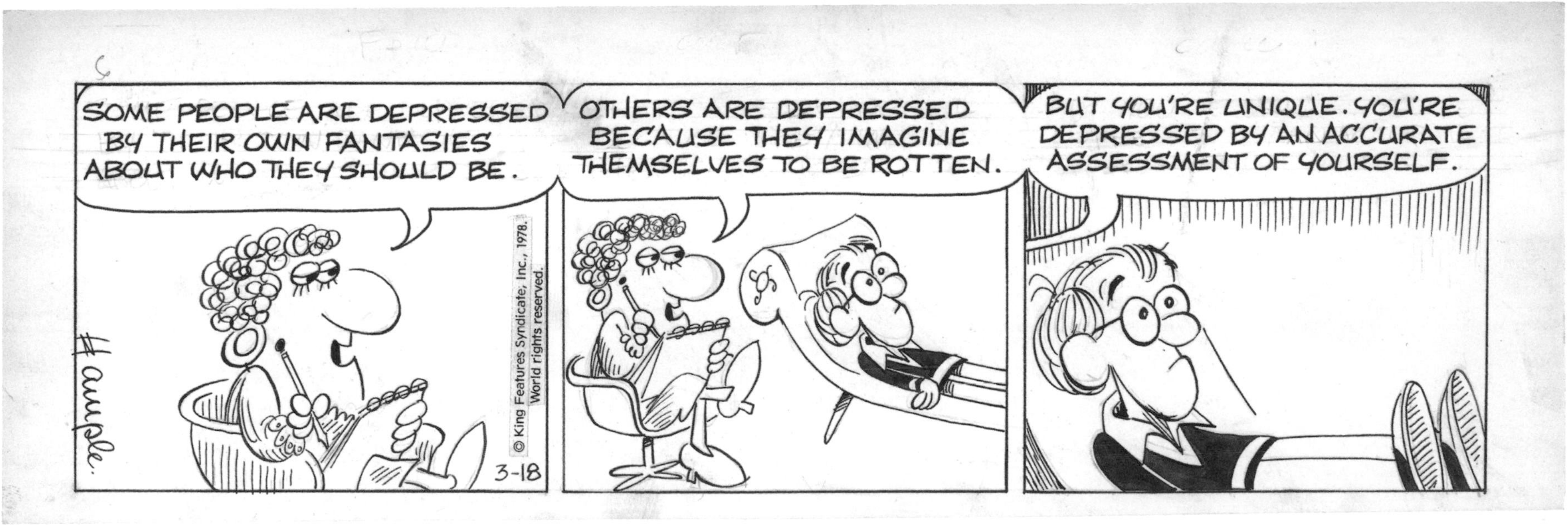
SOME PEOPLE ARE DEPRESSED BY THEIR OWN FANTASIES ABOUT WHO THEY SHOULD BE.
OTHERS ARE DEPRESSED BECAUSE THEY IMAGINE THEMSELVES TO BE ROTTEN.
BUT YOU'RE UNIQUE. YOU'RE DEPRESSED BY AN ACCURATE ASSESSMENT OF YOURSELF.
Hample.
3-18
© King Features Syndicate, Inc., 1978. World rights reserved.

March 18, 1978

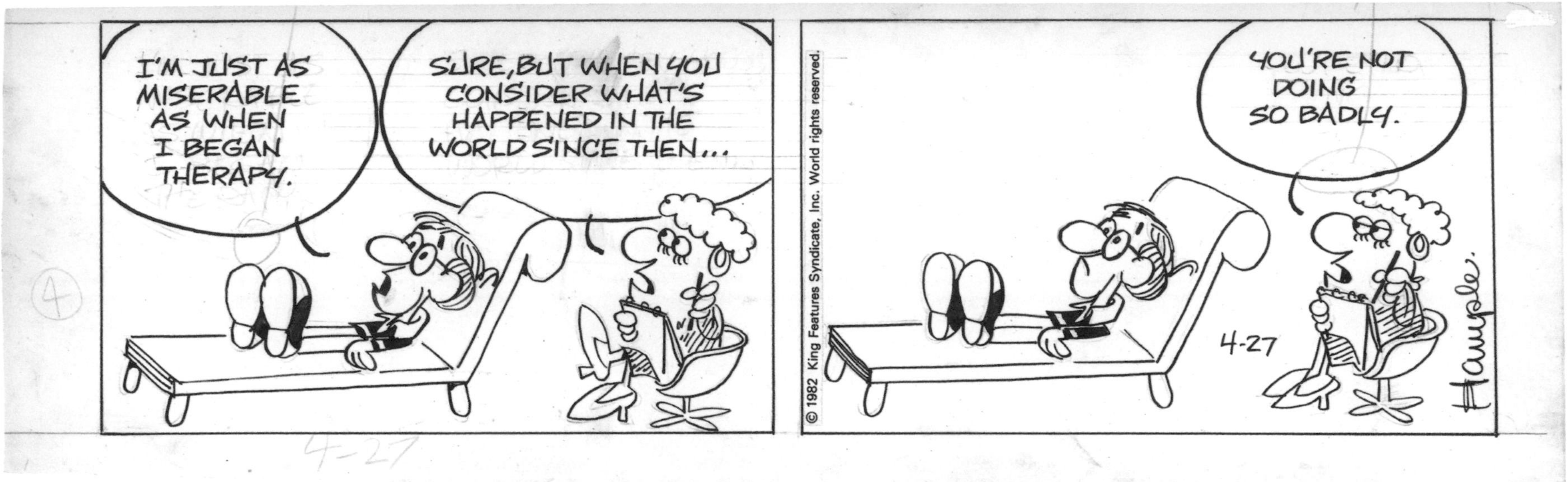
I'M JUST AS MISERABLE AS WHEN I BEGAN THERAPY.
SURE, BUT WHEN YOU CONSIDER WHAT'S HAPPENED IN THE WORLD SINCE THEN...
YOU'RE NOT DOING SO BADLY.
© 1982 King Features Syndicate, Inc. World rights reserved.
4-27
Hample.

April 27, 1982

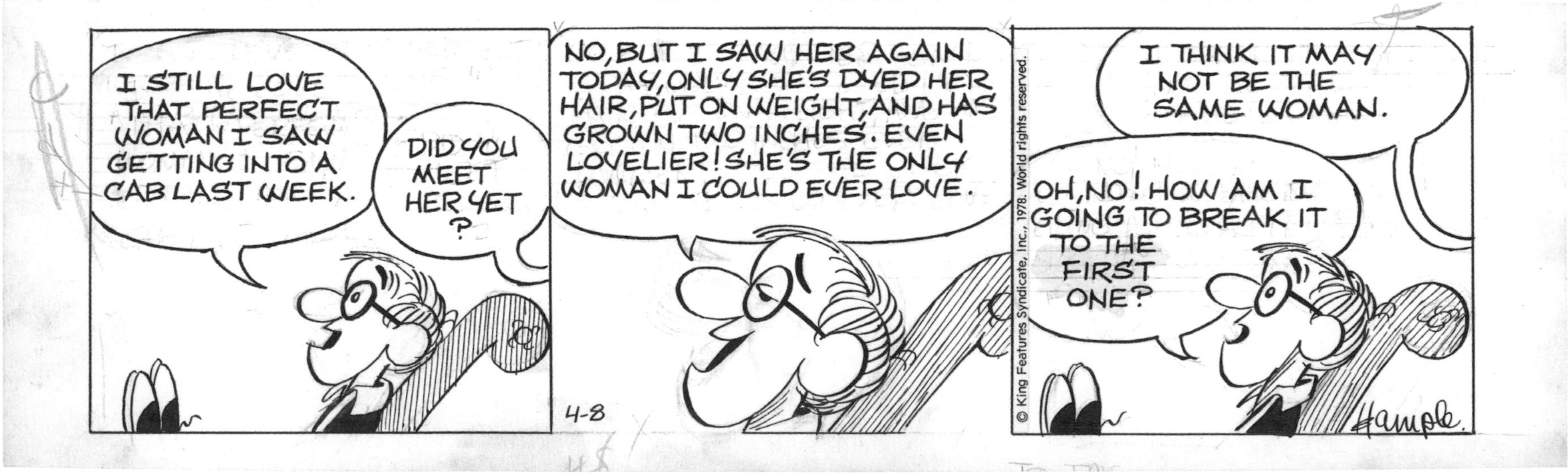
I STILL LOVE THAT PERFECT WOMAN I SAW GETTING INTO A CAB LAST WEEK.
DID YOU MEET HER YET ?
4-8
NO, BUT I SAW HER AGAIN TODAY, ONLY SHE'S DYED HER HAIR, PUT ON WEIGHT, AND HAS GROWN TWO INCHES. EVEN LOVELIER! SHE'S THE ONLY WOMAN I COULD EVER LOVE.
© King Features Syndicate, Inc., 1978. World rights reserved.
I THINK IT MAY NOT BE THE SAME WOMAN.
OH, NO! HOW AM I GOING TO BREAK IT TO THE FIRST ONE?
Hample.

April 8, 1978

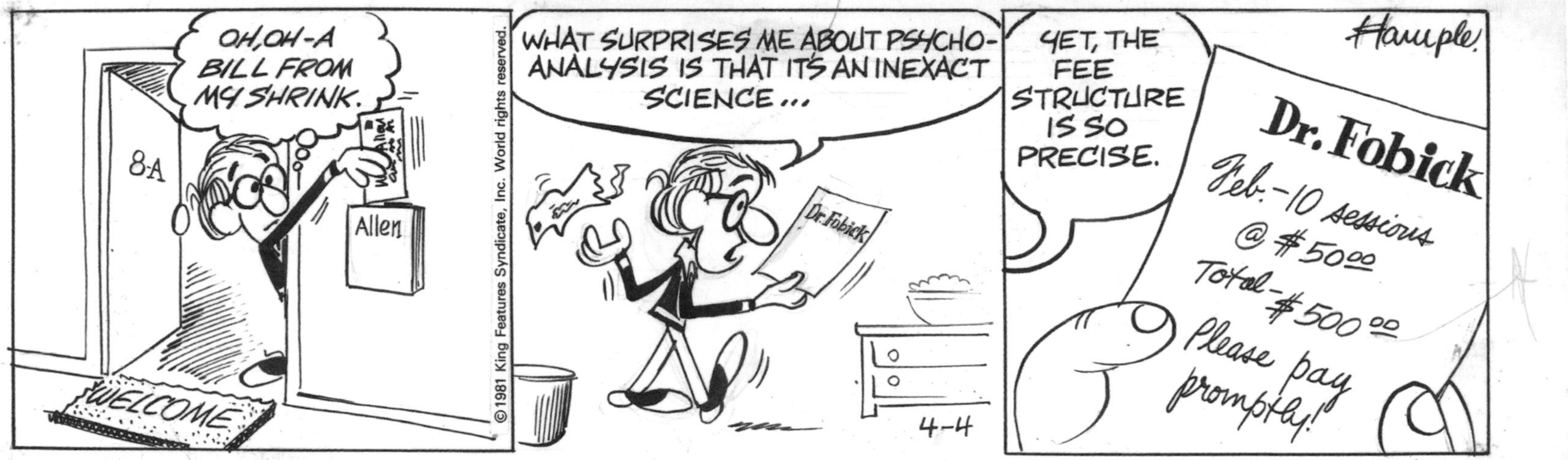
OH, OH-A BILL FROM MY SHRINK.
8-A
Allen
WELCOME
© 1981 King Features Syndicate, Inc. World rights reserved.
WHAT SURPRISES ME ABOUT PSYCHO-ANALYSIS IS THAT IT'S AN INEXACT SCIENCE...
Dr. Fobick
4-4
YET, THE FEE STRUCTURE IS SO PRECISE.
Hample
Dr. Fobick
Feb.-10 sessions
@ $50.00
Total-$500.00
Please pay promptly!

April 4, 1981

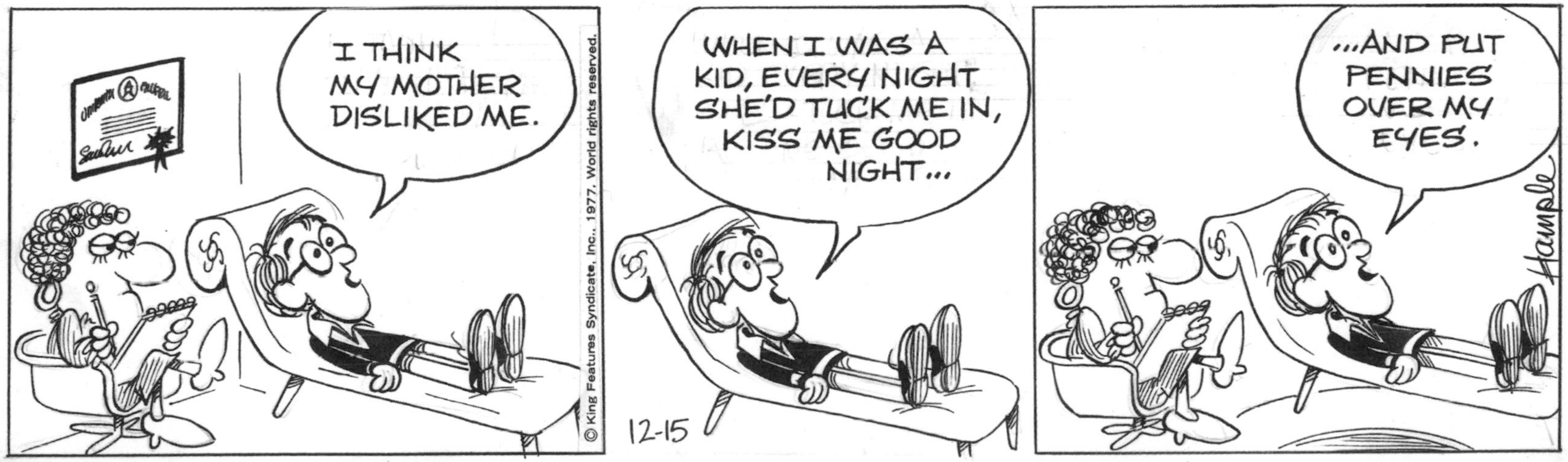
I THINK MY MOTHER DISLIKED ME.
© King Features Syndicate, Inc., 1977. World rights reserved.
WHEN I WAS A KID, EVERY NIGHT SHE'D TUCK ME IN, KISS ME GOOD NIGHT...
12-15
...AND PUT PENNIES OVER MY EYES.
Hample

December 15, 1977

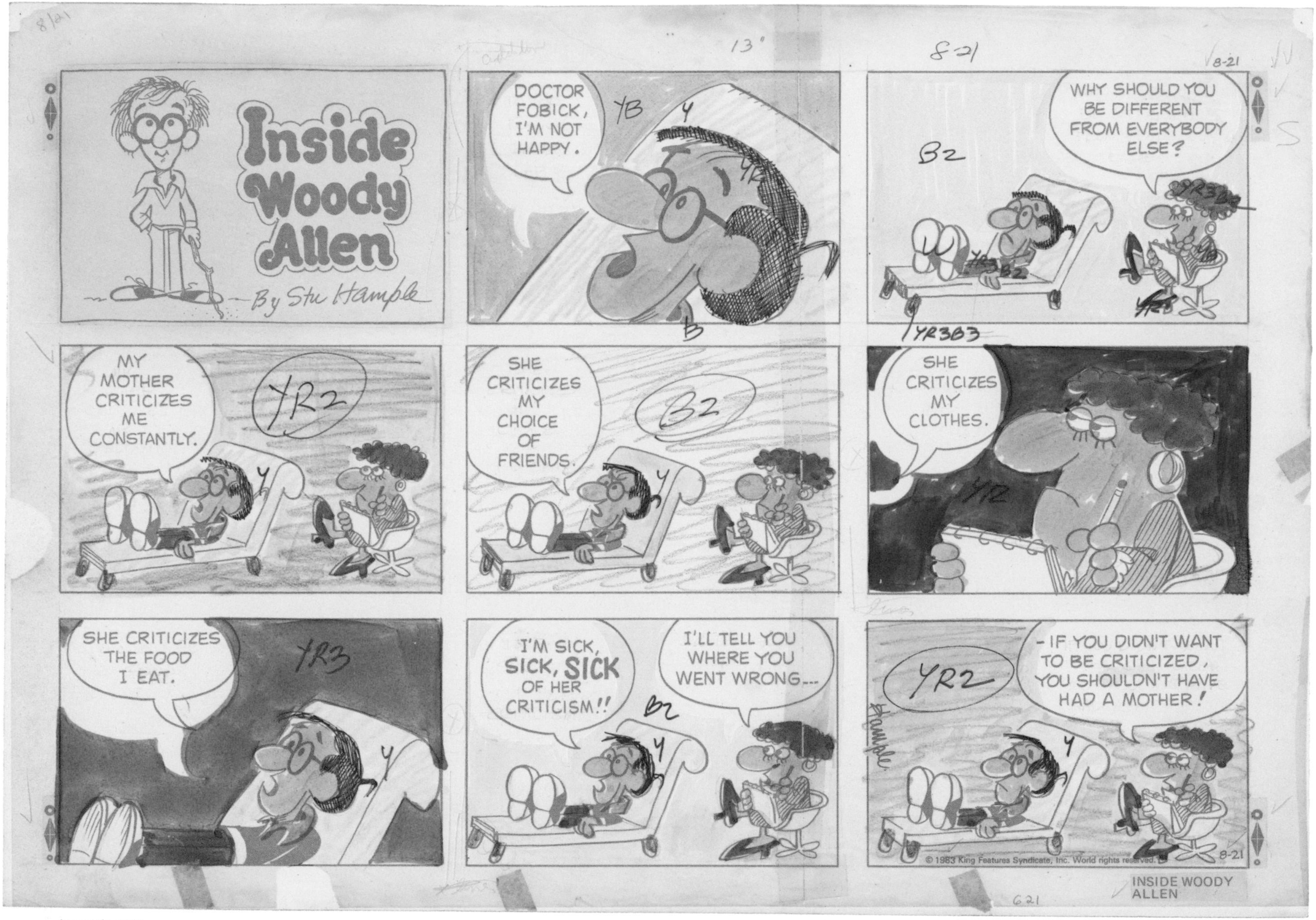
Inside Woody Allen
By Stu Hample
DOCTOR FOBICK, I'M NOT HAPPY.
WHY SHOULD YOU BE DIFFERENT FROM EVERYBODY ELSE?
MY MOTHER CRITICIZES ME CONSTANTLY.
SHE CRITICIZES MY CHOICE OF FRIENDS.
SHE CRITICIZES MY CLOTHES.
SHE CRITICIZES THE FOOD I EAT.
I'M SICK, SICK, SICK OF HER CRITICISM!!
I'LL TELL YOU WHERE YOU WENT WRONG...
- IF YOU DIDN'T WANT TO BE CRITICIZED, YOU SHOULDN'T HAVE HAD A MOTHER!
Hample
© 1983 King Features Syndicate, Inc. World rights reserved.
8-21
INSIDE WOODY ALLEN

August 21, 1983

August 21, 1983

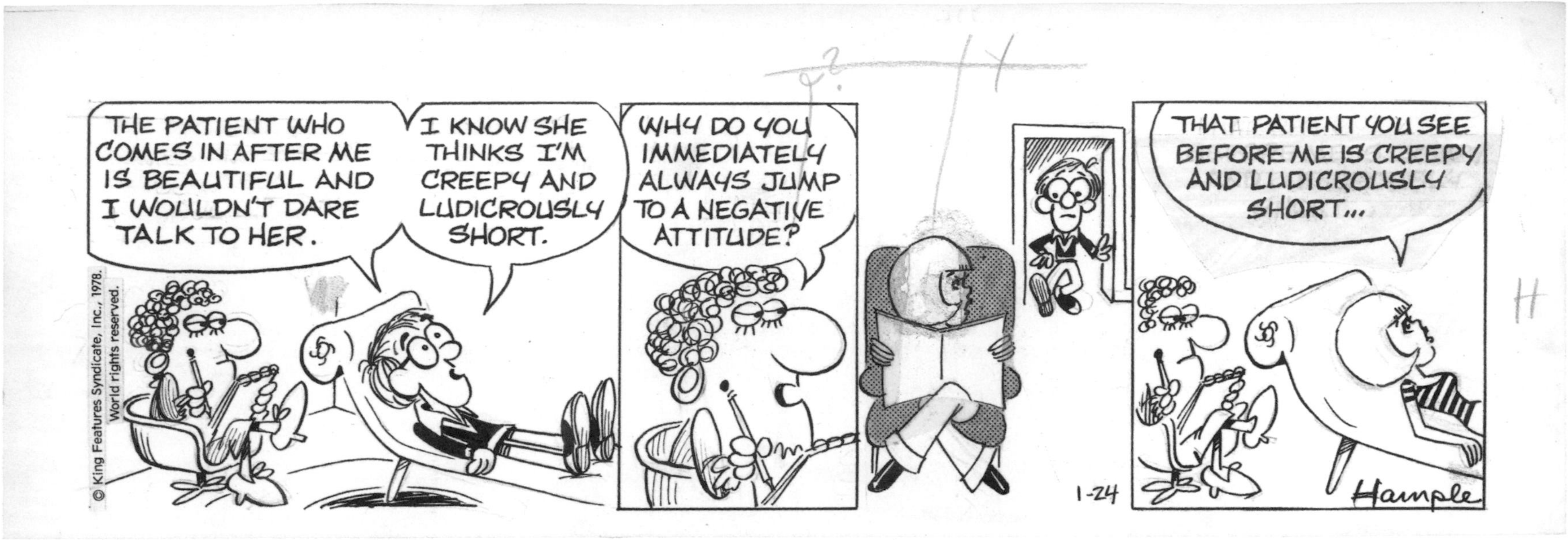
THE PATIENT WHO COMES IN AFTER ME IS BEAUTIFUL AND I WOULDN'T DARE TALK TO HER.
I KNOW SHE THINKS I'M CREEPY AND LUDICROUSLY SHORT.
WHY DO YOU IMMEDIATELY ALWAYS JUMP TO A NEGATIVE ATTITUDE?
THAT PATIENT YOU SEE BEFORE ME IS CREEPY AND LUDICROUSLY SHORT...
© King Features Syndicate, Inc., 1978. World rights reserved.
1-24
Hample

January 24, 1978

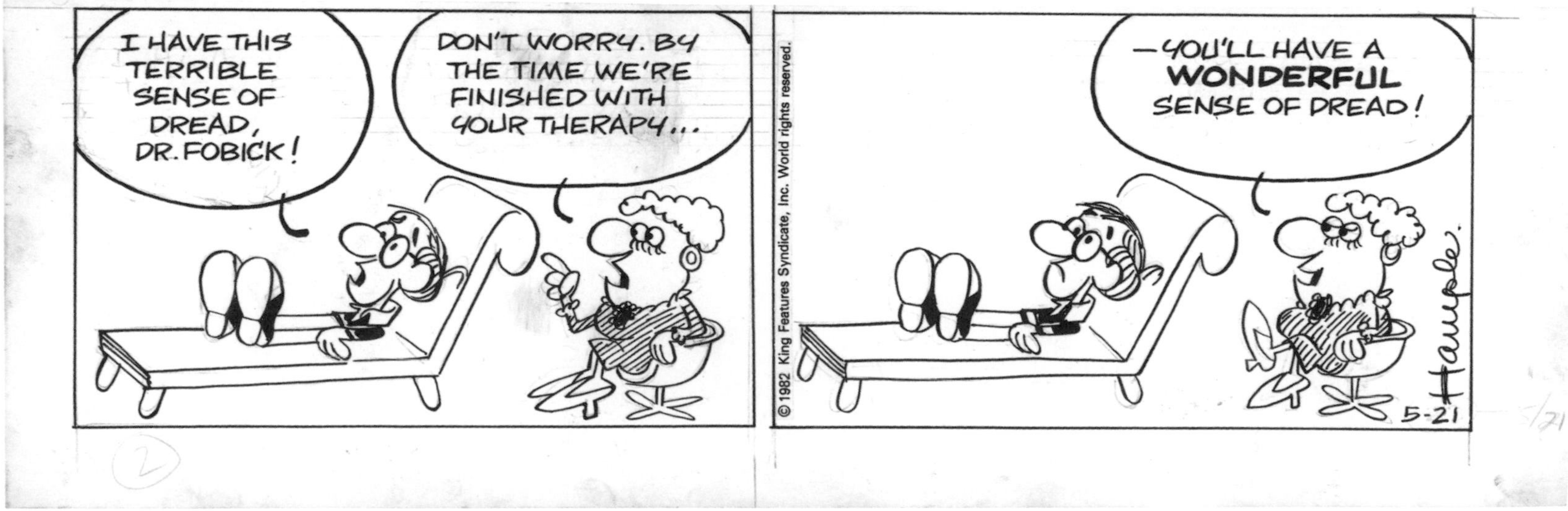
I HAVE THIS TERRIBLE SENSE OF DREAD, DR. FOBICK!
DON'T WORRY. BY THE TIME WE'RE FINISHED WITH YOUR THERAPY...
—YOU'LL HAVE A **WONDERFUL** SENSE OF DREAD!
© 1982 King Features Syndicate, Inc. World rights reserved.
Hample
5-21

May 21, 1982

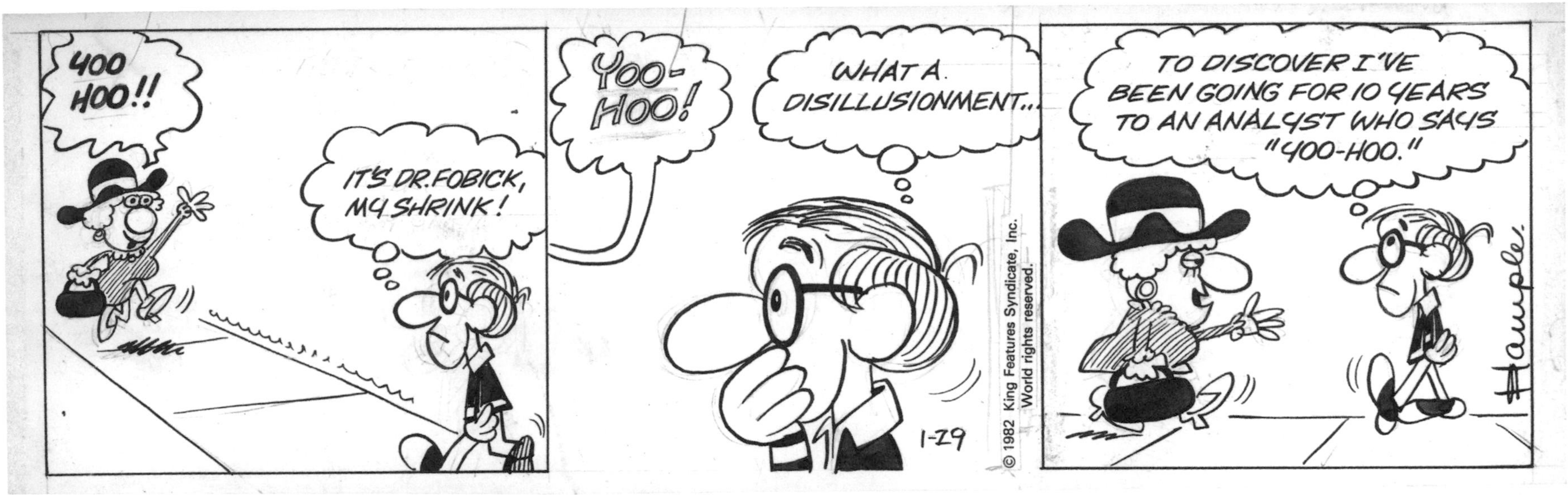
YOO HOO!!
IT'S DR. FOBICK, MY SHRINK!
YOO-HOO!
WHAT A DISILLUSIONMENT...
1-29
© 1982 King Features Syndicate, Inc. World rights reserved.
TO DISCOVER I'VE BEEN GOING FOR 10 YEARS TO AN ANALYST WHO SAYS "YOO-HOO."
Hample

January 29, 1982

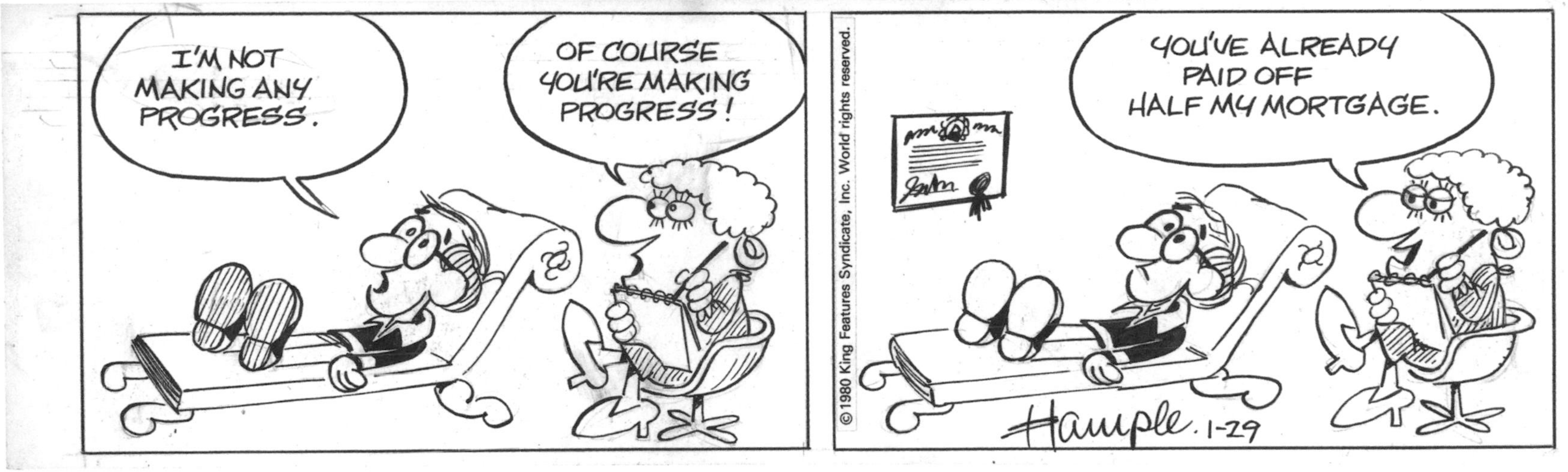
I'M NOT MAKING ANY PROGRESS.
OF COURSE YOU'RE MAKING PROGRESS!
© 1980 King Features Syndicate, Inc. World rights reserved.
YOU'VE ALREADY PAID OFF HALF MY MORTGAGE.
Hample. 1-29

January 29, 1980

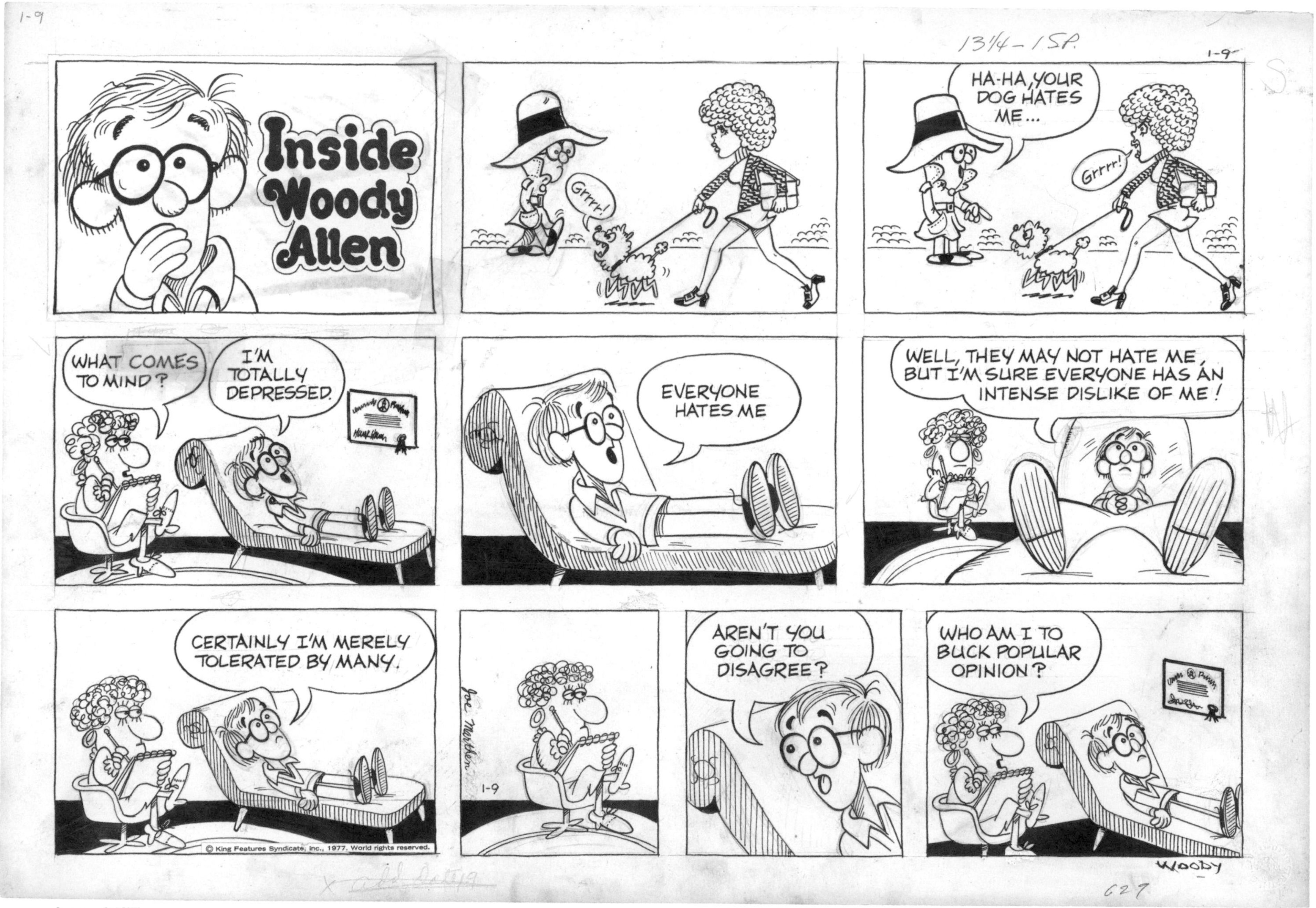
Inside Woody Allen
Grrr!
HA-HA, YOUR DOG HATES ME...
Grrrr!
WHAT COMES TO MIND?
I'M TOTALLY DEPRESSED.
EVERYONE HATES ME
WELL, THEY MAY NOT HATE ME, BUT I'M SURE EVERYONE HAS AN INTENSE DISLIKE OF ME!
CERTAINLY I'M MERELY TOLERATED BY MANY.
© King Features Syndicate, Inc., 1977. World rights reserved.
AREN'T YOU GOING TO DISAGREE?
WHO AM I TO BUCK POPULAR OPINION?
WOODY

January 9, 1977

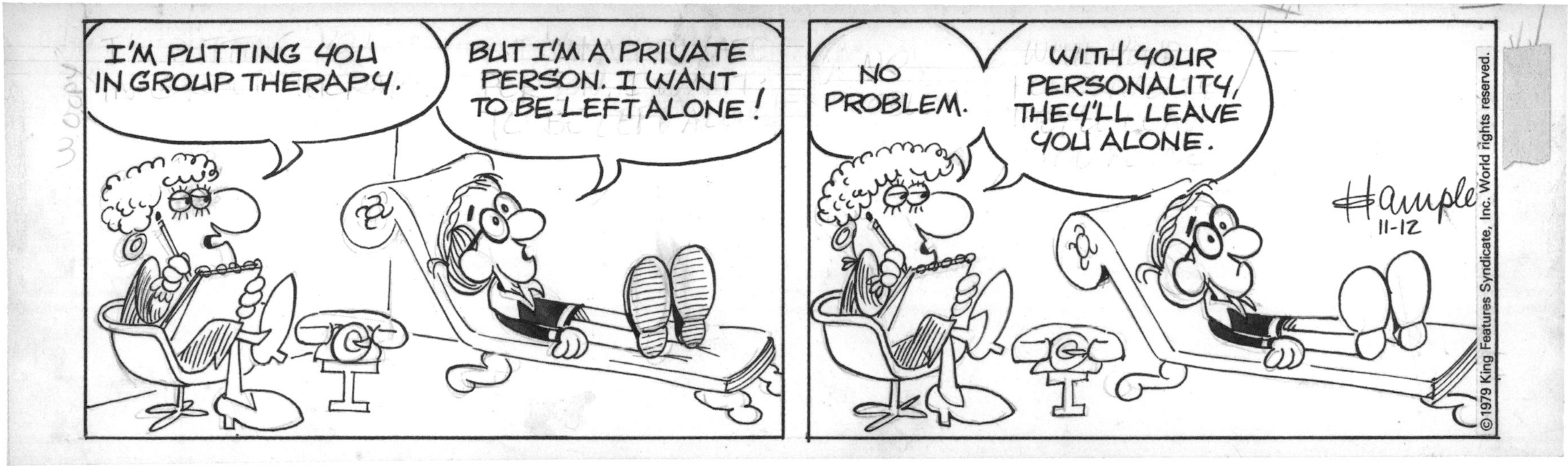
I'M PUTTING YOU IN GROUP THERAPY.
BUT I'M A PRIVATE PERSON. I WANT TO BE LEFT ALONE!
NO PROBLEM.
WITH YOUR PERSONALITY, THEY'LL LEAVE YOU ALONE.
Hample 11-12
©1979 King Features Syndicate, Inc. World rights reserved.

November 12, 1979

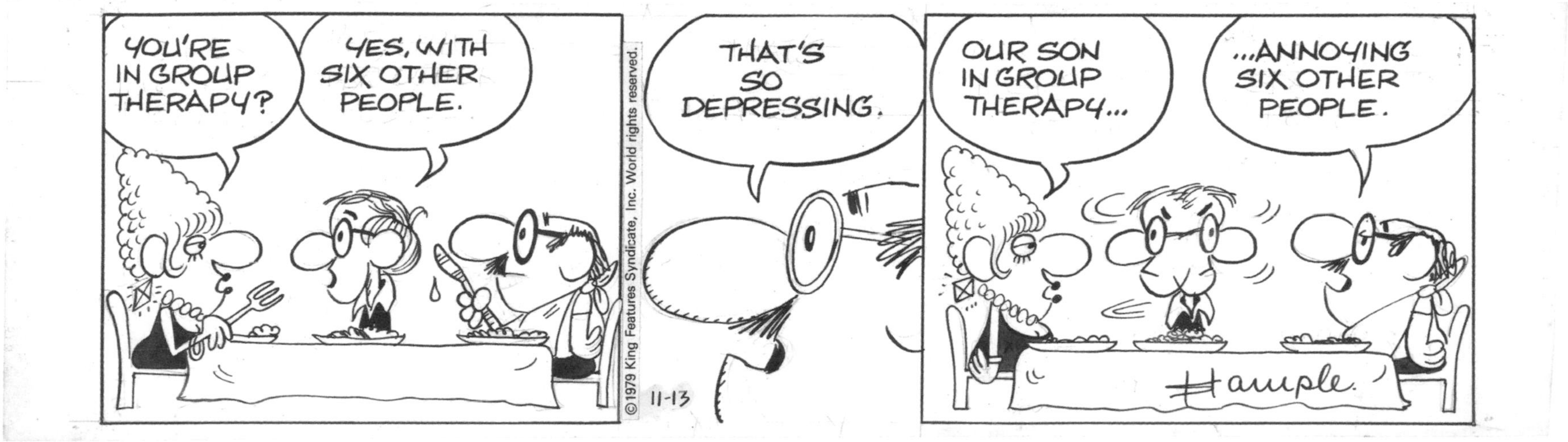
YOU'RE IN GROUP THERAPY?
YES, WITH SIX OTHER PEOPLE.
©1979 King Features Syndicate, Inc. World rights reserved.
11-13
THAT'S SO DEPRESSING.
OUR SON IN GROUP THERAPY...
...ANNOYING SIX OTHER PEOPLE.
Hample.

November 13, 1979

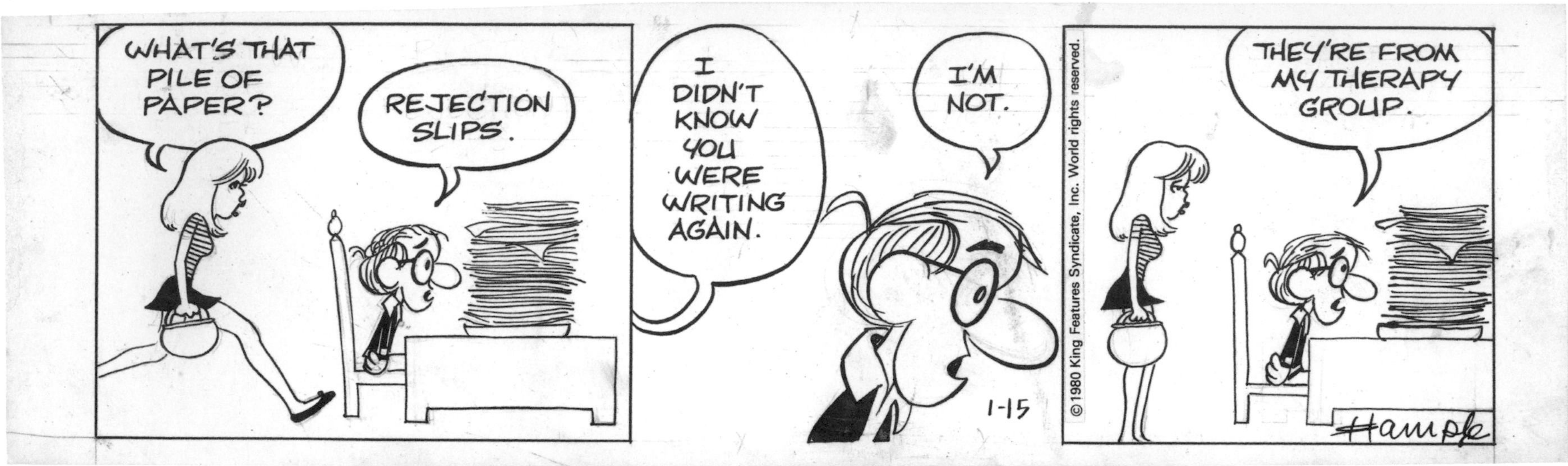
WHAT'S THAT PILE OF PAPER?
REJECTION SLIPS.
I DIDN'T KNOW YOU WERE WRITING AGAIN.
I'M NOT.
THEY'RE FROM MY THERAPY GROUP.
1-15
© 1980 King Features Syndicate, Inc. World rights reserved.
Hample

January 15, 1980

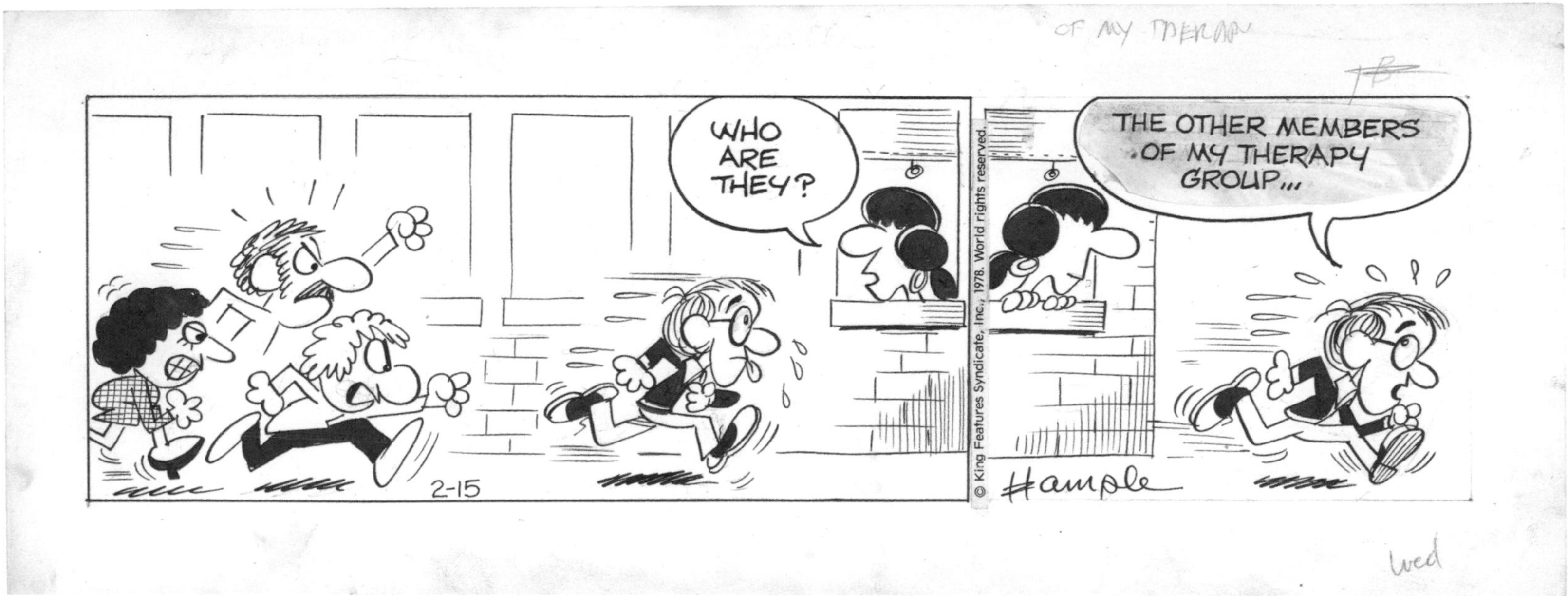
WHO ARE THEY?
THE OTHER MEMBERS OF MY THERAPY GROUP...
2-15
© King Features Syndicate, Inc., 1978. World rights reserved.
Hample

February 15, 1978

In the Mirror World

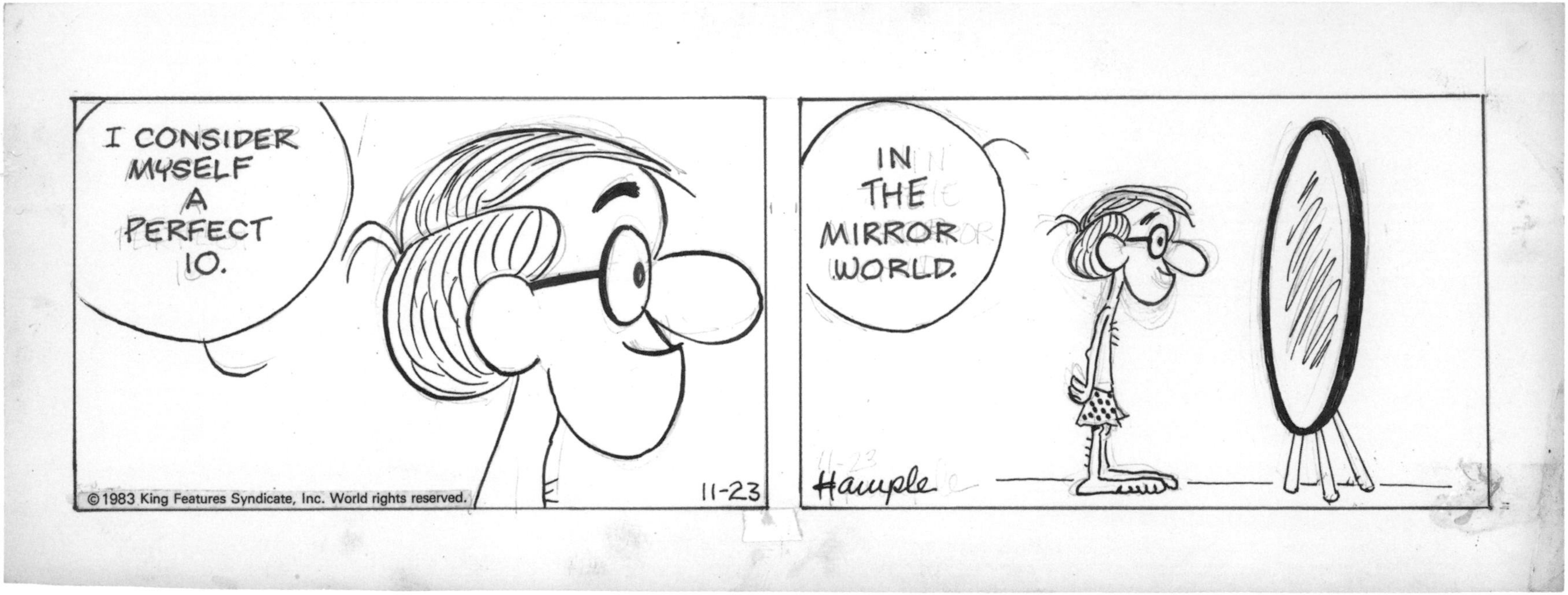
I CONSIDER MYSELF A PERFECT 10.
IN THE MIRROR WORLD.
©1983 King Features Syndicate, Inc. World rights reserved.
11-23
Hample

November 23, 1983

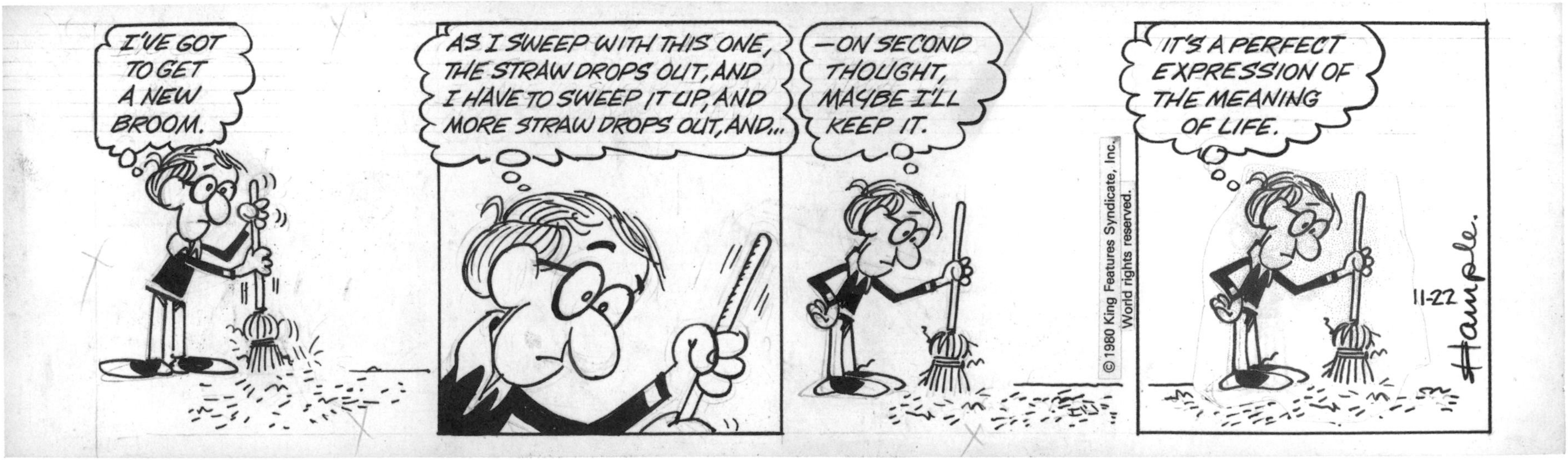
I'VE GOT TO GET A NEW BROOM.
AS I SWEEP WITH THIS ONE, THE STRAW DROPS OUT, AND I HAVE TO SWEEP IT UP, AND MORE STRAW DROPS OUT, AND...
—ON SECOND THOUGHT, MAYBE I'LL KEEP IT.
©1980 King Features Syndicate, Inc. World rights reserved.
IT'S A PERFECT EXPRESSION OF THE MEANING OF LIFE.
11-22
Hample

November 22, 1980

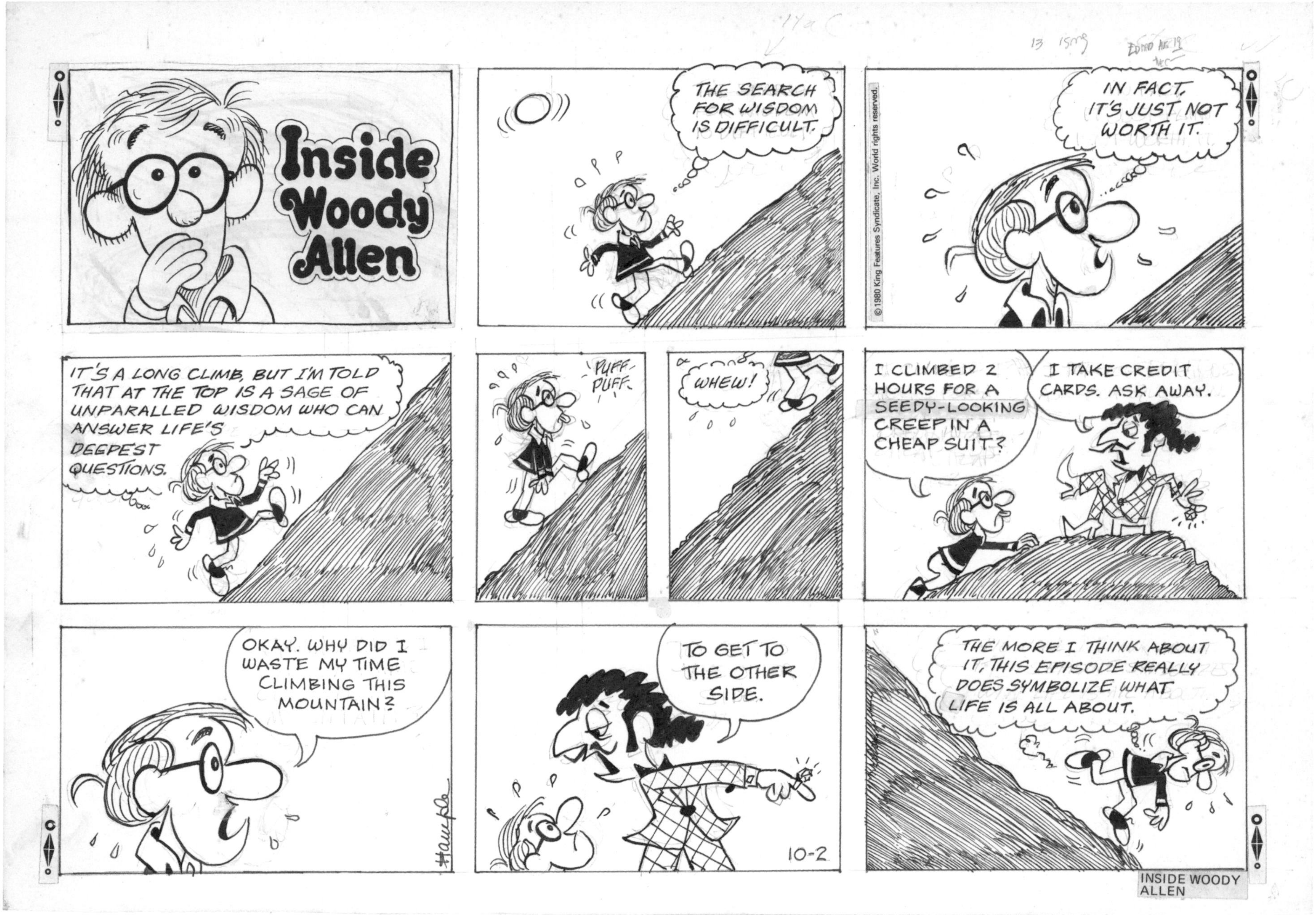
Inside Woody Allen
THE SEARCH FOR WISDOM IS DIFFICULT.
© 1980 King Features Syndicate, Inc. World rights reserved.
IN FACT, IT'S JUST NOT WORTH IT.
IT'S A LONG CLIMB, BUT I'M TOLD THAT AT THE TOP IS A SAGE OF UNPARALLED WISDOM WHO CAN ANSWER LIFE'S DEEPEST QUESTIONS.
PUFF PUFF
WHEW!
I CLIMBED 2 HOURS FOR A SEEDY-LOOKING CREEP IN A CHEAP SUIT?
I TAKE CREDIT CARDS. ASK AWAY.
OKAY. WHY DID I WASTE MY TIME CLIMBING THIS MOUNTAIN?
TO GET TO THE OTHER SIDE.
10-2
THE MORE I THINK ABOUT IT, THIS EPISODE REALLY DOES SYMBOLIZE WHAT LIFE IS ALL ABOUT.
INSIDE WOODY ALLEN

October 2, 1980

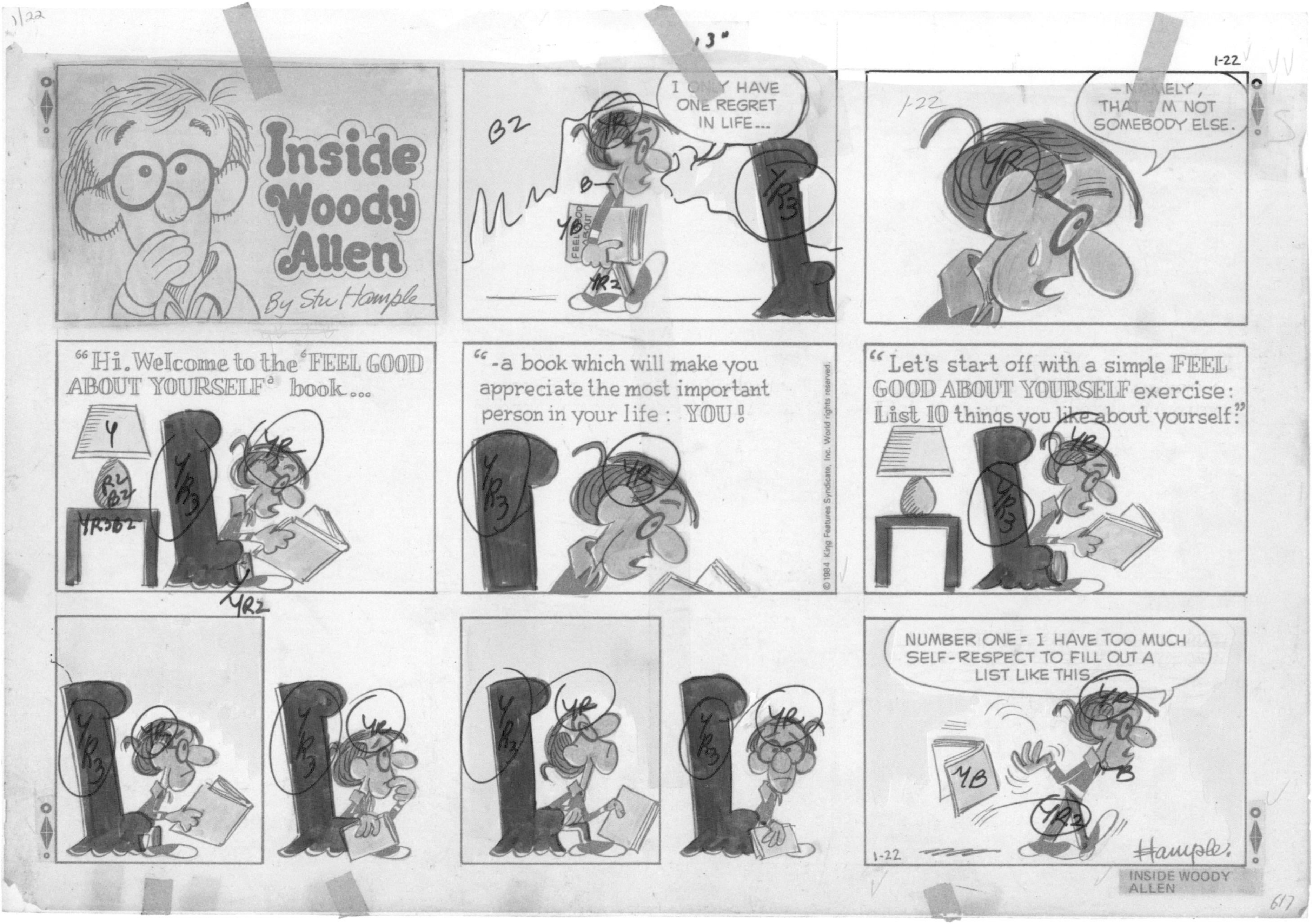
Inside Woody Allen
By Stu Hample
I ONLY HAVE ONE REGRET IN LIFE...
FEEL GOOD ABOUT
–NAMELY, THAT I'M NOT SOMEBODY ELSE.
"Hi. Welcome to the 'FEEL GOOD ABOUT YOURSELF' book...
"-a book which will make you appreciate the most important person in your life: YOU!
© 1984 King Features Syndicate, Inc. World rights reserved.
"Let's start off with a simple FEEL GOOD ABOUT YOURSELF exercise: List 10 things you like about yourself."
NUMBER ONE: I HAVE TOO MUCH SELF-RESPECT TO FILL OUT A LIST LIKE THIS.
Hample.
INSIDE WOODY ALLEN

January 22, 1984

January 22, 1984

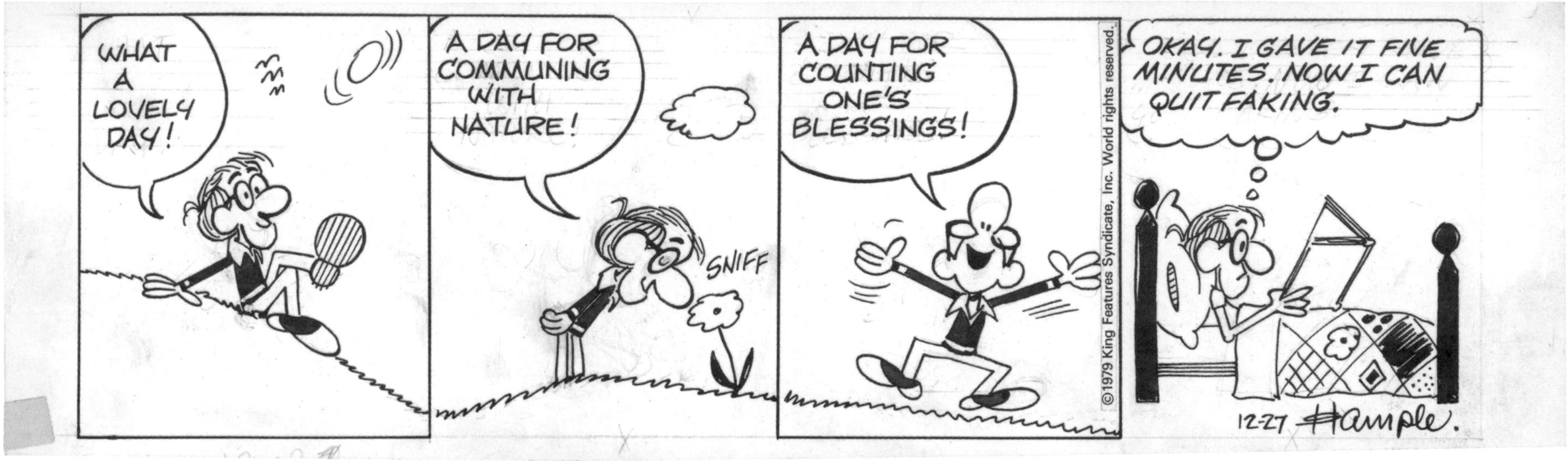
WHAT A LOVELY DAY!
A DAY FOR COMMUNING WITH NATURE!
SNIFF
A DAY FOR COUNTING ONE'S BLESSINGS!
©1979 King Features Syndicate, Inc. World rights reserved.
OKAY. I GAVE IT FIVE MINUTES. NOW I CAN QUIT FAKING.
12-27 Hample.

December 27, 1979

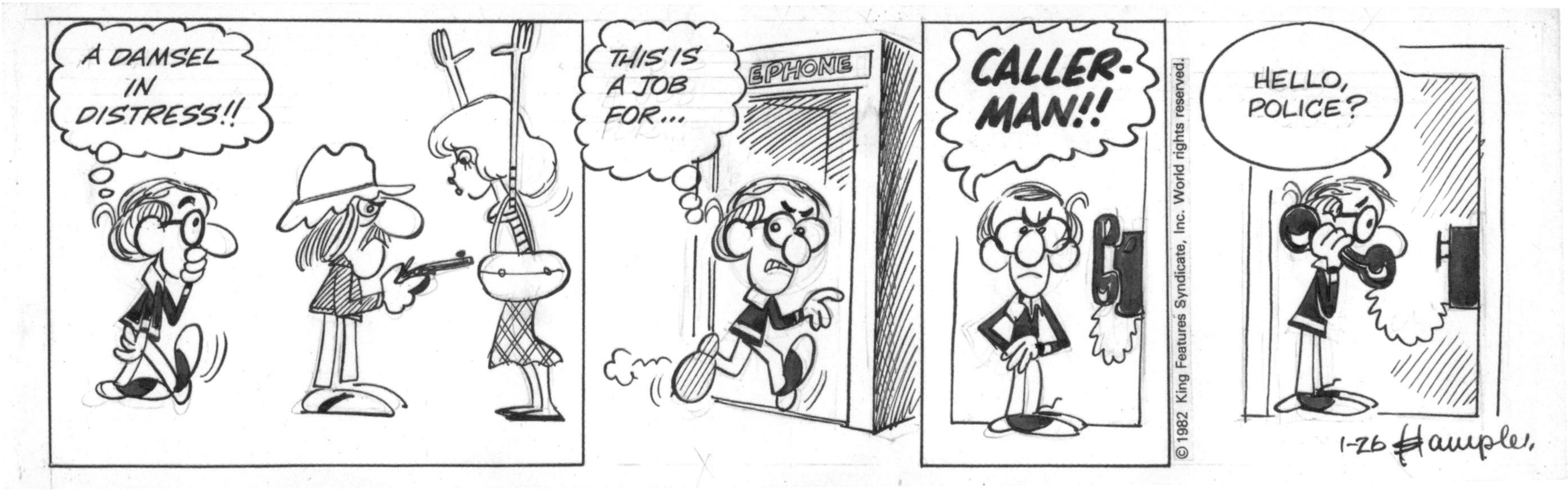
A DAMSEL IN DISTRESS!!
THIS IS A JOB FOR...
EPHONE
CALLER-MAN!!
© 1982 King Features Syndicate, Inc. World rights reserved.
HELLO, POLICE?
1-26 Hample.

January 26, 1982

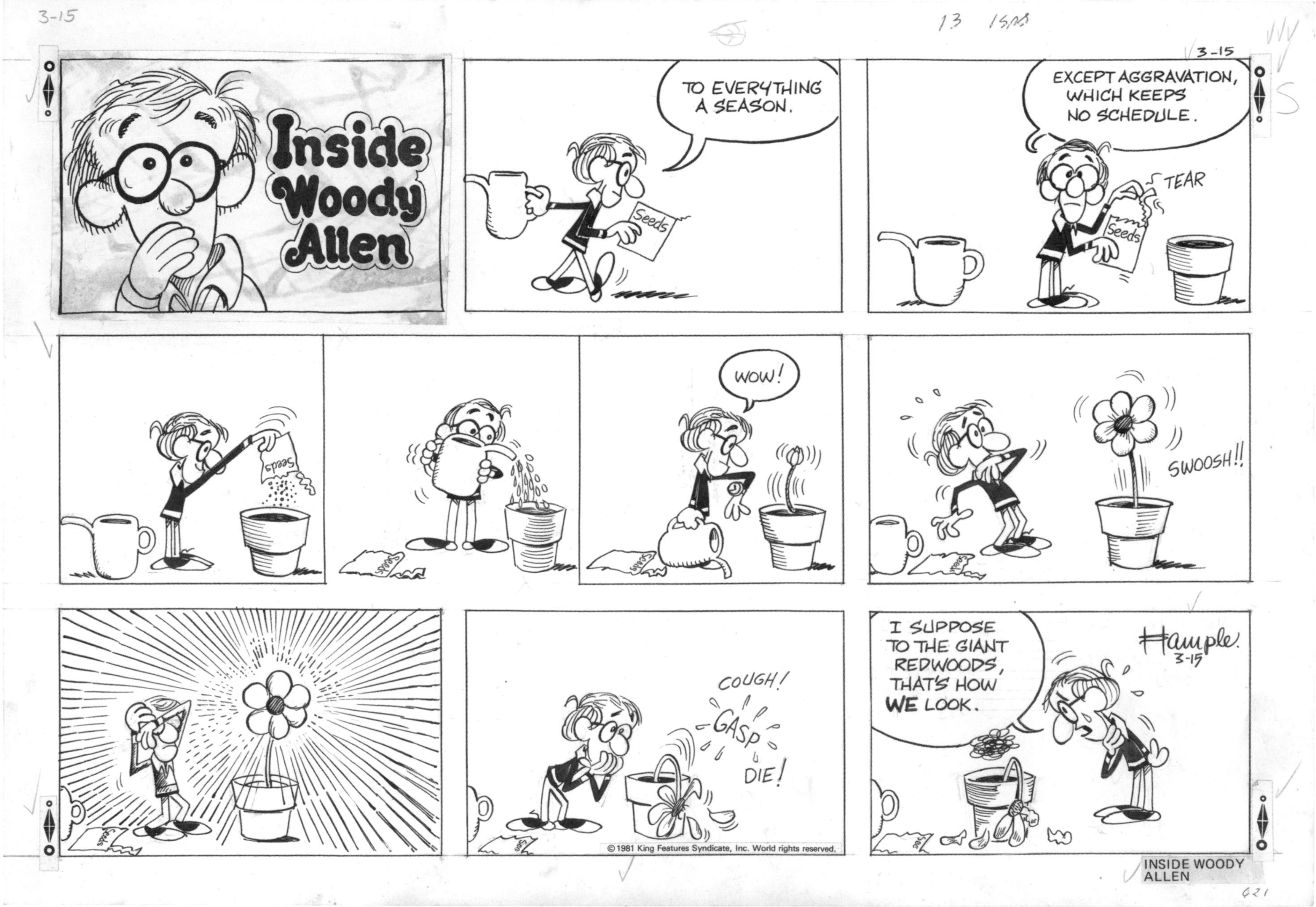
3-15
13 15,25
3-15
Inside Woody Allen
TO EVERYTHING A SEASON.
Seeds
EXCEPT AGGRAVATION, WHICH KEEPS NO SCHEDULE.
TEAR
Seeds
Seeds
WOW!
SWOOSH!!
COUGH!
GASP
DIE!
© 1981 King Features Syndicate, Inc. World rights reserved.
I SUPPOSE TO THE GIANT REDWOODS, THAT'S HOW **WE** LOOK.
Hample 3-15
INSIDE WOODY ALLEN
621

March 15, 1981

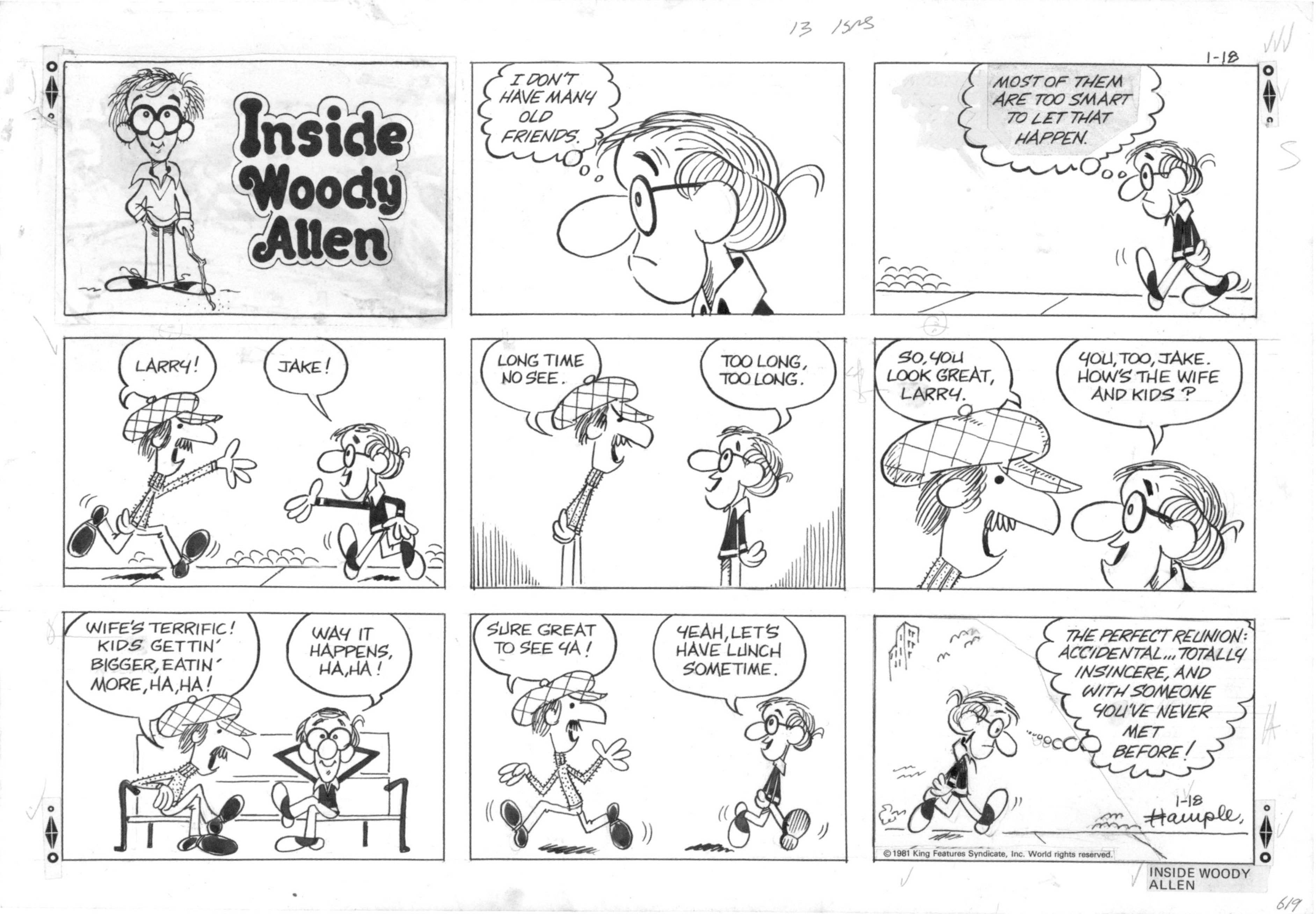
13 ISRS
1-18
Inside Woody Allen
I DON'T HAVE MANY OLD FRIENDS.
MOST OF THEM ARE TOO SMART TO LET THAT HAPPEN.
LARRY!
JAKE!
LONG TIME NO SEE.
TOO LONG, TOO LONG.
SO, YOU LOOK GREAT, LARRY.
YOU, TOO, JAKE. HOW'S THE WIFE AND KIDS?
WIFE'S TERRIFIC! KIDS GETTIN' BIGGER, EATIN' MORE, HA, HA!
WAY IT HAPPENS, HA, HA!
SURE GREAT TO SEE YA!
YEAH, LET'S HAVE LUNCH SOMETIME.
THE PERFECT REUNION: ACCIDENTAL... TOTALLY INSINCERE, AND WITH SOMEONE YOU'VE NEVER MET BEFORE!
1-18
Hample
© 1981 King Features Syndicate, Inc. World rights reserved.
INSIDE WOODY ALLEN
619

January 18, 1981

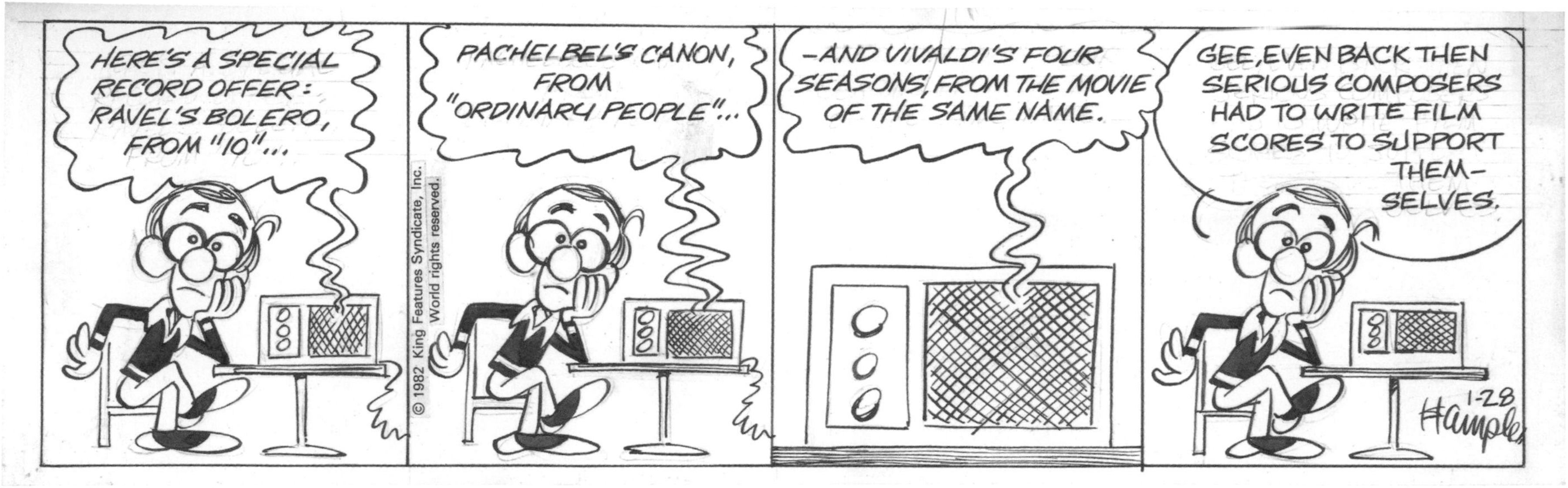
HERE'S A SPECIAL RECORD OFFER: RAVEL'S BOLERO, FROM "10"...
PACHELBEL'S CANON, FROM "ORDINARY PEOPLE"...
© 1982 King Features Syndicate, Inc. World rights reserved.
–AND VIVALDI'S FOUR SEASONS, FROM THE MOVIE OF THE SAME NAME.
GEE, EVEN BACK THEN SERIOUS COMPOSERS HAD TO WRITE FILM SCORES TO SUPPORT THEM-SELVES.
1-28
Hampler

January 28, 1982

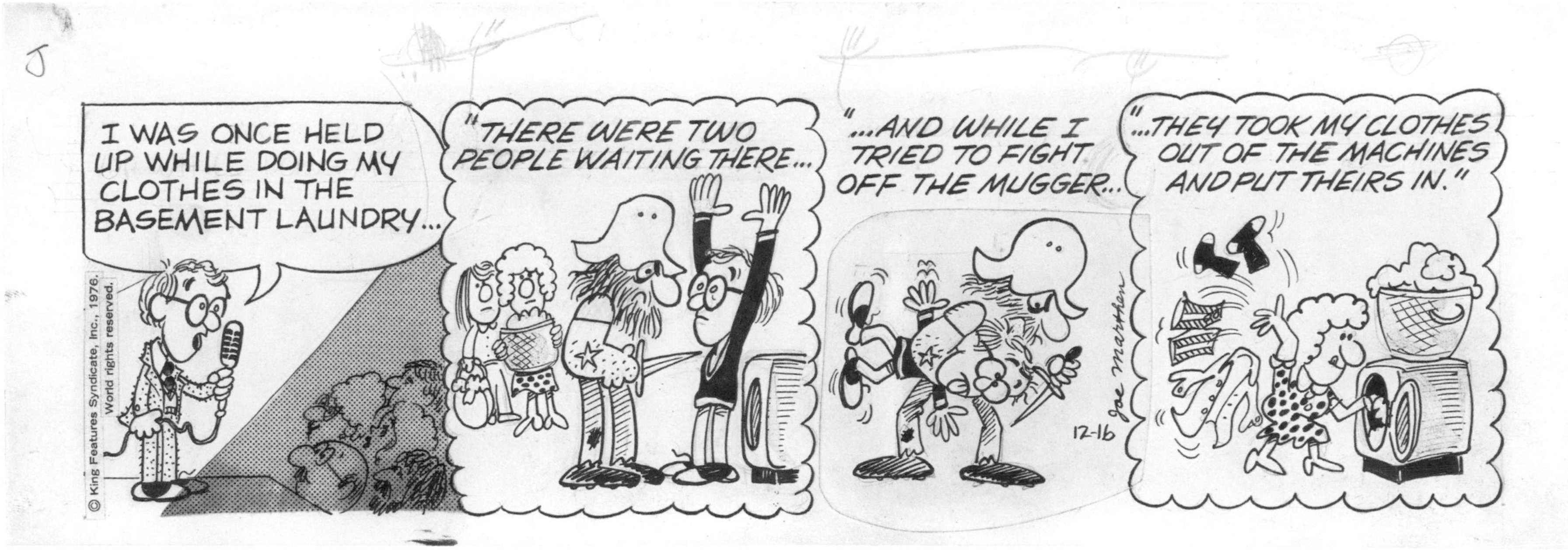
I WAS ONCE HELD UP WHILE DOING MY CLOTHES IN THE BASEMENT LAUNDRY...
© King Features Syndicate, Inc., 1976. World rights reserved.
"THERE WERE TWO PEOPLE WAITING THERE...
"...AND WHILE I TRIED TO FIGHT OFF THE MUGGER...
12-16
Joe Martin
"...THEY TOOK MY CLOTHES OUT OF THE MACHINES AND PUT THEIRS IN."

December 16, 1976

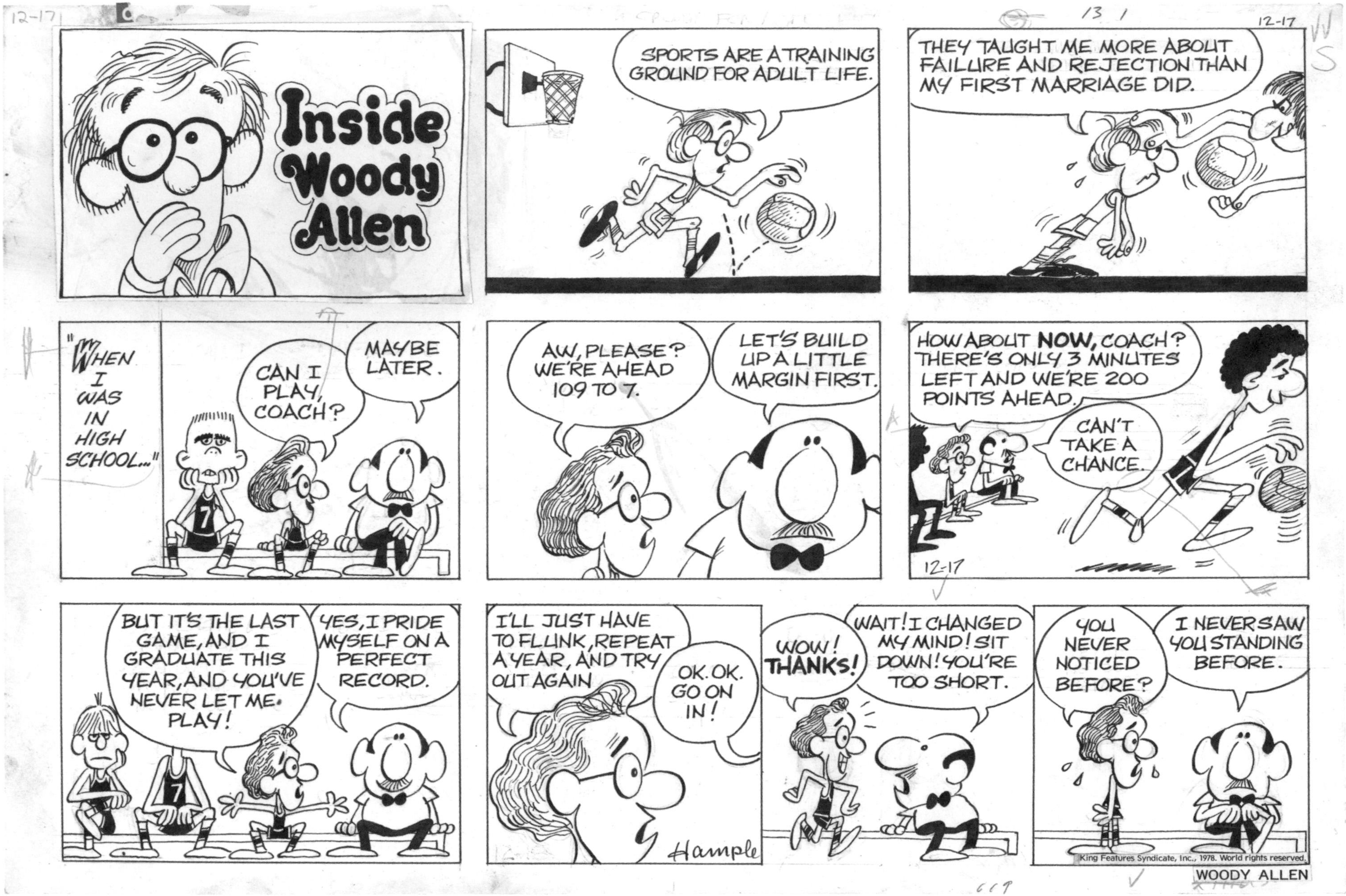
Inside Woody Allen
SPORTS ARE A TRAINING GROUND FOR ADULT LIFE.
THEY TAUGHT ME MORE ABOUT FAILURE AND REJECTION THAN MY FIRST MARRIAGE DID.
"WHEN I WAS IN HIGH SCHOOL..."
CAN I PLAY, COACH?
MAYBE LATER.
AW, PLEASE? WE'RE AHEAD 109 TO 7.
LET'S BUILD UP A LITTLE MARGIN FIRST.
HOW ABOUT NOW, COACH? THERE'S ONLY 3 MINUTES LEFT AND WE'RE 200 POINTS AHEAD.
CAN'T TAKE A CHANCE.
BUT IT'S THE LAST GAME, AND I GRADUATE THIS YEAR, AND YOU'VE NEVER LET ME PLAY!
YES, I PRIDE MYSELF ON A PERFECT RECORD.
I'LL JUST HAVE TO FLUNK, REPEAT A YEAR, AND TRY OUT AGAIN
OK. OK. GO ON IN!
WOW! THANKS!
WAIT! I CHANGED MY MIND! SIT DOWN! YOU'RE TOO SHORT.
YOU NEVER NOTICED BEFORE?
I NEVER SAW YOU STANDING BEFORE.
Hample
King Features Syndicate, Inc., 1978. World rights reserved.
WOODY ALLEN

December 17, 1978

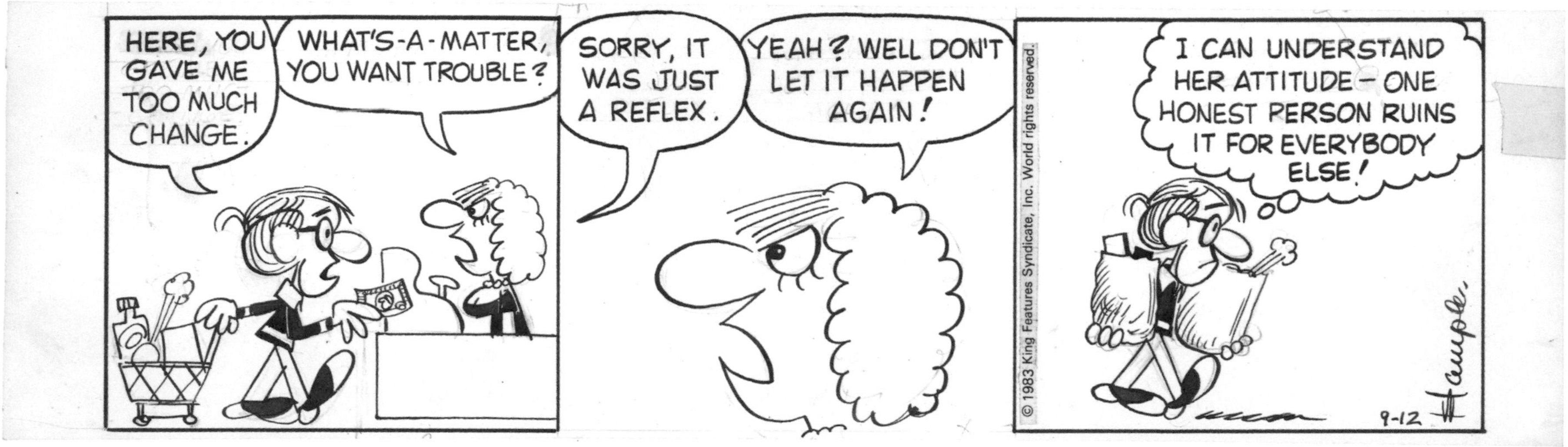
HERE, YOU GAVE ME TOO MUCH CHANGE.
WHAT'S-A-MATTER, YOU WANT TROUBLE?
SORRY, IT WAS JUST A REFLEX.
YEAH? WELL DON'T LET IT HAPPEN AGAIN!
I CAN UNDERSTAND HER ATTITUDE—ONE HONEST PERSON RUINS IT FOR EVERYBODY ELSE!
© 1983 King Features Syndicate, Inc. World rights reserved.
9-12
Hample.

September 12, 1983

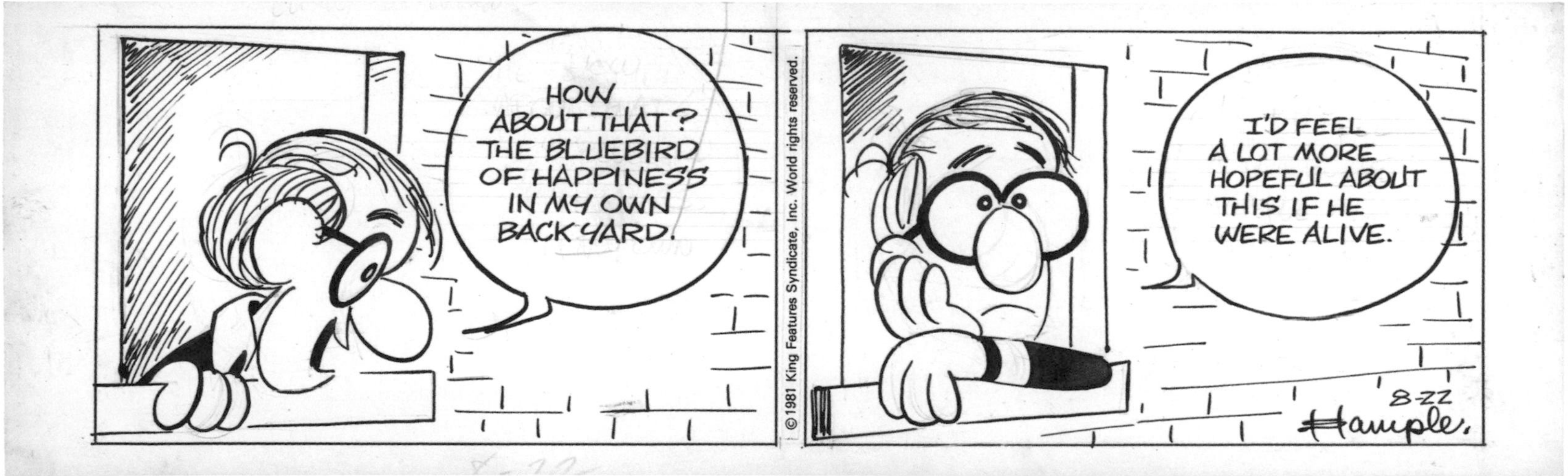
HOW ABOUT THAT? THE BLUEBIRD OF HAPPINESS IN MY OWN BACK YARD.
I'D FEEL A LOT MORE HOPEFUL ABOUT THIS IF HE WERE ALIVE.
© 1981 King Features Syndicate, Inc. World rights reserved.
8-22
Hample.

August 22, 1981

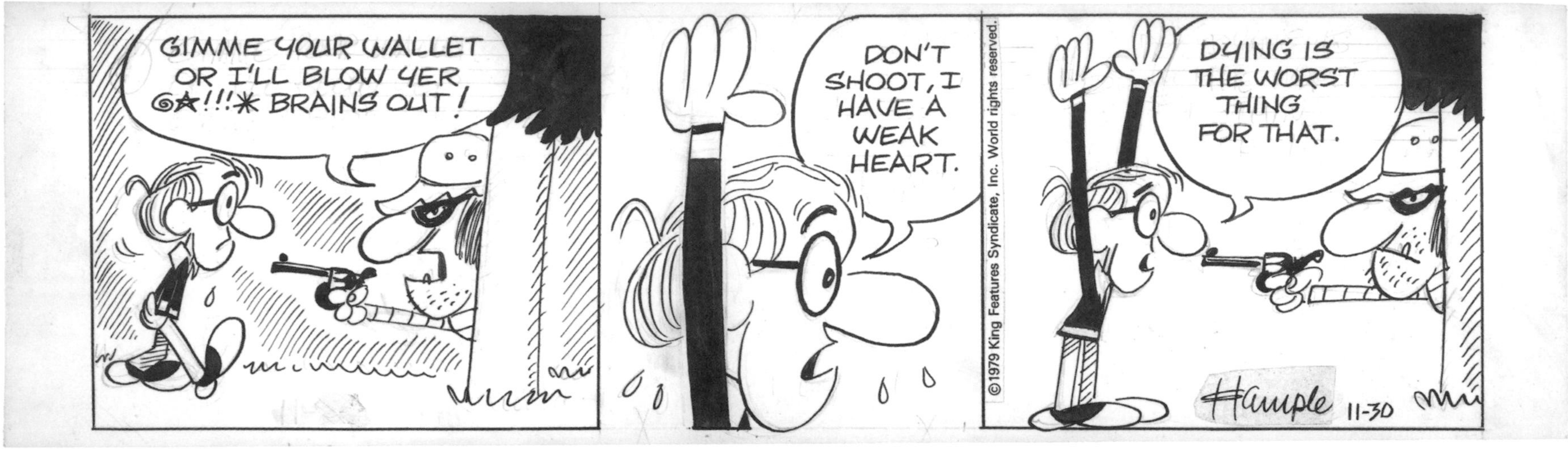
GIMME YOUR WALLET OR I'LL BLOW YER @☆!!!✱ BRAINS OUT!
DON'T SHOOT, I HAVE A WEAK HEART.
©1979 King Features Syndicate, Inc. World rights reserved.
DYING IS THE WORST THING FOR THAT.
Hample
11-30

November 30, 1979

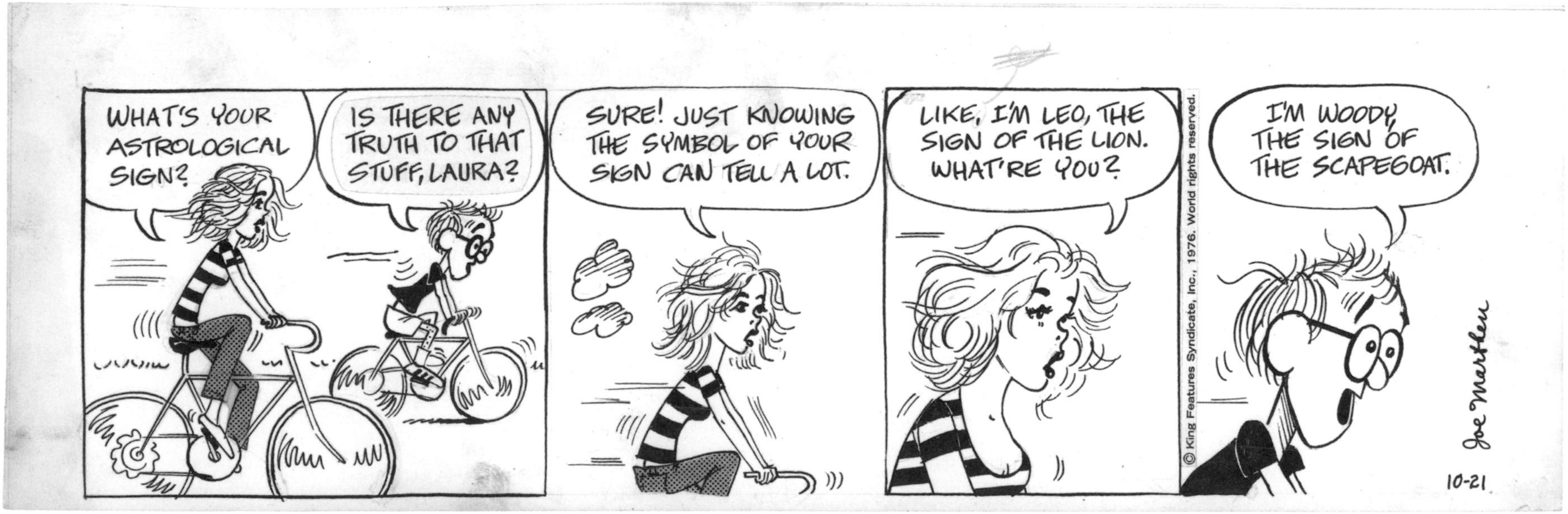
WHAT'S YOUR ASTROLOGICAL SIGN?
IS THERE ANY TRUTH TO THAT STUFF, LAURA?
SURE! JUST KNOWING THE SYMBOL OF YOUR SIGN CAN TELL A LOT.
LIKE, I'M LEO, THE SIGN OF THE LION. WHAT'RE YOU?
© King Features Syndicate, Inc., 1976. World rights reserved.
I'M WOODY, THE SIGN OF THE SCAPEGOAT.
Joe Marthen
10-21

October 21, 1976

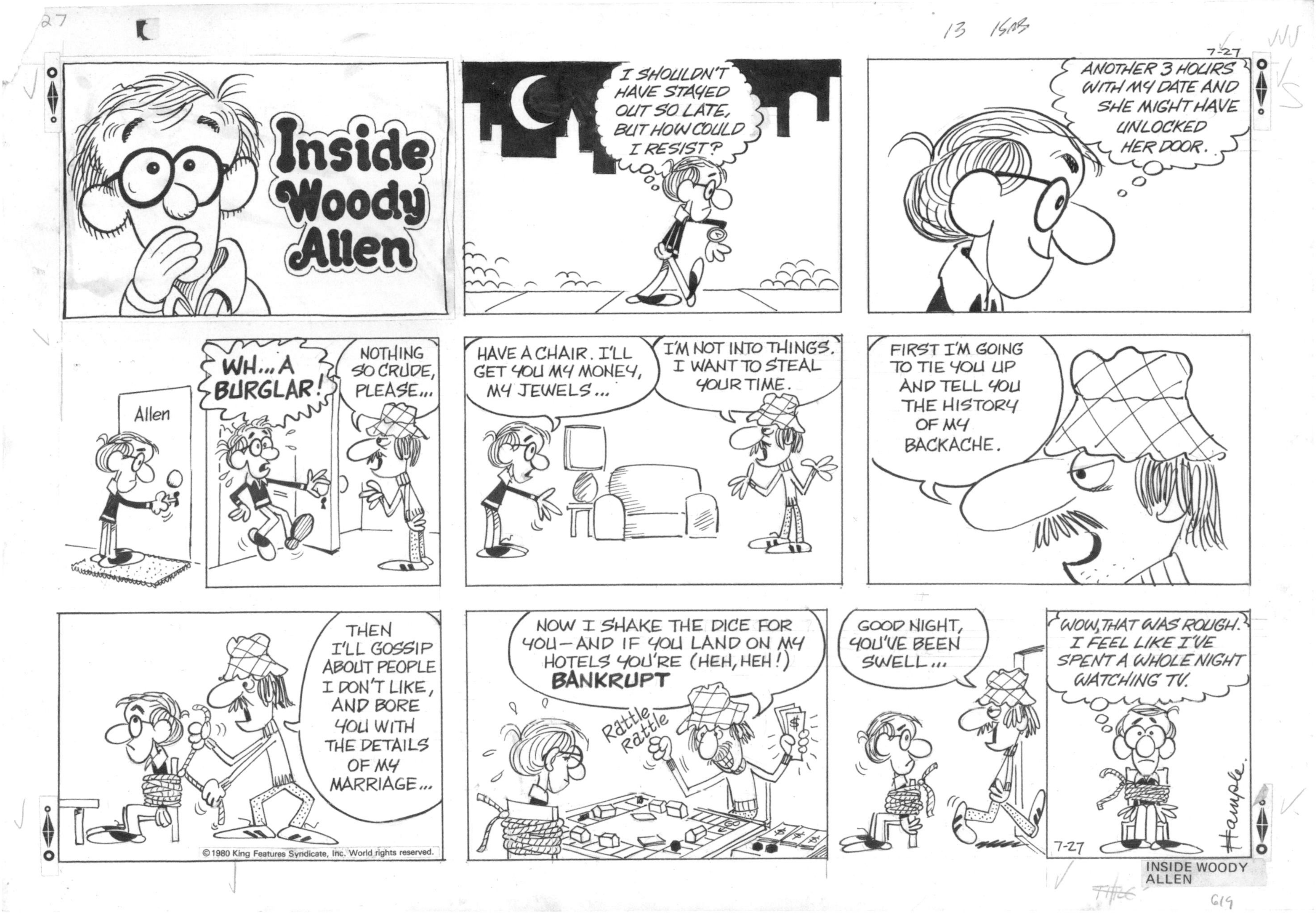
Inside Woody Allen
I SHOULDN'T HAVE STAYED OUT SO LATE, BUT HOW COULD I RESIST?
ANOTHER 3 HOURS WITH MY DATE AND SHE MIGHT HAVE UNLOCKED HER DOOR.
Allen
WH... A BURGLAR!
NOTHING SO CRUDE, PLEASE...
HAVE A CHAIR. I'LL GET YOU MY MONEY, MY JEWELS...
I'M NOT INTO THINGS. I WANT TO STEAL YOUR TIME.
FIRST I'M GOING TO TIE YOU UP AND TELL YOU THE HISTORY OF MY BACKACHE.
THEN I'LL GOSSIP ABOUT PEOPLE I DON'T LIKE, AND BORE YOU WITH THE DETAILS OF MY MARRIAGE...
© 1980 King Features Syndicate, Inc. World rights reserved.
NOW I SHAKE THE DICE FOR YOU—AND IF YOU LAND ON MY HOTELS YOU'RE (HEH, HEH!) BANKRUPT
Rattle Rattle
GOOD NIGHT, YOU'VE BEEN SWELL...
WOW, THAT WAS ROUGH. I FEEL LIKE I'VE SPENT A WHOLE NIGHT WATCHING TV.
7-27
Hample
INSIDE WOODY ALLEN

July 27, 1980

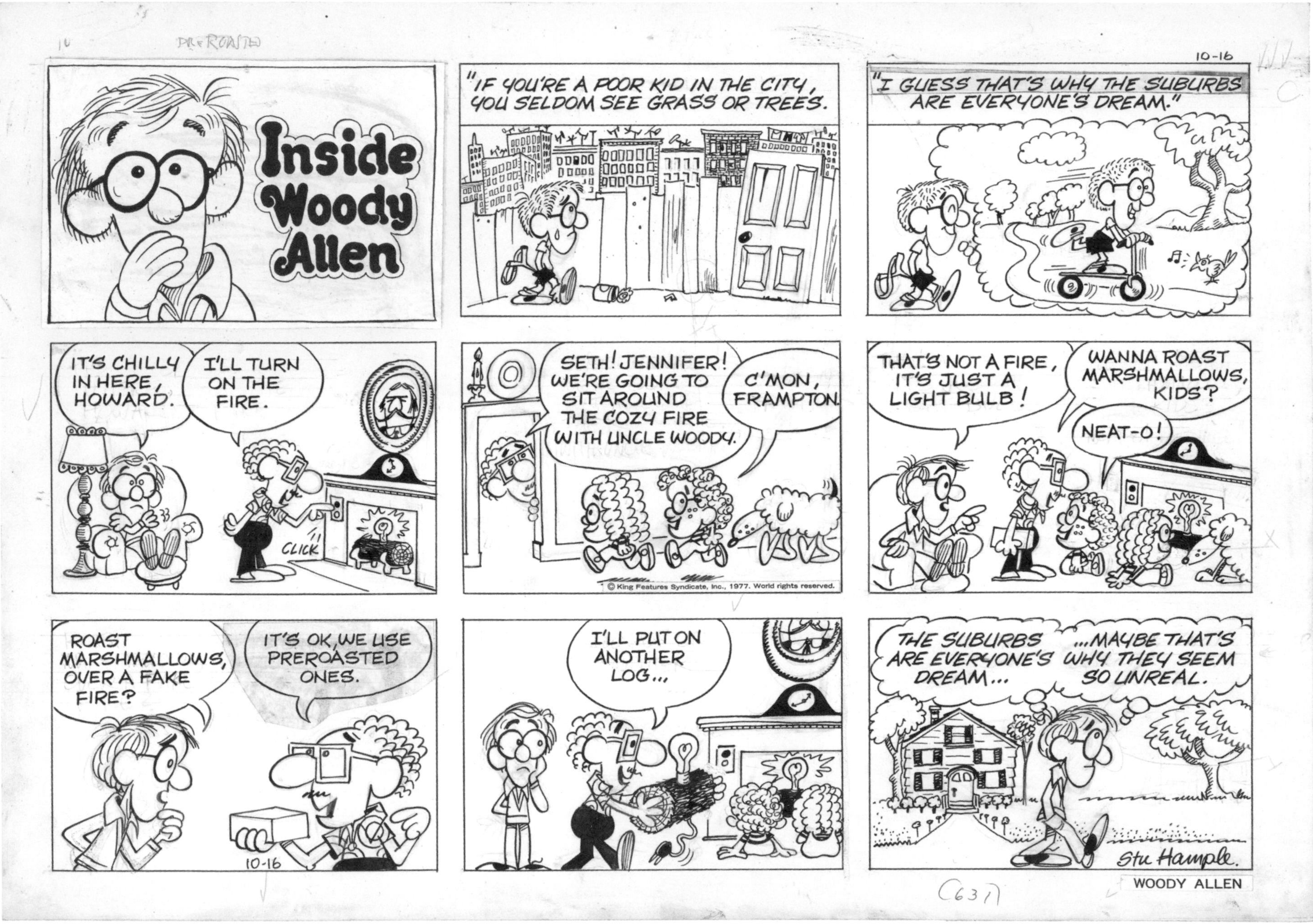
PREROASTED
10-16
Inside Woody Allen
"IF YOU'RE A POOR KID IN THE CITY, YOU SELDOM SEE GRASS OR TREES.
"I GUESS THAT'S WHY THE SUBURBS ARE EVERYONE'S DREAM."
IT'S CHILLY IN HERE, HOWARD.
I'LL TURN ON THE FIRE.
CLICK
SETH! JENNIFER! WE'RE GOING TO SIT AROUND THE COZY FIRE WITH UNCLE WOODY.
C'MON, FRAMPTON.
© King Features Syndicate, Inc., 1977. World rights reserved.
THAT'S NOT A FIRE, IT'S JUST A LIGHT BULB!
WANNA ROAST MARSHMALLOWS, KIDS?
NEAT-O!
ROAST MARSHMALLOWS, OVER A FAKE FIRE?
IT'S OK, WE USE PREROASTED ONES.
10-16
I'LL PUT ON ANOTHER LOG...
THE SUBURBS ARE EVERYONE'S DREAM...
...MAYBE THAT'S WHY THEY SEEM SO UNREAL.
Stu Hample.
(637)
WOODY ALLEN

October 16, 1977

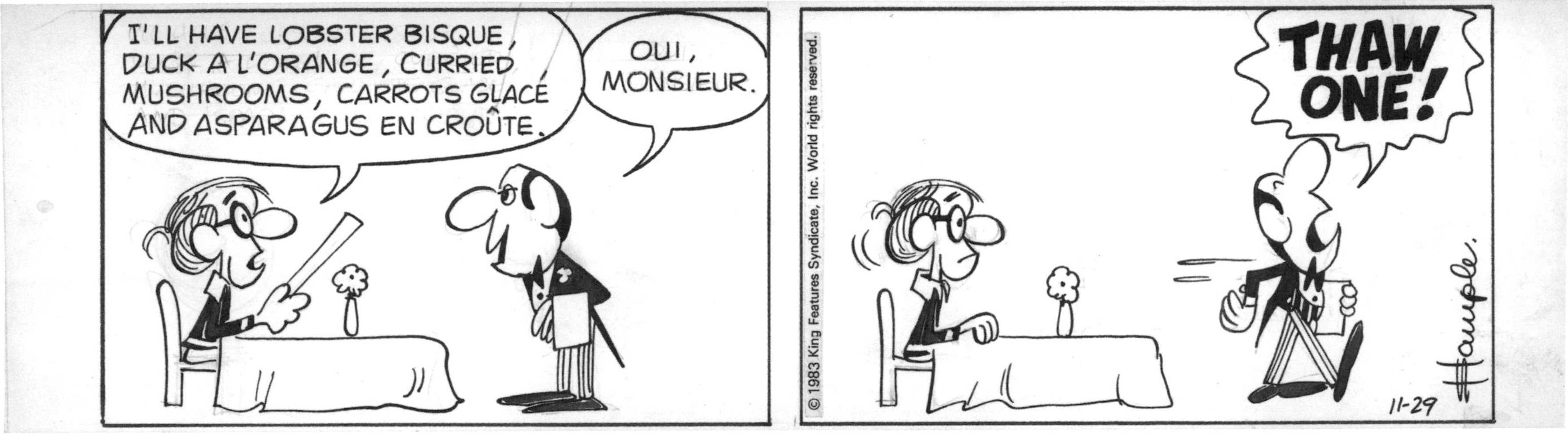
I'LL HAVE LOBSTER BISQUE, DUCK A L'ORANGE, CURRIED MUSHROOMS, CARROTS GLACÉ AND ASPARAGUS EN CROÛTE.
OUI, MONSIEUR.
THAW ONE!
© 1983 King Features Syndicate, Inc. World rights reserved.
11-29

November 29, 1983

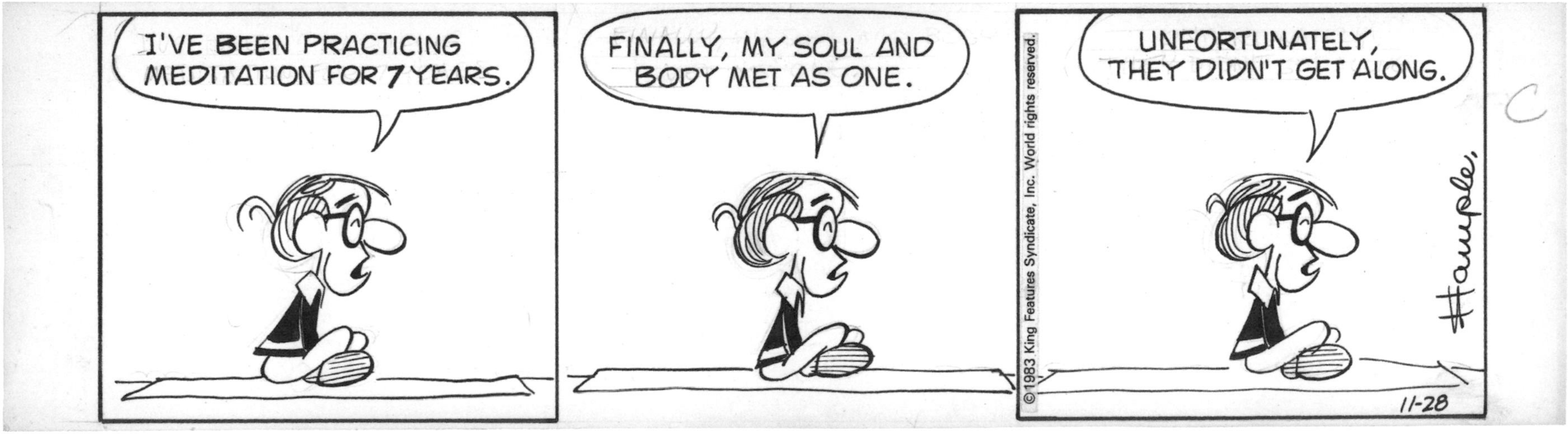
I'VE BEEN PRACTICING MEDITATION FOR 7 YEARS.
FINALLY, MY SOUL AND BODY MET AS ONE.
UNFORTUNATELY, THEY DIDN'T GET ALONG.
© 1983 King Features Syndicate, Inc. World rights reserved.
11-28

November 28, 1983

Inside Woody Allen

Up until now, the subject of flying saucers has been mostly associated with kooks and oddballs.

Frequently, some observers admit to being a member of both groups.

IN MY NIGHTMARE, A BRIGHT YELLOW SPHERE LANDS BESIDE ME....

"THE DOOR OPENS AND SEVERAL CREATURES EMERGE

THEIR LANGUAGE SOUNDS LIKE WHEN YOU BACK A CAR OVER A FAT PERSON

"THEY TAKE ME ABOARD AND GIVE ME WHAT SEEMS LIKE A COMPLETE PHYSICAL EXAM."

we come from another galaxy to tell you that you must learn to live in peace or we will return with special weapons and laminate every firstborn male.

THEY PROMISED TO GET THE RESULTS OF MY BLOOD TEST BACK IN A WEEK, AND IF I DIDN'T HEAR FROM THEM, I COULD GO AHEAD AND MARRY MY ANALYST.

INSIDE WOODY ALLEN

February 21, 1982

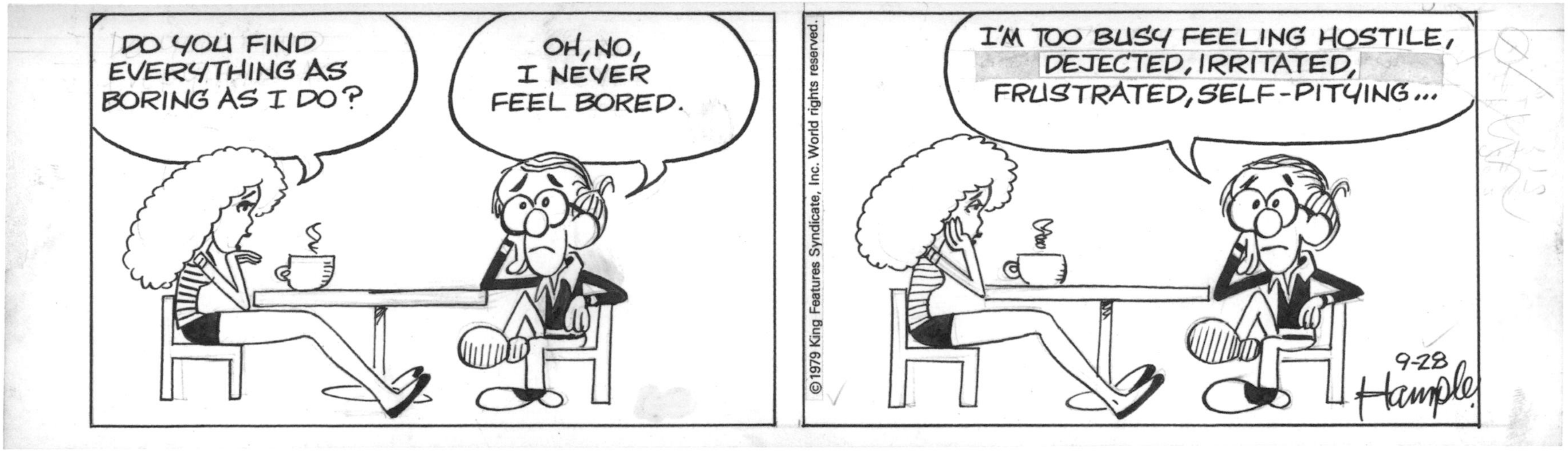
DO YOU FIND EVERYTHING AS BORING AS I DO?
OH, NO, I NEVER FEEL BORED.
I'M TOO BUSY FEELING HOSTILE, DEJECTED, IRRITATED, FRUSTRATED, SELF-PITYING...
9-28
Hample
© 1979 King Features Syndicate, Inc. World rights reserved.

September 28, 1979

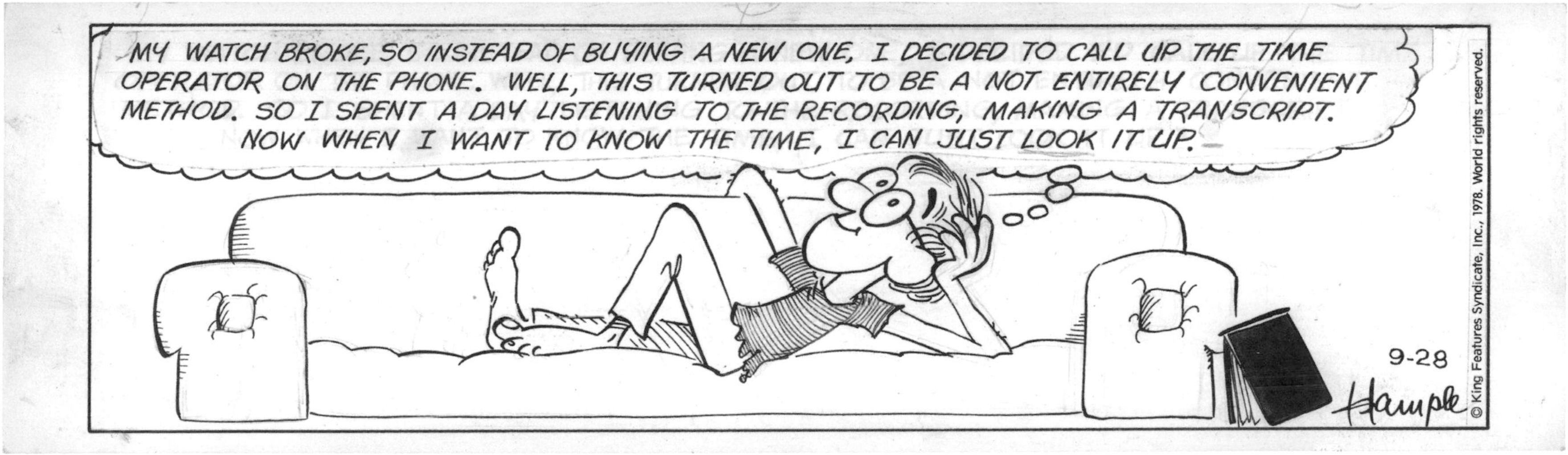
MY WATCH BROKE, SO INSTEAD OF BUYING A NEW ONE, I DECIDED TO CALL UP THE TIME OPERATOR ON THE PHONE. WELL, THIS TURNED OUT TO BE A NOT ENTIRELY CONVENIENT METHOD. SO I SPENT A DAY LISTENING TO THE RECORDING, MAKING A TRANSCRIPT. NOW WHEN I WANT TO KNOW THE TIME, I CAN JUST LOOK IT UP.
9-28
Hample
© King Features Syndicate, Inc., 1978. World rights reserved.

September 28, 1978

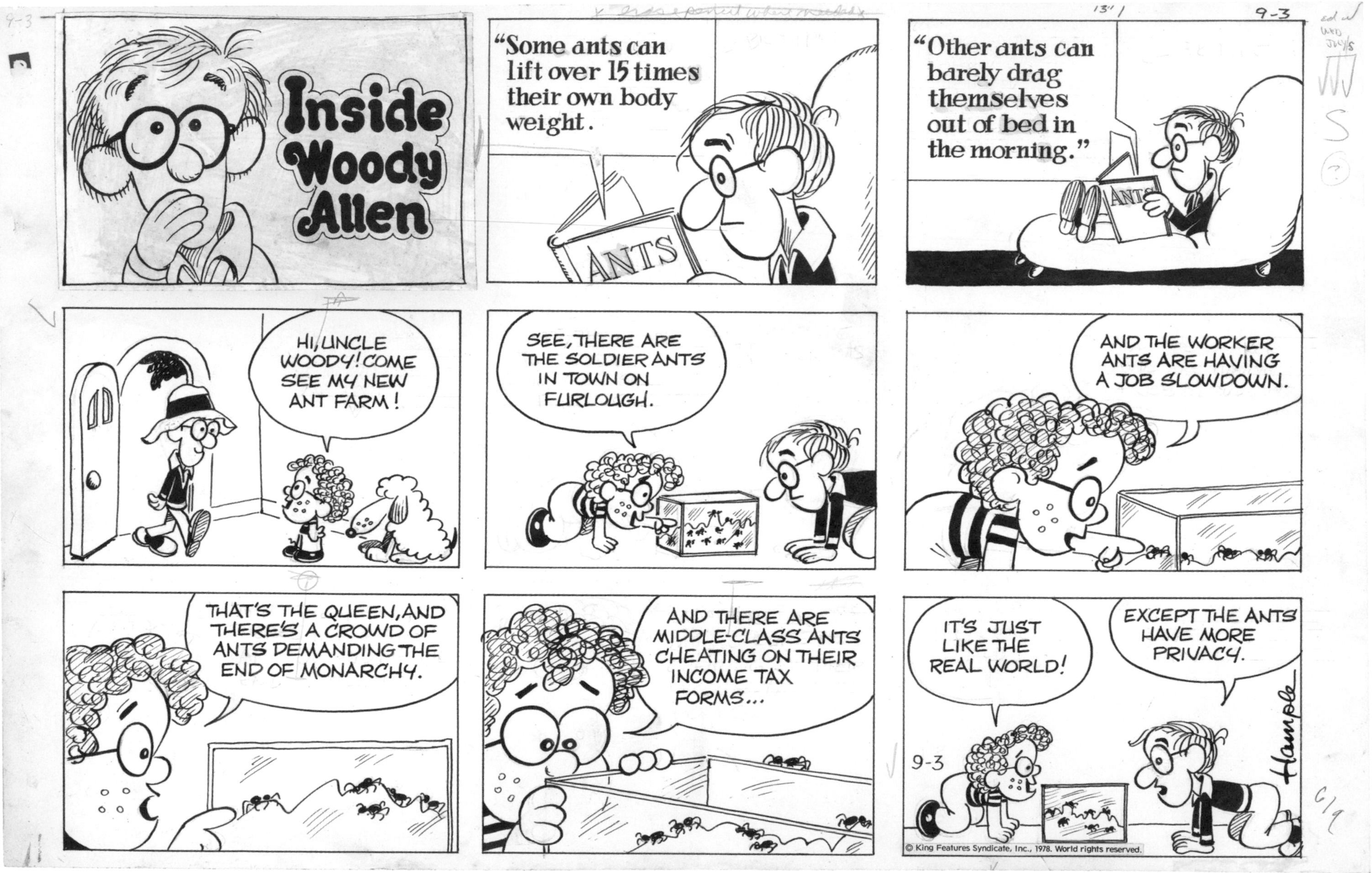
Inside Woody Allen
"Some ants can lift over 15 times their own body weight.
ANTS
"Other ants can barely drag themselves out of bed in the morning."
ANTS
HI, UNCLE WOODY! COME SEE MY NEW ANT FARM!
SEE, THERE ARE THE SOLDIER ANTS IN TOWN ON FURLOUGH.
AND THE WORKER ANTS ARE HAVING A JOB SLOWDOWN.
THAT'S THE QUEEN, AND THERE'S A CROWD OF ANTS DEMANDING THE END OF MONARCHY.
AND THERE ARE MIDDLE-CLASS ANTS CHEATING ON THEIR INCOME TAX FORMS...
IT'S JUST LIKE THE REAL WORLD!
EXCEPT THE ANTS HAVE MORE PRIVACY.
9-3
Hample
© King Features Syndicate, Inc., 1978. World rights reserved.

September 3, 1978

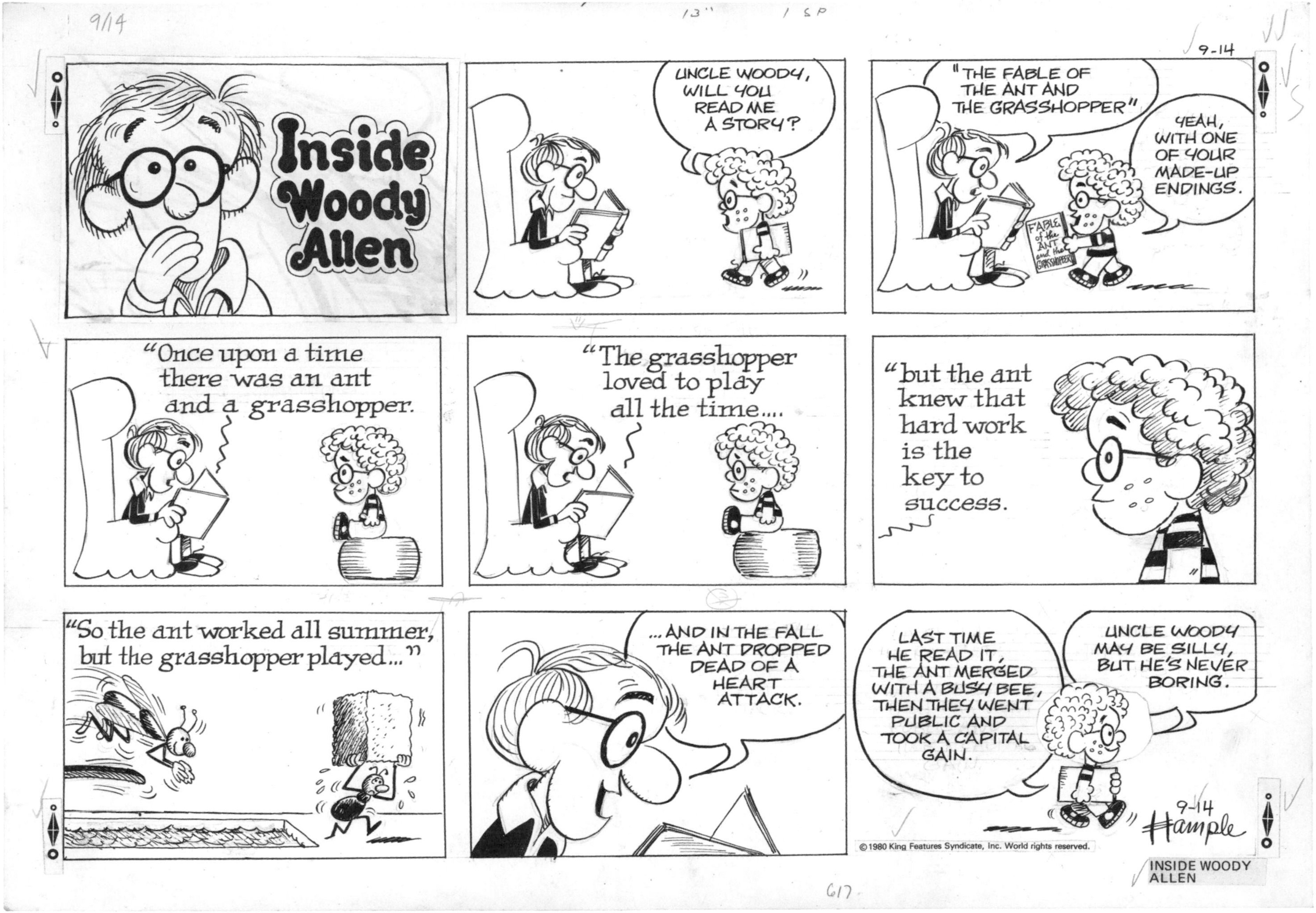
Inside Woody Allen
UNCLE WOODY, WILL YOU READ ME A STORY?
"THE FABLE OF THE ANT AND THE GRASSHOPPER"
YEAH, WITH ONE OF YOUR MADE-UP ENDINGS.
FABLE of the ANT and the GRASSHOPPER
"Once upon a time there was an ant and a grasshopper.
"The grasshopper loved to play all the time....
"but the ant knew that hard work is the key to success.
"So the ant worked all summer, but the grasshopper played..."
...AND IN THE FALL THE ANT DROPPED DEAD OF A HEART ATTACK.
LAST TIME HE READ IT, THE ANT MERGED WITH A BUSY BEE, THEN THEY WENT PUBLIC AND TOOK A CAPITAL GAIN.
UNCLE WOODY MAY BE SILLY, BUT HE'S NEVER BORING.
9-14 Hample
© 1980 King Features Syndicate, Inc. World rights reserved.
INSIDE WOODY ALLEN

September 14, 1980

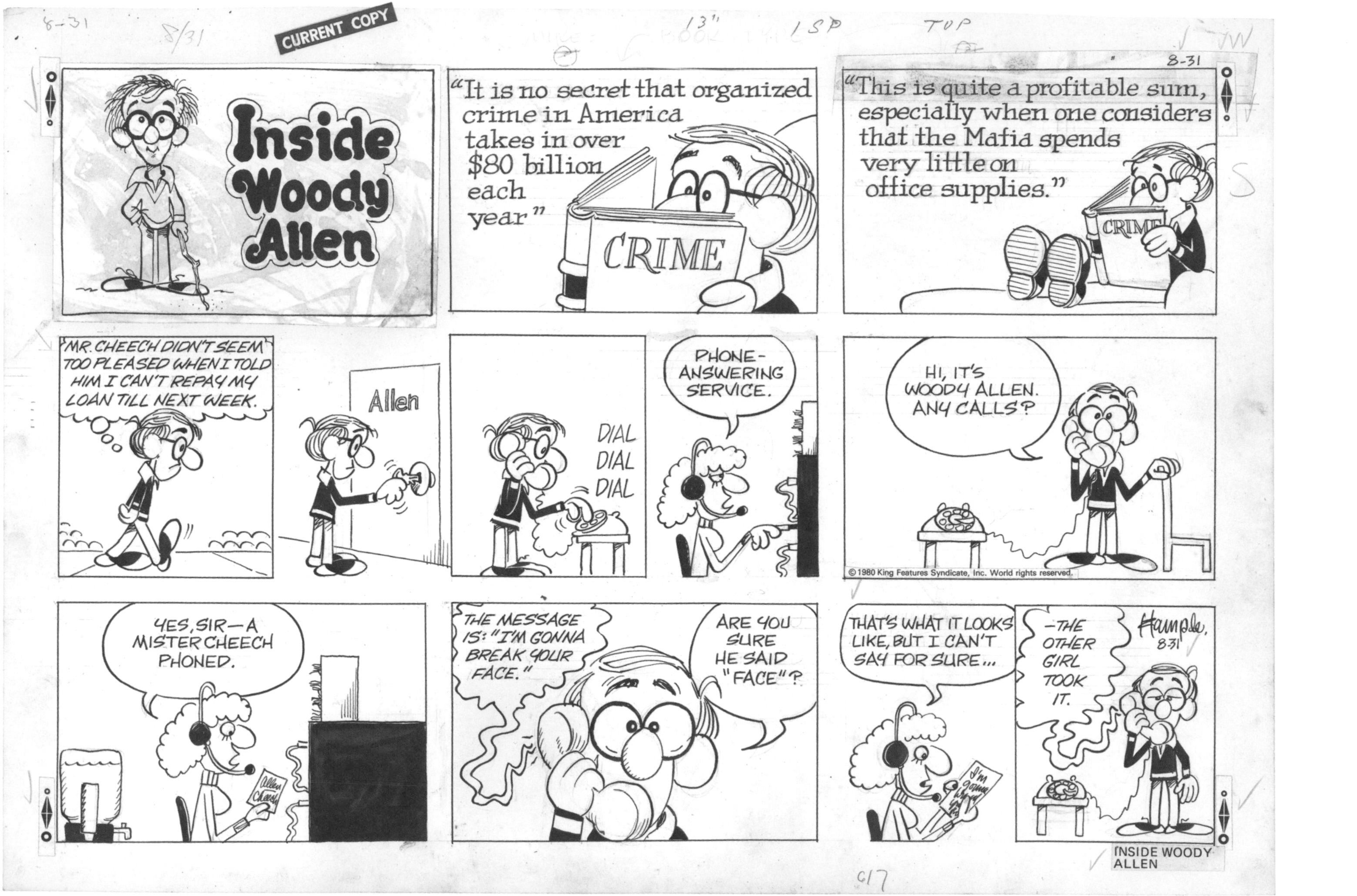
CURRENT COPY
Inside Woody Allen
"It is no secret that organized crime in America takes in over $80 billion each year"
CRIME
"This is quite a profitable sum, especially when one considers that the Mafia spends very little on office supplies."
CRIME
MR. CHEECH DIDN'T SEEM TOO PLEASED WHEN I TOLD HIM I CAN'T REPAY MY LOAN TILL NEXT WEEK.
Allen
DIAL DIAL DIAL
PHONE-ANSWERING SERVICE.
HI, IT'S WOODY ALLEN. ANY CALLS?
© 1980 King Features Syndicate, Inc. World rights reserved.
YES, SIR—A MISTER CHEECH PHONED.
THE MESSAGE IS: "I'M GONNA BREAK YOUR FACE."
ARE YOU SURE HE SAID "FACE"?
THAT'S WHAT IT LOOKS LIKE, BUT I CAN'T SAY FOR SURE...
—THE OTHER GIRL TOOK IT.
Hample 8-31
INSIDE WOODY ALLEN

August 31, 1980

November 21, 1981

CURRENT COPY

November 21, 1977

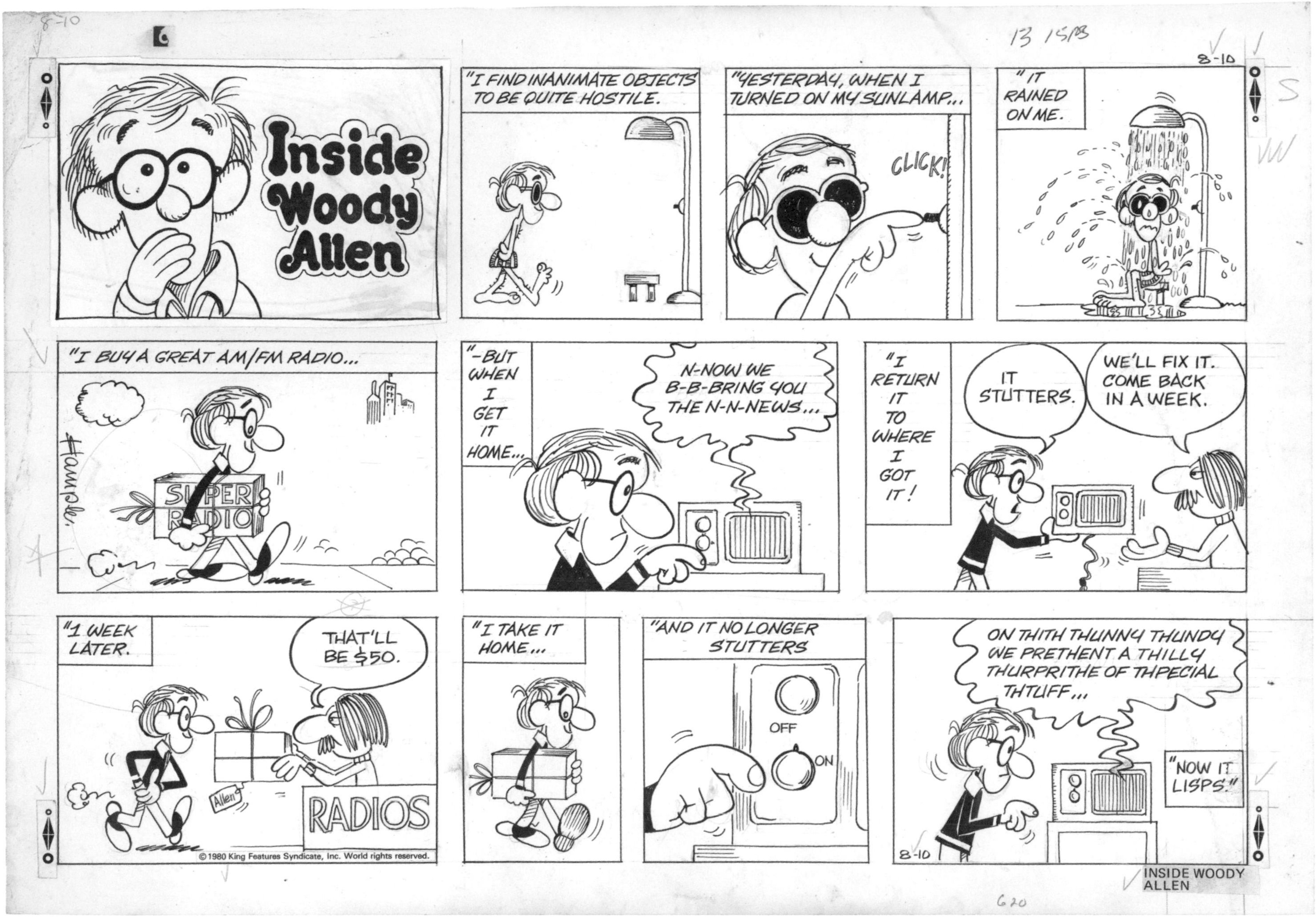
Inside Woody Allen
"I FIND INANIMATE OBJECTS TO BE QUITE HOSTILE.
"YESTERDAY, WHEN I TURNED ON MY SUNLAMP...
CLICK!
"IT RAINED ON ME.
"I BUY A GREAT AM/FM RADIO...
SUPER RADIO
"-BUT WHEN I GET IT HOME...
N-NOW WE B-B-BRING YOU THE N-N-NEWS...
"I RETURN IT TO WHERE I GOT IT!
IT STUTTERS.
WE'LL FIX IT. COME BACK IN A WEEK.
"1 WEEK LATER.
THAT'LL BE $50.
Allen
RADIOS
© 1980 King Features Syndicate, Inc. World rights reserved.
"I TAKE IT HOME...
"AND IT NO LONGER STUTTERS
OFF
ON
ON THITH THUNNY THUNDY WE PRETHENT A THILLY THURPRITHE OF THPECIAL THTUFF...
"NOW IT LISPS!"
INSIDE WOODY ALLEN

August 10, 1980

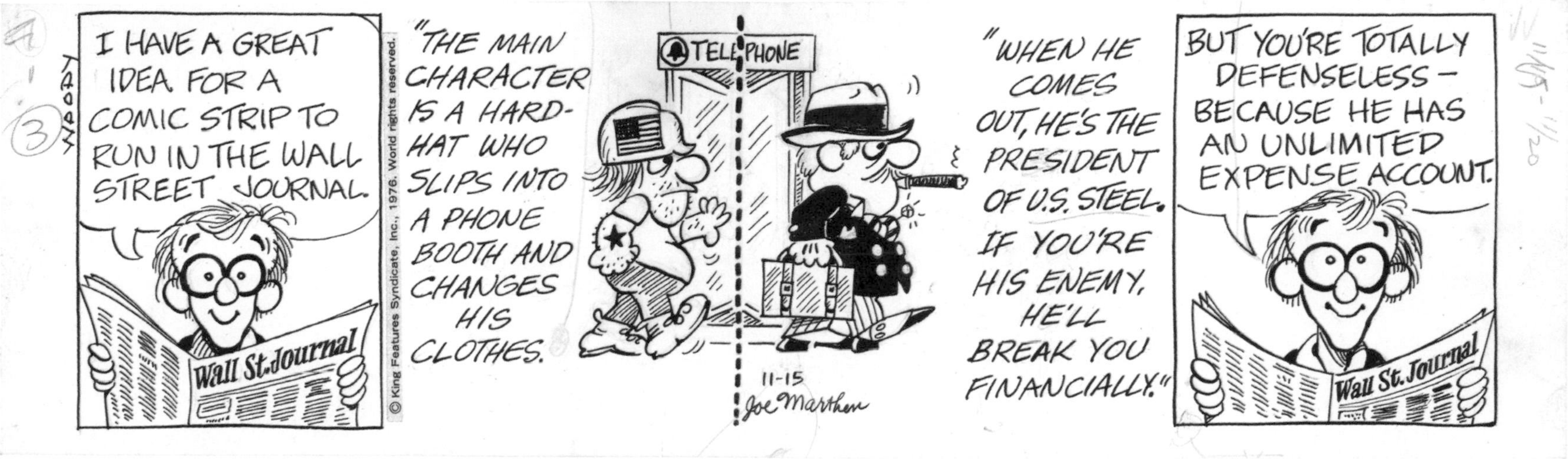
I HAVE A GREAT IDEA FOR A COMIC STRIP TO RUN IN THE WALL STREET JOURNAL.
Wall St. Journal
© King Features Syndicate, Inc., 1976. World rights reserved.
"THE MAIN CHARACTER IS A HARD-HAT WHO SLIPS INTO A PHONE BOOTH AND CHANGES HIS CLOTHES.
TELEPHONE
11-15
"WHEN HE COMES OUT, HE'S THE PRESIDENT OF U.S. STEEL.
IF YOU'RE HIS ENEMY, HE'LL BREAK YOU FINANCIALLY."
BUT YOU'RE TOTALLY DEFENSELESS - BECAUSE HE HAS AN UNLIMITED EXPENSE ACCOUNT.
Wall St. Journal

November 15, 1976

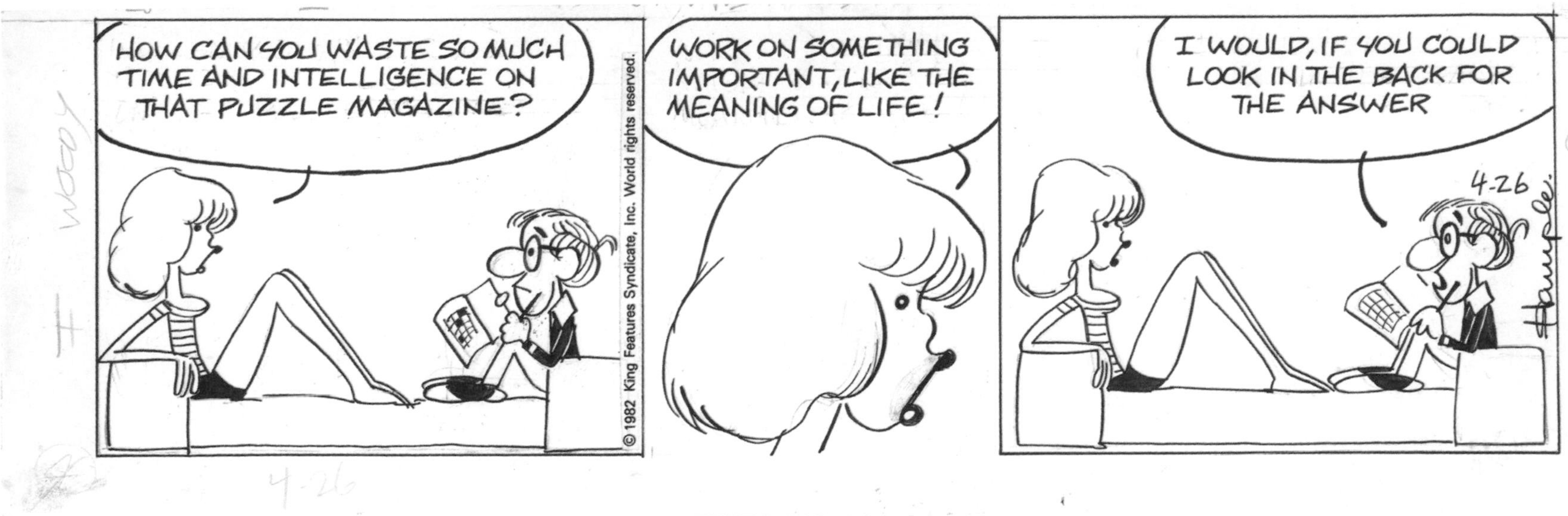
HOW CAN YOU WASTE SO MUCH TIME AND INTELLIGENCE ON THAT PUZZLE MAGAZINE?
© 1982 King Features Syndicate, Inc. World rights reserved.
WORK ON SOMETHING IMPORTANT, LIKE THE MEANING OF LIFE!
I WOULD, IF YOU COULD LOOK IN THE BACK FOR THE ANSWER
4-26

April 26, 1982

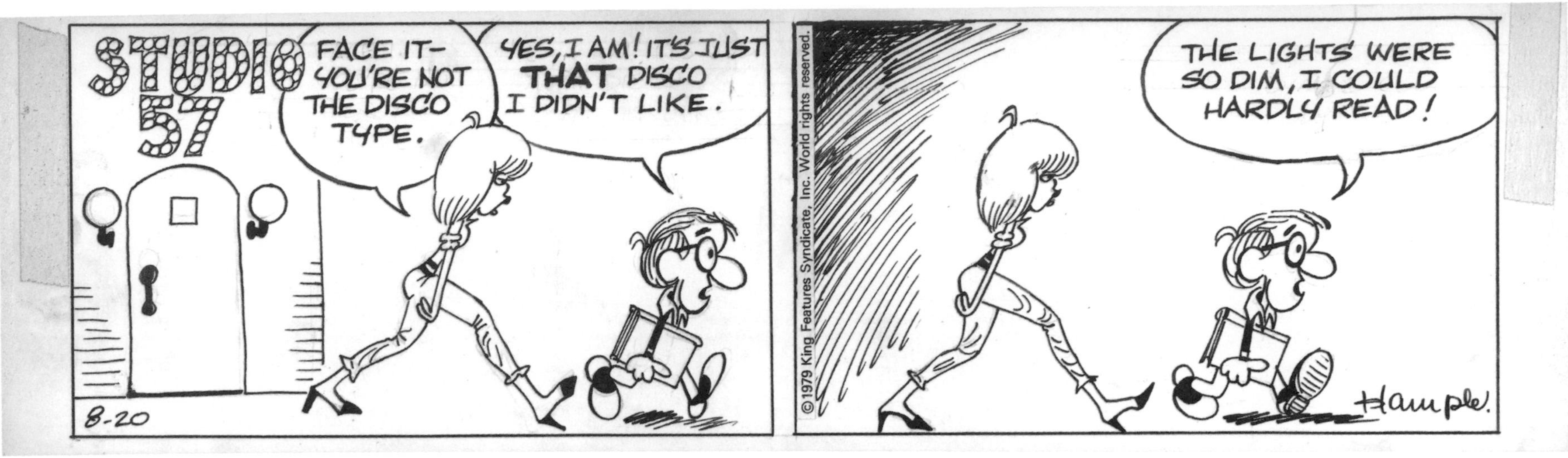
STUDIO 57
FACE IT– YOU'RE NOT THE DISCO TYPE.
YES, I AM! IT'S JUST THAT DISCO I DIDN'T LIKE.
8-20
© 1979 King Features Syndicate, Inc. World rights reserved.
THE LIGHTS WERE SO DIM, I COULD HARDLY READ!
Hample

August 20, 1979

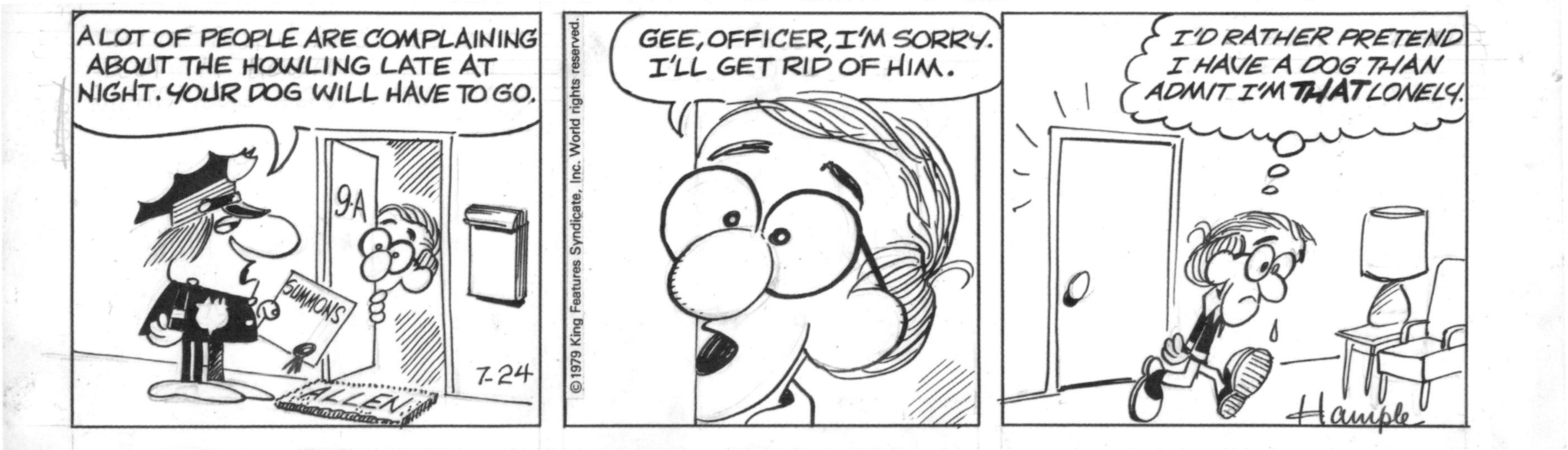
A LOT OF PEOPLE ARE COMPLAINING ABOUT THE HOWLING LATE AT NIGHT. YOUR DOG WILL HAVE TO GO.
9-A
SUMMONS
ALLEN
7-24
© 1979 King Features Syndicate, Inc. World rights reserved.
GEE, OFFICER, I'M SORRY. I'LL GET RID OF HIM.
I'D RATHER PRETEND I HAVE A DOG THAN ADMIT I'M THAT LONELY.
Hample

July 24, 1979

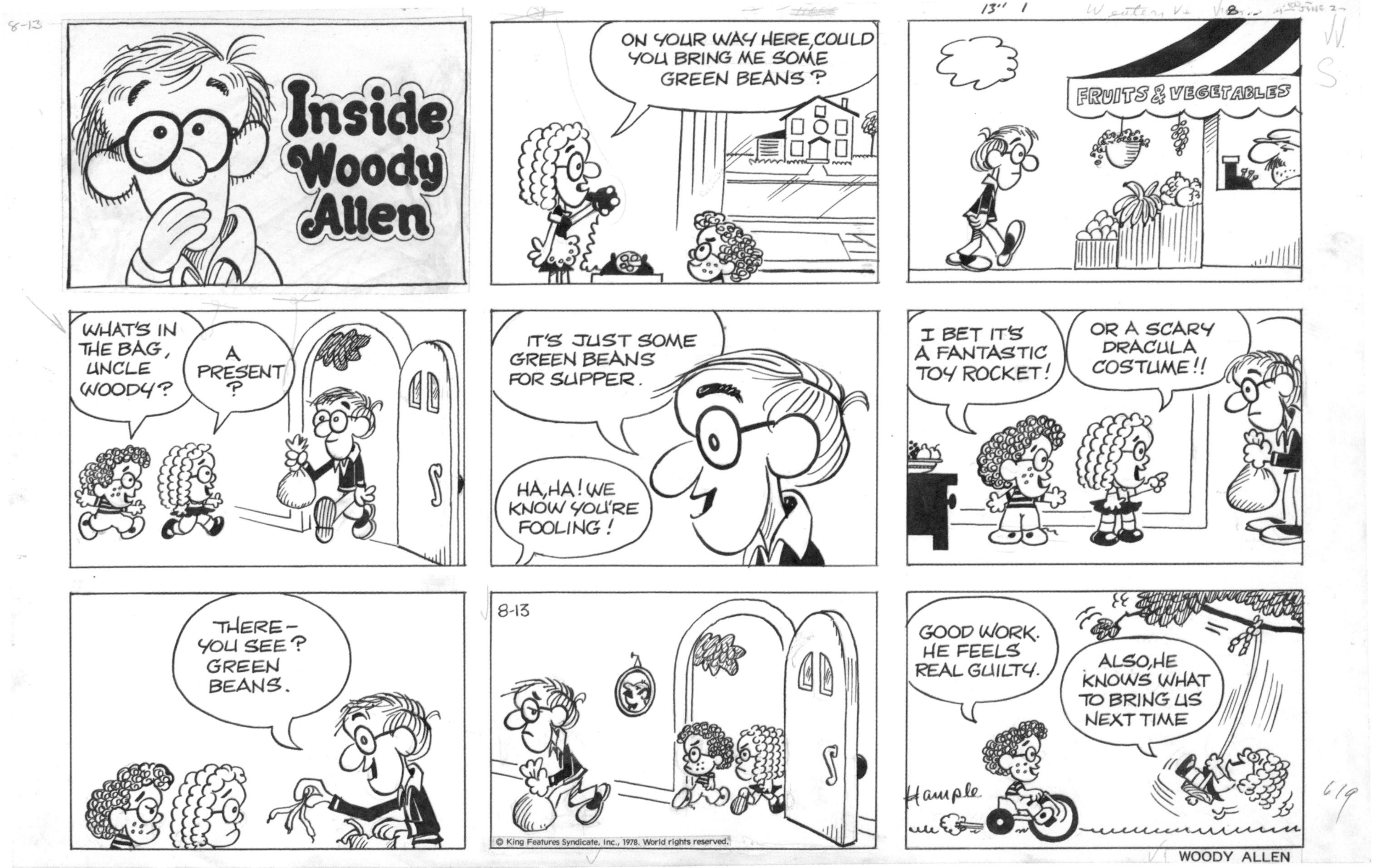
8-13
Inside Woody Allen
ON YOUR WAY HERE, COULD YOU BRING ME SOME GREEN BEANS?
FRUITS & VEGETABLES
WHAT'S IN THE BAG, UNCLE WOODY?
A PRESENT?
IT'S JUST SOME GREEN BEANS FOR SUPPER.
HA, HA! WE KNOW YOU'RE FOOLING!
I BET IT'S A FANTASTIC TOY ROCKET!
OR A SCARY DRACULA COSTUME!!
THERE- YOU SEE? GREEN BEANS.
8-13
© King Features Syndicate, Inc., 1978. World rights reserved.
GOOD WORK. HE FEELS REAL GUILTY.
ALSO, HE KNOWS WHAT TO BRING US NEXT TIME
Hample
WOODY ALLEN

August 13, 1978

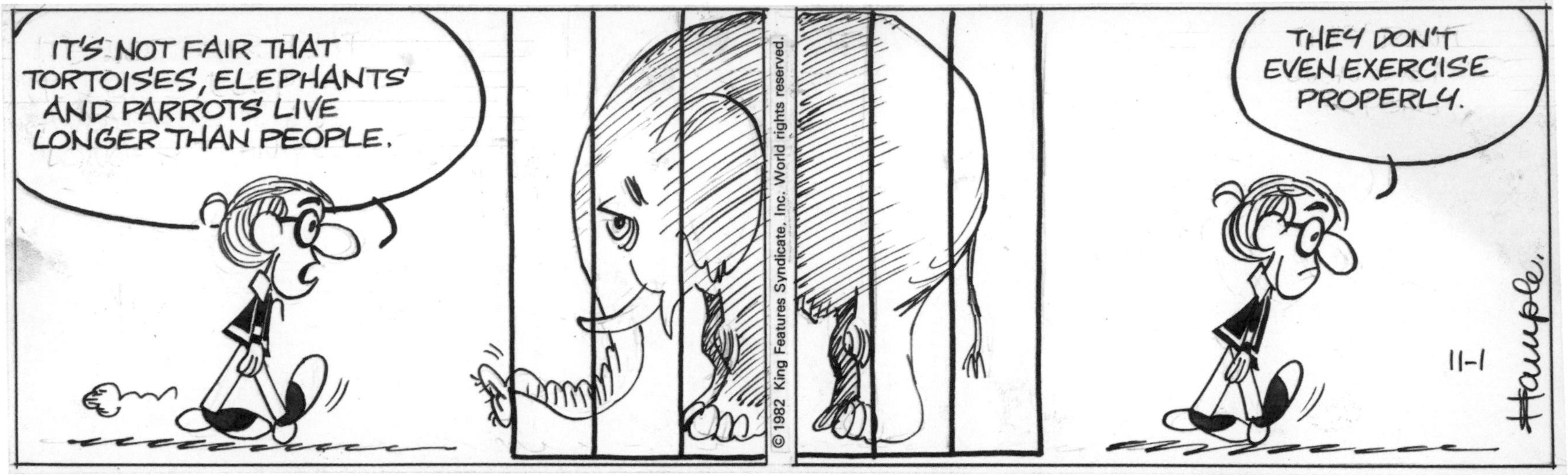
IT'S NOT FAIR THAT TORTOISES, ELEPHANTS AND PARROTS LIVE LONGER THAN PEOPLE.
© 1982 King Features Syndicate, Inc. World rights reserved.
THEY DON'T EVEN EXERCISE PROPERLY.
11-1
Hample

November 1, 1982

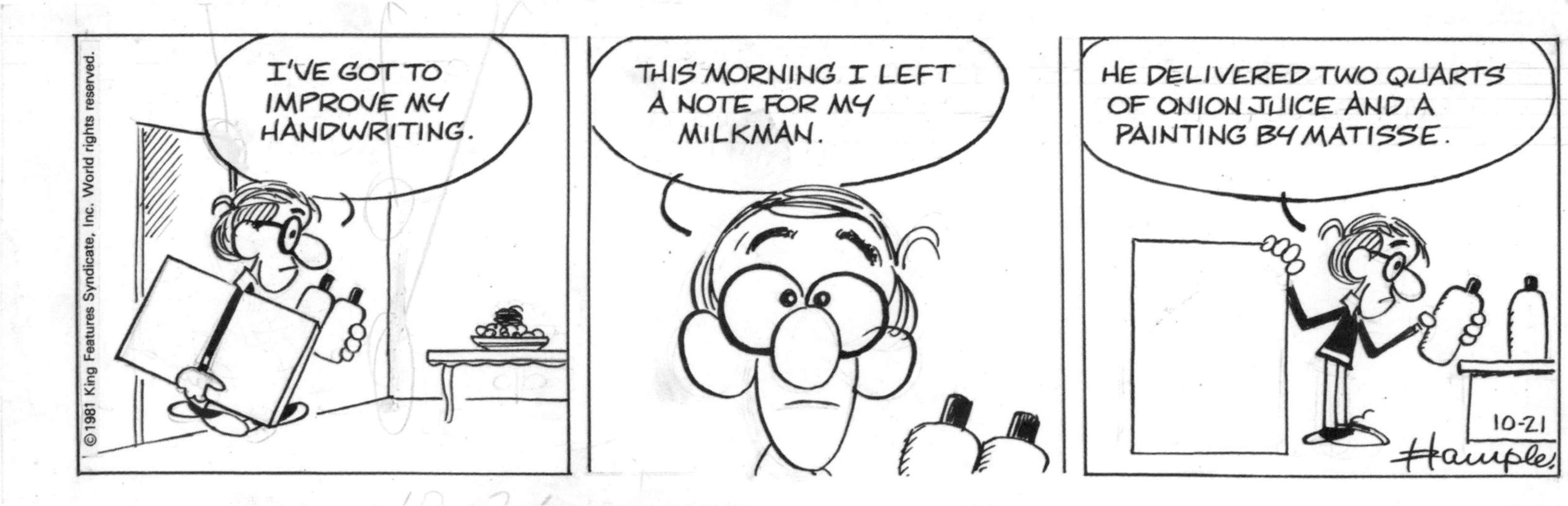
© 1981 King Features Syndicate, Inc. World rights reserved.
I'VE GOT TO IMPROVE MY HANDWRITING.
THIS MORNING I LEFT A NOTE FOR MY MILKMAN.
HE DELIVERED TWO QUARTS OF ONION JUICE AND A PAINTING BY MATISSE.
10-21
Hample

October 21, 1981

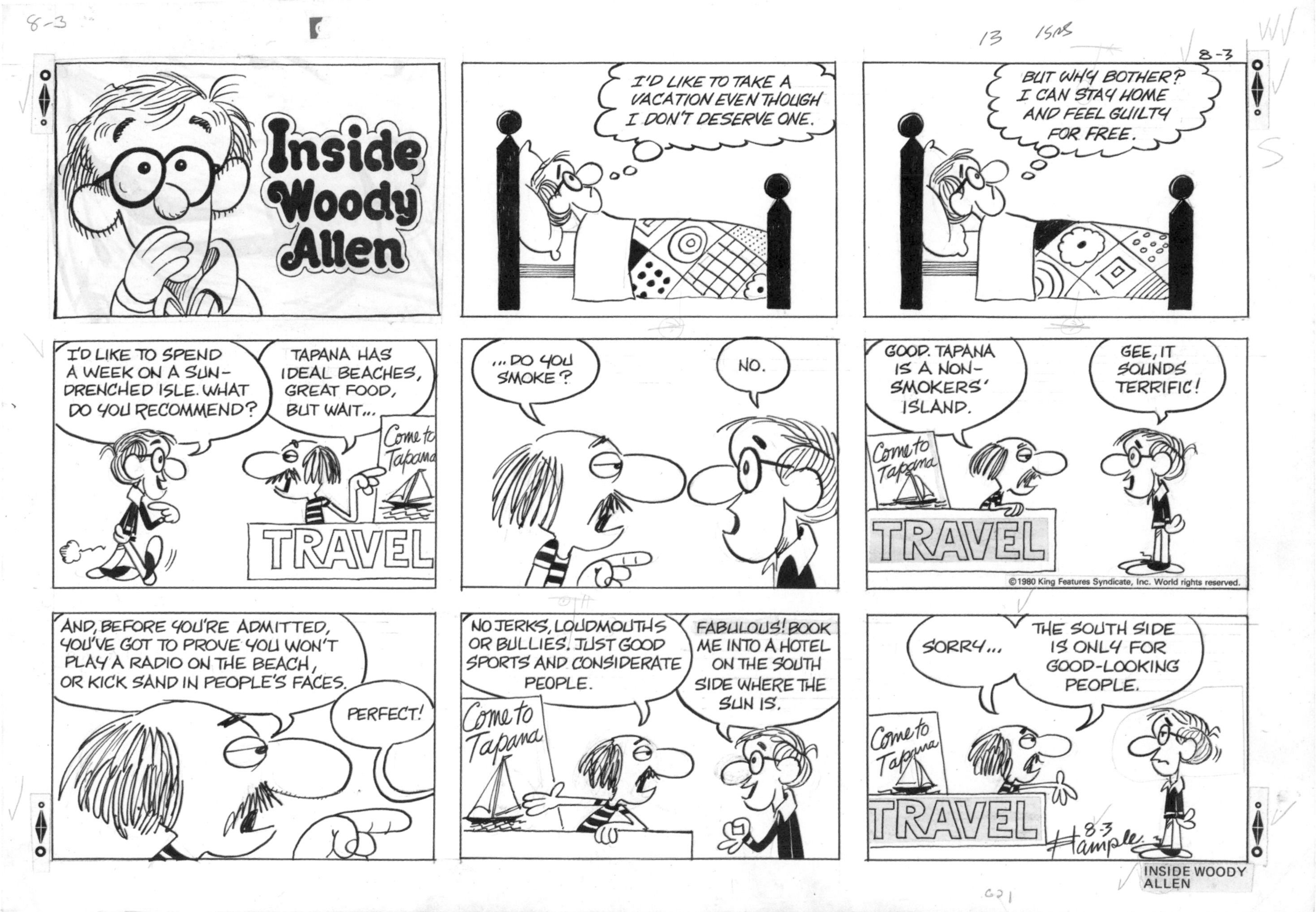
Inside Woody Allen
I'D LIKE TO TAKE A VACATION EVEN THOUGH I DON'T DESERVE ONE.
BUT WHY BOTHER? I CAN STAY HOME AND FEEL GUILTY FOR FREE.
I'D LIKE TO SPEND A WEEK ON A SUN-DRENCHED ISLE. WHAT DO YOU RECOMMEND?
TAPANA HAS IDEAL BEACHES, GREAT FOOD, BUT WAIT...
Come to Tapana
TRAVEL
...DO YOU SMOKE?
NO.
GOOD. TAPANA IS A NON-SMOKERS' ISLAND.
GEE, IT SOUNDS TERRIFIC!
Come to Tapana
TRAVEL
©1980 King Features Syndicate, Inc. World rights reserved.
AND, BEFORE YOU'RE ADMITTED, YOU'VE GOT TO PROVE YOU WON'T PLAY A RADIO ON THE BEACH, OR KICK SAND IN PEOPLE'S FACES.
PERFECT!
NO JERKS, LOUDMOUTHS OR BULLIES. JUST GOOD SPORTS AND CONSIDERATE PEOPLE.
Come to Tapana
FABULOUS! BOOK ME INTO A HOTEL ON THE SOUTH SIDE WHERE THE SUN IS.
SORRY...
THE SOUTH SIDE IS ONLY FOR GOOD-LOOKING PEOPLE.
Come to Tapana
TRAVEL
8-3
Hample
INSIDE WOODY ALLEN

August 3, 1980

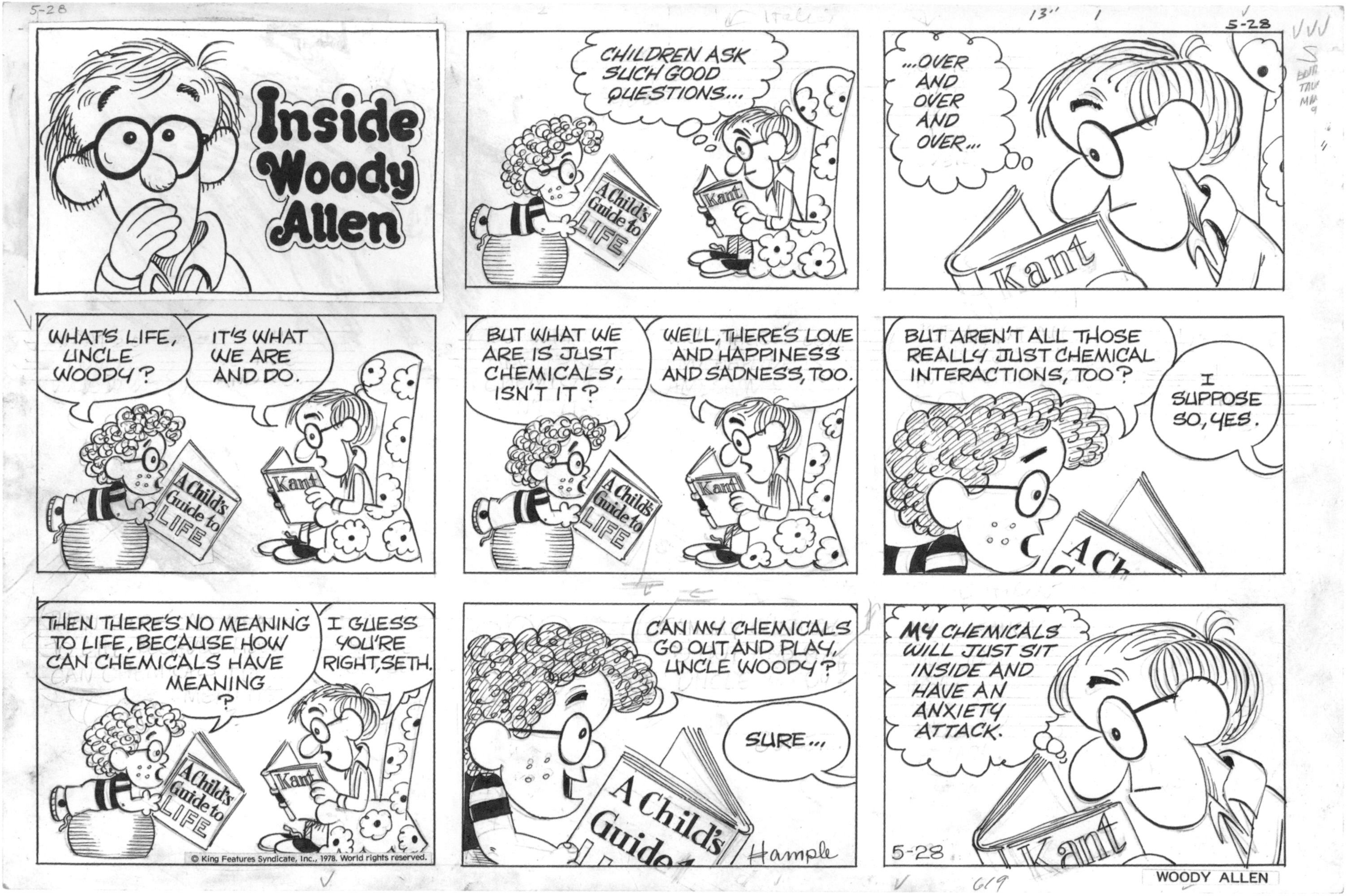
Inside Woody Allen
CHILDREN ASK SUCH GOOD QUESTIONS...
A Child's Guide to LIFE
Kant
...OVER AND OVER AND OVER...
Kant
WHAT'S LIFE, UNCLE WOODY?
IT'S WHAT WE ARE AND DO.
BUT WHAT WE ARE IS JUST CHEMICALS, ISN'T IT?
WELL, THERE'S LOVE AND HAPPINESS AND SADNESS, TOO.
BUT AREN'T ALL THOSE REALLY JUST CHEMICAL INTERACTIONS, TOO?
I SUPPOSE SO, YES.
THEN THERE'S NO MEANING TO LIFE, BECAUSE HOW CAN CHEMICALS HAVE MEANING?
I GUESS YOU'RE RIGHT, SETH.
© King Features Syndicate, Inc., 1978. World rights reserved.
CAN MY CHEMICALS GO OUT AND PLAY, UNCLE WOODY?
SURE...
A Child's Guide
Hample
MY CHEMICALS WILL JUST SIT INSIDE AND HAVE AN ANXIETY ATTACK.
Kant
5-28
WOODY ALLEN

May 28, 1978

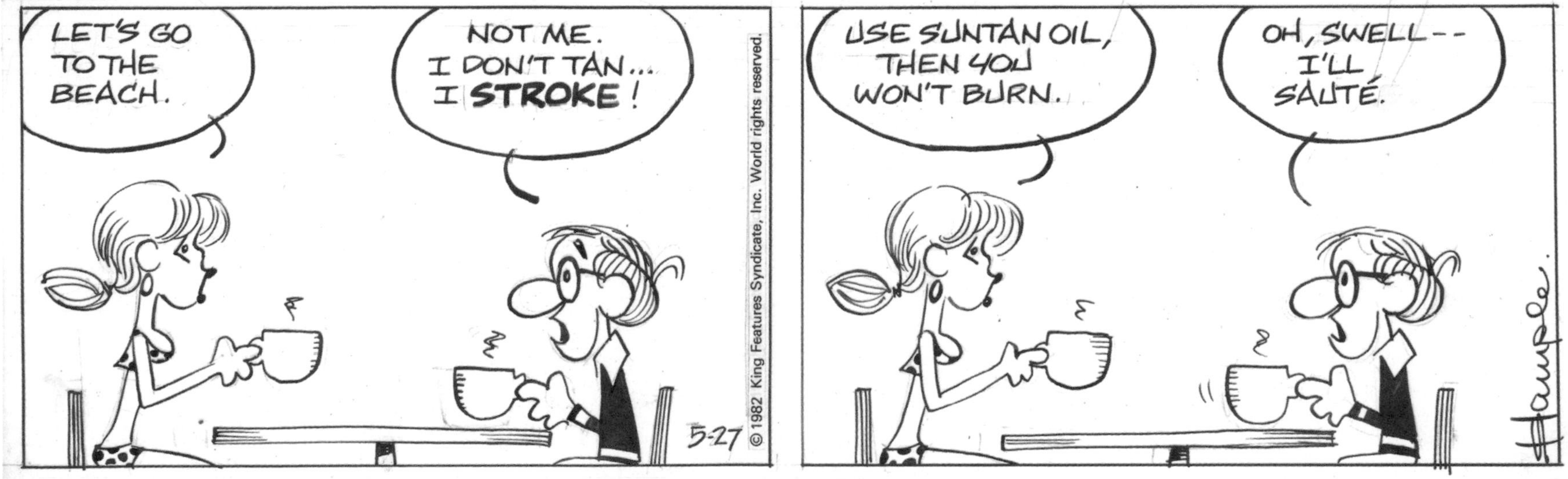
LET'S GO TO THE BEACH.
NOT ME. I DON'T TAN... I STROKE!
USE SUNTAN OIL, THEN YOU WON'T BURN.
OH, SWELL-- I'LL SAUTÉ.
© 1982 King Features Syndicate, Inc. World rights reserved.
5-27
Hample

May 27, 1982

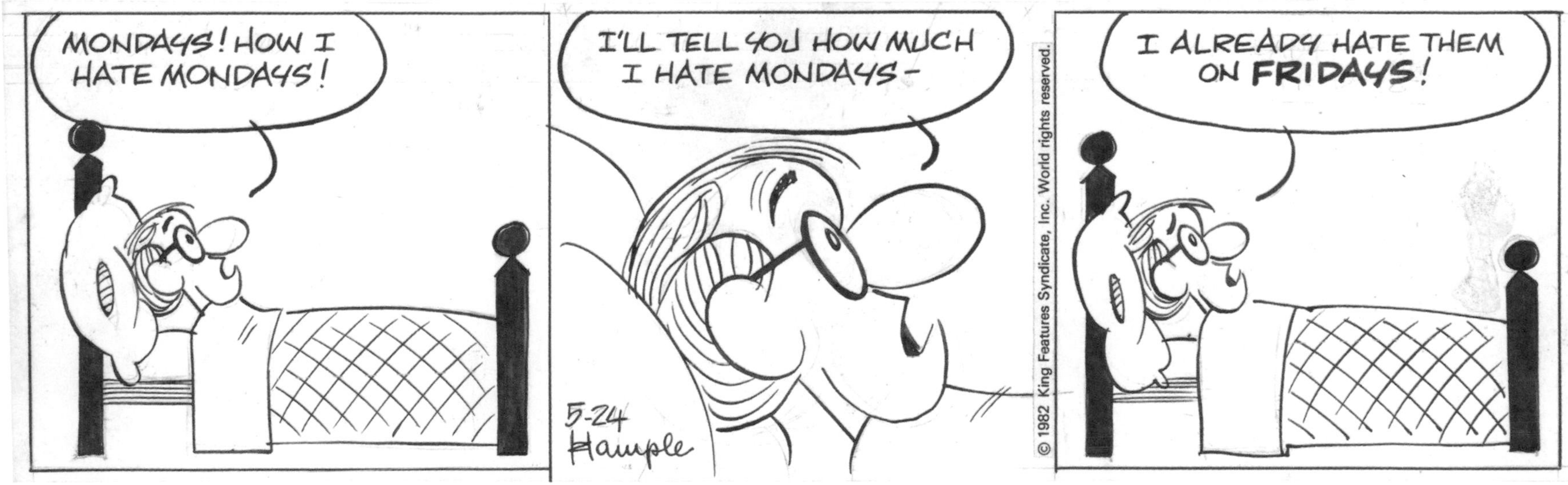
MONDAYS! HOW I HATE MONDAYS!
I'LL TELL YOU HOW MUCH I HATE MONDAYS-
I ALREADY HATE THEM ON FRIDAYS!
5-24
Hample
© 1982 King Features Syndicate, Inc. World rights reserved.

May 24, 1982

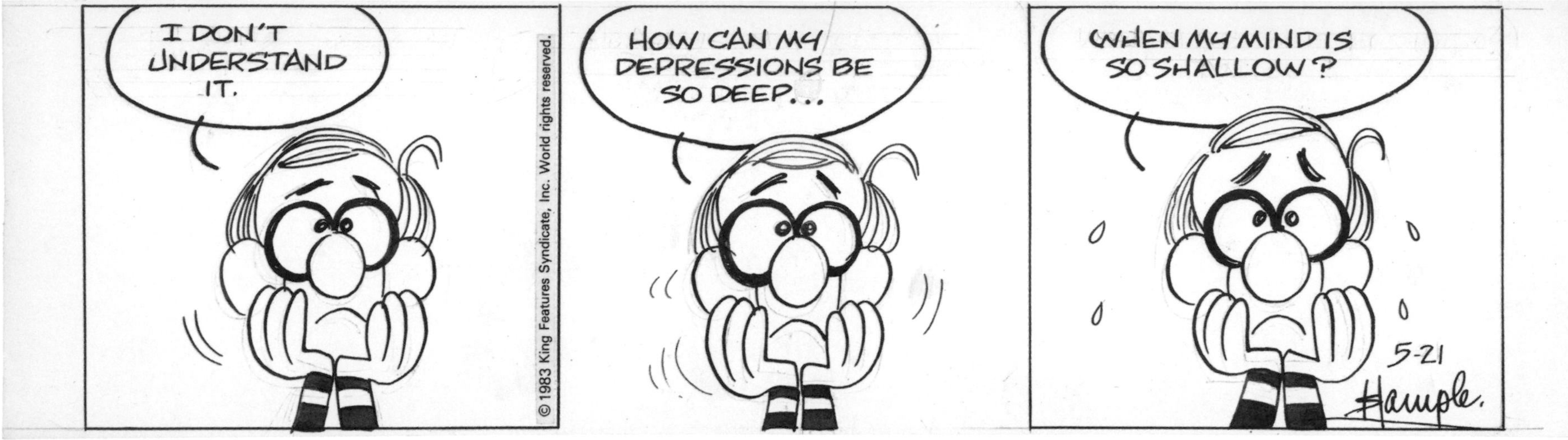
I DON'T UNDERSTAND IT.
© 1983 King Features Syndicate, Inc. World rights reserved.
HOW CAN MY DEPRESSIONS BE SO DEEP...
WHEN MY MIND IS SO SHALLOW?
5-21
Hample.

May 21, 1983

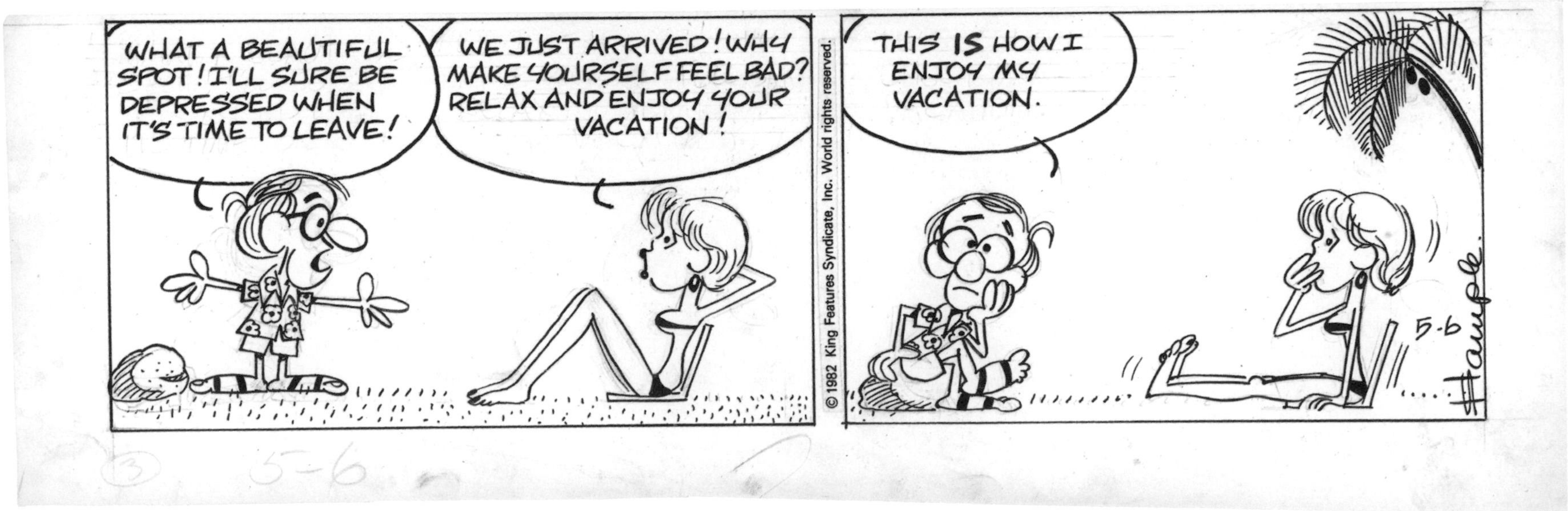
WHAT A BEAUTIFUL SPOT! I'LL SURE BE DEPRESSED WHEN IT'S TIME TO LEAVE!
WE JUST ARRIVED! WHY MAKE YOURSELF FEEL BAD? RELAX AND ENJOY YOUR VACATION!
© 1982 King Features Syndicate, Inc. World rights reserved.
THIS **IS** HOW I ENJOY MY VACATION.
5-6
Hample

May 6, 1982

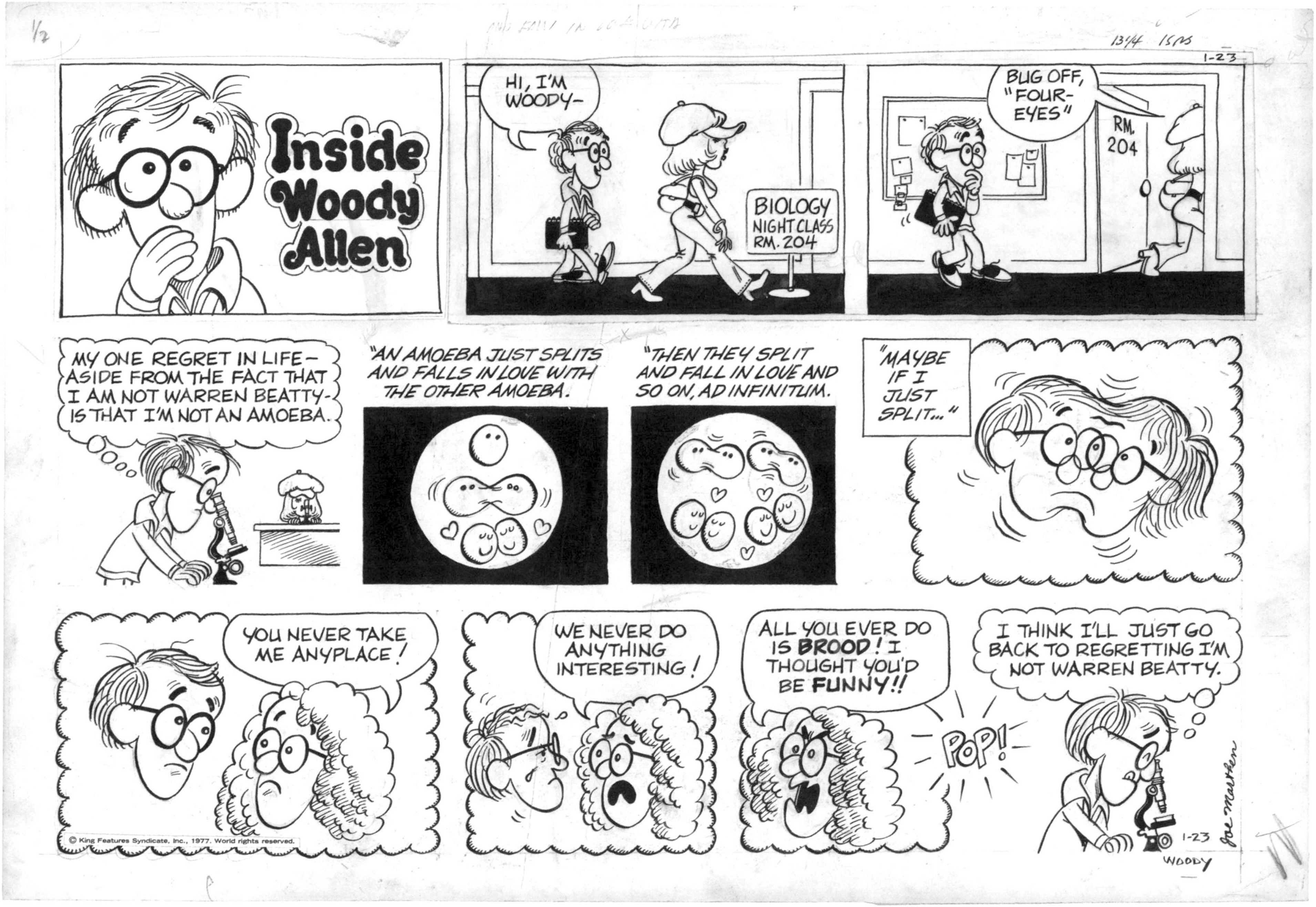
Inside Woody Allen
HI, I'M WOODY-
BIOLOGY NIGHT CLASS RM. 204
BUG OFF, "FOUR-EYES"
RM. 204
MY ONE REGRET IN LIFE- ASIDE FROM THE FACT THAT I AM NOT WARREN BEATTY- IS THAT I'M NOT AN AMOEBA.
"AN AMOEBA JUST SPLITS AND FALLS IN LOVE WITH THE OTHER AMOEBA.
"THEN THEY SPLIT AND FALL IN LOVE AND SO ON, AD INFINITUM.
"MAYBE IF I JUST SPLIT..."
YOU NEVER TAKE ME ANYPLACE!
WE NEVER DO ANYTHING INTERESTING!
ALL YOU EVER DO IS BROOD! I THOUGHT YOU'D BE FUNNY!!
POP!
I THINK I'LL JUST GO BACK TO REGRETTING I'M NOT WARREN BEATTY.
© King Features Syndicate, Inc., 1977. World rights reserved.
1-23
Joe Marthen
WOODY

January 23, 1977

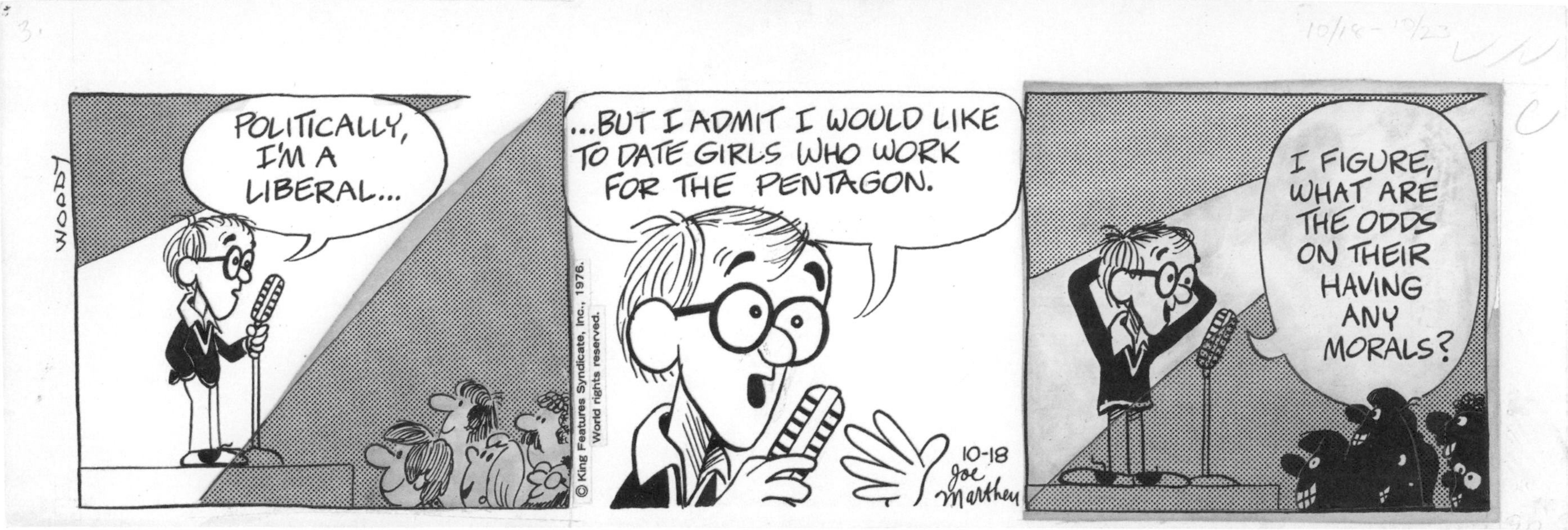
WOOD
POLITICALLY, I'M A LIBERAL...
...BUT I ADMIT I WOULD LIKE TO DATE GIRLS WHO WORK FOR THE PENTAGON.
© King Features Syndicate, Inc., 1976. World rights reserved.
10-18 Joe Martin
I FIGURE, WHAT ARE THE ODDS ON THEIR HAVING ANY MORALS?

October 18, 1976

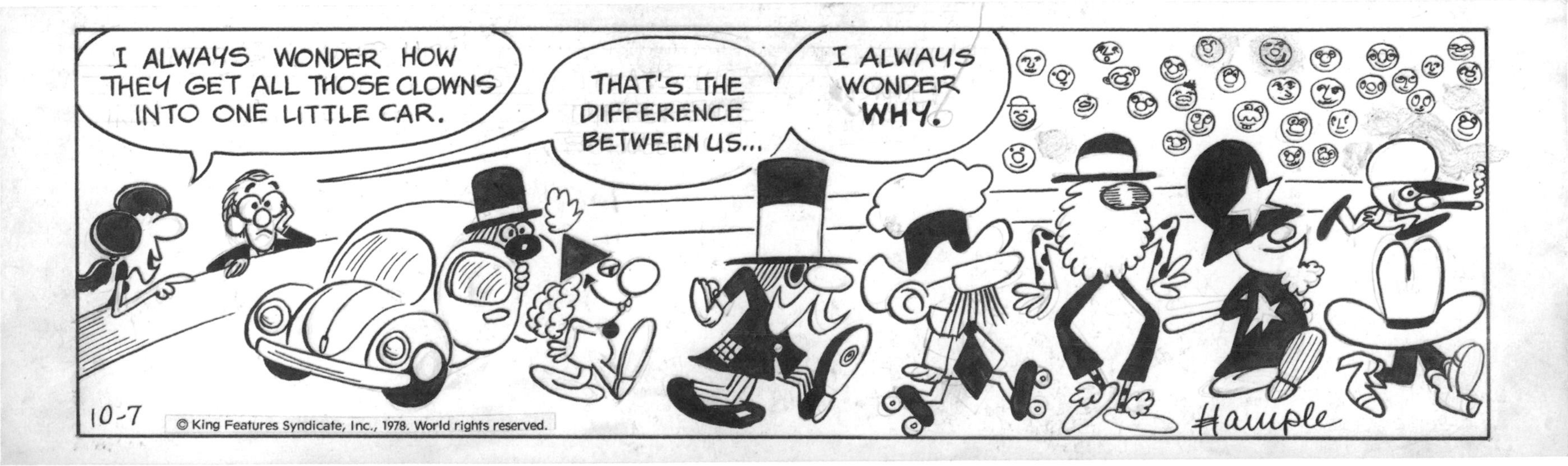
I ALWAYS WONDER HOW THEY GET ALL THOSE CLOWNS INTO ONE LITTLE CAR.
THAT'S THE DIFFERENCE BETWEEN US...
I ALWAYS WONDER WHY.
10-7
© King Features Syndicate, Inc., 1978. World rights reserved.
Hample

October 7, 1978

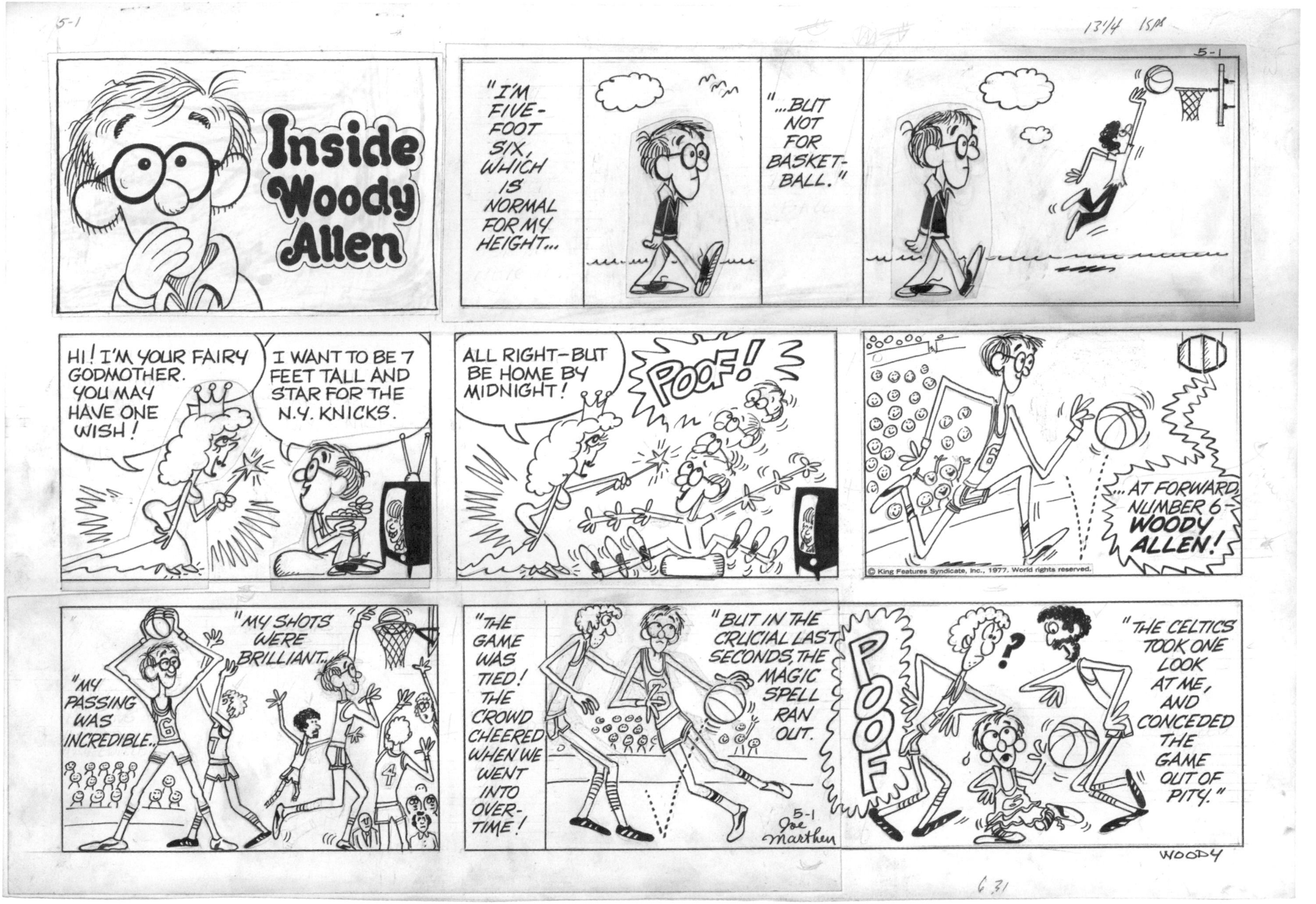
Inside Woody Allen
"I'M FIVE-FOOT SIX, WHICH IS NORMAL FOR MY HEIGHT...
"...BUT NOT FOR BASKET-BALL."
HI! I'M YOUR FAIRY GODMOTHER. YOU MAY HAVE ONE WISH!
I WANT TO BE 7 FEET TALL AND STAR FOR THE N.Y. KNICKS.
ALL RIGHT—BUT BE HOME BY MIDNIGHT!
POOF!
...AT FORWARD NUMBER 6—WOODY ALLEN!
© King Features Syndicate, Inc., 1977. World rights reserved.
"MY PASSING WAS INCREDIBLE...
"MY SHOTS WERE BRILLIANT...
"THE GAME WAS TIED! THE CROWD CHEERED WHEN WE WENT INTO OVER-TIME!
"BUT IN THE CRUCIAL LAST SECONDS, THE MAGIC SPELL RAN OUT.
5-1 Joe Marthen
POOF
"THE CELTICS TOOK ONE LOOK AT ME, AND CONCEDED THE GAME OUT OF PITY."
WOODY

May 1, 1977

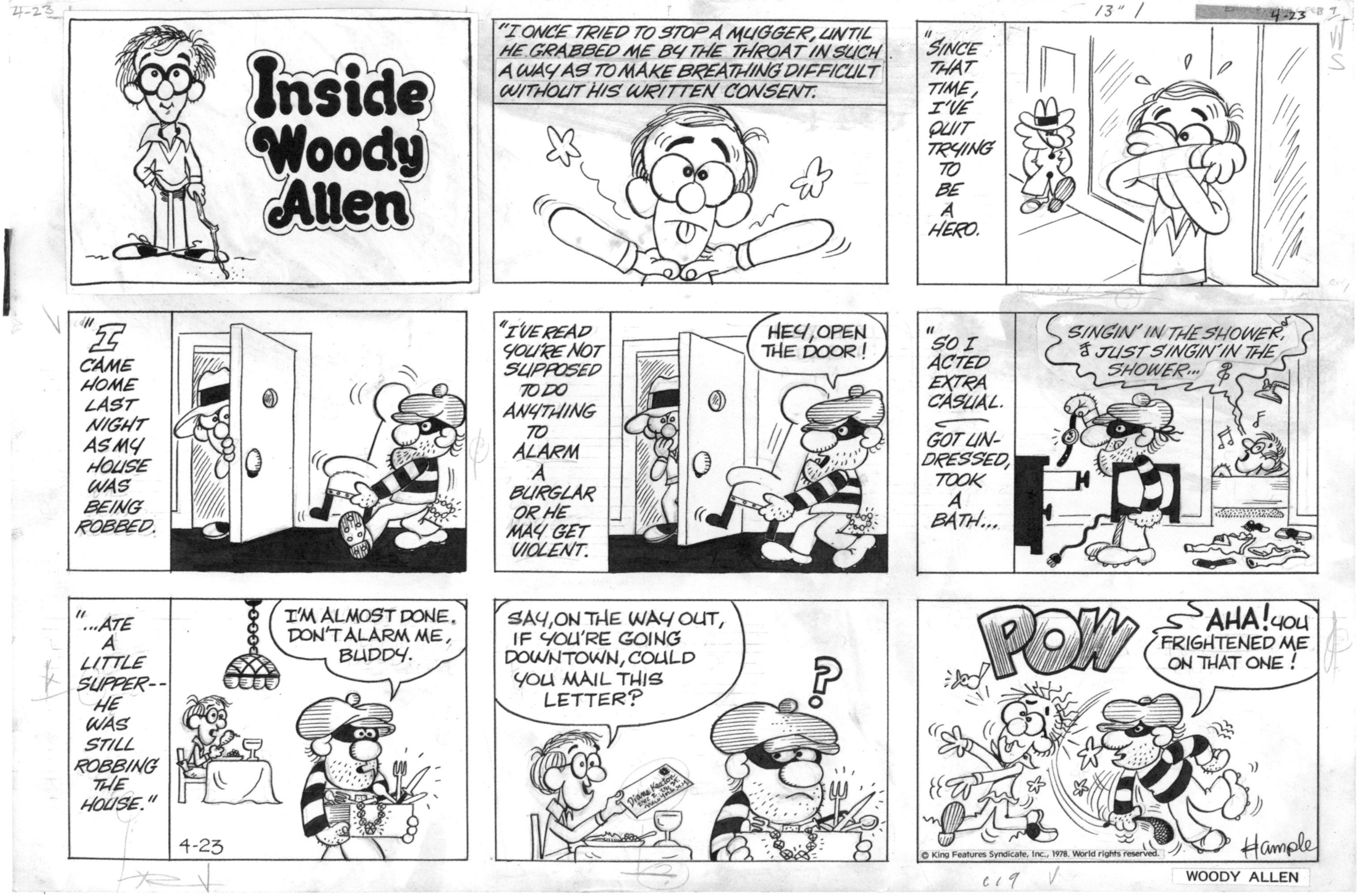
Inside Woody Allen
"I ONCE TRIED TO STOP A MUGGER, UNTIL HE GRABBED ME BY THE THROAT IN SUCH A WAY AS TO MAKE BREATHING DIFFICULT WITHOUT HIS WRITTEN CONSENT.
"SINCE THAT TIME, I'VE QUIT TRYING TO BE A HERO.
"I CAME HOME LAST NIGHT AS MY HOUSE WAS BEING ROBBED.
"I'VE READ YOU'RE NOT SUPPOSED TO DO ANYTHING TO ALARM A BURGLAR OR HE MAY GET VIOLENT.
HEY, OPEN THE DOOR!
"SO I ACTED EXTRA CASUAL.
GOT UNDRESSED, TOOK A BATH...
SINGIN' IN THE SHOWER, ♫ JUST SINGIN' IN THE SHOWER...
"...ATE A LITTLE SUPPER-- HE WAS STILL ROBBING THE HOUSE."
I'M ALMOST DONE. DON'T ALARM ME, BUDDY.
4-23
SAY, ON THE WAY OUT, IF YOU'RE GOING DOWNTOWN, COULD YOU MAIL THIS LETTER?
?
POW
AHA! YOU FRIGHTENED ME ON THAT ONE!
© King Features Syndicate, Inc., 1978. World rights reserved.
Hample
WOODY ALLEN

April 23, 1978

"IT IS ILLEGAL TO STRIKE PRISONERS IN JAILS—BUT THE SUPREME COURT RULES IT IS PERMISSIBLE TO BEAT SCHOOL CHILDREN."

THAT'S SURE GOING TO DISCOURAGE HARDENED CRIMINALS FROM GOING BACK TO SCHOOL.

April 17, 1982

WHAT'S THAT BIRD?

A CRESTED FINCH, WHICH LIVES ON NUTS AND BERRIES, WALKS UPSIDE-DOWN, AND CAN FLY RINGS AROUND THE COMMON JAY...

ACCORDING TO THIS BOOK, IT **IS** A COMMON JAY!

IT ALSO DOES IMITATIONS.

April 16, 1982

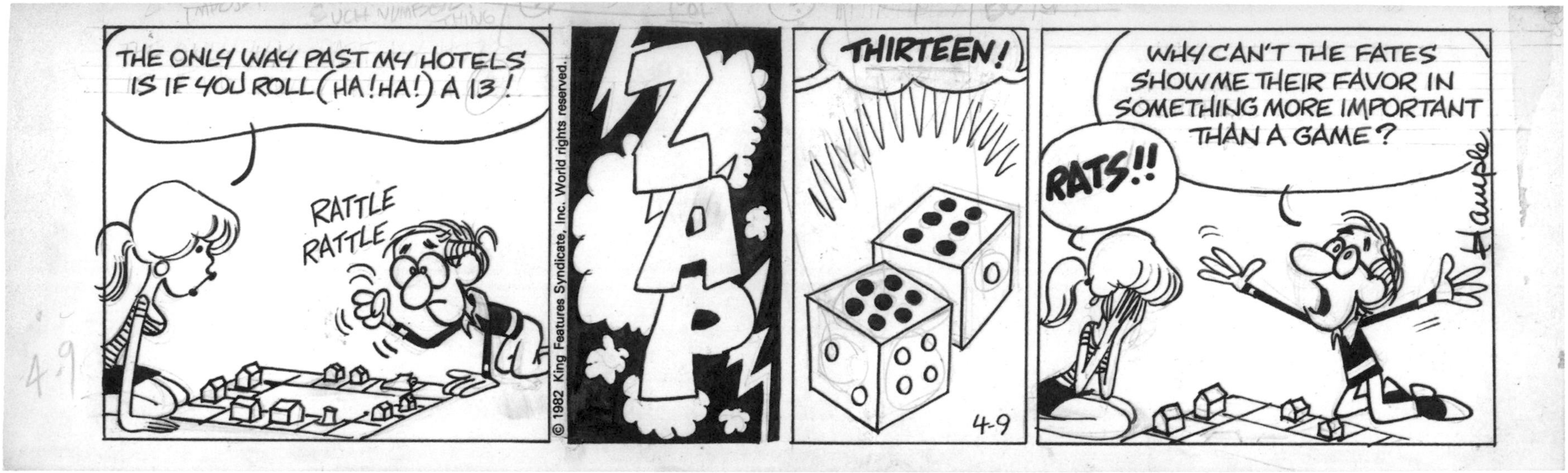
THE ONLY WAY PAST MY HOTELS IS IF YOU ROLL (HA! HA!) A 13!
RATTLE RATTLE
ZAP
THIRTEEN!
RATS!!
WHY CAN'T THE FATES SHOW ME THEIR FAVOR IN SOMETHING MORE IMPORTANT THAN A GAME?
© 1982 King Features Syndicate, Inc. World rights reserved.
4-9
Hample

April 9, 1982

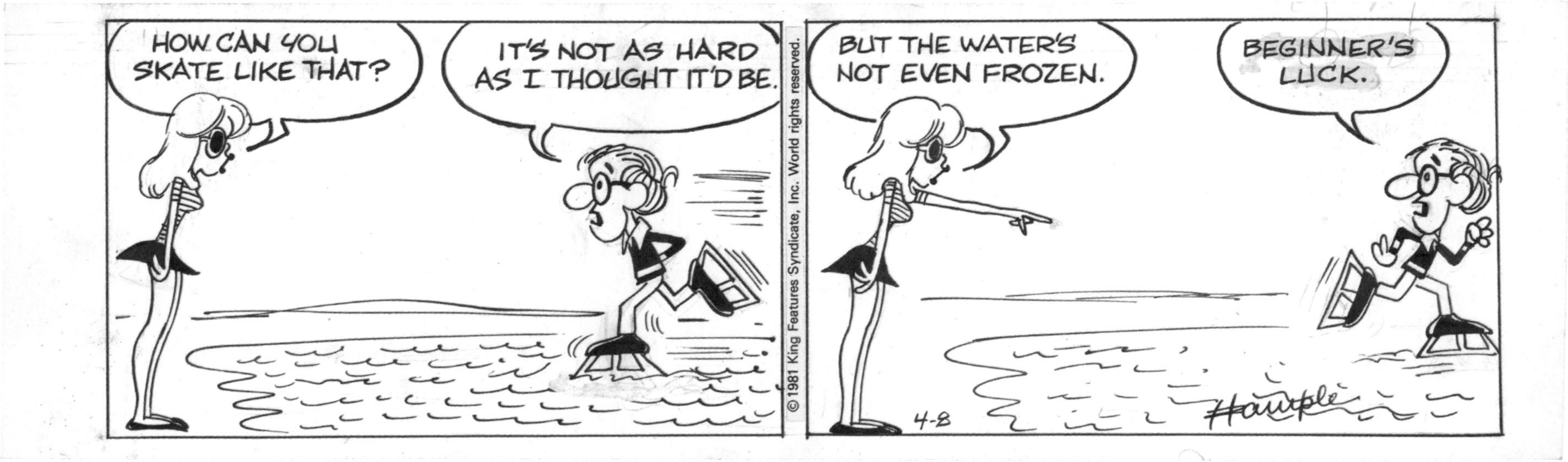
HOW CAN YOU SKATE LIKE THAT?
IT'S NOT AS HARD AS I THOUGHT IT'D BE.
BUT THE WATER'S NOT EVEN FROZEN.
BEGINNER'S LUCK.
© 1981 King Features Syndicate, Inc. World rights reserved.
4-8
Hample

April 8, 1981

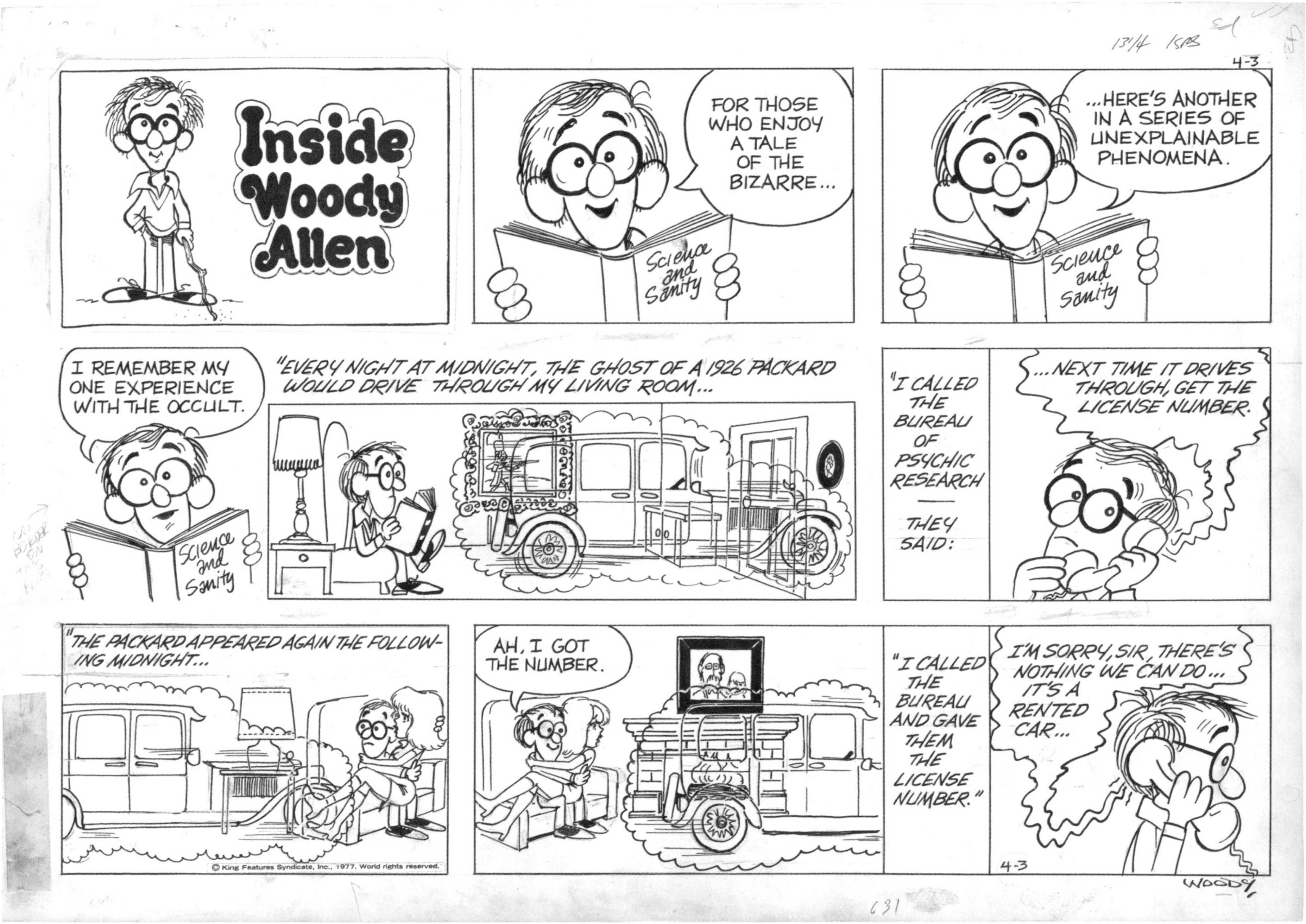
Inside Woody Allen
FOR THOSE WHO ENJOY A TALE OF THE BIZARRE...
Science and Sanity
...HERE'S ANOTHER IN A SERIES OF UNEXPLAINABLE PHENOMENA.
I REMEMBER MY ONE EXPERIENCE WITH THE OCCULT.
"EVERY NIGHT AT MIDNIGHT, THE GHOST OF A 1926 PACKARD WOULD DRIVE THROUGH MY LIVING ROOM...
"I CALLED THE BUREAU OF PSYCHIC RESEARCH — THEY SAID:
...NEXT TIME IT DRIVES THROUGH, GET THE LICENSE NUMBER.
"THE PACKARD APPEARED AGAIN THE FOLLOWING MIDNIGHT...
© King Features Syndicate, Inc., 1977. World rights reserved.
AH, I GOT THE NUMBER.
"I CALLED THE BUREAU AND GAVE THEM THE LICENSE NUMBER."
I'M SORRY, SIR, THERE'S NOTHING WE CAN DO... IT'S A RENTED CAR...
4-3
WOODY

April 3, 1977

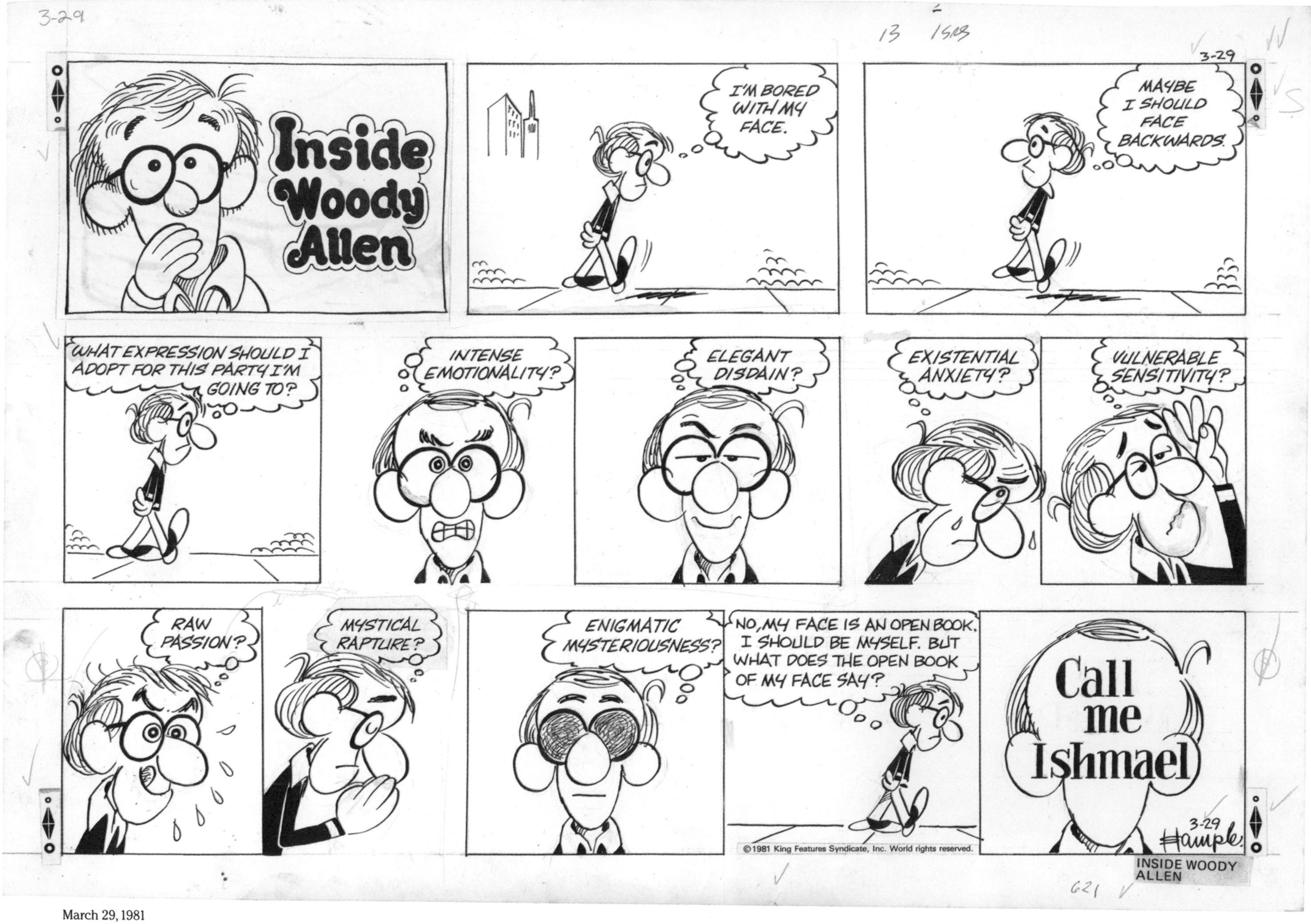

Inside Woody Allen
I'M BORED WITH MY FACE.
MAYBE I SHOULD FACE BACKWARDS.
WHAT EXPRESSION SHOULD I ADOPT FOR THIS PARTY I'M GOING TO?
INTENSE EMOTIONALITY?
ELEGANT DISDAIN?
EXISTENTIAL ANXIETY?
VULNERABLE SENSITIVITY?
RAW PASSION?
MYSTICAL RAPTURE?
ENIGMATIC MYSTERIOUSNESS?
NO, MY FACE IS AN OPEN BOOK. I SHOULD BE MYSELF. BUT WHAT DOES THE OPEN BOOK OF MY FACE SAY?
Call me Ishmael
©1981 King Features Syndicate, Inc. World rights reserved.
3-29
Hample
INSIDE WOODY ALLEN

March 29, 1981

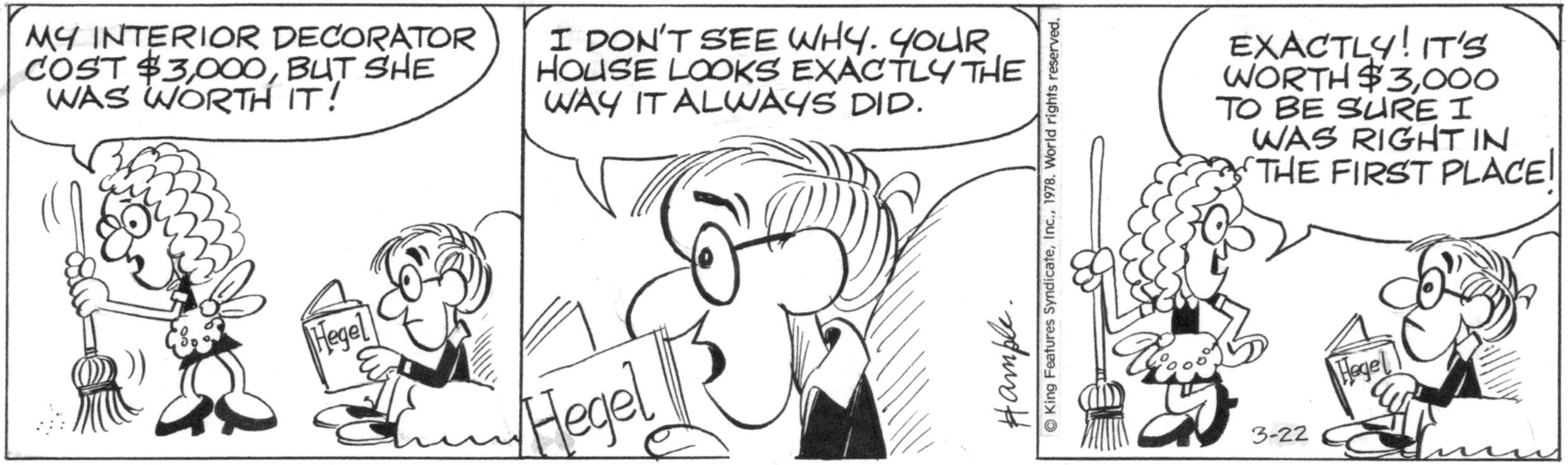
MY INTERIOR DECORATOR COST $3,000, BUT SHE WAS WORTH IT!
Hegel
I DON'T SEE WHY. YOUR HOUSE LOOKS EXACTLY THE WAY IT ALWAYS DID.
Hegel
Hample
© King Features Syndicate, Inc., 1978. World rights reserved.
EXACTLY! IT'S WORTH $3,000 TO BE SURE I WAS RIGHT IN THE FIRST PLACE!
Hegel
3-22

March 22 , 1978

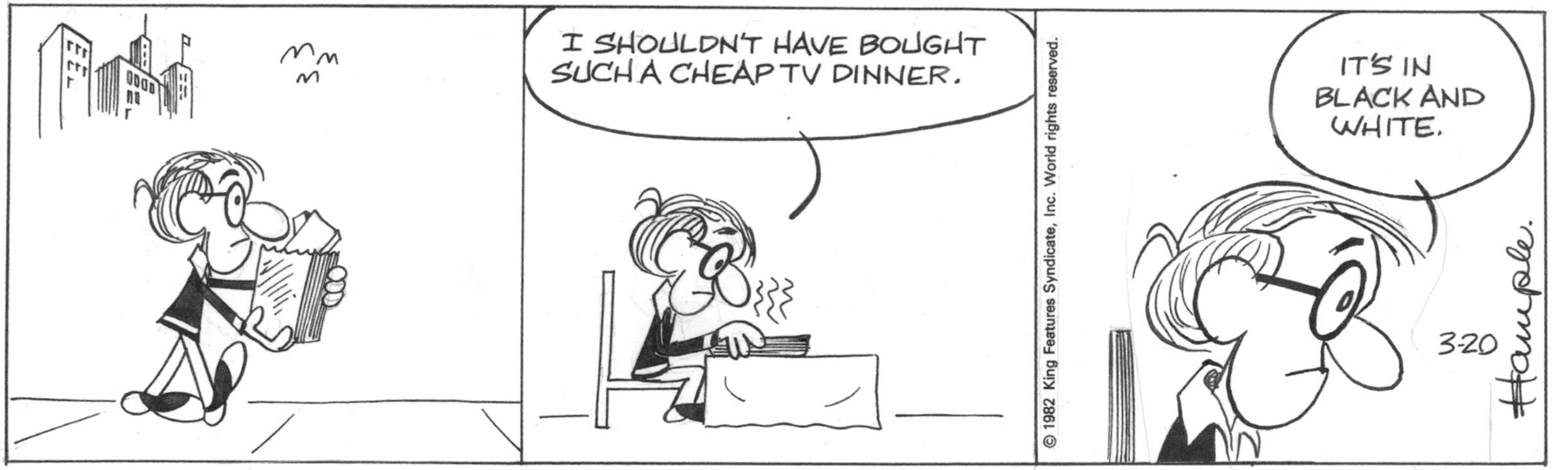
I SHOULDN'T HAVE BOUGHT SUCH A CHEAP TV DINNER.
© 1982 King Features Syndicate, Inc. World rights reserved.
IT'S IN BLACK AND WHITE.
3-20
Hample

March 20, 1982

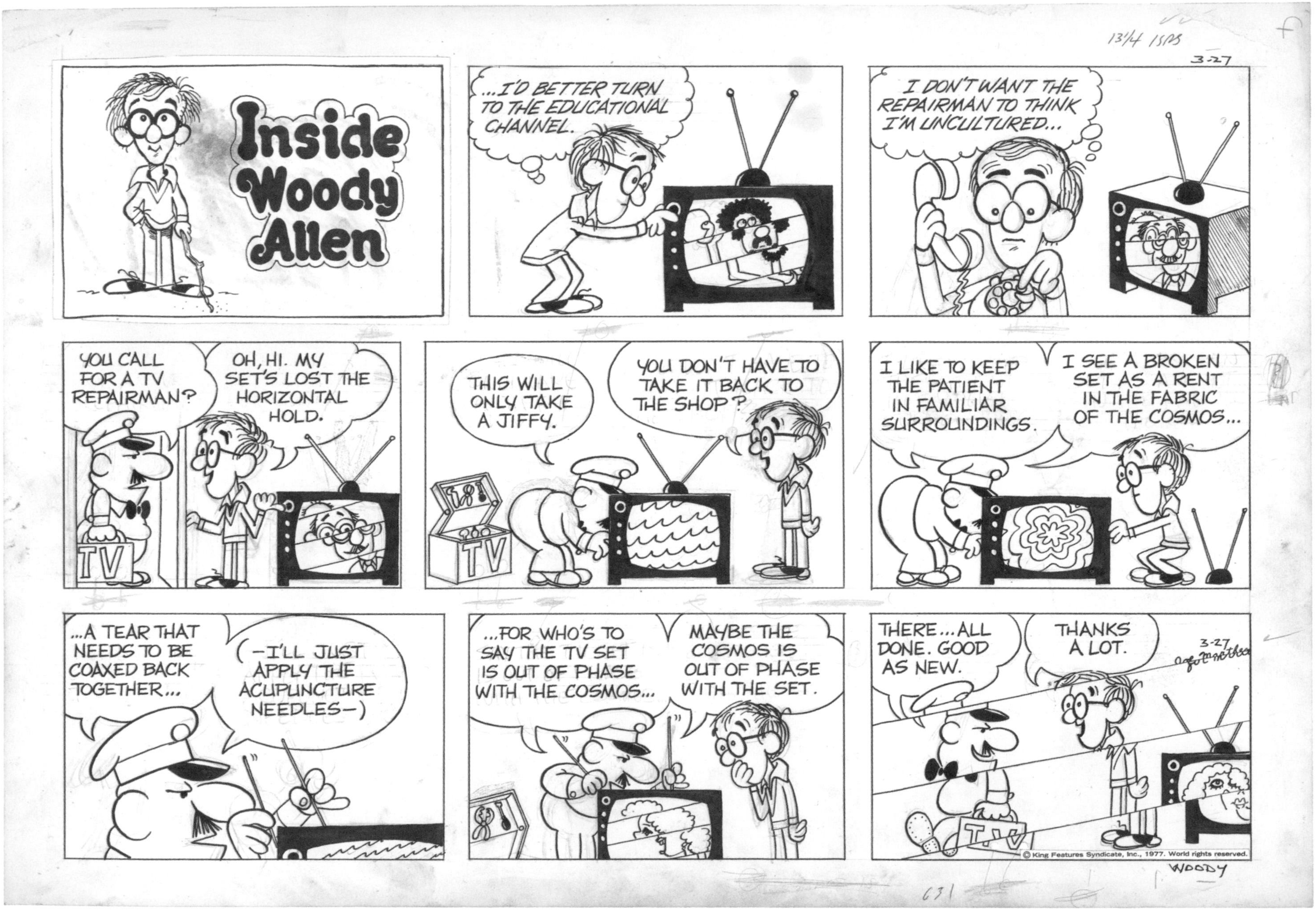
13 1/4 ISPS
3-27
Inside Woody Allen
...I'D BETTER TURN TO THE EDUCATIONAL CHANNEL.
I DON'T WANT THE REPAIRMAN TO THINK I'M UNCULTURED...
YOU CALL FOR A TV REPAIRMAN?
OH, HI. MY SET'S LOST THE HORIZONTAL HOLD.
TV
THIS WILL ONLY TAKE A JIFFY.
YOU DON'T HAVE TO TAKE IT BACK TO THE SHOP?
TV
I LIKE TO KEEP THE PATIENT IN FAMILIAR SURROUNDINGS.
I SEE A BROKEN SET AS A RENT IN THE FABRIC OF THE COSMOS...
...A TEAR THAT NEEDS TO BE COAXED BACK TOGETHER...
(-I'LL JUST APPLY THE ACUPUNCTURE NEEDLES-)
...FOR WHO'S TO SAY THE TV SET IS OUT OF PHASE WITH THE COSMOS...
MAYBE THE COSMOS IS OUT OF PHASE WITH THE SET.
THERE... ALL DONE. GOOD AS NEW.
THANKS A LOT.
3-27
TV
© King Features Syndicate, Inc., 1977. World rights reserved.
WOODY
631

March 27, 1977

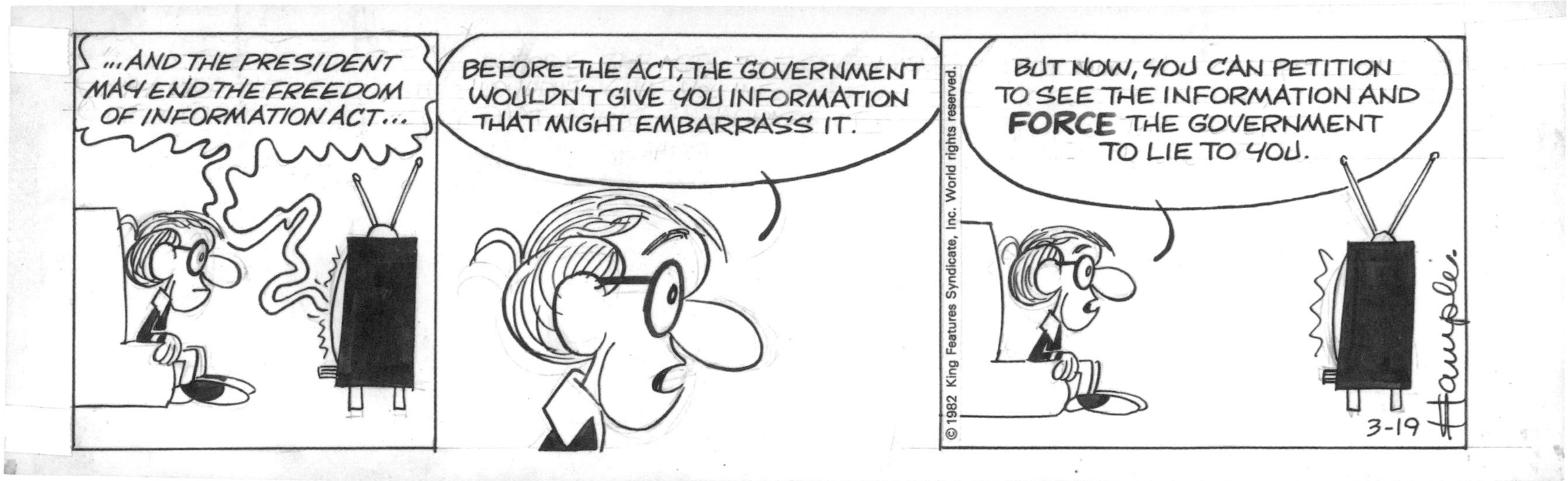
...AND THE PRESIDENT MAY END THE FREEDOM OF INFORMATION ACT...
BEFORE THE ACT, THE GOVERNMENT WOULDN'T GIVE YOU INFORMATION THAT MIGHT EMBARRASS IT.
BUT NOW, YOU CAN PETITION TO SEE THE INFORMATION AND **FORCE** THE GOVERNMENT TO LIE TO YOU.
© 1982 King Features Syndicate, Inc. World rights reserved.
3-19
Hample

March 19, 1982

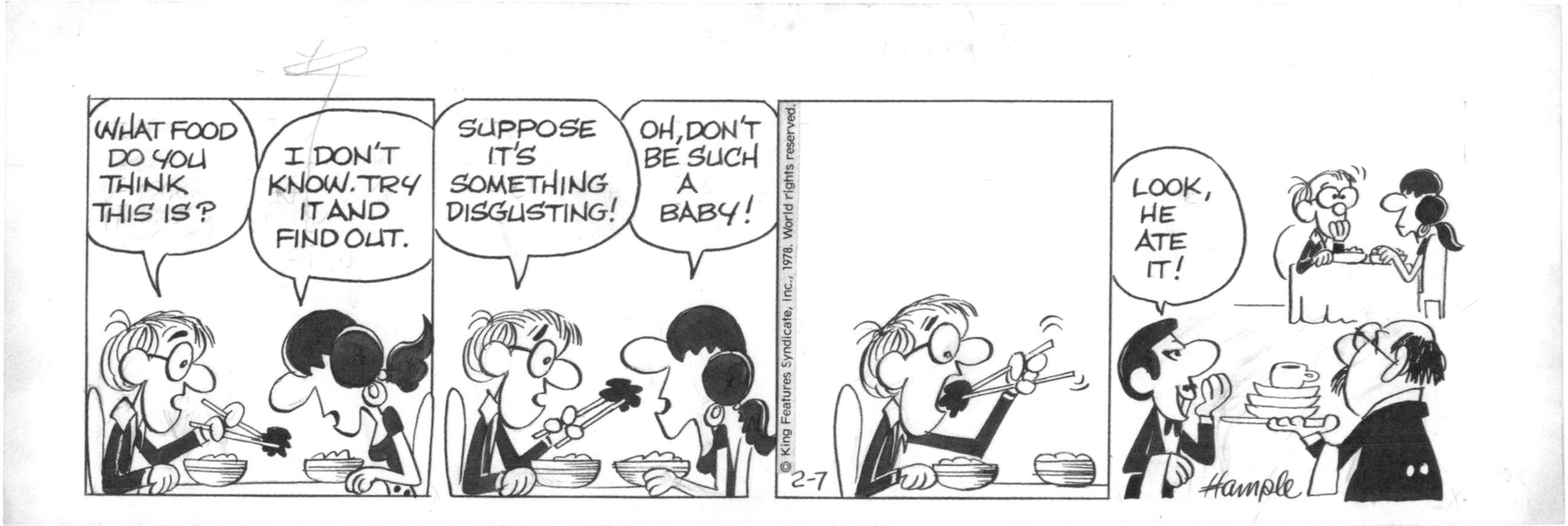
WHAT FOOD DO YOU THINK THIS IS?
I DON'T KNOW. TRY IT AND FIND OUT.
SUPPOSE IT'S SOMETHING DISGUSTING!
OH, DON'T BE SUCH A BABY!
© King Features Syndicate, Inc., 1978. World rights reserved.
2-7
LOOK, HE ATE IT!
Hample

February 7, 1978

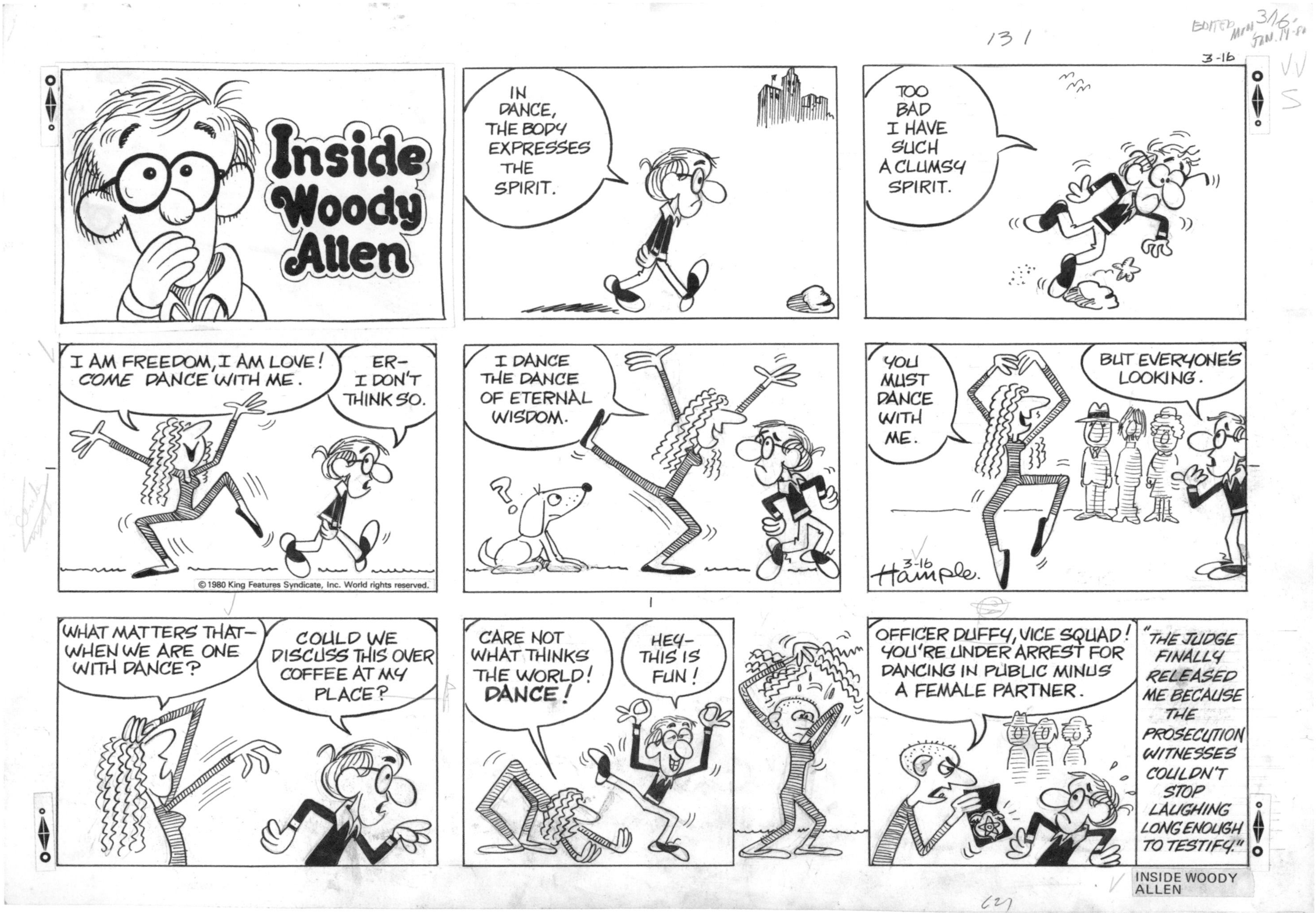

131
EDITED MRN 3/16 JAN. 14-80
3-16
Inside Woody Allen
IN DANCE, THE BODY EXPRESSES THE SPIRIT.
TOO BAD I HAVE SUCH A CLUMSY SPIRIT.
I AM FREEDOM, I AM LOVE! COME DANCE WITH ME.
ER- I DON'T THINK SO.
© 1980 King Features Syndicate, Inc. World rights reserved.
I DANCE THE DANCE OF ETERNAL WISDOM.
YOU MUST DANCE WITH ME.
BUT EVERYONE'S LOOKING.
3-16 Hample.
WHAT MATTERS THAT- WHEN WE ARE ONE WITH DANCE?
COULD WE DISCUSS THIS OVER COFFEE AT MY PLACE?
CARE NOT WHAT THINKS THE WORLD! DANCE!
HEY- THIS IS FUN!
OFFICER DUFFY, VICE SQUAD! YOU'RE UNDER ARREST FOR DANCING IN PUBLIC MINUS A FEMALE PARTNER.
"THE JUDGE FINALLY RELEASED ME BECAUSE THE PROSECUTION WITNESSES COULDN'T STOP LAUGHING LONG ENOUGH TO TESTIFY."
INSIDE WOODY ALLEN

March 16, 1980

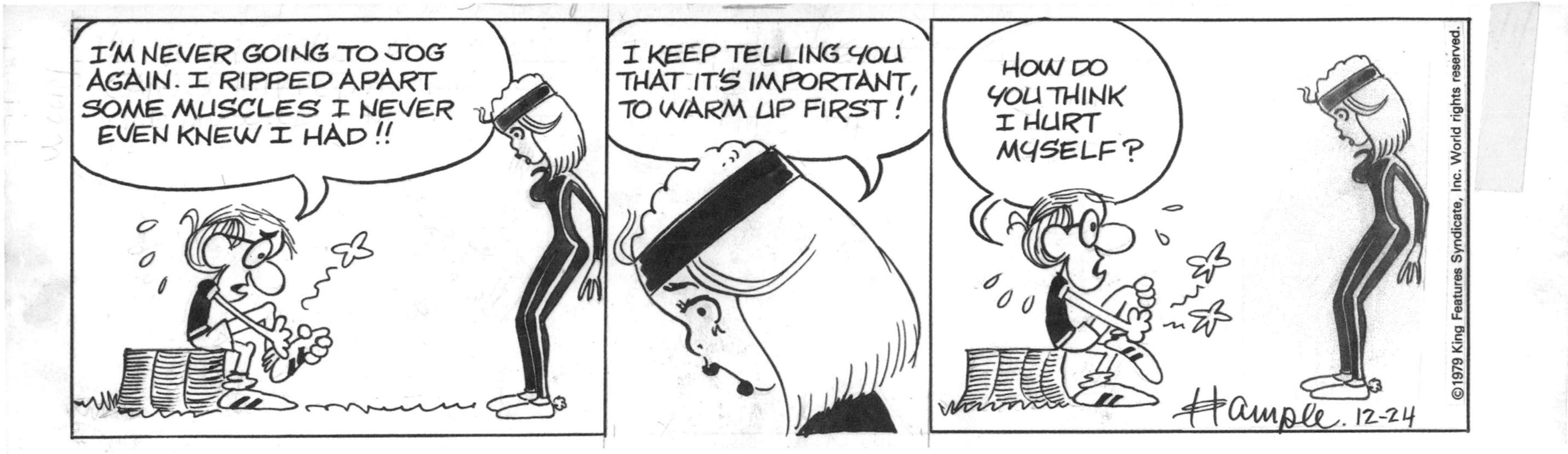

I'M NEVER GOING TO JOG AGAIN. I RIPPED APART SOME MUSCLES I NEVER EVEN KNEW I HAD!!
I KEEP TELLING YOU THAT IT'S IMPORTANT, TO WARM UP FIRST!
HOW DO YOU THINK I HURT MYSELF?
Hample. 12-24
©1979 King Features Syndicate, Inc. World rights reserved.

December 24, 1979

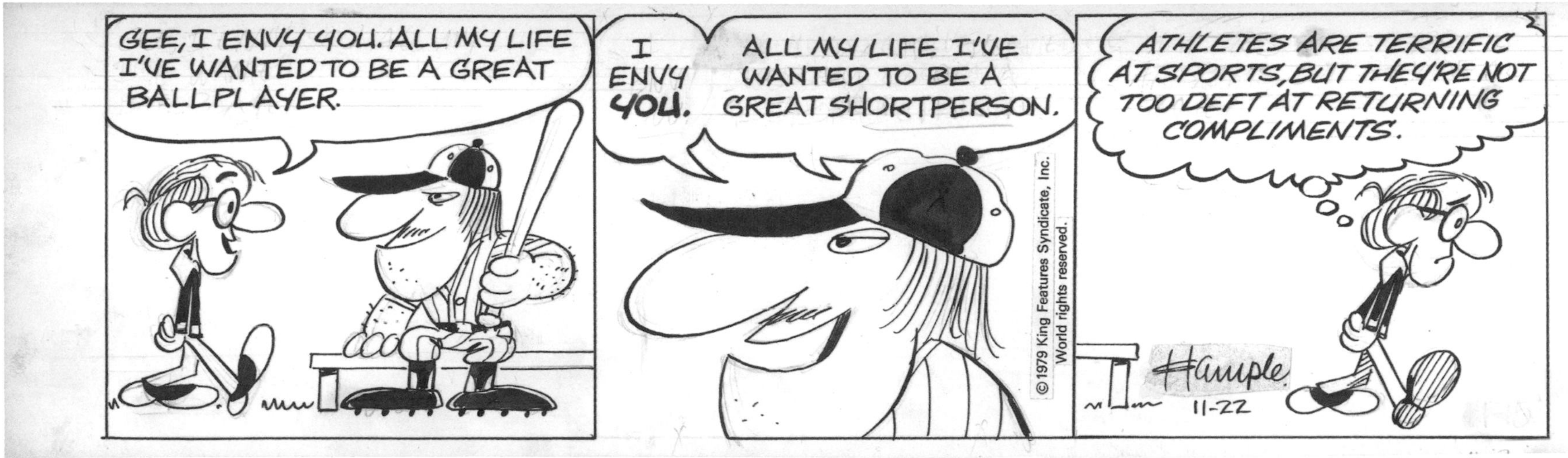

GEE, I ENVY YOU. ALL MY LIFE I'VE WANTED TO BE A GREAT BALLPLAYER.
I ENVY **YOU**.
ALL MY LIFE I'VE WANTED TO BE A GREAT SHORTPERSON.
ATHLETES ARE TERRIFIC AT SPORTS, BUT THEY'RE NOT TOO DEFT AT RETURNING COMPLIMENTS.
Hample
11-22
©1979 King Features Syndicate, Inc. World rights reserved.

November 22, 1979

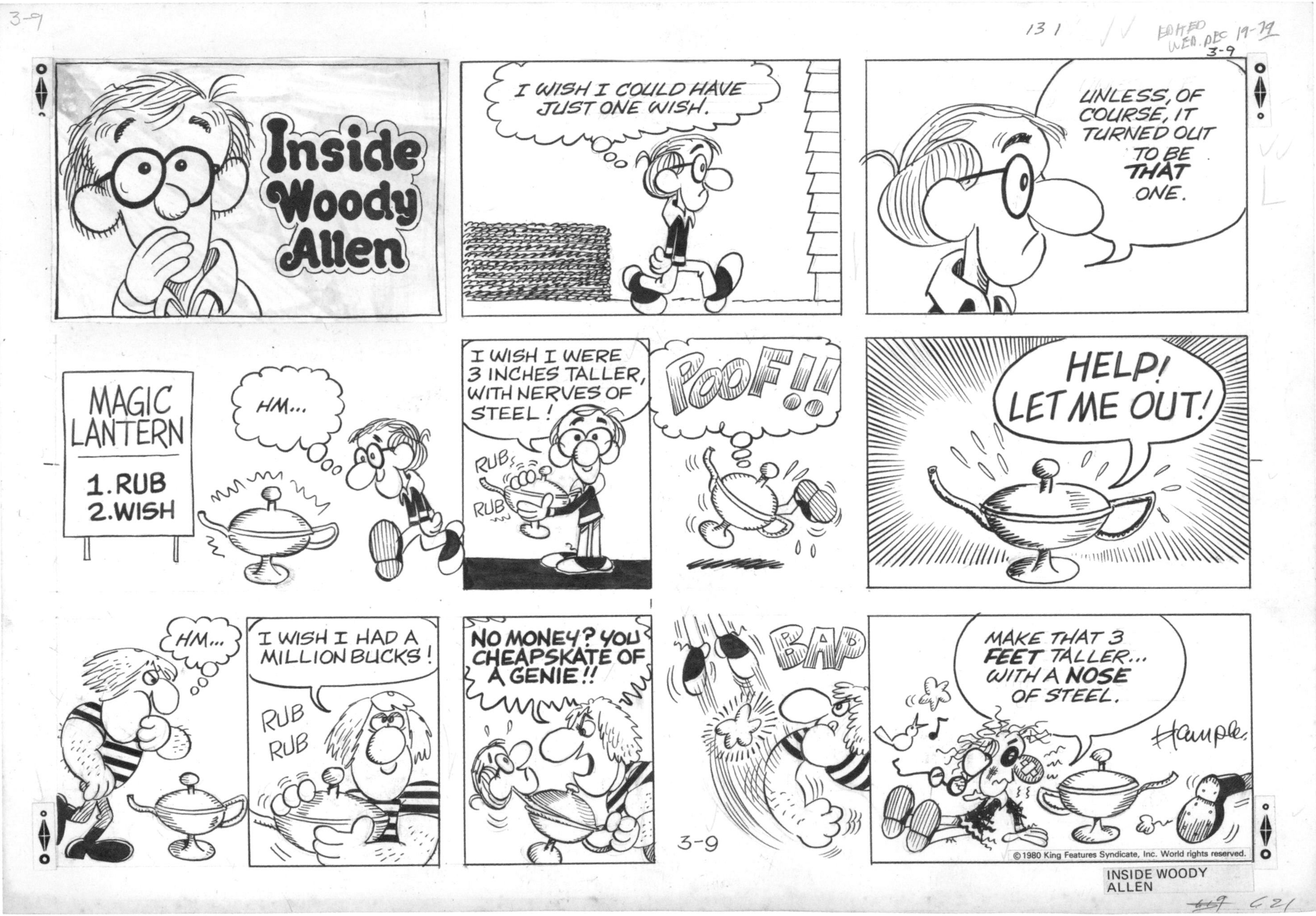
3-9
131
EDITED WED. DEC 19-79
3-9
Inside Woody Allen
I WISH I COULD HAVE JUST ONE WISH.
UNLESS, OF COURSE, IT TURNED OUT TO BE THAT ONE.
MAGIC LANTERN
1. RUB
2. WISH
HM...
I WISH I WERE 3 INCHES TALLER, WITH NERVES OF STEEL!
RUB RUB RUB
POOF!!
HELP! LET ME OUT!
HM...
I WISH I HAD A MILLION BUCKS!
RUB RUB
NO MONEY? YOU CHEAPSKATE OF A GENIE!!
3-9
BAP
MAKE THAT 3 FEET TALLER... WITH A NOSE OF STEEL.
Hample
© 1980 King Features Syndicate, Inc. World rights reserved.
INSIDE WOODY ALLEN
March 9, 1980

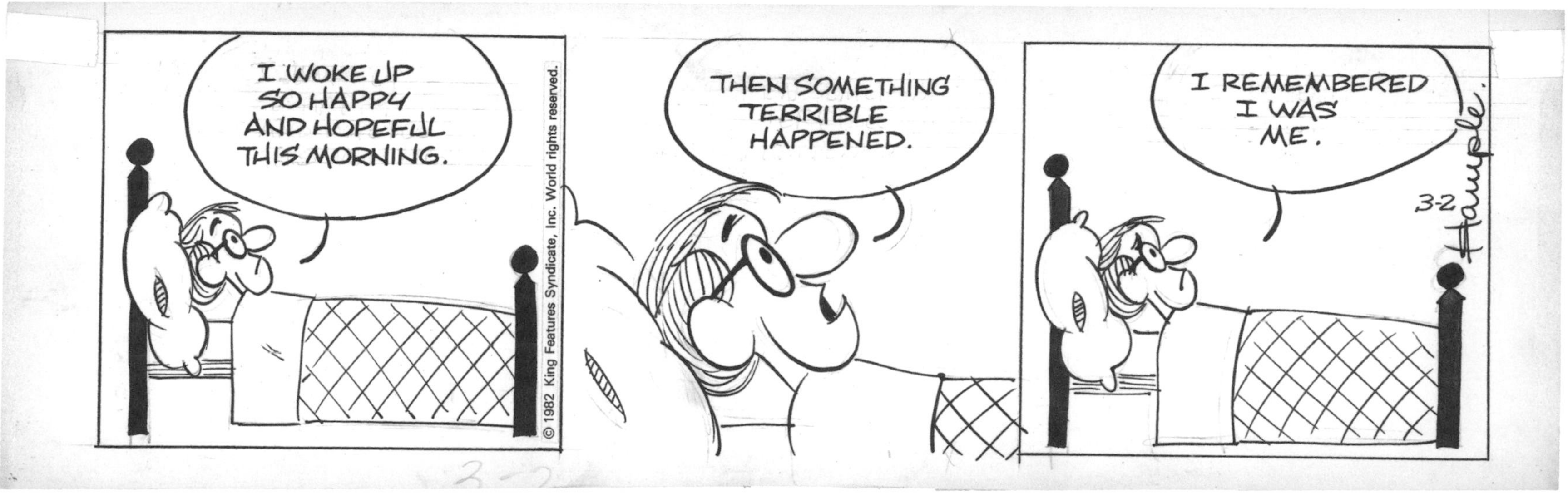
I WOKE UP SO HAPPY AND HOPEFUL THIS MORNING.
© 1982 King Features Syndicate, Inc. World rights reserved.
THEN SOMETHING TERRIBLE HAPPENED.
I REMEMBERED I WAS ME.
3-2
Hample

March 2, 1982

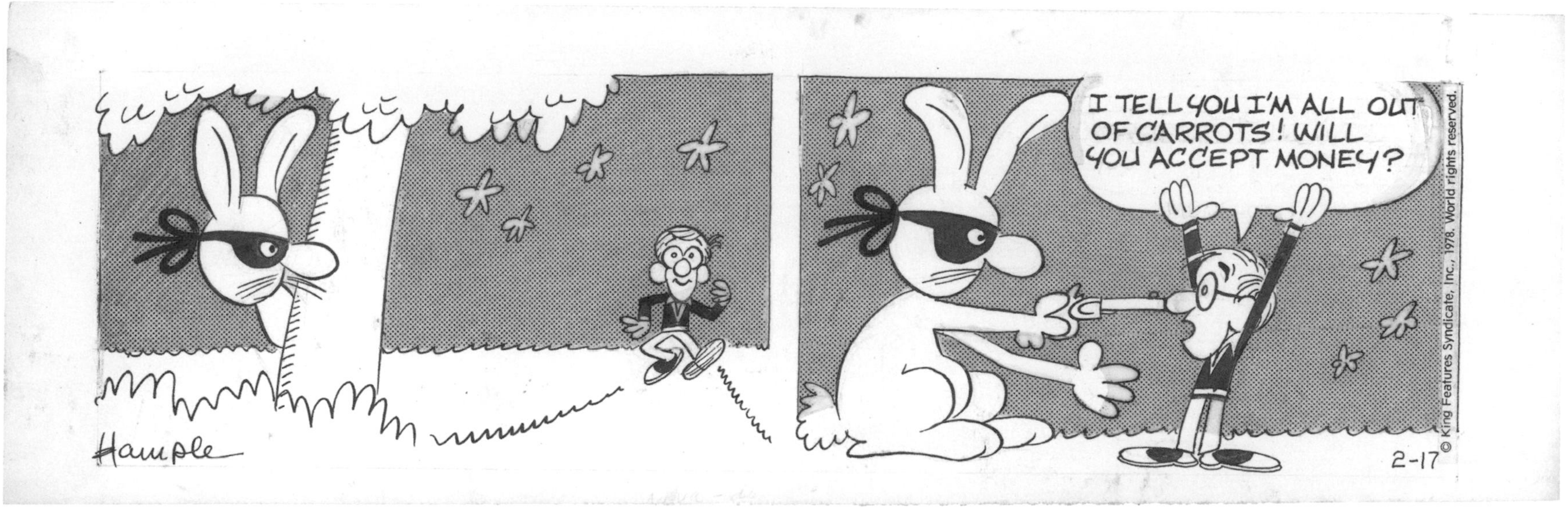
Hample
I TELL YOU I'M ALL OUT OF CARROTS! WILL YOU ACCEPT MONEY?
© King Features Syndicate, Inc., 1978. World rights reserved.
2-17

February 17, 1978

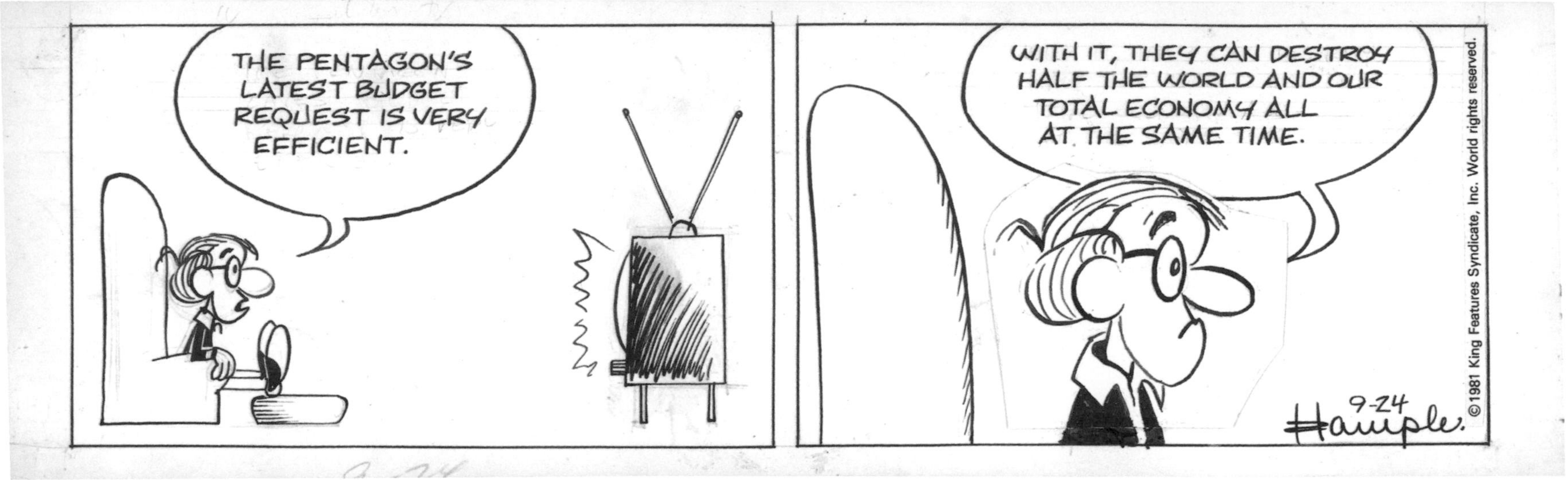
THE PENTAGON'S LATEST BUDGET REQUEST IS VERY EFFICIENT.
WITH IT, THEY CAN DESTROY HALF THE WORLD AND OUR TOTAL ECONOMY ALL AT THE SAME TIME.
9-24
Hample.
©1981 King Features Syndicate, Inc. World rights reserved.

September 24, 1981

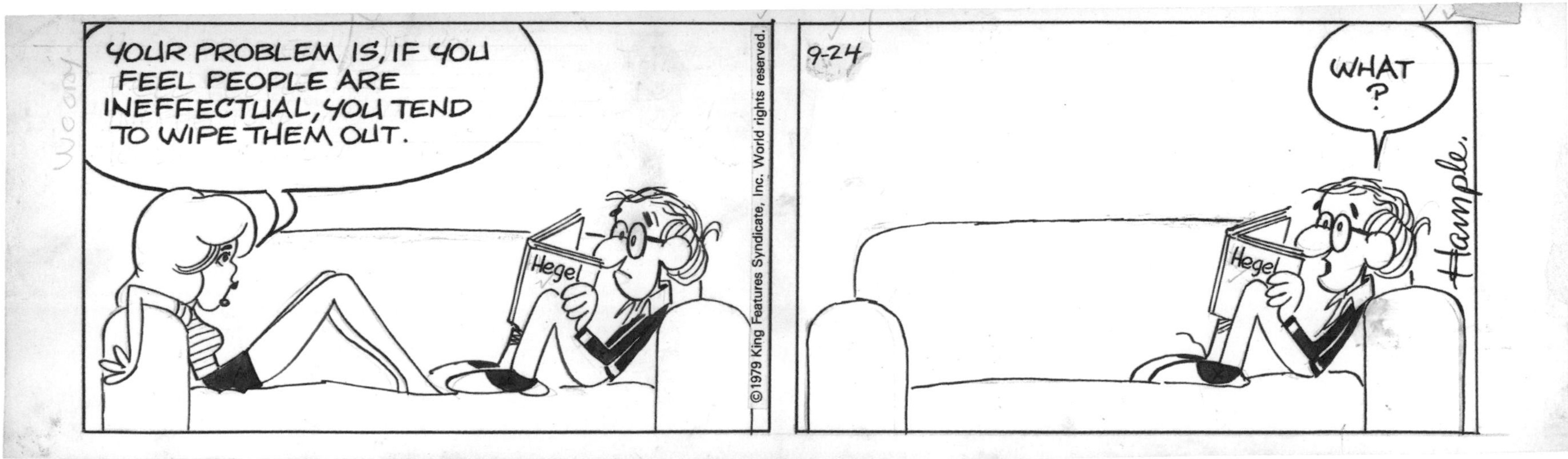
YOUR PROBLEM IS, IF YOU FEEL PEOPLE ARE INEFFECTUAL, YOU TEND TO WIPE THEM OUT.
Hegel
©1979 King Features Syndicate, Inc. World rights reserved.
9-24
WHAT ?
Hegel
Hample.

September 24, 1979

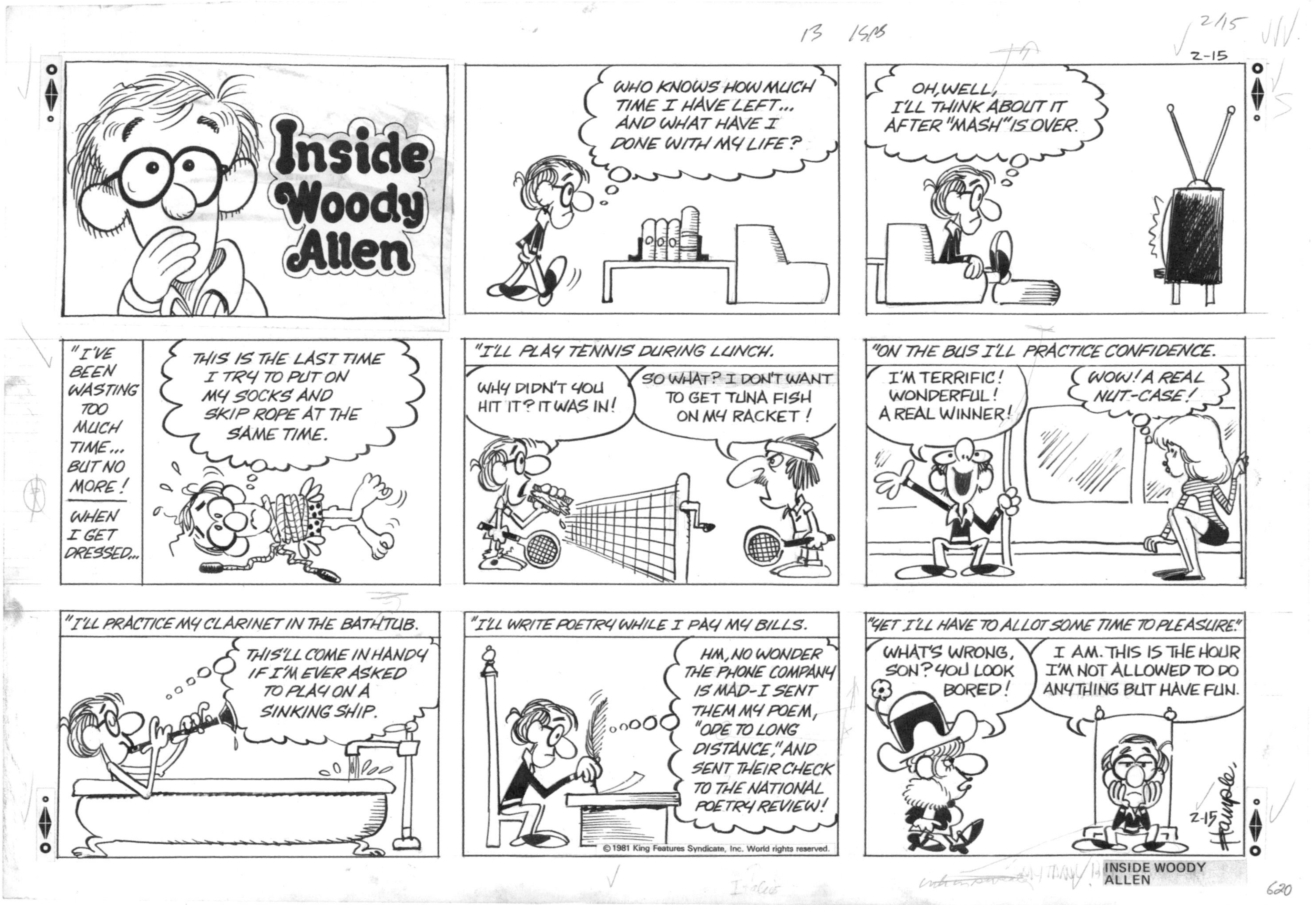

Inside Woody Allen
WHO KNOWS HOW MUCH TIME I HAVE LEFT... AND WHAT HAVE I DONE WITH MY LIFE?
OH, WELL, I'LL THINK ABOUT IT AFTER "MASH" IS OVER.
"I'VE BEEN WASTING TOO MUCH TIME... BUT NO MORE!
WHEN I GET DRESSED...
THIS IS THE LAST TIME I TRY TO PUT ON MY SOCKS AND SKIP ROPE AT THE SAME TIME.
"I'LL PLAY TENNIS DURING LUNCH.
WHY DIDN'T YOU HIT IT? IT WAS IN!
SO WHAT? I DON'T WANT TO GET TUNA FISH ON MY RACKET!
"ON THE BUS I'LL PRACTICE CONFIDENCE.
I'M TERRIFIC! WONDERFUL! A REAL WINNER!
WOW! A REAL NUT-CASE!
"I'LL PRACTICE MY CLARINET IN THE BATHTUB.
THIS'LL COME IN HANDY IF I'M EVER ASKED TO PLAY ON A SINKING SHIP.
"I'LL WRITE POETRY WHILE I PAY MY BILLS.
HM, NO WONDER THE PHONE COMPANY IS MAD-I SENT THEM MY POEM, "ODE TO LONG DISTANCE," AND SENT THEIR CHECK TO THE NATIONAL POETRY REVIEW!
© 1981 King Features Syndicate, Inc. World rights reserved.
"YET I'LL HAVE TO ALLOT SOME TIME TO PLEASURE."
WHAT'S WRONG, SON? YOU LOOK BORED!
I AM. THIS IS THE HOUR I'M NOT ALLOWED TO DO ANYTHING BUT HAVE FUN.
2-15
Hample
INSIDE WOODY ALLEN
620

February 15, 1981

February 13, 1978. Woody's comic strip sister.

March 15, 1978

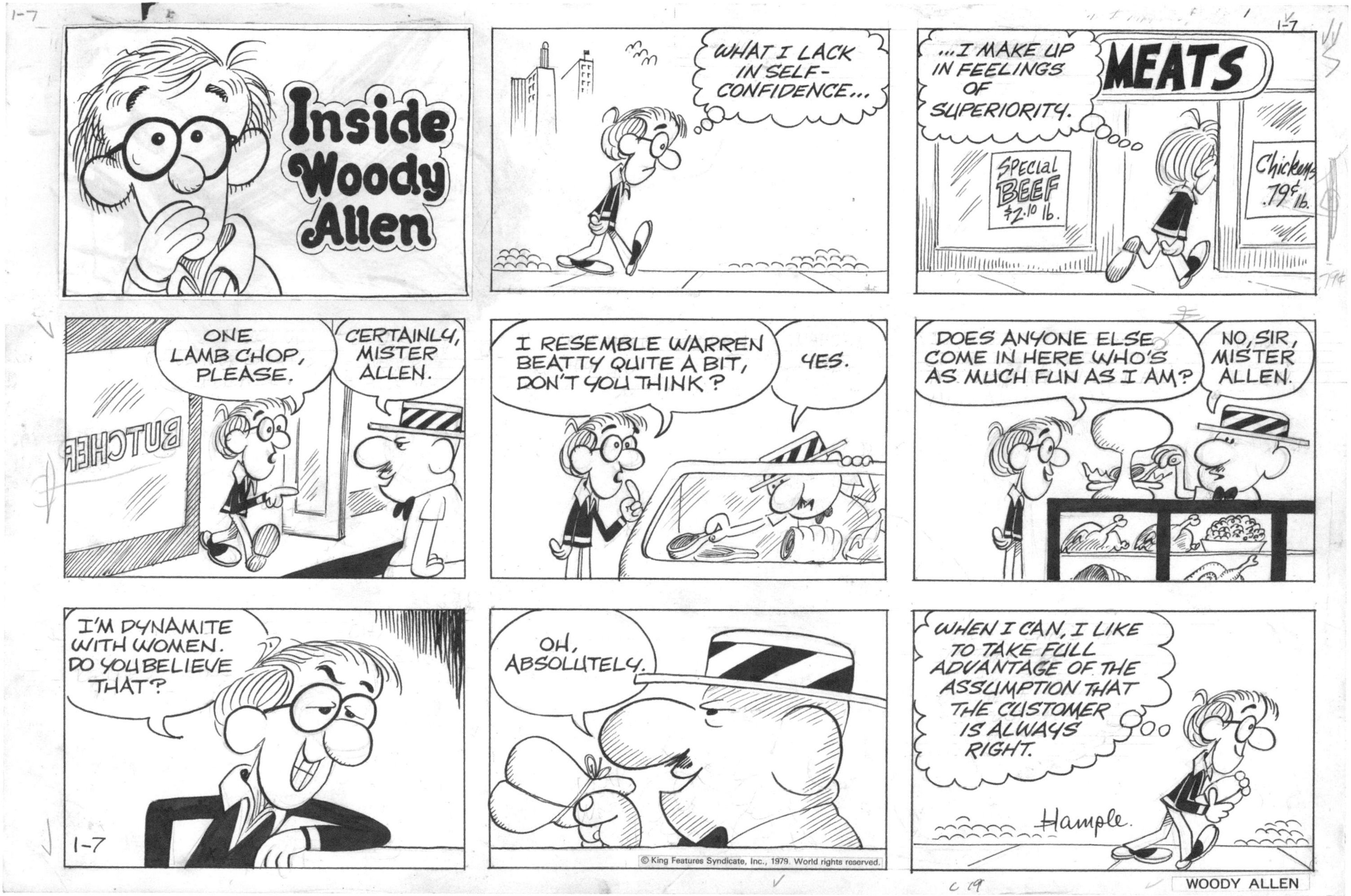
1-7
Inside Woody Allen
WHAT I LACK IN SELF-CONFIDENCE...
...I MAKE UP IN FEELINGS OF SUPERIORITY.
MEATS
Special BEEF $2.10 lb.
Chickens .79¢ lb.
1-7
BUTCHER
ONE LAMB CHOP, PLEASE.
CERTAINLY, MISTER ALLEN.
I RESEMBLE WARREN BEATTY QUITE A BIT, DON'T YOU THINK?
YES.
DOES ANYONE ELSE COME IN HERE WHO'S AS MUCH FUN AS I AM?
NO, SIR, MISTER ALLEN.
I'M DYNAMITE WITH WOMEN. DO YOU BELIEVE THAT?
1-7
OH, ABSOLUTELY.
© King Features Syndicate, Inc., 1979. World rights reserved.
WHEN I CAN, I LIKE TO TAKE FULL ADVANTAGE OF THE ASSUMPTION THAT THE CUSTOMER IS ALWAYS RIGHT.
Hample.
WOODY ALLEN

January 7, 1979

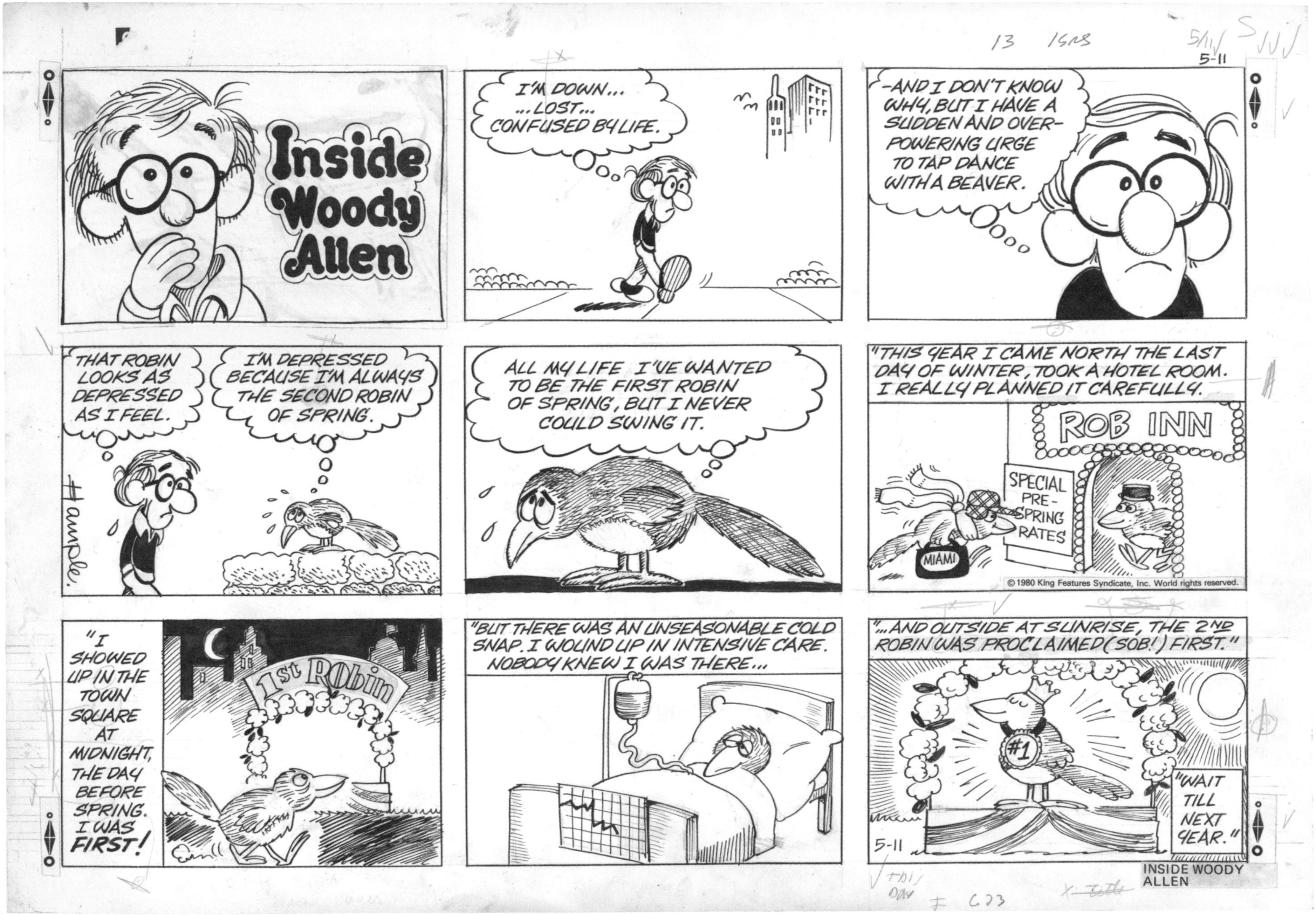

Inside Woody Allen
I'M DOWN... ...LOST... CONFUSED BY LIFE.
-AND I DON'T KNOW WHY, BUT I HAVE A SUDDEN AND OVER-POWERING URGE TO TAP DANCE WITH A BEAVER.
THAT ROBIN LOOKS AS DEPRESSED AS I FEEL.
I'M DEPRESSED BECAUSE I'M ALWAYS THE SECOND ROBIN OF SPRING.
ALL MY LIFE I'VE WANTED TO BE THE FIRST ROBIN OF SPRING, BUT I NEVER COULD SWING IT.
"THIS YEAR I CAME NORTH THE LAST DAY OF WINTER, TOOK A HOTEL ROOM. I REALLY PLANNED IT CAREFULLY.
ROB INN
SPECIAL PRE-SPRING RATES
MIAMI
© 1980 King Features Syndicate, Inc. World rights reserved.
"I SHOWED UP IN THE TOWN SQUARE AT MIDNIGHT, THE DAY BEFORE SPRING. I WAS FIRST!
1st Robin
"BUT THERE WAS AN UNSEASONABLE COLD SNAP. I WOUND UP IN INTENSIVE CARE. NOBODY KNEW I WAS THERE...
"...AND OUTSIDE AT SUNRISE, THE 2ND ROBIN WAS PROCLAIMED (SOB!) FIRST."
#1
"WAIT TILL NEXT YEAR."
5-11
INSIDE WOODY ALLEN

May 11, 1980

7

They Exchanged Gunfire Daily

Inside Woody Allen

I USED TO WONDER WHY I DIDN'T RESEMBLE MY PARENTS...

—UNTIL I FOUND OUT THEY WERE ADOPTED.

MY PARENTS WERE NOT HAPPY TOGETHER.

DUMMY!

IDIOT!

"BITTERNESS SLOWLY CREPT INTO THE MARRIAGE, AND BY THE TIME I WAS 9, THEY EXCHANGED GUNFIRE DAILY.

BANG!

POW!

"THIS ATMOSPHERE TOOK ITS TOLL, AND SOON I BEGAN TO SUFFER THE FIRST OF MY MANY MOODS AND 'ANXIETIES'...

WHAT A GRIM COSMOS

"—RENDERING ME (FOR 4 YEARS) UNABLE TO PASS A ROAST CHICKEN WITHOUT TIPPING MY HAT.

"MY PSYCHIATRIST SUGGESTED THAT THE TENSION BETWEEN MY PARENTS WAS RESPONSIBLE FOR MY DEPRESSIONS

DON'T KICK THE LITTLE @*!!*MM. OVER HERE! CAN'T YOU SEE I'M BUSY?

"WHEN I TOLD THAT TO MY MOTHER SHE TRIED TO DO HERSELF IN BY TAKING AN OVERDOSE OF WARM MILK."

INSIDE WOODY ALLEN

September 7, 1980

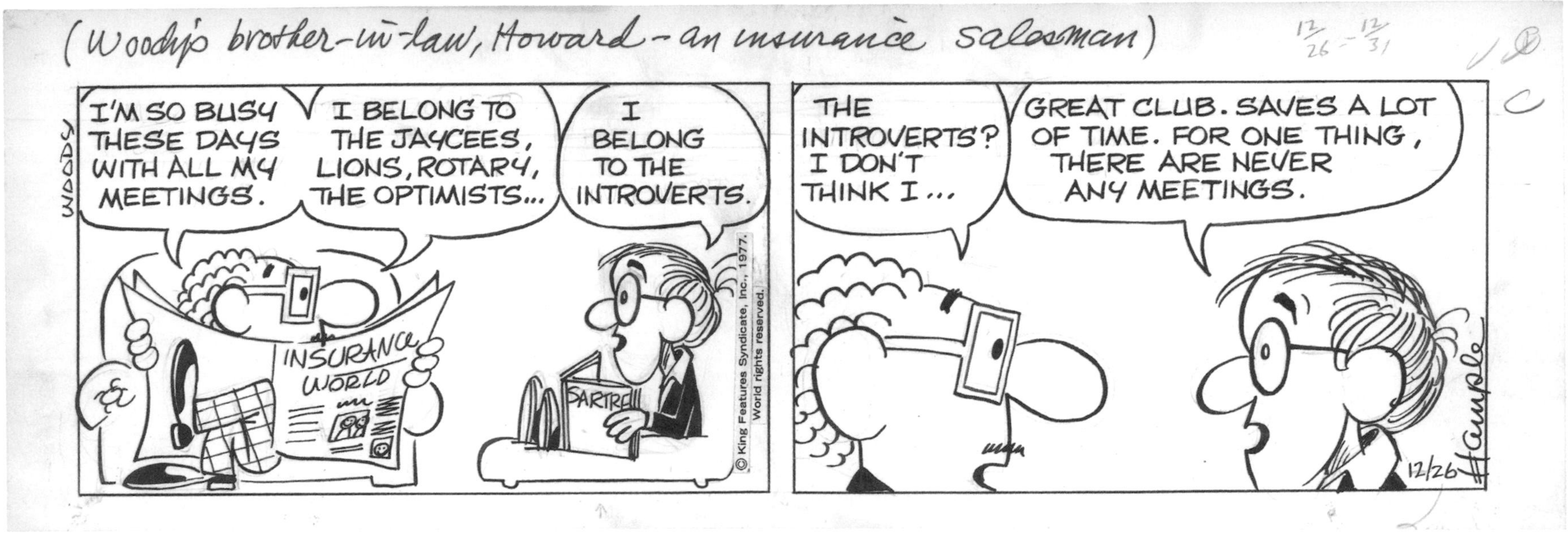
(Woody's brother-in-law, Howard - an insurance salesman)
12/26 - 12/31
WOODY
I'M SO BUSY THESE DAYS WITH ALL MY MEETINGS.
I BELONG TO THE JAYCEES, LIONS, ROTARY, THE OPTIMISTS...
I BELONG TO THE INTROVERTS.
INSURANCE WORLD
SARTRE
© King Features Syndicate, Inc., 1977. World rights reserved.
THE INTROVERTS? I DON'T THINK I...
GREAT CLUB. SAVES A LOT OF TIME. FOR ONE THING, THERE ARE NEVER ANY MEETINGS.
12/26
Hample

December 26, 1977

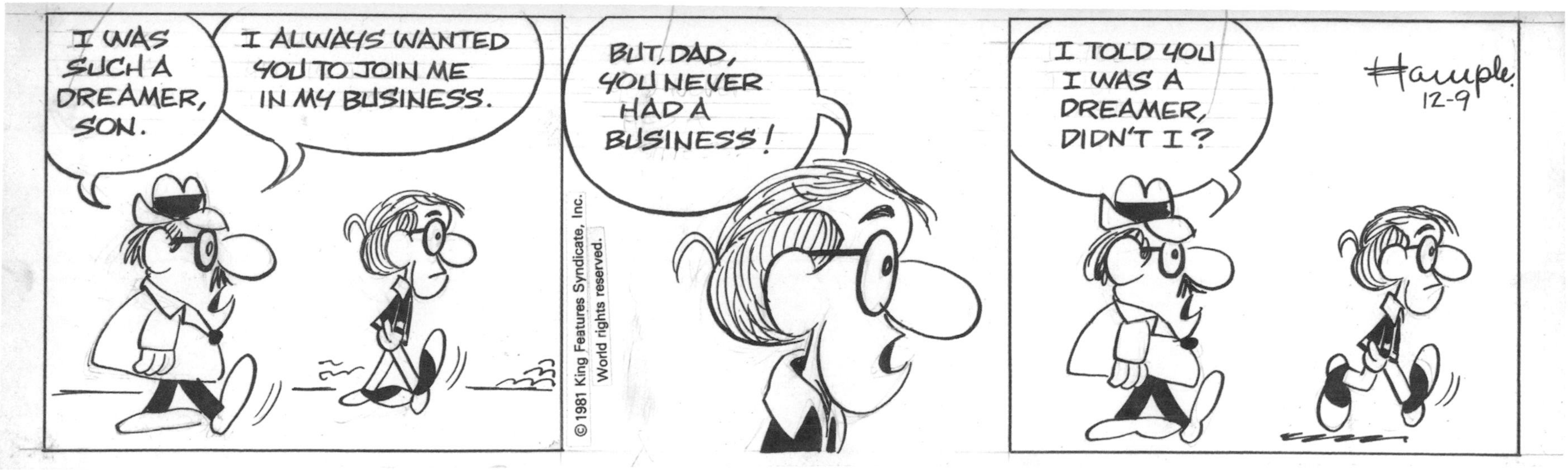
I WAS SUCH A DREAMER, SON.
I ALWAYS WANTED YOU TO JOIN ME IN MY BUSINESS.
©1981 King Features Syndicate, Inc. World rights reserved.
BUT, DAD, YOU NEVER HAD A BUSINESS!
I TOLD YOU I WAS A DREAMER, DIDN'T I?
Hample 12-9

December 9, 1981

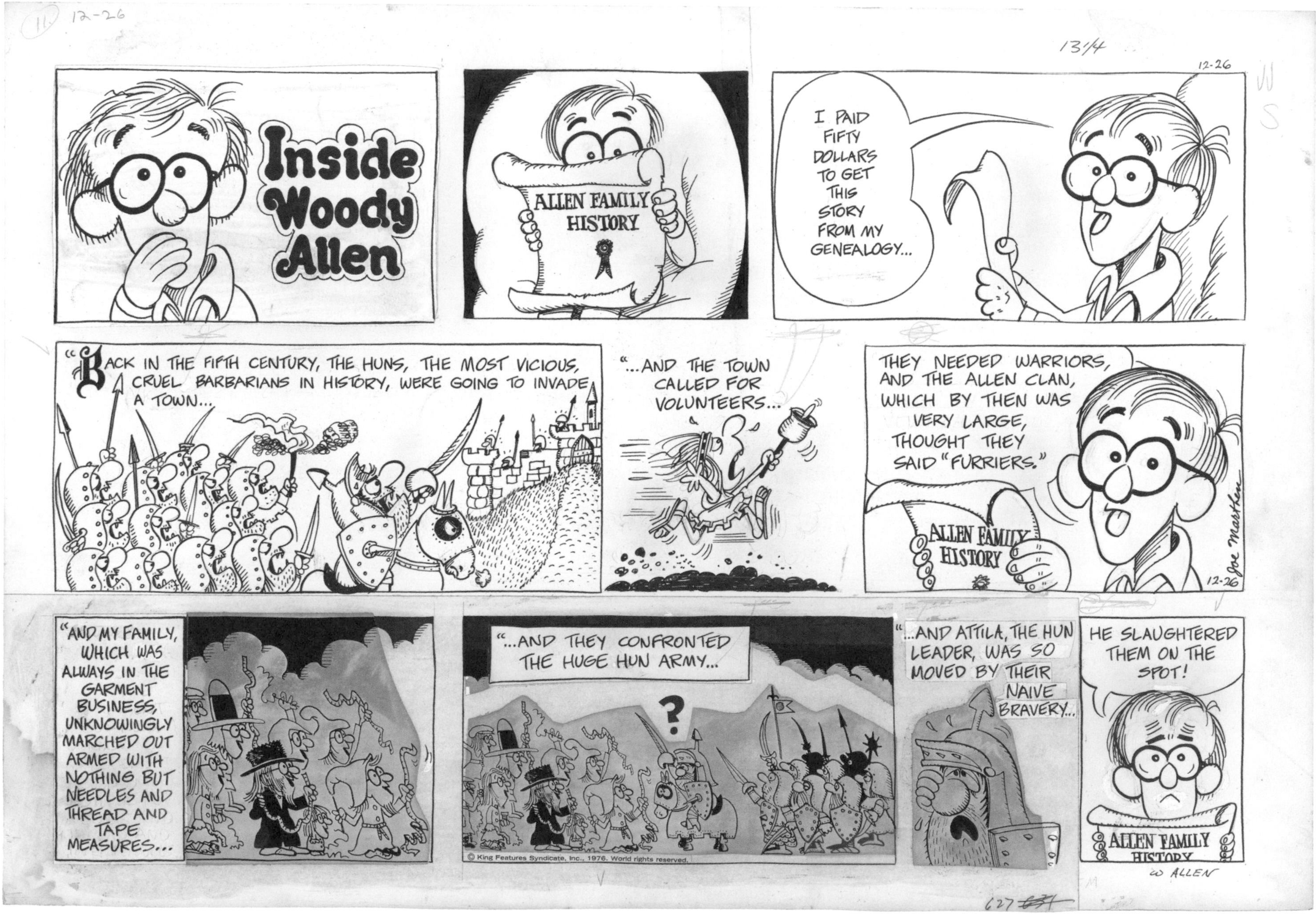
12-26
13 1/4
12-26
Inside Woody Allen
ALLEN FAMILY HISTORY
I PAID FIFTY DOLLARS TO GET THIS STORY FROM MY GENEALOGY...
"BACK IN THE FIFTH CENTURY, THE HUNS, THE MOST VICIOUS, CRUEL BARBARIANS IN HISTORY, WERE GOING TO INVADE A TOWN...
"...AND THE TOWN CALLED FOR VOLUNTEERS...
THEY NEEDED WARRIORS, AND THE ALLEN CLAN, WHICH BY THEN WAS VERY LARGE, THOUGHT THEY SAID "FURRIERS."
ALLEN FAMILY HISTORY
Joe Marthen
12-26
"AND MY FAMILY, WHICH WAS ALWAYS IN THE GARMENT BUSINESS, UNKNOWINGLY MARCHED OUT ARMED WITH NOTHING BUT NEEDLES AND THREAD AND TAPE MEASURES...
"...AND THEY CONFRONTED THE HUGE HUN ARMY...
?
© King Features Syndicate, Inc., 1976. World rights reserved.
"...AND ATTILA, THE HUN LEADER, WAS SO MOVED BY THEIR NAIVE BRAVERY...
HE SLAUGHTERED THEM ON THE SPOT!
ALLEN FAMILY HISTORY
W ALLEN
627

December 26, 1976

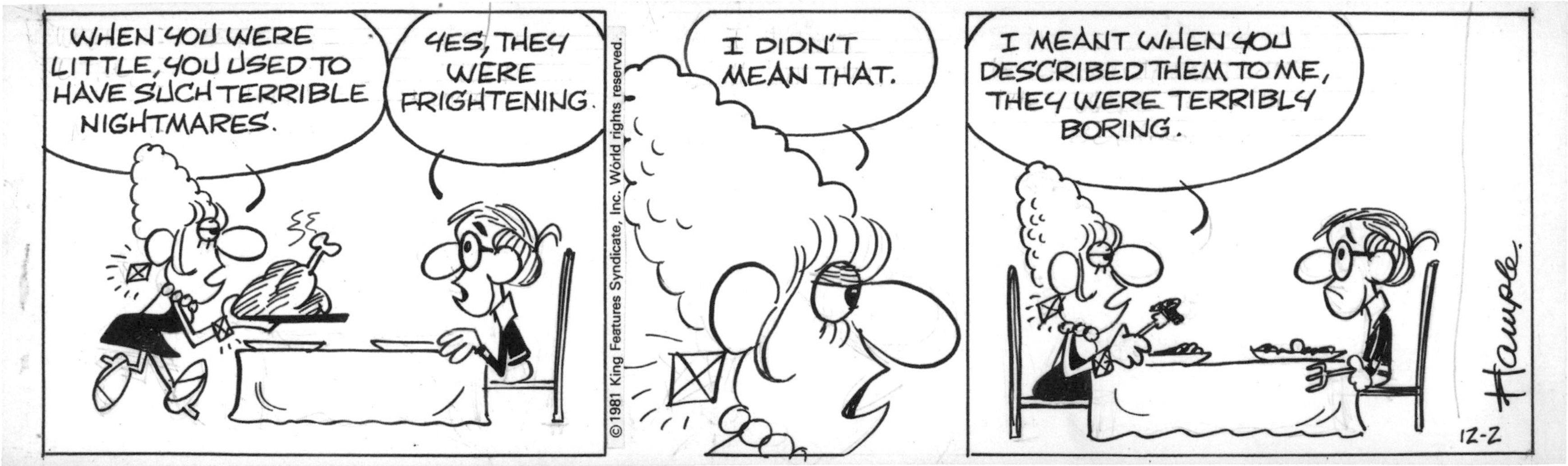
WHEN YOU WERE LITTLE, YOU USED TO HAVE SUCH TERRIBLE NIGHTMARES.
YES, THEY WERE FRIGHTENING.
I DIDN'T MEAN THAT.
I MEANT WHEN YOU DESCRIBED THEM TO ME, THEY WERE TERRIBLY BORING.
©1981 King Features Syndicate, Inc. World rights reserved.
Hample.
12-2

December 2, 1981

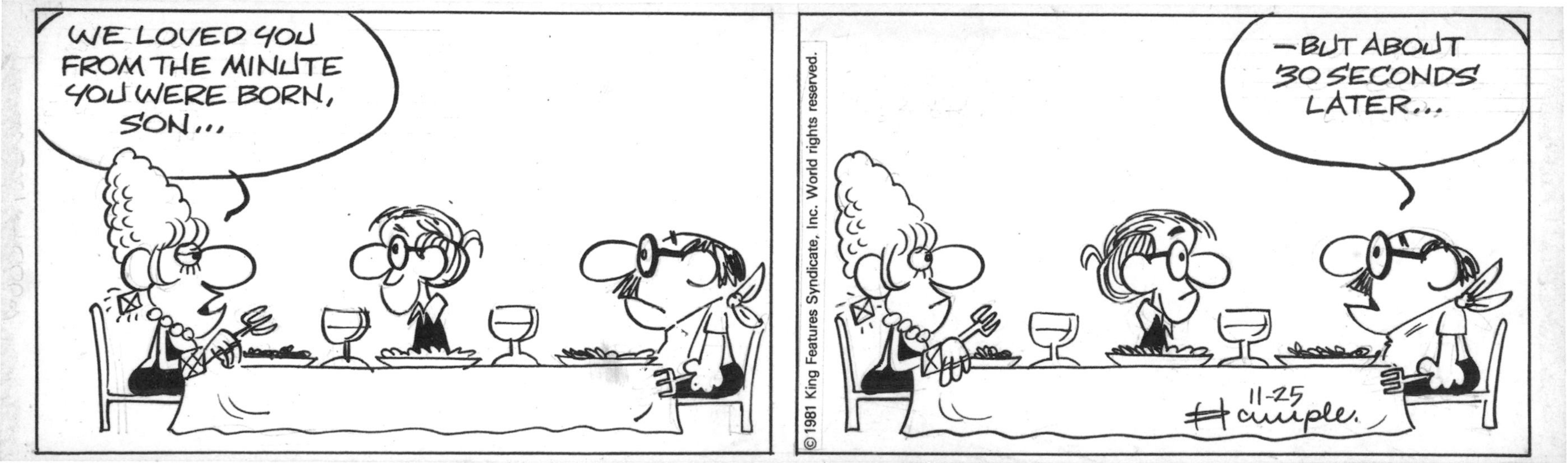
WE LOVED YOU FROM THE MINUTE YOU WERE BORN, SON...
—BUT ABOUT 30 SECONDS LATER...
©1981 King Features Syndicate, Inc. World rights reserved.
11-25
Hample.

November 25, 1981

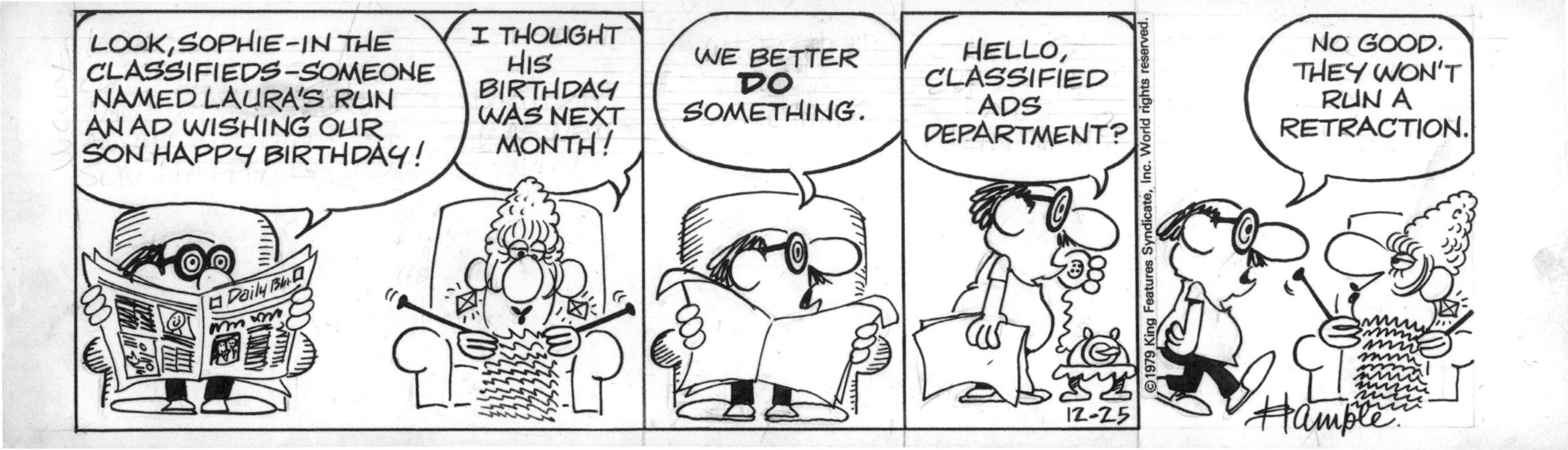
LOOK, SOPHIE-IN THE CLASSIFIEDS-SOMEONE NAMED LAURA'S RUN AN AD WISHING OUR SON HAPPY BIRTHDAY!
I THOUGHT HIS BIRTHDAY WAS NEXT MONTH!
WE BETTER DO SOMETHING.
HELLO, CLASSIFIED ADS DEPARTMENT?
NO GOOD. THEY WON'T RUN A RETRACTION.
Daily Bl
12-25
© 1979 King Features Syndicate, Inc. World rights reserved.
Hample

December 25, 1979

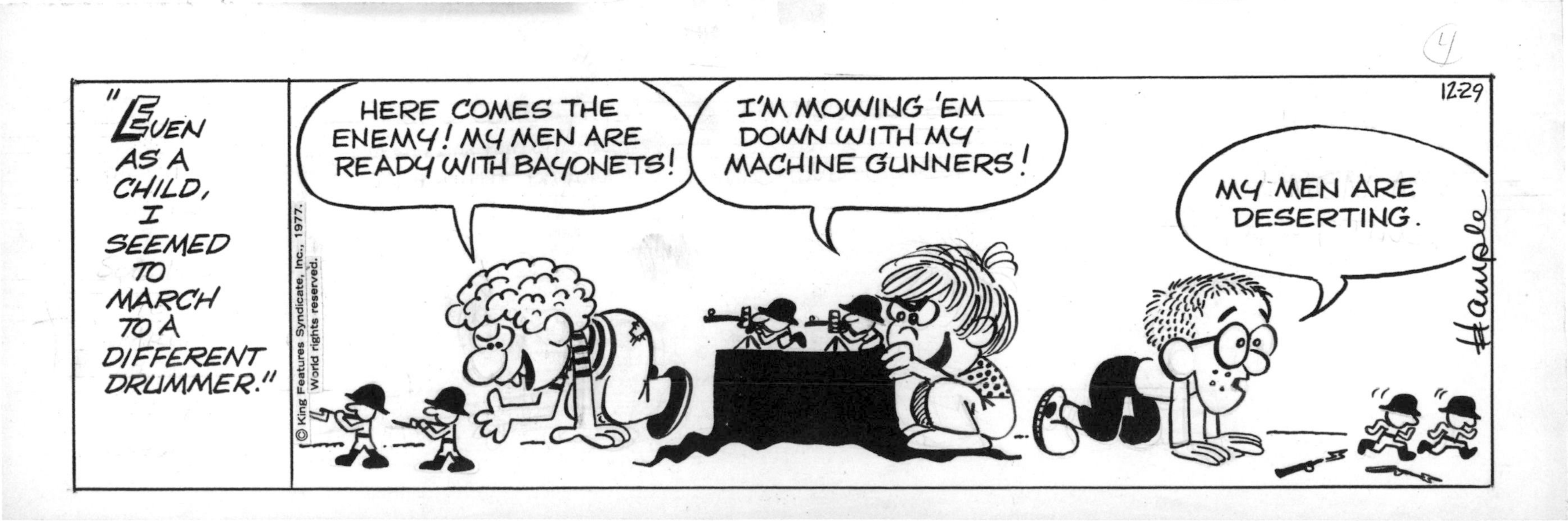
"EVEN AS A CHILD, I SEEMED TO MARCH TO A DIFFERENT DRUMMER."
HERE COMES THE ENEMY! MY MEN ARE READY WITH BAYONETS!
I'M MOWING 'EM DOWN WITH MY MACHINE GUNNERS!
MY MEN ARE DESERTING.
12-29
© King Features Syndicate, Inc., 1977. World rights reserved.
Hample

December 29, 1977

Inside Woody Allen

"MY GRANDFATHER ONCE TRIED TO VISIT THE PRESIDENT OF THE UNITED STATES.

WHITE HOUSE Keep out

"HE WANTED TO DISCUSS HIS IDEA OF HAVING ALL GOVERN-MENT OFFICIALS DRESS LIKE HENS.

"YEARS AGO, ON A FAMILY TRIP TO WASHINGTON, D.C., MY GRAND-FATHER WANDERED OFF.

WOODY, WHERE'S GRANDPA?

BAW! HE TOOK MY BALLOON!!

©1980 King Features Syndicate, Inc. World rights reserved.

"IT TURNED OUT HE GOT LOST ON THE ROOF OF THE TREASURY DEPARTMENT...

TREASURY DEPT.

"..WHERE THEY WERE BURNING PAPER CURRENCY WHICH WAS OUT OF CIRCULATION.

"GRANDPA INHALED, AND GOT A TREMEN-DOUS HIGH ON THE MONEY SMOKE.

HEE, HEE...

"FIRST, HE ATTEMPTED TO HIJACK AN ELEVATOR...

THIS BALLOON IS FILLED WITH DEADLY NERVE GAS. FLY ME TO CUBA OR ELSE...!!

"THEN HE BROKE TWO TEETH TRYING TO GIVE A HICKEY TO THE WASHINGTON MONUMENT."

I LOVE YOU!

Hample 6-8

INSIDE WOODY ALLEN

June 8, 1980

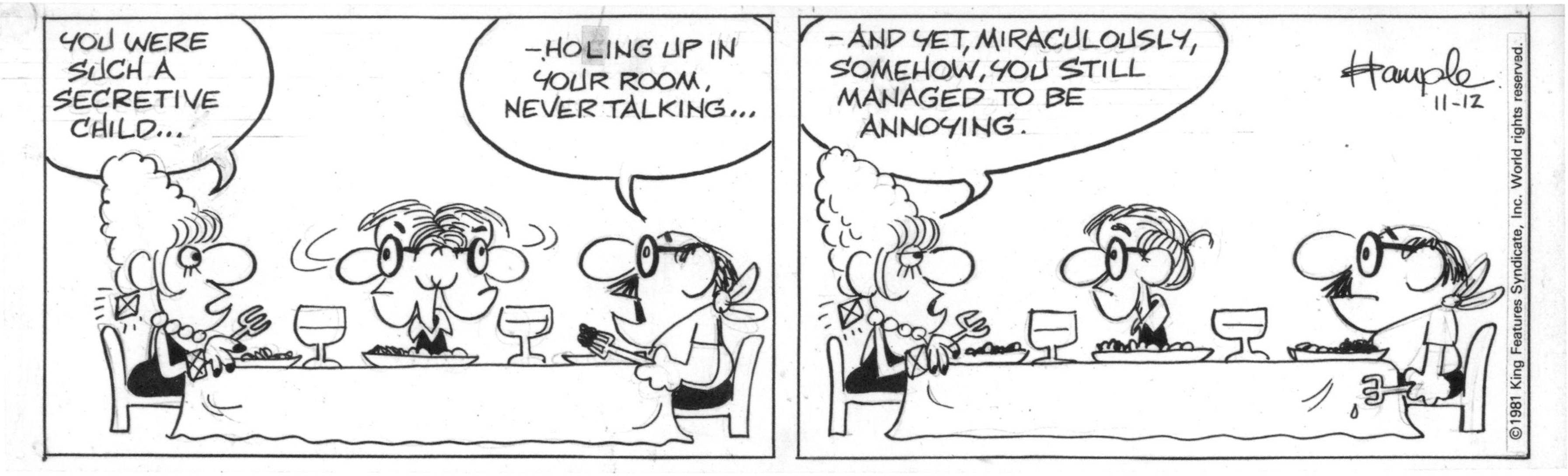
YOU WERE SUCH A SECRETIVE CHILD...
-HOLING UP IN YOUR ROOM, NEVER TALKING...
-AND YET, MIRACULOUSLY, SOMEHOW, YOU STILL MANAGED TO BE ANNOYING.
Hample 11-12
© 1981 King Features Syndicate, Inc. World rights reserved.

November 12, 1981

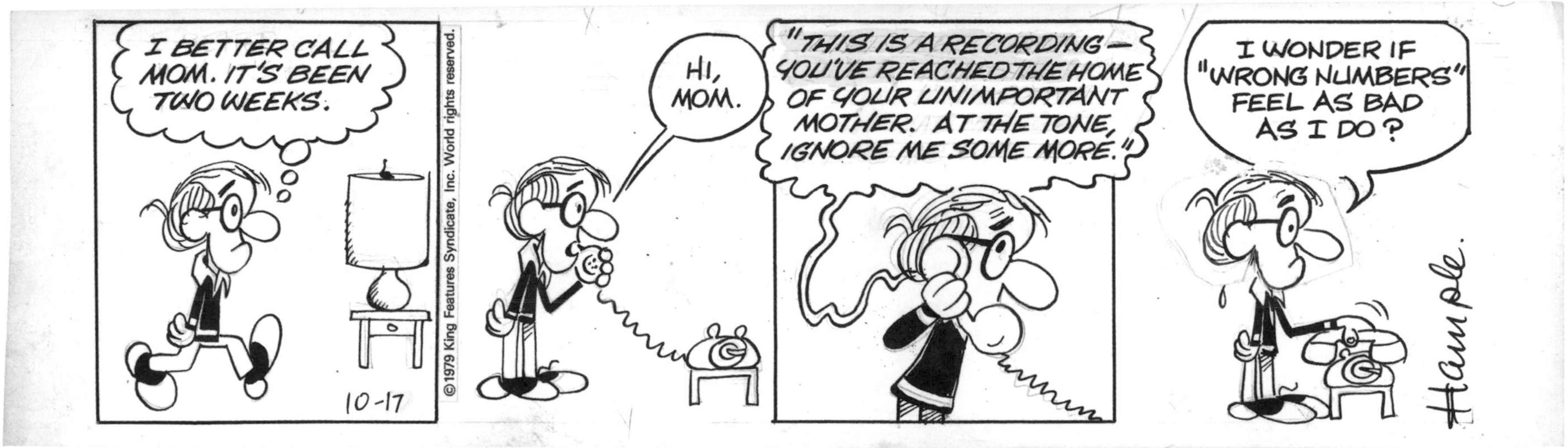
I BETTER CALL MOM. IT'S BEEN TWO WEEKS.
10-17
© 1979 King Features Syndicate, Inc. World rights reserved.
HI, MOM.
"THIS IS A RECORDING— YOU'VE REACHED THE HOME OF YOUR UNIMPORTANT MOTHER. AT THE TONE, IGNORE ME SOME MORE."
I WONDER IF "WRONG NUMBERS" FEEL AS BAD AS I DO?
Hample

October 17, 1979

Inside Woody Allen

I MAY WRITE A NOVEL ABOUT WHY I DIDN'T BECOME A JAZZ GREAT...

...OR, I MAY NOT.

"I WANTED TO PLAY AN INSTRUMENT AS A BOY— BUT MY FATHER WAS SO POOR HE GAVE ME A STICK PAINTED BLACK AND TOLD ME IT WAS A CLARINET.

TRUST ME.

"WHEN I PRACTICED, THE NEIGHBORS COMPLAINED ABOUT THE NOISE, BUT EVENTUALLY I GOT A PRETTY GOOD TONE OUT OF IT.

"WHEN I WENT TO AUDITION FOR THE SCHOOL BAND THEY LAUGHED AND SAID, AS FAR AS THEY KNEW, NO MUSICAL PARTS HAD EVER BEEN WRITTEN FOR A STICK.

"BUT I SOLVED THE PROBLEM— BECAUSE IN MY CLASS WAS A RICH KID.

"WHEN HE WANTED TO PLAY STICKBALL HIS RICH PARENTS DIDN'T HAVE A STICK BECAUSE THEY NEVER HAD USE FOR ONE...

"INSTEAD, SO HE COULD PLAY STICKBALL, THEY BOUGHT HIM A CLARINET—

AND WE MADE A TRADE.

"AFTER SCHOOL, HE WENT TO MUSIC CLASS WITH MY STICK...

"...AND I PLAYED BALL WITH HIS CLARINET."

Joe Marthen
10-10

WOODY ALLEN

October 10, 1976

Inside Woody Allen

THE OUTDOORS WOULD BE GREAT...

—IF IT WAS INDOORS.

"WHEN I WAS A BOY SCOUT..."

SMITH, YOU'RE IN HAWK PATROL.

DUKAS, FALCON PATROL.

ALLEN, BUNNY RABBIT PATROL.

REMEMBER THE BASIC SURVIVAL TECHNIQUES IF LOST: MOSS GROWS ON THE NORTH SIDE OF TREES. STREAMS FLOW DOWNHILL. AND IN CASE OF DANGER, REMAIN MOTIONLESS AND BLEND INTO THE TERRAIN.

"NEXT MORNING."

THEY COULD HAVE AWAKENED ME BEFORE THEY LEFT.

I'M LOST! LET'S SEE...

—MOSS FLOWS UP TREES...

—STREAMS GO NORTH FOR THE WINTER...

I SUPPOSE THERE'S NO HOPING IT'S STUFFED.

I BETTER BLEND IN WITH THE TERRAIN.

"WINTER CAME, AND I BLENDED IN SO WELL, THE BEAR HIBERNATED BETWEEN MY LEGS."

Hample. 9-21

INSIDE WOODY ALLEN

September 21, 1980

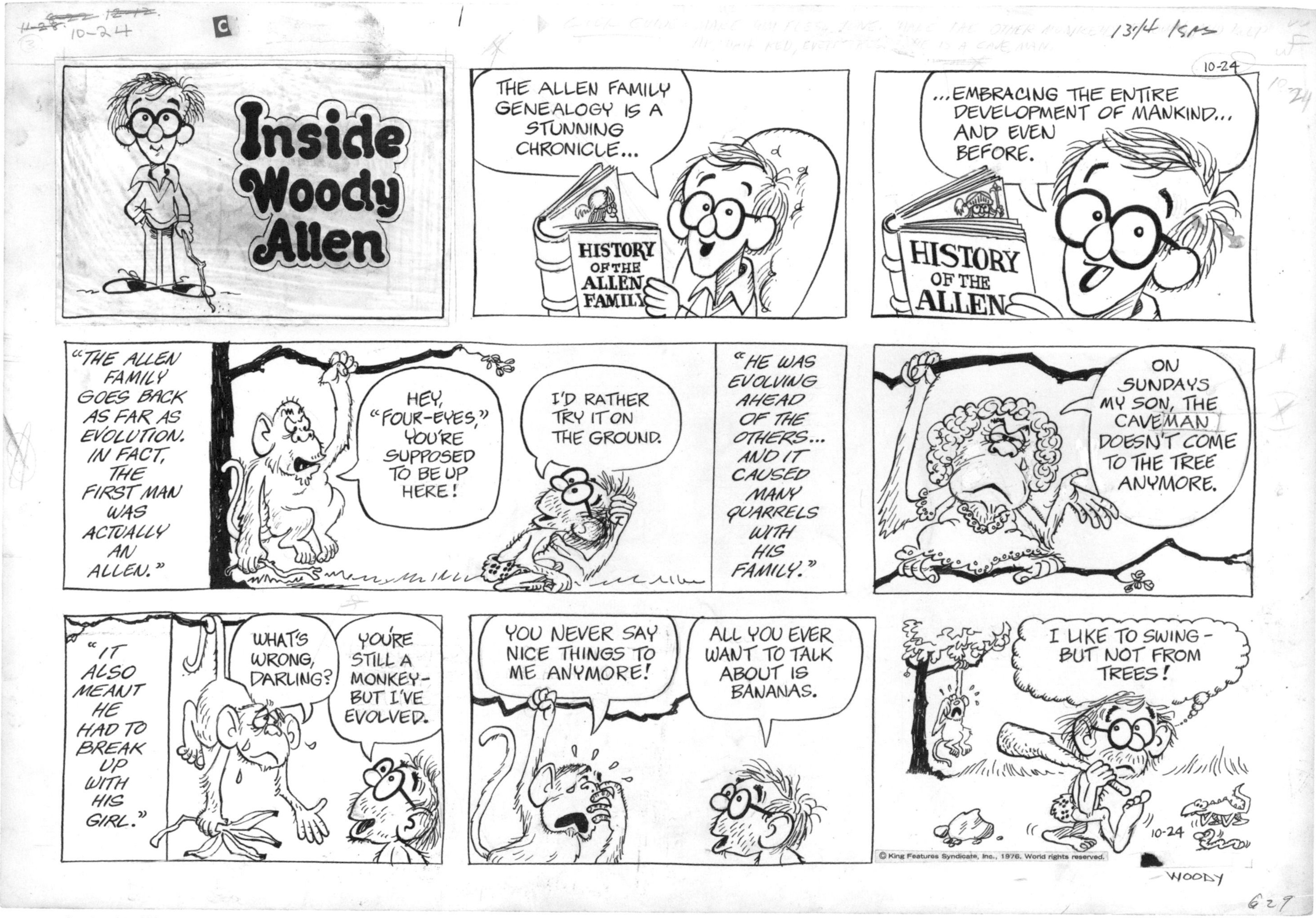
Inside Woody Allen
THE ALLEN FAMILY GENEALOGY IS A STUNNING CHRONICLE...
HISTORY OF THE ALLEN FAMILY
...EMBRACING THE ENTIRE DEVELOPMENT OF MANKIND... AND EVEN BEFORE.
HISTORY OF THE ALLEN
"THE ALLEN FAMILY GOES BACK AS FAR AS EVOLUTION. IN FACT, THE FIRST MAN WAS ACTUALLY AN ALLEN."
HEY, "FOUR-EYES," YOU'RE SUPPOSED TO BE UP HERE!
I'D RATHER TRY IT ON THE GROUND.
"HE WAS EVOLVING AHEAD OF THE OTHERS... AND IT CAUSED MANY QUARRELS WITH HIS FAMILY."
ON SUNDAYS MY SON, THE CAVEMAN DOESN'T COME TO THE TREE ANYMORE.
"IT ALSO MEANT HE HAD TO BREAK UP WITH HIS GIRL."
WHAT'S WRONG, DARLING?
YOU'RE STILL A MONKEY- BUT I'VE EVOLVED.
YOU NEVER SAY NICE THINGS TO ME ANYMORE!
ALL YOU EVER WANT TO TALK ABOUT IS BANANAS.
I LIKE TO SWING- BUT NOT FROM TREES!
10-24
© King Features Syndicate, Inc., 1976. World rights reserved.
WOODY

October 24, 1976

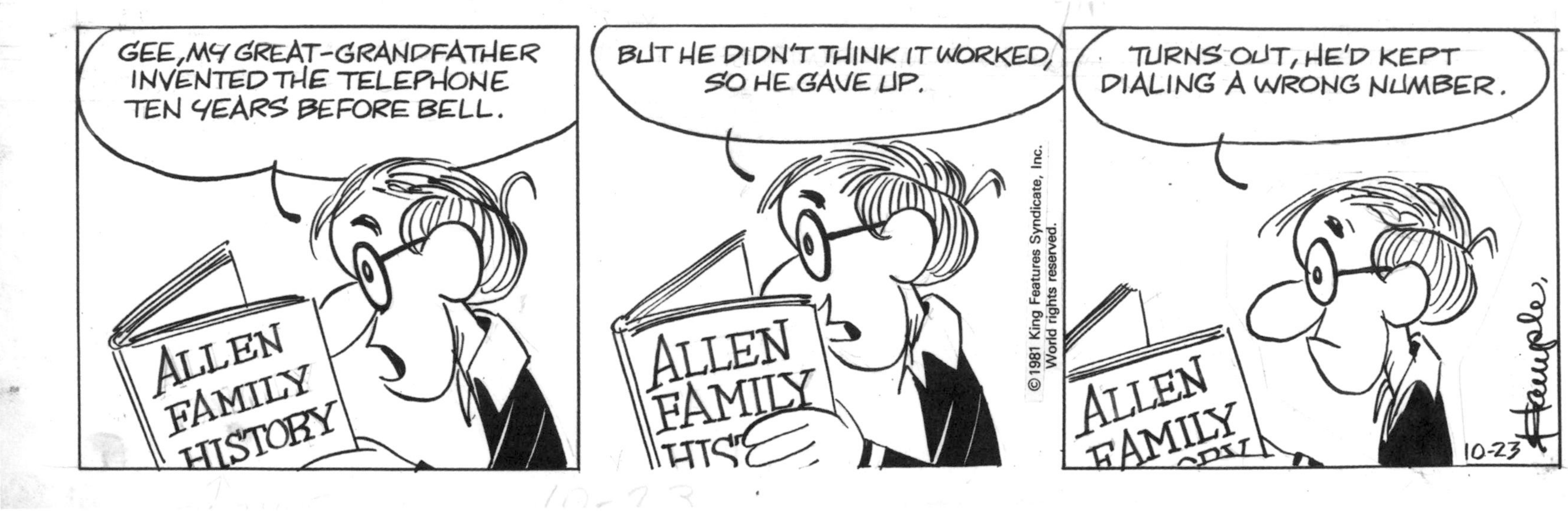
GEE, MY GREAT-GRANDFATHER INVENTED THE TELEPHONE TEN YEARS BEFORE BELL.
ALLEN FAMILY HISTORY
BUT HE DIDN'T THINK IT WORKED, SO HE GAVE UP.
© 1981 King Features Syndicate, Inc. World rights reserved.
TURNS OUT, HE'D KEPT DIALING A WRONG NUMBER.
10-23
Hampele

October 23, 1981

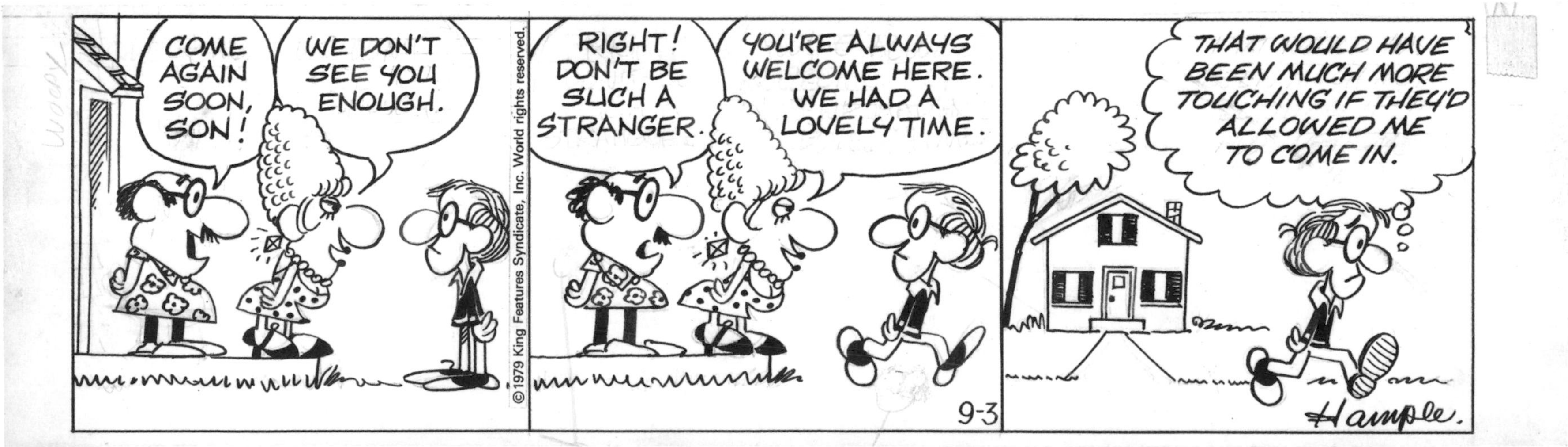
COME AGAIN SOON, SON!
WE DON'T SEE YOU ENOUGH.
© 1979 King Features Syndicate, Inc. World rights reserved.
RIGHT! DON'T BE SUCH A STRANGER.
YOU'RE ALWAYS WELCOME HERE. WE HAD A LOVELY TIME.
9-3
THAT WOULD HAVE BEEN MUCH MORE TOUCHING IF THEY'D ALLOWED ME TO COME IN.
Hample.

September 3, 1979

Inside Woody Allen

"I VISITED MY OLD NEIGHBORHOOD, AND THERE WAS A PARKING LOT WHERE THE PIZZA PARLOR ONCE STOOD."

WOODY

I USED TO TAKE ALL MY DATES THERE.

"I FIRST LEARNED ABOUT INGRATITUDE AT MACHIAVELLI'S PIZZA PARLOR IN BROOKLYN."

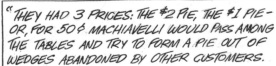

"THEY HAD 3 PRICES: THE $2 PIE, THE $1 PIE— OR, FOR 50¢ MACHIAVELLI WOULD PASS AMONG THE TABLES AND TRY TO FORM A PIE OUT OF WEDGES ABANDONED BY OTHER CUSTOMERS."

"ONCE I TOOK A GIRL THERE AND THE PIE CAME OUT IN 7 SLICES, WHICH MEANT 3 APIECE AND 1 EXTRA."

"IT WAS A PROBLEM, BECAUSE I LOVED HER VERY MUCH, SO I FINALLY DECIDED TO GIVE HER THE EXTRA SLICE."

"FOUR YEARS LATER, WHEN I PROPOSED TO HER, SHE TURNED ME DOWN."

"AND WHEN I BROUGHT UP THE INCIDENT OF THE EXTRA SLICE, SHE CLAIMED TO HAVE FORGOTTEN IT."

A LIKELY STORY!

WOODY

January 2, 1977

August 27, 1979

June 16, 1977

They Exchanged Gunfire Daily

Inside Woody Allen

ONE OF MY CHILDHOOD FANTASIES WAS TO WEAR A UNIFORM...

I HAVE ALWAYS HAD A PREDILECTION TOWARD UNIFORMS.

"AS A KID, I TOLD MY PARENTS I DESPERATELY WANTED TO BE A BOY SCOUT...

BOY SCOUT? YOU? YOU WOULDN'T MAKE IT!

YOU'VE NEVER DONE A GOOD DEED

"TO PROVE THEM WRONG, I SET OUT TO HELP OLD LADIES CROSS THE STREET.

ARE YOU A BOY SCOUT?

I'M FREE-LANCING.

CAN I HELP YOU CROSS THE STREET?

WHAT'S IT WORTH TO YOU, KID?

"I HELPED THEM ACROSS AT 25¢ APIECE.

DON'T SHOVE!

I'M GOING AS FAST AS I CAN. HERE'S YOUR QUARTER.

"FACES STARTED BECOMING FAMILIAR.

DIDN'T I HELP YOU ACROSS THIS MORNING?

YES, BUT I'M COMING HOME NOW. GIMME MY QUARTER!

"NEWS OF MY VENTURE SPREAD.

FOR 50¢ YOU CAN HELP **ME** CROSS THE STREET!

"NOT ONLY DIDN'T I GET INTO THE BOY SCOUTS, BUT THEY ENDED UP SUING ME FOR RESTRAINT OF TRADE."

WOODY ALLEN

August 7, 1977

Inside Woody Allen

"AS A KID, I WAS A TRUANT. WHENEVER MY FATHER ASKED ME TO DO SOMETHING, I KICKED HIM.

CLEAN YOUR ROOM...

NO!

"THEN HE'D TELL MY MOTHER—AND SHE WOULD KICK HIM.

"I HAD A TERRIBLE CHILDHOOD, MAINLY BECAUSE I WAS SUCH A TERRIBLE CHILD.

PUSH

"WHEN I WAS A BABY I REFUSED TO SLEEP IN A CRIB.

NOO GOO GLUCK!!

"MY FATHER WOULD GET IN THE CRIB TO SHOW ME IT WAS SAFE.

SEE HOW NICE?

"THEN MY MOTHER WOULD TRY TO PUT ME IN, BUT MY FATHER WOULDN'T GET OUT.

I WANT CRIB!

NOO GOO GLUCK

"HE LIKED THE CRIB HIMSELF AND GOT USED TO IT.

Rattle!

Rattle!

"TO GET EVEN I'D BREAK HIS RATTLE.

"WE HAD TO TAKE HIM TO A CHILD PSYCHOLOGIST.

"HE SAID MY FATHER WAS IN HIS SECOND CHILDHOOD."

I WASN'T TOO CRAZY ABOUT MY FIRST.

6-22 Hample.

INSIDE WOODY ALLEN

June 22, 1980

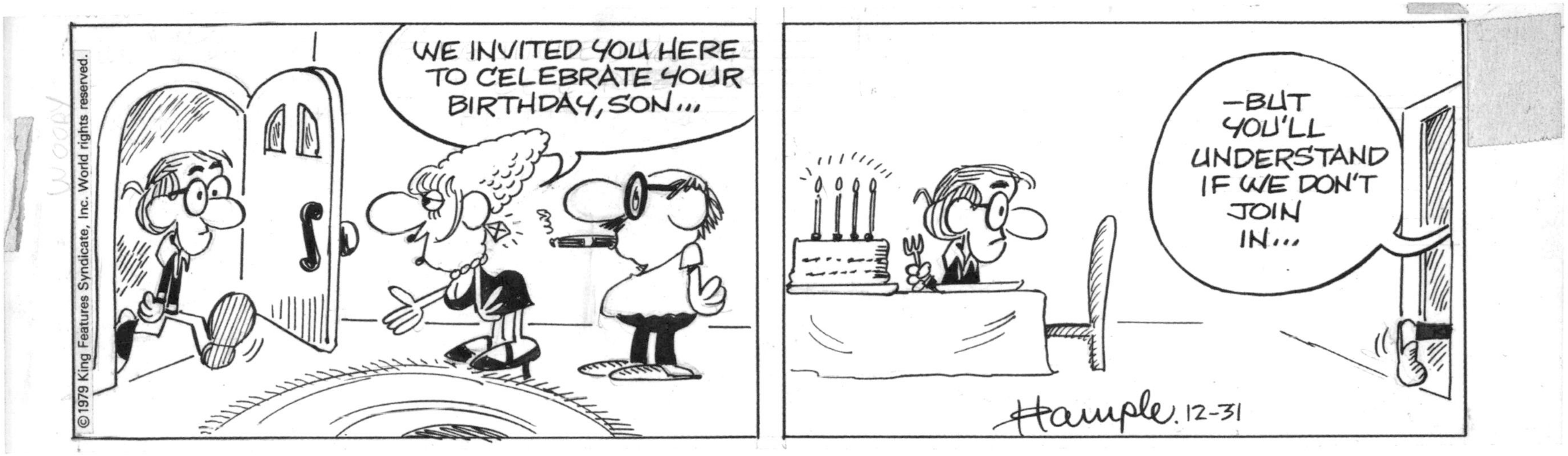

© 1979 King Features Syndicate, Inc. World rights reserved.
WE INVITED YOU HERE TO CELEBRATE YOUR BIRTHDAY, SON...
—BUT YOU'LL UNDERSTAND IF WE DON'T JOIN IN...
Hample. 12-31

December 31, 1979

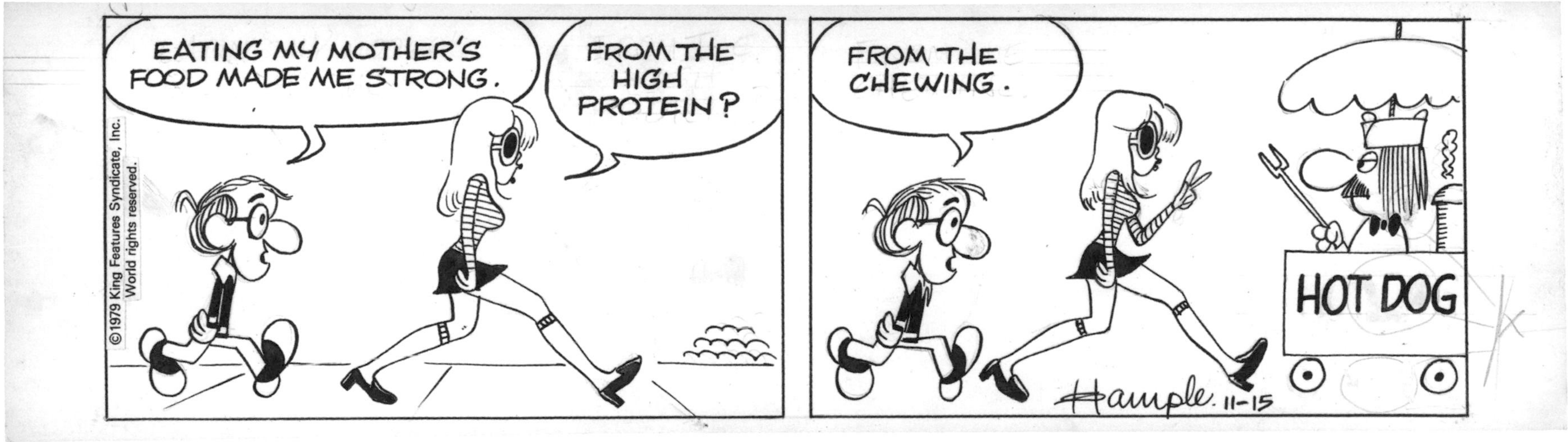

© 1979 King Features Syndicate, Inc. World rights reserved.
EATING MY MOTHER'S FOOD MADE ME STRONG.
FROM THE HIGH PROTEIN?
FROM THE CHEWING.
HOT DOG
Hample. 11-15

November 15, 1979

Inside Woody Allen

"I INHERITED SHORTNESS FROM BOTH OF MY PARENTS...

"PROBABLY BECAUSE MY FATHER IS SHORTER THAN MY MOTHER AND VICE VERSA.

"FROM THE TIME I WAS A KID, MY DREAM WAS TO JOIN THE POLICE OR THE F.B.I.

"I SENT FOR THE REQUIREMENTS, BUT I GOT TURNED DOWN BECAUSE YOU HAD TO BE 5'8" WITH 20-20 VISION.

F.B.I. Dear Sir: No.

"THEN I TOYED WITH THE IDEA OF BECOMING A MASTER CRIMINAL, AND I WROTE TO SOME CRIMINALS.

TAP TAP

"BUT...

The Mob, Inc.
Dear Sir:
In order to be a gangster, you must be 5'8" and have 20-20 vision.
However

"ONE MOB FAMILY IN NEW JERSEY WAS SHORT OF MEMBERS...

...WE'LL TAKE YA, KID, BUT YA GOTTA WEAR PLATFORM SHOES...

GEE, IT'S TEMPTING...

"BUT I DECIDED AGAINST IT BECAUSE I DIDN'T WANT TO LIVE IN THE SUBURBS."

WOODY

June 5, 1977

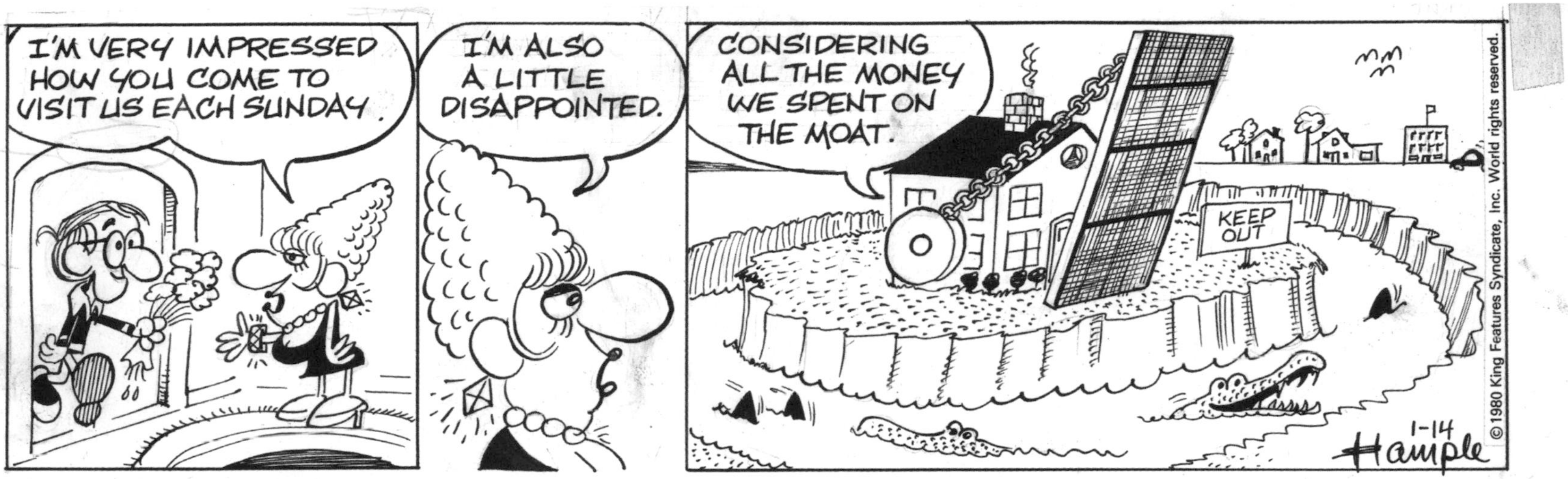
I'M VERY IMPRESSED HOW YOU COME TO VISIT US EACH SUNDAY.
I'M ALSO A LITTLE DISAPPOINTED.
CONSIDERING ALL THE MONEY WE SPENT ON THE MOAT.
KEEP OUT
1-14 Hample
© 1980 King Features Syndicate, Inc. World rights reserved.

January 14, 1980

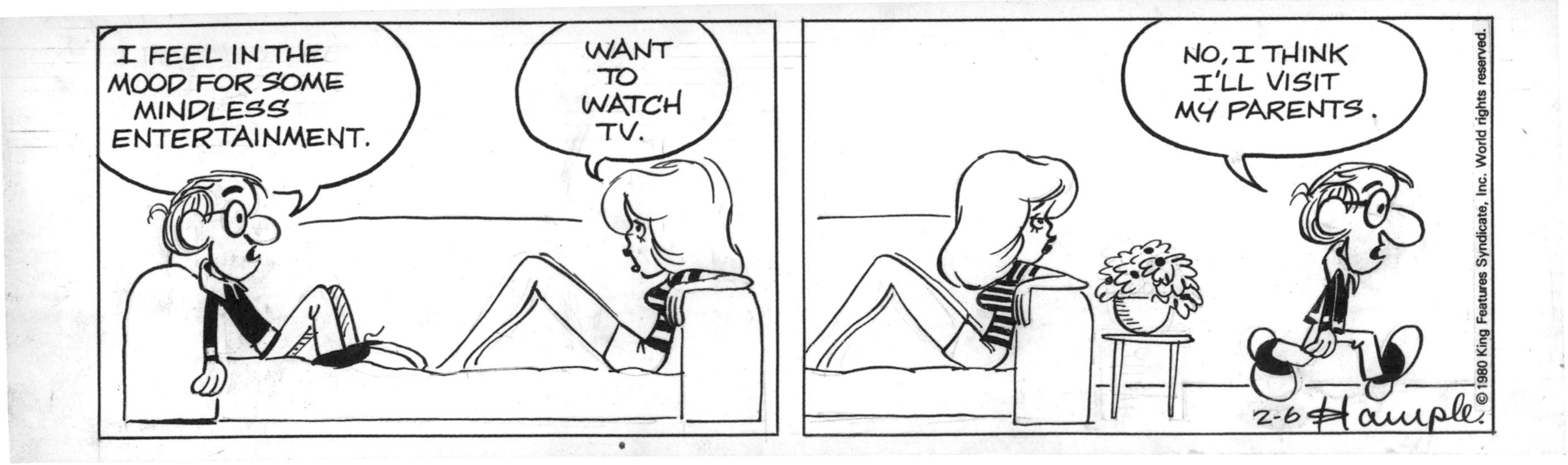
I FEEL IN THE MOOD FOR SOME MINDLESS ENTERTAINMENT.
WANT TO WATCH TV.
NO, I THINK I'LL VISIT MY PARENTS.
2-6 Hample.
© 1980 King Features Syndicate, Inc. World rights reserved.

February 6, 1980

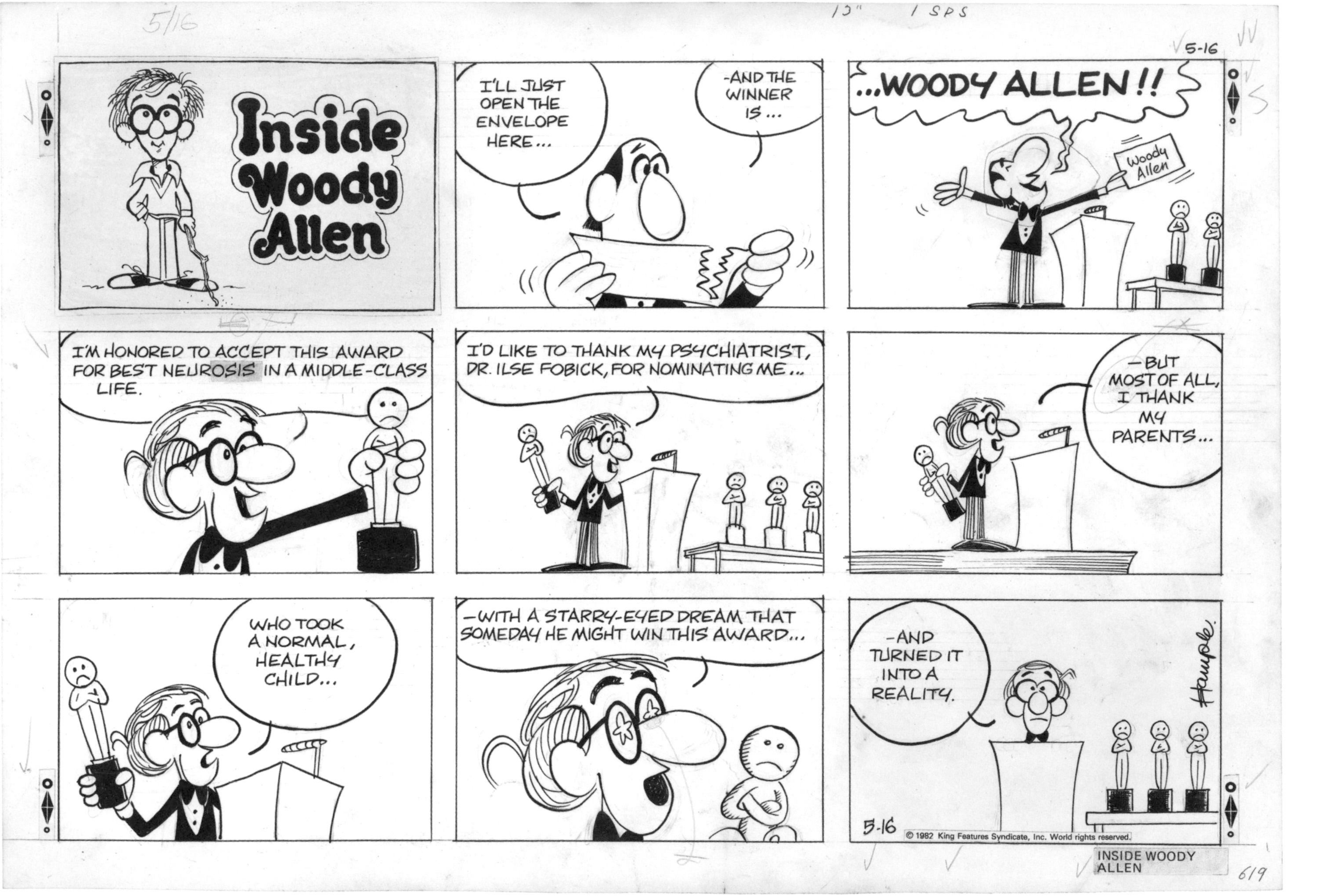
5/16
13" 1 SPS
5-16
Inside Woody Allen
I'LL JUST OPEN THE ENVELOPE HERE...
-AND THE WINNER IS...
...WOODY ALLEN!!
Woody Allen
I'M HONORED TO ACCEPT THIS AWARD FOR BEST NEUROSIS IN A MIDDLE-CLASS LIFE.
I'D LIKE TO THANK MY PSYCHIATRIST, DR. ILSE FOBICK, FOR NOMINATING ME...
-BUT MOST OF ALL, I THANK MY PARENTS...
WHO TOOK A NORMAL, HEALTHY CHILD...
-WITH A STARRY-EYED DREAM THAT SOMEDAY HE MIGHT WIN THIS AWARD...
-AND TURNED IT INTO A REALITY.
Hample
5-16
© 1982 King Features Syndicate, Inc. World rights reserved.
INSIDE WOODY ALLEN
619

May 16, 1982

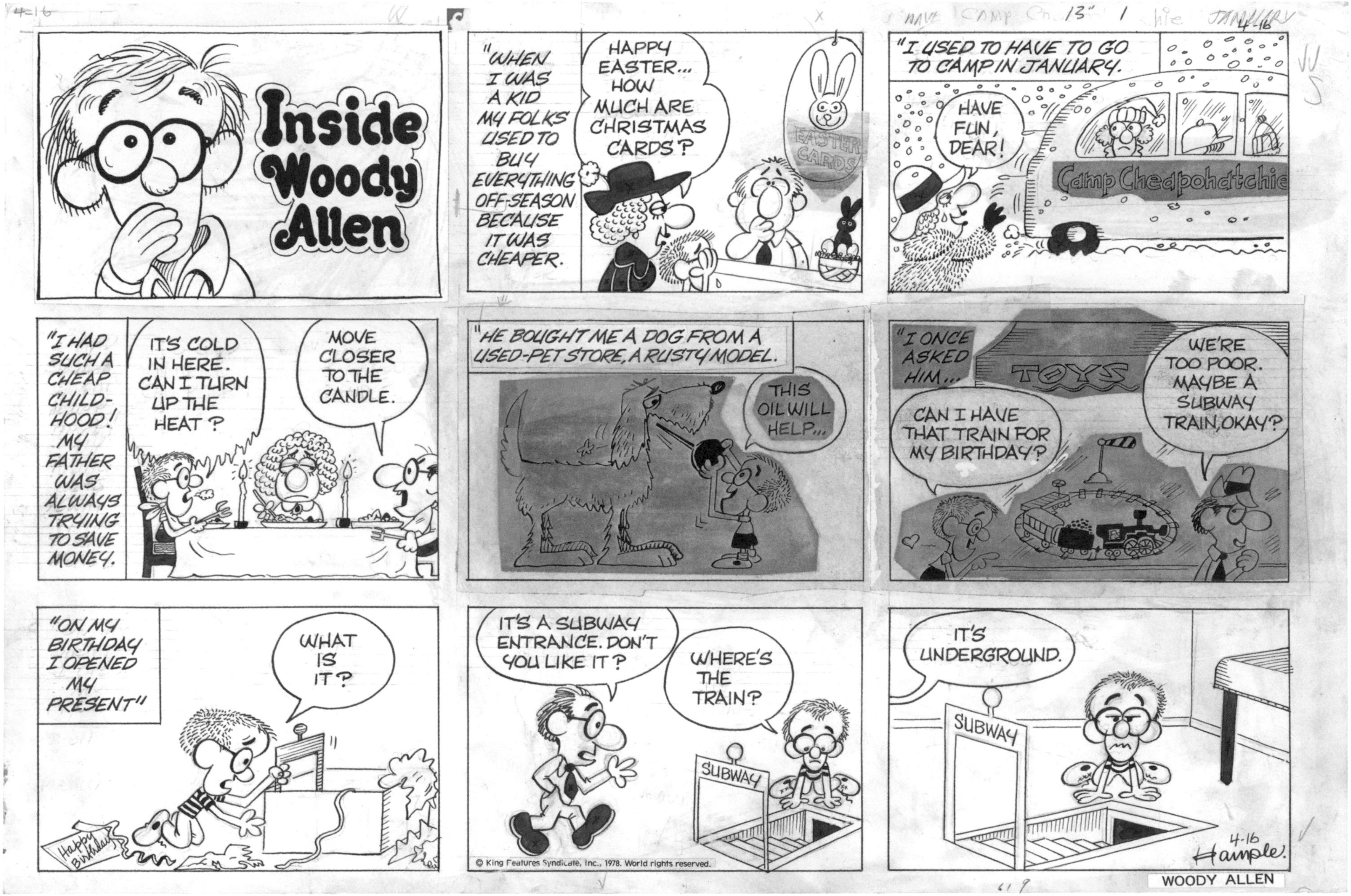
Inside Woody Allen
"WHEN I WAS A KID MY FOLKS USED TO BUY EVERYTHING OFF-SEASON BECAUSE IT WAS CHEAPER.
HAPPY EASTER... HOW MUCH ARE CHRISTMAS CARDS?
EASTER CARDS
"I USED TO HAVE TO GO TO CAMP IN JANUARY.
HAVE FUN, DEAR!
Camp Cheapohatchie
"I HAD SUCH A CHEAP CHILDHOOD! MY FATHER WAS ALWAYS TRYING TO SAVE MONEY.
IT'S COLD IN HERE. CAN I TURN UP THE HEAT?
MOVE CLOSER TO THE CANDLE.
"HE BOUGHT ME A DOG FROM A USED-PET STORE, A RUSTY MODEL.
THIS OIL WILL HELP...
"I ONCE ASKED HIM...
TOYS
CAN I HAVE THAT TRAIN FOR MY BIRTHDAY?
WE'RE TOO POOR. MAYBE A SUBWAY TRAIN, OKAY?
"ON MY BIRTHDAY I OPENED MY PRESENT"
WHAT IS IT?
Happy Birthday
IT'S A SUBWAY ENTRANCE. DON'T YOU LIKE IT?
WHERE'S THE TRAIN?
SUBWAY
© King Features Syndicate, Inc., 1978. World rights reserved.
IT'S UNDERGROUND.
SUBWAY
4-16
Hample
WOODY ALLEN
April 16, 1978

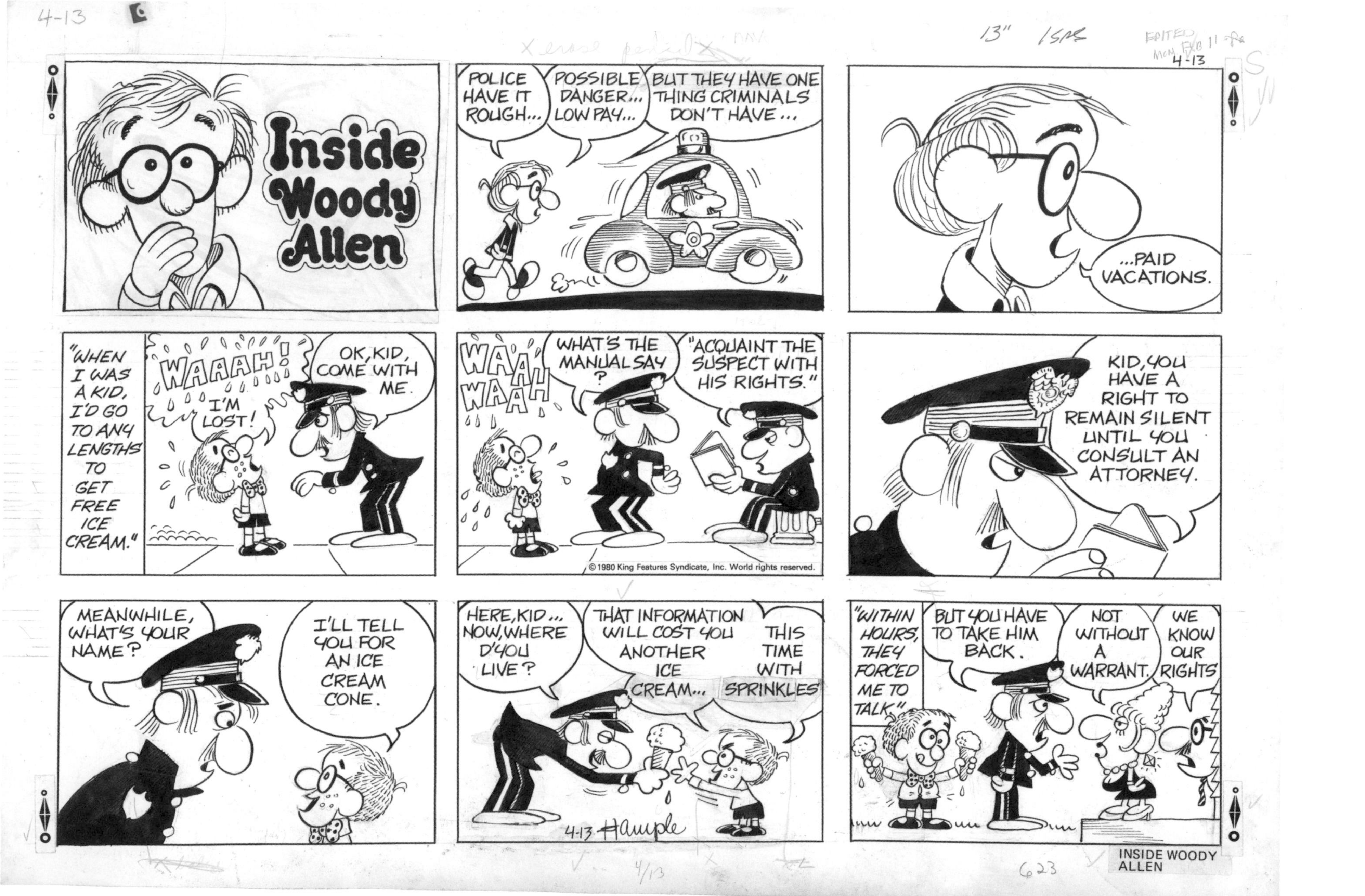
Inside Woody Allen
POLICE HAVE IT ROUGH...
POSSIBLE DANGER... LOW PAY...
BUT THEY HAVE ONE THING CRIMINALS DON'T HAVE...
...PAID VACATIONS.
"WHEN I WAS A KID, I'D GO TO ANY LENGTHS TO GET FREE ICE CREAM."
WAAAH!
I'M LOST!
OK, KID, COME WITH ME.
WAAAH WAAAH
WHAT'S THE MANUAL SAY?
"ACQUAINT THE SUSPECT WITH HIS RIGHTS."
© 1980 King Features Syndicate, Inc. World rights reserved.
KID, YOU HAVE A RIGHT TO REMAIN SILENT UNTIL YOU CONSULT AN ATTORNEY.
MEANWHILE, WHAT'S YOUR NAME?
I'LL TELL YOU FOR AN ICE CREAM CONE.
HERE, KID... NOW, WHERE D'YOU LIVE?
THAT INFORMATION WILL COST YOU ANOTHER ICE CREAM...
THIS TIME WITH SPRINKLES
4-13 Hample
"WITHIN HOURS, THEY FORCED ME TO TALK."
BUT YOU HAVE TO TAKE HIM BACK.
NOT WITHOUT A WARRANT.
WE KNOW OUR RIGHTS
INSIDE WOODY ALLEN

April 13, 1980

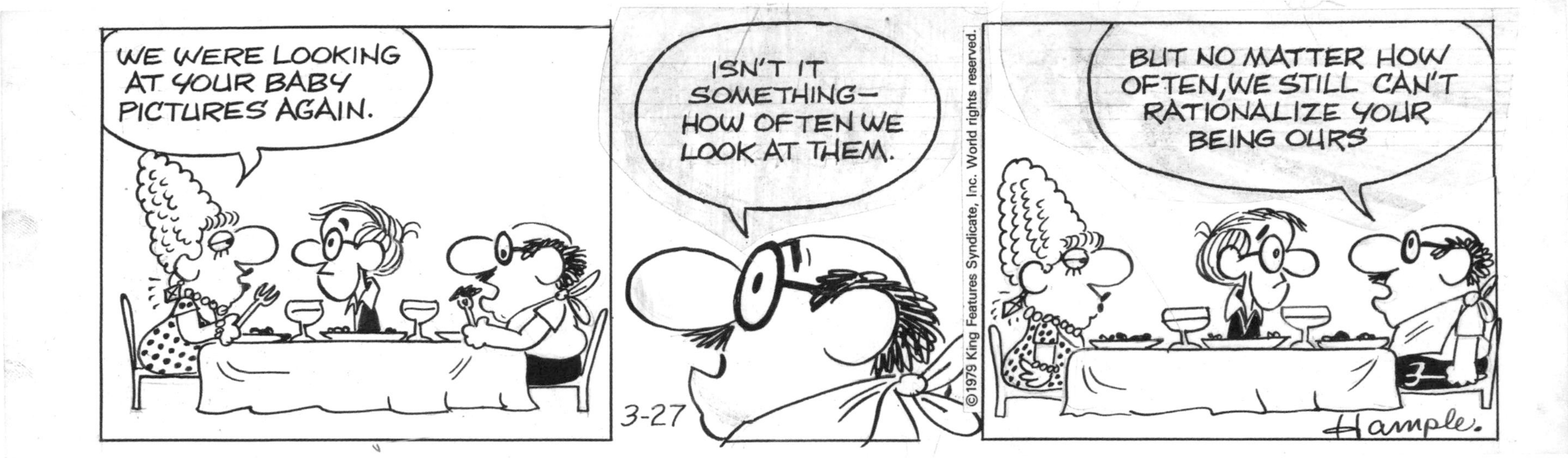
WE WERE LOOKING AT YOUR BABY PICTURES AGAIN.
ISN'T IT SOMETHING— HOW OFTEN WE LOOK AT THEM.
3-27
© 1979 King Features Syndicate, Inc. World rights reserved.
BUT NO MATTER HOW OFTEN, WE STILL CAN'T RATIONALIZE YOUR BEING OURS
Hample.

March 27, 1979

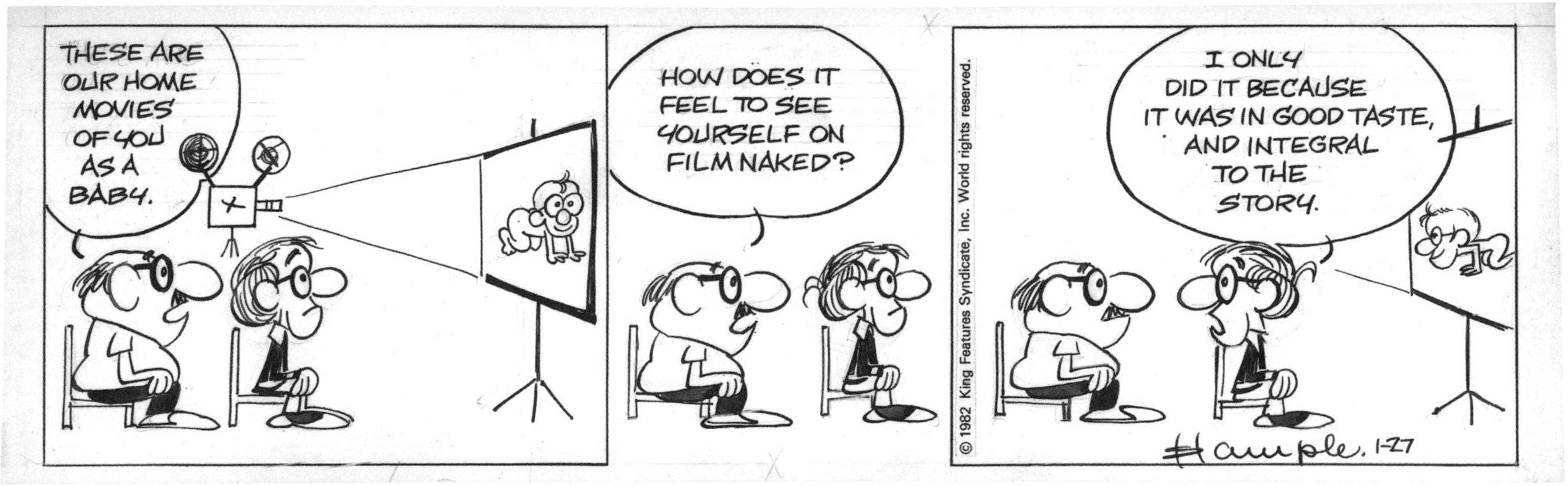
THESE ARE OUR HOME MOVIES OF YOU AS A BABY.
HOW DOES IT FEEL TO SEE YOURSELF ON FILM NAKED?
© 1982 King Features Syndicate, Inc. World rights reserved.
I ONLY DID IT BECAUSE IT WAS IN GOOD TASTE, AND INTEGRAL TO THE STORY.
Hample. 1-27

January 27, 1982

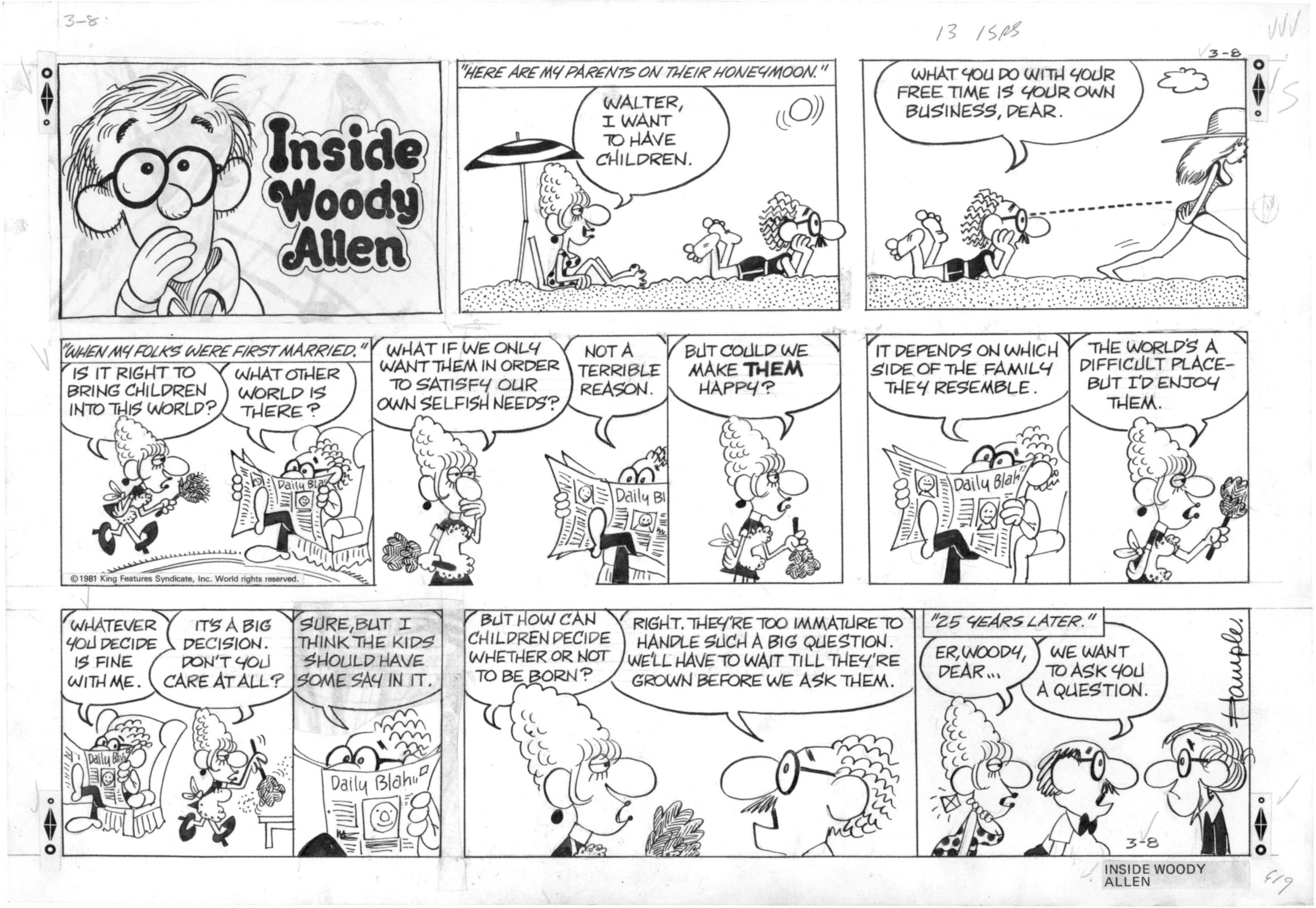
3-8
13 1SRS
3-8
Inside Woody Allen
"HERE ARE MY PARENTS ON THEIR HONEYMOON."
WALTER, I WANT TO HAVE CHILDREN.
WHAT YOU DO WITH YOUR FREE TIME IS YOUR OWN BUSINESS, DEAR.
"WHEN MY FOLKS WERE FIRST MARRIED."
IS IT RIGHT TO BRING CHILDREN INTO THIS WORLD?
WHAT OTHER WORLD IS THERE?
Daily Blah
WHAT IF WE ONLY WANT THEM IN ORDER TO SATISFY OUR OWN SELFISH NEEDS?
NOT A TERRIBLE REASON.
BUT COULD WE MAKE THEM HAPPY?
IT DEPENDS ON WHICH SIDE OF THE FAMILY THEY RESEMBLE.
Daily Blah
THE WORLD'S A DIFFICULT PLACE–BUT I'D ENJOY THEM.
© 1981 King Features Syndicate, Inc. World rights reserved.
WHATEVER YOU DECIDE IS FINE WITH ME.
IT'S A BIG DECISION. DON'T YOU CARE AT ALL?
SURE, BUT I THINK THE KIDS SHOULD HAVE SOME SAY IN IT.
Daily Blah
BUT HOW CAN CHILDREN DECIDE WHETHER OR NOT TO BE BORN?
RIGHT. THEY'RE TOO IMMATURE TO HANDLE SUCH A BIG QUESTION. WE'LL HAVE TO WAIT TILL THEY'RE GROWN BEFORE WE ASK THEM.
"25 YEARS LATER."
ER, WOODY, DEAR...
WE WANT TO ASK YOU A QUESTION.
Hample
3-8
INSIDE WOODY ALLEN

March 8, 1981

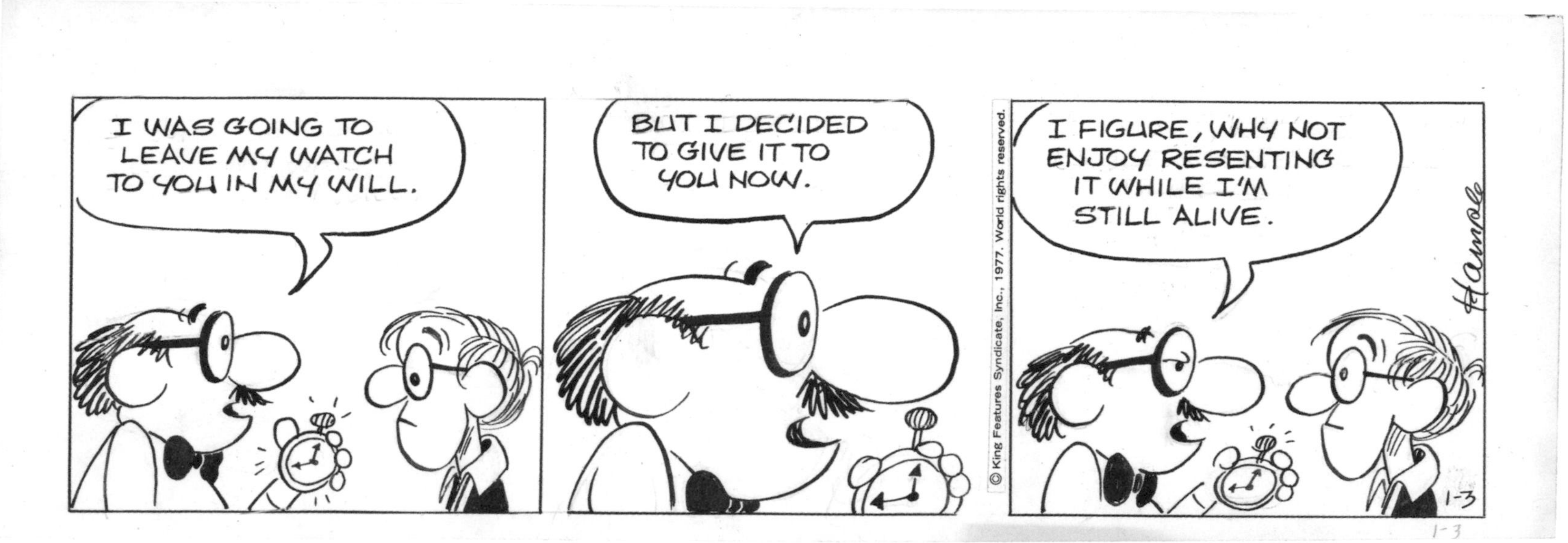
I WAS GOING TO LEAVE MY WATCH TO YOU IN MY WILL.
BUT I DECIDED TO GIVE IT TO YOU NOW.
© King Features Syndicate, Inc., 1977. World rights reserved.
I FIGURE, WHY NOT ENJOY RESENTING IT WHILE I'M STILL ALIVE.
Hample
1-3

January 3, 1977

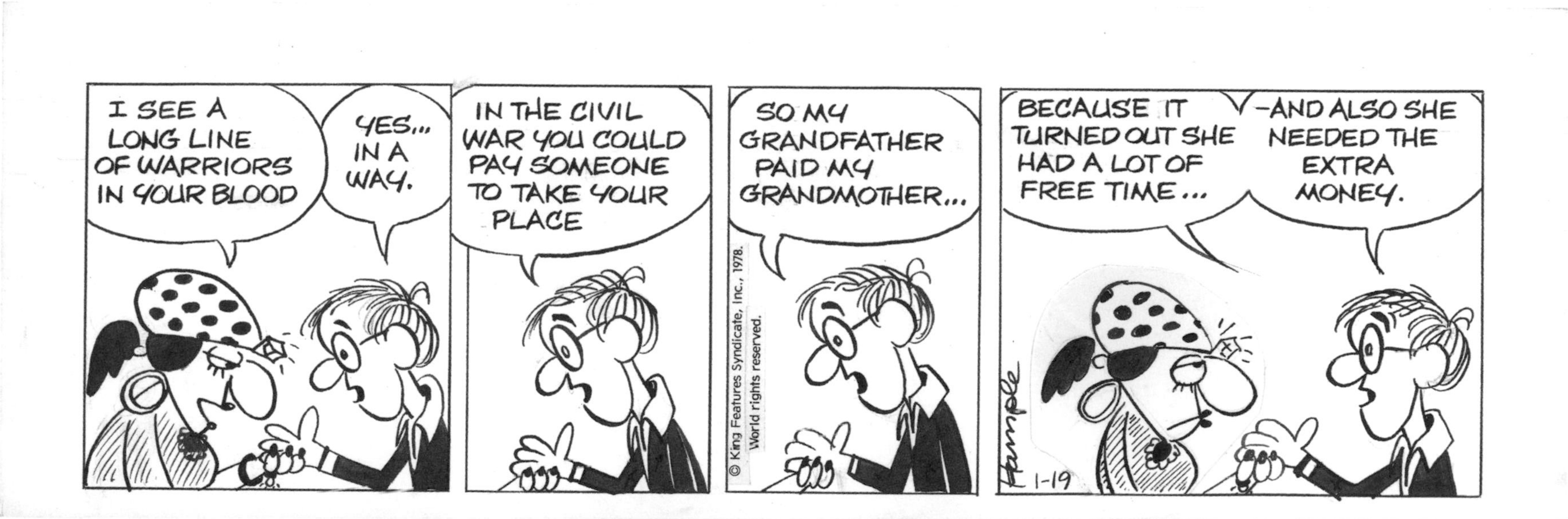
I SEE A LONG LINE OF WARRIORS IN YOUR BLOOD
YES... IN A WAY.
IN THE CIVIL WAR YOU COULD PAY SOMEONE TO TAKE YOUR PLACE
© King Features Syndicate, Inc., 1978. World rights reserved.
SO MY GRANDFATHER PAID MY GRANDMOTHER...
Hample
1-19
BECAUSE IT TURNED OUT SHE HAD A LOT OF FREE TIME...
—AND ALSO SHE NEEDED THE EXTRA MONEY.

January 19, 1978

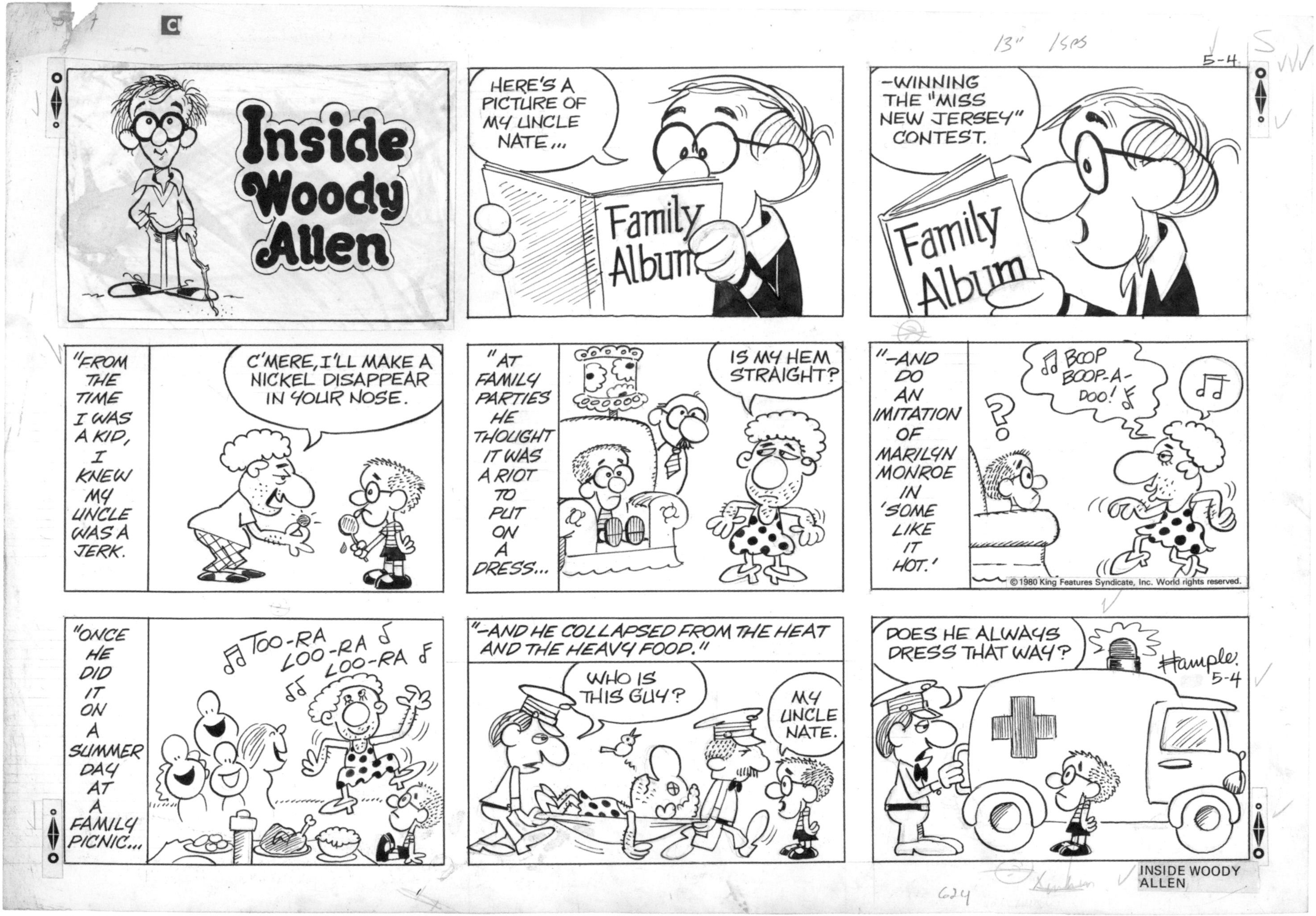
Inside Woody Allen
HERE'S A PICTURE OF MY UNCLE NATE...
Family Album
-WINNING THE "MISS NEW JERSEY" CONTEST.
Family Album
"FROM THE TIME I WAS A KID, I KNEW MY UNCLE WAS A JERK.
C'MERE, I'LL MAKE A NICKEL DISAPPEAR IN YOUR NOSE.
"AT FAMILY PARTIES HE THOUGHT IT WAS A RIOT TO PUT ON A DRESS...
IS MY HEM STRAIGHT?
"-AND DO AN IMITATION OF MARILYN MONROE IN 'SOME LIKE IT HOT.'
BOOP BOOP-A-DOO!
?
© 1980 King Features Syndicate, Inc. World rights reserved.
"ONCE HE DID IT ON A SUMMER DAY AT A FAMILY PICNIC...
TOO-RA LOO-RA LOO-RA
"-AND HE COLLAPSED FROM THE HEAT AND THE HEAVY FOOD."
WHO IS THIS GUY?
MY UNCLE NATE.
DOES HE ALWAYS DRESS THAT WAY?
Hample 5-4
INSIDE WOODY ALLEN

May 4, 1980

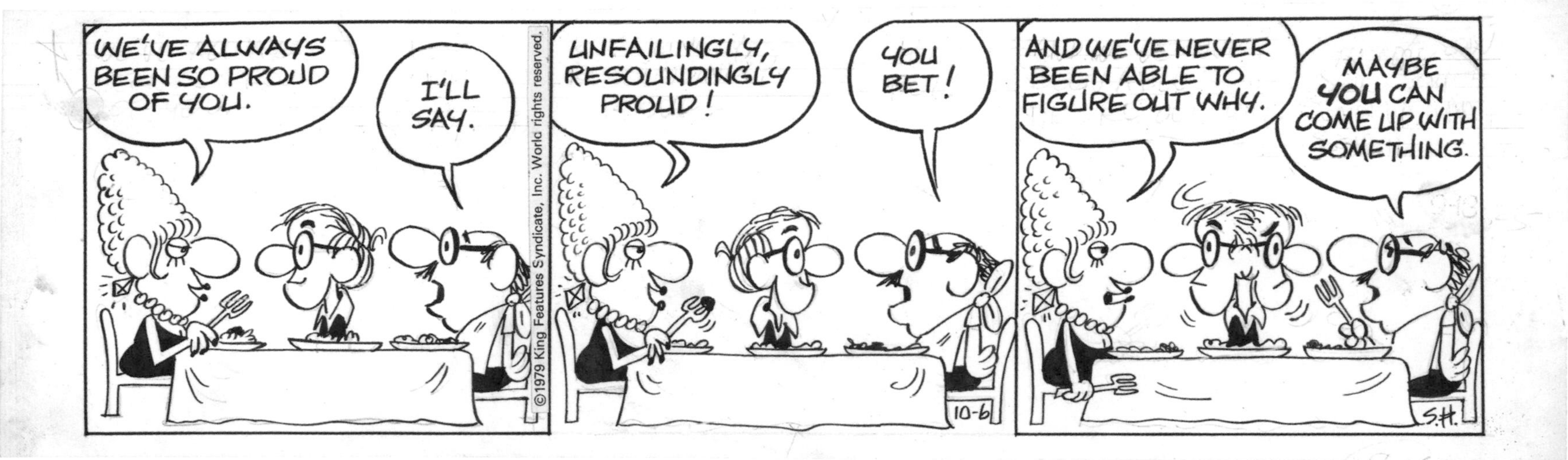
WE'VE ALWAYS BEEN SO PROUD OF YOU.
I'LL SAY.
©1979 King Features Syndicate, Inc. World rights reserved.
UNFAILINGLY, RESOUNDINGLY PROUD!
YOU BET!
10-6
AND WE'VE NEVER BEEN ABLE TO FIGURE OUT WHY.
MAYBE YOU CAN COME UP WITH SOMETHING.
S.H.

October 6, 1979

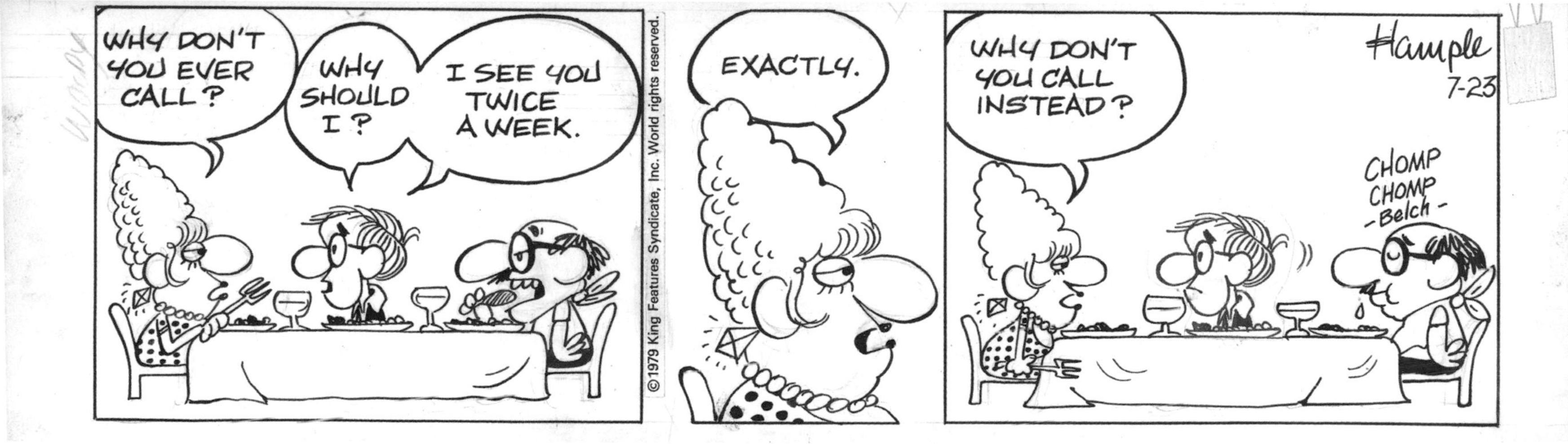
WHY DON'T YOU EVER CALL?
WHY SHOULD I?
I SEE YOU TWICE A WEEK.
©1979 King Features Syndicate, Inc. World rights reserved.
EXACTLY.
Hample
7-23
WHY DON'T YOU CALL INSTEAD?
CHOMP
CHOMP
-Belch-

July 23, 1979

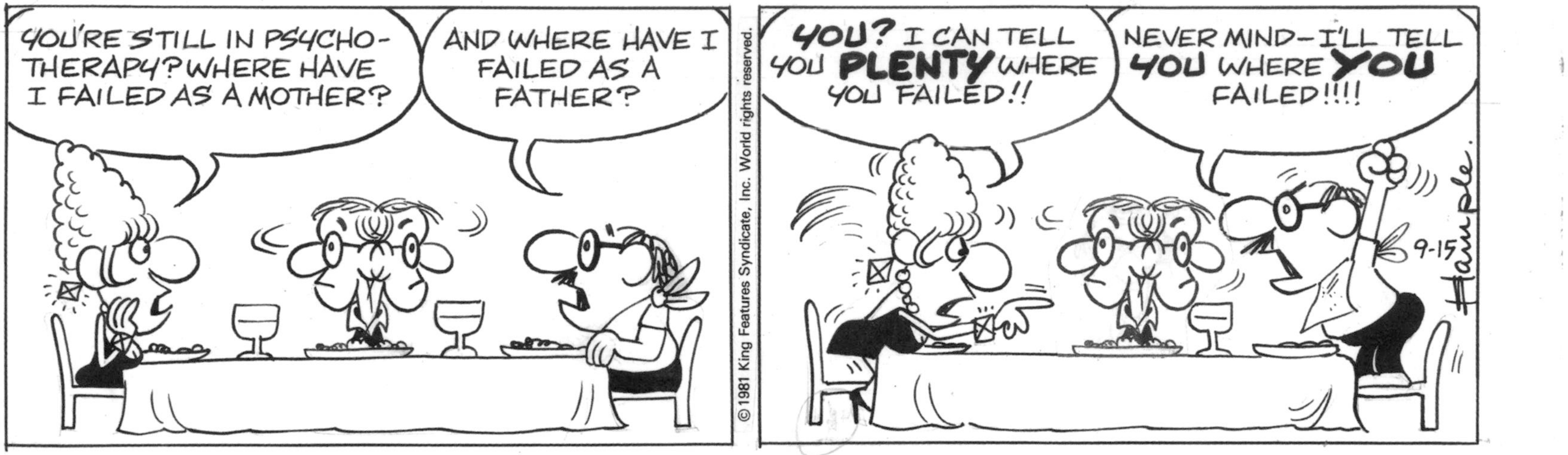
YOU'RE STILL IN PSYCHO-THERAPY? WHERE HAVE I FAILED AS A MOTHER?
AND WHERE HAVE I FAILED AS A FATHER?
© 1981 King Features Syndicate, Inc. World rights reserved.
YOU? I CAN TELL YOU PLENTY WHERE YOU FAILED!!
NEVER MIND—I'LL TELL YOU WHERE YOU FAILED!!!!
9-15
Hample

September 15, 1981

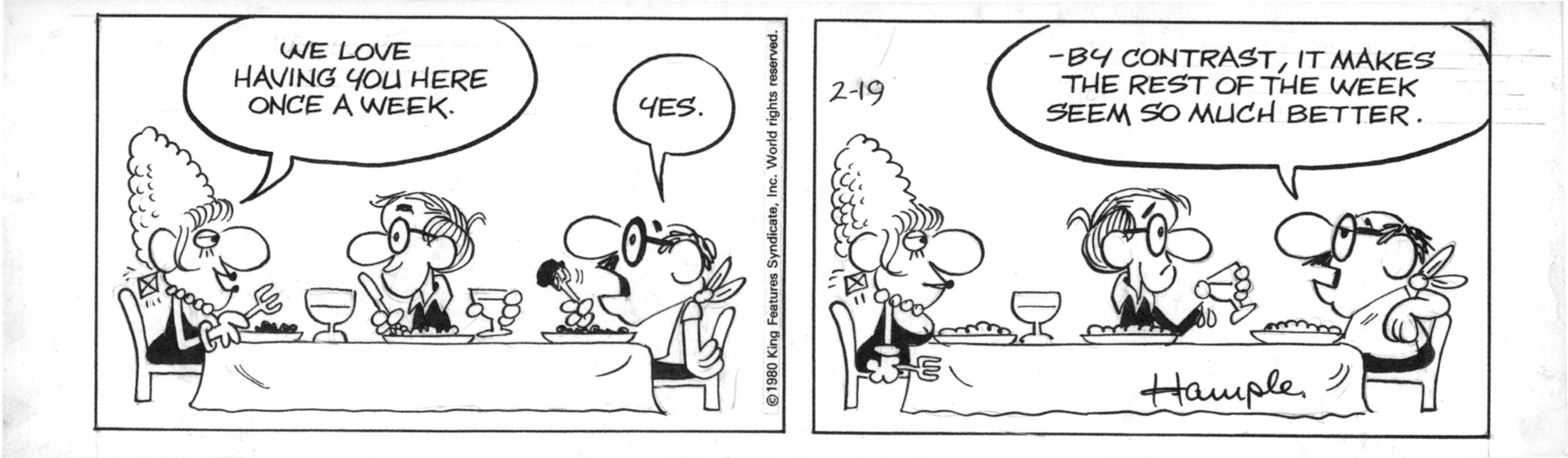
WE LOVE HAVING YOU HERE ONCE A WEEK.
YES.
© 1980 King Features Syndicate, Inc. World rights reserved.
2-19
-BY CONTRAST, IT MAKES THE REST OF THE WEEK SEEM SO MUCH BETTER.
Hample.

February 19, 1980

Inside Woody Allen

LIKE TO SEE SOME FAMILY MOVIES I TOOK YEARS AGO, SON?

NOT REALLY.

GOOD! PUT OUT THE LIGHTS.

AREN'T THESE OLD HOME MOVIES GREAT?

YES, BUT UNCLE MILO SURE WAS WEIRD.

LET'S HAVE SOME FUN! RUN THEM BACKWARDS.

ISN'T IT FUNNY? EVERYBODY'S DOING EVERYTHING BACKWARDS NOW.

YES, EXCEPT FOR UNCLE MILO.

© 1980 King Features Syndicate, Inc. World rights reserved.

2-10

IT SEEMS ODD—HIM DOING THINGS FORWARD!

Hample.

INSIDE WOODY ALLEN

February 10, 1980

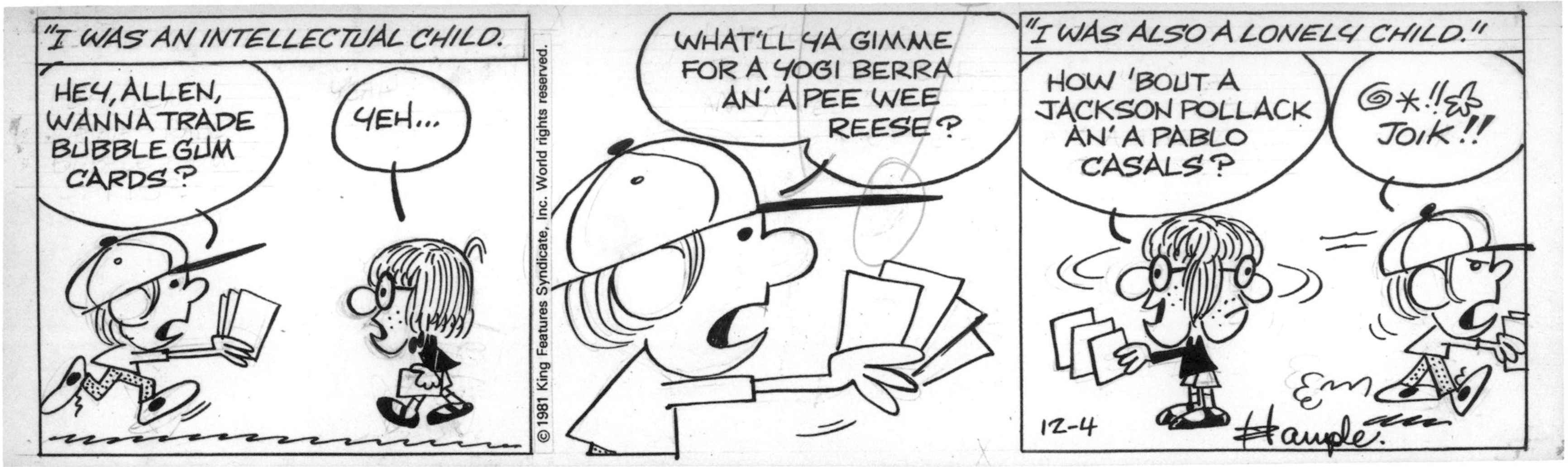
"I WAS AN INTELLECTUAL CHILD.
HEY, ALLEN, WANNA TRADE BUBBLE GUM CARDS?
YEH...
© 1981 King Features Syndicate, Inc. World rights reserved.
WHAT'LL YA GIMME FOR A YOGI BERRA AN' A PEE WEE REESE?
"I WAS ALSO A LONELY CHILD."
HOW 'BOUT A JACKSON POLLACK AN' A PABLO CASALS?
JOIK!!
12-4
Hample

December 4, 1981

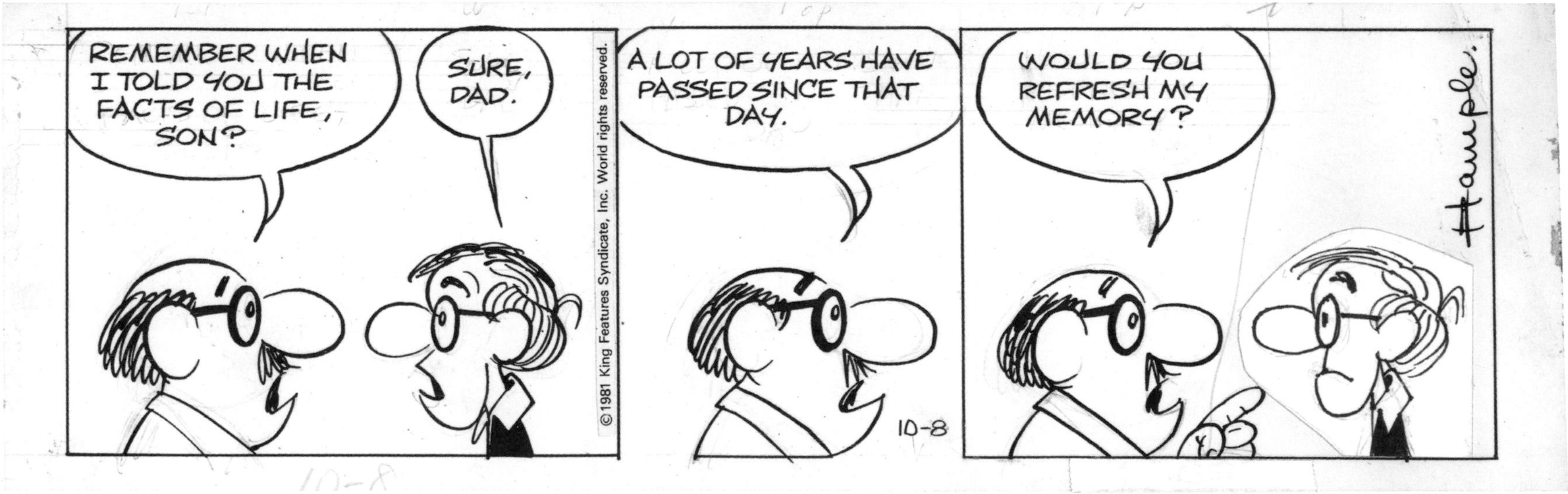
REMEMBER WHEN I TOLD YOU THE FACTS OF LIFE, SON?
SURE, DAD.
© 1981 King Features Syndicate, Inc. World rights reserved.
A LOT OF YEARS HAVE PASSED SINCE THAT DAY.
WOULD YOU REFRESH MY MEMORY?
10-8
Hample

October 8, 1981

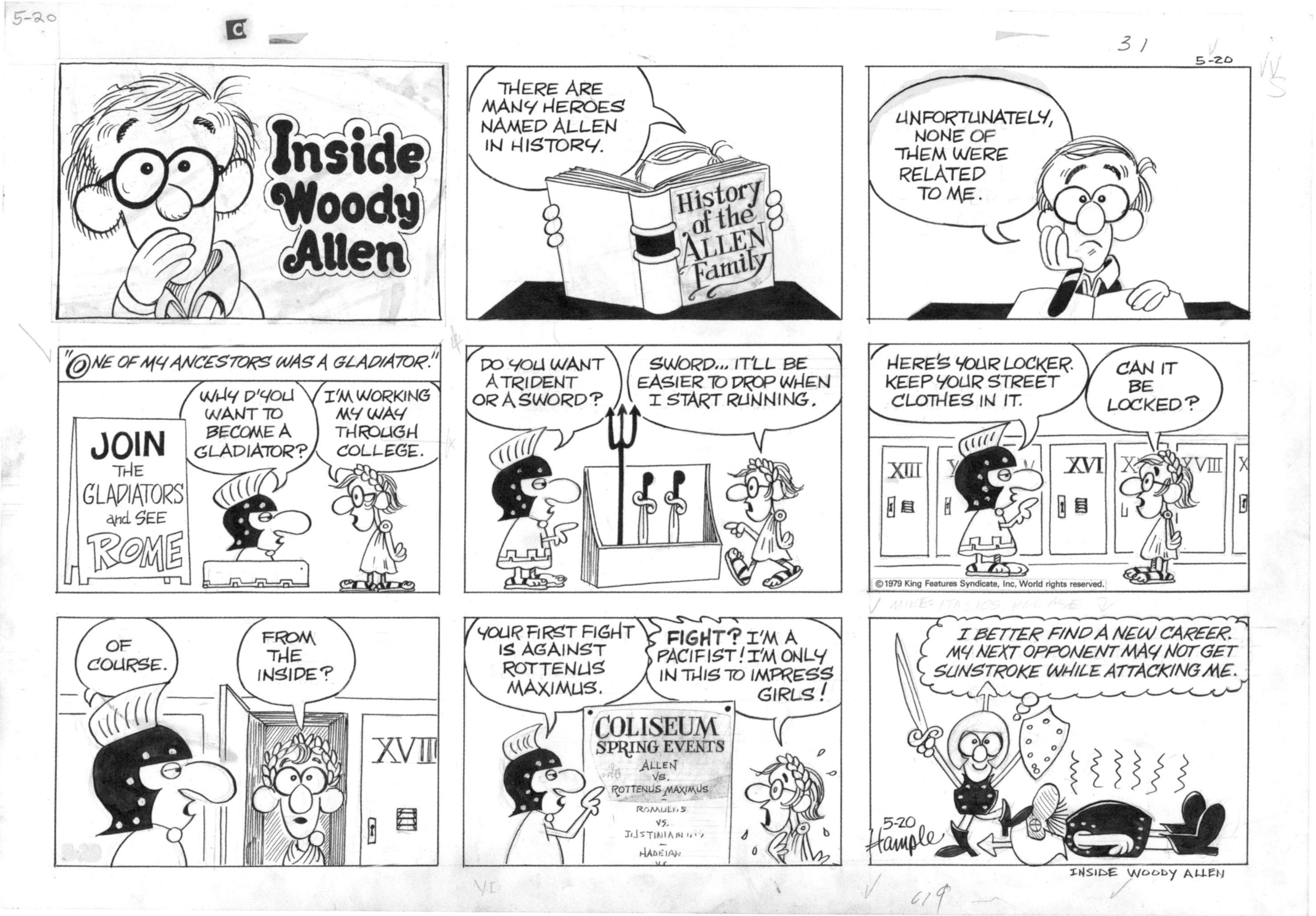

Inside Woody Allen
THERE ARE MANY HEROES NAMED ALLEN IN HISTORY.
History of the ALLEN Family
UNFORTUNATELY, NONE OF THEM WERE RELATED TO ME.
"ONE OF MY ANCESTORS WAS A GLADIATOR."
JOIN THE GLADIATORS and SEE ROME
WHY D'YOU WANT TO BECOME A GLADIATOR?
I'M WORKING MY WAY THROUGH COLLEGE.
DO YOU WANT A TRIDENT OR A SWORD?
SWORD... IT'LL BE EASIER TO DROP WHEN I START RUNNING.
HERE'S YOUR LOCKER. KEEP YOUR STREET CLOTHES IN IT.
CAN IT BE LOCKED?
XIII
XVI
XVIII
© 1979 King Features Syndicate, Inc, World rights reserved.
OF COURSE.
FROM THE INSIDE?
XVII
YOUR FIRST FIGHT IS AGAINST ROTTENUS MAXIMUS.
FIGHT? I'M A PACIFIST! I'M ONLY IN THIS TO IMPRESS GIRLS!
COLISEUM SPRING EVENTS
ALLEN VS. ROTTENUS MAXIMUS
I BETTER FIND A NEW CAREER. MY NEXT OPPONENT MAY NOT GET SUNSTROKE WHILE ATTACKING ME.
5-20 Hample
INSIDE WOODY ALLEN

May 20, 1979

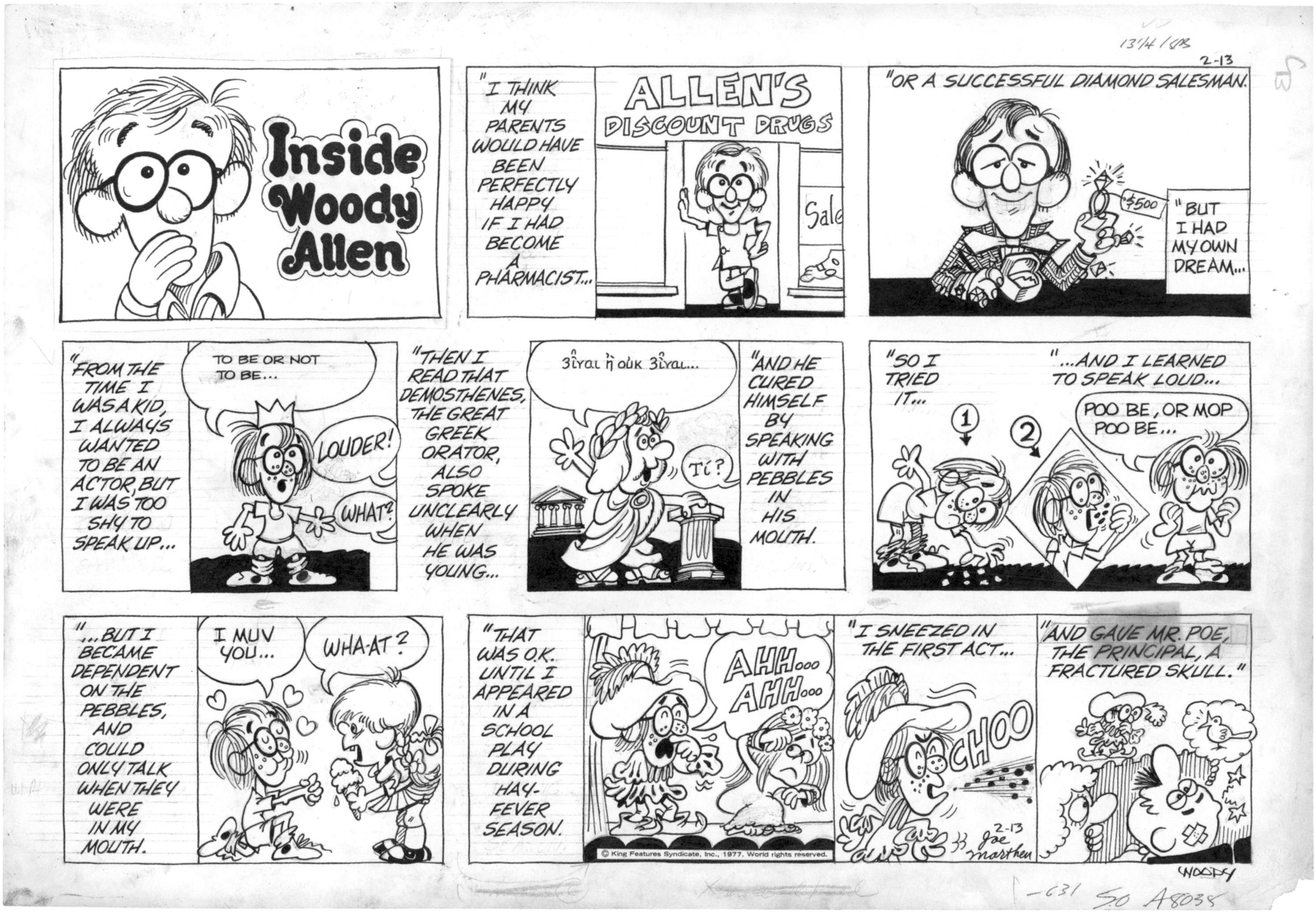
Inside Woody Allen
"I THINK MY PARENTS WOULD HAVE BEEN PERFECTLY HAPPY IF I HAD BECOME A PHARMACIST...
ALLEN'S DISCOUNT DRUGS
Sale
"OR A SUCCESSFUL DIAMOND SALESMAN.
$500
"BUT I HAD MY OWN DREAM...
"FROM THE TIME I WAS A KID, I ALWAYS WANTED TO BE AN ACTOR, BUT I WAS TOO SHY TO SPEAK UP...
TO BE OR NOT TO BE...
LOUDER!
WHAT?
"THEN I READ THAT DEMOSTHENES, THE GREAT GREEK ORATOR, ALSO SPOKE UNCLEARLY WHEN HE WAS YOUNG...
εἶναι ἢ οὐκ εἶναι...
Τί?
"AND HE CURED HIMSELF BY SPEAKING WITH PEBBLES IN HIS MOUTH.
"SO I TRIED IT...
1
2
"...AND I LEARNED TO SPEAK LOUD...
POO BE, OR MOP POO BE...
"...BUT I BECAME DEPENDENT ON THE PEBBLES, AND COULD ONLY TALK WHEN THEY WERE IN MY MOUTH.
I MUV YOU...
WHA-AT?
"THAT WAS O.K. UNTIL I APPEARED IN A SCHOOL PLAY DURING HAY-FEVER SEASON.
AHHooo AHHooo
© King Features Syndicate, Inc., 1977. World rights reserved.
"I SNEEZED IN THE FIRST ACT...
CHOO
2-13 Joe Marthen
"AND GAVE MR. POE, THE PRINCIPAL, A FRACTURED SKULL."
WOODY

February 13, 1977

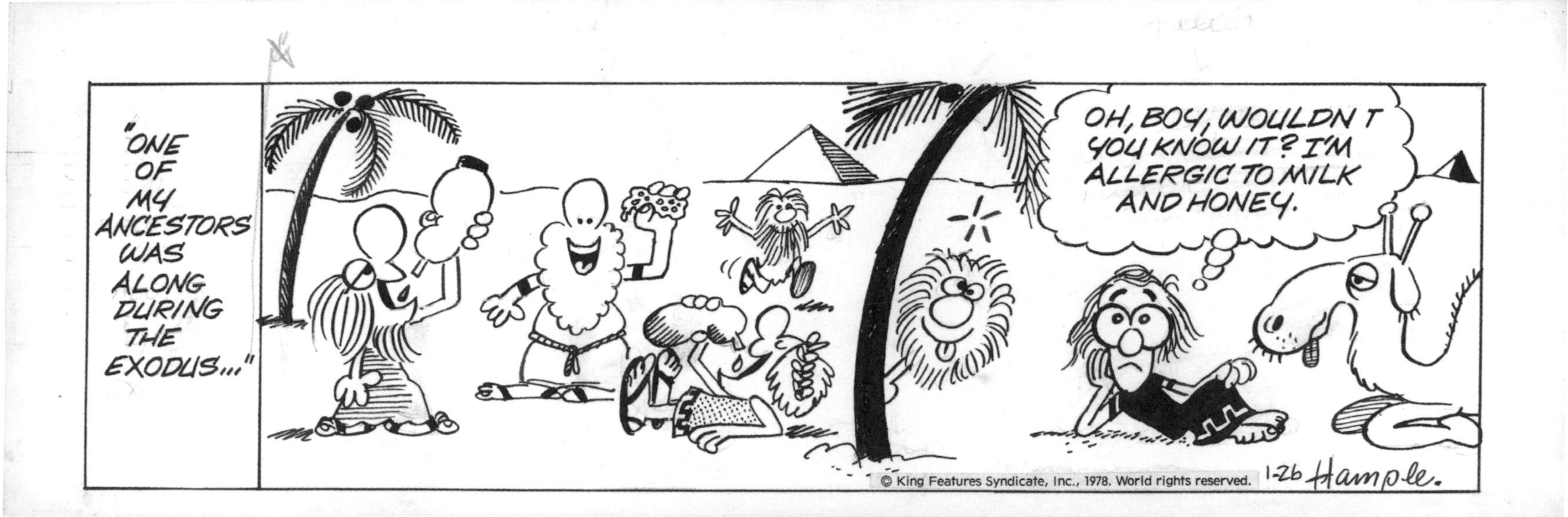
"ONE OF MY ANCESTORS WAS ALONG DURING THE EXODUS..."
OH, BOY, WOULDN T YOU KNOW IT? I'M ALLERGIC TO MILK AND HONEY.
© King Features Syndicate, Inc., 1978. World rights reserved.
1-26 Hample.

January 26, 1978

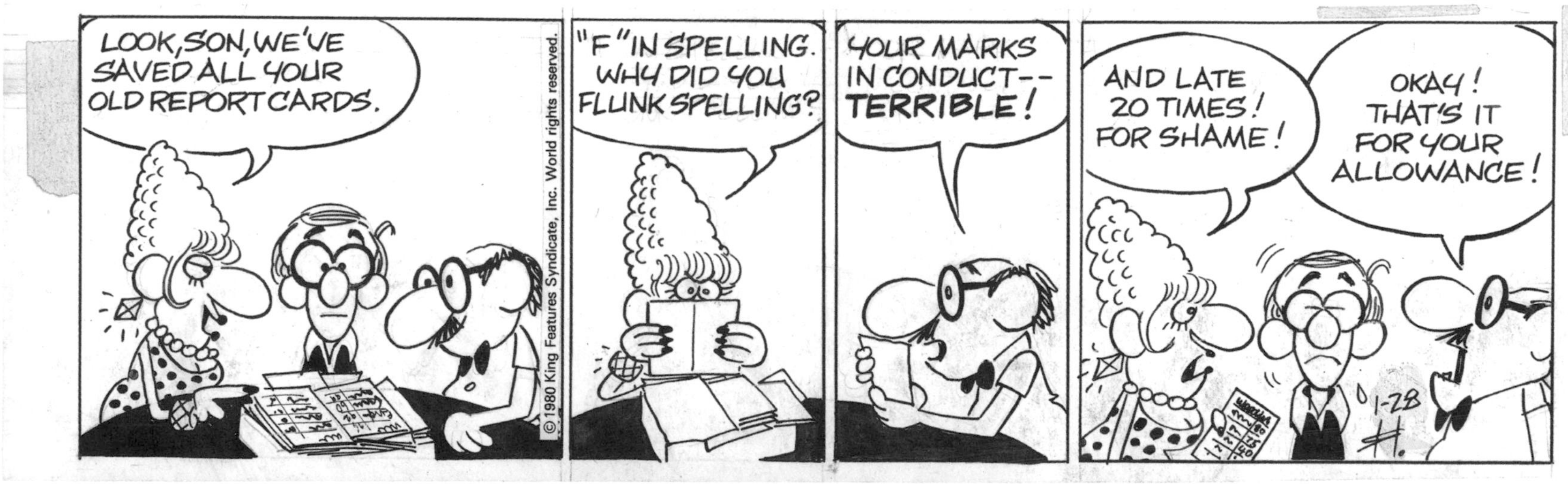
LOOK, SON, WE'VE SAVED ALL YOUR OLD REPORT CARDS.
©1980 King Features Syndicate, Inc. World rights reserved.
"F" IN SPELLING. WHY DID YOU FLUNK SPELLING?
YOUR MARKS IN CONDUCT-- **TERRIBLE**!
AND LATE 20 TIMES! FOR SHAME!
OKAY! THAT'S IT FOR YOUR ALLOWANCE!
1-28

January 28, 1980

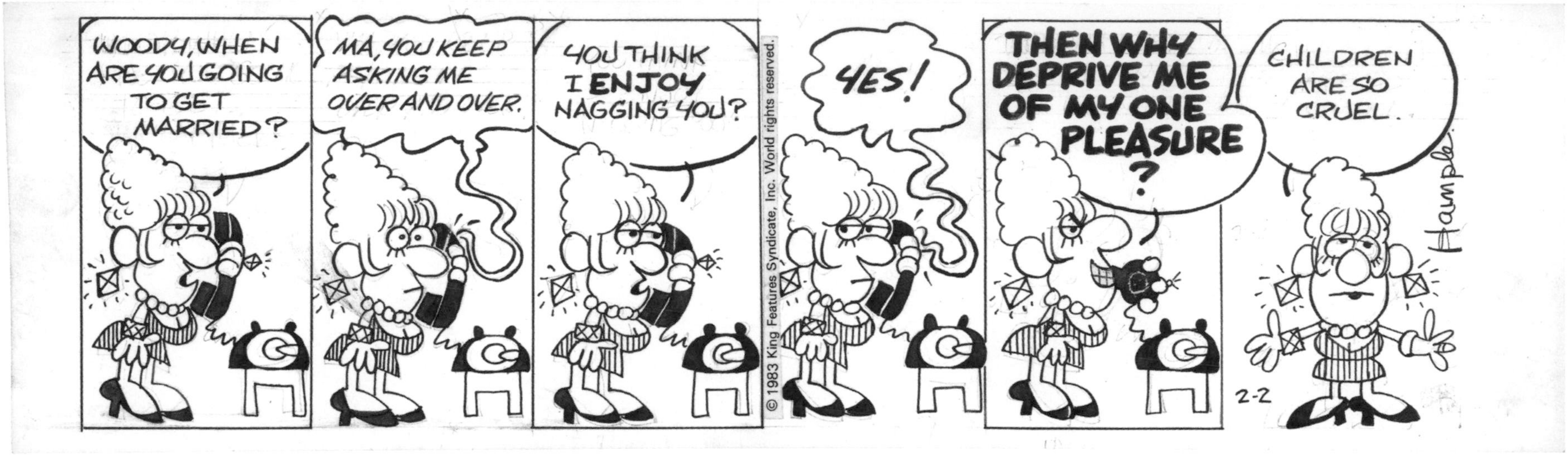
WOODY, WHEN ARE YOU GOING TO GET MARRIED?
MA, YOU KEEP ASKING ME OVER AND OVER.
YOU THINK I ENJOY NAGGING YOU?
YES!
THEN WHY DEPRIVE ME OF MY ONE PLEASURE?
CHILDREN ARE SO CRUEL.
© 1983 King Features Syndicate, Inc. World rights reserved.
Hample
2-2

February 2, 1983

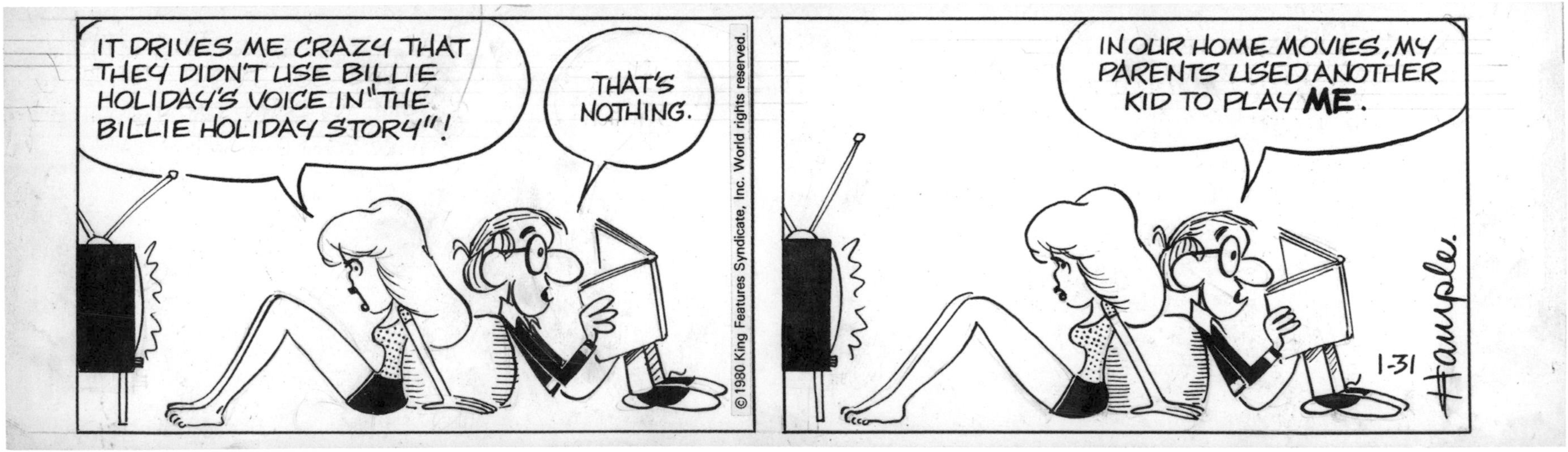
IT DRIVES ME CRAZY THAT THEY DIDN'T USE BILLIE HOLIDAY'S VOICE IN "THE BILLIE HOLIDAY STORY"!
THAT'S NOTHING.
IN OUR HOME MOVIES, MY PARENTS USED ANOTHER KID TO PLAY ME.
© 1980 King Features Syndicate, Inc. World rights reserved.
1-31
Hample

January 31, 1980

Inside Woody Allen

I'M GLAD MY PARENTS ARE TAKING A TRIP.

I CAN USE THE VACATION!

MOM! POP! YOU'RE TAKING A TRIP AROUND THE WORLD?

ALL THOSE YEARS OF PLAYING HOST TO FOREIGN STUDENTS...

ARE FINALLY GOING TO PAY OFF!

FIRST WE'LL VISIT LITTLE CECILY IN ENGLAND.

SHE'S THE ONE WHO BROKE THE CRYSTAL VASE!

THEN KURT, IN GERMANY.

HE STILL OWES US $12 FOR TV PRIVILEGES.

NIRMAL IN INDIA COMES NEXT! THE LITTLE RAT NEVER MADE HIS BED!

THEN THERE'S KATO, THE FLOOR SCUFFER, LARS, THE SPOON LOSER...

"A WEEK LATER."

BACK ALREADY?

WE NEVER LEFT. OUR PASSPORTS WERE REVOKED!

AT THE LAST MINUTE, SOMEONE LEAKED OUR PLANS TO THE STATE DEPARTMENT!

INSIDE WOODY ALLEN

May 30, 1982

Editor: **Charles Kochman**
Assistant Editor: **Sofia Gutiérrez**
Designer: **Neil Egan**
Layout & Composition: **Arlene Lee**
Production Managers: **Anet Sirna-Bruder** with **Ankur Ghosh**

Library of Congress Cataloging-in-Publication Data

Hample, Stuart E.
      Dread & superficiality : Woody Allen as comic strip / by
Stuart Hample ; with an introduction by R. Buckminster Fuller.
          p. cm.
      "This collection of classic Woody Allen newspaper
comics from 1976–1984 are shot off the original art, and
includes sketches, photographs, and development work,
offering a rare glimpse into a facet of Allen's career that has
long been overlooked." —Provided by publisher.
          ISBN 978-0-8109-5742-8
          I. Allen, Woody. II. Title.

      PN6728.I5H36 2009
      741.5'973—dc22
                        2008054349

Additional photography by Geoff Spear
German editions on pages 16–17 courtesy of Robert S. Bader
        and Erich Allinger

Printed and bound in China
10 9 8 7 6 5 4 3 2 1

Abrams ComicArts books are available at special discounts
when purchased in quantity for premiums and promotions
as well as fundraising or educational use. Special editions
can also be created to specification. For details, contact
specialmarkets@abramsbooks.com or the address below.

THE ART OF BOOKS SINCE 1949
115 West 18th Street
New York, NY 10011
www.abramsbooks.com